T0180875

Lecture Notes in Computer Science   12811

More information about this subseries at http://www.springer.com/series/7407

Nelma Moreira · Rogério Reis (Eds.)

Developments in Language Theory

25th International Conference, DLT 2021
Porto, Portugal, August 16–20, 2021
Proceedings

 Springer

Editors
Nelma Moreira 🆔
University of Porto
Porto, Portugal

Rogério Reis 🆔
University of Porto
Porto, Portugal

ISSN 0302-9743   ISSN 1611-3349 (electronic)
Lecture Notes in Computer Science
ISBN 978-3-030-81507-3   ISBN 978-3-030-81508-0 (eBook)
https://doi.org/10.1007/978-3-030-81508-0

LNCS Sublibrary: SL1 – Theoretical Computer Science and General Issues

This Springer imprint is published by the registered company Springer Nature Switzerland AG
The registered company address is: Gewerbestrasse 11, 6330 Cham, Switzerland

Preface

The 25th International Conference on Developments in Language Theory (DLT 2021) was held in Porto, Portugal, during August 16–20, 2021. The conference took place in an hybrid format with both in-person and online participation. It was organized by the Center of Mathematics of the University of Porto (Centro de Matemática da Universidade do Porto, CMUP) and the Faculty of Science of the University of Porto (FCUP).

The DLT conference series provides a forum for presenting current developments in formal languages and automata. Its scope is very general and includes, among others, the following topics and areas: grammars, acceptors, and transducers for words, trees and graphs; algebraic theories of automata; algorithmic, combinatorial, and algebraic properties of words and languages; variable length codes; symbolic dynamics; cellular automata; polyominoes and multidimensional patterns; decidability questions; image manipulation and compression; efficient text algorithms; relationships to cryptography, concurrency, complexity theory, and logic; bio-inspired computing; quantum computing.

Since its establishment by Grzegorz Rozenberg and Arto Salomaa in Turku (1993), the DLT conference had been held biennially, taking place in Magdeburg (1995), Thessaloniki (1997), Aachen (1999), and Vienna (2001). Since 2001 the conference has been held annually, taking place in Europe in every odd year and outside Europe in every even year: Kyoto (2002), Szeged (2003), Auckland (2004), Palermo (2005), Santa Barbara (2006), Turku (2007), Kyoto (2008), Stuttgart (2009), London (2010), Milano (2011), Taipei (2012), Marne-la-Vallée (2013), Ekaterinburg (2014), Liverpool (2015), Montréal (2016), Liège (2017), Tokyo (2018), and Warsaw (2019). In 2020, the DLT conference was planned to be held in Tampa, Florida, but due to the COVID-19 pandemic it was canceled. However, accepted papers of DLT 2020 were published in volume 12086 of Lecture Notes in Computer Science. Authors of these papers were welcome to present their work at DLT 2021.

In 2018, the DLT conference series instituted the Salomaa Prize, to honour the work of Arto Salomaa, as well as the success of automata and formal languages theory. The prize is founded by the University of Turku. The ceremony for the Salomaa Prize 2020 took place during DLT 2021, and we here by congratulate the winners Joël Ouaknine and James Worrell.

This volume contains the invited contributions and the accepted papers of DLT 2021. There were 48 submissions by 101 authors from 18 countries: Belgium, Czech Republic, Ecuador, Finland, France, Germany, India, Italy, Japan, Latvia, Netherlands, Poland, Russia, Slovakia, South Korea, Switzerland, UK and USA. Each of the submissions was reviewed by three referees, except for three submissions that only had two reviews each. All submissions were thoroughly discussed by the Program Committee (PC) who decided to accept 27 papers (56% acceptance rate) to be presented at the conference. We would like to thank the members of the Program Committee, and all external referees, for their work in evaluating the papers and the valuable comments that led to the selection of the contributed papers.

There were five invited talks, that were presented by the following speakers:

- Jean-Paul Allouche (CNRS, IMJ-PRG, and UPMC, France)
- Henning Fernau (Universität Trier, Germany)
- Michal Koucký (Charles University, Czech Republic)
- Alexandra Silva (University College London, UK)
- Benjamim Steinberg (City College of New York, USA)

We warmly thank the invited speakers, as well as all authors of submitted papers. Their efforts were the basis for the success of the conference.

The EasyChair conference system provided excellent support in the selection of the papers, the preparation of these proceedings, and the production of the conference schedule. We would like to thank Springer's editorial staff, and in particular Anna Kramer, Guido Zosimo-Landolfo, Christine Reiss, and Raghuram Balasubramanian for their help during the process of publishing this volume.

We are grateful to the Organizing Committee members: Sabine Broda, Bruno Loff, António Machiavelo, and Shinnosuke Seki. A special thank goes to Inês Maia from Pé de Cabra, Lda. Thanks are also due to our colleague Samuel Lopes, head of CMUP.

DLT 2021 was financially supported by Fundação para a Ciência e Tecnologia (FCT) through Centro de Matemática da Universidade do Porto (UIDB/00144/ 2020), Universidade do Porto, CRACS (INESC-TEC), Turismo de Portugal, and Câmara Municipal do Porto.

Finally, we would like to thank all participants who, either in-person or virtually, made the 25th edition of DLT a scientific and successful event, and the departure point for new research and collaborations.

We look forward to DLT 2022 at the University of South Florida, Tampa, USA.

June 2021   Nelma Moreira
                                                                   Rogério Reis

Organization

Steering Committee

Marie-Pierre Béal	Université Paris-Est, Marne-la-Vallée, France
Cristian S. Calude	University of Auckland, New Zealand
Volker Diekert	Universität Stuttgart, Germany
Yo-Sub Han	Yonsei University, South Korea
Juraj Hromkovic	ETH Zürich, Switzerland
Oscar H. Ibarra	University of California, Santa Barbara, USA
Nataša Jonoska	University of South Florida, Tampa, USA
Juhani Karhumäki	University of Turku, Finland
Martin Kutrib	Universität Giessen, Germany
Giovanni Pighizzini (Chair)	Università degli Studi di Milano, Italy
Michel Rigo	University of Liège, Belgium
Antonio Restivo	Università degli Studi di Palermo, Italy
Wojciech Rytter	University of Warsaw, Poland
Kai Salomaa	Queen's University, Kingston, Canada
Shinnosuke Seki	The University of Electro-Communications, Japan
Mikhail Volkov	Ural Federal University, Ekaterinburg, Russia
Takashi Yokomori	Waseda University, Tokyo, Japan

Program Committee

Szilárd Zsolt Fazekas	Akita University, Japan
Dora Giammarresi	Università degli Studi di Roma "Tor Vergata", Italy
Yo-Sub Han	Yonsei University, South Korea
Juraj Hromkovic	ETH Zürich, Switzerland
Oscar Ibarra	University of California, Santa Barbara, USA
Nataša Jonoska	University of South Florida, Tampa, USA
Christos Kapoutsis	Carnegie Mellon University, Qatar
Jarkko Kari	University of Turku, Finland
Martin Kutrib	Universität Giessen, Germany
Andreas Maletti	University of Leipzig, Germany
Tomáš Masopust	Palacky University Olomouc, Czech Republic
Ian McQuillan	University of Saskatchewan, Canada
Carlo Mereghetti	Università degli Studi di Milano, Italy
Nelma Moreira (Co-chair)	University of Porto, Portugal
Giovanni Pighizzini	Università degli Studi di Milano, Italy
Rogério Reis (Co-chair)	University of Porto, Portugal
Michael Rigo	University of Liège, Belgium
Kai Salomaa	Queen's University, Canada

Marinella Sciortino   Università di Palermo, Italy
Philippe Schnoebelen   Université Paris-Saclay, France
Helmut Seidl   Technical University Munich, Germany
Shinnosuke Seki   The University of Electro-Communications, Japan
Jeffrey Shallit   University of Waterloo, Canada
György Vaszil   University of Debrecen, Hungary
Mikhail Volkov   Ural Federal University, Ekaterinburg, Russia
Marc Zeitoun   University of Bordeaux, France

Organizing Committee

Sabine Broda   University of Porto, Portugal
Bruno Loff   University of Porto, Portugal
António Machiavelo   University of Porto, Portugal
Inês Maia   Pé de Cabra, Lda, Portugal
Nelma Moreira   University of Porto, Portugal
Rogério Reis   University of Porto, Portugal
Shinnosuke Seki   The University of Electro-Communications, Japan

Additional Reviewers

Anselmo, Marcella
Bannai, Hideo
Berglund, Martin
Björklund, Johanna
Boehm, Martin
Bordihn, Henning
Broda, Sabine
Cadilhac, Michaël
Castiglione, Giuseppa
Cisternino, Célia
Edwin, Hamel-De Le Court
Endrullis, Joerg
Fici, Gabriele
Glen, Amy
Hoffmann, Stefan
Holzer, Markus
Hospodár, Michal
Ivan, Szabolcs
Karhumaki, Juhani
Keeler, Chris
Kim, Hwee
Ko, Sang-Ki
Konstantinidis, Stavros

Kufleitner, Manfred
Köppl, Dominik
Leroy, Julien
Liptak, Zsuzsanna
Loff, Bruno
Lombardy, Sylvain
Löding, Christof
Machiavelo, António
Madonia, Maria
Malcher, Andreas
Mandrali, Eleni
Mercas, Robert
Mráz, František
Okhotin, Alexander
Parreaux, Julie
Paul, Erik
Pinchinat, Sophie
Prigioniero, Luca
Ravikumar, Balasubramanian
Rodaro, Emanuele
Rubtsov, Alexander
Schiffer, Lena Katharina
Smith, Taylor

Stier, Kevin
Subramanian, K. G.
Teh, Wen Chean
Truthe, Bianca

Wendlandt, Matthias
Yakaryilmaz, Abuzer
Yamakami, Tomoyuki

Sponsors

Abstracts of Invited Talks

Computing Edit Distance

Michal Koucký

Computer Science Institute of Charles University,
Malostranské nám. 25, 118 00 Praha 1, Czech Republic
koucky@iuuk.mff.cuni.cz
https://iuuk.mff.cuni.cz/koucky/

Abstract. Edit distance (or Levenshtein distance) is a measure of similarity of strings. The edit distance of two strings x, y is the minimum number of character insertions, deletions, and substitutions needed to convert x into y. It has numerous applications in various fields from text processing to bioinformatics so algorithms for edit distance computation attract lot of attention. In this talk I will survey recent progress on computational aspects of edit distance in several contexts: computing edit distance approximately, computing edit distance in streaming model, and exchanging similar strings in communication complexity model. I will point out many problems that are still open in those areas.

Keywords: Edit distance · Approximation algorithms · Streaming algorithms · Document Exchange Problem

Guarded Kleene Algebra with Tests

Alexandra Silva

University College London, UK
alexandra.silva@ucl.ac.uk
https://alexandrasilva.org

Abstract. Guarded Kleene Algebra with Tests (GKAT) is an efficient fragment of KAT, as it allows for almost linear decidability of equivalence. In this talk, we will review the basics of GKAT and describe its (co)algebraic properties. We will describe two completeness results and an automaton model that plays a key role in their proof. We will show examples of different models of GKAT that can be used in program verification and discuss future directions of research.

Keywords: Kleene algebra · Program verification · Decision procedures · Program equivalence · Coequations

The material in this talk is based on the publications [1, 2].

References

1. Schmid, T., Kappé, T., Kozen, D., Silva, A.: Guarded Kleene algebra with tests: coequations, coinduction, and completeness. In: 48th International Colloquium on Automata, Languages, and Programming, ICALP 2021. LIPIcs (2021)
2. Smolka, S., Foster, N., Hsu, J., Kappé, T., Kozen, D., Silva, A.: Guarded Kleene algebra with tests: verification of uninterpreted programs in nearly linear time. Proc. ACM Program. Lang. 4(POPL), 61:1–61:28 (2020). https://doi.org/10.1145/3371129

Contents

Invited Talks

Morphic Sequences Versus Automatic Sequences

Jean-Paul Allouche[(✉)]

CNRS, IMJ-PRG, Sorbonne, 4 Place Jussieu, 75005 Paris, France
`jean-paul.allouche@imj-prg.fr`

Abstract. Two classical families of infinite sequences with some regularity properties are the families of *morphic* and of *automatic* sequences. After recalling their definitions, we survey some recent work trying to "separate" between them.

Keywords: Automatic sequences · Morphic sequences · Combinatorics on words

1 Introduction

Combinatorics on Words is the study of finite or infinite sequences, usually taking their values in a finite set of symbols. To learn more about the history of Combinatorics on Words, the reader can look at the nice paper by Berstel and Perrin [6]. We will only mention the pioneering 1906 and 1912 papers by Thue [18,19]: Thue was interested in infinite sequences that contain no "squares" or no "cubes", where a square (resp., a cube) is a block of two (resp., three) identical consecutive blocks of symbols.

We will concentrate on two classes of (infinite) sequences with many properties that are studied in Combinatorics on Words: the class of *morphic sequences* and its subclass of *automatic sequences*. Actually these two kinds of sequences are both easy to generate, "reasonably regular", and, for the non-periodic ones, they can simulate some sort of disorder: some authors have spoken of a "controlled disorder".

We will quickly revisit the definition of these two classes of sequences. To learn more about the subject the reader can consult the books [1,7,10,11,13–16], where one can read in particular that these sequences are used in many domains: e.g., Combinatorics on Words, Number Theory (transcendence, continued fractions, Dirichlet series, distribution modulo 1, ...), Iteration of continuous maps of the interval, Fractals, Theoretical Physics (quasicrystals), ...

Then we will discuss how one can "separate" these two classes—namely, both contain sequences with some kind of "regularity properties", but automatic sequences have more precise properties, including arithmetic properties. In particular, some sequences given as morphic happen to be automatic: which ones? Also most morphic sequences are not automatic: given a morphic sequence, how can it be proved that it is not automatic? We will in particular try to propose a synthesis of three recent papers [2–4].

© Springer Nature Switzerland AG 2021
N. Moreira and R. Reis (Eds.): DLT 2021, LNCS 12811, pp. 3–11, 2021.
https://doi.org/10.1007/978-3-030-81508-0_1

2 Words, Morphisms, Sequences

We start with a few basic definitions in Combinatorics on Words.

Definition 1.
- *An* alphabet *is a finite set. Its elements are called* letters. *A finite sequence of elements taken from an alphabet* $\mathcal{A}$ *is called a* word *on* $\mathcal{A}$. *The word* $a_1, a_2, \ldots, a_d$ *over* $\mathcal{A}$ *is denoted* $a_1 a_2 \cdots a_d$, *and* d *is called its* length: *notation* $d = |a_1 a_2 \cdots a_d|$. *The* empty word *is the word with no letter: its length is defined to be* 0.
- *If* $w = a_1 a_2 \cdots a_d$ *and* $z = b_1 b_2 \cdots b_e$ *are two words over* $\mathcal{A}$, *the* concatenation *of* w *and* z, *denoted* $w.z$ *or* wz, *is the word defined by*

$$wz := a_1 a_2 \cdots a_d \ b_1 b_2 \cdots b_e.$$

Its length is $d + e$, *i.e.,* $|wz| = |w| + |z|$.
- *We let* $\mathcal{A}^*$ *denote the set of all words (including the empty word) over the alphabet* $\mathcal{A}$.
- *If* u, v, w, z *are four words over some alphabet such that* $z = uvw$, *then* u *is called a* prefix *of* z *and* w *is called a* sufix *of* z. *Any of the words* u, v, w, z *is called a* factor *of* z. *If* $(u_n)_{n \geq 0}$ *is a sequence over some alphabet, then the finite sequence* $u_0 u_1 \cdots u_{k-1}$ *can be also considered as a word (of length* k) *over this alphabet: it is called a* prefix *(of length* k) *of the sequence* $(u_n)_{n \geq 0}$; *the finite sequence* $u_j u_{j+1} \cdots u_{k-1}$ *is called a* factor *of the sequence* $(u_n)_{n \geq 0}$.

Remark 1. A word is equal to the concatenation of its letters.

Remark 2. The set $\mathcal{A}^*$ equipped with the concatenation operation is a *monoid* (actually a *free* monoid).

Remark 3. Some authors use the term "words" for either a finite or for an infinite sequence: we will use "word" for a finite sequence only. What some authors call "infinite word" will always be called a *sequence*.

Definition 2. *Let* $\mathcal{A}$ *and* $\mathcal{B}$ *be two alphabets. A* morphism φ *from* $\mathcal{A}^*$ *to* $\mathcal{B}^*$ *is a map from* $\mathcal{A}^*$ *to* $\mathcal{B}^*$ *such that* $\varphi(wz) = \varphi(w)\varphi(z)$, *for all words* w *and* z *over* $\mathcal{A}$. *A morphism* φ *is called* uniform *if all the words* $\varphi(a)$ *for* $a \in \mathcal{A}$ *have the same length. If this length is equal to* $q \geq 1$, *the morphism is called* q-uniform. *If* $\mathcal{A} = \mathcal{B}$: *a morphism from* $\mathcal{A}^*$ *to itself is called a* morphism on $\mathcal{A}$.

Remark 4. Note that concatenation is written in the same way for the two monoids $\mathcal{A}^*$ and $\mathcal{B}^*$.

Remark 5. A morphism φ is completely defined by its values on letters.

Example 1. Let $\mathcal{A} := \{0, 1\}$.

– Define the morphism φ on $\mathcal{A}$ by

$$\varphi(0) = 01, \; \varphi(1) = 10.$$

This morphism is called the *Thue-Morse morphism* on $\{0,1\}$. It is 2-uniform. To compute, e.g., $\varphi(001)$, one writes

$$\varphi(001) = \varphi(0.0.1) = \varphi(0).\varphi(0).\varphi(1) = 01.01.10 = 010110.$$

– Define the morphism ψ on $\mathcal{A}$ by

$$\psi(0) = 01, \; \psi(1) = 0.$$

This morphism is called the *Fibonacci morphism* on $\{0,1\}$. It is not uniform (the terminology "Fibonacci morphism" will be explained later on).

Definition 3. *Let φ be a morphism on A, with $A := \{a_0, a_1, \ldots, a_{r-1}\}$. Its adjacency matrix (or transition matrix) is the matrix $M = (m_{i,j})$, where, for all i and j in $\{0, 1, \ldots, r-1\}$, $m_{i,j}$ is the number of letters a_i in the word $\varphi(a_j)$. The length vector of φ is the vector $L = (L_0, L_1, \ldots, L_{r-1})$, where $L_j := |\varphi(a_j)|$, i.e., L_j is the sum of the entries of the column indexed by j of the adjacency matrix of φ.*

3   (Purely) Morphic Sequences. Automatic Sequences

Taking the Thue-Morse morphism above, one can iterate it starting from 0:

$$\varphi^0(0) := 0$$
$$\varphi^1(0) := \varphi(0) = 01$$
$$\varphi^2(0) := \varphi(\varphi(0)) = \varphi(01) = 0110$$
$$\varphi^3(0) := \varphi(\varphi^2(0)) = \varphi(0110) = 01101001$$
$$\vdots$$

It is not difficult to see that there exists a unique sequence $(a_n)_{n \geq 0}$ such that, for all $k \geq 0$, the word $\varphi^k(0)$ is a prefix of the sequence $(a_n)_{n \geq 0}$. Thinking a bit more shows that this is due to the fact that $\varphi(0)$ begins with 0, and that $|\varphi^k(0)|$ tends to infinity when $k \to \infty$. We say that the sequence of words $\varphi^k(0)$ *tends to* this infinite sequence $(a_n)_{n \geq 0} = 011010011001\ldots$. Note that it is possible to interpret this with the usual topological meaning by equipping the set of all finite and infinite sequences with a topology, but we will not give more details here.

Here is another example. Take the Fibonacci morphism ψ defined above ($\psi(0) = 01$, $\psi(1) = 0$). Iterating ψ starting from 0, we obtain the set of words:

$$\psi^0(0) := 0$$
$$\psi^1(0) := \psi(0) = 01$$
$$\psi^2(0) := \psi(\psi(0)) = \psi(01) = 010$$
$$\psi^3(0) := \psi(\psi^2(0)) = \psi(010) = 01001$$
$$\vdots$$

which, as previously, tends to an infinite sequence $01001010010\ldots$ This sequence is called the binary Fibonacci sequence: the reason for calling "Fibonacci" this sequence and the morphism ψ is because the lengths of the successive words $\psi^0(0), \psi(0), \psi^2(0)\ldots$ are the usual Fibonacci numbers.

Definition 4. *Let φ be a morphism on the alphabet $\mathcal{A}$. Suppose that there exists $a \in \mathcal{A}$ such that $\varphi(a)$ begins with a, and such that $|\varphi^k(a)|$ tends to infinity when $k \to \infty$, where φ^k denotes the k-th iterate of φ. There exists a unique infinite sequence over $\mathcal{A}$ admitting all words $\varphi^k(a)$ as its prefixes (of length $|\varphi^k(a)|$). This sequence is called the* fixed point beginning with a *of the morphism φ. We let $\lim_{k\to\infty} \varphi^k(a)$ denote this fixed point.*

If a sequence is a fixed point of some morphism, it is called purely morphic.

Remark 6. The terminology comes from the fact that the infinite sequence obtained by iterating φ is a fixed point of the extension of φ to infinite sequences defined by: $\varphi(a_0a_1\ldots a_n \ldots) := \varphi(a_0)\varphi(a_1)\ldots\varphi(a_n)\ldots$ (in the topological terminology that we skipped, this is an extension of φ by continuity).

We can extend a bit the notion of purely morphic sequences.

Example 2. Let $\mathcal{B} := \{a, b, c, d\}$. Define a morphism φ on $\mathcal{B}$ by

$$\varphi(a) = ab, \quad \varphi(b) = (ac), \quad \varphi(c) = db, \quad \varphi(d) = dc.$$

The fixed point of φ beginning with a is: $\lim_{k\to\infty} \varphi^k(a) = a\ b\ a\ c\ a\ b\ d\ b\ldots$.

Let f denote the map: $a \to 0,\ b \to 0,\ c \to 1,\ d \to 1$. This map can be considered as a 1-morphism from $\mathcal{B}$ to $\{0,1\}$. The Golay-Shapiro sequence (also called the Rudin-Shapiro sequence) is then defined as the sequence:

$$f\left(\lim_{k\to\infty} \varphi^k(a)\right) = 0\ 0\ 0\ 1\ 0\ 0\ 1\ 0\ \ldots$$

Definition 5. *Let φ be a morphism on the alphabet $\mathcal{B}$. Suppose that there exists $a \in \mathcal{B}$ such that $\varphi(a)$ begins with a, and such that $|\varphi^k(a)|$ tends to infinity when $k \to \infty$, where φ^k denotes the k-th iterate of φ. Let f be a map (a 1-morphism) from $\mathcal{B}$ to some alphabet $\mathcal{A}$. The sequence $f\left(\lim_{k\to\infty} \varphi^k(a)\right)$ is called a* morphic *sequence over $\mathcal{A}$.*

Remark 7. Every purely morphic sequence is a morphic sequence.

We end this lengthy set of definitions with the following one.

Definition 6. *A sequence is said to be* q-automatic *if it is morphic and if the morphism in the definition has constant length $q \geq 2$. A sequence that is q-automatic for some $q \geq 2$ is called* automatic *(or* uniformly morphic*).*

Remark 8. The term "automatic" comes from the fact that a sequence is q-automatic if and only if there exists a deterministic finite automaton with output, whose transitions are labelled by $0, 1, \ldots, q-1$, that generates the n-th term of the sequence when fed with the base-q digits of n.

Example 3. The Thue-Morse sequence (fixed point beginning with 0 of the Thue-Morse morphism seen above: $\varphi(0) = 01$, $\varphi(1) = 10$) is 2-automatic. So is the Golay-Shapiro sequence seen in Example 2.

Definition 7. *We will say that a sequence is* non-uniformly morphic *if it is morphic, and if the morphism involved in the definition is not uniform.*

Remark 9. Note that the property of being "non-uniformly morphic" is not the same as being "not uniformly morphic". In the first case, the sequence is the image by a 1-morphism of a fixed point of a non-uniform morphism, but it may happen that this sequence is also the image by a 1-morphism of a fixed point of some uniform morphism. In the second case, there is no uniform morphism such that the sequence is the image by a 1-morphism of this uniform morphism (such a sequence can also be called a "non-automatic" sequence).

4   Comparing the Classes of Morphic and of Automatic Sequences

This section will expand on Remark 9 above. It contains the main result of [2]. Let us begin with an example (the details are taken from [3]): the Thue-Morse sequence, fixed point of the morphism $\varphi(0) = 01$, $\varphi(1) = 10$, is also the fixed point of φ^3. We define two letters different from 0 and 1, say b and c. We also define two words on the alphabet $\{0, 1, b, c\}$: $z = 0, t = 110100110010110$. (Note that z and t have different lengths, and that $zt = \varphi^3(0)$.) Now let γ be the morphism defined on $\{0, 1, b, c\}$ by

$$\gamma(0) = 011bc001, \ \gamma(1) = \gamma(1), \ \gamma(b) = z, \ \gamma(c) = t.$$

Finally define D by: $D(0) = 0, D(1) = 1, D(b) = 0, D(c) = 1$. It is easy to see that the image by D of the infinite fixed point of γ starting with 0 is also the fixed point of φ^3 starting with 0, hence is equal to the Thue-Morse sequence.

Actually, this situation is quite general as proven in the following theorem.

Theorem 1 ([2]). *Let $(a_n)_{n \geq 0}$ be an automatic sequence taking its values in the alphabet $\mathcal{A}$. Then $(a_n)_{n \geq 0}$ is also non-uniformly morphic. Furthermore, if $(a_n)_{n \geq 0}$ is a fixed point of a uniform morphism, then there exist an alphabet $\mathcal{B}$ of cardinality $(3 + \#\mathcal{A})$ and a sequence $(a'_n)_{n \geq 0}$ with values in $\mathcal{B}$, such that $(a'_n)_{n \geq 0}$ is a fixed point of some non-uniform morphism on $\mathcal{B}$ and $(a_n)_{n \geq 0}$ is the image of $(a'_n)_{n \geq 0}$ under a 1-morphism.*

This result may seem surprising. Automatic sequences have a somehow more rigid structure, but they can also be generated in a seemingly strictly less

demanding way. In other words the family of all morphic sequences is equal
to its subfamily of non-uniformly morphic sequences. This immediately implies
a natural question: given a morphic (or even a pure morphic) sequence, how can
we see whether it is automatic or how can we prove that it is *not* automatic?
This will be the subject of the next two sections.

5   Hidden Automatic Sequences

One of the first unexpected examples of a morphic sequence that happens to
be also automatic was given by Berstel [5], who discovered and proved that the
Istrail squarefree sequence [12], defined as the fixed point beginning with 1 of
the morphism σ_{IS}, given by

$$\sigma_{\text{IS}}(0) = 12, \ \sigma_{\text{IS}}(1) = 102 \ , \sigma_{\text{IS}}(2) = 0,$$

can also be obtained by first considering the fixed point beginning with 1 of the
uniform morphism $0 \to 12, \ 1 \to 13, \ 2 \to 20, \ 3 \to 21$, then taking its image by
the 1-morphism that consists in reducing modulo 3.

As asked at the end of Sect. 4, is it possible, given a morphic sequence, to
"recognize" whether it is automatic? A 1978-result of Dekking gives a sufficient
condition.

Theorem 2 ([9]). *Let σ be a morphism on $\{0, \ldots, r-1\}$ with length vector
$L = (|\sigma(0)|, \ldots, |\sigma(r-1)|)$, for some integer $r > 1$. Suppose that σ is non-erasing
(i.e., for all i in $\{0, \ldots, r-1\}$, one has $|\sigma(i)| \geq 1$). Let x be a fixed point of σ,
and let M be the adjacency matrix of σ. If L is a left eigenvector of M, then x
is q-automatic, where q is the spectral radius of M.*

Weaker but more "visual" conditions are given in the following two theorems.

Theorem 3 ([3], "Rank 1 Theorem"). *Let σ be a morphism as in Theorem 2
above. Let x be a fixed point of σ. If M has rank 1, then x is q-automatic, where
q is the spectral radius of M.*

Theorem 4 ([3], "Anagram Theorem"). *Let $\mathcal{A}$ be a finite set. Let W be a
set of anagrams over $\mathcal{A}$ (the words in W are also said to be abelian equivalent).
Let ψ be a morphism on $\mathcal{A}$ such that the image of each letter is a concatenation
of words in W. Then, if a sequence is a fixed point of ψ, it must be q-automatic,
where q is the quotient of the length of $\psi(w)$ by the length of w, which is the
same for all $w \in W$.*

Several "hidden automatic sequences", i.e., morphic sequences that happen
to be automatic, can be found in the literature:

Example 4. The following examples are taken from [3].

- The fixed point beginning with a of the Lysënok morphism $a \to aca, \ b \to d,$
  $c \to b, \ d \to c$ is 2-automatic. It is the fixed point beginning with a of the
  morphism $a \to ac, \ b \to ad, \ c \to ab, \ d \to ac$.
- The four sequences A284878, A284905, A285305, and A284912 in [17] are
  3-automatic.

6 How to Prove that a Sequence Is Not Automatic

Theorem 2 and Theorem 3 give a sufficient condition for a pure morphic sequence to be automatic. We can also explore necessary conditions. More precisely, looking at various properties of automatic sequences, we can state conditions implying that a given sequence (and in particular a morphic sequence) is not automatic. Below we give a catalog of such statements (more details, proofs, and references can be found in [4]).

Let $\mathbf{u} = (u_n)_{n \geq 0}$ a fixed point of a non-uniform morphism φ, whose adjacency matrix M has spectral radius ρ.

- First suppose that the morphism φ is *primitive*, i.e., the matrix M is primitive, which means that there exists an integer d such that all entries of M^d are positive.

  - If ρ is not an integer, then $\mathbf{u}$ is not q-automatic for any $q \geq 2$.
  - Compute the dynamical eigenvalues of the dynamical system $X_{\mathbf{u}}$ *(this aspect is not studied here; see [4] for a definition and some results)*.

- Now suppose that there is no primitivity hypothesis for the morphism φ, and that ρ^d is never an integer for d positive integer.

  - Then the sequence $(u_n)_{n \geq 0}$ is not q-automatic for any $q \geq 2$. Note that this is in particular the case if there exists some integer $t \geq 1$ such that ρ^t is a rational number but not an integer.

- Finally suppose that there is no primitivity hypothesis for the morphism φ, and that $\rho^k = d$ for some integer $d \geq 2$. Then, from a result of Durand [8], proving that the sequence $(u_n)_{n \geq 0}$ is not q-automatic for $q \geq 2$ is the same as proving that it is not d-automatic. Up to replacing φ with φ^k, one can suppose that $\rho = d$ for some integer $d \geq 2$. In order to prove that $(u_n)_{n \geq 0}$ is not d-automatic, one can try one of the following strategies.

  - Exhibit infinitely many distinct elements in the *d-kernel* of $(u_n)_{n \geq 0}$, i.e., the set of subsequences $\mathrm{Ker}_d\, \mathbf{u} = \{(u_{d^k n + r})_{n \geq 0},\ k \geq 0,\ r \in [0, d^k - 1]\}$.
  - Prove that some factor occurs in $(u_n)_{n \geq 0}$ with irrational frequency.
  - Prove that the *factor-complexity* of $(u_n)_{n \geq 0}$ (i.e., the number of factors occurring in $(u_n)_{n \geq 0}$) is not in $\mathcal{O}(n)$.
  - Find gaps of "wrong" size in the sequence of integers $\{n,\ u_n = a\}$ for some value a.
  - Look at the poles of the (continuation of the) Dirichlet series associated with $(u_n)_{n \geq 0}$.
  - Study the closed orbit of $(u_n)_{n \geq 0}$ under the shift *(we skip this aspect in this survey; see, e.g., [4])*.

Example 5. The following examples are taken from [4].

- The binary Fibonacci sequence, fixed point of $0 \to 01$, $1 \to 0$ is not q-automatic for any $q \geq 2$. Namely the adjacency matrix is minimal, and its dominant eigenvalue is not an integer.

– The infinite fixed point $\mathbf{v} = (v_n)_{n \geq 0}$ of the morphism $a \to aab$, $b \to b$ is not 2-automatic: it can be proved that its 2-kernel is infinite; more precisely that the sequences $(v_{2^k n + 2^k - k})_{n \geq 0}$ for $k \geq 1$ are all distinct.

7 Towards a (Partially) Automated Approach?

Is it possible to test in an automated (or semi-automated) way whether a (purely) morphic sequence is automatic? While the general question of recognizing whether a morphic sequence is automatic is probably undecidable, some of the conditions listed above can be tested in an automated way. For example, it is decidable whether the dominant eigenvalue of a matrix is an integer. Some other conditions that are not listed above might also be tested in some semi-automated way: for example J. Shallit suggested a way of proving that the fixed point of the morphism $a \to aab$, $b \to b$ is not automatic as follows. Define the function f by: $f(n)$ is the index of the leftmost term of the first occurrence of a run of length n in this fixed point. If the fixed point were q-automatic then f would be q-synchronized, and hence in $\mathcal{O}(n)$. But the first occurrence of a run of length n begins at position $2^{n+1} - n - 1$, which is clearly not in $\mathcal{O}(n)$ (see [4] for details).

Acknowledgements. We warmly thank F. Durand and J. Shallit for discussions and comments.

References

1. Allouche, J.-P., Shallit, J.: Automatic Sequences. Theory, Applications, Generalizations. Cambridge University Press, Cambridge (2003)
2. Allouche, J.-P., Shallit, J.: Automatic sequences are also non-uniformly morphic. In: Raigorodskii, A.M., Rassias, M.Th. (eds.) Discrete Mathematics and Applications. SOIA, vol. 165, pp. 1–6. Springer, Cham (2020). https://arxiv.org/abs/1910.08546
3. Allouche, J.-P., Dekking, F.M., Queffélec, M.: Hidden automatic sequences. Preprint (2020). https://arxiv.org/abs/2010.00920
4. Allouche, J.-P., Shallit, J., Yassawi, R.: How to prove that a sequence is not automatic. Preprint (2021). https://arxiv.org/abs/2104.13072
5. Berstel, J.: Sur la construction de mots sans carré. Sém. Théorie Nombres Bordeaux **8**, 1–16 (1978–1979)
6. Berstel, J., Perrin, D.: The origins of combinatorics on words. Eur. J. Combin. **28**, 996–1022 (2007)
7. Berthé, V., Rigo, M. (eds.): Combinatorics, Words and Symbolic Dynamics. Encyclopedia of Mathematics and its Applications, vol. 159. Cambridge University Press, Cambridge (2016)
8. Durand, F.: Cobham's theorem for substitutions. J. Eur. Math. Soc. **13**, 1799–1814 (2011)
9. Dekking, F.M.: The spectrum of dynamical systems arising from substitutions of constant length. Z. Wahrscheinlichkeitstheorie und Verw. Gebiete **41**, 221–239 (1977/78)

10. Pytheas Fogg, N.: Substitutions in Dynamics, Arithmetics and Combinatorics. Lecture Notes in Mathematics, vol. 1794. Springer, Berlin (2002). https://doi.org/10.1007/b13861
11. von Haeseler, F.: Automatic Sequences. De Gruyter Expositions in Mathematics, vol. 36. Walter de Gruyter & Co., Berlin (2003)
12. Istrail, S.: On irreducible [sic] languages and nonrational numbers. Bull. Math. Soc. Sci. Math. R. S. Roumanie **21**(69), 301–308 (1977)
13. Lothaire, M.: Combinatorics on Words. Encyclopedia of Mathematics and its Applications, vol. 17, , 2nd edn. Cambridge University Press, Cambridge (1997)
14. Lothaire, M.: Algebraic Combinatorics on Words. Cambridge University Press, Cambridge (2002)
15. Lothaire, M.: Applied Combinatorics on Words. Encyclopedia of Mathematics and its Applications, vol. 105. Cambridge University Press, Cambridge (2005)
16. Rigo, M.: Formal Languages, Automata and Numeration Systems, vol. 1. Introduction to Combinatorics on Words. ISTE, Wiley (2014)
17. Sloane, N.J.A.: On-Line Encyclopedia of Integer Sequences. http://oeis.org
18. Thue, A.: Über unendliche Zeichenreihen. Norske vid. Selsk. Skr. Mat. Nat. Kl. **7**, 1–22 (1906). Reprinted in Nagell, T., (ed.) Selected mathematical papers of Axel Thue, pp. 139–158. Universitetsforlaget, Oslo (1977)
19. Thue, A.: Über die gegenseitige Lage gleicher Teile gewisser Zeichenreihen. Norske vid. Selsk. Skr. Mat. Nat. Kl. **1**, 1–67 (1912). Reprinted in Nagell, T., (ed.) Selected mathematical papers of Axel Thue, pp. 413–478. Universitetsforlaget, Oslo (1977)

Parsimonious Computational Completeness

Henning Fernau[(✉)] [iD]

FB 4 – Informatikwissenschaften, Universität Trier, 54286 Trier, Germany
fernau@uni-trier.de

Abstract. Throughout the history of Formal Languages, one of the research directions has always been to describe computational completeness using only a small amount of possibly scarce resources. We review some of these results in the form of an essay.

Keywords: Normal forms · Computational completeness · Descriptional complexity

1 Introduction: A Historical Perspective

Automata. Nearly from the beginning of the development of the theory of Formal Languages, the question was raised if computational completeness can be reached by restricting available resources. For instance, Claude Shannon [69] has shown that, concerning Turing machines, 2-element state sets or 2-element tape alphabets suffice for this purpose. Also, Shannon argued that singleton state sets are not sufficient to allow for arbitrarily complex computations.

Shannon is probably best known for his "invention" of information theory [68], and so is Marvin Minsky, our next protagonist in this historical essay, nowadays rather hailed for his contributions to the foundations of Artificial Intelligence, maybe starting out from [54], than for his contributions in Formal Languages. In videos 72&73[1], Minsky describes how a problem of Emil Post that he was told by his former advisor Martin Davis led him to the "invention" of what is nowadays often called a Minsky machine, or a register machine, or a counter automaton. But as Minsky acknowledges in the description of "program machines" (as he called them) in his textbook [55], his line of research was highly influenced by Hao Wang. Wang wrote in the introduction of his paper [76]: *The principle purpose of this paper is to offer a theory which is closely related to Turing's but is more economical in the basic operations.* Here, *economy* refers to a very reduced instruction set, combined with a 2-way infinite tape: moving the 'Turing head' left or right (shifting), marking a square (i.e., there is a single non-blank tape symbol) or a conditional jump (if the current tape symbol is marked, go to instruction n). But, just by definition, the computational completeness of

---

[1] Out of a series of 151 short videos showing interviews with Minsky within the Web of Stories - Life Stories of Remarkable People.

© Springer Nature Switzerland AG 2021
N. Moreira and R. Reis (Eds.): DLT 2021, LNCS 12811, pp. 12–26, 2021.
https://doi.org/10.1007/978-3-030-81508-0_2

Wang's machine re-proves the mentioned completeness result of Shannon about binary tape alphabets.

Although this *economy* or *parsimony* was first introduced more out of mathematical curiosity, and this kind of intrinsic motivation continues to exist until today, there is also another (more practical) aspect to the word *economy*: It could well be that certain resources of computational devices are very expensive, so it would literally pay off to save on these resources. To substantiate this claim with a modern example, consider existing quantum computers: qbits are still a rare and expensive resource.

Let us return to the reduced instruction set machines of Wang and Minsky: in their most parsimonious form, 2-counter machines can simulate Turing machines, as Minsky proved [55].[2] However, there is a caveat to this assertion (if it comes to using it for proving other computational completeness results): it is not that clear how input is first fed into these machines; this has to be done first 'somehow'. A similar problem is faced with Wang's B-machines (as he called them), and Wang clearly pronounced it in his treatment [76]. Interestingly enough, a similar problem is faced nowadays with quantum computers: before running them, a 'classical input' has to be fed into them, which is kind of destroying the idea of running sub-linear algorithms. So, this aspect is not just a mathematical artefact.

Another variety of computationally complete devices are tag systems [53,62]. Also here, the parsimony principle was applied: it is known that it is sufficient to remove a prefix of two symbols and append two encoded words at the end to describe a Turing-equivalent mechanism [5]. Again, this leads to a reduced set of instructions for this type of machinery, and it is possibly no coincidence that the first author of this paper, John Cocke, then working with the IBM Research Division, reported on the *evolution of RISC technology at IBM* in [4], a processor architecture that was literally implementing this parsimony idea.

Grammars. While the benefits of parsimony in machine models is pretty obvious, this might be less the case with grammatical models, as there is no direct hardware implementation. This starts by their very motivation, that was purely linguistic, as elaborated by Noam Chomsky in [2]. Chomsky later proved [3] that phrase structure grammars can be used to describe all recursively enumerable languages, this way linking his linguistic theory with the already developed theory of recursive functions via Turing machines. But what should now take the

---

[2] If somebody wonders about how one of the 'fathers of AI' and the philosophy behind could write one of the first textbooks on Automata Theory, let Minsky himself make the link in the preface of his book: *The abstract theory—as described in this book— tells us in no uncertain terms that the machines' potential range is enormous, and that its theoretical limitations are of the subtlest and most elusive sort. There is no reason to suppose machines have any limitations not shared by man.* But this role of Minsky created some peculiar situations until today; for instance, the said book is collected within the 'methodological books' in the part of our university library dedicated to psychology. Presumably, this was because one part of the book explains a mathematical model of neural networks.

role of internal states or of tape symbols, two quantities discussed above for Turing machines?

In a sense, both combine into one entity in phrase structure grammars, namely, into *nonterminal symbols*. This very fact is already interesting, as it also (implicitly) raises the question if one could limit both the number of internal states and the number of tape symbols with Turing machines; for instance, Shannon's constructions [69] discussed above limit either of these quantities but not both at the same time. This question for Turing machines is, in a sense, answered by constructing small *universal* Turing machines; see [57] for a survey. There is also an answer in a different direction: Turing machines that both have a small number of states and a small number of tape symbols can only accept very restricted languages, mostly regular ones, as shown in [8,47] (giving also quite some references to other, often Russian, publications in this direction).

As the *nonterminal complexity* forms quite an interesting topic of its own interest, we defer its discussion to Sect. 2.

From a historical perspective, it should be also noted that normal forms that restrict the *structure* of rules in grammars are what has been considered next. Concerning context-free grammars, the possibly best known examples (also taught in classical textbooks on Formal Languages) are the Chomsky and the Greibach normal forms. However, more important for the present discussion are normal forms for type-1 or type-0 grammars. Here, the linguist Sige-Yuki Kuroda proved [48] that for each type-1 grammar (without erasing productions), there is an equivalent grammar[3] that uses only rules of the following forms: $A \rightarrow a$, $A \rightarrow B$, $A \rightarrow BC$, $AB \rightarrow CD$, where A, B, C, D are nonterminals and a is a terminal symbol. Notice that the first three types of rules are 'simple' in the sense of being context-free. We could therefore consider rules of the fourth type as being an expensive resource. We are not aware of any results that bound the number of rules of the form $AB \rightarrow CD$ for monotone grammars. However, when admitting erasing rules, we also get a Kuroda normal form for type-0 grammars. As detailed in Sect. 2, it is possible to bring down the number of rules of the form $AB \rightarrow CD$ to two. It seems to be unknown if one such rule suffices for describing every recursively enumerable language.

Let us return to the Kuroda normal form. There have been several attempts to further simplify it. For instance, Kuroda himself [48] suggested on page 211 to replace rules of the form $AB \rightarrow CD$ by $AB \rightarrow A'B$, $A'B \rightarrow A'D$ and $A'D \rightarrow CD$ (where A' is a fresh nonterminal) in order to turn Kuroda normal form grammars into context-sensitive grammars. This is a tempting construction, but unfortunately, it is wrong, as observed by György E. Révész in [64]. He suggested to consider the following set of rules as a basis for a counter-example: $S \rightarrow AB$, $B \rightarrow DE$, $AB \rightarrow CD$. Clearly, $S \Rightarrow^* CDE$ is not possible with these rules. However, after the replacements suggested by Kuroda,

$$S \Rightarrow AB \Rightarrow A'B \Rightarrow A'DE \Rightarrow CDE$$

---

[3] A further restricted form thereof Kuroda himself termed *linear-bounded grammar*, but our definition corresponds to what is nowadays called *Kuroda normal form*.

is a possible derivation. This mistake is quite instructive and shows that one has to be quite careful with checking 'simple constructions'. Révész also offered a fix in his paper, sometimes referred to as "Révész's trick". One has to take two fresh nonterminals A', B' and four replacement rules for $AB \to CD$: $AB \to A'B$, $A'B \to A'B'$, $A'B' \to CB'$ and $CB' \to CD$. Furthermore, Révész explained how to get rid of the chain rules $A \to B$. Again, this is not completely trivial, and an incorrect idea was published before. Further improvements of this normal form are due to Martti Penttonen: each type-1 grammar (without erasing productions) can be replaced by a context-sensitive grammar only having rules of the forms $A \to a, A \to BC, AB \to AC$, where A, B, C are nonterminals and a is a terminal symbol. Here, not only chain rules were eliminated and all rules are context-sensitive, but also context-sensitivity is only used in a left context. Again, when admitting additional erasing rules, we arrive at a Penttonen normal form for recursively enumerable languages. However, it is open if it is possible to delimit the number of context-sensitive rules of the form $AB \to AC$ in a Penttonen normal form grammar.

Another type of normal form was achieved by Walter A. Savitch [67]: He showed that every recursively enumerable languages can be generated by some type-0 grammar that contains, apart from context-free rules, only erasing rules of the form $AB \to \lambda$. The natural question if one can delimit the number of these erasing non-context-free rules. Again, this question will be answered affirmatively in Sect. 2.[4] Notice that Savitch's normal form also implies Kuroda's for type-0 grammars, as one can choose a fresh nonterminal Λ with a rule $\Lambda \to \lambda$ and then replace $AB \to \lambda$ by $AB \to \Lambda\Lambda$.

2 Nonterminal Complexity

In [66], it was shown that three nonterminals suffice to describe every recursively enumerable language with a type-0 grammar. However, this proof is a bit cheating, because it heavily uses possible replacements of terminal symbols. Can we achieve similar results if further replacements of terminal symbols are not allowed? This question was solved by Villiam Geffert in his PhD thesis [38]. For our exposition, the most important material can be also found in [40]. As also the intermediate results of Geffert are quite interesting in our context, let us present these in some more breadth.

Extended Post Correspondences. Geffert's construction starts with so-called g-systems, a computationally complete mechanism introduced by Geffert's PhD advisor Branislav Rovan [65]. By simulating g-systems, it is then shown that also so-called *extended Post correspondences* (or EPC for short) characterize the recursively enumerable languages. They are defined by a language alphabet Σ

---

[4] With different arguments, the fact that two such erasing non-context-free rules suffice to reach computational completeness was also explained in [41], pointing to several earlier papers. We also refer to [38,39].

and a tuple $P = (\{(u_i, v_i) \mid 1 \le i \le r\}, \{z_a \mid a \in \Sigma\})$, where the elements u_i, v_i, z_a are all words over the binary alphabet $\{0, 1\}$. This also defines a homomorphism $h : \Sigma \to \{0, 1\}^*, a \mapsto z_a$. Then, the language $L(P) \subseteq \Sigma^*$ is defined as

$$L(P) = \{w \in \Sigma^* \mid \exists i_1, \dots i_\ell : v_{i_1} \cdots v_{i_\ell} = u_{i_1} \cdots u_{i_\ell} h(w)\}.$$

The classical Post correspondence problem (also known as PCP) was introduced by Post [63] and, interestingly enough, one of its motivations that helped introduce the PCP in any standard textbook on Automata Theory and Formal Languages was the particular simplicity of the PCP as an undecidable problem.[5] The PCP could be formally introduced as the question if, for a given EPC P (with $\Sigma = \emptyset$), $L(P) \ne \emptyset$. It is known that PCPs with two word pairs (i.e., $\ell = 2$) give a decidable problem, but with five (and more) word pairs, PCP is (already) undecidable, while the case of three or four word pairs is still open; see [9,56]. Also, it is unclear if these bounds on the number of word pairs translate to EPC.

Geffert Normal Form. The computational completeness result for EPC is then used by Geffert to prove that each recursively enumerable language can be generated by a type-0 grammar that contains only five nonterminals, say, S, A, B, C, D and only context-free rules (of the form $S \to v$) but the two erasing rules $AB \to \lambda$ and $CD \to \lambda$. This is also known as *Geffert normal form*. To show this result, consider an EPC $P = (\{(u_i, v_i) \mid 1 \le i \le r\}, \{z_a \mid a \in \Sigma\})$ and the homomorphisms $g_1 : 0 \mapsto A, 1 \mapsto C$ and $g_2 : 0 \mapsto B, 1 \mapsto D$. For each $a \in \Sigma$, introduce the rule $S \to \overleftarrow{g_1(z_a)}Sa$.[6] For each i, $1 \le i \le r$, introduce $S \to \overleftarrow{g_1(u_i)}Sg_2(v_i)$ and $S \to \overleftarrow{g_1(u_i)}g_2(v_i)$. Together with the mentioned erasing rules, this specifies a type-0 grammar G_P. Now, $v_{i_1} \cdots v_{i_\ell} = u_{i_1} \cdots u_{i_\ell} h(w)$ means that the sentential form $\overleftarrow{g_1(h(w))}\overleftarrow{g_1(u_{i_\ell})} \cdots \overleftarrow{g_1(u_{i_1})}g_2(v_{i_1}) \cdots g_2(v_{i_\ell})w$ can be derived in G_P, and then the erasing rules test if, indeed, $v_{i_1} \cdots v_{i_\ell} = u_{i_1} \cdots u_{i_\ell} h(w)$. If the test succeeds, then the terminal word w is produced. For the reverse direction, it is important to show that indeed first the rules $S \to \overleftarrow{g_1(z_a)}Sa$ have to be used and then the other rules with left-hand side S. When simulating Geffert normal form grammars, this has to be taken into account, to avoid malicious derivations.

Coding Tricks. Recall the role of the two morphisms g_1 and g_2 whose purpose was to differentiate between left and right sides with respect to the 'central' nonterminal S, this way preparing the matching test with the rules $AB \to \lambda$ and $CD \to \lambda$. With using different morphisms, possibly forgoing the distinction between left and right sides concerning S, Geffert could show further computational completeness results.

---

[5] Observe that according to our definition, PCPs are collections of word pairs over a binary alphabet; of course, one could also consider such word pair collections over arbitrary alphabets, but we stick to this simpler case in our treatment.

[6] We use $\overleftarrow{w}$ to denote the mirror (or reversal) of word w.

G'_P with the morphisms $g'_1 : 0 \mapsto CAA, 1 \mapsto CA$ and $g'_2 : 0 \mapsto CBB, 1 \mapsto CB$: sentential forms like $\overleftarrow{g'_1(h(w))} \; \overleftarrow{g'_1(u_{i_\ell})} \cdots \overleftarrow{g'_1(u_{i_1})} g'_2(v_{i_1}) \cdots g'_2(v_{i_\ell}) w$ can be derived in G'_P that can be checked with rules $AB \to \lambda$ and $CC \to \lambda$.

G''_P with the morphisms $g''_1 : 0 \mapsto BBA, 1 \mapsto BA$ and $g''_2 : 0 \mapsto BA, 1 \mapsto BBA$: sentential forms like $\overleftarrow{g''_1(h(w))} \; \overleftarrow{g''_1(u_{i_\ell})} \cdots \overleftarrow{g''_1(u_{i_1})} g''_2(v_{i_1}) \cdots g''_2(v_{i_\ell}) w$ can be derived in G''_P that can be checked with rules $AA \to \lambda$ and $BBB \to \lambda$, or, alternatively, with the single (but longer) erasing rule $ABBBA \to \lambda$.

G'''_P with the morphisms $g'''_1 : 0 \mapsto BA, 1 \mapsto A$ and $g'''_2 : 0 \mapsto C, 1 \mapsto BC$: sentential forms like $\overleftarrow{g'''_1(h(w))} \; \overleftarrow{g'''_1(u_{i_\ell})} \cdots \overleftarrow{g'''_1(u_{i_1})} g'''_2(v_{i_1}) \cdots g'''_2(v_{i_\ell}) w$ can be derived in G'''_P that can be checked with the single erasing rule $ABC \to \lambda$.

Although G''_P offers the strongest normal form result for type-0 grammars with respect to nonterminal complexity (three nonterminals suffice to generate every recursively enumerable language), other normal forms offer some 'structural advantages', so that it is not always advisable to choose G''_P in order to prove computational completeness results, as shown below. For the ease of reference, we write (n, r)-GNF to refer to the Geffert normal form that uses n nonterminals and r non-context-free (erasing) rules. Hence, so far we presented $(5, 2)$-GNF, $(4, 2)$-GNF, $(3, 2)$-GNF, $(3, 1)$-GNF, and $(4, 1)$-GNF, in this order.

We strongly conjecture that one single nonterminal is not sufficient to describe every recursively enumerable language with some type-0 grammar, but as far as we know, neither this question is settled nor the question if two nonterminals suffice to generate every recursively enumerable language.

Sometimes, further modifications are necessary to produce useful normal forms. For instance, correctness proofs might become easier when the two 'uses' of the nonterminal S in $S \to \overleftarrow{g_1(z_a)} Sa$ and $S \to \overleftarrow{g_1(u_i)} S g_2(v_i)$ are separated by introducing a further nonterminal, as made explicit in [32]. Tomas Masopust and Alexander Meduna [51] developed the idea to forgo the use of the coding functions g_i (i.e., they are the identity) but to rather use a new nonterminal $\$$ to indicate the test phase that is maintained (and finally left) with the rules $0\$0 \to \$, 1\$1 \to \$, \$ \to \lambda$. Now, sentential forms like $\overleftarrow{h(w)} \overleftarrow{u_{i_\ell}} \cdots \overleftarrow{u_{i_1}} \$ v_{i_1} \cdots v_{i_\ell} w$ can be derived and then tested. We call this normal form MMNF for short. We even found an application of the variant where the morphism $\neg : 0 \mapsto 1, 1 \mapsto 0$ is used, in combination with the rules $0\$1 \to \$, 1\$0 \to \$, \$ \to \lambda$. Sentential forms like $\overleftarrow{h(w)} \overleftarrow{u_{i_\ell}} \cdots \overleftarrow{u_{i_1}} \$ \neg v_{i_1} \cdots \neg v_{i_\ell} w$ can be derived and then tested. We called this variant *modified Masopust-Meduna normal form*, or MMMNF for short, in [32].

Special Geffert Normal Form. The idea of this normal form, also called SGNF for short, was due to Rudi Freund et al. [36]; it is particularly useful in the context of insertion-deletion systems (see Sect. 3). In that context, maybe surprisingly, the challenging part of the simulation is often posed by the context-free rules. Here, it is important to have right-hand sides of length at most two, only. This can be enforced by 'spelling out' longer strings, but then, one clearly pays with additional nonterminals. So, this story-line is more about structural simplicity.

Regulated Rewriting. There are only rare occasions of grammatical mechanisms where the exact borderline between computational completeness and computational incompleteness is known with respect to the nonterminal complexity. For instance, it is shown in [16] that any recursively enumerable language can be generated by some graph-controlled grammar (using context-free core rules) with only two nonterminals, while we also proved that one nonterminal is insufficient.

These results come with some anecdotes that fit into this essay. Jürgen Dassow showed in [6] that eleven nonterminals suffice to generate each recursively enumerable set with a programmed grammar, based on [66]. In the same year, Gheorghe Păun proved in [59] that six nonterminals are sufficient for computational completeness in matrix grammars. As programmed and matrix grammars are special cases of graph-controlled grammars (also see [12,15,35]), corresponding results for graph-control hold. Then, on my first flight to Australia, more than 20 years ago, I had an idea how to further bring down the number of nonterminals. I took my laptop computer and started typing my ideas, and when touching down-under, most of the paper was ready, so that I could still submit it [13] to MCU 2001. What I did not know at that time was that, independently, Freund and Păun worked on this topic and also sent another paper to the same conference [37]. The approaches were different: while I started out with simulating Turing machines [13,14], Freund and Păun took register machines. However, with hindsight, the approaches were not that different. Namely, the Turing machine simulation used the nonterminals to store numbers encoding configurations, switching between different nonterminal representations to access and move the head position. Although I was not aware of this fact by that time, this is quite similar to Minsky's constructions [55] of 'program machines' using few registers (as discussed in Sect. 1), the basis of the approach of Freund and Păun. Then, we joined forces [16], and with two more colleagues we could further improve these descriptional complexity results, partially to provable optimality.

3   Indian Connections

Recently, I have been pretty active and involved in various aspects of descriptional complexity concerning especially computational complete variations of insertion-deletion systems. How did I get involved? About five years ago, I was visiting India. More precisely, I delivered some talks on invitation of Madras Christian College (MCC), the university where my (at that time) PhD student Meenakshi Paramasivan [58] graduated. Also, I traveled to Kerala to present a paper on a completely different topic [1]. Actually shortly before traveling to India, I started being in contacts with Lakshmanan Kuppusamy. Hence, together with his family, he came down from Vellore to Chennai to talk to me. This was triggering quite some active collaboration, both on insertion-deletion systems [17,20–25,27,29–31,33,72] and on more classical regulated rewriting [18,19,26,28,32]. As the (growing) list of co-authors indicates, the collaboration was later enriched and deepened by meeting with Sergey Verlan in Paris (in fact, a trip to Paris could be quite an adventure, as Kuppusamy and me experienced, but this is another story) and by visits in Trier both of Kuppusamy, of

Indhumathi Raman, and of Rufus Oladele from Nigeria. We now report on the connections of these research projects to the topics discussed so far in this essay.

Insertion-Deletion Systems. Since the 1990s, there have been various attempts to create a formal basis of models for DNA computing; see [45,61]. One of the key observations here is that insertions and deletions play a central role in such formalisms [44]. Research of formal systems based on these operations was initiated by Lila Kari [42]. For the ease of possible implementations *in vitro*, quite from the early days of this area onwards, one of the main research questions was to look into the simplest possible models that can still achieve computational completeness, giving further motivation to study the parsimony principle.[7]

An *insertion-deletion system*, or *ins-del system* for short, is a construct $\gamma = (V, T, A, R)$, where V is an alphabet, $T \subseteq V$ is the terminal alphabet, A is a finite language over V, R is a finite set of triplets of the form $(u, \eta, v)_{ins}$ or $(u, \delta, v)_{del}$, where $(u, v) \in V^* \times V^*$ denotes the left and right context and $\eta, \delta \in V^+$ are the strings that are inserted or deleted. For $x, y \in V^*$, we write $x \Rightarrow y$ if y can be obtained from x by using either an insertion rule or a deletion rule. More formally, applying $(u, \eta, v)_{ins}$ on $x \in V^*$ means to find the substring uv in x, i.e., $x = x_1 uv x_2$, resulting in $y = x_1 u \eta v x_2$. To apply $(u, \delta, v)_{del}$ on $x \in V^*$, we have to find the substring $u\delta v$ in x, i.e., $x = x_1 u \delta v x_2$, and the result is $y = x_1 uv x_2$. The language generated by γ is $L(\gamma) = \{w \in T^* \mid x \Rightarrow^* w, \text{ for some } x \in A\}$, where $\Rightarrow^*$ denotes the reflexive and transitive closure of the relation $\Rightarrow$. A tuple $(n, i', i''; m, j', j'')$ is associated with an ins-del system to denote its size, where n denotes the maximal length of the insertion string, i' denotes the maximal length of the left context for insertion, i'' the maximal length of the right context for insertion; m is the maximal length of the deletion string, j' is the maximal length of the left context for deletion, and j'' is the maximal length of the right context for deletion. For instance, it is known that insertion-deletion systems of sizes $(1, 1, 1; 1, 1, 1)$, $(1, 1, 1; 2, 0, 0)$, $(2, 0, 0; 1, 1, 1)$, $(2, 0, 0; 3, 0, 0)$ or $(3, 0, 0; 2, 0, 0)$ are computationally complete (see [50,70]), while upon decreasing any of the non-zero size parameter bounds, we arrive at systems that are not capable to simulate every Turing machine; see [46,52]. We also refer to Verlan's survey [71]. Some of the proofs make use of Kuroda normal form grammars, as described above.

To further improve on the size bounds, the effect of regulation mechanisms put on ins-del systems has been studied. For instance, matrix control can be seen as (small) program fragments that prescribe in which order certain rules have to be executed. For instance, in [24], it was shown that with matrices containing at most three ins-del rules, for all $c_1, c_2, c_3, c_4 \in \{0, 1\}$ with $c_1 + c_2 + c_3 + c_4 = 2$, matrix ins-del systems of size $(1, c_1, c_2; 1, c_3, c_4)$ characterize the recursively enumerable languages. For matrix ins-del systems with at most two rules per matrix, sizes $(2, 0, 0; 1, c, c')$, $(1, 1, 1; 1, c, c')$, $(1, c, c'; 2, 0, 0)$ and $(1, c, c'; 1, 1, 1)$,

---

[7] For a discussion of programming languages tailored towards DNA computing, we refer to the study [49] conducted by Microsoft Research.

with $c, c' \in \{0, 1\}$ and $c + c' = 1$, reach computational completeness. All proofs were based on simulating type-0 grammars in SGNF.

Alternatively, one could allow further operations. Based on suggestions contained in [43], we studied the effect of adding so-called substitutions (allowing to replace a symbol a by another symbol b in a certain context) to ins-del systems. Indeed, they allow to decrease some of the mentioned descriptional complexity measures; we refer to [73–75] for the precise progress both compared to traditional ins-del systems and to matrix ins-del systems. This detour also allowed us to obtain new variations of Penttonen-style normal forms.

Back to Regulated Rewriting. About a quarter of a century ago, I was quite interested in this branch of Formal Languages, also, because it is focused on grammatical mechanisms that are 'kind of context-free' (and hence appear to be simple), yet they (often) reach the power of Turing machines. One variant, namely semi-conditional grammars, was introduced by Păun in 1985 [60]. Here, to each context-free rule $A \to w$, two strings w_+ and w_- are (possibly) attached, and the rule can only be applied to a sentential form x (in the usual manner) if w_+ is a substring (factor) of x (i.e., w_+ is a permitting string) and w_- is not a substring of x, (i.e., w_- is a forbidding string). Apart from the number n of nonterminals, also the so-called degree (d_+, d_-) is a natural measure of descriptional complexity, where d_+ upper-bounds the length of any w_+, and d_- upper-bounds the length of any w_-. Also, it is interesting to upper-bound the number c of rules that are conditional, i.e., at least one permitting or one forbidding string is attached to a conditional rule. In order to bound (n, d_+, d_-, c) so that semi-conditional grammars are still computationally complete, various Geffert normal forms turned out to be useful. For instance, the $(4, 2)$-GNF was the starting point to simulate the rule $AB \to \lambda$ by the rules labeled $1, 2, 3, 6, 6, 7$ and the rule $CC \to \lambda$ by the rules labeled $4, 5, 6, 6, 7$ in the following list of rules from [18]. This corresponds to a bound of $(6, 2, 1, \infty)$. There is no finite bound on the number of conditional rules, because the start symbol S was 'recycled'.

$$1: (A \to \$S, \ AB, \ S) \qquad 2: (B \to \#, \ \$S \ , \ \#)$$
$$3: (S \to \$ \ , \ S\#, \ 0 \ ) \qquad 4: (C \to \$\$, \ CC, \ \$ \ )$$
$$5: (C \to \# \ , \ \$\$ \ , \ \#) \qquad 6: (\$ \to \lambda \ , \ \$\#, \ 0 \ )$$
$$7: (\# \to \lambda \ , \ 0 \ \ , \ \$ \ ) \qquad w: (S \to w \ , \ 0 \ \ , \ \$ \ )$$

Here, 0 indicates that there is no context needed in the rule. It is clearly tempting to further 'optimize' this grammar by taking, say,

$$1: (A \to \$, \ AB, \ S) \qquad 2: (B \to \#, \ \$B, \ \#)$$

as the first two rules. So, we are hoping for a bound like $(6, 2, 1, 6)$, as the start symbol S is not re-used. However, consider a sentential form with a factor of the form $CCCB$. Such sentential forms might be derivable in the original type-0 grammar G, but (as Geffert has proved) they would never lead to terminal strings. Yet, in the simulating grammar G', we might apply the rules $4, 2, 6, 6, 7$, converting the factor $CCCB$ into CC, so that from now on, a terminal string might be derivable in G'. This explains how subtle these simulations could be.

All Geffert-like normal forms that we described are useful in simulations, having their pros and cons. We employed (nearly) all of them in our papers. More specifically, $(5, 2)$-GNF was used in [19], $(4, 2)$-GNF in [18, 28], $(3, 1)$-GNF in [18, 28], $(4, 1)$-GNF in [19, 28, 32], MMNF in [19], and MMMNF in [32].

4   Some Weird Grammars to Conclude

Finally, I would like to point to some grammatical mechanisms that were proven to be computationally complete, but which have, for instance, a decidable emptiness problem. This sounds weird, as the said mechanisms look quite innocent. For me, this adventure started out when proving that so-called 1-limited ET0L systems (introduced in [77]) have an undecidable membership problem [10], a result that is also true for k-limited ET0L systems in general [11]. (It is unknown if the language classes that can be described by 1-limited ET0L systems and by 2-limited ET0L systems coincide.) By [7, 12], there are a number of characterizations of the class of languages describable by 1-limited ET0L systems by regulated grammars with unconditional transfer. Yet, it is unknown if 1-limited ET0L systems characterize the recursively enumerable languages. This could only be achieved when adding a certain form of leftmost derivations [34]. Without going into details, it is at least possible to give a high-level explanation how computational completeness can be proved in such a situation. Namely, the trick is to use Higman's Lemma to infer that every language L can be decomposed in a finite collection of languages, each of which contains a certain subsequence (sparse subword) that is contained in L. Then, if a certain type of mistake in a simulation is detected, the derivation will continue and deliver the mentioned subsequence. The only non-constructive part of this 'construction' is indeed the mentioned decomposition. The descriptional complexity of these devices has not yet been investigated. Notice, however, that although the mentioned construction starts out with a traditional programmed grammar, we cannot use the fact that we might assume that they only have three nonterminals, because we must use different sets of nonterminals for the grammar parts forming the decomposition of L and there is no universal bound on the number of sets in this decomposition. Hence, this offers ample room to investigate the parsimony principle.

References

1. Bazgan, C., Brankovic, L., Casel, K., Fernau, H.: On the complexity landscape of the domination chain. In: Govindarajan, S., Maheshwari, A. (eds.) CALDAM 2016. LNCS, vol. 9602, pp. 61–72. Springer, Cham (2016). https://doi.org/10.1007/978-3-319-29221-2_6
2. Chomsky, N.: Three models for the description of language. IRE Trans. Inf. Theory **2**(3), 113–124 (1956)

3. Chomsky, N.: On certain formal properties of grammars. Inf. Control **2**, 137–167 (1959)
4. Cocke, J., Markstein, V.: The evolution of RISC technology at IBM. IBM J. Res. Dev. **34**(1), 4–11 (1990)
5. Cocke, J., Minsky, M.: Universality of tag systems with $P = 2$. J. ACM **11**(1), 15–20 (1964)
6. Dassow, J.: Remarks on the complexity of regulated rewriting. Fund. Inform. **7**, 83–103 (1984)
7. Dassow, J.: A remark on limited 0L systems. J. Inf. Process. Cybern. EIK **24**(6), 287–291 (1988)
8. Diekert, V., Kudlek, M.: Small deterministic turing machines. In: Gecseg, F., Peák, I. (eds.) Proceedings of 2nd Conference on Automata, Languages and Programming Systems, Salgótarján (Hungary) 1988, pp. 77–87. No. DM 88-4 in Technical report, Department of Mathematics, Karl Marx University of Economics (1988)
9. Ehrenfeucht, A., Karhumäki, J., Rozenberg, G.: The (generalized) Post correspondence problem with lists consisting of two words is decidable. Theoret. Comput. Sci. **21**, 119–144 (1982)
10. Fernau, H.: Membership for 1-limited ET0L languages is not decidable. J. Inf. Process. Cybern. EIK **30**(4), 191–211 (1994)
11. Fernau, H.: Membership for k-limited ET0L languages is not decidable. J. Autom. Lang. Comb. **1**, 243–245 (1996)
12. Fernau, H.: Unconditional transfer in regulated rewriting. Acta Informatica **34**, 837–857 (1997)
13. Fernau, H.: Nonterminal complexity of programmed grammars. In: Margenstern, M., Rogozhin, Y. (eds.) MCU 2001. LNCS, vol. 2055, pp. 202–213. Springer, Heidelberg (2001). https://doi.org/10.1007/3-540-45132-3_13
14. Fernau, H.: Nonterminal complexity of programmed grammars. Theoret. Comput. Sci. **296**, 225–251 (2003)
15. Fernau, H.: An essay on general grammars. J. Autom. Lang. Comb. **21**, 69–92 (2016)
16. Fernau, H., Freund, R., Oswald, M., Reinhardt, K.: Refining the nonterminal complexity of graph-controlled, programmed, and matrix grammars. J. Autom. Lang. Comb. **12**(1/2), 117–138 (2007)
17. Fernau, H., Kuppusamy, L.: Parikh images of matrix ins-del systems. In: Gopal, T.V., Jäger, G., Steila, S. (eds.) TAMC 2017. LNCS, vol. 10185, pp. 201–215. Springer, Cham (2017). https://doi.org/10.1007/978-3-319-55911-7_15
18. Fernau, H., Kuppusamy, L., Oladele, R.O.: New nonterminal complexity results for semi-conditional grammars. In: Manea, F., Miller, R.G., Nowotka, D. (eds.) CiE 2018. LNCS, vol. 10936, pp. 172–182. Springer, Cham (2018). https://doi.org/10.1007/978-3-319-94418-0_18
19. Fernau, H., Kuppusamy, L., Oladele, R.O., Raman, I.: Improved descriptional complexity results on generalized forbidding grammars. Discret. Appl. Math. (2021). https://doi.org/10.1016/j.dam.2020.12.027
20. Fernau, H., Kuppusamy, L., Raman, I.: Graph-controlled insertion-deletion systems generating language classes beyond linearity. In: Pighizzini, G., Câmpeanu, C. (eds.) DCFS 2017. LNCS, vol. 10316, pp. 128–139. Springer, Cham (2017). https://doi.org/10.1007/978-3-319-60252-3_10
21. Fernau, H., Kuppusamy, L., Raman, I.: On the computational completeness of graph-controlled insertion-deletion systems with binary sizes. Theor. Comput. Sci. **682**, 100–121 (2017). Special Issue on Languages and Combinatorics in Theory and Nature

22. Fernau, H., Kuppusamy, L., Raman, I.: On the generative power of graph-controlled insertion-deletion systems with small sizes. J. Autom. Lang. Comb. **22**, 61–92 (2017)
23. Fernau, H., Kuppusamy, L., Raman, I.: Computational completeness of simple semi-conditional insertion-deletion systems. In: Stepney, S., Verlan, S. (eds.) UCNC 2018. LNCS, vol. 10867, pp. 86–100. Springer, Cham (2018). https://doi.org/10.1007/978-3-319-92435-9_7
24. Fernau, H., Kuppusamy, L., Raman, I.: Investigations on the power of matrix insertion-deletion systems with small sizes. Nat. Comput. **17**(2), 249–269 (2018)
25. Fernau, H., Kuppusamy, L., Raman, I.: On describing the regular closure of the linear languages with graph-controlled insertion-deletion systems. RAIRO Informatique théorique et Applications/Theor. Inform. Appl. **52**(1), 1–21 (2018)
26. Fernau, H., Kuppusamy, L., Raman, I.: Properties of language classes between linear and context-free. J. Autom. Lang. Comb. **23**(4), 329–360 (2018)
27. Fernau, H., Kuppusamy, L., Raman, I.: Computational completeness of simple semi-conditional insertion-deletion systems of degree (2, 1). Nat. Comput. **18**(3), 563–577 (2019)
28. Fernau, H., Kuppusamy, L., Raman, I.: Descriptional complexity of matrix simple semi-conditional grammars. In: Hospodár, M., Jirásková, G., Konstantinidis, S. (eds.) DCFS 2019. LNCS, vol. 11612, pp. 111–123. Springer, Cham (2019). https://doi.org/10.1007/978-3-030-23247-4_8
29. Fernau, H., Kuppusamy, L., Raman, I.: On matrix ins-del systems of small sum-norm. In: Catania, B., Královič, R., Nawrocki, J., Pighizzini, G. (eds.) SOFSEM 2019. LNCS, vol. 11376, pp. 192–205. Springer, Cham (2019). https://doi.org/10.1007/978-3-030-10801-4_16
30. Fernau, H., Kuppusamy, L., Raman, I.: On path-controlled insertion-deletion systems. Acta Informatica **56**(1), 35–59 (2019)
31. Fernau, H., Kuppusamy, L., Raman, I.: On the power of generalized forbidding insertion-deletion systems. In: Jirásková, G., Pighizzini, G. (eds.) DCFS 2020. LNCS, vol. 12442, pp. 52–63. Springer, Cham (2020). https://doi.org/10.1007/978-3-030-62536-8_5
32. Fernau, H., Kuppusamy, L., Raman, I.: Generalized forbidding matrix grammars and their membrane computing perspective. In: Freund, R., Ishdorj, T.-O., Rozenberg, G., Salomaa, A., Zandron, C. (eds.) CMC 2020. LNCS, vol. 12687, pp. 31–45. Springer, Cham (2021). https://doi.org/10.1007/978-3-030-77102-7_3
33. Fernau, H., Kuppusamy, L., Verlan, S.: Universal matrix insertion grammars with small size. In: Patitz, M.J., Stannett, M. (eds.) UCNC 2017. LNCS, vol. 10240, pp. 182–193. Springer, Cham (2017). https://doi.org/10.1007/978-3-319-58187-3_14
34. Fernau, H., Stephan, F.: Characterizations of recursively enumerable languages by programmed grammars with unconditional transfer. J. Autom. Lang. Comb. **4**(2), 117–142 (1999)
35. Freund, R.: A general framework for sequential grammars with control mechanisms. In: Hospodár, M., Jirásková, G., Konstantinidis, S. (eds.) DCFS 2019. LNCS, vol. 11612, pp. 1–34. Springer, Cham (2019). https://doi.org/10.1007/978-3-030-23247-4_1
36. Freund, R., Kogler, M., Rogozhin, Y., Verlan, S.: Graph-controlled insertion-deletion systems. In: McQuillan, I., Pighizzini, G. (eds.) Proceedings Twelfth Annual Workshop on Descriptional Complexity of Formal Systems, DCFS. EPTCS, vol. 31, pp. 88–98 (2010)

24		H. Fernau

37. Freund, R., Păun, G.: On the number of non-terminal symbols in graph-controlled, programmed and matrix grammars. In: Margenstern, M., Rogozhin, Y. (eds.) MCU 2001. LNCS, vol. 2055, pp. 214–225. Springer, Heidelberg (2001). https://doi.org/10.1007/3-540-45132-3_14
38. Geffert, V.: Problémy zložitosti generatívnych systémov (in Slovak). Ph.D. thesis, Katedra teoretickej kybernetiky, Matematicko-fyzikálnej fakulty UK, Bratislava (1987)
39. Geffert, V.: How to generate languages using only two pairs of parentheses. J. Inf. Process. Cybern. EIK **27**(5/6), 303–315 (1991)
40. Geffert, V.: Normal forms for phrase-structure grammars. RAIRO Informatique théorique et Applications/Theor. Inform. Appl. **25**, 473–498 (1991)
41. Jantzen, M., Kudlek, M., Lange, K.-J., Petersen, H.: $Dyck_1$-reductions of context-free languages. In: Budach, L., Bukharajev, R.G., Lupanov, O.B. (eds.) FCT 1987. LNCS, vol. 278, pp. 218–227. Springer, Heidelberg (1987). https://doi.org/10.1007/3-540-18740-5_45
42. Kari, L.: On insertions and deletions in formal languages. Ph.D. thesis, University of Turku, Finland (1991)
43. Kari, L.: DNA computing: arrival of biological mathematics. Math. Intell. **19**(2), 9–22 (1997)
44. Kari, L., Daley, M., Gloor, G., Siromoney, R., Landweber, L.F.: How to compute with DNA. In: Rangan, C.P., Raman, V., Ramanujam, R. (eds.) FSTTCS 1999. LNCS, vol. 1738, pp. 269–282. Springer, Heidelberg (1999). https://doi.org/10.1007/3-540-46691-6_21
45. Kari, L., Păun, Gh., Thierrin, G., Yu, S.: At the crossroads of DNA computing and formal languages: characterizing recursively enumerable languages using insertion-deletion systems. In: Rubin, H., Wood, D.H. (eds.) DNA Based Computers III, DIMACS Series in Discrete Mathematics and Theretical Computer Science, vol. 48, pp. 329–338. AMS (1999)
46. Krassovitskiy, A., Rogozhin, Y., Verlan, S.: Computational power of insertion-deletion (P) systems with rules of size two. Nat. Comput. **10**, 835–852 (2011)
47. Kudlek, M.: Small deterministic Turing machines. Theoret. Comput. Sci. **168**(2), 241–255 (1996)
48. Kuroda, S.Y.: Classes of languages and linear-bounded automata. Inf. Control **7**, 207–223 (1964)
49. Lakin, M.R., Phillips, A.: Domain-specific programming languages for computational nucleic acid systems. ACS Synth. Biol. **9**(7), 1499–1513 (2020)
50. Margenstern, M., Păun, Gh., Rogozhin, Y., Verlan, S.: Context-free insertion-deletion systems. Theoret. Comput. Sci. **330**(2), 339–348 (2005)
51. Masopust, T., Meduna, A.: Descriptional complexity of generalized forbidding grammars. In: Geffert, V., Pighizzini, G. (eds.) 9th International Workshop on Descriptional Complexity of Formal Systems - DCFS, pp. 170–177. University of Kosice, Slovakia (2007)
52. Matveevici, A., Rogozhin, Y., Verlan, S.: Insertion-deletion systems with one-sided contexts. In: Durand-Lose, J., Margenstern, M. (eds.) MCU 2007. LNCS, vol. 4664, pp. 205–217. Springer, Heidelberg (2007). https://doi.org/10.1007/978-3-540-74593-8_18
53. Minsky, M.L.: Recursive unsolvability of post's problem of "tag" and other topics in theory of Turing machines. Ann. Math. **74**(3), 437–455 (1961)
54. Minsky, M.L.: Steps toward artificial intelligence. Proc. IRE **49**, 8–30 (1961)
55. Minsky, M.L.: Computation: Finite and Infinite Machines. Prentice Hall, Hoboken (1967)

56. Neary, T.: Undecidability in binary tag systems and the Post correspondence problem for five pairs of words. In: Mayr, E.W., Ollinger, N. (eds.) 32nd International Symposium on Theoretical Aspects of Computer Science, STACS. LIPIcs, vol. 30, pp. 649–661. Schloss Dagstuhl - Leibniz-Zentrum für Informatik (2015)
57. Neary, T., Woods, D.: The complexity of small universal Turing machines: a survey. In: Bieliková, M., Friedrich, G., Gottlob, G., Katzenbeisser, S., Turán, G. (eds.) SOFSEM 2012. LNCS, vol. 7147, pp. 385–405. Springer, Heidelberg (2012). https://doi.org/10.1007/978-3-642-27660-6_32
58. Paramasivan, M.: Operations on graphs, arrays and automata. Ph.D. thesis, Fachbereich IV, Universität Trier, Germany (2017)
59. Păun, Gh.: Six nonterminals are enough for generating each R.E. language by a matrix grammar. Int. J. Comput. Math. **15**(1–4), 23–37 (1984)
60. Păun, Gh.: A variant of random context grammars: semi-conditional grammars. Theoret. Comput. Sci. **41**, 1–17 (1985)
61. Păun, Gh., Rozenberg, G., Salomaa, A.: DNA Computing: New Computing Paradigms. Springer, Heidelberg (1998). https://doi.org/10.1007/978-3-662-03563-4
62. Post, E.L.: Formal reductions of the general combinatorial decision problem. Am. J. Math. **65**(2), 197–215 (1943)
63. Post, E.L.: A variant of a recursively unsolvable problem. Bull. Am. Math. Soc. **52**(4), 264–268 (1946)
64. Révész, G.E.: Comment on the paper "error detection in formal languages". J. Comput. Syst. Sci. **8**(2), 238–242 (1974)
65. Rovan, B.: A framework for studying grammars. In: Gruska, J., Chytil, M. (eds.) MFCS 1981. LNCS, vol. 118, pp. 473–482. Springer, Heidelberg (1981). https://doi.org/10.1007/3-540-10856-4_115
66. Rozenberg, G., Vermeir, D.: On the effect of the finite index restriction on several families of grammars; Part 2: context dependent systems and grammars. Found. Control Eng. **3**(3), 126–142 (1978)
67. Savitch, W.J.: How to make arbitrary grammars look like context-free grammars. SIAM J. Comput. **2**(3), 174–182 (1973)
68. Shannon, C.E.: A mathematical theory of communication. Bell Syst. Tech. J. **27**, 379–423 & 623–656 (1948)
69. Shannon, C.E.: A universal Turing machine with two internal states. In: Shannon, C.E., McCarthy, J. (eds.) Automata Studies, Annals of Mathematics Studies, vol. 34, pp. 157–165. Princeton University Press, Princeton (1956)
70. Takahara, A., Yokomori, T.: On the computational power of insertion-deletion systems. Nat. Comput. **2**(4), 321–336 (2003)
71. Verlan, S.: Recent developments on insertion-deletion systems. Comput. Sci. J. Moldova **18**(2), 210–245 (2010)
72. Verlan, S., Fernau, H., Kuppusamy, L.: Universal insertion grammars of size two. Theoret. Comput. Sci. **843**, 153–163 (2020)
73. Vu, M., Fernau, H.: Insertion-deletion systems with substitutions I. In: Anselmo, M., Della Vedova, G., Manea, F., Pauly, A. (eds.) CiE 2020. LNCS, vol. 12098, pp. 366–378. Springer, Cham (2020). https://doi.org/10.1007/978-3-030-51466-2_33
74. Vu, M., Fernau, H.: Insertion-deletion with substitutions II. In: Jirásková, G., Pighizzini, G. (eds.) DCFS 2020. LNCS, vol. 12442, pp. 231–243. Springer, Cham (2020). https://doi.org/10.1007/978-3-030-62536-8_19
75. Vu, M., Fernau, H.: Adding matrix control: insertion-deletion systems with substitutions III. Algorithms **14**(5) (2021). https://doi.org/10.3390/a14050131

76. Wang, H.: A variant to Turing's theory of computing machines. J. ACM **4**(1), 63–92 (1957)
77. Wätjen, D.: k-limited 0L systems and languages. J. Inf. Process. Cybern. EIK **24**(6), 267–285 (1988)

Pointlike Sets and Separation: A Personal Perspective

Benjamin Steinberg[✉]

Department of Mathematics, City College of New York,
Convent Avenue at 138th Street, New York, NY 10031, USA
bsteinberg@ccny.cuny.edu

Abstract. This is a personal survey about pointlike sets since their
inception to roughly the present. Personal means that I make no attempt
to be exhaustive, but rather to highlight things that have affected my
research in the area or that I consider fundamental to the area. Pointlike
sets, in the language of separation and covering problems, have become
very popular now in Computer Science because of the truly amazing
work of Place and Zeitoun on dot-depth and related hierarchies. I believe
revisiting some of the older results will revive interest and provide perspective.

Keywords: Pointlike sets · Separation

1 Pointlike Sets: Definitions and Reformulations

This article is a short survey on old and new results about pointlike sets and
separation, focusing primarily on areas in which I have worked, and including
occasional personal anecdotes. My first paper [47] was on pointlike sets and I
have revisited the topic many times since. In the early seventies, motivated by
the question of computing the Krohn-Rhodes complexity of a semigroup [27],
John Rhodes introduced the notion of a pointlike set. First let me recall some
preliminary notions. The power set $P(S)$ of a semigroup S is again a semigroup
under the usual operation $XY = \{xy \mid x \in X, y \in Y\}$. A *relational morphism*
of semigroups $\varphi \colon S \to T$ is a mapping $\varphi \colon S \to P(T)$ such that $\varphi(s) \neq \emptyset$ for all
$s \in S$ and $\varphi(s)\varphi(s') \subseteq \varphi(ss')$ for all $s, s' \in S$. A *pseudovariety* is a class of finite
semigroups closed under subsemigroups, finite direct products and homomorphic
images.

If $\mathbf{V}$ is a pseudovariety of semigroups, then a subset X of a finite semigroup
S is $\mathbf{V}$-*pointlike* if it is covered by a point with respect to any relational morphism into $\mathbf{V}$; that is, if $\varphi \colon S \to V$ is a relational morphism with $V \in \mathbf{V}$, then
there is $v \in V$ with $X \subseteq \varphi^{-1}(v)$. For example, any subgroup of S is pointlike
with respect to the pseudovariety of aperiodic semigroups (semigroups with only
trivial subgroups). Rhodes believed that to compute Krohn-Rhodes complexity,

The author was supported by a PSC CUNY grant.

N. Moreira and R. Reis (Eds.): DLT 2021, LNCS 12811, pp. 27–40, 2021.
https://doi.org/10.1007/978-3-030-81508-0_3

it would be important to be able to compute aperiodic pointlikes and possibly group pointlikes.

Note that the decidability of **V**-pointlike pairs (two-element pointlikes) implies the decidability of membership in **V** since S belongs to **V** if and only if no two-element subset of S is **V**-pointlike. What makes this work is the following observation. Because S has only finitely many subsets and **V** is closed under finite direct products, one can show that there exists a relational morphism $\varphi\colon S \to V$ with $V \in \mathbf{V}$ that *witnesses* **V**-pointlikes in the sense that $X \subseteq S$ is **V**-pointlike if and only if $X \subseteq \varphi^{-1}(v)$ for some $v \in V$. More precisely, for each non-pointlike subset $X \subseteq S$, we can find a relational morphism $\varphi_X\colon S \to V_X$ with $V_X \in \mathbf{V}$ and with no element $v \in V_X$ such that $X \subseteq \varphi^{-1}(v)$. Then take $\varphi\colon S \to \prod V_X$ to be the product of these relational morphisms over all non-pointlike subsets X; this φ will witness **V**-pointlikes. A witnessing relational morphism will be a division when there are no **V**-pointlike pairs. The reader is referred to [40, Chapter 2] for background on pointlike sets and their various generalizations, and for proofs of the witnessing argument. Note that if one can compute the **V**-pointlikes, then one can effectively find a witnessing relational morphism via an enumeration of relational morphisms argument (which has no reasonable time complexity bound). Many proofs that pointlike sets are computable explicitly produce a witnessing relational morphism, but not all do.

In the late nineties, when I was a Ph. D. student under John Rhodes, he told me that he had this proof he had shown Pascal Weil a few years earlier, but had never written up, that there is a profinite interpretation of pointlike sets. Namely, if S is an A-generated semigroup and $\widehat{F}_{\mathbf{V}}(A)$ is the free pro-**V** semigroup on A [4,40] (the inverse limit of all A-generated semigroups in **V**), then there is a natural 'continuous' relational morphism $\rho_{\mathbf{V}}\colon S \to \widehat{F}_{\mathbf{V}}(A)$ respecting the generating set A. Rhodes observed that $X \subseteq S$ is **V**-pointlike if and only if there is $v \in \widehat{F}_{\mathbf{V}}(A)$ with $X \subseteq \rho_{\mathbf{V}}^{-1}(v)$, that is, $\rho_{\mathbf{V}}$ witnesses **V**-pointlike sets. Since $\widehat{F}_{\mathbf{V}}(A)$ is usually uncountable, this is not often feasible to use. But it shows immediately that pointlike sets are decidable with respect to (order computable) locally finite pseudovarieties (ones where $\widehat{F}_{\mathbf{V}}(A)$ is finite and you can algorithmically compute this semigroup). I also showed in my thesis [46], using that the free pro-**J** semigroup is countable with a decidable word problem [4], that the **J**-pointlikes could be computed using this approach [47,53]. Here **J** is the pseudovariety of $\mathscr{J}$-trivial semigroups. Rhodes's observation was independently made by Jorge Almeida, whose work on profinite semigroups was pioneering, and Almeida and Marc Zeitoun also computed the **J**-pointlikes [3]. The profinite method is a powerful tool in understanding pointlikes although making things algorithmic can be difficult from that perspective.

In the nineties, Almeida gave a translation of the notions of pointlike pairs and pointlike sets into formal language theory [5]. I'll stick here to the case of pointlike pairs. If $L_1, L_2 \subseteq A^+$ are regular languages, then they can be **V**-*separated* if there is a **V**-recognizable language L with $L_1 \subseteq L$ and $L \cap L_2 = \emptyset$. Recall that L is **V**-*recognizable* if its syntactic semigroup belongs to **V**. Almeida showed that decidability of **V**-separation is equivalent to decidability of

V-pointlike pairs. So, for example, since the pseudovariety **J** recognizes the piecewise testable languages by Simon's theorem [45], decidability of **J**-pointlikes implies the decidability of separation by piecewise testable languages. The decidability of **V**-pointlike sets is equivalent to what Thomas Place and Zeitoun call the covering problem [35].

2 Aperiodic Pointlikes

A semigroup is *aperiodic* if all its subgroups are trivial, that is, it satisfies $x^\omega = x^{\omega+1}$ where x^ω denotes the idempotent power of x. Schützenberger's theorem says that the aperiodic languages are the first order definable languages [44]; see Straubing's book for a nice introduction [54]. The pseudovariety of aperiodic semigroups is denoted **A**.

The first major result about pointlike sets was by Karsten Henckell, in his thesis under John Rhodes (published in [22]), who proved the decidability of aperiodic pointlikes and hence the decidability of separation of regular languages by first order definable languages.

The collection $\mathrm{PL}_\mathbf{V}(S)$ of **V**-pointlike subsets of S is a subsemigroup of $P(S)$, closed downwards in the order. Note that the power semigroup construction is a monad [28]. There is a semigroup homomorphism

$$\bigcup \colon P(P(S)) \to P(S),$$

natural in S, given by $X \mapsto \bigcup X$ and a natural inclusion $\eta \colon S \to P(S)$ sending s to $\{s\}$, which is the unit of the monad. Rhodes observed that $\mathrm{PL}_\mathbf{V}$ is a submonad, meaning

$$\bigcup \colon \mathrm{PL}_\mathbf{V}(\mathrm{PL}_\mathbf{V}(S)) \to \mathrm{PL}_\mathbf{V}(S)$$

and singletons are pointlikes. This is useful because, for example, any subgroup is aperiodic pointlike. Therefore, if H is a subgroup of $\mathrm{PL}_\mathbf{A}(S)$, then $\bigcup H \in \mathrm{PL}_\mathbf{A}(S)$. The general philosophy used by Henckell and Rhodes for computing pointlikes in the early days was to find some obvious types of subsets that are always **V**-pointlike (like subgroups are **A**-pointlike) and prove that $\mathrm{PL}_\mathbf{V}(S)$ is the smallest subsemigroup of $P(S)$ containing the singletons, closed downward in the order and closed under unions of obvious **V**-pointlikes. A similar philosophy also appears in Place and Zeitoun [32,34], both in the context of ordered and unordered semigroups.

Henckell proved that $\mathrm{PL}_\mathbf{A}(S)$ is the smallest subsemigroup of $P(S)$ that contains the singletons, is closed downward in the order and is closed under taking unions of subgroups. In fact, he showed it is enough to take unions of cyclic subgroups. So, in other words, if $X \subseteq S$ is **A**-pointlike, then so is $X^\omega \cdot \bigcup_{n \geq 0} X^n$.

Henckell's proof explicitly constructs a relational morphism witnessing aperiodic pointlikes and is based on the holonomy proof of the Krohn-Rhodes theorem [23]. Henckell's proof is notoriously difficult to read, and so Henckell, Rhodes and I provided a simpler proof that Henckell's construction works in [21]. We also expanded on his result. Let π be a set of prime numbers. Then the semigroups satisfying an identity of the form $x^\omega = x^{\omega+n}$ for some n whose prime factors belong to π is a pseudovariety. When $\pi = \emptyset$, this is the pseudovariety of aperiodic semigroups. The result of [21] shows that pointlikes for the pseudovariety corresponding to π are decidable if and only if π is recursive. Although our proof is simpler to follow and shorter than Henckell's, it is still not so easy. Nonetheless, it is one of the few papers I have ever written that the referee completely understood; the referee even found a nice trick to shave off a page of the most technical part of the argument. A simplified version of the argument, covering just the aperiodic case, is given in the book [40, Chapter 4.18].

Recently, Place and Zeitoun used a different approach to prove Henckell's theorem [33]. Their main idea is based on a pointlike analogue of the inductive approach to the Krohn-Rhodes theorem that uses groups and cyclic semigroups as the base case and then uses the ideal structure for induction [26,40]. (Place and Zeitoun cite Wilke [59] for their idea, but Wilke is using exactly the Krohn-Rhodes scheme.) Place and Zeitoun's result uses the language theoretic formulation of the covering problem and essentially gives an upper bound on the quantifier depth of first order languages needed to witness the covering problem (or separation). In particular, they make explicit use of Schützenberger's theorem [44], and at a certain point perform constructions on first order definable languages and give a high level description of how to build sentences showing that the result is still first order definable.

Sam van Gool and I took Place and Zeitoun's inductive scheme, but replaced the use of logic and languages by a new bilateral semidirect product decomposition [20]. We showed that this decomposition leads to extremely short (and we would argue readable) proofs of both the two-sided Krohn-Rhodes theorem and Henckell's aperiodic pointlike theorem. Our proof leads to a slightly better bound on the quantifier depth of formulas witnessing the covering problem than that of Place and Zeitoun. Although the proof does not explicitly construct a relational morphism witnessing aperiodic pointlikes, the bound on quantifier depth implicitly provides such a relational morphism.

3   Group Pointlikes

For the Krohn-Rhodes complexity problem, the decidability of group pointlikes seemed like an important step. Let $\mathbf{G}$ denote the pseudovariety of finite groups. Henckell and Rhodes formulated a conjectural (algorithmic) description of the $\mathbf{G}$-pointlike sets in [25] that was proved by Ash in his famous solution to the Rhodes Type II conjecture [12]. An alternative, independent proof of Ash's theorem was obtained by Ribes and Zalesskii [42] using the theory of profinite groups acting on profinite graphs. These are truly deep results; see [24] for a survey.

From the algorithmic point of view, the most elegant and efficient approach to computing $\mathbf{G}$-pointlikes was given by me twenty years ago in [51]. I'll explain the algorithm for the case of separation. The case of separation is also handled in book form in [40, Chapter 4.17] (see, in particular, Exercise 4.17.27). Let L

be a regular language over the alphabet A given by a not necessarily deterministic automaton $\mathcal{A}$ computing L. First we modify $\mathcal{A}$ to make each strongly connected component both deterministic and codeterministic by identifying edges in a strong component with the same label beginning or ending at the same state to get a new automaton $\mathcal{A}'$. Then whenever there is an edge labelled by a in a strong component of $\mathcal{A}'$ from a state v to a state w, we add a reverse edge from w to v labelled by a^{-1}. This results in a new automaton $\mathcal{A}''$ over the alphabet $A \cup A^{-1}$. There is a well-known construction, due to Benois [15], that builds an automaton $\mathcal{A}_L$ over $A \cup A^{-1}$ accepting exactly the freely reduced words accepted by $\mathcal{A}''$. It is shown in [40,51] that $\mathcal{A}_L$ accepts precisely the closure of L in the profinite topology on the free group on A. Now two languages L, L' can be separated by a group language if and only if their closures in the profinite topology on the free group do not intersect, that is, the intersection of the languages accepted by $\mathcal{A}_L$ and $\mathcal{A}_{L'}$ is empty; this can, of course, be tested algorithmically. My proof of correctness of the algorithm uses the Ribes and Zalesskii theorem [42]; a more elementary proof (avoiding profinite groups) is given by me and Karl Auinger in [14], and a textbook variant appears in [40, Chapter 4.19].

If p is a prime, let $\mathbf{G}_p$ denote the pseudovariety of finite p-groups. The results of Ribes and Zalesskii [43] imply that $\mathbf{G}_p$-pointlikes are decidable. I considered pseudovarieties of abelian groups in [48], but will discuss this in detail at a later point in the survey. More recently, Almeida, Shahzamanian and I proved separation is decidable for the pseudovariety of nilpotent groups [2]; pointlike sets in general remain open for nilpotent groups.

4   Join Results and Tameness

In my thesis [46] (and the resulting papers [47,53]) I proved that the join $\mathbf{J} \vee \mathbf{G}$ of the pseudovarieties $\mathbf{J}$ of $\mathscr{J}$-trivial monoids and $\mathbf{G}$ of finite groups has decidable pointlikes. At the time, membership in this pseudovariety was an open question posed by Rhodes 10 years earlier. Almeida, Assis and Zeitoun solved the separation problem for $\mathbf{J} \vee \mathbf{G}$ independently, slightly afterward [6].

My approach was based on a criterion I discovered for a set to be pointlike with respect to a join. Namely, I showed [47,53] that a subset X of a finite semigroup S is $\mathbf{V} \vee \mathbf{W}$-pointlike, if and only if, for each relational morphism $\varphi \colon S \to W$ with $W \in \mathbf{W}$, there is $w \in W$ with $X \subseteq \varphi^{-1}(w)$ and the slice subset $X \times \{w\}$ a $\mathbf{V}$-pointlike subset of the graph of the relation φ (the graph is a subsemigroup of $S \times W$). Rhodes dubbed this the "Slice Theorem." It was the first result I ever proved. This result immediately implies that if $\mathbf{W}$ is an order computable locally finite pseudovariety, then $\mathbf{V} \vee \mathbf{W}$ has decidable pointlikes (or pointlike pairs) whenever $\mathbf{V}$ does because one need only test the slice condition when W is the relatively free semigroup in $\mathbf{W}$ on a generating set of S and φ is the relational morphism respecting generators. For example, any pseudovariety of bands (semigroups with all elements idempotent) is order computable locally finite [4, Chapter 5.5]. Zeitoun showed in his thesis [60] that the join of the pseudovariety of bands with $\mathbf{J}$ is decidable. But since $\mathbf{J}$ has decidable pointlikes, one can deduce from the Slice Theorem that the join of $\mathbf{J}$ with any pseudovariety of bands has decidable pointlikes and hence membership.

The proof of decidability of $\mathbf{J} \vee \mathbf{G}$ was via an enumeration procedure. The idea is that since the pseudovariety $\mathbf{J} \vee \mathbf{G}$ is obviously recursively enumerable, we can enumerate all relational morphisms from a finite semigroup S to semigroups in $\mathbf{J} \vee \mathbf{G}$ and if a subset of X is not $\mathbf{J} \vee \mathbf{G}$-pointlike we will eventually find a relational morphism showing this to be the case. That is, the $\mathbf{J} \vee \mathbf{G}$-pointlike sets form a corecursively enumerable set. To show that the pointlike sets are recursively enumerable, I introduced a certain relational morphism from S to the direct product of the free pro-$\mathbf{J}$-semigroup and the free group on the generating set of S. I showed that this relational morphism to a countable semigroup with decidable word problem witnesses $\mathbf{J} \vee \mathbf{G}$-pointlikes using the Slice Theorem and Ash's Theorem [12]. One can then recursively enumerate the $\mathbf{J} \vee \mathbf{G}$-pointlike subsets of a finite semigroup using this computable relational morphism.

This approach was explored in an axiomatic fashion by me and Jorge Almeida during my postdoc in Portugal, leading to the notion of tameness of pseudovarieties [10,11]; see [40, Chapter 3] for further developments. Roughly speaking, a decidable pseudovariety of semigroups $\mathbf{V}$ is tame with respect to pointlikes if we can find some reasonably nice set σ of implicit operations [4,38] (like the ω-power) so that if we view finite semigroups as universal algebras with signature consisting of σ and multiplication, then the free σ-semigroup in the variety of σ-semigroups generated by $\mathbf{V}$ on any finite set has a decidable word problem and the natural relational morphism of σ-semigroups from a finite semigroup S to this free σ-semigroup in $\mathbf{V}$ witnesses $\mathbf{V}$-pointlikes. Tameness implies decidability of $\mathbf{V}$-pointlikes via an enumeration algorithm.

A number of other pseudovariety joins were computed using the tameness approach, e.g. [7,16].

5   Undecidability of Pointlikes

Decidability of pointlikes or separation implies decidability of membership, so it is natural to ask about the converse direction.

Albert, Baldinger and Rhodes showed that the identity problem is undecidable for finite semigroups [1]. They show that there is a fixed finite set E of identities over an alphabet A, for which there is no algorithm which given input $(u, v) \in A^+$ can determine whether $u = v$ is a consequence of E in finite semigroups, that is, whether every finite semigroup that satisfies all the identities in E must also satisfy the identity $u = v$. Let $\mathbf{V}(E)$ be the pseudovariety defined by the identities E. Then it is shown in [1] that $\mathbf{V}(E) \vee \mathbf{ACom}$ has undecidable membership where $\mathbf{ACom}$ is the pseudovariety of aperiodic commutative semigroups. In light of my results [47,53] relating membership in joins to the separation problem via the Slice Theorem, Rhodes conjectured that $\mathbf{V}(E)$ has undecidable pointlike pairs; since it obviously has decidable membership, this conjecture, if true, would yield an example where the separation and pointlike problems are undecidable, but the membership problem is decidable.

At the excursion for the Conference on Algebraic Engineering for Rhodes's 60th birthday, held in Aizu-Wakematsu, Japan, in 1997, there was a trip to the public baths. Rhodes and I skipped out on the baths and instead proved the following theorem [39].

Theorem 1. *If* **V** *is a variety of semigroup and* $u, v \in A^+$ *with* $n = \max\{|u|, |v|\}$, *then every semigroup in* **V** *satisfies the identity* $u = v$ *if and only if* $\{u, v\}$ *is a* **V**-*pointlike subset of* $S = A^+/I_n$ *where* I_n *is the ideal of words of length greater than* n.

The proof of the theorem is quite simple since under the generator preserving relational morphism $\rho_{\mathbf{V}} \colon S \to \widehat{F}_{\mathbf{V}}(A)$, $\rho_{\mathbf{V}}(u) = \{u\}$ and $\rho_{\mathbf{V}}(v) = \{v\}$ as these words belong to singleton congruence classes in A^+/I_n. Therefore, $\rho_{\mathbf{V}}(u) \cap \rho_{\mathbf{V}}(v) \neq \emptyset$ if and only if $u = v$ in $\widehat{F}_{\mathbf{V}}(A)$, which is the same as saying that **V** satisfies the identity $u = v$. It follows that if E is a finite set of identities with undecidable identity problem as per [1], then $\mathbf{V}(E)$ has decidable membership but undecidable pointlike pairs (i.e., separation).

Incidentally, I first spoke about this theorem during a workshop in Kyoto in 1999. Volker Diekert, who I met then for the first time, came up to me after the talk to tell me that he now finally understood why people like Jean-Éric Pin were interested in pointlike sets.

I observed in my thesis that if **H** is any decidable pseudovariety of finite groups, then the **H**-pointlikes subsets of a finite group are computable. In fact, relational morphisms of groups were studied by Wedderburn in 1941 [58]. I had essentially rediscovered his results, and so I guess I missed my chance for an Annals paper by 57 years.

It was then natural to ask if there are pseudovarieties of groups with decidable membership but undecidable pointlikes. I proved in [48] that such examples can not be found among pseudovarieties of abelian groups.

Theorem 2. *A pseudovariety of finite abelian groups has decidable pointlikes if and only if it has decidable membership.*

The decidability of pointlikes for the pseudovariety of all finite abelian groups was first obtained by Delgado [17].

A group is *metabelian* (or two-step solvable) if its commutator subgroup is abelian. With Auinger, I proved the following result [13].

Theorem 3. *There is a pseudovariety of metabelian groups with decidable membership and undecidable pointlike pairs (separation).*

The proof uses a diagonalization argument to construct the pseudovariety directly from a Turing machine which computes a recursively enumerable but nonrecursive set of prime numbers.

6 Transference Results

There has been a lot of work on pseudovarieties of the form $\mathbf{V} * \mathbf{D}$ with $\mathbf{V}$ a nontrivial pseudovariety of monoids and $\mathbf{D}$ the pseudovariety of semigroups whose idempotents are right zeros (i.e., satisfying $xy^\omega = y^\omega$). Here $*$ denotes the semidirect product of pseudovarieties of semigroups [4,18,40]. Roughly speaking, $\mathbf{V} * \mathbf{D}$ can recognize inverse images of $\mathbf{V}$-recognizable languages under sliding block codes. For example, the locally testable languages are recognized by $\mathbf{SL} * \mathbf{D}$ where $\mathbf{SL}$ is the pseudovariety of semilattices.

The earliest result on pseudovarieties of the form $\mathbf{V} * \mathbf{D}$ is a result in Eilenberg [18], due to Bret Tilson, called Tilson's Trace-Delay Theorem. Howard Straubing then improved upon the result [55] and finally Tilson proved the definitive Delay Theorem [57], relating membership in $\mathbf{V} * \mathbf{D}$ to category membership in $\mathbf{V}$. It follows from Tilson's results that under very weak assumptions on $\mathbf{V}$, the decidability of $\mathbf{V}$ is equivalent to that of $\mathbf{V} * \mathbf{D}$. This is important because it provides the connection between the quantifier alternation hierarchy for first order definable languages and the classical dot-depth hierarchy of Brzozowski and Cohen.

Note that $\mathbf{V} * \mathbf{D}$ can have undecidable membership, even if $\mathbf{V}$ has decidable membership. Auinger used our results on group pseudovarieties with undecidable pointlikes and a construction of Kad'ourek to give an example of a decidable pseudovariety of monoids $\mathbf{V}$ such that $\mathbf{V} * \mathbf{D}$ has undecidable membership. The pseudovariety $\mathbf{V}$ consists of all finite monoids whose regular $\mathcal{J}$-classes are groups belonging to a certain decidable pseudovariety of groups with undecidable pointlikes constructed by me and Auinger in [13].

In [50], I proved the following transference result.

Theorem 4 (Delay Theorem for Pointlikes). *If $\mathbf{V}$ is a pseudovariety of monoids, then $\mathbf{V} * \mathbf{D}$ had decidable pointlikes (or separation) if and only if $\mathbf{V}$ does.*

So the operation $\mathbf{V} \mapsto \mathbf{V} * \mathbf{D}$ is better behaved at the level of pointlikes than at the level of membership. This theorem was recently reproved by Place and Zeitoun [37] in the language theoretic formulation, with the added feature that $\mathbf{V}$ is allowed to be a pseudovariety of ordered semigroups. I'm fairly confident that my original argument can also be easily adapted to this more general setting using the results of [29] in place of those of Tilson [57], although I have not verified all the details.

Since semilattices are locally finite, and hence have decidable pointlikes, my result yields decidability of separation and the covering problem for locally testable languages (and also locally threshold testable languages), which was later reproved by Place and Zeitoun [31].

Place and Zeitoun [36] have proven recently a beautiful transference result for hierarchies associated to group pseudovarieties. I showed in [49] that if $\mathbf{H}$ is a pseudovariety of groups, then the pseudovariety of semigroups corresponding to the Boolean polynomial closure of the $\mathbf{H}$-recognizable languages is $\mathbf{J} * \mathbf{H}$. As a consequence of this and the results of [36] one can deduce the following.

Theorem 5 (Place and Zeitoun). *Let* $\mathbf{H}$ *be a pseudovariety of groups with decidable pointlikes (separation). Then* $\mathbf{J} * \mathbf{H}$ *has decidable pointlikes (separation).*

In particular, $\mathbf{J} * \mathbf{G}$ is the pseudovariety of block groups, which plays an important role in semigroup theory [24]. Ash's theorem, combined with the theorem of Place and Zeitoun, gives that pointlikes are decidable for block groups. It should be mentioned that I had proven long ago [51,52] that decidability of separation for $\mathbf{H}$ implies decidability of membership in $\mathbf{J} * \mathbf{H}$, which can be viewed as a forerunner of this result. Decidability of $\mathbf{H}$ is not enough to guarantee decidability of $\mathbf{J} * \mathbf{H}$ since Auinger and I showed that for our decidable pseudovariety $\mathbf{H}$ of metabelian groups with undecidable separation, the pseudovariety $\mathbf{J} * \mathbf{H}$ has undecidable membership problem [13].

7   A New Result: Separation for Modular Quantifiers

If $\mathbf{H}$ is a pseudovariety of finite groups, then $\overline{\mathbf{H}}$ denotes the pseudovariety of semigroups all of whose subgroups belong to $\mathbf{H}$. For example, if $\mathbf{1}$ is the pseudovariety containing just the trivial group, then $\overline{\mathbf{1}}$ is the pseudovariety of aperiodic semigroups.

Recall that modular quantifiers allow you to form logical sentences of the form: the number of positions x in a word w for which the formula $\phi(x)$ is true is congruent to k modulo n. Details can be found in [56].

Straubing showed that if $\mathbf{G}_{\mathrm{sol}}$ is the pseudovariety of solvable groups, then the $\overline{\mathbf{G}_{\mathrm{sol}}}$ recognizes those languages that can be defined in first order logic enhanced with modular quantifiers [56]. Straubing showed that $\overline{\mathbf{G}_p}$, for a prime p, recognizes those languages definable in first order logic enhanced with mod-p quantifiers [56]. The classes of solvable groups and p-groups are closed under wreath product.

The paper [21] showed that $\overline{\mathbf{G}_p}$-pointlikes are decidable and hence the problem of separation by languages defined in first order logic with mod-p quantifiers is decidable.

The two-sided Krohn-Rhodes theorem [40, Chapter 5] implies that if $\mathbf{H}$ is closed under wreath product, then $\overline{\mathbf{H}}$ is the smallest pseudovariety containing the finite simple groups in $\mathbf{H}$ and the two-element semilattice that is closed under bilateral semidirect product (or block product).

Originally, van Gool and I had hoped that our proof of Henckell's aperiodic pointlikes theorem and the two-sided Krohn-Rhodes theorem, using bilateral semidirect product decompositions [20], could be extended to compute $\overline{\mathbf{H}}$-pointlikes when $\mathbf{H}$ is closed under wreath product. But the base case of the induction turned out to become quite complicated at this level of generality (although the inductive step worked fine).

Instead, we found a simplification in the proof in [21] of Henckell's theorem that allowed us to make things works for any pseudovariety $\mathbf{H}$ of finite groups. If $\mathbf{H}$ is a pseudovariety of finite groups, then ever finite group G has a smallest normal subgroup $K_{\mathbf{H}}(G)$ (called the $\mathbf{H}$-kernel) such that $G/K_{\mathbf{H}}(G) \in \mathbf{H}$. For example, if $\mathbf{H}$ is the pseudovariety of abelian groups, then the $\mathbf{H}$-kernel is the commutator subgroup. If $\mathbf{1}$ is the trivial pseudovariety, then $K_{\mathbf{1}}(G) = G$. The $\mathbf{H}$-kernel is clearly computable if and only if $\mathbf{H}$ has decidable membership.

I proved with van Gool the following theorem describing the $\overline{\mathbf{H}}$-pointlikes [19]. The monad property for pointlikes once again played a crucial role.

Theorem 6. *Let $\mathbf{H}$ be a pseudovariety of finite groups and S a finite semigroup. Then $\mathrm{PL}_{\overline{\mathbf{H}}}(S)$ is the smallest subsemigroup T of the power semigroup $P(S)$ such that:*

1. *T contains the singletons;*
2. *T is closed downward under the inclusion ordering;*
3. *if G is a subgroup of T, then $\bigcup K_{\mathbf{H}}(G) \in T$.*

Clearly, we can effectively construct $\mathrm{PL}_{\overline{\mathbf{H}}}(S)$ from the above description if we can solve the membership problem for $\mathbf{H}$. The proof explicitly constructs a witness to $\overline{\mathbf{H}}$-pointlikes. Notice that $\overline{\mathbf{H}}$ can have decidable pointlikes while $\mathbf{H}$ has undecidable pointlikes.

A related result, involving modular predicates, was proved by Place *et al.* in [30]. As far as I understand, their results give conditions on a pseudovariety $\mathbf{V}$ of (possibly ordered) semigroups so that $\mathbf{V} * \mathbf{Ab}$ has decidable separation or covering problem, where $\mathbf{Ab}$ is the pseudovariety of abelian groups.

8   Two More of My Favorite Results About Pointlike Sets

It was shown by Almeida and Silva [9] that pointlikes sets are decidable for the pseudovariety of $\mathscr{R}$-trivial semigroups. A cleaner argument for $\mathscr{R}$-trivial and $\mathscr{J}$-trivial semigroups is given in [8]. I was impressed by this result because I had tried very hard to prove it in my thesis and failed utterly.

My favorite recent result on pointlike sets is the famous Place-Zeitoun result on separation (and later pointlikes) for the pseudovariety of dot-depth two semi-groups [34]. Their brilliant realization that separation was crucial for going up the dot-depth hierarchy (or equivalently the quantifier alternation hierarchy for first order definable languages) allowed them to solve the very old open question of membership in dot-depth two in their seminal paper [32]. Place and Zeitoun have done an excellent job of showing the importance and applicability of pointlike sets in Computer Science and have generated renewed interest and enthusiasm in the subject. Their work certainly re-inspired me to revisit this subject, which I had stopped thinking about for a number of years.

9   Some Open Problems

Decidability of separation and pointlikes is still open for most of the dot-depth (quantifier alternation) hierarchy and is an active area of research, in particular, by Place and Zeitoun, and I am probably behind on the state of the art of this rapidly developing subject.

One of the most intriguing open problems concerning pointlikes and separation is that of deciding pointlikes (or separation) for the semidirect product $\mathbf{G} * \mathbf{A}$ of finite groups $\mathbf{G}$ and finite aperiodic semigroups $\mathbf{A}$. This is generated by all wreath products $G \wr A = G^A \rtimes A$ with G a finite group and A a finite aperiodic semigroup. Using the Presentation Lemma [40, Chapter 4.14], it was shown in [41] that decidability of whether a semigroup has Krohn-Rhodes complexity one reduces to the separation problem for $\mathbf{G} * \mathbf{A}$, that is, decidability of $\mathbf{G} * \mathbf{A}$-pointlike pairs. In fact, it is enough to compute pointlike pairs restricted to a special class of finite semigroups called group mapping semigroups. An algorithm to compute the $\mathbf{G} * \mathbf{A}$-pointlikes of a group mapping semigroup is proposed in [41], where soundness is proved but not completeness.

References

1. Albert, D., Baldinger, R., Rhodes, J.: Undecidability of the identity problem for finite semigroups. J. Symb. Logic **57**(1), 179–192 (1992)
2. Almeida, J., Shahzamanian, M.H., Steinberg, B.: The pro-nilpotent group topology on a free group. J. Algebra **480**, 332–345 (2017)
3. Almeida, J., Zeitoun, M.: The pseudovariety **J** is hyperdecidable. RAIRO Inform. Théor. Appl. **31**(5), 457–482 (1997)
4. Almeida, J.: Finite Semigroups and Universal Algebra. Series in Algebra, vol. 3. World Scientific Publishing Co., Inc., River Edge (1994). Translated from the 1992 Portuguese original and revised by the author
5. Almeida, J.: Some algorithmic problems for pseudovarieties. Publ. Math. Debrecen **54**, 531–552 (1999). Automata and formal languages, VIII (Salgótarján, 1996)
6. Almeida, J., Azevedo, A., Zeitoun, M.: Pseudovariety joins involving $\mathscr{J}$-trivial semigroups. Internat. J. Algebra Comput. **9**(1), 99–112 (1999)
7. Almeida, J., Costa, J.C., Zeitoun, M.: Tameness of pseudovariety joins involving R. Monatsh. Math. **146**(2), 89–111 (2005)
8. Almeida, J., Costa, J.C., Zeitoun, M.: Pointlike sets with respect to **R** and **J**. J. Pure Appl. Algebra **212**(3), 486–499 (2008)
9. Almeida, J., Silva, P.V.: SC-hyperdecidability of **R**. Theoret. Comput. Sci. **255**(1–2), 569–591 (2001)
10. Almeida, J., Steinberg, B.: On the decidability of iterated semidirect products with applications to complexity. Proc. London Math. Soc. (3) **80**(1), 50–74 (2000)
11. Almeida, J., Steinberg, B.: Syntactic and global semigroup theory: a synthesis approach. In: Algorithmic problems in groups and semigroups (Lincoln, NE, 1998), pp. 1–23. Trends Math., Birkhäuser Boston, Boston (2000)
12. Ash, C.J.: Inevitable graphs: a proof of the type II conjecture and some related decision procedures. Internat. J. Algebra Comput. **1**(1), 127–146 (1991)
13. Auinger, K., Steinberg, B.: On the extension problem for partial permutations. Proc. Amer. Math. Soc. **131**(9), 2693–2703 (2003)
14. Auinger, K., Steinberg, B.: A constructive version of the Ribes-Zalesskiĭ product theorem. Math. Z. **250**(2), 287–297 (2005)

15. Benois, M.: Descendants of regular language in a class of rewriting systems: algorithm and complexity of an automata construction. In: Lescanne, P. (ed.) RTA 1987. LNCS, vol. 256, pp. 121–132. Springer, Heidelberg (1987). https://doi.org/10.1007/3-540-17220-3_11

16. Costa, J.C., Nogueira, C.: Tameness of joins involving the pseudovariety of local semilattices. Internat. J. Algebra Comput. **22**(7), 1250060, 35 (2012)

17. Delgado, M.: Abelian pointlikes of a monoid. Semigroup Forum **56**(3), 339–361 (1998)

18. Eilenberg, S.: Automata, languages, and machines. Vol. B. Academic Press, New York (1976). With two chapters ("Depth decomposition theorem" and "Complexity of semigroups and morphisms") by Bret Tilson, Pure and Applied Mathematics, vol. 59

19. Gool, S.J.V., Steinberg, B.: Pointlike sets for varieties determined by groups. Adv. Math. **348**, 18–50 (2019)

20. van Gool, S.J., Steinberg, B.: Merge decompositions, two-sided Krohn-Rhodes, and aperiodic pointlikes. Canad. Math. Bull. **62**(1), 199–208 (2019)

21. Henckell, K., Rhodes, J., Steinberg, B.: Aperiodic pointlikes and beyond. Int. J. Algebra Comput. **20**(2), 287–305 (2010)

22. Henckell, K.: Pointlike sets: the finest aperiodic cover of a finite semigroup. J. Pure Appl. Algebra **55**(1–2), 85–126 (1988)

23. Henckell, K., Lazarus, S., Rhodes, J.: Prime decomposition theorem for arbitrary semigroups: general holonomy decomposition and synthesis theorem. J. Pure Appl. Algebra **55**(1–2), 127–172 (1988)

24. Henckell, K., Margolis, S.W., Pin, J.E., Rhodes, J.: Ash's type II theorem, profinite topology and Mal′ cev products. I. Int. J. Algebra Comput. **1**(4), 411–436 (1991)

25. Henckell, K., Rhodes, J.: The theorem of Knast, the $PG = BG$ and type-II conjectures. In: Monoids and Semigroups with Applications (Berkeley, CA, 1989), pp. 453–463. World Scientific Publishing, River Edge (1991)

26. Krohn, K., Rhodes, J., Tilson, B.: Algebraic theory of machines, languages, and semigroups. Edited by Michael A. Arbib. With a major contribution by Kenneth Krohn and John L. Rhodes. Academic Press, New York (1968). Chapters 1, 5–9

27. Krohn, K., Rhodes, J.: Complexity of finite semigroups. Ann. Math. **2**(88), 128–160 (1968)

28. Mac Lane, S.: Categories for the Working Mathematician. Graduate Texts in Mathematics, vol. 5. Springer, New York (1998)

29. Pin, J.E., Pinguet, A., Weil, P.: Ordered categories and ordered semigroups. Commun. Algebra **30**(12), 5651–5675 (2002)

30. Place, T., Ramanathan, V., Weil, P.: Covering and separation for logical fragments with modular predicates. Log. Methods Comput. Sci. **15**(2), Paper No. 11, 32 (2019)

31. Place, T., van Rooijen, L., Zeitoun, M.: On separation by locally testable and locally threshold testable languages. Log. Methods Comput. Sci. **10**(3), 3:24, 28 (2014)

32. Place, T., Zeitoun, M.: Going higher in the first-order quantifier alternation hierarchy on words. In: Esparza, J., Fraigniaud, P., Husfeldt, T., Koutsoupias, E. (eds.) ICALP 2014. LNCS, vol. 8573, pp. 342–353. Springer, Heidelberg (2014). https://doi.org/10.1007/978-3-662-43951-7_29

33. Place, T., Zeitoun, M.: Separating regular languages with first-order logic. Log. Methods Comput. Sci. **12**(1), Paper No. 5, 31 (2016)

34. Place, T., Zeitoun, M.: Separation for dot-depth two. In: 2017 32nd Annual ACM/IEEE Symposium on Logic in Computer Science (LICS), p. 12. IEEE, Piscataway (2017)

35. Place, T., Zeitoun, M.: The covering problem. Log. Methods Comput. Sci. **14**(3), Paper No. 1, 54 (2018)

36. Place, T., Zeitoun, M.: Separation and covering for group based concatenation hierarchies. In: 2019 34th Annual ACM/IEEE Symposium on Logic in Computer Science (LICS), pp. Paper No. 17, 13. IEEE, Piscataway (2019)

37. Place, T., Zeitoun, M.: Adding successor: a transfer theorem for separation and covering. ACM Trans. Comput. Log. **21**(2), Art. 9, 45 (2020)

38. Reiterman, J.: The Birkhoff theorem for finite algebras. Algebra Universalis **14**(1), 1–10 (1982)

39. Rhodes, J., Steinberg, B.: Pointlike sets, hyperdecidability and the identity problem for finite semigroups. Internat. J. Algebra Comput. **9**(3–4), 475–481 (1999). Dedicated to the memory of Marcel-Paul Schützenberger

40. Rhodes, J., Steinberg, B.: The q-theory of Finite Semigroups. Springer Monographs in Mathematics, Springer, New York (2009)

41. Rhodes, J., Tilson, B.R.: Improved lower bounds for the complexity of finite semigroups. J. Pure Appl. Algebra **2**, 13–71 (1972)

42. Ribes, L., Zalesskii, P.A.: On the profinite topology on a free group. Bull. London Math. Soc. **25**(1), 37–43 (1993)

43. Ribes, L., Zalesskii, P.A.: The pro-p topology of a free group and algorithmic problems in semigroups. Int. J. Algebra Comput. **4**(3), 359–374 (1994)

44. Schützenberger, M.P.: On finite monoids having only trivial subgroups. Inf. Control **8**, 190–194 (1965)

45. Simon, I.: Piecewise testable events. In: Brakhage, H. (ed.) GI-Fachtagung 1975. LNCS, vol. 33, pp. 214–222. Springer, Heidelberg (1975). https://doi.org/10.1007/3-540-07407-4_23

46. Steinberg, B.: Decidability and hyperdecidability of joins of pseudovarieties. ProQuest LLC, Ann Arbor, MI, thesis (Ph.D.)-University of California, Berkeley (1998)

47. Steinberg, B.: On pointlike sets and joins of pseudovarieties. Int. J. Algebra Comput. **8**(2), 203–234 (1998). With an addendum by the author

48. Steinberg, B.: Monoid kernels and profinite topologies on the free abelian group. Bull. Austral. Math. Soc. **60**(3), 391–402 (1999)

49. Steinberg, B.: Polynomial closure and topology. Int. J. Algebra Comput. **10**(5), 603–624 (2000)

50. Steinberg, B.: A delay theorem for pointlikes. Semigroup Forum **63**(3), 281–304 (2001)

51. Steinberg, B.: Finite state automata: a geometric approach. Trans. Amer. Math. Soc. **353**(9), 3409–3464 (2001)

52. Steinberg, B.: Inevitable graphs and profinite topologies: some solutions to algorithmic problems in monoid and automata theory, stemming from group theory. Int. J. Algebra Comput. **11**(1), 25–71 (2001)

53. Steinberg, B.: On algorithmic problems for joins of pseudovarieties. Semigroup Forum **62**(1), 1–40 (2001)

54. Straubing, H.: Aperiodic homomorphisms and the concatenation product of recognizable sets. J. Pure Appl. Algebra **15**(3), 319–327 (1979)

55. Straubing, H.: Finite semigroup varieties of the form $\mathbf{V} * \mathbf{D}$. J. Pure Appl. Algebra **36**(1), 53–94 (1985)

56. Straubing, H.: Finite automata, formal logic, and circuit complexity. Progress in Theoretical Computer Science, Birkhäuser Boston Inc., Boston (1994)
57. Tilson, B.: Categories as algebra: an essential ingredient in the theory of monoids. J. Pure Appl. Algebra **48**(1–2), 83–198 (1987)
58. Wedderburn, J.H.M.: Homomorphism of groups. Ann. Math. **2**(42), 486–487 (1941)
59. Wilke, T.: Classifying discrete temporal properties. In: Meinel, C., Tison, S. (eds.) STACS 1999. LNCS, vol. 1563, pp. 32–46. Springer, Heidelberg (1999). https://doi.org/10.1007/3-540-49116-3_3
60. Zeitoun, M.: On the decidability of the membership problem of the pseudovariety **J** ∨ **B**. Int. J. Algebra Comput. **5**(1), 47–64 (1995)

Regular Papers

A Strong Non-overlapping Dyck Code

Elena Barcucci[ID], Antonio Bernini[(✉)][ID], and Renzo Pinzani

Dipartimento di Matematica e Informatica "U. Dini", Università degli Studi di
Firenze, Viale G.B. Morgagni 65, 50134 Firenze, Italy
{elena.barcucci,antonio.bernini,renzo.pinzani}@unifi.it

Abstract. We propose a strong non-overlapping set of Dyck paths having variable length. First, we construct a set starting from an elevated Dyck path by cutting it in a specific point and inserting suitable Dyck paths (not too long...) in this cutting point. Then, we increase the cardinality of the set by replacing the first and the second factor of the original elevated Dyck path with suitable sets of prefixes and suffixes.

Keywords: Variable length non-overlapping codes · Dyck paths · Cross bifix-free codes

1 Introduction

Non-overlapping codes (or cross bifix-free codes) have been widely studied since their introduction by scientists and engineers [5,6,8], motivated by applications in telecommunication systems theory and engineering. Typically, a non-overlapping code is a set of words, over a given finite alphabet, where any two words have some specific properties relating to the overlap between them. For example, one can require that one of them is not a prefix or a suffix of the other one, in this case the set is either a *prefix-free code* or a *suffix-free code*. Often, the constraint requires that any prefix of any word must be different from any suffix of any other word in the set (*cross bifix-free set* or equivalently *non-overlapping set*) as in [1,11], where issues about frame synchronization in digital communication systems are investigated.

In [3] different approaches for the construction of non-overlapping sets are presented. One of them provides a non-overlapping set of words such that any its word does not occur as an inner factor in any other word of the set (a set having this property is said to be *strong non-overlapping code*). The elements of this set are constructed using the notion of forbidden consecutive patterns: each word is not allowed to contain particular consecutive sequences (*patterns*). A different method uses the well known elevated Dyck paths with restricted length: the author shows that the set $\mathcal{ED}_n$ (see Sect. 2) of elevated Dyck path having length less than $2n$ constitutes a *non-overlapping* set of binary words (each Dyck path can be easily encoded by a binary word) but it is not a *strong non-overlapping* set. For example, the two words $w = 110100$ e $w' = \mathbf{11101000}$

© Springer Nature Switzerland AG 2021
N. Moreira and R. Reis (Eds.): DLT 2021, LNCS 12811, pp. 43–53, 2021.
https://doi.org/10.1007/978-3-030-81508-0_4

encode two elevated Dyck paths, then they are non-overlapping words but w is an inner factor of w' (in bold).

Nevertheless, the set $\mathcal{ED}_n$ has two important features: it is a non-expandable set and each element has the same number of 0's and 1's, which constitute the alphabet which Dyck paths are constructed with. This last property is interesting since non-overlapping codes are used in the study of DNA-based storage system [12,13], where the balance between the letters of the codewords is crucial (see Theorem 3 in [12]).

In this paper we are interested in the construction of a variable-length strong non-overlapping set of binary words. We also use elevated Dyck paths having constraints on the length but we also require some properties on their prefixes and suffixes. We could carry on our discussion always referring to Dyck words (which are a subset of binary words), nevertheless, throughout the paper, we prefer to refer to Dyck paths since in our opinion most of the treated arguments will be better understood. We are also interested in the cardinality of such à set. The motivation for it is twofold. Firstly, it is interesting by itself by a combinatorics point of view, moreover it could be useful to a potential user about a choice among the various existing sets.

2   Preliminary Notations

A Dyck path is a lattice path in $\mathbb{Z}^2$ from $(0,0)$ to $(2n,0)$ with steps in $\{(1,1),(1,-1)\}$ (up and down step, respectively) never crossing the x-axis. The number of up steps in any prefix of a Dyck path is greater or equal to the number of down steps and the total number of steps (the *length* of the path) is $2n$. We denote the set of Dyck paths having length $2n$ by $\mathcal{D}_n$.

A Dyck path can be codified by a binary word, replacing the up steps by 1's and the down steps by 0's, so that the set $\mathcal{D}_n$ of all $2n$-length Dyck paths is a subset of $\mathcal{B} = \{1,0\}^*$ where $\mathcal{B}$ is the set of all the binary words.

If $P \in \mathcal{D}_n$, then $1P0$ is said to be an *elevated* Dyck path (the only points on the x- axis are the first one and the last one). We collect the elevated Dyck paths in the set $\mathcal{ED}_n = \{1P0 | P \in \mathcal{D}_i, \ 0 \leq i \leq n-1\}$, having length greater than or equal to 2 and less than $2n$.

If P is a path (not necessarily a Dyck path), we denote its length by $|P|$ and, given a prefix A of P, we denote by h_A its final height which is the ordinate of its final point. If S is a lattice point, its height is its ordinate y_S.

If $P \in \mathcal{D}_n$, then for any prefix A of P, we have $|A|_1 \geq |A|_0$ where $|A|_1$ and $|A|_0$ denote the numbers of 1's and 0's in A, respectively. Clearly, for any $P \in \mathcal{D}_n$, it is $|P|_1 = |P|_0$ and $|P| = 2n$. Moreover, it is straightforward that $h_A = |A|_1 - |A|_0$. A pattern of k consecutive 1's (0's) can be denoted by 1^k (0^k), therefore if $P = 1110110000$, we could use the notation $P = 1^301^20^4$ to refer to P.

The set $\mathcal{D}_n$ is enumerated by the n-th Catalan number $C_n = \frac{1}{n+1}\binom{2n}{n}$ (sequence A000108 in [9]).

Given a finite alphabet Σ, a word $v \in \Sigma^*$ is said to be *bifix-free* (often said *unbordered* or equivalently *self non-overlapping*) if any proper prefix of v is different from any proper suffix of v (a prefix (suffix) u of v is a proper prefix (suffix) if $u \neq v$ and $u \neq \varepsilon$, where ε is the empty word).

Two bifix-free words $v, v' \in \Sigma^*$ are said to be *cross bifix-free* (or equivalently *non-overlapping*) if any proper prefix of v is different from any proper suffix of v', and vice versa. A set of words is said to be a *cross bifix-free set* (or *non-overlapping set*) of words if each element of the set is a bifix-free word and if any two words are cross bifix-free.

The cross bifix-free property does not exclude that the word v is an inner factor of v' (or vice versa). For example, the words $v = 1100$ and $v' = \mathbf{1100}100$ are cross bifix-free and v' contains an occurrence of v (in bold). For our purpose, we require that this is not allowed as follows. Two cross bifix-free words are said to be *strong non-overlapping* if the smallest one does not occur as inner factor in the largest one. More precisely, the word v is an inner factor of v' if $v' = \alpha v \beta$ for some α, β, possibly empty but not both.

A set of words is said to be a *strong non-overlapping set* if any two words are strong non-overlapping. For the sake of clearness, we point out that any element of a strong non-overlapping set is a self non-overlapping word, and any two elements of the set are strong non-overlapping.

In the next section we are going to define a strong non-overlapping set of Dyck paths. The notions of self non-overlapping, non-overlapping, and strong non-overlapping words can be easily transferred to Dyck paths, thanks to the above mentioned encoding of a Dyck path in a binary word.

3   The Construction

The leading idea moves from the simple guess that, given an elevated Dyck path P, if you split P in some point and insert in the cutting point two different Dyck paths, one at a time, say D and D', then two new different Dyck paths Q and Q' are obtained which surely are non-overlapping paths (since they are still two elevated Dyck paths [3]) and most likely are strong non-overlapping paths. In other words, it is not easy to find an occurrence of the shortest one inside the longest one since these two new paths (Q and Q') have been generated by the inflation of P by means of two different Dyck paths (D and D'). Our aim is the investigation on the hypothesis under which the strong non-overlapping property is guaranteed.

First of all, we observe that the length of the inserted paths can not be too large, otherwise in the construction of the second path Q' one could insert in P the whole path Q obtained with the first inflation. We illustrate this remark with an example.

If $P = 111000$, consider the factorization $P = A_1 A_2$ with $A_1 = 1110$ and $A_2 = 00$. The choice $D = 10$ (which is the only Dyck path with minimal length) leads to the first path $Q = 1110\mathbf{10}00$. If $D' = Q$, then the second path $Q' = 110\mathbf{1110100}000$ clearly contains Q.

Which is the maximal length for D' such that the above fact can not occur? Clearly, it is $|D'| < |Q|$ and to be sure we have to consider the minimal length that Q can have. For this purpose, note that, given a Dyck prefix A_1, the shortest suffix A_2 useful to complete the Dyck path $P = A_1 A_2$ is $A_2 = 0^k$, with $k = h_{A_1}$. Moreover, the minimal length of a Dyck path is 2, given by $D = 10$. Therefore, the minimal length for $Q = A_1 D A_2$ is $|Q| = |A_1| + 2 + h_{A_1}$.

A second consideration concerns with the feature of the prefix A_1 of P. It is illustrated in the following example, where P is factorized in two different ways.

Let P be the Dyck path $P = 1101110000$ and let factorize it in $P = A_1 A_2$ where $A_1 = 1101110$ and $A_2 = 000$. We choose $D = 10$ and $D' = 11101000$. The Dyck paths Q and Q' we obtain after inflating P with D and D' are $Q = 110111010000$ and $Q' = 110$**11101110**1000000. As the reader can easily check, the path Q' contains an occurrence of Q, highlighted in bold.

Nevertheless, if $P = A_1 A_2$ with $A_1 = 11011100$ and $A_2 = 00$, using the same Dyck paths D and D' as before, we obtain $Q = 110111001000$ and $Q' = 1101111001110100000$ which are strong non-overlapping paths. The reason why in this second case Q does not occur as a subpath in Q' lies in the fact that A_1 is a bifix-free prefix, differently from the previous factorization.

In the following proposition we formalize the two arguments above.

Proposition 1. *Let $P = A_1 A_2$ be an elevated Dyck path such that A_1 is a bifix-free prefix of P. Let $|A_1|$ be the length of A_1 and h_{A_1} its final height. If D, D' (with $|D| < |D'|$) denote two Dyck path such that $|D|, |D'| \leq |A_1| + h_{A_1}$, then the Dyck paths*

$$Q = A_1 D A_2$$

and

$$Q' = A_1 D' A_2$$

are strong non-overlapping.

Proof. The paths Q and Q' are elevated Dyck paths, then they are non-overlapping [3]. Since $|D| < |D'|$ (so that $|Q| < |Q'|$), we have to prove that there is not any occurrence of Q inside Q'.

We proceed *ad absurdum*, supposing that there exists an occurrence of Q in Q'. We denote by S the starting point of Q. Then, recalling that Q starts with the prefix A_1, the point S cannot be an inner point of A_1 in Q' since A_1 is a bifix-free prefix, by hypothesis. Moreover, the point S can not coincide with the first point of A_1 in Q' since, in this case, the final point E of Q would be a point in Q' with height $y_E = 0$. This is not possible since Q' is an elevated Dyck path where the only points with height 0 are the first one and the last one.

A different possibility for S is that S coincides with an inner point of D'. First, suppose that $y_S > h_{A_1}$. The final point E of Q can neither coincide with the final point B of D' nor coincide with a point in A_2, since $y_B = h_{A_1} < y_S$ and Q would not be a Dyck path. Therefore, there are two cases:

1. E is an inner point of D';
2. $y_S = h_{A_1}$.

The former one can not occur since in this case $|Q| < |D'| \leq |A_1| + h_{A_1}$ while $|Q| > |A_1| + h_{A_1}$, by construction. If the latter one would occur, then E could neither coincide with an inner point of D' nor coincide with B for the argument above. Moreover, the point E can not lie in A_2 since, in this case, the path Q would not be an elevated Dyck path, due to the presence of B whose height is $y_B = y_S = y_E$.

The last possibility for S is that S is either an inner point of A_2 or coincides with its first point. Clearly, this is not possible since $|A_2| < |Q|$.

■

We can now define the set $W_{A_1 A_2}$ collecting all the Dyck paths we can obtain by the described construction and give the following proposition.

Proposition 2. *Let P be an elevated Dyck path and consider a factorization $P = A_1 A_2$ where A_1 is a bifix-free prefix with $|A_1| = \ell$ and $h_{A_1} = h$. The set*

$$W_{A_1 A_2} = \{A_1 D A_2 | D \in \mathcal{D}_i, \; i \leq (\ell + h)/2\}$$

is a strong non-overlapping set of paths whose cardinality is

$$|W_{A_1 A_2}| = \sum_{i=1}^{(\ell+h)/2} C_i \; .$$

Proof. For any two paths in $W_{A_1 A_2}$ we can apply Proposition 1 so that the set is strong non-overlapping. Easily, the cardinality is given by the sum of the cardinality of the sets of Dyck paths having length from 2 up to $\ell + h$. Note that ℓ and h have the same parity, so that $\ell + h$ is even.

■

The set $W_{A_1 A_2}$ clearly depends on the factorization of P and all the elevated Dyck paths contained in $W_{A_1 A_2}$ have the same prefix A_1 and the same suffix A_2. In the next section we expand the set by working at first on the suffixes, then on the prefixes.

4   Expansion of the Set

A deeper inspection shows that, given a path in $W_{A_1 A_2}$, it is possible to replace the suffix A_2 with other different and suitable ones, in order to construct a new set W_{A_1}. Clearly, the new suffixes have to be suffixes of elevated Dyck paths. Moreover, roughly speaking, they can not be too long, otherwise it would be possible to choose one that contains some other Dyck path of W_{A_1}. In other words, there is a maximum length for the new suffixes.

We start by considering the set $F = \{A_1 D 0^h \mid D \in \mathcal{D}_i, \; i \leq (\ell + h)/2\}$ which is surely strong non-overlapping thanks to Proposition 2 (in this case $A_2 = 0^h$). Note that 0^h is the smallest suffix to append after $A_1 D$ in order to have an (elevated) Dyck path. The smallest $Q \in F$ is obtained with $D = 10$ and it is $Q = A_1 10 0^h$ whose length is $|Q| = \ell + 2 + h$.

Which is the length of one largest suffix R useful to replace 0^h in F in order to keep the non-overlapping property? Let T be the smallest suffix containing Q. The path $G = A_1 10T$ (obtained by replacing 0^h with T), clearly, contains Q, so that $F \cup \{G\}$ is not strong non-overlapping. But if the suffix 0^h is replaced with a smaller suffix than T, then the new path H is such that $F \cup \{H\}$ is strong non-overlapping (see next Proposition). Therefore it is $|R| < |T|$.

It is not difficult to see that $T = Q0^h$ where the factor 0^h is the shortest which can be appended to Q in order to make G a Dyck path. Since $|T| = \ell + 2 + h + h$, it must be $|R| \le \ell + 2h + 1$. Note that it can not be $|R| = \ell + 2h + 1$ since $|R|$ and h must have the same parity (recall that ℓ has the same parity of h). Then, $|R| \le \ell + 2h$.

Let $\mathcal{A}_2$ be the set containing the suffixes of the elevated Dyck paths starting with a down step. We summarize the expansion of $W_{A_1 A_2}$: starting from $W_{A_1 A_2}$, where A_1 is a bifix-free prefix, we replace the fixed suffix A_2 with any suffix $R \in \mathcal{A}_2$ with $|R| \le \ell + 2h + 1$, in order to obtain the new set

$$W_{A_1} = \{A_1 DR | D \in \mathcal{D}_i, \ i \le (\ell + h)/2, \ R \in \mathcal{A}_2, \ h \le |R| \le \ell + 2h\} \ .$$

The suffix must start with a down step since, otherwise, we can get an identical path twice. Indeed, if $Z = A_1 DR$ and $D = D_1 D_2$ with D_1, D_2 Dyck paths, then Z can be obtained also by considering $Z = A_1 D'R'$ with $D' = D_1$ and $R' = D_2 R$. If the suffix starts with a down step, it is not possible to get $R' = D_2 R$.

Proposition 3. *The set W_{A_1} is strong non-overlapping and its cardinality is*

$$|W_{A_1}| = \sum_{i=1}^{(\ell + h)/2} C_i \sum_{j=h}^{\ell + 2h} s_j^{(h)} \ ,$$

where $s_j^{(h)}$ is the number of the suffixes of length j of elevated Dyck paths, starting at height h with a down step.

Proof. Given two paths $V, V' \in W_{A_1}$, with $V = A_1 DR$ and $V' = A_1 D'R'$ suppose that $|V| < |V'|$. We have to exclude a consecutive occurrence of V in V'. Again, we proceed ad absurdum.

As in Proposition 1, the starting point S of V can not be in A_1 in V', since A_1 is a bifix-free prefix.

Suppose that the point S is an inner point of R'. Then, the final point E of V is either an inner point of R' or coincides with its final point. This latter case can not occur, otherwise V would not be a Dyck path. Suppose E is an inner point of R'. Recalling that $|R'| \le \ell + 2h$ and $|V| \ge \ell + 2 + h$, we have that $|R| - |V| < h$ is the number of steps in R' not involved in the occurrence of V. But they are not sufficient to reach the x-axis even if they would be all down steps, since the suffix R' starts from height h.

It can not even be that S is an inner point of D', since in this case, by arguments similar to the ones used in Proposition 1, the path V either would not be an elevated Dyck path (in the case we suppose that E is inside R'), or would not be contained in D' (in the case we suppose E is inside D').

As far as the cardinality is concerned, we observe that we can append all the suffixes $\mathcal{A}_2$ to the paths $A_1 D$ having length from h up to $\ell + 2h$. The number of these suffixes is $\sum_{j=2}^{\ell+2h} s_j^{(h)}$. The thesis easily follows.

■

A similar method can be applied starting from W_{A_1} in order to replace the fixed prefix A_1 with other different and suitable ones, obtaining a new set W. In this case, we fix only the height h reached by the prefixes, rather than a particular prefix as in the set W_{A_1}.

As before, we consider the set $F' = \{1^{h+1}0D0^h \mid D \in \mathcal{D}_i, \ i \leq (\ell + h)/2\}$ which is strong non-overlapping by Proposition 2. Note that the bifix-free prefix $1^{h+1}0$ is the smallest bifix-free prefix useful to reach a point with height h, starting from the x-axis. The smallest $Q \in F'$ is obtained with $D = 10$ and it is $Q = 1^{h+1}0100^h$ whose length is $|Q| = 2h + 4$.

Which is the length $|L|$ of a largest bifix-free prefix L useful to replace $1^{h+1}0$ in F' in order to keep the non-overlapping property? A similar argument to the one used for the construction of W_{A_1} shows that $|L| \leq 3h + 2$. Moreover, all the bifix-free prefixes one can use to replace $1^{h+1}0$ must be non-overlapping one each other, i.e. they must form up a cross bifix-free set of Dyck prefixes ending at height h.

Let $\mathcal{A}_1$ be the set containing the bifix-free prefixes of the elevated Dyck paths ending at height h. Let $X \subset \mathcal{A}_1$ be a cross bifix-free subset of $\mathcal{A}_1$. We define the set

$$W^{(h)} = \{LDR \mid L \in X, \ h + 2 \leq |L| \leq 3h + 2, \ D \in \mathcal{D}_i, \ i \leq (|L| + h)/2,$$
$$R \in \mathcal{A}_2, \ h \leq |R| \leq |L| + 2h, \} \ .$$

We have the following

Proposition 4. *The set $W^{(h)}$ is strong non-overlapping and its cardinality is*

$$|W^{(h)}| = \sum_{k=h+2}^{3h+2} p_k^{(h)} \sum_{i=1}^{(k+h)/2} C_i \sum_{j=h}^{k+2h} s_j^{(h)} \ , \tag{1}$$

where $p_k^{(h)}$ is the number of prefixes of length k belonging to X.

Proof. Recalling that $|L| \leq 3h + 2$, the arguments used in the prof of Proposition 3 can be easily adapted to exclude that a prefix L could contain an occurrence of an element of $W^{(h)}$.

For each allowed length k for a prefix, there are $p_k^{(h)}$ possible prefixes, so that the total number of the choices for the prefixes L is $\sum_{k=h+2}^{3h+2} p_k^{(h)}$.

■

Finally we provide a cross bifix-free subset $X \subset \mathcal{A}_1$. Its definition is

$$X = \{1^h1D0 \mid D \in \mathcal{D}_t, t \geq 0\} .$$

Clearly, each $x \in X$ is a prefix of an elevated Dyck path, having final height h. We will prove that X is a non-overlapping set.

First, we recall the following Lemma [7]:

Lemma 1. *Given a word p of length n over a finite alphabet, a necessary and sufficient condition for p to be bifix-free is that it does not have any bifix b having length $|b| \leq \lfloor \frac{n}{2} \rfloor$.*

We have the following

Proposition 5. *The set X is a non-overlapping set.*

Proof. We first prove that $x \in X$ is bifix-free. Let d be the length of a prefix α and a suffix β of x. Note that $|\alpha|_1 > |\alpha|_0$ and this is true for each prefix of x.

If $d \leq 2t + 2$, then $|\beta|_0 \geq |\beta|_1$ (the equality holds when β coincides with the elevated Dyck path $1D0$), than $\alpha \neq \beta$. If $2t+2 < d \leq \lfloor |x|/2 \rfloor$, then $\alpha = 1^d$ while β surely contains some 0's, so that $\alpha \neq \beta$, again. Then, for Lemma 1, the prefix x is bifix-free.

Given two distinct prefixes $x, x' \in X$, with $x = 1^h1D0$ and $x' = 1^h1D'0$, let β' be a proper suffix of x'. If $|\beta'| \leq 2 + |D'|$, then $\alpha \neq \beta'$ for a similar argument on the number of 1's in α and 0's in β', as in the previous paragraph. Then, suppose $|\beta'| > 2 + |D'|$, so that $\beta' = 1^r1D'0$, with $r < h$. If $\alpha = \beta'$, then x would have the prefix α ending at height $r < h$, so that it should be $\alpha = 1^r$, since the only prefixes of x ending under the line $y = h$ are constituted only by a certain number of 1's. Therefore, $\alpha \neq \beta'$.

With similar arguments we can exclude that x is a proper prefix or a proper suffix of x'. Then, x and x' are cross bifix-free and X is non-overlapping. ∎

Moreover, we can prove that it is a *non-expandable* set in $\mathcal{A}_1$. In other words, for each prefix $a \in \mathcal{A}_1 \setminus X$, there exists a prefix $x \in X$ such that a and x are not non-overlapping (or, equivalently, such that $X \cup a$ is not a non-overlapping set).

Proposition 6. *The set X is non-expandable in $\mathcal{A}_1$.*

Proof. Let $a \in \mathcal{A}_1 \setminus X$, then $a = 1^r0\beta$ with $r > 1$ and β (possibly empty) ending with 0. There are two possibilities: either $r \leq h + 1$ or $r \geq h + 2$. In the former case, the prefix 1^r0 of a coincides with a suffix of $1^{h+1}0 \in X$, so that $X \cup a$ is not non-overlapping.

If $r \geq h + 2$, then the element a, after crossing the line $y = h + 1$ with the first $h+2$ consecutive up steps, must cross this line at least once (actually twice) more, otherwise a would be an element of X. Therefore a can be factorized in $a = a'\gamma$ with $h_{a'} = h$. Then a' would be an element of X since it is a prefix starting with at least $h+2$ up steps and ending at height h. Again, the set $X \cup a$ is not non-overlapping. ∎

5   Enumeration

Let us consider the subset $X^{(3h+2)} \subset X$ with

$$X^{(3h+2)} = \{1^h 1 D 0 \mid D \in \mathcal{D}_t, \ 0 \le t \le h\}$$

containing prefixes x of length $h+2 \le |x| \le 3h+2$, we focus on the enumeration of the subset $W' \subset W$ where

$$W'^{(h)} = \{LDR \mid L \in X^{(3h+2)}, D \in \mathcal{D}_i, \ i \le (|L| + h)/2,$$
$$R \in \mathcal{A}_2, \ h \le |R| \le |L| + 2h, \} .$$

Obviously, it is $|X^{(3h+2)}| = \sum_{t=0}^{h} C_t$, and if $x \in X^{(3h+2)}$ we have $|x| = 2t+h+2$, so that the expression for $|W'|$, recalling expression (1) for $|W^{(h)}|$, is

$$|W'^{(h)}| = \sum_{t=0}^{h} C_t \sum_{i=1}^{t+h+1} C_i \sum_{j=h}^{2t+3h+2} s_j^{(h)} . \tag{2}$$

The number $\bar{s}_j^{(h)}$ of the suffixes of Dyck paths of length j starting at height h is given by (sequence A053121 in [9])

$$\bar{s}_j^{(h)} = \begin{cases} 0, & \text{if either } j < h \text{ or } j - h \text{ is odd,} \\ \dfrac{h+1}{j+1} \dbinom{j+1}{\frac{j-h}{2}}, & \text{otherwise} \end{cases} ,$$

then, the number $s_j^{(h)}$ of the suffixes of elevated Dyck path of length j starting at height h with a down step is

$$s_j^{(h)} = \begin{cases} 0, & \text{if either } j < h \text{ or } j - h \text{ is odd,} \\ \dfrac{h-1}{j-1} \dbinom{j-1}{\frac{j-h}{2}}, & \text{otherwise} \end{cases} ,$$

since $s_j^{(h)} = \bar{s}_{j-2}^{(h-2)}$ (just add a down step at the beginning and at the end of a Dyck suffix to obtain a suffix of an elevated Dyck path starting with a down step).

We now look for a lower bound for $|W'^{(h)}|$ as a function of the parameter h, on which the lengths d of the paths of $W'^{(h)}$ depend. From Proposition 4 it is $2h + 2 \le d \le 12h + 6$.

$$|W'^{(h)}| \ge \sum_{t=0}^{h} C_t \sum_{i=1}^{t+h+1} C_i \cdot s_{2t+3h+2}^{(h)} \ge \sum_{t=1}^{h} C_t \sum_{i=1}^{t+h+1} C_i \cdot \frac{h-1}{2t+3h+1} \binom{2t+3h+1}{t+h+1} . \tag{3}$$

It is known [4] that $C_t > \dfrac{2^{2t-1}}{t(t+1)\sqrt{\pi/(4t-1)}}$ for $t \geq 1$ and that $\binom{n}{k} \geq \left(\dfrac{n}{k}\right)^k$. Moreover, from [10], we have $\sum_{i=1}^{n} C_i > \dfrac{4^{n+1}}{3(n+1)\sqrt{\pi n^3}}$. After some manipulations on the above expression for $|W'|$ it is possible to deduce:

$$|W'^{(h)}| \geq \Theta_1(h) = \frac{128}{45\pi} \cdot \frac{h+1}{(2h+1)^5} \cdot 4^h(16^h - 1) . \tag{4}$$

If the binomial coefficient in expression (3) is estimated by using the Stirling's approximation for factorial $\sqrt{2\pi}\, n^{n+\frac{1}{2}}e^{-n} \leq n! \leq e\, n^{n+\frac{1}{2}}e^{-n}$ we obtain:

$$|W'^{(h)}| \geq \Theta_2(h) = \frac{128}{45e} \cdot (h+3)^{h-5} \cdot \frac{16^h - 1}{e^h} \tag{5}$$

which holds for $h \geq 2$.

It is possible to show that $\Theta_2(h) > \Theta_1(h)$ for $h \geq 8$ so that we can estimate $|W'^{(h)}|$ for small values of h using expression (4). Experimental results show that for $h = 7$ the cardinality of $|W'^{(7)}|$ is larger than $4,2 \times 10^7$, while using expression (5) for $h = 30$, we find that $|W'^{(30)}| > 1,6 \times 10^{61}$.

The above discussion surely does not complete the analysis of the cardinality of our set. It should be more deeply investigated by means of analytic techniques similar to the ones used in [3] and [2], in order to better evaluate its asymptotic behaviour. Here, our aim in this direction is only providing a first evaluation of $|W'^{(h)}|$ which may indicate useful information for applications even if loose. We also point out that the computations of this section are referred to a particular subset $X^{(3h+2)} \subset \mathcal{A}_1$ and that a more general discussion could reveal even more useful indications.

6   Conclusions and Further Developments

The aim of the present paper is the construction of a strong non-overlapping set $W'^{(h)}$ of binary words by using elevated Dyck paths. Given $h \geq 1$, the length d of the words is $2h + 2 \leq d \leq 12h + 6$. Moreover, in each word the number of 1's is equal to the number of 0's. Any element of the set is essentially constituted by three parts: an elevated Dyck prefix (belonging to a cross bifix-free set), a Dyck path, and an elevated Dyck suffix. After the details for the generation of that set, we provide a non-overlapping set X which the prefixes can be chosen from, also proving that X is a non-expandable set. The construction allows to find the formula (2) for the cardinality of the set. We give also a lower bound for the cardinality of $W'^{(h)}$.

Surely, a further development should concern the search for the generating function of the sequence $\{|W'^{(h)}|\}_{h\geq 1}$, depending on h. The extraction of each generic coefficient would let to compare the cardinality of the set herein developed against the other ones in the literature.

References

1. Bajic, D., Stojanovic, J.: Distributed sequences and search process. In: 2004 IEEE International Conference on Communications, Paris, vol. 1, pp. 514–518 (2004)
2. Barcucci, E., Bernini, A., Bilotta, S., Pinzani, R.: A 2D non-overlapping code over a q-ary alphabet. Cryptogr. Commun. **10**, 667–683 (2018)
3. Bilotta, S.: Variable-length non-overlapping codes. IEEE Trans. Inform. Theory **63**, 6530–6537 (2017)
4. Dutton, R., Brigham, R.: Computationally efficient bounds for the catalan numbers. Eur. J. Combin. **7**, 211–213 (1986)
5. Gilbert, E.N., Moore, E.F.: Variable-length binary encodings. Bell Syst. Tech. J. **38**, 933–967 (1959)
6. Levenshtein, V.: Decoding automata which are invariant with respect to their initial state. Probl. Cybern. **12**, 125–136 (1964)
7. Nielsen, P.: A note on bifix-free sequences. IEEE Trans. Inf. Theory **19**, 704–706 (1973)
8. Schützenberger, M.P.: On an application of semi groups methods to some problems in coding. IRE Trans. Inf. Theory **IT-2**, 47–60 (1956)
9. Sloane, N.J.A.: The online encyclopedia of integer sequences. http://oeis.org/
10. Topley, K.: Computationally efficient bounds for the sum of catalan numbers. Fund. J. Math. Math. Sci. **5**, 27–36 (2016)
11. van Wijngaarden, A.J.D.L., Willink, T.J.: Frame synchronization using distributed sequences. IEEE Trans. Commun. **48**, 2127–2138 (2000)
12. Yazdi, S.M.H.T., Kiah, H.M., Garcia-Ruiz, E., Ma, J., Milenkovic, O.: DNA-based storage: trends and methods. IEEE Trans. Mol. Biol. Multi-Scale Commun. **1**, 230–248 (2015)
13. Yazdi, S.M.H.T., Yuan, Y., Ma, J., Zhao, H., Milenkovic, O.: A rewritable, random-access DNA-based storage system. Sci. Rep. **5**, Art. no. 14138 (2015)

Active Learning of Sequential Transducers with Side Information About the Domain

Raphaël Berthon[1,2], Adrien Boiret[1(✉)], Guillermo A. Pérez[2],
and Jean-François Raskin[1]

[1] Université libre de Bruxelles, Brussels, Belgium
adrien.boiret@ulb.be
[2] University of Antwerp – Flanders Make, Antwerp, Belgium

Abstract. Active learning is a setting in which a student queries a teacher, through membership and equivalence queries, in order to learn a language. Performance on these algorithms is often measured in the number of queries required to learn a target, with an emphasis on costly equivalence queries. In graybox learning, the learning process is accelerated by foreknowledge of some information on the target. Here, we consider graybox active learning of subsequential string transducers, where a regular overapproximation of the domain is known by the student. We show that there exists an algorithm to learn subsequential string transducers with a better guarantee on the required number of equivalence queries than classical active learning.

1 Introduction

Active learning is a way for a non-expert user to describe a formal object through behavioral examples and counterexamples, or to obtain formal models for the behavior of legacy or black-box systems which can subsequently be formally verified [14]. In this context, additional information about black-box systems can make learning more efficient in practice [7,13].

The L^* algorithm from [2] has been extended to learn various classes of formal object, e.g. probabilistic automata [5] and, more relevant to this paper, (subsequential deterministic) transducers on words [15]. In this work, we aim to learn transducers, and focus on a specific class of side information: an upper bound on the domain of the transduction. The advantage of this *graybox* model is twofold. First and more directly, it can be used to skip some membership queries outside the transformation's domain. Second, by looking for transducers with the proper behavior when limited to the upper bound, we allow for solutions that are smaller than the canonical objects learned by L^*. This, in turn, offers better guarantees than L^* when we consider the number of equivalence queries required to learn a target. This is relevant, as in cases like non-expert description or legacy-system

This work was supported by the ARC "Non-Zero Sum Game Graphs" project (Fédération Wallonie-Bruxelles), the EOS "Verilearn" project (F.R.S.-FNRS & FWO), and the FWO "SAILor" project (G030020N).

© Springer Nature Switzerland AG 2021
N. Moreira and R. Reis (Eds.): DLT 2021, LNCS 12811, pp. 54–65, 2021.
https://doi.org/10.1007/978-3-030-81508-0_5

learning, the equivalence test is realistically unreliable, or prohibitively costly, when compared to the rest of the operations.

One motivation to focus on learning transducers, and more specifically Mealy machines, with an upper bound on the domain comes from games. In multi-player verification games, assumptions about other players have been proposed to facilitate strategy synthesis [4,6, for instance]. Such assumptions also make sense when a strategy has already been obtained (via synthesis [3] or some alternative means) and one wishes to "minimize" it or its encoding. A simple way to do so is to restrict the domain of the strategy to the reachable set of game configurations (under the assumptions made about the adversaries). Finally, when the game formalism considered allows for delays or multiple choices made unilaterally by some player—as is the case in regular infinite games [8]—strategies are not implementable by Mealy machines but rather require general transducers.

Related Work. The classical algorithm for active learning is L^* [2]. It saturates a table of observations with membership queries, then building a minimal deterministic automaton compatible with those observations to send as candidate for an equivalence query. A polynomial number of membership queries and at most n equivalence queries are always sufficient to learn the automaton.

For transducers, the OSTIA algorithm [15] generalizes L^*, follows a similar structure, and offers comparable guarantees. Like in L^*, the number of queries is polynomial in the size of the minimal normal form of the target transducer.

In the case of graybox learning, the methods differ and this alters the complexity guarantees. For instance, when learning languages from so-called "inexperienced teachers" [11], one considers a case where the teacher sometimes answers a membership query with "I don't know". Under those circumstance, it is impossible to learn a unique minimal automaton. This leads to a trade-off in complexity. On the one hand, finding the minimal automaton compatible with an incomplete table of observations necessitates calls to **NP** oracles (a SAT encoding is used in [11]). On the other hand, obscuring a regular language by replacing some information with "I don't know" will always make the size of the minimal solution smaller or equal to the canonical minimal DFA.

Another work on the topic [1] concerns Mealy machines, i.e. transducers that write one letter exactly for each letter they read. It is shown that one can learn a composition of two Mealy machines if the first one is already known. Just like in [11], the L^*-type algorithm uses oracles to find minimal machines compatible with an incomplete table of observations (as we can only know the behavior of the second machine on the range of the first) and offers a guarantee in the number of equivalence queries bound to the number of states of the minimal second machine, rather than that of the composition in whole.

Contributions. We show how to use string equations that can be encoded into SAT to find a minimal transducer compatible with incomplete observations, and to use this in an L^*-like algorithm to learn transducers. Our algorithm is guaranteed to issue a number of equivalence query that is bounded by the minimal compatible transducer, rather than the canonical one. This difference can be a huge benefit when our upper bound is the result of known complex logical properties or elaborate formats respected by the input, and the transformation we wish to learn is simple.

We note the differences with [1,11] in objects learned, learning frameworks, and available queries. We focus on transducers, a class that subsumes automata and Mealy machine. As an added benefit, transducers are as compact as automata, and as or more compact than Mealy machines they are equivalent to. This compactness preserves or improves the equivalence queries guarantees. In our learning framework, the upper bound is supposed to be known by the student. This is in contrast to the inexperienced teacher case, where the scope of possible observations is unknown, and has to be assumed regular and learned on the fly. When it comes to available queries, [11] assumes the student has access to containment queries i.e. student can ask teacher if the candidates' language contains or is contained in the target, this to obtain better the guarantees. In our model, a simple equivalence query is considered. Conversely, in [1], the only way to do a membership query is to do so on the composition of both machines. In that regard, learning a composition is more constraining than learning with a domain upper bound. However, since finding a reverse image to an output word through a transducer is possible with good complexity, our algorithm can be adapted to learn a composition of two transducers, in the framework of [1].

2 Preliminaries

A *(subsequential string) transducer* $\mathcal{M}$ is a tuple $(\Sigma, \Gamma, Q, q_0, w_0, \delta, \delta_F)$ where Σ is the finite input alphabet, Γ is the finite output alphabet, Q is the finite set of states, $q_0 \in Q$ is the initial state, $w_0 \in \Gamma^*$ is an initial production, δ is the transition function, a partial function $Q \times \Sigma \to Q \times \Gamma^*$ and δ_F is the final function, a partial function $Q \to \Gamma^*$. If $\delta(q,a) = (q', w)$ we note $q \xrightarrow{a|w} q'$. If $\delta_F(q) = w$ we say that q is final, and note $q \xrightarrow{w} \top$. We define the relation $\to^*$ by combining the input and output of several transitions: $\to^*$ is the smallest relation such that $q \xrightarrow{\varepsilon|\varepsilon}^* q$, and if $q \xrightarrow{u|w}^* q'$ and $q' \xrightarrow{a|w'} q''$ then $q \xrightarrow{ua|w \cdot w'}^* q''$. We write $q_0 \xrightarrow{u|w}^* q$ when u reaches the state q with partial output w.

For every state $q \in Q$, we associate a partial function $[\![\mathcal{M}^q]\!](u)$ to $\mathcal{M}$ from input words over Σ to output words over Γ. Formally, $[\![\mathcal{M}^q]\!](u) = w \cdot w'$ if $q \xrightarrow{u|w}^* q_F$ and $q_F \xrightarrow{w'} \top$ for some $q_F \in Q$ and is undefined otherwise. Finally, we define $[\![\mathcal{M}]\!] := w_0 \cdot [\![\mathcal{M}^{q_0}]\!]$ and write that $\mathcal{M}$ implements $[\![\mathcal{M}]\!]$.

We write $\mathrm{dom}([\![\mathcal{M}]\!])$ to denote the domain of $[\![\mathcal{M}]\!]$, that is the set of all $u \in \Sigma^*$ that reach a final state $q_F \in Q$. We often consider the restriction of $[\![\mathcal{M}]\!]$ to a given domain $D \subseteq \Sigma^*$, and denote it $[\![\mathcal{M}]\!]_{|D}$.

Example 1. Consider the function τ_{abc} with domain $Up_{abc} = (a + bc)c^*$ and $\tau_{abc}(ac^n) = \tau_{abc}(bc^n) = 1^n$. It is implemented by the left transducer in Fig. 1.

We note that if we want to restrict a transducer's function to a regular language L for which we have a deterministic word automaton $\mathcal{A}$, a classic construction is to build the product transducer $\mathcal{M} \times \mathcal{A}$, where the states are the

Fig. 1. On the left, a transducer compatible with the merging map in the center, on the right the transducer resulting from this merging map.

Cartesian products of both state spaces, and the final function δ_F is only defined for pairs (q, p) where q is in the domain of the final function of $\mathcal{M}$ and p is final in $\mathcal{A}$. This transducer implements the function $[\![\mathcal{M}]\!]_{\mathcal{A}}$.

We write $|\mathcal{M}|$ to denote the *size* of $\mathcal{M}$, i.e. its number of states. For convenience, we only consider *trim* transducers, that is to say that every state q is reachable from q_0 and co-reachable from a final state. This is no loss of generality, as every transducer is equivalent to a trimmed one with as many or fewer states, and we only consider minimal transducers.

Active Learning. Let Σ and Γ be finite input and output alphabets respectively. Further, let $\tau\colon \Sigma^* \to \Gamma^*$ be a partial function implementable by a transducer. In this work we will be interested in *actively learning* a transducer implementing τ by interacting with a *teacher* who knows τ and can answer questions our algorithm asks about τ. Formally, the teacher is an oracle that can answer *membership* and *equivalence* queries.

Given $u \in \Sigma^*$, a membership query answers $\tau(u)$ if $u \in \mathrm{dom}(\tau)$, and $\perp$ otherwise. Given $\mathcal{M}$ a transducer, an equivalence query answer *true* if $[\![\mathcal{M}]\!] = \tau$, otherwise it provides $u \in \Sigma^*$, a non-equivalence witness such that $u \in \mathrm{dom}([\![\mathcal{M}]\!])\backslash\mathrm{dom}(\tau)$, or $u \in \mathrm{dom}(\tau)\backslash\mathrm{dom}([\![\mathcal{M}]\!])$, or $u \in \mathrm{dom}([\![\mathcal{M}]\!]) \cap \mathrm{dom}(\tau)$ but $[\![\mathcal{M}]\!](u) \neq \tau(u)$. The goal of a learning algorithm in this context is to produce a transducer $\mathcal{M}$ such that $[\![\mathcal{M}]\!] = \tau$.

Side Information About the Domain. We generalize the active learning problem by introducing side information available to the learning algorithm. Concretely, we assume that an *upper bound* on the domain of τ is known in advance. That is, we are given a DFA $\mathcal{A}_{Up}$ whose language Up is such that $\mathrm{dom}(\tau) \subseteq Up$. The goal of the learning algorithm is to produce a transducer $\mathcal{M}$ such that $[\![\mathcal{M}]\!]_{|Up} = \tau$.

The domain upper bound Up may allow us to learn simpler transducers $\mathcal{M}$ than the canonical minimal transducer describing τ—i.e. the class of transducers learnt by OSTIA. For instance, consider the domain Up is the set of BibTeX references where n different properties appear (title, author, year...), but in any order. The automaton recognizing this domain has $\mathcal{O}(2^n)$ states. Learning it, or any transformation on this domain, with a blackbox algorithm may thus require $\mathcal{O}(2^n)$ equivalence tests. However, if the transformation we want to learn is just to extract the title, ignoring every other property, then there exists a very simple transducer, whose size does not increase with n and that, when restricted to Up, performs the desired transformation.

3   Learning Transducers with Side Information

Our algorithm uses an *observation table* T based on a finite prefix-closed subset P of Σ^* and a finite suffix-closed subset S of Σ^*. Formally, we define T as a function $(P \cup P \cdot \Sigma) \cdot S \to \Gamma^* \cup \{\#, \bot\}$ and maintain the following invariant for all $u \in (P \cup P \cdot \Sigma)$ and all $v \in S$. If $u \cdot v \notin Up$ then $T(u \cdot v) = \#$. If $u \cdot v \in Up \setminus \mathrm{dom}(\tau)$ then $T(u \cdot v) = \bot$, otherwise $T(u \cdot v) = \tau(u \cdot v)$. For technical reasons, proper to graybox learning [11], we often consider the set P_T of prefixes of the elements of $(P \cup P\Sigma) \cdot S$.

Definition 2 (Compatible transducer). *Let T be an observation table and $\mathcal{M}$ a transducer of input alphabet Σ and output alphabet Γ. We say that $\mathcal{M}$ is compatible with T when for all $u, v \in P \cup P\Sigma$, if $T(u \cdot v) \in \Gamma^*$ then $[\![\mathcal{M}]\!](u \cdot v) = T(u, v)$ whereas if $T(u \cdot v) = \bot$ then $u \cdot v \notin \mathrm{dom}([\![\mathcal{M}]\!])$.*

To "fill" the table so as to satisfy the invariant, we pose membership queries to the teacher. Once T has certain satisfactory properties (as defined in the OSTIA algorithm and elaborated upon briefly), we are able to construct a transducer $\mathcal{M}$ from it. As a table T can be filled with $\#$, multiple minimal transducers may be compatible with T. To minimize the number of equivalence queries posed, we will send an equivalence query only if there is a unique minimal transducer $\mathcal{M}$ (up to equivalence in Up) compatible with T.

Instead of searching directly for transducers, we work only with the information on how those transducers behave on P_T. We represent this information using objects we call merging maps. We show that we can characterize when there exist two competing minimal transducers with two different merging maps, or two competing minimal transducers with the same merging map. If neither is the case, then there is a unique minimal compatible transducer $\mathcal{M}$, and we build it by guessing its merging map. We then pose an equivalence query to the teacher in order to determine whether $A_{Up} \times \mathcal{M}$ implements the target function τ.

Satisfactory Properties. The following properties are those that allow the OSTIA algorithm [15] to work. Under these properties, we are sure that a transducer can be derived from the table T. They are defined on a specific table $T : (P \cup P\Sigma) \cdot S \to \Gamma^* \cup \{\bot\}$. Given $u \in P \cup P\Sigma$, we call $\mathrm{lcp}_T(u)$ the longest common prefix of all the $T(u \cdot v)$ in Γ^*. For $u, u' \in P \cup P\Sigma^*$, we say that $u \equiv_T u'$ iff for all $v \in S$, we have both $T(u \cdot v) = \bot \iff T(u' \cdot v) = \bot$ and if $T(u \cdot v) \in \Gamma^*$ then $\mathrm{lcp}_T(u)^{-1} T(u \cdot v) = \mathrm{lcp}_T(u')^{-1} T(u' \cdot v)$. A table T is *closed* if for all $ua \in P\Sigma$ there exists $u' \in P$ such that $ua \equiv_T u'$; *$\equiv$-consistent*, if for all $u, u' \in P$, $a \in \Sigma$ such that $ua, u'a \in P \cup P\Sigma^*$, then $u \equiv_T u' \implies ua \equiv_T u'a$; *lcp-consistent*, if for all $ua \in P \cup P\Sigma$, we have that $\mathrm{lcp}_T(u)$ is a prefix of $\mathrm{lcp}_T(ua)$.

The role of these notions in Algorithm 2 is twofold. First, it guarantees that the algorithm could, at worst, find the same transducer as the OSTIA algorithm [15] as a candidate for an equivalence query from a closed, $\equiv$-consistent, lcp-consistent table. Second, it can be seen as an efficient way to acquire information for a learner, as the set of words witnessing non-closure (resp. non-consistency) gives new elements to add to P (resp. S). We can see closed, $\equiv$-consistent, lcp-consistent tables as those that are saturated with membership queries, such that no further information can be obtained by a learner without resorting to more costly operations, e.g. an equivalence query.

Difficulties to Overcome. For any given table T there are infinitely many compatible transducers. This was already the case in automata or Mealy Machines [1,11]. However, where transducers differ, is that even when limiting ourselves to transducers with a minimal number of states, this might still be the case. Indeed, on some transitions, the output can be arbitrary (see Example 9). As a consequence, the method we will use to obtain a compatible transducer from a finite search space combines the methods of [11] with the addition of partial output information and an additional constraint on the output of transitions.

We want to obtain concomitantly an equivalence $\equiv$ on P_T that describes the set of states of the transducer and a *partial output* function $f : P_T \to \Gamma^*$ that describe which output is produced while reading an input. In the context of transducers, side information adds another restriction: a transducer can contain transitions that link together elements of P_T for which we have no output information in T. This is a problem, as the output of such transitions is arbitrary and leads to an infinite number of candidates.

We will represent the behavior of a transducer on P_T but keep only the output information that can be corroborated in T. We call $P_\Gamma \subseteq P_T$ the set of all $u \in P_T$ such that there exists $v \in \Sigma^*$ for which $T(u \cdot v) \in \Gamma^*$. We call $P_\emptyset \subseteq P_T$ the set of all $u \in P_T$ such that there is no $v \in \Sigma^*$ for which $T(u \cdot v) \in \Gamma^*$.

Definition 3 (Merging map). *Let T be an observation table. A merging map (MM) on T is a pair $(\equiv, f)$ where $\equiv$ is an equivalence relation on P_T, and f is a partial function from P_T to Γ^*, such that for all $u, u' \in P_T$ and $a \in \Sigma$:*

1. *P_T is a single equivalence class of $\equiv$.*
2. *If $f(ua)$ exists, then $f(u)$ exists and is a prefix of $f(ua)$.*
3. *If $T(u) \in \Gamma^*$ then $f(u)$ is a prefix of $T(u)$.*
4. *If we have that $f(u)$ exists, $u \equiv u'$ and $ua, u'a \in P_T$ then $ua \equiv u'a$. Furthermore, if $f(ua)$ exists then $f(u)^{-1}f(ua) = f(u')^{-1}f(u'a)$.*
5. *If $T(u) \in \Gamma^*$, $u \equiv u'$ then $T(u') \neq \bot$. Furthermore, if $T(u') \in \Gamma^*$ then $f(u)^{-1}T(u) = f(u')^{-1}T(u')$.*
6. *If $f(ua)$ exists, but there is no $v \in P_T$ such that $v \equiv u$, and $va \in P_\Gamma$, then $f(ua) = f(u)$.*

The intuition is that a MM $(\equiv, f)$ contains the information necessary to model the behavior on P_T of a transducer compatible with T. Rule 1 defines an equivalence class for all elements of P_T that would end up in a sink state. Rule 2 and 3 ensure that the output function f only grows with each transition and the final function respectively. Rule 4 and 5 ensure that the output value is properly defined for each transition and the final function respectively. Finally, rule 6 ensures we only keep output information from P_Γ. If such a pair (u, a) exists, we say that it is *muted*.

Every transducer $\mathcal{M}$ compatible with T has an underlying MM $(\equiv, f)$, and conversely, every MM $(\equiv, f)$ can be used to build a transducer $\mathcal{M}$ compatible with T. The size of a MM is the number of equivalence classes of $\equiv$ in $\mathrm{dom}(f)$. Below, we write q_u for the state associated with $u \in P_T$.

Definition 4 (Resulting Transducer). *Let T be an observation table and $(\equiv, f)$ a MM on T. In the transducer $\mathcal{M}$ resulting from $(\equiv, f)$ the set of states is the set of equivalence classes of $\equiv$ in $\mathrm{dom}(f)$, the initial state is q_ε, the initial production is $f(\varepsilon)$, the transitions are $q_u \xrightarrow{a|f(u)^{-1}f(ua)} q_{ua}$ for $u, ua \in \mathrm{dom}(f)$, and for each u such that $T(u) \in \Gamma^*$, we have $\delta_F(q_u) = f(u)^{-1}T(u)$.*

Definition 5 (Induced MM). *Let T be an observation table and $\mathcal{M}$ a transducer compatible with T. The MM $(\equiv, f)$ induced by the transducer $\mathcal{M}$ is such that we have (A) $u \equiv v$ iff u and v reach the same state of $\mathcal{M}$; (B) for all $u \in P_T$, $a \in \Sigma$ such that $ua \in P_T$ reaches a state q of $\mathcal{M}$: (B.I) if there exists $v \in P_T$ such that $v \equiv u$, and $va \in P_T$, then $f(ua) = f(u) \cdot \delta(q, a)$ (B.II) and if (u, a) is muted, then $f(ua) = f(u)$.*

We note that these transformations are not one-to-one: some transducers compatible with T cannot be obtained with this method. For instance, let us consider a table full of $\#$. Since no $T(u)$ is ever in Γ^*, there is no final state in any transducer created with this method. This is the goal of projecting the transducers' behavior on P_T: the MM induced by $\mathcal{M}$ only contains information on its behavior on P_T, and the transducer resulting from a MM is the transducer with the smallest amount of states and transitions whose behavior on P_T matches what is described in the MM.

Learning Algorithm. Our learning algorithm works as follows: (1) We build up T until it is closed and $\equiv$ and lcp-consistent. (2) If two minimal compatible transducers exist, we find them and a word u to tell them apart. We use a membership query on u and start again. (3) If only one minimal compatible transducer $\mathcal{M}$ remains, we find it. We use an equivalence query on $\mathcal{A}_{Up} \times \mathcal{M}$. Such an algorithm allows using the knowledge of Up to propose more compact candidates, as the minimal transducer compatible with a table T is always smaller than the canonical transducer that can be derived from T if we substitute $\perp$ for the $\#$. This smaller model size leads to a better guarantee when it comes to the number of required equivalence queries. The full algorithm is in Algorithm 2. It uses the subprocedures CompetingMingGen and MinGen which we elaborate upon later.

Theorem 6. *Algorithm 2 terminates and makes a number of equivalence queries bounded by the number of states of a minimal $\mathcal{M}$ such that $[\![\mathcal{M}]\!]_{|Up} = \tau$.*

Proof (Sketch). We first assume termination and focus on the bound on equivalence queries. Note that, by construction of the tables, any minimal $\mathcal{M}$ such that $[\![\mathcal{M}]\!]_{|Up} = \tau$ is compatible with all of them. Thus, it suffices to argue that every equivalence query our algorithm poses increases the size of a minimal transducer compatible with it. For termination, it remains to bound the number

---

Algorithm 2 MinTransducerUp($\mathcal{A}_{Up}$)

Input: The DFA $\mathcal{A}_{Up}$ of an upper-bound
Output: A minimal DFA $\mathcal{M}$ such that $L = \mathcal{M} \cap \mathcal{A}_{Up}$
1: Let $P = S = \{\varepsilon\}$ and $T(P, S)$ the associated table
2: **while** True **do**   ▷ With $u, u' \in P$, $a \in \Sigma$, $v, v' \in S$
3:    **if** (u, a, v, v') is a witness of non-lcp-consistency **then** add av, av' to S
4:    **else if** (u, u', a, v) is a witness of non-$\equiv$-consistency **then** add av to S
5:    **else if** ua is a witness of non-closure **then** add ua to P
6:    **else if** $u := \text{CompetingMinGen}(T(P, S)) \neq \emptyset$ **then** add u and its suffixes to S
7:    **else** $\mathcal{M} := \text{MinGen}(T(P, S))$
8:       **if** u is a non-equiv. witness for $\mathcal{A}_{Up} \times \mathcal{M}$ **then** add all its suffixes to S
9:       **else** return $\mathcal{M}$

---

of membership queries and calls to the subprocedures. Note that it is impossible to enumerate all n-state transducers compatible with an observation table. Termination will follow from the fact that we enumerate a finite subset of them. □

4 Merging Maps to Guess a Minimal Transducer

Algorithm 2 relies on CompetingMinGen(T) and MinGen(T) to find one or several competing transducers compatible with an observation table. This type of procedures is absent from blackbox learning algorithms, but central to graybox learning algorithm [11]. In the automata case, an oracle that guesses a minimal compatible automaton only needs to guess an equivalence relation on P_T. For transducers, we guess a function f that associates to each element of P_T an output in Γ^*. Since this is not a finite search space, we aim to restrict ourselves to a finite subspace that allows us to find one unique or two non-equivalent minimal candidates. We will limit the scope of this search with Definition 10 and 11 of *muted* and *open* transitions, to fix arbitrary outputs at ε.

To combine the two subprocedures, we characterize a necessary and sufficient condition for two possible minimal candidates to exist. This condition is tested by CompetingMinGen(T). When the minimal candidate is unique up to equivalence on Up, we use MinGen(T) to generate it, then send an equivalence query.

MinGen(T) Using MMs. Recall that there are transducers compatible with a table T that do not result from a MM on T. We will show that to implement MinGen(T) and CompetingMinGen(T), it is enough to focus on minimal MMs and to take the resulting transducers as candidates. To justify that this method provides the right result, we prove that it provides valid candidates.

Lemma 7. *Let $(f, \equiv)$ be a minimal MM on a table T and $\mathcal{M}$ its resulting transducer. Then, $\mathcal{M}$ is compatible with T.*

Among the minimal transducers compatible with T, there is one resulting from a MM. Indeed, from a transducer $\mathcal{M}$ compatible with T one can create a smaller one using the MM induced by $\mathcal{M}$ and Definition 4.

Proposition 8. *Let T be a table, $\mathcal{M}$ a transducer compatible with T. There is a transducer $\mathcal{M}'$, with as many states, compatible with T resulting from a MM.*

CompetingMinGen(T) Using MMs. While guessing a MM is enough to guess a minimal transducer, it does not provide a reliable way to decide whether two non-equivalent minimal compatible transducers exist. For the subroutine CompetingMinGen(T), we must find a way to detect whether this is the case. A natural first step is to say that if we can find minimal MMs whose resulting transducers are non-equivalent on Up, then we have found a solution to CompetingMinGen(T). Unfortunately, this condition is not necessary. Indeed, there are minimal MM induced by several non-equivalent transducers. This arises when a transition going out of the state associated to some $u \in P_T$ can have an arbitrarily defined output, because $ua \in P_\emptyset$, or $ua \notin P_T$.

Example 9. In Fig. 1, we note the special case of two transitions in the left transducer: the transition $q_a \xrightarrow{c|1} q_a$ linking $a \in P_\Gamma$ to $ac \in P_\varepsilon$, and the transition $q_b \xrightarrow{a|\varepsilon} q_a$ linking $b \in P_\Gamma$ to $ba \notin P_T$. In both cases, the transition is never used by any $u \in P_T$ such that $T(u) \in \Gamma^*$. The right transducer is also compatible with T, but the output of $q_a \xrightarrow{c|1} q_a$ is ε and $q_b \xrightarrow{a|\varepsilon} q_a$ has been deleted.

The first case, $ua \in P_\emptyset$, is the one we aimed to eliminate by erasing the output in muted pairs (u, a). We call muted transitions those whose output has to be ε in a transducer induced from a MM.

Definition 10. *Let T be a table, $(\equiv, f)$ a MM, and $\mathcal{M}$ its resulting transducer. For all $u \in P_T$, $a \in \Sigma$, (u, a) is a muted pair of $(\equiv, f)$, and $q_u \xrightarrow{a|\varepsilon} q_{ua}$ is a muted transition of $\mathcal{M}$, if $u, ua \in dom(f)$ but there is no $v \in P_T$ such that $u \equiv v$ and $va \in P_\Gamma$.*

The second case, $ua \notin P_T$, is new. We formalize this as follows: An open end is a place where a transition could be added without influencing the behavior of the resulting transducer on P_T. We fix the output of such transitions to ε.

Definition 11. *Let T be a table and $(\equiv, f)$ a MM. For all $u \in P_T$, $a \in \Sigma$, (u, a) is an open end of the map if there is no $v \in P_T$ s.t. $v \equiv u$ and $va \in P_T$. Let $\mathcal{M}$ be the resulting transducer of $(\equiv, f)$. We say that $\mathcal{M}'$ is an open completion of $(\equiv, f)$ (or of $\mathcal{M}$) if it is the transducer with at most one additional transition $u \xrightarrow{a|\varepsilon} u'$ per open end (u, a). We call such transitions open transitions.*

Muted and open transitions allow arbitrary output: if there exists a word $u \in Up$ that goes through a muted transition, that is sufficient to build several compatible transducers that give different outputs on u. This condition together with the existence of competing minimal MMs give a necessary, sufficient and effective, condition for CompetingMinGen(T).

Lemma 12. *Let T be an observation table, $(\equiv, f)$ a MM on T and $\mathcal{M}$ its resulting transducer. If there exists an open completion $\mathcal{M}'$ and an element $u \in Up$ such that $u \in dom(\llbracket \mathcal{M}' \rrbracket)$ and u uses a muted or open transition in its run in $\mathcal{M}'$, then there exist competing minimal transducers compatible with T.*

Implementation: We prove that the following is a possible implementation of CompetingMinGen(T). (1) Search for two minimal MMs with non-equivalent corresponding transducers, (2) if these do not exist, search for a minimal MM and an open completion as in Lemma 12; (3) otherwise, we have a unique minimal transducer up to equivalence on Up.

Proposition 13. *Let T be a table. If there exist two minimal transducers $\mathcal{M}_1$ and $\mathcal{M}_2$ compatible with T but not equivalent on Up, one of the following exists: (i) two minimal MMs with non-equivalent resulting transducers $\mathcal{M}'_1, \mathcal{M}'_2$, or (ii) an open completion $\mathcal{M}'$ of a minimal MM compatible with T and a word $u \in dom(\llbracket \mathcal{M}' \rrbracket) \cap Up$ using at least one open or muted transition of $\mathcal{M}'$.*

5   Encoding into String Equations

Algorithm 2 would work as long as its subroutines return the desired results. While it is impossible to enumerate all compatible transducers, one way to find compatible transducers would be to enumerate all MM. For complexity's sake and to align our result with other graybox algorithms [1,11], we encode the minimal generation subroutines into an **NP** problem like SAT. While a direct encoding is possible, it is easier to go through a first encoding into string equations. We only use operations that are easily encoded into SAT: word (in)equality, concatenation, Boolean operators, and a restricted use of quantifiers.

This setting has the advantage of being more directly relevant to the notions we consider, while keeping the **NP** theoretical bound. Furthermore, SMT solvers have specialized tools [12,16] to solve such equations, that may yield better practical results than a direct SAT encoding.

We encode a table T, merging maps ($\equiv, f$), and runs of $u \in Up$ with output $w \in \Gamma^*$ in the resulting transducer of T. We use word variables T_u for $T(u)$, booleans $E_{u,v}$ for $u \equiv v$, word variables f_u for $f(u)$, word variable u and letter variables $a_i \in [1, k]$ with $u = a_1 \cdots \cdots a_k$ for an input word of length k, and word variables $w = w_0 \cdot w_1 \cdots \cdots w_k \cdot w_{k+1}$ for their output step by step. The bounds on the size of u is given by small model theorems in automata and transducers.

We use string equation formulae to encode the properties we combine in the minimal generation subroutines. We classically build ϕ_{eq} that ensures $E_{u,v}$ denotes an equivalence. Then, each point of Definition 3 can be seen as a simple combination of string equations on T_u and f_u using the binary variables $E_{u,v}$ for $u, v \in P_T$. We can thus build ϕ_{mm} that ensures $E_{u,v}$ and f_u denote a MM.

For the transducer resulting from ($\equiv, f$), and its open completions, we add booleans $m_{u,a}$, $o_{u,a}$ that indicate leaving q_u with a is a muted or open transition.

To model runs, we use $\phi_{run}(u, w)$ ensuring u has a run with output w in the transducer resulting from $E_{u,v}$ and f_u. We build it by making sure the run starts in the initial state with production w_0, ends in a final state with production w_{k+1}, and at the ith step, the input letter is a_i and the output word is w_i.

To encode MinGen(T) we only need to find $E_{u,v}, f_u$ that respect ϕ_{mm} with n states, where n starts at 1 and increases until a solution is found.

For CompetingMinGen(T), we use Proposition 13 to split the encoding in two. To encode the case where there exist two non-equivalent MMs, we use variables $E_{u,v}$ and f_u respecting ϕ_{mm} for a first MM, copies $E'_{u,v}$ and f'_u respecting ϕ_{mm} for a second MM, and ϕ_{Up} and ϕ_{run} to encode the existence of $u \in Up$ whose run differs in the transducers resulting from both MMs.

It is easy to encode the case where there exist an open completion and a word $u \in Up$ that uses an open or muted transition, by using $m_{u,a}$ and $o_{u,a}$ on the run of u in the transducer resulting from the MM of $E_{u,v}$ and f_u.

Combined together, they encode the minimal generating subroutines in string equations, that could then be encoded in SAT, leading to our result:

Proposition 14. *Let T be an observation table. The subroutines MinGen(T) and CompetingMinGen(T) can be effectively implemented.*

Note on Complexity: As this string-equation encoding is a polynomial shorthand for a SAT encoding, each oracle call solves an **NP** problem. Coarsely, MinGen(T) and CompetingMinGen(T) are of complexity $\mathbf{P^{NP}}$. To find a minimal MM of size n, we need $n - 1$ of those oracles to fail on sizes $1 \leq i < n$. If we take Algorithm 2 in its entirety, each call to MinGen(T) and CompetingMinGen(T) need not make use of n oracle calls since we can cache current minimal size for future calls.

6   Conclusion

Adapting graybox learning to transducers revealed more complex than expected. Our solution relies on merging maps, muted and open transitions while offering better bounds on equivalence queries than OSTIA. Two main questions remain open: (1) The bound on the number of equivalence queries was the aim of this paper, but the number of membership queries or call to string equations solvers are not considered. Providing tight bounds or proposing a potential tradeoff, like the one described in [1], would increase the viability of the implementation of such an algorithm. (2) We could consider other classes of side information like general upper bound that cut sections of $\Sigma^* \times \Gamma^*$.

As practical future work, we plan to apply our learning algorithm to the minimization of strategies synthesized by tools participating in the *Reactive Synthesis Competition* [9]. In one of the tracks from the competition, specifications are even given in a format where assumptions about the environment are explicit [10]. We expect our algorithm to work best for that setup.

References

1. Abel, A., Reineke, J.: Gray-box learning of serial compositions of mealy machines. In: Rayadurgam, S., Tkachuk, O. (eds.) NFM 2016. LNCS, vol. 9690, pp. 272–287. Springer, Cham (2016). https://doi.org/10.1007/978-3-319-40648-0_21
2. Angluin, D.: Learning regular sets from queries and counterexamples. Inf. Comput. **75**(2), 87–106 (1987)

3. Bloem, R., Chatterjee, K., Jobstmann, B.: Graph games and reactive synthesis. In: Clarke, E., Henzinger, T., Veith, H., Bloem, R. (eds.) Handbook of Model Checking, pp. 921–962. Springer, Cham (2018). https://doi.org/10.1007/978-3-319-10575-8_27
4. Brenguier, R., Raskin, J., Sankur, O.: Assume-admissible synthesis. Acta Informatica **54**(1), 41–83 (2017). https://doi.org/10.1007/s00236-016-0273-2
5. de la Higuera, C., Oncina, J.: Learning stochastic finite automata. In: Paliouras, G., Sakakibara, Y. (eds.) ICGI 2004. LNCS (LNAI), vol. 3264, pp. 175–186. Springer, Heidelberg (2004). https://doi.org/10.1007/978-3-540-30195-0_16
6. Fisman, D., Kupferman, O., Lustig, Y.: Rational synthesis. In: Esparza, J., Majumdar, R. (eds.) TACAS 2010. LNCS, vol. 6015, pp. 190–204. Springer, Heidelberg (2010). https://doi.org/10.1007/978-3-642-12002-2_16
7. Garhewal, B., Vaandrager, F., Howar, F., Schrijvers, T., Lenaerts, T., Smits, R.: Grey-box learning of register automata. In: Dongol, B., Troubitsyna, E. (eds.) IFM 2020. LNCS, vol. 12546, pp. 22–40. Springer, Cham (2020). https://doi.org/10.1007/978-3-030-63461-2_2
8. Holtmann, M., Kaiser, L., Thomas, W.: Degrees of lookahead in regular infinite games. Log. Methods Comput. Sci. **8**(3) (2012). https://doi.org/10.2168/LMCS-8(3:24)2012
9. Jacobs, S., et al.: The 4th reactive synthesis competition (SYNTCOMP 2017): benchmarks, participants & results. In: Fisman, D., Jacobs, S. (eds.) Proceedings Sixth Workshop on Synthesis, SYNT@CAV 2017, Heidelberg, Germany, 22 July 2017. EPTCS, vol. 260, pp. 116–143 (2017). https://doi.org/10.4204/EPTCS.260.10
10. Jacobs, S., Klein, F., Schirmer, S.: A high-level LTL synthesis format: TLSF v1.1. In: Piskac, R., Dimitrova, R. (eds.) Proceedings Fifth Workshop on Synthesis, SYNT@CAV 2016, Toronto, Canada, 17–18 July 2016. EPTCS, vol. 229, pp. 112–132 (2016). https://doi.org/10.4204/EPTCS.229.10
11. Leucker, M., Neider, D.: Learning minimal deterministic automata from inexperienced teachers. In: Margaria, T., Steffen, B. (eds.) ISoLA 2012. LNCS, vol. 7609, pp. 524–538. Springer, Heidelberg (2012). https://doi.org/10.1007/978-3-642-34026-0_39
12. Liang, T., Reynolds, A., Tsiskaridze, N., Tinelli, C., Barrett, C., Deters, M.: An efficient SMT solver for string constraints. FMSD **48**(3), 206–234 (2016)
13. Neider, D., Smetsers, R., Vaandrager, F., Kuppens, H.: Benchmarks for automata learning and conformance testing. In: Margaria, T., Graf, S., Larsen, K.G. (eds.) Models, Mindsets, Meta: The What, the How, and the Why Not? LNCS, vol. 11200, pp. 390–416. Springer, Cham (2019). https://doi.org/10.1007/978-3-030-22348-9_23
14. Vaandrager, F.W.: Model learning. Commun. ACM **60**(2), 86–95 (2017). https://doi.org/10.1145/2967606
15. Vilar, J.M.: Query learning of subsequential transducers. In: Miclet, L., de la Higuera, C. (eds.) ICGI 1996. LNCS, vol. 1147, pp. 72–83. Springer, Heidelberg (1996). https://doi.org/10.1007/BFb0033343
16. Zheng, Y., Zhang, X., Ganesh, V.: Z3-str: a z3-based string solver for web application analysis. In: Proceedings of the 2013 9th Joint Meeting on Foundations of Software Engineering, pp. 114–124 (2013)

Compositions of Constant Weighted Extended Tree Transducers

Malte Blattmann$^{(\boxtimes)}$ and Andreas Maletti

Universität Leipzig, Faculty of Mathematics and Computer Science, PO Box 100 920,
04009 Leipzig, Germany
malteblattmann@gmx.de, andreas.maletti@uni-leipzig.de

Abstract. Conjecture 11 of [Lagoutte, Maletti: Survey—Weighted extended top-down tree transducers—Part III: Composition. Proc. AFCS, LNCS 7020, p. 272–308, Springer 2011] is confirmed. It is demonstrated that the composition of a constant weighted extended tree transducer with a linear weighted top-down tree transducer can be computed by a single weighted extended tree transducer. Whereas linearity and the top-down property are syntactic, the constant property is semantic. The decidability of the constant property is investigated in several restricted settings.

Keywords: Weighted tree transducer · Top-down tree transducer · Extended tree transducer · Composition · Decidability

1 Introduction

Weighted tree transducers [5, 7, 16] are a straightforward generalization of classical tree transducers [23–25] such that each rule carries a weight from a semiring. They compute a weighted relation on trees, which assigns a weight to each pair of an input and an output tree. Overall, they thus allow a much more fine-grained classification of the input-output relation. A good overview of weighted tree transducers is presented in [8].

The weighted extended tree transducers [12, 18, 20] have been introduced to model certain syntax-based translation systems in machine translation [15] and have also been utilized in that capacity [12]. Whereas (non-extended) tree transducers permit only a single input symbol in the left-hand side of each rule, the extended variants allow arbitrary many input symbols in the left-hand side of their rules, which makes the model more symmetric. In the unweighted case, this asymmetry was noted much earlier and has been thoroughly investigated [2, 3].

In this contribution we study compositions of certain weighted extended tree transducers. Composition is one of the basic operations on relations and can straightforwardly be extended to weighted relations. More precisely, given weighted relations $\tau_1 \colon A \times B \to \mathbb{Q}$ and $\tau_2 \colon B \times C \to \mathbb{Q}$ with weights in the rational numbers $\mathbb{Q}$, their composition is the weighted relation $\tau_1 \, ; \, \tau_2$ given for every $a \in A$ and $c \in C$ by

$$(\tau_1 \, ; \, \tau_2)(a, c) = \sum_{b \in B} \tau_1(a, b) \cdot \tau_2(b, c) \ .$$

© Springer Nature Switzerland AG 2021
N. Moreira and R. Reis (Eds.): DLT 2021, LNCS 12811, pp. 66–77, 2021.
https://doi.org/10.1007/978-3-030-81508-0_6

Note that this composition is essentially a matrix product. Compositions of weighted relations naturally occur in the development of speech recognition systems [22], where the standard methodology composes from right-to-left a language-model transducer, a lexicon transducer, a context-dependency trans-ducer, and a final HMM transducer each computing corresponding weighted relations. While the transducers for speech recognition usually work on strings, the transducers in syntax-based machine translation operate on trees [27] and individual components of the cascade reorder the subtrees of the input, insert additional subtrees, and finally translate the lexical entries. Representing the composed weighted relation computed by the cascade by just a single trans-ducer offers significant advantages [1,12,21].

We continue the investigation started in [17] and confirm [17, Conjecture 11]. To this end, we show how to compose an arbitrary constant weighted extended tree transducer with a linear weighted top-down tree transducer. In other words, we require that the first transducer is constant, which is a semantic property and essentially states that a certain weight total does not depend on the actual input tree, but only on the state of the transducer. The second transducer needs to be linear (i.e., is not allowed to copy subtrees) and non-extended (i.e., handles a single input symbol in each rule). However, we place no constraints on the utilized weight structure. Our construction works for any commutative semiring [11,14]. Both main features, commutativity and distributivity, of the weight structure are heavily utilized in the construction. The history and corresponding unweighted composition results are discussed at length in [17].

Besides the construction, we offer an illustration of the problem that occurs in the standard composition construction of [17] and motivate the adjustment in this manner. A proof sketch for the correctness of the composition construction is provided. Since the constant property is semantic, it is not trivially decidable whether a given transducer is constant. In the final section, we explore a few cases, in which decidability of the constant property can be established.

2   Preliminaries

The nonnegative integers are $\mathbb{N}$, and we let $[n] = \{i \in \mathbb{N} \mid 1 \leq i \leq n\}$ for every $n \in \mathbb{N}$. We use the countable set $X = \{x_i \mid i \in \mathbb{N}\}$ of (formal) variables and its finite subsets $X_k = \{x_i \mid i \in [k]\}$ for every $k \in \mathbb{N}$. Given relations $R \subseteq A \times B$ and $S \subseteq B \times C$ their composition $R \,;\, S$ is

$$R \,;\, S = \{(a,c) \in A \times C \mid \exists b \in B \colon (a,b) \in R, \ (b,c) \in S\}.$$

The inverse R^{-1}, domain $\mathrm{dom}(R)$, and range $\mathrm{ran}(R)$ of R are $R^{-1} = \{(b,a) \mid (a,b) \in R\}$, $\mathrm{dom}(R) = \{a \in A \mid \exists b \in B \colon (a,b) \in R\}$ and $\mathrm{ran}(R) = \mathrm{dom}(R^{-1})$.

For any set A we let A^* be the set of all finite words (i.e. sequences) over A including the empty word ε. Finite sets are also called alphabets. The length of a word $w \in A^*$ is written as $|w|$, and for all $k \in \mathbb{N}$ we let $A^{\leq k} = \{w \in A^* \mid k \geq |w|\}$ be the words of length at most k.

A ranked alphabet (Σ, rk) consists of an alphabet Σ together with a mapping $\mathrm{rk} \colon \Sigma \to \mathbb{N}$ that assigns a *rank* to each element of Σ. For every $k \in \mathbb{N}$ we let $\Sigma^{(k)} = \{\sigma \in \Sigma \mid \mathrm{rk}(\sigma) = k\}$ be the set of all symbols of Σ that have rank k. We write $\sigma^{(k)}$ to indicate that $\mathrm{rk}(\sigma) = k$. To simplify the notation, we often refer to the ranked alphabet (Σ, rk) by Σ alone. The set $T_\Sigma(A)$ of all trees is the smallest set T such that $A \subseteq T$ and $\sigma(t_1, \dots, t_k) \in T$ for all $k \in \mathbb{N}$, $\sigma \in \Sigma^{(k)}$, and $t_1, \dots, t_k \in T$. Instead of $T_\Sigma(\emptyset)$ we simply write T_Σ. Given a finite set Q and a subset $T \subseteq T_\Sigma(A)$, we let $Q(T) = \{q(t) \mid q \in Q, t \in T\} \subseteq T_{\Sigma \cup Q}(A)$, where each element of q is considered as a unary symbol. The *positions* of a tree $t \in T_\Sigma(A)$ are inductively defined by $\mathrm{pos}(a) = \{\varepsilon\}$ for all $a \in A$ and

$$\mathrm{pos}(\sigma(t_1, \dots, t_k)) = \{\varepsilon\} \cup \{iw \mid i \in [k], w \in \mathrm{pos}(t_i)\}$$

for all $k \in \mathbb{N}$, $\sigma \in \Sigma^{(k)}$, and $t_1, \dots, t_k \in T_\Sigma(A)$. Note that the positions $\mathrm{pos}(t)$ are totally ordered by the usual lexicographic order $\leq_{\mathrm{lex}}$. We write $t(w)$, $t|_w$, and $t[u]_w$ to refer to the symbol at position $w \in \mathrm{pos}(t)$ in the tree $t \in T_\Sigma(A)$, the subtree of t rooted in w, and the tree obtained from t by replacing the subtree rooted in w by the tree $u \in T_\Sigma(A)$, respectively. Formally, $a(\varepsilon) = a|_\varepsilon = a$ and $a[u]_\varepsilon = u$ for all $a \in A$ and for $t = \sigma(t_1, \dots, t_k)$

$$t(\varepsilon) = \sigma \qquad t(iw) = t_i(w) \qquad t|_\varepsilon = t \qquad t|_{iw} = t_i|_w$$

$$t[u]_\varepsilon = u \qquad t[u]_{iw} = \sigma(t_1, \dots, t_{i-1}, t_i[u]_w, t_{i+1}, \dots, t_k)$$

for all $k \in \mathbb{N}$, $\sigma \in \Sigma^{(k)}$, $t_1, \dots, t_k \in T_\Sigma(A)$, $i \in [k]$, and $w \in \mathrm{pos}(t_i)$. Given labels $L \subseteq \Sigma \cup A$ we let $\mathrm{pos}_L(t) = \{w \in \mathrm{pos}(t) \mid t(w) \in L\}$ be the set of positions of t labeled by elements of L, and $\mathrm{pos}_a(t) = \mathrm{pos}_{\{a\}}(t)$ for all $a \in A$. We let $\mathrm{var}(t) = \{x \in X \mid \mathrm{pos}_x(t) \neq \emptyset\}$ for every tree $t \in T_\Sigma(A \cup X)$. The tree t is called *linear* if $|\mathrm{pos}_x(t)| \leq 1$ for all $x \in X$. For every $V \subseteq X$, we let $C_\Sigma(V) = \{t \in T_\Sigma(V) \mid \mathrm{var}(t) = V, t \text{ linear}\}$ be the set of those trees that contain exactly one position labeled v for every $v \in V$. Given a *substitution* $\theta \colon V \to T_\Sigma(A \cup X)$ with $V \subseteq X$ finite, its application to a tree $t \in T_\Sigma(A \cup X)$ is given by $v\theta = \theta(v)$ for all $v \in V$, $x\theta = x$ for all $x \in X \setminus V$, $a\theta = a$ for all $a \in A$, and $\sigma(t_1, \dots, t_k)\theta = \sigma(t_1\theta, \dots, t_k\theta)$ for all $k \in \mathbb{N}$, $\sigma \in \Sigma^{(k)}$, and $t_1, \dots, t_k \in T_\Sigma(A \cup X)$. For every $t \in T_\Sigma$ we let

$$\mathrm{match}(t) = \{(c, \theta) \mid k \in \mathbb{N}, c \in C_\Sigma(X_k), \theta \colon X_k \to T_\Sigma, t = c\theta\} \ .$$

A (commutative) *semiring* [11,14] is an algebraic structure $(S, +, \cdot, 0, 1)$, in which $(S, +, 0)$ and $(S, \cdot, 1)$ are both commutative monoids, $s \cdot 0 = 0$ for all $s \in S$, and multiplication $\cdot$ distributes over addition $+$. The semiring is *idempotent* if $1 + 1 = 1$. Moreover, the semiring is *zero-sum free* if $s + s' = 0$ implies $s = 0$ for all $s, s' \in S$, and *zero-divisor free* if $s \cdot s' = 0$ implies $0 \in \{s, s'\}$ for all $s, s' \in S$. Note that every idempotent semiring is zero-sum free. If there exists $(-1) \in S$ such that $1 + (-1) = 0$, then S is a *ring*. Finally, given a mapping $f \colon A \to S$, we let $\mathrm{supp}(f) = \{a \in A \mid f(a) \neq 0\}$.

3   Weighted Extended Tree Transducers

Let us start by introducing the main tree transducer model, the weighted extended tree transducer [12,18,20], for which we want to study composition.

It is the weighted version of the bimorphism model studied in [2,3]. For convenience we use the minor syntactic variant of [17, Definition 3], which introduces an additional indirection via rule identifiers. For the rest of the contribution, let $(S, +, \cdot, 0, 1)$ be an arbitrary commutative semiring.

Definition 1 (see [17, Definition 3]). *A* weighted extended tree transducer *(for short: wxtt) is a tuple* $(Q, \Sigma, \Delta, Q_0, I, \chi)$, *in which*

- Q *is a finite set of* states
- Σ *and* Δ *are ranked alphabets of* input *and* output *symbols, respectively, such that* $Q \cap (\Sigma \cup \Delta) = \emptyset$,
- $Q_0 \subseteq Q$ *is a set of* initial states,
- I *is a finite set of* rule identifiers, *and*
- $\chi : I \to Q(T_\Sigma(X)) \times S \times T_\Delta(Q(X))$ *assigns a weighted rule* $\chi(i) = \langle \ell, s, r \rangle$ *to each identifier* $i \in I$ *such that* $\ell \notin Q(X)$, ℓ *is linear, and* $var(r) \subseteq var(\ell)$.

In the following, let $M = (Q, \Sigma, \Delta, Q_0, I, \chi)$ be a wxtt. To simplify the notation, we also write $\ell \xrightarrow{s} r$ instead of $\langle \ell, s, r \rangle$. Moreover, for every $i \in I$ we let ℓ_i, s_i, and r_i be such that $\chi(i) = \langle \ell_i, s_i, r_i \rangle$. Since we can select the identifiers such that they uniquely determine M (i.e., different wxtt have disjoint sets of identifiers), the notation ℓ_i, s_i, and r_i should not lead to confusion. The wxtt M is called *linear* if r_i is linear for every $i \in I$, and it is called BOOLEAN if $s_i \in \{0, 1\}$ for every $i \in I$. Finally, M is a *weighted top-down tree transducer* (for short: wtdtt), if $|\mathrm{pos}_\Sigma(\ell_i)| = 1$ for all $i \in I$.

Next, we introduce the semantics of M. Later in our composition construction it proves to be convenient to handle symbols and states of another wxtt. To this end, we consider ranked alphabets Σ' and Δ' such that $\Sigma \subseteq \Sigma'$ and $\Delta \subseteq \Delta'$. Moreover, let $q \in Q$, $i \in I$, and $\xi \in T_{\Delta'}(Q(T_{\Sigma'}(X)))$, which we treat as a tree of $T_{\Delta' \cup Q \cup \Sigma'}(X)$. This treatment entails certain technical difficulties since the rank of each symbol needs to be unique, but we largely ignore those issues here in the interest of clarity. A position $w \in \mathrm{pos}_q(\xi)$ is i-*reducible* if there exists a substitution $\theta : var(\ell_i) \to T_{\Sigma'}(X)$ such that $\xi|_w = \ell_i \theta$. Note that if such a substitution exists, then it is unique. Let $w \in \mathrm{pos}_Q(\xi)$ be the lexicographically least position labeled by a state. If w is i-reducible, then we let $i(\xi) = \xi[r_i \theta]_w$, which we also write as $\xi \xRightarrow{i}_M [r_i \theta]_w$. Otherwise, $i(\xi)$ is undefined. Given $i_1, \ldots, i_n \in I$ we let $(i_1 \cdots i_n)(\xi) = i_n(\cdots i_1(\xi) \cdots)$, which we also write as $\xi \xRightarrow{i_1 \cdots i_n}_M (i_1 \cdots i_n)(\xi)$. A sequence $d \in I^*$ is called *derivation* for ξ if $d(\xi)$ is defined, and the finite set of all such derivations is denoted by $D_M(\xi)$. Moreover, we let

$$D_M^\perp(\xi) = \{d \in D_M(\xi) \mid d(\xi) \in T_\Delta\}$$

be the subset of terminal derivations. Given a derivation $i_1 \cdots i_n \in D_M(\xi)$ with $n \in \mathbb{N}$ and $i_1, \ldots, i_n \in I$ we let $\mathrm{wt}_M(i_1 \cdots i_n) = \prod_{j=1}^{n} s_{i_j}$. Finally, we define the mapping $\tau'_M : T_{\Delta'}(Q(T_{\Sigma'}(X))) \times T_{\Delta'}(Q(T_{\Sigma'}(X))) \to S$ by

$$\tau'_M(\xi, \zeta) = \sum_{\substack{d \in D_M(\xi) \\ d(\xi) = \zeta}} \mathrm{wt}_M(d)$$

Fig. 1. Rules of the wtdtt M' of Example 3.

for all $\xi, \zeta \in T_{\Delta'}(Q(T_{\Sigma'}(X)))$. The semantics of M is the *weighted relation* $\tau_M \colon T_\Sigma \times T_\Delta \to S$ given by

$$\tau_M(t,u) = \sum_{q \in Q_0} \tau'_M(q(t), u)$$

for all trees $t \in T_\Sigma$ and $u \in T_\Delta$. The wxtt M is *total* if for all states $q \in Q$ and input trees $t \in T_\Sigma$ there is an output tree $u \in T_\Delta$ such that $(q(t), u) \in \mathrm{supp}(\tau'_M)$. Finally, M is *unambiguous* if for every state q and input tree $t \in T_\Sigma$ there exists at most one derivation $d \in D^\perp_M(q(t))$.

Next, let us introduce the special property, for which we provide a composition construction. The property *constant* was introduced in [17, Definition 9] and essentially says that for any given state $q \in Q$ there exists a constant c_q such that for every input tree $t \in T_\Sigma$ the sum of all weights of derivations $d \in D^\perp_M(q(t))$ is exactly c_q.

Definition 2 (see [17, Definition 9]). *Let* $q \in Q$ *and* $c \in S$. *State* q *is* c-*constant if* $c = \sum_{d \in D^\perp_M(q(t))} \mathit{wt}_M(d)$ *for every* $t \in T_\Sigma$. *The wxtt* M *is constant if for every state* $q \in Q$ *there exists* $c_q \in S$ *such that* q *is* c_q-*constant.*

To conclude this section, let us quickly discuss a small example to illustrate the notions introduced in this section.

Example 3. Let $M' = (\{q'\}, \Sigma, \Delta, \{q'\}, \{1,2,3\}, \chi')$ be the wtdtt over the semi-ring $(\mathbb{R}, +, \cdot, 0, 1)$ with $\Sigma = \{\gamma^{(1)}, \alpha^{(0)}\}$, $\Delta = \{\gamma^{(1)}, \alpha^{(0)}, \beta^{(0)}\}$ and χ' presented in Fig. 1. Then for

$$t = \underbrace{\gamma(\cdots \gamma(\alpha) \cdots)}_{n \text{ times } \gamma} \qquad \text{we have} \qquad D^\perp_{M'}(q'(t)) = \{\underbrace{1 \cdots 1}_{n \text{ times}} 2, \underbrace{1 \cdots 1}_{n \text{ times}} 3\}$$

and those derivations have weight $s_1 \cdot \ldots \cdot s_1 \cdot s_2 = .5$ and $s_1 \cdot \ldots \cdot s_1 \cdot s_3 = .5$. The derivations are illustrated in Fig. 2 for $n = 2$. This illustrates that state q' is 1-constant, which also proves that M' is constant.

4   Composition

Our overall goal is to settle [17, Conjecture 11], which deals with compositions of the weighted relations computed by certain wxtt. Before stating the

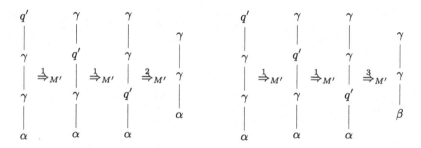

Fig. 2. Illustration of derivations of M' discussed in Example 3.

conjecture let us settle the relevant notion of composition first. A weighted relation $\tau \colon T_\Sigma \times T_\Delta \to S$ is *finitary* if the set $\{u \in T_\Delta \mid (t,u) \in \mathrm{supp}(\tau)\}$ is finite for every $t \in T_\Sigma$. The weighted relation τ_M computed by a wxtt M is always finitary by [6, Note before Lemma 2], which also applies to nonlinear wxtt. Now, let us first formally introduce the composition of 2 weighted relations. Let $\tau' \colon T_\Sigma \times T_\Delta \to S$ and $\tau \colon T_\Delta \times T_\Gamma \to S$ be weighted relations such that τ' is finitary. Their composition $\tau' \,;\, \tau \colon T_\Sigma \times T_\Gamma \to S$ is given by

$$(\tau' \,;\, \tau)(t, t'') = \sum_{t' \in T_\Delta} \tau'(t, t') \cdot \tau(t', t'')$$

for all $t \in T_\Sigma$ and $t'' \in T_\Gamma$, where the sum is finite since τ' is finitary. Now we can state the conjecture. Given a constant wxtt M' and a linear wtdtt M, [17, Conjecture 11] claims that the composition $\tau_{M'} \,;\, \tau_M$ can be computed by a wxtt.

Let us first provide some insight into the difficulties that arise when attempting the standard composition constructions. Let $M' = (Q', \Sigma, \Delta, Q'_0, I', \chi')$ be the constant wxtt and $M = (Q, \Delta, \Gamma, Q_0, I, \chi)$ be the linear wtdtt. Moreover, for every state $q' \in Q'$, let $c_{q'} \in S$ be such that q' is $c_{q'}$-constant. We first investigate the composition of M' and M using the generic composition construction of [17, Definition 6] to highlight the problem. Afterwards we provide a solution and prove that it is correct. We start with the exposition of the generic construction and an illustration of the inherent problem on a simplistic example.

Example 4. We reconsider the constant wtdtt $M' = (Q', \Sigma, \Delta, Q', I', \chi')$ of Example 3 together with the linear wtdtt $M = (\{q\}, \Delta, \{\alpha^{(0)}\}, \{q\}, \{4\}, \chi)$, where $\chi(4) = q\big(\gamma(x_1)\big) \xrightarrow{1} \alpha$. For the sake of illustration, we adjust M' such that $s_2 = s_3 = 2$; i.e., the weight of rules 2 and 3 is adjusted to weight 2. It can be verified as in Example 3 that q' is 4-constant in the adjusted wtdtt M'. Now, let us consider the input tree $t = \gamma\big(\gamma(\alpha)\big)$. As illustrated in Example 3 there are exactly 2 derivations in $D_{M'}^\perp(q'(t))$, which are 112 and 113 as demonstrated in Fig. 2. Their weights are $s_1 \cdot s_1 \cdot s_2 = 1 \cdot 1 \cdot 2 = 2$ and $s_1 \cdot s_1 \cdot s_3 = 1 \cdot 1 \cdot 2 = 2$. There exists a single derivation $d_1 \in D_M^\perp\big(q(\gamma(\gamma(\gamma(\alpha))))\big)$ on the output tree $\gamma\big(\gamma(\alpha)\big)$ of derivation 112 and a single derivation $d_2 \in D_M^\perp\big(q(\gamma(\gamma(\gamma(\beta))))\big)$ on the output tree $\gamma\big(\gamma(\beta)\big)$ of derivation 113. In both cases the derivation is $d_1 = d_2 = 4$, and it is illustrated in Fig. 3. Its weight is obviously $s_4 = 1$.

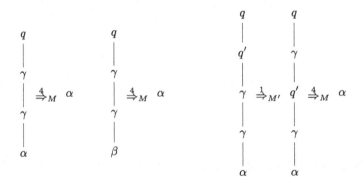

Fig. 3. Illustration of derivations discussed in Example 4.

The main idea of the generic composition construction is to apply rules of M immediately after the input symbol it consumes has been produced by a rule of M'. In this manner we avoid the explicit construction of the intermediate trees, which were $\gamma(\gamma(\alpha))$ and $\gamma(\gamma(\beta))$ in our example. Every rule i' of M' together with the rules of M that consume the symbols output by i' will form a new rule in the composed wxtt. In this manner we mix the rule applications of M' and M and obtain the derivation 14 starting at $q(q'(t))$, which is illustrated right-most in Fig. 3. Note that since rule identifier 1 belongs to M', it will select the least occurrence of a state in the set $\{q'\}$ of states of M'. This derivation 14 has weight $s_1 \cdot s_4 = 1 \cdot 1 = 1$. It is evident that applications of rules 1, 2, and 3 are missing since the subtree $q'(\gamma(\alpha))$ is deleted by the application of rule 4. This has no impact on the generated output tree, but the missing application of rules 1, 2, and 3 impacts the weight. Indeed the rule weights might even contain a factor 0 (directly or as a product of factors), which would potentially remove the pair of the input and output tree from the support of the computed weighted relation altogether.

This change of weight, which in our case always amounts to missing factors due to missing rule applications, needs to be corrected in an adjusted composition construction. We also remark that in the derivation presented the subtree $\gamma(\alpha)$ in the input tree was never processed and could potentially been processed utilizing different rules. As presented in the example, we could utilize derivation 12 or 13 to process the remaining subtree $q'(\gamma(\alpha))$. The newly constructed rule needs to account for all derivations that would have been possible starting in $q'(\gamma(\alpha))$, which have total weight $c_{q'}$ by the definition of $c_{q'}$-constant. Moreover, due to the definition of $c_{q'}$-constant, we know that $c_{q'}$ is the total weight irrespective of the actual subtree that would need to still be processed.

The solution is relatively straightforward. Whenever M deletes a subtree (i.e., a variable $x \in X$ occurs in the left-hand side of a rule, but does not occur in the corresponding right-hand side), we charge the weight $c_{q'}$ for every occurrence of state q' in the deleted part. Since the wtdtt M is linear, it will not copy subtrees and thus not duplicate occurrences of states $q' \in Q'$. This motivates the following composition of the given wxtt.

Definition 5. (see [17, Definition 6]). *Let* $M' = (Q', \Sigma, \Delta, Q'_0, I', \chi')$ *be a constant wxtt and* $M = (Q, \Delta, \Gamma, Q_0, I, \chi)$ *be a linear wtdtt. Moreover, for every* $q' \in Q'$, *let* $c_{q'} \in S$ *be such that* q' *is* $c_{q'}$-*constant. Finally, let* $b \in \mathbb{N}$ *be such that* $|pos(r_{i'})| \leq b$ *for every* $i' \in I'$. *The composed wxtt* M' ; M *is the wxtt* $(Q \times Q', \Sigma, \Gamma, Q_0 \times Q'_0, P, \rho)$ *such that* $P = I' \times Q \times I^{\leq b}$ *and*

$$\rho(\langle i', q, d\rangle) = \begin{cases} (q(\ell_{i'}),\ s,\ r) & \text{if } r = d\big(q(r_{i'})\big) \in T_\Delta\big(Q(Q'(X))\big) \\ 0 & \text{otherwise} \end{cases}$$

for every identifier $i' \in I'$, *state* $q \in Q$, *and identifier sequence* $d \in I^{\leq b}$, *where*

$$s = s_{i'} \cdot wt_M(d) \cdot \prod_{q' \in Q'} c_{q'}^{|pos_{q'}(r_{i'})| - |pos_{q'}(r)|} .$$

Note that we identify $Q\big(Q'(T)\big)$ *with* $(Q \times Q')(T)$.

For the given example derivation in Fig. 3 we observe that the application of rule 4 deletes a subtree containing 1 occurrence of state q', for which $c_{q'} = 4$. Hence the newly constructed rule with identifier $\langle 1, q, 4\rangle$ would be assigned weight $s_1 \cdot s_4 \cdot c_{q'}$. Let us state the main result, which confirms [17, Conjecture 11].

Theorem 6. *Let* M' *be a constant wxtt and* M *be a linear wtdtt. Then there exists a wxtt* N *such that* $\tau_N = \tau_{M'}$; τ_M.

Proof (sketch). Let $M' = (Q', \Sigma, \Delta, Q'_0, I', \chi')$. Without loss of generality, we can assume that for every $i' \in I'$ there exists $k_{i'} \in \mathbb{N}$ such that $var(\ell_{i'}) = X_{k_{i'}}$. We call a tree $c \in C_\Sigma(X_k)$ *normalized* if the leafs labeled $x_1, \ldots, x_k$ occur exactly in this order when read left-to-right. Following [19, Definition 3] we define the mapping $h_{M'} \colon Q'(T_\Sigma) \times T_\Delta \to S$ for every $\xi \in Q'(T_\Sigma)$ and $u \in T_\Delta$ by

$$h_{M'}(\xi, u) = \sum_{\substack{i' \in I' \\ (l_{i'}, \theta') \in \text{match}(\xi) \\ (c, \theta'') \in \text{match}(u) \\ c \text{ normalized} \\ \theta: \text{var}(c) \to Q'(X_{k_{i'}}) \\ r_{i'} = c\theta}} s_{i'} \cdot \prod_{x \in \text{var}(c)} h_{M'}(x\theta\theta', x\theta'') .$$

The proof of [19, Theorem 5] shows that $h_{M'}(\xi, u) = \tau'_{M'}(\xi, u)$ for all $\xi \in Q'(T_\Sigma)$ and $u \in T_\Delta$. The same alternative semantics also applies to M and N naturally. The following statement can be proven for every $t \in T_\Sigma$ and $t'' \in T_\Gamma$ by induction on t

$$h_N(\langle q, q'\rangle(t), t'') = \sum_{t' \in T_\Delta} h_{M'}(q'(t), t') \cdot h_M(q(t'), t'') .$$

This directly yields

$$\tau_N(t, t'')$$

$$= \sum_{\langle q,q' \rangle \in Q_0 \times Q_0'} \tau_N'(\langle q,q' \rangle(t), t'') = \sum_{\substack{\langle q,q' \rangle \in Q_0 \times Q_0' \\ t' \in T_\Delta}} \tau_{M'}'(q'(t), t') \cdot \tau_M'(q(t'), t'')$$

$$= \sum_{t' \in T_\Delta} \left(\sum_{q' \in Q_0'} \tau_{M'}'(q'(t), t') \right) \cdot \left(\sum_{q \in Q_0} \tau_M'(q(t'), t'') \right) = \sum_{t' \in T_\Delta} \tau_{M'}(t, t') \cdot \tau_M(t', t'')$$

$$= (\tau_{M'} ; \tau_M)(t, t'')$$

and thus the desired $\tau_N = \tau_{M'} ; \tau_M$. An alternative argumentation based on the original derivation semantics is provided in the appendix. □

5   Decidability of Constant Property

To make Theorem 6 effective, we would like to decide whether a given state is c-constant for a given $c \in S$ and, more generally, whether a given wxtt is constant. In the following let $M = (Q, \Sigma, \Delta, Q_0, I, \chi)$ be a wxtt, for which we want to check whether it is constant. Some straightforward results are already mentioned in [17, Example 10] for wtdtt, which we generalize easily to wxtt here.

Lemma 7 (see [17, Example 10]). *Every state $q \in Q$ is 1-constant if*

1. *M is BOOLEAN and total and the semiring S is idempotent, or*
2. *M is BOOLEAN, total, and unambiguous.*

Clearly, totality of M is necessary for every state $q \in Q$ to be 1-constant because otherwise there exists a state $q \in Q$ and input tree $t \in T_\Sigma$ such that $\tau_M'(q(t), u) = 0$ for all output trees $u \in T_\Delta$. Consequently, for that q and t the sum in the definition of 1-constant (see Definition 2) is 0, which shows that q is not 1-constant. Already [17] mentions that totality is not sufficient. Next, we demonstrate that none of the properties mentioned in Lemma 7 besides totality are necessary for every state $q \in Q$ to be 1-constant.

Example 8. Recall the wxtt M' over the semiring $(\mathbb{R}, +, \cdot, 0, 1)$ of Example 3. We already observed in Example 3 that q' is 1-constant, but M' is neither unambiguous nor BOOLEAN. In addition, the semiring $(\mathbb{R}, +, \cdot, 0, 1)$ is clearly not idempotent.

Next we investigate some special cases, for which we can decide the constant property. We start with the BOOLEAN semiring as a starting point. Clearly, the Boolean semiring $(\{0, 1\}, \max, \min, 0, 1)$ is idempotent and all wxtt over the BOOLEAN semiring are trivially BOOLEAN, so according to Lemma 7 we only need to check totality. We present a slightly more general statement, which states decidability of totality for all BOOLEAN wxtt over an idempotent semiring.

Lemma 9. *Totality of BOOLEAN wxtt over an idempotent semiring is decidable.*

Proof. Clearly, rules with weight 0 are useless, so without loss of generality, let $M = (Q, \Sigma, \Delta, Q_0, I, \chi)$ be a BOOLEAN wxtt such that $s_i = 1$ for all $i \in I$; i.e., all rules have weight 1. For every state $q \in Q$ we also consider the variant $M_q = (Q, \Sigma, \Delta, \{q\}, I, \chi)$, which is essentially M but with the single initial state q. Clearly, the subsemiring of S generated by $\{0, 1\}$, which are the only weights permitted in M (as well as M_q for all $q \in Q$), is isomorphic to the BOOLEAN semiring $(\{0, 1\}, \max, \min, 0, 1)$ because S is idempotent. Let $q \in Q$ be an arbitrary state. Hence M_q is essentially a wxtt over the BOOLEAN semiring, and thus also an (unweighted) extended tree transducer of [20]. By [20, Theorem 4.8] such a transducer can equivalently be presented as a top-down tree transducer N_q with regular look-ahead [4]. It is well-known [4, Corollary 2.7] that the domain $\mathrm{dom}(\tau_{N_q})$ of the tree transformation $\tau_{N_q} \subseteq T_\Sigma \times T_\Delta$ computed by N_q is a recognizable tree language [9,10].

Obviously, M is total if and only if $\mathrm{dom}(\tau_{N_q}) = T_\Sigma$ for every $q \in Q$. Since $\mathrm{dom}(\tau_{N_q})$ is recognizable and universality is decidable [9,10] for recognizable tree languages, totality is also decidable.

A closer analysis of the proof shows that a (semiring) homomorphism [11,14] from the subsemiring S' of S generated by the weights in M into the BOOLEAN semiring would be sufficient. Such a homomorphism exists if S' is not a ring by [26, Theorem 2.1]. Additionally, the restrictions on the addition can be avoided, if the wxtt is restricted such that multiple derivations for the same state, input and output tree are impossible. Using similar techniques we can thus also show that totality is decidable for

- BOOLEAN wxtt over zero-sum free semirings,
- wxtt over zero-sum and zero-divisor free semirings,
- BOOLEAN unambiguous wxtt, and
- unambiguous wxtt over zero-divisor free semirings.

Thus the conditions of the first item of Lemma 7 can effectively be checked in an idempotent semiring. It is beyond the scope of this contribution to develop general decidability results for unambiguity. However, a simpler condition exists for wtdtt. Suppose that M is a wtdtt. It is called *deterministic* if for every state $q \in Q$ and $\sigma \in \Sigma$ there exists at most one rule identifier $i \in I$ such that $\ell_i(\varepsilon) = q$ and $\ell_i(1) = \sigma$. Every deterministic wtdtt is guaranteed to be unambiguous.

Let us provide another relevant scenario. Let M be a deterministic wtdtt without useless rules, which can efficiently be checked, and no rules of weight 0 (i.e., $s_i \neq 0$ for all $i \in I$). Moreover, suppose that S is multiplicatively cancellative (i.e., $s \cdot s' = s \cdot s''$ implies $s' = s''$ for all $s, s', s'' \in S$ with $s \neq 0$). For example, every field S is multiplicatively cancellative. Then S is zero-divisor free and by the last item of the previous list, totality is decidable. In fact, due to the special shape of left-hand sides of a wtdtt it suffices to check whether for every state $q \in Q$ and $\sigma \in \Sigma$ there exists a rule identifier $i \in I$ with $\ell_i(\varepsilon) = q$ and $\ell_i(1) = \sigma$. Together with determinism there is thus exactly one rule identifier $i \in I$ with $\ell_i(\varepsilon) = q$ and $\ell_i(1) = \sigma$ for every state $q \in Q$ and $\sigma \in \Sigma$.

Due to the cancellation property of S we can now utilize the weight pushing strategy [13, 22] to determine whether a given state $q \in Q$ is c-constant for some $c \in S$. The standard pushing strategy cannot be applied directly since M might copy or delete. We consider it interesting to extend the existing pushing strategies to these scenarios where (i) weights might not be applied due to deletion or (ii) weights might be applied multiple times due to copying. We leave the details of this adaptation to future work, but believe that this avenue allows an efficient test of the constant property in this relevant scenario (without requiring the wtdtt to be BOOLEAN).

References

1. Allauzen, C., Riley, M., Schalkwyk, J., Skut, W., Mohri, M.: OpenFst – a general and efficient weighted finite-state transducer library. In: Proceedings of 12th International Conference Implementation and Application of Automata. Lecture Notes in Computer Science, vol. 4783, pp. 11–23. Springer (2007). https://doi.org/10.1007/978-3-540-76336-9_3

2. Arnold, A., Dauchet, M.: Morphismes et bimorphismes d'arbres. Theor. Comput. Sci. **20**(4), 33–93 (1982). https://doi.org/10.1016/0304-3975(82)90098-6

3. Dauchet, M.: Transductions inversibles de forêts. Thèse 3ème cycle, Université de Lille (1975). http://ori.univ-lille1.fr/notice/view/univ-lille1-ori-70098

4. Engelfriet, J.: Top-down tree transducers with regular look-ahead. Math. Syst. Theory **10**, 289–303 (1977). https://doi.org/10.1007/BF01683280

5. Engelfriet, J., Fülöp, Z., Vogler, H.: Bottom-up and top-down tree series transformations. J. Autom. Lang. Comb. **7**(1), 11–70 (2002). https://doi.org/10.25596/jalc-2002-011

6. Fülöp, Z., Maletti, A.: Composition closure of linear weighted extended top-down tree transducers. In: Hospodár, M., Jirásková, G. (eds.) CIAA 2019. LNCS, vol. 11601, pp. 133–145. Springer, Cham (2019). https://doi.org/10.1007/978-3-030-23679-3_11

7. Fülöp, Z., Vogler, H.: Tree series transformations that respect copying. Theory Comput. Syst. **36**(3), 247–293 (2003). https://doi.org/10.1007/s00224-003-1072-z

8. Fülöp, Z., Vogler, H.: Weighted tree automata and tree transducers. In: Droste, M., Kuich, W., Vogler, H. (eds.) Handbook of Weighted Automata, chap. 9, pp. 313–403. Springer (2009). https://doi.org/10.1007/978-3-642-01492-5_9

9. Gécseg, F., Steinby, M.: Tree Automata. Akadémiai Kiadó, Budapest 2nd revision (1984). https://arxiv.org/abs/1509.06233

10. Gécseg, F., Steinby, M.: Tree languages. In: Rozenberg, G., Salomaa, A. (eds.) Handbook of Formal Languages, pp. 1–68. Springer, Heidelberg (1997). https://doi.org/10.1007/978-3-642-59126-6_1

11. Golan, J.S.: Semirings and their applications. Kluwer Acad. Publishers (1999). https://doi.org/10.1007/978-94-015-9333-5

12. Graehl, J., Knight, K., May, J.: Training tree transducers. Comput. Linguist. **34**(3), 391–427 (2008). https://doi.org/10.1162/coli.2008.07-051-R2-03-57

13. Hanneforth, T., Maletti, A., Quernheim, D.: Pushing for weighted tree automata. Logical Meth. Comput. Sci. **14**(1:5), 1–16 (2018). https://doi.org/10.23638/LMCS-14(1:5)

14. Hebisch, U., Weinert, H.J.: Semirings – algebraic theory and applications in computer science. World Sci. Publishing (1998). https://doi.org/10.1142/3903

15. Koehn, P.: Statistical Machine Translation. Cambridge University Press (2010). https://doi.org/10.1017/CBO9780511815829
16. Kuich, W.: Tree transducers and formal tree series. Acta Cybernetica **14**(1), 135–149 (1999). https://cyber.bibl.u-szeged.hu/index.php/actcybern/article/view/3516
17. Lagoutte, A., Maletti, A.: *Survey*: weighted extended top-down tree transducers part III — composition. In: Kuich, W., Rahonis, G. (eds.) Algebraic Foundations in Computer Science. LNCS, vol. 7020, pp. 272–308. Springer, Heidelberg (2011). https://doi.org/10.1007/978-3-642-24897-9_13
18. Maletti, A.: Compositions of extended top-down tree transducers. Inf. Comput. **206**(9–10), 1187–1196 (2008). https://doi.org/10.1016/j.ic.2008.03.019
19. Maletti, A.: Survey: weighted extended top-down tree transducers – part I: basics and expressive power. Acta Cybernetica **20**(2), 223–250 (2011). https://doi.org/10.14232/actacyb.20.2.2011.2
20. Maletti, A., Graehl, J., Hopkins, M., Knight, K.: The power of extended top-down tree transducers. SIAM J. Comput. **39**(2), 410–430 (2009). https://doi.org/10.1137/070699160
21. May, J., Knight, K., Vogler, H.: Efficient inference through cascades of weighted tree transducers. In: Proceedings 48th Annual Meeting Association for Computational Linguistics, pp. 1058–1066. Association for Computational Linguistics (2010). https://www.aclweb.org/anthology/P10-1108
22. Mohri, M., Pereira, F., Riley, M.: Weighted finite-state transducers in speech recognition. Comput. Speech Lang. **16**(1), 69–88 (2002). https://doi.org/10.1006/csla.2001.0184
23. Rounds, W.C.: Mappings and grammars on trees. Math. Syst. Theory **4**(3), 257–287 (1970). https://doi.org/10.1007/BF01695769
24. Thatcher, J.W.: Generalized^2 sequential machine maps. J. Comput. Syst. Sci. **4**(4), 339–367 (1970). https://doi.org/10.1016/S0022-0000(70)80017-4
25. Thatcher, J.W.: Tree automata: an informal survey. In: Aho, A.V. (ed.) Currents in the Theory of Computing, chap. 4, pp. 143–172. Prentice Hall (1973)
26. Wang, H.: On characters of semirings. Houston J. Math. **23**(3), 391–405 (1997). https://www.math.uh.edu/~hjm/restricted/archive/v023n3/0391WANG.pdf
27. Yamada, K., Knight, K.: A decoder for syntax-based statistical MT. In: Proceedings of 40th Annual Meeting Association for Computational Linguistics, pp. 303–310. Association for Computational Linguistics (2002). https://doi.org/10.3115/1073083.1073134

Extremal Binary PFAs in a Černý Family

Stijn Cambie, Michiel de Bondt, and Henk Don[(✉)]

Department of Mathematics, Radboud University, Postbus 9010,
6500 GL Nijmegen, The Netherlands
{s.cambie,m.debondt,h.don}@math.ru.nl

Abstract. The largest known reset thresholds for DFAs are equal to $(n-1)^2$, where n is the number of states. This is conjectured to be the maximum possible. PFAs (with partial transition function) can have exponentially large reset thresholds. This is still true if we restrict to binary PFAs. However, asymptotics do not give conclusions for fixed n. We prove that the maximal reset threshold for binary PFAs is strictly greater than $(n-1)^2$ if and only if $n \geq 6$.

These results are mostly based on the analysis of synchronizing word lengths for a certain family of binary PFAs. This family has the following properties: it contains the well-known Černý automata; for $n \leq 10$ it contains a binary PFA with maximal possible reset threshold; for all $n \geq 6$ it contains a PFA with reset threshold larger than the maximum known for DFAs.

Analysis of this family reveals remarkable patterns involving the Fibonacci numbers and related sequences such as the Padovan sequence. We prove that the family asymptotically still gives reset thresholds of polynomial order. For a few sequences in the family, we derive explicit formulas for the reset thresholds, which turn out to be no pure polynomials.

Keywords: Finite automata · Synchronization · Černý conjecture

1 Introduction and Preliminaries

The diagram on the right depicts the *deterministic finite automaton* (DFA) C_4. Starting in any state q and reading the word ba^3ba^3b leads to state 1. Therefore, w is called a synchronizing word for C_4. It is also the only synchronizing word of length at most 9.

Formally, a DFA A is defined as a triple (Q, Σ, δ). Here Σ is a finite alphabet, Q a finite set of states, which we generally choose to be $[n] = \{1, 2, \ldots, n\}$ and $\delta : Q \times \Sigma \to Q$ the transition function. For $w \in \Sigma^*$ and $q \in Q$, we define qw inductively by $q\varepsilon = q$ and

The DFA C_4

The first author has been supported by a Vidi Grant of the Netherlands Organization for Scientific Research (NWO), grant number 639.032.614.

N. Moreira and R. Reis (Eds.): DLT 2021, LNCS 12811, pp. 78–89, 2021.
https://doi.org/10.1007/978-3-030-81508-0_7

$qwa = \delta(qw, a)$ for $a \in \Sigma$, where ε is the empty word. So qw is the state where one ends, when starting in q and reading the symbols in w consecutively, and qa is a short hand notation for $\delta(q, a)$. We extend the transition function to sets $S \subseteq Q$ by $Sw := \{qw : q \in S\}$. A word $w \in \Sigma^*$ is called *synchronizing*, if a state $q_s \in Q$ exists such that $qw = q_s$ for all $q \in Q$. The length of a shortest word with this property is the *reset threshold* of A.

A central conjecture in the field (standing since 1964) is due to Černý [2]:

Conjecture 1. Every synchronizing DFA on n states admits a synchronizing word of length $\leq (n-1)^2$.

We denote the maximal possible reset threshold for a DFA on n states by $d(n)$, rephrasing the conjecture to $d(n) = (n-1)^2$. The best known upper bounds are still cubic in n. In 1983 Pin [4] established the bound $\frac{1}{6}(n^3 - n)$, using a combinatorial result by Frankl [3]. More than thirty years later, the leading constant was improved to 0.1664 by Szykuła, and subsequently to 0.1654 by Shitov [5]. For a survey on synchronizing automata and Černý's conjecture, we refer to [6].

If Conjecture 1 holds true, the bound is sharp. The DFA C_4 is one in a sequence found by Černý [2]. For $n \geq 2$, the DFA C_n has n states which we denote by $Q = [n]$, a symbol a sending q to $q+1 \pmod n$ and a symbol b sending n to 1 and being the identity in all other states. The shortest synchronizing word for C_n is $b(a^{n-1}b)^{n-2}$ of length $(n-1)^2$, so that $d(n) \geq (n-1)^2$.

The picture changes drastically if we consider *partial finite automata* (PFAs). In a PFA, the transition function is allowed to be partial. This means that qa may be undefined for $q \in Q$ and $a \in \Sigma$. In this case a word w is called synchronizing for a PFA if there exists $q_s \in Q$ such that qw is defined and $qw = q_s$ for all $q \in Q$. In the literature this is sometimes called *careful synchronization*, while also other notions of synchronization exist.

For PFAs the maximal reset thresholds grow asymptotically like an exponential function of n, in contrast with the polynomial growth for DFAs. Also the behaviour in terms of alphabet size is different. The upper bound of Conjecture 1 is attained by binary DFAs. For PFAs there is evidence that the alphabet size has to grow with n to attain the maximal reset thresholds [1]. Still, also binary PFAs give exponentially growing reset thresholds. We denote the maximal values by $p(n, 2)$. For $2 \leq n \leq 10$ the values as found in [1] are given below. For $n \geq 11$, the maximum is unknown.

n	2	3	4	5	6	7	8	9	10
$p(n, 2)$	1	4	9	16	26	39	55	73	94

For all $2 \leq n \leq 10$, these reset thresholds are attained by members of what we will call the *Černý family*. This family will be introduced in Sect. 2. In Sect. 3 we relate the problem of finding reset thresholds for this family to a minimization problem involving racing pawns. A recursive solution for this problem is presented in Sect. 4, from which it follows that the maximal reset thresholds in the family grow like $n^2 \log(n)$. Finally, in Sect. 5, we give explicit formulas for the reset thresholds of a few sequences in the family.

2   Extending the Černý Sequence to a Family

This family of binary PFAs, denoted by C_n^c, contains the Černý sequence $C_n = C_n^0$ of binary DFAs. For fixed $c \in \mathbb{N}$ and $n \geq c + 2$, we define the PFA C_n^c with n states and alphabet $\Sigma = \{a, b\}$ by

$$qa = \begin{cases} q+1 & 1 \leq q \leq n-c-1 \\ \bot & n-c \leq q \leq n-1 \\ 1 & q = n \end{cases} \qquad qb = \begin{cases} q & 1 \leq q \leq n-c-1 \\ q+1 & n-c \leq q \leq n-1 \\ 1 & q = n \end{cases}$$

The PFA C_n^c is depicted in Fig. 1 for $n = 8$ and $c = 2$, next to the DFA C_n^0 of Černý. By analyzing this family, we obtain our main results. In particular, we will conclude that $p(n, 2) > (n-1)^2$ if and only if $n \geq 6$.

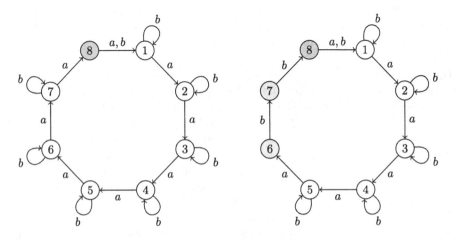

Fig. 1. The DFA C_8^0 and the PFA C_8^2

Before deriving general formulas for the reset thresholds, we present the values for $2 \leq n \leq 15$ and $0 \leq c \leq 4$ in the following table. Independent of the analysis that will follow, these values were found by an algorithm computing the reset threshold for a given PFA.

n	2	3	4	5	6	7	8	9	10	11	12	13	14	15
$c = 0$	1	4	9	16	25	36	49	64	81	100	121	144	169	196
$c = 1$		2	7	**26**	**39**	**55**	**73**	93	116	141	168	197	228
$c = 2$			3	10	21	35	52	72	**94**	**119**	**146**	**176**	208	242
$c = 3$				4	13	27	44	65	89	115	144	**176**	**211**	**248**
$c = 4$					5	16	33	53	78	106	136	169	206	246

Values in boldface represent the maximal reset threshold in the family for a given n. Later we will see that for large n, the optimal c is close to $n/2$. For $2 \leq n \leq 10$, these maxima exactly match the values of $p(n, 2)$. This means that the Černý family contains a binary PFA on n states with maximal possible reset threshold for all $2 \leq n \leq 10$. In fact, for $6 \leq n \leq 10$, there exists only one binary PFA reaching this maximum [1].

The first line of the table shows the squares $(n-1)^2$ for the Černý sequence C_n^0. To give explicit expressions for subsequent lines is much harder. The order of growth is still quadratic for every c, but no formula of the form $a_2 n^2 + a_1 n + a_0$ exists in general, as we will see later in this paper.

We now turn to the analytic derivation of reset thresholds for the Černý family. We use the following interpretation of synchronization: let a pawn be placed in every state of a PFA, let them simultaneously follow the same word w and let two of them merge if they are in the same state after reading some prefix of w. A synchronizing word is then a word that merges all pawns.

3   Reduction to a Pawn Race Problem

Our first result reduces the question of synchronizing C_n^c to the following problem.

Problem 1 (Pawn race problem). We have n pawns on the *integers* $1, 2, \ldots, n$. In every iteration, every pawn has the choice to move from its location k to $k+1$ or to stay at k. Moving costs $c+1$, staying costs c. After every iteration, if two pawns are in the same position, they merge. What is the minimum cost for which it is possible to merge all the pawns?

Theorem 1. *Let $f_c(n)$ be the solution to Problem 1 and denote $n' = n - c - 1$. The reset threshold of C_n^c is equal to*

$$n'(n'-1) + c + 1 + f_c(n').$$

The rest of this section will be devoted to the proof of Theorem 1.

Lemma 1. $C_n^c = (Q, \Sigma, \delta)$ *has a synchronizing word.*

Proof. We denote $[k] := \{1, 2, \ldots, k\}$ and note that $Qb^{c+1} = [n-c-1] \subset [n-c]$. Define $\tilde{a} = b^c a$ and $\tilde{b} = b^{c+1}$. Then $\tilde{a}$ acts as a cyclic permutation on $[n-c]$ and $\tilde{b}$ sends $n-c$ to 1 and is the identity otherwise. Here we recognize the Černý automaton C_{n-c}^0, so that C_n^c is synchronizing.   □

Inspired by the proof of Lemma 1, we define the PFA C_{n-c}^* with state set $[n-c]$, alphabet $\Gamma = \{a, \tilde{a}, \tilde{b}\}$, and the transition function of C_n^c restricted to $[n-c]$. We define the *weighted length* $|w|$ of a word $w \in \Gamma^*$ as the sum of the weights of the symbols, counting multiplicities, with weight 1 for a and weight $c+1$ for $\tilde{a}$ and $\tilde{b}$.

Lemma 2. *Let w be a shortest synchronizing word for $S \subseteq Q$ with $|S| > 1$.*

(i) If $S = Q$, then w starts with b^{c+1}.
(ii) If $S \subseteq [n-c]$ and $n-c \in S$, then w starts with $b^c a$ or b^{c+1}.

(iii) If $S \subseteq [n - c]$ and $n - c \notin S$, then w starts with a.
(iv) If $S = Q$ or $S \subseteq [n - c]$, then w corresponds to a synchronizing word of minimum weighted length in C^*_{n-c}, for $[n - c]$ or S respectively.

Proof. Since $qb^{c+2} = qb^{c+1}$ for all states q, the word w can not contain b^{c+2}. Furthermore, $(n - c)b^m a$ is not defined for $m = 0, 1, \ldots, c - 1$. These observations together with $|Sb^c| = |S|$ imply the second statement. It also follows that w starts with b^c if $S = Q$. If it starts with $b^c a$, then it has (by the second statement) to start with $b^c ab^c$ since $Qb^c a = [n - c]$. But this contradicts the assumption that w is a shortest synchronizing word, since $Qb^c = Qb^c ab^c$. So w starts with b^{c+1}. The third statement follows by observing that $Sb = S$ in this case. The last statement follows by induction from the first three statements and the proof of Lemma 1. □

We see a subset of the state set $[n - c]$ as a collection of pawns on those states. Symbols a and $\tilde{a}$ move these pawns without merging, but if both $n - c$ and 1 are occupied by a pawn, then symbol $\tilde{b}$ merges both pawns. We call a pawn a *chaser* if its next merge will be with a pawn in front of it, and a resigner otherwise. So a chaser is on state $n - c$ when it merges and a resigner on state 1.

If a pawn which results from a merge advances as a chaser, then we see the chaser assigned to the merge as the continuation of it, so the resigner dies. But if a pawn which results from a merge advances as a resigner, then the chaser dies. We call the resigner of the last merge the *yellow jersey*, and the chaser of the last merge the *lanterne rouge*.

Lemma 3. *Let $n - c \in S \subseteq [n - c]$ and let $w \in \Gamma^*$ be synchronizing for S with $|w|$ minimal. If the pawn in $n - c$ is a chaser, w starts with $\tilde{b}$ or $c = 0$. If the pawn in $n - c$ is a resigner, w starts with $\tilde{a}$.*

Proof. Write $w = w^*_1 \ldots w^*_k$ with $w^*_i \in \Gamma$. Assume that the pawn in $n - c$ is the lanterne rouge (so it is a chaser) and that $w^*_1 = \tilde{a}$. After reading w^*_1, it is in state 1. Each time it visits $n - c$, it chooses $\tilde{a}$ or $\tilde{b}$. The last time before merging, it chooses $w^*_m = \tilde{b}$ for some m to merge with the pawn in 1. We will construct a shorter synchronizing word starting with $\tilde{b}$. This gives a contradiction, so that $w^*_1 = \tilde{b}$.

Starting with $\tilde{b}a$ instead of $\tilde{a}$, the lanterne rouge would already be in state 2, while it makes no difference for any of the other pawns. By keeping the choices of the lanterne rouge in subsequent visits to $n - c$ the same as in w, it will stay one step ahead of its original position. We can therefore replace w^*_m by ε, saving c letters in total. The yellow jersey can be treated similarly.

Now suppose the pawn in $n - c$ is a chaser, but not the lanterne rouge. Let v be any synchronizing word for all other pawns. We can make this into a synchronizing word u for all pawns as follows. Start reading v and each time the chaser is in $n - c$, either insert $\tilde{b}$ or replace a by $\tilde{a}$. Inserting $\tilde{b}$ minimizes the length of u, since it always brings the chaser one step closer to its target, thus reduces the number of visits to $n - c$. Since u still synchronizes the lanterne rouge and the yellow jersey, it synchronizes S. Finally, note that w has to be the extension of some word v as above, completing the proof in this case. If the pawn starting in $n - c$ is a resigner, a similar (slightly simpler) proof works. □

Suppose the yellow jersey starts in $j \in [n']$. To simplify the further investigation, we will first look to the *shortest full synchronizing word*, which is the shortest word that synchronizes all pawns into state j. Now consider an arbitrary set $S \subseteq [n']$. By Claim 2(ii) and (iii) a shortest full synchronizing word for S has a prefix of the form

$$w = aw_{n'}aw_{n'-1}a \ldots aw_3 aw_2 aw_1 aw_n, \quad \text{with} \quad w_k \in \{\varepsilon, b^c, b^{c+1}\}. \quad (1)$$

A word of this form will be called an iteration word. If w is a prefix of a shortest full synchronizing word for S and wb is not, then w is an optimal iteration word.

Lemma 4. *Let w be an optimal iteration word for $S \subseteq [n']$ which agrees with the strategy of Lemma 3. Then*

(i) For $k \notin S$, we have $w_k = \varepsilon$. For $k \in S$, we have $w_k = b^c$ or $w_k = b^{c+1}$.
(ii) For all $k \in S$,

$$kw = \begin{cases} k & \text{if } w_k = b^c, \\ k+1 \mod n' & \text{if } w_k = b^{c+1}. \end{cases}$$

(iii) If $w_{n'} = b^{c+1}$, then $w_n = b^{c+1}$. If $w_{n'} \neq b^{c+1}$, then $w_n = \varepsilon$.

Proof. The word w has the following properties for $1 \leq k \leq n'$:

$$kw = \begin{cases} \perp & \text{if } w_k = \varepsilon \\ k & \text{if } w_k = b^c \\ k+1 & \text{if } w_k = b^{c+1}, k \neq n'. \end{cases} \quad (2)$$

Since w_k only can affect a pawn in state k, we observe that $w_k = \varepsilon$ if and only if $k \notin S$, proving the first statement. Now consider a pawn starting in state n'. If $w_{n'} = b^{c+1}$, then it follows from Lemma 3 that this pawn is a chaser. Write $w = vw_n$. Then $n'v = n - c$ and $kv = kw \neq n - c$ for all $k \neq n'$. Therefore, the pawn under consideration did not merge yet and is still chasing. Hence, again using Lemma 3, it is optimal to choose $w_n = b^{c+1}$. This means that $n'w = n'vw_n = (n - c)b^{c+1} = 1$. Together with Eq. (2), this proves the second statement.

If $w_{n'} = b^c$ or $w_{n'} = \varepsilon$, then $Sv \subseteq [n']$. By Lemma 2 (iii), a shortest synchronizing word for S then starts with va so that $w_n = \varepsilon$. $\square$

Proof (of Theorem 1). The idea of Lemma 4 is that an iteration word can be used to decide for every pawn if it has to move one step (at the cost of $c + 1$ letters b and possible more if we needed $w_n = b^{c+1}$), or to stay where it is (at the cost of c letters b). The optimal choice depends on the pawn being a chaser or a resigner. After applying an optimal iteration word, all pawns will be located on a subset of $[n']$. Consequently, every shortest full synchronizing word can be partitioned into iteration words.

As the yellow jersey starts in $j \in [n']$, the lanterne rouge starts in $j + 1$ mod n'. Observe that after each iteration, the lanterne rouge (being a chaser) will have moved from ℓ to $\ell + 1$ (mod n'), while the yellow jersey is still at j. After $n' - 1$ iterations, both the lanterne rouge and the yellow jersey and hence all initial pawns are in j. For the shortest synchronizing word, we can delete a^{j-1} from the shortest full synchronizing word.

Hence the number of letters a in a shortest synchronizing word equals $(n'-1) \cdot (n'+1) - (j-1)$. We have used $c+1$ letters b in the beginning and at least $f_c(n')$ letters b in all iteration words. By Lemma 4 (iii), there is an additional cost of $c + 1$ letters b for each iteration word with $w_{n'} = b^{c+1}$. Now suppose the yellow jersey starts in $j = n'$. This minimizes the number of a's. Furthermore, since the yellow jersey is always a resigner, $w_{n'} = b^c$ in each iteration. Consequently, there will be no additional costs for w_n, so that the minimal possible length as given in Theorem 1 is attained for $j = n'$. □

4 Recursive and Asymptotic Results

We will now turn our attention to the analysis of Problem 5. The following proposition gives a recursive formula for the solution.

Proposition 1. *The function f_c satisfies $f_c(1) = 0$ and $f_c(n) = \min\{f_c(i) + f_c(n-i) + (c+1)n - i \mid \frac{n}{2} \le i \le n-1\}$.*

Proof. In Problem 1, we define chasers and resigners as before. Since we now work on $\mathbb{Z}$, the pawn at 1 is the lanterne rouge and the pawn at n is the yellow jersey. In total we will need $n - 1$ iterations. Let $\sigma_j(k)$ be the position after j iterations of the pawn that starts in k. After $n - 2$ iterations, all pawns are merged into the lanterne rouge at $n - 1$ and the yellow jersey at n. Let $I = \sigma_{n-2}^{-1}(n-1) = \{1, 2, \ldots, i\}$ (being the peloton) and $J = \sigma_{n-2}^{-1}(n) = \{i+1, \ldots, n\}$ (being the first group). See also Fig. 2.

Now note that i is a resigner until the full peloton has merged into one pawn in position i. The minimal cost for this is equal to $f_c(i)$. In each of the remaining $n - i$ iterations, this pawn will be a chaser at cost $c + 1$. Similarly, the pawn starting in $i + 1$ is a chaser until the first group has merged into one pawn in position n. This takes $n - i - 1$ iterations and the minimal cost to merge the first group is $f_c(n - i)$. In the remaining i iterations, the pawn at n is a resigner at cost c.

So the minimum cost is indeed $f_c(i) + f_c(n-i) + (c+1)n - i$, where we have to minimize over all possible $1 \le i \le n-1$. Since $f_c(i) + f_c(n-i)$ is a symmetric function around $\frac{n}{2}$ and $(c+1)n - i$ is decreasing in i, we also know $\frac{n}{2} \le i \le n-1$, Hence we have determined the recursion for the function f_c. □

In Fig. 2 we have presented three ways in which the minimum cost can be attained when $c = 1$ and $n = 7$ (the pawn at place 3 having two choices in the right part). Here resigners are drawn amber (light) and chasers red (dark). In the optimal races in this example, there are either 8 chasers and 13 resigners or 9 chasers and 11 resigners. The total cost $f_1(7)$ therefore is

$$f_1(7) = 8 \cdot 2 + 13 \cdot 1 = 9 \cdot 2 + 11 \cdot 1 = 29.$$

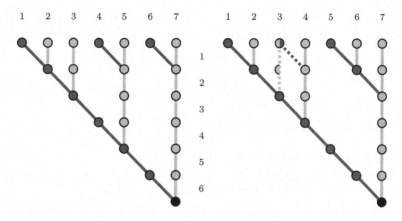

Fig. 2. The three optimal races for $n = 7$ and $c = 1$. The positions are indicated above and the iterations are numbered in the middle. The peloton has size 5 in the left race and size 4 in the other two races.

Computing $f_1(1), \ldots, f_1(5)$ by the recursion gives 0, 3, 7, 12, 17 which can be used to alternatively express the total cost $f_1(7)$ by

$$f_1(7) = f_1(5) + f_1(2) + 2 \cdot 7 - 5 = f_1(4) + f_1(3) + 2 \cdot 7 - 4 = 29.$$

We will not solve the recursion analytically for all c, but the next result does determine the order of growth of the function $f_c(n)$.

Proposition 2. *For all $c \geq 0$ and $n \geq 1$, we have*

$$cn \log_2(n) \leq f_c(n) \leq (c+1)n\lceil \log_2(n)\rceil.$$

Proof. Both bounds can be proven by induction, the base case for $n = 1$ being true. For the lower bound, fix n and assume that $ci \log_2 i \leq f_c(i)$ for $i < n$. This implies that for every $1 \leq i \leq n - 1$ we have that

$$f_c(i) + f_c(n - i) + (c+1)n - i \geq c\left(i \log_2 i + (n - i) \log_2(n - i) + n\right).$$

Note that $i \log_2 i + (n-i) \log_2(n-i)$ is minimized when $i = \frac{n}{2}$ since its derivative (as a function of i for n fixed) is $\log_2 i - \log_2(n - i)$. Plugging in $i = \frac{n}{2}$ gives $cn \log_2 n$ on the right hand side. So, we have $cn \log_2 n \leq f_c(n)$ and we conclude by mathematical induction.

For the upper bound, assuming it is true for values strictly smaller than n (where $n > 1$), we have

$$f_c(n) \leq f_c\left(\left\lfloor \frac{n}{2}\right\rfloor\right) + f_c\left(\left\lceil \frac{n}{2}\right\rceil\right) + (c+1)n$$
$$\leq (c+1)n\left\lceil \log_2\left(\left\lceil \frac{n}{2}\right\rceil\right)\right\rceil + (c+1)n$$
$$= (c+1)n\lceil \log_2(n)\rceil.$$

So again by mathematical induction the bound does hold for every n. $\square$

As a corollary of this result, we determine the asymptotic growth of maximal reset thresholds in the Černý family.

Theorem 2. *Denoting the reset threshold of C_n^c by $r(C_n^c)$, we have*

$$\max_c r(C_n^c) \sim \frac{n^2}{4} \log_2(n).$$

The optimal choice for c satisfies $c = \frac{n}{2} - o(n)$.

Proof. By Theorem 1 and the fact that $n'(n'-1) + c + 1 \leq n^2 = o(n^2 \log_2(n))$ for $n' = n - c - 1$, it is sufficient to prove that $\max_c f_c(n-c-1) \sim \frac{n^2}{4} \log_2(n)$.

By Proposition 2, we have for the upper bound that

$$f_c(n-c-1) \leq (c+1)(n-c-1)\lceil \log_2(n-c-1)\rceil \leq \frac{n^2}{4}\lceil \log_2(n)\rceil = (1+o(1))\frac{n^2}{4}\log_2(n).$$

For the lower bound, we choose $c = \lfloor \frac{n-1}{2} \rfloor$ and from the lower bound in Proposition 2 we get that

$$\begin{aligned}
f_c(n-c-1) &\geq c(n-c-1)\log_2(n-c-1) \\
&\geq \frac{(n-1)^2 - 1}{4}\log_2(n/2 - 1) \\
&= (1-o(1))\frac{n^2}{4}\log_2(n).
\end{aligned}$$

The two bounds together imply the result. It is not hard to see from these computations that the optimal choice for c satisfies $c = \frac{n}{2} - o(n)$. $\qquad\square$

5   Explicit Solution of the Pawn Race Problem for Small c

In this section, we determine the exact solution of Problem 1 for small c, from which by Theorem 1 the exact expressions for the reset thresholds of C_n^c for all n follow as well.

When $c = 0$, we see that the lanterne rouge has to move $n-1$ times and if the other pawns do not move, we get the minimum cost of $n-1$, i.e. $f_0(n) = n-1$. This result can also immediately be derived from Proposition 1. Theorem 1 now gives that the reset threshold of C_n^0 is indeed equal to $(n-1)(n-2)+1+(n-2) = (n-1)^2$, thus giving an alternative proof for the well-known reset thresholds of the Černý sequence.

When $c = 1$, our approach is based on solving the recursion given in Proposition 1 for $f_1(n)$, which will be abbreviated to $f(n)$. The Fibonacci numbers $(F_n)_n$ play an important role in the analysis. They are recursively defined by $F_0 = 0, F_1 = F_2 = 1$ and $F_n = F_{n-1} + F_{n-2}$ for every $n \geq 3$.

Lemma 5. *For any integer $n \geq 1$ and the unique corresponding m such that $F_{m-1} < n \leq F_m$, we have $f(n) = nm - F_{m+1}$.*

We illustrate the statement for $n = 7$. Since $F_5 = 5$, $F_6 = 8$ and $F_7 = 13$, we find $m = 6$ and therefore $f(7) = 7 \cdot 6 - 13 = 29$, in agreement with the example in the previous section.

Proof. We will prove this lemma by induction.

Induction Basis. Proposition 1 gives $f(1) = 0$ and $f(2) = 3$. We verify the result of Lemma 5. When $n = 1$, we find $m = 1$ and $f(n) = 1 \cdot 1 - F_2 = 0$. When $n = 2$, we find $m = 3$ and $f(n) = 2 \cdot 3 - F_4 = 3$. So the base case is true.

Induction Hypothesis. For any integer $2 \leq m \leq k - 1$ and any n with $F_{m-1} < n \leq F_m$, we have $f(n) = nm - F_{m+1}$.

Induction Step. Take any n for which $F_{k-1} < n \leq F_k$. We first prove that $f(n) \geq nk - F_{k+1}$. For this, we have to do some case distinction. By observing that $F_{k-3} < \frac{n}{2} \leq i \leq n - 1 < F_k$, there are only three cases to consider.

1. Case $F_{k-3} < i \leq F_{k-2}$. Note that $F_{k-3} = F_{k-1} - F_{k-2} < n - i \leq i \leq F_{k-2}$ and hence

$$
\begin{aligned}
f(i) + f(n - i) + 2n - i &= (k - 2)i - F_{k-1} + (k - 2)(n - i) - F_{k-1} + 2n - i \\
&= (k - 2)n - 2F_{k-1} + 2n - i \\
&= nk - 2F_{k-1} - i \geq nk - F_{k+1},
\end{aligned}
$$

with equality if and only if $i = F_{k-2}$.

2. Case $F_{k-2} < i \leq F_{k-1}$. We have $F_{k'-1} < n - i \leq F_{k'}$ for some $1 \leq k' \leq k - 1$ in this case. If $k' = k - 1$, we have

$$
f(i) + f(n - i) + 2n - i = kn - 2F_k + n - i > kn - 2F_k + F_{k-2} = kn - F_{k+1}.
$$

If $k' \leq k - 2$, we note that

$$
\begin{aligned}
f(i) + f(n - i) + 2n - i &= (k - 1)i - F_k + k'(n - i) - F_{k'+1} + 2n - i \\
&= nk - F_k - F_{k'+1} - (k - 2 - k')(n - i) \\
&\geq nk - F_k - F_{k'+1} - (k - 2 - k')F_{k'} \\
&\geq nk - F_k - F_{k'+1} - (F_{k'} + F_{k'+1} + \ldots + F_{k-3}) \\
&= nk - F_k - F_{k'+1} - \sum_{i=k'+2}^{k-1}(F_i - F_{i-1}) \\
&= nk - F_k - F_{k-1} = nk - F_{k+1}.
\end{aligned}
$$

Equality holds if $k' = k - 2$ or if $k' = k - 3$ and $n - i = F_{k'}$. Also $k' = k - 4$ can still give equality if $2(n - i) = 2F_{k-4} = F_{k-4} + F_{k-3}$, which gives $k = 5$, $k' = 1$, $n = 4$ and $i = 3$. To have equality for $k' \leq k - 5$, we would need at least three consecutive terms in the Fibonacci sequence to be equal. So no more cases of equality exist.

88   S. Cambie et al.

3. Case $F_{k-1} < i < F_k$. Choose k' such that $F_{k'-1} < n - i \leq F_{k'}$ (note $k' \leq k - 2$), we have

$$
\begin{aligned}
f(i) + f(n-i) + 2n - i &= ki - F_{k+1} + k'(n-i) - F_{k'+1} + 2n - i \\
&= nk - F_{k+1} - (k - k' - 2)(n-i) - F_{k'+1} + i \\
&> nk - F_{k+1} - (k - k' - 2)F_{k'} - F_{k'+1} + F_{k-1} \\
&= nk - F_k - F_{k'+1} - (k - 2 - k')F_{k'} \geq nk - F_{k+1},
\end{aligned}
$$

where the last inequality was already proved in the previous case.

We conclude that $f(n) = \min\{f(i) + f(n-i) + 2n - i \mid \frac{n}{2} \leq i \leq n - 1\} \geq nk - F_{k+1}$ and since equality occurs for $i = F_{k-2}$ when $n \leq 2F_{k-2}$ and for $i = n - F_{k-2}$ when $n > 2F_{k-2}$, we have $f(n) = nk - F_{k+1}$. By mathematical induction, the result holds for all positive integers. □

Furthermore one can observe that there is a unique i such that $f(n) = f(i) + f(n-i) + 2n - i$ if and only if n is of the form F_k, in which case $i = F_{k-1}$.

This result leads to the following theorem, which appeared in [1] without proof and without the uniqueness claim. As a corollary, it follows that for every $n \geq 6$ there is a binary PFA with reset threshold larger than the maximum known for DFAs. To our best knowledge, so far this was only proved to hold asymptotically and for $6 \leq n \leq 10$, see [1].

Theorem 3. *For $n \geq 3$, let m be the unique integer for which $F_{m-1} < n - 2 \leq F_m$. If w is a shortest synchronizing word for C_n^1, then*

$$
|w| = n^2 + mn - 5n - F_{m+1} - 2m + 8 = n^2 + \frac{n\log(n)}{\log(\phi)} - \Theta(n).
$$

Furthermore, $|w| > (n-1)^2$ for $n \geq 6$ and the shortest synchronizing word is unique if and only if $n - 2$ is a Fibonacci number.

Proof. The exact expression follows from Theorem 1 and Lemma 5. Hence

$$
\begin{aligned}
|w| - (n-1)^2 &= (m-3)n - F_{m+1} - 2m + 7 \\
&\geq (m-3)(F_{m-1} + 3) - F_{m+1} - 2m + 7 \\
&= (m-6)F_{m-1} + F_{m-3} + m - 2 \geq 1
\end{aligned}
$$

whenever $m \geq 5$. This is the case for $n \geq F_4 + 3 = 6$.

A closed form for the Fibonacci numbers can be given by Binet's formula, $F_k = (\phi^k - (-\phi)^{-k})/\sqrt{5}$, where $\phi = (1 + \sqrt{5})/2$ is the golden ratio. We therefore obtain $m = \frac{\log(n)}{\log(\phi)} + O(1)$ from which the asymptotic expression can be derived by checking the coefficients of the linear terms. □

Corollary 1. *If the Černý conjecture holds, then $p(n, 2) > d(n)$ for all $n \geq 6$.*

For $c = 2$, it turns out that the Padovan sequence is the key for the analysis of the pawn race problem. The Padovan sequence is defined by $P_1 = 0, P_2 = P_3 = P_4 = 1$ and $P_n = P_{n-2} + P_{n-3}$ for every $n \geq 4$. This sequence grows exponentially with a rate equal to ψ which is the real solution for $x^3 = x + 1$. An analogous case analysis as has been done for Lemma 5 can be executed to obtain the following results, presented without proof due to space limitations.

Lemma 6. *For any integer $n \geq 1$ and corresponding m such that $P_{m-1} < n \leq P_m$, we have $f_2(n) = nm - P_{m+4}$.*

Theorem 4. *For $n \geq 4$, let m be the unique integer for which $P_{m-1} < n - 3 \leq P_m$. If w is a shortest synchronizing word for C_n^2, then*

$$|w| = n^2 + mn - 7n - P_{m+4} - 3m + 15 = n^2 + \frac{n\log(n)}{\log(\psi)} + O(n).$$

We wrap up with some concluding remarks. We are working on an extended version of this paper, in which we give a more insightful proof of Lemma 5 which works for all c. The Černý family presented in this paper contains for all $n \leq 10$ a binary PFA with n states and maximal possible reset threshold. The asymptotic growth in the family can be bounded by a polynomial in n (Theorem 2). On the other hand, constructions with exponential growth are known to exist. So for n large enough, the PFAs in this family are not extremal. In our forthcoming extended version, we will show that for every $n \geq 41$, there exists a binary PFA with n states and larger reset threshold than the PFAs with n states in this family. This still leaves a significant range open.

References

1. de Bondt, M., Don, H., Zantema, H.: Lower bounds for synchronizing word lengths in partial automata. Int. J. Found. Comput. Sci. **30**(1), 29–60 (2019). https://doi. org/10.1142/S0129054119400021
2. Černý, J.: Poznámka k homogénnym experimentom s konečnými automatmi. Matematicko-fyzikálny časopis, Slovensk. Akad. Vied **14**(3), 208–216 (1964)
3. Frankl, P.: An extremal problem for two families of sets. Eur. J. Comb. **3**, 125–127 (1982)
4. Pin, J.E.: On two combinatorial problems arising from automata theory. Ann. Discrete Math. **17**, 535–548 (1983)
5. Shitov, Y.: An improvement to a recent upper bound for synchronizing words of finite automata. J. Autom. Lang. Comb. **24**(2–4), 367–373 (2019). https://doi.org/ 10.15388/na.2019.3.3
6. Volkov, M.V.: Synchronizing automata and the Černý conjecture. In: Martín-Vide, C., Otto, F., Fernau, H. (eds.) LATA 2008. LNCS, vol. 5196, pp. 11–27. Springer, Heidelberg (2008). https://doi.org/10.1007/978-3-540-88282-4_4

Variations on the Post Correspondence Problem for Free Groups

Laura Ciobanu$^{(\boxtimes)}$ (ID) and Alan D. Logan (ID)

Heriot-Watt University, Edinburgh EH14 4AS, Scotland
{L.Ciobanu,A.Logan}@hw.ac.uk

Abstract. The Post Correspondence Problem is a classical decision problem about equalisers of free monoid homomorphisms. We prove connections between several variations of this classical problem, but in the setting of free groups and free group homomorphisms. Among other results, and working under certain injectivity assumptions, we prove that computing the rank of the equaliser of a pair of free group homomorphisms can be applied to computing a basis of this equaliser, and also to solve the "generalised" Post Correspondence Problem for free groups.

Keywords: Post Correspondence Problem · Free group · Rational constraint

1 Introduction

In this article we connect several variations of the classical Post Correspondence Problem in the setting of free groups. The problems we consider have been open since the 1980s, and understanding how they relate and compare to their analogues in free monoids could bring us closer to their resolution. All problems are defined in Table 1, while their status in free groups and monoids is given in Table 2. However, three of these problems deserve proper introductions.

We first consider the Post Correspondence Problem (PCP) for free groups. This is analogous to the classical Post Correspondence Problem, which is about free monoids rather than free groups and has numerous applications in mathematics and computer science [11]. The PCP for other classes of groups has been successfully studied (see for example [17, Theorem 5.8]), but it remains open for free groups, where it is defined as follows. Let Σ and Δ be two alphabets, let $g, h : F(\Sigma) \to F(\Delta)$ be two group homomorphisms from the free group over Σ to the free group over Δ, and store this data in a four-tuple $I = (\Sigma, \Delta, g, h)$, called an *instance* of the PCP. The PCP is the decision problem:

Given $I = (\Sigma, \Delta, g, h)$, is there $x \in F(\Sigma) \setminus \{1\}$ such that $g(x) = h(x)$?

That is, if we consider the *equaliser* $\mathrm{Eq}(g, h) = \{x \in F(\Sigma) \mid g(x) = h(x)\}$ of g and h, which is a subgroup of $F(\Sigma)$, the PCP asks if $\mathrm{Eq}(g, h)$ is nontrivial. Determining the decidability of this problem is an important question [6, Problem 5.1.4] [17, Section 1.4].

Work supported by EPSRC grant EP/R035814/1.

N. Moreira and R. Reis (Eds.): DLT 2021, LNCS 12811, pp. 90–102, 2021.
https://doi.org/10.1007/978-3-030-81508-0_8

Our second problem asks not just about the triviality of $\mathrm{Eq}(g,h)$, but for a finite description of it. We write $\mathrm{PCP}^{\mathrm{inj}}$ (see Table 1) for the PCP with at least one map injective, in which case the subgroup $\mathrm{Eq}(g,h)$ is finitely generated [10] and a finite description relates to bases (as defined in Sect. 2): The *Basis Problem* (BP) takes as input an instance $I = (\Sigma, \Delta, g, h)$ of the $\mathrm{PCP}^{\mathrm{inj}}$ and outputs a basis for $\mathrm{Eq}(g,h)$. In Sect. 8 we show that the BP is equivalent to the *Rank Problem* (RP), which seeks the number of elements in a basis, and was asked by Stallings in 1984. Recent results settle the BP for certain classes of free group maps [2–4,8], but despite this progress its solubility remains open in general. The analogous problem for free monoids, which we call the *Algorithmic Equaliser Problem* (AEP) (see [4, page 2]) because it aims to describe the equaliser in terms of automata rather than bases, is insoluble [14, Theorem 5.2].

Our third problem is the *generalised* Post Correspondence Problem (GPCP), which is an important generalisation of the PCP for both free groups and monoids from 1982 [7]. For group homomorphisms $g, h : F(\Sigma) \to F(\Delta)$ and fixed elements u_1, u_2, v_1, v_2 of $F(\Delta)$, an instance of the GPCP is an 8-tuple $I_{\mathrm{GPCP}} = (\Sigma, \Delta, g, h, u_1, u_2, v_1, v_2)$ and the GPCP itself is the decision problem:

$$\text{Given } I_{\mathrm{GPCP}} = (\Sigma, \Delta, g, h, u_1, u_2, v_1, v_2),$$
$$\text{is there } x \in F(\Sigma) \setminus \{1\} \text{ such that } u_1 g(x) u_2 = v_1 h(x) v_2?$$

Table 1. Summary of certain decision problems related to the PCP

Problems (for free groups)	Fixed: finite alphabets Σ and Δ and free groups $F(\Sigma)$, $F(\Delta)$. Input: homomorphisms $g, h : F(\Sigma) \to F(\Delta)$
	Additional input for GPCP: $u_1, u_2, v_1, v_2 \in F(\Delta)$
	Additional input for $\mathrm{PCP}_{\mathcal{R}}$: rational set $\mathcal{R} \subseteq F(\Sigma)$
	Additional input for $\mathrm{PCP}_{\mathcal{EL}}$: $a, b \in \Sigma^{\pm 1}$, $\Omega \subset \Sigma$
	Is it decidable whether:
PCP	there exists $x \in F(\Sigma) \setminus \{1\}$ s.t. $g(x) = h(x)$?
GPCP	there exists $x \in F(\Sigma) \setminus \{1\}$ s.t. $u_1 g(x) u_2 = v_1 h(x) v_2$?
$\mathrm{PCP}_{\mathcal{R}}$	there exists $x \neq 1$ in $\mathcal{R}$ s.t. $g(x) = h(x)$?
$\mathrm{PCP}_{\mathcal{EL}}$	there exists $x \in F(\Sigma) \setminus \{1\}$ s.t. $g(x) = h(x)$ and x decomposes as a freely reduced word ayb for some $y \in F(\Omega)$
$\mathrm{PCP}^{(\neg\mathrm{inj}, \neg\mathrm{inj})}$	PCP with neither g, nor h injective
$\mathrm{PCP}^{(\neg\mathrm{inj}, \mathrm{inj})}$	PCP with exactly one of g, h injective
$\mathrm{PCP}^{(\mathrm{inj}, \mathrm{inj})}$	PCP with both g, h injective
$\mathrm{PCP}^{\mathrm{inj}}$	$\mathrm{PCP}^{(\neg\mathrm{inj}, \mathrm{inj})} \cup \mathrm{PCP}^{(\mathrm{inj}, \mathrm{inj})}$ (i.e. PCP with at least one of g, h injective)
$\mathrm{PCP}^{\mathrm{CI}}$	PCP with g, h s.t. $g(y) \neq u^{-1} h(y) u$ for all $u \in F(\Delta), y \in F(\Sigma) \setminus \{1\}$
$\mathrm{PCP}^{\mathrm{inj} + \mathrm{CI}}$	$\mathrm{PCP}^{\mathrm{inj}} \cap \mathrm{PCP}^{\mathrm{CI}}$
$\mathrm{PCP}(n)$	$\mathrm{PCP}(n)$ for alphabet size $|\Sigma| = n$
variants for $\mathrm{GPCP} \& \mathrm{PCP}_{\mathcal{EL}}$	$\mathrm{GPCP}^{\mathrm{inj}}$, $\mathrm{PCP}_{\mathcal{EL}}^{\mathrm{inj}}$, $\mathrm{GPCP}^{\mathrm{inj} + \mathrm{CI}}$, $\mathrm{GPCP}(n)$, $\mathrm{PCP}_{\mathcal{EL}}(n)$, etc. analogue to PCP variants

For free monoids, the PCP is equivalent to the GPCP [11, Theorem 8]. The corresponding connection for free groups is more complicated, and explaining this connection is the main motivation of this article. In particular, the GPCP for free groups is known to be undecidable [17, Corollary 4.2] but this proof does not imply that the PCP for free groups is undecidable (because of injectivity issues; see Sect. 3). In Theorem 4 we connect the PCP with the GPCP via a sequence of implications, and require at least one map to be injective.

Main Theorem. Theorem A summarises the connections established in this paper (arrows are labeled by the section numbers where the implications are proven), and Sect. 9 brings all the results together. Given two algorithmic problems $\mathcal{P}$ and $\mathcal{Q}$, we write $\mathcal{P} \implies \mathcal{Q}$ to mean that $\mathcal{Q}$ is Turing reducible to $\mathcal{P}$ (that is, if we can solve $\mathcal{P}$ then we can solve $\mathcal{Q}$). Note that asking for both maps to be injective refines the results in this theorem, as does restricting the size of the source alphabet Σ (see Theorem 9). All our result are for finitely generated free groups, which we abbreviate to *f.g. free groups*.

Theorem A (Theorem 9). *The following implications hold in f.g free groups.*

Rank Problem (RP)

$\Big\updownarrow 8$

Basis Problem (BP) $\xoverset{6}{\Longrightarrow}$ GPCP^{inj} $\xoverset{6}{\Longrightarrow}$ PCP $\xoverset{7.2}{\Longrightarrow}$ GPCP$^{\text{inj + CI}}$

$\Big\downarrow 4$

PCP$^{\text{inj}}_{\mathcal{R}}$

Establishing the decidability of Stallings' Rank Problem is thus of central importance, as the chain RP $\Rightarrow$ GPCP^{inj} $\Rightarrow$ PCP obtained above would lead to the decidability of the PCP.

Rational Constraints. The proof of the implication BP $\Rightarrow$ GPCP^{inj} above uses the PCP^{inj} with a certain rational constraint, namely the problem PCP$^{\text{inj}}_{\mathcal{EL}}$ (see Table 1). The relationship between the GPCP and the PCP$_{\mathcal{EL}}$ still holds if neither map is injective. As the GPCP for free groups is undecidable in general, this connection yields Theorem B, which specifies a rational constraint $\mathcal{R}$ such that the PCP$_{\mathcal{R}}$ is undecidable.

Theorem B (Theorem 3). *The PCP$_{\mathcal{EL}}$ is undecidable in f.g. free groups.*

Random Homomorphisms and Generic Behaviour. A different perspective on the PCP and its variations is to consider the behaviour of these problems when the pairs of homomorphisms are picked randomly (while the two alphabets $\Sigma = \{x_1, \ldots, x_m\}$ and Δ, and ambient free groups $F(\Sigma)$ and $F(\Delta)$ remain fixed). Any map is completely determined by how it acts on the generators, and so picking g and h randomly is to be interpreted as picking $(g(x_1), \ldots, g(x_m))$ and $(h(x_1), \ldots, h(x_m))$ as random tuples of words in $F(\Delta)$ (see Sect. 7 for details). There is a vast literature (see for example [13]) on the types of objects and behaviours which appear with probability 1, called *generic*, in infinite groups. In this spirit, the *generic* PCP refers to the PCP applied to a generic set (of pairs) of maps, that is, a set of measure 1 in the set of all (pairs of) homomorphisms, and we say that the generic PCP is decidable if the PCP is decidable for 'almost all' instances, that is, for a set of measure 1 of pairs of homomorphisms.

In Sect. 7 we describe the setup used to count pairs of map and compute probabilities, and show that among all pairs of homomorphisms g, h, the property of being *conjugacy inequivalent* (that is, for every $u \in F(\Delta)$ there is no $x \neq 1$ in $F(\Sigma)$ such that $g(x) = u^{-1}h(x)u$; defined in Table 1 as $\mathrm{PCP}^{\mathrm{CI}}$) occurs with probability 1; that is, conjugacy inequivalent maps are generic. This follows from the fact that 'most' pairs of maps are injective *and* conjugacy inequivalent:

Theorem C (Theorem 5). *With probability 1, an arbitrary pair of homomorphisms consists of injective homomorphisms that are conjugacy inequivalent. That is, instances of the $\mathrm{PCP}^{\mathrm{inj}+\mathrm{CI}}$ are generic instances of the PCP.*

Theorem C shows that the implication $\mathrm{PCP} \Rightarrow \mathrm{GPCP}^{\mathrm{inj}+\mathrm{CI}}$ in Theorem A is the generic setting, and hence for 'almost all maps' we have $\mathrm{PCP} \Leftrightarrow \mathrm{GPCP}$.

We conclude the introduction with a summary of the status of the PCP and its variations for free monoids and groups. We aim to study the computational complexity of these problems and how this complexity behaves with respect to the implications proved in this paper in future work.

Table 2. Status of results for free monoids and free groups

Problems	In free monoids	References for free monoids	In free groups	References for free groups
general PCP	undecidable	[19]	unknown	[4]
general AEP / BP	undecidable	[14, Theorem 5.2]	unknown	[4]
$\mathrm{PCP}^{(\neg\,\mathrm{inj},\neg\,\mathrm{inj})}$	undecidable	[19]	decidable	Lemma 1
$\mathrm{PCP}^{\mathrm{inj}}$	undecidable	[15]	unknown	
GPCP	undecidable	[11, Theorem 8]	undecidable	[17, Corollary 4.2]
$\mathrm{GPCP}^{(\neg\,\mathrm{inj},\neg\,\mathrm{inj})}$	undecidable	[11, Theorem 8]	undecidable	Lemma 2
$\mathrm{GPCP}^{\mathrm{inj}}$	undecidable	[15]	unknown	
$\mathrm{GPCP}^{\mathrm{inj}+\mathrm{CI}}$	N/A		unknown	
$\mathrm{PCP}_{\mathcal{R}}$	undecidable	[19]	undecidable	Theorem B
$\mathrm{PCP}^{\mathrm{inj}+\mathrm{CI}}$	N/A		unknown	
generic PCP	decidable	[9, Theorem 4.4]	decidable	[5]

2   Free Group Preliminaries

For an alphabet Σ, let Σ^{-1} be the set of formal inverses of Σ, and write $\Sigma^{\pm 1} = \Sigma \cup \Sigma^{-1}$. For example, if $\Sigma = \{a, b\}$ then $\Sigma^{\pm 1} = \{a, b, a^{-1}, b^{-1}\}$.

We denote the free group with finite generating set Σ by $F(\Sigma)$, and view it as the set of all *freely reduced words* over $\Sigma^{\pm 1}$, that is, words not containing xx^{-1} or $x^{-1}x$ as subwords, where $x \in \Sigma^{\pm 1}$, together with the operations of concatenation and free reduction (that is, the removal of any xx^{-1} that might occur when concatenating two words). If $S \subset F(\Sigma)$ is a set in the free group, then $\langle S \rangle$ denotes the *subgroup generated by* S, which is the minimal subgroup of $F(\Sigma)$ containing S (equivalently, it is the subgroup of $F(\Sigma)$ consisting of elements corresponding to words over $S^{\pm 1}$). If S has minimal cardinality among all generating sets of $\langle S \rangle$ then S is a *basis* for $\langle S \rangle$, and $|S|$ is the *rank* of $\langle S \rangle$, written $\mathrm{rk}(\langle S \rangle)$; in particular, Σ is a basis for $F(\Sigma)$ and $\mathrm{rk}(F(\Sigma)) = |\Sigma|$. We will often use the fact that a homomorphism $f : F(\Sigma) \to F(\Delta)$ is injective if and only if the image $\mathrm{Im}(f)$ has rank $|\Sigma|$ as a subgroup of $F(\Delta)$.

The above definition of free groups is similar to the definition of the free monoid Σ^* as words over Σ under concatenation. However, the presence of inverse elements is an important difference and gives rise to specific notation: If $u, v \in F(\Sigma)$ then v^u denotes the element $u^{-1}vu$, and we say that v and v^u are *conjugate*, while if $H \subseteq F(\Sigma)$ then H^u denotes the set $\{x^u \mid x \in H\}$. If $u, v \in F(\Sigma)$ then we write $[u, v] := u^{-1}v^{-1}uv$ for their *commutator*.

3   Non-injective Maps: $\mathrm{PCP}^{(\neg\,\mathrm{inj},\neg\,\mathrm{inj})}$ and $\mathrm{GPCP}^{(\neg\,\mathrm{inj},\neg\,\mathrm{inj})}$

The PCP for Non-injective Maps. We first prove that the $\mathrm{PCP}^{(\neg\,\mathrm{inj},\neg\,\mathrm{inj})}$ is trivially decidable, with the answer always being "yes".

Lemma 1. *If $g, h : F(\Sigma) \to F(\Delta)$ are both non-injective homomorphisms then $\mathrm{Eq}(g, h)$ is non-trivial.*

Proof. We prove that $\ker(g) \cap \ker(h)$ is non-trivial, which is sufficient. Let $u \in \ker(g)$ and $v \in \ker(h)$ be non-trivial elements. If $\langle u, v \rangle \cong \mathbb{Z} = \langle x \rangle$, there exist integers k, l such that $u = x^k$ and $v = x^l$. Then $g(x^{kl}) = 1 = h(x^{kl})$ so $x^{kl} \in \ker(g) \cap \ker(h)$ with x^{kl} non-trivial, as required. If $\langle u, v \rangle \not\cong \mathbb{Z}$ then $g([u, v]) = 1 = h([u, v])$, so $[u, v] \in \ker(g) \cap \ker(h)$ with $[u, v]$ non-trivial, as required. □

As we can algorithmically determine if a free group homomorphism is injective (e.g. via Stallings' foldings), Lemma 1 gives us that $\mathrm{PCP} \Leftrightarrow \mathrm{PCP}^{\mathrm{inj}}$ for fixed alphabet sizes:

Proposition 1. $\mathrm{PCP}(n) \iff \mathrm{PCP}^{\mathrm{inj}}(n)$

The GPCP for Non-injective Maps. Myasnikov, Nikolaev and Ushakov defined the PCP and GPCP for general groups in [17]. Due to this more general setting their formulation is slightly different to ours but, from a decidability point of view, the problems are equivalent for free groups. They proved that the GPCP is undecidable for free groups; however, from their proof we observe that it assumes both maps are non-injective. Therefore, GPCP^{inj} remains open.

Lemma 2. *The* GPCP$^{(\neg\,\mathrm{inj},\neg\,\mathrm{inj})}$ *is undecidable.*

Proof. Let H be a group with undecidable word problem and let $\langle \mathbf{x} \mid \mathbf{r} \rangle$ be a finite presentation of H. Let $\Delta := \mathbf{x}$, and let $F(\Sigma)$ have basis

$$\Sigma := \{(x, x^{-1}) \mid x \in \mathbf{x}\} \cup \{(x^{-1}, x) \mid x \in \mathbf{x}\} \cup \{(R, 1) \mid R \in \mathbf{r}\} \cup \{(R^{-1}, 1) \mid R \in \mathbf{r}\}.$$

Define maps $g : (p, q) \mapsto p$ and $h : (p, q) \mapsto q$ for $(p, q) \in \Sigma$. Neither g nor h is injective as the product $(x, x^{-1})(x^{-1}, x) \in F(\Sigma)$ is in the kernel of both g and h. Taking $w \in F(\Delta)$, the instance $(\Sigma, \Delta, g, h, w, 1, 1, 1)$ of the GPCP$^{(\neg\,\mathrm{inj},\neg\,\mathrm{inj})}$ has a solution if and only if the word w defines the identity of H [17, Proof of Proposition 4.1]. The result now follows as H has undecidable word problem. □

4 The PCP Under Rational Constraints: PCP$_\mathcal{R}$

For an alphabet A, a language $L \subseteq A^*$ is *regular* if there exists some finite state automaton over A which accepts exactly the words in L. Let $\pi : (\Sigma^{\pm 1})^* \to F(\Sigma)$ be the natural projection that maps any word over $\Sigma^{\pm 1}$ to the corresponding element in the free group $F(\Sigma)$. A subset $R \subseteq F(\Sigma)$ is *rational* if $R = \pi(L)$ for some regular language $L \subseteq (\Sigma^{\pm 1})^*$.

In this section we consider the PCP$_\mathcal{R}^{\mathrm{inj}}$, which is the PCP^{inj} subject to a rational constraint $\mathcal{R}$ (see Table 1). We prove that the PCP$_\mathcal{R}^{\mathrm{inj}}$ under any rational constraint $\mathcal{R}$ can be solved via the Basis Problem (BP) (so BP $\Rightarrow$ PCP$_\mathcal{R}^{\mathrm{inj}}$ from Theorem A). In Sect. 5 we apply this to prove BP $\Rightarrow$ GPCP^{inj} from Theorem A, as the PCP$_{\mathcal{EL}}^{\mathrm{inj}}$ is simply the PCP^{inj} under a specific rational constraint.

Our results here, as in much of the rest of the paper, are broken down in terms of injectivity, and also alphabet sizes; see Table 1. Understanding for which sizes of alphabet Σ the classical Post Correspondence Problem is decidable/undecidable is an important research theme [7,11,18].

Theorem 1. *The following implications hold in f.g. free groups.*

1. BP$^{(\neg\,\mathrm{inj},\mathrm{inj})}(n) \implies$ PCP$_\mathcal{R}^{(\neg\,\mathrm{inj},\mathrm{inj})}(n)$
2. BP$^{(\mathrm{inj},\mathrm{inj})}(n) \implies$ PCP$_\mathcal{R}^{(\mathrm{inj},\mathrm{inj})}(n)$

Proof. Let g, h be homomorphisms from $F(\Sigma)$ to $F(\Delta)$ such that at least one of them is injective. Their equaliser Eq(g, h) is a finitely generated subgroup of $F(\Sigma)$ [10], so Eq(g, h) is a rational set (see for example Sect. 3.1 in [1]).

By assumption the Basis Problem is soluble, so we can compute a basis for $\text{Eq}(g, h)$. This is equivalent to finding a finite state automaton $\mathcal{A}$ (called a "core graph" in the literature on free groups; see [12]) that accepts the set $\text{Eq}(g, h)$.

Let $\mathcal{R}$ be a rational set in $F(\Sigma)$. The $\text{PCP}_{\mathcal{R}}$ for g and h is equivalent to determining if there exists any non-trivial $x \in \mathcal{R} \cap \text{Eq}(g, h)$. Since the intersection of two rational sets is rational, and an automaton recognising this intersection is computable by the standard product construction of automata, one can determine whether $\mathcal{R} \cap \text{Eq}(g, h)$ is trivial or not, and thus solve $\text{PCP}_{\mathcal{R}}$. $\square$

In the next section we consider the $\text{PCP}_{\mathcal{EL}}$, which is the PCP under a certain rational constraint, and so is a specific case of $\text{PCP}_{\mathcal{R}}$.

5   The GPCP and Extreme-Letter Restrictions

In this section we connect the GPCP and the $\text{PCP}_{\mathcal{EL}}$, as defined in Table 1. This connection underlies Theorem B, as well as the implications BP $\Rightarrow$ GPCP^{inj} and PCP $\Rightarrow$ GPCP$^{\text{inj}+\text{CI}}$ in Theorem A.

Connecting the GPCP and the PCP. We start with an instance $I_{\text{GPCP}} = (\Sigma, \Delta, g, h, u_1, u_2, v_1, v_2)$ of the GPCP and consider the instance

$$I_{\text{PCP}} = (\Sigma \sqcup \{B, E\}, \Delta \sqcup \{B, E, \#\}, g', h')$$

of the PCP, where g' and h' are defined as follows.

$$g'(z) := \begin{cases} \#^{-1}g(z)\# & \text{if } z \in \Sigma \\ B\#u_1\# & \text{if } z = B \\ \#^{-1}u_2\#E & \text{if } z = E \end{cases} \qquad h'(z) := \begin{cases} \#h(z)\#^{-1} & \text{if } z \in \Sigma \\ B\#v_1\#^{-1} & \text{if } z = B \\ \#v_2\#E & \text{if } z = E \end{cases}$$

Injectivity is preserved by this construction as $\text{rk}(\text{Im}(g')) = \text{rk}(\text{Im}(g)) + 2$ (see Sect. 2 for the connection between injectivity and rank): this can be seen via Stallings' foldings [12], or directly by noting that the image of g' restricted to $F(\Sigma)$ is isomorphic to $\text{Im}(g)$, that B only occurs in $g'(d)$ and E only occurs in $g'(e)$. Analogously, h' is an injection if and only if h is, as again $\text{rk}(\text{Im}(h)) + 2 = \text{rk}(\text{Im}(h'))$. Thus we get:

Lemma 3. *The map g' is injective if and only if g is, and the map h' is injective if and only if h is.*

We now connect the solutions of I_{GPCP} to those of I_{PCP}.

Lemma 4. *A word $y \in F(\Sigma)$ is a solution to I_{GPCP} if and only if the word 'ByE' is a solution to I_{PCP}.*

Proof. Starting with y being a solution to I_{GPCP}, we obtain the following sequence of equivalent identities:

$$u_1 g(y) u_2 = v_1 h(y) v_2$$
$$B\#(u_1 g(y) u_2)\#E = B\#(v_1 h(y) v_2)\#E$$
$$B\#u_1\# \cdot \#^{-1} g(y)\# \cdot \#^{-1} u_2 \#E = B\#v_1\#^{-1} \cdot \#h(y)\#^{-1} \cdot \#v_2 \#E$$
$$g'(B)g'(y)g'(E) = h'(B)h'(y)h'(E)$$
$$g'(ByE) = h'(ByE).$$

Therefore ByE is a solution to I_{PCP}, so the claimed equivalence follows. □

We now have that $\text{PCP}^{\text{inj}}_{\mathcal{EL}}(n+2) \implies \text{GPCP}^{\text{inj}}(n)$.

Theorem 2. *The following implications hold in f.g. free groups.*

1. $\text{PCP}^{(\neg\text{inj},\text{inj})}_{\mathcal{EL}}(n+2) \implies \text{GPCP}^{(\neg\text{inj},\text{inj})}(n)$
2. $\text{PCP}^{(\text{inj},\text{inj})}_{\mathcal{EL}}(n+2) \implies \text{GPCP}^{(\text{inj},\text{inj})}(n)$

Proof. Let I_{GPCP} be an instance of the GPCP^{inj}, and construct from it the instance $I_{\text{PCP}_{\mathcal{EL}}} = (\Sigma \sqcup \{B,E\}, \Delta \sqcup \{B,E,\#\}, g', h', B, \Sigma, E)$ of the $\text{PCP}_{\mathcal{EL}}$, which is the instance I_{PCP} defined above under the constraint that solutions have the form ByE for some $y \in F(\Sigma)$.

By Lemma 3, $I_{\text{PCP}_{\mathcal{EL}}}$ is an instance of the $\text{PCP}^{(\neg\text{inj},\text{inj})}_{\mathcal{EL}}(n+2)$ if and only if I_{GPCP} is an instance of $\text{GPCP}^{(\neg\text{inj},\text{inj})}(n)$, and similarly for $\text{PCP}^{(\text{inj},\text{inj})}_{\mathcal{EL}}(n+2)$ and $\text{GPCP}^{(\text{inj},\text{inj})}(n)$. The result then follows from Lemma 4. □

The above does not prove that $\text{PCP}^{\text{inj}} \Leftrightarrow \text{GPCP}^{\text{inj}}$, because I_{PCP} might have solutions of the form BxB^{-1} or $E^{-1}xE$. For example, if we let $I_{\text{GPCP}} = (\{a\}, \{a,c,d\}, g, h, c, \epsilon, \epsilon, d)$ with $g(a) = a$ and $h(a) = cac^{-1}$, then there is no $x \in F(a)$ such that $cg(a) = h(a)d$, but defining g', h' as above then $BaB^{-1} \in \text{Eq}(g', h')$. In Sect. 7.2 we consider maps where such solutions are impossible, and there the equivalence $\text{PCP}^{\text{inj}} \Leftrightarrow \text{GPCP}^{\text{inj}}$ does hold.

Undecidability of $\text{PCP}_{\mathcal{EL}}$. The link between the GPCP and $\text{PCP}_{\mathcal{EL}}$ yields the following theorem, which immediately implies Theorem B.

Theorem 3 (Theorem B). $\text{PCP}^{(\neg\text{inj},\neg\text{inj})}_{\mathcal{EL}}$ *is undecidable in f.g. free groups.*

Proof. We have $\text{PCP}^{(\neg\text{inj},\neg\text{inj})}_{\mathcal{EL}} \Rightarrow \text{GPCP}^{(\neg\text{inj},\neg\text{inj})}$ by Lemmas 3 and 4. The result follows as $\text{GPCP}^{(\neg\text{inj},\neg\text{inj})}$ is undecidable by Lemma 2. □

6   Main Results: Part 1

Here we combine results from the previous sections to prove certain of the implications in Theorem A. The implications we prove refine Theorem A, as they additionally contain information on alphabet sizes and on injectivity.

Theorem 4. *The following implications hold in f.g. free groups.*

1. $\mathrm{BP}^{(\neg\,\mathrm{inj},\mathrm{inj})}(n+2) \implies \mathrm{GPCP}^{(\neg\,\mathrm{inj},\mathrm{inj})}(n) \implies \mathrm{PCP}^{(\neg\,\mathrm{inj},\mathrm{inj})}(n)$
2. $\mathrm{BP}^{(\mathrm{inj},\mathrm{inj})}(n+2) \implies \mathrm{GPCP}^{(\mathrm{inj},\mathrm{inj})}(n) \implies \mathrm{PCP}^{(\mathrm{inj},\mathrm{inj})}(n)$

Proof. As $\mathrm{PCP}_{\mathcal{EL}}^{(\neg\,\mathrm{inj},\mathrm{inj})}$ is an instance of the $\mathrm{PCP}^{\mathrm{inj}}$ under a rational constraint, Theorem 1 gives us that $\mathrm{BP}^{(\neg\,\mathrm{inj},\mathrm{inj})}(n+2) \Rightarrow \mathrm{PCP}_{\mathcal{EL}}^{(\neg\,\mathrm{inj},\mathrm{inj})}(n+2)$, while Theorem 2 gives us that $\mathrm{PCP}_{\mathcal{EL}}^{(\neg\,\mathrm{inj},\mathrm{inj})}(n+2) \Rightarrow \mathrm{GPCP}^{(\neg\,\mathrm{inj},\mathrm{inj})}(n)$, and the implication $\mathrm{GPCP}^{(\neg\,\mathrm{inj},\mathrm{inj})}(n) \Rightarrow \mathrm{PCP}^{(\neg\,\mathrm{inj},\mathrm{inj})}(n)$ is obvious as instances of the PCP are instances of the GPCP but with empty constants u_i, v_i. Sequence (1), with one map injective, therefore holds, while the proof of sequence (2) is identical. □

Removing the injectivity assumptions gives the following corollary; the implications $\mathrm{BP} \Rightarrow \mathrm{GPCP}^{\mathrm{inj}} \Rightarrow \mathrm{PCP}$ of Theorem A follow immediately.

Corollary 1. $\mathrm{BP}(n+2) \implies \mathrm{GPCP}^{\mathrm{inj}}(n) \implies \mathrm{PCP}(n)$

Proof. Theorem 4 gives that $\mathrm{BP}(n+2) \Rightarrow \mathrm{GPCP}^{\mathrm{inj}}(n) \Rightarrow \mathrm{PCP}^{\mathrm{inj}}(n)$, while $\mathrm{PCP}(n) \Leftrightarrow \mathrm{PCP}^{\mathrm{inj}}(n)$ by Proposition 1. □

7   Conjugacy Inequivalent Maps: $\mathrm{PCP}^{\mathrm{CI}}$ and $\mathrm{PCP}^{\mathrm{inj}+\mathrm{CI}}$

In this section we prove genericity results and give conditions under which the PCP implies the GPCP. In particular, we prove Theorem C, and we prove the implication $\mathrm{PCP} \Rightarrow \mathrm{GPCP}^{\mathrm{inj}+\mathrm{CI}}$ from Theorem A.

A pair of maps $g, h : F(\Sigma) \to F(\Delta)$ is said to be *conjugacy inequivalent* if for every $u \in F(\Delta)$ there does not exist any non-trivial $x \in F(\Sigma)$ such that $g(x) = u^{-1}h(x)u$ (see Table 1). For example, if the images of $g, h : F(\Sigma) \to F(\Delta)$ are *conjugacy separated*, that is, if $\mathrm{Im}(g) \cap u^{-1}\mathrm{Im}(h)u$ is trivial for all $u \in F(\Delta)$, then g and h are conjugacy inequivalent. We write $\mathrm{PCP}^{\mathrm{inj}+\mathrm{CI}}/\mathrm{GPCP}^{\mathrm{inj}+\mathrm{CI}}$ for those instances of the $\mathrm{GPCP}^{\mathrm{inj}}/\mathrm{PCP}^{\mathrm{inj}}$ where the maps are conjugacy inequivalent.

7.1   Random Maps and Genericity

Here we show that among all pairs of homomorphisms $g, h : F(\Sigma) \to F(\Delta)$, the property of being conjugacy inequivalent occurs with probability 1; that is, conjugacy inequivalent maps are *generic*. In fact, a stronger result holds: *injective* conjugacy inequivalent maps are already generic, as we show below.

Theorem 5 (Theorem C). *With probability 1, an arbitrary pair of maps consists of injective maps that are conjugacy inequivalent. That is, instances of the $\mathrm{PCP}^{\mathrm{inj}+\mathrm{CI}}$ are generic instances of the PCP.*

Before we prove the theorem, we need to describe the way in which probabilities are computed. We consider maps sending generators to words of length $\leq n$, and consider asymptotics as $n \to \infty$. Formally: Fix the two alphabets

$\Sigma = \{x_1, \ldots, x_m\}$ and $\Delta = \{y_1, \ldots, y_k\}$, $m, k \geq 2$, and ambient free groups $F(\Sigma)$ and $F(\Delta)$, and pick g and h randomly by choosing $(g(x_1), \ldots, g(x_m))$ and $(h(x_1), \ldots, h(x_m))$ independently at random, as tuples of words of length bounded by n in $F(\Delta)$. If $\mathcal{P}$ is a property of tuples (or subgroups) of $F(\Delta)$, we say that *generically many* tuples (or finitely generated subgroups) of $F(\Delta)$ satisfy $\mathcal{P}$ if the proportion of m-tuples of words of length $\leq n$ in $F(\Delta)$ which satisfy $\mathcal{P}$ (or generate a subgroup satisfying $\mathcal{P}$), among all possible m-tuples of words of length $\leq n$, tends to 1 when n tends to infinity.

Proof. Let $n > 0$ be an integer, and let $(a_1, \ldots, a_m)$ and $(b_1, \ldots, b_m)$ be two tuples of words in $F(\Sigma)$ satisfying length inequalities $|a_i| \leq n$ and $|b_i| \leq n$ for all i. We let the maps $g, h : F(\Sigma) \to F(\Delta)$ that are part of an instance of PCP be defined as $g(x_i) = a_i$ and $h(x_i) = b_i$, and note that the images $\mathrm{Im}(g)$ and $\mathrm{Im}(h)$ in $F(\Delta)$ are subgroups generated by $(a_1, \ldots, a_m)$ and $(b_1, \ldots, b_m)$, respectively.

We claim that among all $2m$-tuples $(a_1, \ldots, a_m, b_1, \ldots, b_m)$ with $|a_i|, |b_i| \leq n$, a proportion of them tending to 1 as $n \to \infty$ satisfy (1) the subgroups $L = \langle a_1, \ldots, a_m \rangle$ and $K = \langle b_1, \ldots, b_m \rangle$ are both of rank m, and (2) for every $u \in F(\Delta)$ we have $L^u \cap K = \{1\}$. Claim (1) is equivalent to g, h being generically injective, and follows from [16], while claim (2) is equivalent to $\mathrm{Im}(g)^u \cap \mathrm{Im}(h) = \{1\}$ for every $u \in F(\Delta)$, which implies g and h are generically conjugacy separated, and follows from [5, Theorem 1]. More specifically, [5, Theorem 1] proves that for any tuple $(a_1, \ldots, a_m)$, 'almost all' (precisely computed) tuples $(b_1, \ldots, b_m)$, with $|b_i| \leq n$, give subgroups $L = \langle a_1, \ldots, a_m \rangle$ and $K = \langle b_1, \ldots, b_m \rangle$ with trivial pullback, that is, for every $u \in F(\Delta)$, $K^u \cap L = \{1\}$. Going over all $(a_1, \ldots, a_m)$ with $|a_i| \leq n$ and counting the tuples $(b_1, \ldots, b_m)$ (as in [5]) satisfying property (2) gives the genericity result for all $2m$-tuples. $\square$

7.2   The GPCP for Conjugacy Inequivalent Maps

We now prove that the PCP implies the GPCP$^{\mathrm{inj}+\mathrm{CI}}$ and hence that, generically, the PCP implies the GPCP. Recall that if I_{GPCP} is a specific instance of the GPCP we can associate to it a specific instance $I_{\mathrm{PCP}} = (\Sigma \sqcup \{B, E\}, \Delta \sqcup \{B, E, \#\}, g', h')$, as in Sect. 5. We start by classifying the solutions to I_{PCP}.

Lemma 5. *Let I_{GPCP} be an instance of the GPCP^{inj}, with associated instance I_{PCP} of the PCP^{inj}. Every solution to I_{PCP} is a product of solutions of the form $(BxE)^{\pm 1}$, $E^{-1}xE$ and BxB^{-1}, for $x \in F(\Sigma)$.*

We now have:

Theorem 6. *Let $I_{\mathrm{GPCP}} = (\Sigma, \Delta, g, h, u_1, u_2, v_1, v_2)$ be an instance of GPCP^{inj}, such that there is no non-trivial $x \in F(\Sigma)$ with $u_1 g(x) u_1^{-1} = v_1 h(x) v_1^{-1}$ or $u_2^{-1} g(x) u_2 = v_2^{-1} h(x) v_2$. Then I_{GPCP} has a solution (possibly trivial) if and only if the associated instance I_{PCP} of the PCP^{inj} has a non-trivial solution.*

Proof. By Lemma 4, if I_{GPCP} has a solution then I_{PCP} has a non-trivial solution. For the other direction, note that the assumptions in the theorem are equivalent to I_{GPCP} having no solutions of the form BxB^{-1} or $E^{-1}xE$, and so by Lemma 5, every non-trivial solution to I_{GPCP} has the form $Bx_1E\cdots Bx_nE$ for some $x_i \in F(\Sigma)$. The Bx_iE subwords block this word off into chunks, and we see that each such word is a solution to I_{PCP}. By Lemma 4, each x_i is a solution to I_{GPCP}. Hence, if I_{PCP} has a non-trivial solution then I_{GPCP} has a solution.   □

Theorem 6 depends both on the maps g and h and on the constants u_i, v_i. The definition of conjugacy inequivalent maps implies that the conditions of Theorem 6 hold always, independent of the u_i, v_i. We therefore have:

Theorem 7. *The following implications hold in f.g. free groups.*

1. $\mathrm{PCP}^{(\neg\,\mathrm{inj},\mathrm{inj})}(n+2) \implies \mathrm{GPCP}^{(\neg\,\mathrm{inj},\mathrm{inj})+\mathrm{CI}}(n)$
2. $\mathrm{PCP}^{(\mathrm{inj},\mathrm{inj})}(n+2) \implies \mathrm{GPCP}^{(\mathrm{inj},\mathrm{inj})+\mathrm{CI}}(n)$

Removing the injectivity assumptions gives the following corollary; the implication $\mathrm{PCP} \Rightarrow \mathrm{GPCP}^{\mathrm{inj}+\mathrm{CI}}$ of Theorem A follows immediately.

Corollary 2. $\mathrm{PCP}(n+2) \implies \mathrm{GPCP}^{\mathrm{inj}+\mathrm{CI}}(n)$

Proof. Theorem 7 gives us that $\mathrm{PCP}^{\mathrm{inj}}(n+2) \Rightarrow \mathrm{GPCP}^{\mathrm{inj}+\mathrm{CI}}(n)$, while the $\mathrm{PCP}(n)$ and $\mathrm{PCP}^{\mathrm{inj}}(n)$ are equivalent by Proposition 1.   □

8   The Basis Problem and Stallings' Rank Problem

In this section we link the Basis Problem to Stallings' Rank Problem. Clearly the Basis Problem solves the Rank Problem, as the rank is simply the size of the basis. We prove that these problems are equivalent, with Lemma 6 providing the non-obvious direction of the equivalence. Combining this equivalence with Corollary 1 gives: $\mathrm{RP} \Rightarrow \mathrm{GPCP}^{\mathrm{inj}} \Rightarrow \mathrm{PCP}$.

Lemma 6 is proven using the "derived graph" construction of Goldstein–Turner [10].

Lemma 6. *There exists an algorithm with input an instance $I = (\Sigma, \Delta, g, h)$ of the $\mathrm{PCP}^{\mathrm{inj}}$ and the rank $\mathrm{rk}(\mathrm{Eq}(g,h))$ of the equaliser of g and h, and output a basis for $\mathrm{Eq}(g,h)$.*

The following shows that Stallings' Rank Problem is equivalent to the BP.

Theorem 8. *The following implications hold in f.g. free groups.*

1. $\mathrm{BP}^{(\neg\,\mathrm{inj},\mathrm{inj})}(n) \iff \mathrm{RP}^{(\neg\,\mathrm{inj},\mathrm{inj})}(n)$
2. $\mathrm{BP}^{(\mathrm{inj},\mathrm{inj})}(n) \iff \mathrm{RP}^{(\mathrm{inj},\mathrm{inj})}(n)$

Proof. Let I_{PCP} be an instance of the $\mathrm{PCP}^{\mathrm{inj}}$. As the rank of a free group is precisely the size of some (hence any) basis for it, if we can compute a basis for $\mathrm{Eq}(g,h)$ then we can compute the rank of $\mathrm{Eq}(g,h)$. On the other hand, by Lemma 6 if we can compute the rank of $\mathrm{Eq}(g,h)$ then we can compute a basis of $\mathrm{Eq}(g,h)$.   □

9   Main Results: Part 2

We now combine results from the previous sections to the following result, from which Theorem A follows immediately.

Theorem 9. *The following implications hold in f.g. free groups.*

$$\mathrm{RP}(n+2)$$

$$\Updownarrow$$

$$\mathrm{BP}(n+2) \Longrightarrow \mathrm{GPCP}^{\mathrm{inj}}(n) \Longrightarrow \mathrm{PCP}(n) \Longrightarrow \mathrm{GPCP}^{\mathrm{inj}+\mathrm{CI}}(n-2)$$

$$\Downarrow$$

$$\mathrm{PCP}^{\mathrm{inj}}_{\mathcal{R}}(n+2)$$

Proof. The proof is a summary of the results already established in the rest of the paper, and we give a schematic version of it here.

$\mathrm{RP}(n+2) \Leftrightarrow \mathrm{BP}(n+2)$ holds by Theorem 8.

$\mathrm{BP}(n+2) \Rightarrow \mathrm{PCP}^{\mathrm{inj}}_{\mathcal{R}}(n+2)$ holds by Theorem 1.

$\mathrm{BP}(n+2) \Rightarrow \mathrm{GPCP}^{\mathrm{inj}}(n) \Rightarrow \mathrm{PCP}(n)$ holds by Corollary 1.

$\mathrm{PCP}(n) \Rightarrow \mathrm{GPCP}^{\mathrm{inj}+\mathrm{CI}}(n-2)$ holds by Corollary 2.   □

Removing the $\mathrm{GPCP}^{\mathrm{inj}}(n)$-term gives a different picture of alphabet sizes:

Theorem 10. $\mathrm{BP}(n+2) \Longrightarrow \mathrm{PCP}(n+2) \Longrightarrow \mathrm{GPCP}^{\mathrm{inj}+\mathrm{CI}}(n)$

References

1. Bartholdi, L., Silva, P.V.: Rational subsets of groups. arXiv:1012.1532 (2010)
2. Bogopolski, O., Maslakova, O.: An algorithm for finding a basis of the fixed point subgroup of an automorphism of a free group. Int. J. Algebra Comput. **26**(1), 29–67 (2016)
3. Ciobanu, L., Logan, A.: Fixed points and stable images of endomorphisms for the free group of rank two. arXiv:2009.04937 (2020)
4. Ciobanu, L., Logan, A.: The Post correspondence problem and equalisers for certain free group and monoid morphisms. In: 47th International Colloquium on Automata, Languages, and Programming (ICALP 2020), pp. 120:1–120:16 (2020)
5. Ciobanu, L., Martino, A., Ventura, E.: The generic hanna neumann conjecture and post correspondence problem (2008). http://www-eupm.upc.es/~ventura/ventura/files/31t.pdf
6. Diekert, V., Kharlampovich, O., Lohrey, M., Myasnikov, A.: Algorithmic problems in group theory. Dagstuhl seminar report 19131 (2019). https://drops.dagstuhl.de/opus/volltexte/2019/11293/pdf/dagrep_v009_i003_p083_19131.pdf
7. Ehrenfeucht, A., Karhumäki, J., Rozenberg, G.: The (generalized) Post correspondence problem with lists consisting of two words is decidable. Theoret. Comput. Sci. **21**(2), 119–144 (1982)
8. Feighn, M., Handel, M.: Algorithmic constructions of relative train track maps and CTs. Groups Geom. Dyn. **12**(3), 1159–1238 (2018)

9. Gilman, R., Miasnikov, A.G., Myasnikov, A.D., Ushakov, A.: Report on generic case complexity. arXiv:0707.1364v1 (2007)

10. Goldstein, R.Z., Turner, E.C.: Fixed subgroups of homomorphisms of free groups. Bull. London Math. Soc. **18**(5), 468–470 (1986)

11. Harju, T., Karhumäki, J.: Morphisms. In: Rozenberg, G., Salomaa, A. (eds.) Handbook of Formal Languages, pp. 439–510. Springer, Heidelberg (1997)

12. Kapovich, I., Myasnikov, A.: Stallings foldings and subgroups of free groups. J. Algebra **248**(2), 608–668 (2002)

13. Kapovich, I., Myasnikov, A., Schupp, P., Shpilrain, V.: Generic-case complexity, decision problems in group theory, and random walks. J. Algebra **264**(2), 665–694 (2003)

14. Karhumäki, J., Saarela, A.: Noneffective regularity of equality languages and bounded delay morphisms. Discrete Math. Theoret. Comput. Sci. **12**(4), 9–17 (2010)

15. Lecerf, Y.: Récursive insolubilité de l'équation générale de diagonalisation de deux monomorphismes de monoïdes libres $\varphi x = \psi x$. C. R. Acad. Sci. Paris **257**, 2940–2943 (1963)

16. Martino, A., Turner, E., Ventura, E.: The density of injective endomorphisms of a free group (2006). http://www-eupm.upc.es/~ventura/ventura/files/23t.pdf

17. Myasnikov, A., Nikolaev, A., Ushakov, A.: The Post correspondence problem in groups. J. Group Theory **17**(6), 991–1008 (2014)

18. Neary, T.: Undecidability in binary tag systems and the post correspondence problem for five pairs of words. In: 32nd International Symposium on Theoretical Aspects of Computer Science, LIPIcs. Leibniz International Proceedings in Informatics, vol. 30, pp. 649–661. Schloss Dagstuhl. Leibniz-Zent. Inform., Wadern (2015)

19. Post, E.L.: A variant of a recursively unsolvable problem. Bull. Am. Math. Soc. **52**, 264–268 (1946)

Reducing Local Alphabet Size
in Recognizable Picture Languages

Stefano Crespi Reghizzi[1], Antonio Restivo[2], and Pierluigi San Pietro[1(✉)]

[1] Politecnico di Milano - DEIB, Milan, Italy
{stefano.crespireghizzi,pierluigi.sanpietro}@polimi.it
[2] Dipartimento di Matematica e Informatica, Università di Palermo, Palermo, Italy
antonio.restivo@unipa.it

Abstract. A recognizable picture language is defined as the projection of a local picture language defined by a set of two-by-two tiles, i.e. by a strictly-locally-testable (SLT) language of order 2. The family of recognizable picture languages is also defined, using larger k by k tiles, $k > 2$, by the projection of the corresponding SLT language. A basic measure of the descriptive complexity of a picture language is given by the size of the SLT alphabet using two-by-two tiles, more precisely by the so-called alphabetic ratio of sizes: SLT-alphabet/picture-alphabet. We study how the alphabetic ratio changes moving from two to larger tile sizes, and we obtain the following result: any recognizable picture language over an alphabet of size n is the projection of an SLT language over an alphabet of size $2n$. Moreover, two is the minimal alphabetic ratio possible in general. This result reproduces into two dimensions a similar property (known as Extended Medvedev's theorem) of the regular word languages, concerning the minimal alphabetic ratio needed to define a language by means of a projection of an SLT word language.

1   Introduction

To present our research in the framework of formal language studies, we observe that language families can be defined by means of different approaches, primarily by automata, by generative rules, by logical formulas, and by mapping one language family into another one. Within the Chomsky hierarchy, the regular language family, originally defined by means of finite automata and regular expressions, has been later supplemented with other definitions, in particular by means of the homomorphic image of the simpler language family known as *local* languages. The latter definition is also referred to as Medvedev's theorem [9,10], for short *MT*. Each local language is characterized by stating that a word is valid if and only if, its 2-factors, i.e., its substrings of length two, are included in a given set. Then, Medvedev's theorem says that for each regular language R over an alphabet Σ there exists a local language L over an alphabet Λ and a letter-to-letter morphism $h : \Lambda \to \Sigma$ such that $R = h(L)$.

The present work deals with languages whose elements, called *pictures*, are rectangular arrays of cells each one containing a letter. Clearly, a word language is

© Springer Nature Switzerland AG 2021
N. Moreira and R. Reis (Eds.): DLT 2021, LNCS 12811, pp. 103–116, 2021.
https://doi.org/10.1007/978-3-030-81508-0_9

also a picture language that only comprises rectangles with unitary (say) height. A well-known family of picture languages, named *tiling recognizable* REC [6], has its natural definition through the analog of MT. The definition relies on a *tiling system* (TS), consisting of a local picture language and of a morphism from the local alphabet Λ to the picture alphabet Σ. More precisely, the local language is specified by a set of tiles, that are pictures of size two-by-two and play the role of the 2-factors of the local word languages. Other definitions of the REC family, by means of automata and logical formulas [6], are less convenient than the corresponding definitions for word languages.

Returning to the MT definition of a regular word language, the letters of the local alphabet Λ correspond to the elements of the state set Q of a finite automaton (FA) recognizing the regular language. Hence, the *ratio* $|\Lambda|/|\Sigma|$ is a meaningful measure of the descriptive complexity of the FA, and obviously induces an infinite hierarchy under set inclusion, for certain series of regular languages. For REC the situation is similar, but less investigated. What we have to retain is that any limitation of the alphabetic ratio of tiling systems would restrict the language family.

Local word languages are located at the lowest level of an infinite language hierarchy (under set inclusion) called *k-strictly locally testable* (SLT) [8], each level $k \geq 2$ using of a sliding window of width k that scans the input and checks that each k-factor belongs to a given set of allowed factors. A similar hierarchy for picture languages [5] uses k-by-k tiles instead of k-factors. The corresponding picture language family is here called *k-strictly locally testable* (k-SLT), simply SLT when the value k is unspecified.

The first basic question one can address is: if in the tiling system definition of REC we allow k-SLT languages with $k > 2$, do we obtain a language family larger than REC? The answer is known to be negative [5,7]. Then, the next interesting question is: using k-by-k tiles with $k > 2$, can we reduce the alphabetic ratio, and how much?

In the case of word languages, the answer to the latter question is known [3], and we refer to it as *Extended Medvedev's Theorem* (EMT): the minimal alphabetic ratio is 2 and can always be achieved by assigning to the SLT parameter k a value in the order of the logarithm of the FA recognizer size. We hint to its proof, which is the starting point of the present development for pictures. Given an FA, the construction in the proof samples in each computation the subsequences made by a series of k state-transitions. Then, a binary code of length k suffices to encode all such FA sub-sequences. To prevent mistakes, the proof resorts to *comma-free* codes [2], that can be decoded without synchronization by using a $2k$-SLT DFA as decoder.

Moving from words to pictures complicates matters, but we succeeded in lifting EMT from regular word languages to REC: any picture language is the projection, by means of a letter-to-letter morphism, of an SLT picture language, with a (minimal) alphabetic ratio 2. We may rephrase the result in an artistic vein for binary pictures: any black and white picture is the projection of an SLT picture using just four colors.

Outline. Section 2 contains the basic notions of picture languages. Section 3 deals with k-SLT picture languages and their use in tiling systems. It also introduces the comma-free codes in picture. Section 4 proves the main result on the alphabetic ratio and its minimality. The Conclusions raise a general question about the validity of similar results for other families of languages. The Appendix presents an example.

2 Preliminaries

All the alphabets to be considered are finite. The following concepts and notations for picture languages follow mostly [6]. A *picture* is a rectangular array of letters over an alphabet. Given a picture p, $|p|_{row}$ and $|p|_{col}$ denote the number of rows and columns, respectively; $|p| = (|p|_{row}, |p|_{col})$ denotes the *picture size*. Pictures of identical size are called *isometric*. The set of all pictures over Σ of size (m, n) is denoted by $\Sigma^{m,n}$. The set of all non-empty pictures over Σ is denoted by Σ^{++}. This notation is naturally extended from an alphabet to a finite set X of pictures, by writing X^{++}.

A *picture language* over Σ is a subset of Σ^{++}. In the following, the term "language" always stands for picture language, and word languages are qualified as such.

A picture of size (r, c) over an alphabet Γ will be also denoted as $[\gamma_{i,j}]$, with every $\gamma_{i,j} \in \Gamma$, which stands for the picture $\begin{bmatrix} \gamma_{1,1} \cdots \gamma_{1,c} \\ \cdots \\ \gamma_{r,1} \cdots \gamma_{r,c} \end{bmatrix}$. We extend the notation to denote a picture of size (kr, kc) in X^{++} with $X \in \Gamma^{++}$ as follows: $[x_{i,j}]$, with $x_{i,j} \in \Gamma^{k,k}$, stands for the picture $(x_{1,1} \oplus \ldots x_{1,c}) \ominus \cdots \ominus (x_{r,1} \oplus \ldots x_{r,c})$.

A *subpicture of* p, denoted by $p_{(i,j;i',j')}$ is the portion of p defined by the top-left coordinates (i, j) and by the bottom right coordinates $(i'j')$, with $1 \le i \le i' \le |p|_{row}$, and $1 \le j \le j' \le |p|_{col}$.

Bordered Pictures and k-tiles. Since the symbols on the boundary of picture p play often a special role for recognition, it is convenient to surround them by a frame of width one comprising only the special symbol $\# \notin \Sigma$. The *bordered picture* $\widehat{p}$ has size $(|p|_{row} + 2)$, $(|p|_{col} + 2)$ and domain $\{0, 1, \cdots, |p|_{row} + 1\} \times \{0, 1, \cdots, |p|_{col} + 1\}$.

We denote by $B_{k,k}(p)$, $k \ge 2$, the set of all subpictures, named *k-tiles*, of picture p having size (k, k). When one or both dimensions of p are smaller than k, we posit $B_{k,k}(p) = \emptyset$. The set of all subpictures of size (k, k) of a language L is defined as $B_{k,k}(L) = \bigcup_{p \in L} B_{k,k}(\widehat{p})$.

Concatenations. Let $p, q \in \Sigma^{++}$. The *horizontal* (or *column*) *concatenation* $p \oplus q$ is defined when $|p|_{row} = |q|_{row}$ as: $\boxed{\text{p q}}$. The *vertical* (or *row*) *concatenation* $p \ominus q$ is defined when $|p|_{col} = |q|_{col}$ as: $\boxed{\begin{smallmatrix} p \\ q \end{smallmatrix}}$. We also use the power operations $p^{\ominus k}$ and $p^{\oplus k}$, $k \ge 1$, and we extend the concatenations to languages in the obvious way.

Definition 1 (picture morphism). *Given two alphabets* Γ, Λ, *a (picture) morphism is a mapping* $\varphi : \Gamma^{++} \to \Lambda^{++}$ *such that, for all* $p, q \in \Gamma^{++}$:

$$\begin{cases} i) \; \varphi(p \oplus q) = \varphi(p) \oplus \varphi(q) \\ ii) \; \varphi(p \ominus q) = \varphi(p) \ominus \varphi(q) \end{cases}$$

Since $\oplus$ is a partial operation, to satisfy *i)* we need that for all $p, q \in \Gamma^{++}$, $p \oplus q$ is satisfied iff $\varphi(p) \oplus \varphi(q)$; and similarly for $\ominus$ to satisfy *ii)*. This implies that the images by φ of the elements of alphabet Γ are isometric, i.e., for any $x, y \in \Gamma$, $|\varphi(x)|_{row} = |\varphi(y)|_{row}$ and $|\varphi(x)|_{col} = |\varphi(y)|_{col}$.

Tiling Recognition. Let Γ and Σ be alphabets; given a mapping $\pi : \Gamma \to \Sigma$, to be termed *projection*, we extend π to isometric pictures $p' \in \Gamma^{++}$, $p \in \Sigma^{++}$ by: $p = \pi(p')$ such that $p_{i,j} = \pi(p'_{i,j})$ for all $(i, j) \in \text{dom}(p')$. Then, p' is called the *pre-image* of p.

Definition 2 (tiling system). *A tiling system (TS) is a quadruple* $\mathcal{T} = (\Sigma, \Gamma, T, \pi)$ *where* Σ *and* Γ *are alphabets,* T *is a finite 2-tile set over* $\Gamma \cup \{\#\}$, *and* $\pi : \Gamma \to \Sigma$ *is a projection. A language* $L \subseteq \Sigma^{++}$ *is recognized by such a TS if* $L = \pi(L(T))$. *We also write* $L = L(\mathcal{T})$. *The family of all tiling recognizable languages is denoted by REC.*

3   Strictly Locally Testable Picture Languages

Definition 3. *Given* $k \geq 2$, *a language* $L \subseteq \Sigma^{++}$ *is* k-*strictly-locally-testable* (k-*SLT*) *if there exists a finite set* T_k *of* k-*tiles   in* $(\Sigma \cup \{\#\})^{k,k}$ *such that* $L = \{p \in \Sigma^{++} \mid B_{k,k}(\widehat{p}) \subseteq T_k\}$; *we also write* $L = L(T_k)$. *A language* L *is called strictly-locally-testable (SLT) if it is* k-*SLT for some* $k \geq 2$.

In other words, to check that a picture is in a k-SLT language, we check that each subpicture of size (k, k) of the bordered picture is included in a given set of k-tiles. Local languages correspond to the special case $k = 2$. This definition ignores pictures with size less than (k, k), which anyway amount to a finite language, to be ignored in the following, when we compare k-SLT languages.

Since k-SLT picture languages include as a special case k-SLT word languages, the following proposition derives immediately from known properties.

Proposition 1. *The family of* k-*SLT languages for* $k \geq 2$ *is strictly included in the family of* $(k + 1)$-*SLT languages, when ignoring pictures smaller than* $(k + 1, k + 1)$.

If we apply a projection to k-SLT languages, the hierarchy of Proposition 1 collapses (proved in [5,7]). We state it to prepare the concepts needed in later developments.

Theorem 1. *Given a* k-*SLT language* $L \subseteq \Sigma^{++}$ *defined by a set of* k-*tiles* T_k *(i,e,* $L = L(T_k)$*), there exists an alphabet* Γ, *a local language* $L' \subseteq \Gamma^{++}$ *and a projection* $\pi : \Gamma \to \Sigma$ *such that* $L = \pi(L')$.

Remark 1. Both proofs in [5,7] consider an alphabet Γ of size $|\Gamma| = |\Sigma| \cdot |T_k|$. Since T_k is a subset of $(\Sigma \cup \{\#\})^{k,k}$, one has $|T_k| \leq (|\Sigma| + 1)^{k^2}$ and $|\Gamma| \leq (|\Sigma| + 1)^{k^2+1}$.

The family of SLT languages is strictly included in REC [6]. An immediate consequence of Theorem 1 is that the use of larger tiles does not enlarge the family REC.

Corollary 1. *The family of languages obtained by projections of SLT languages coincides with the family REC of tiling recognizable languages.*

Thus any REC language over Σ can be obtained both as a projection of a local language over the alphabet Γ_2, and as a projection of a k-SLT language (with $k > 2$) over an alphabet Γ_k. However, if we use 2-tiles instead of k-tiles, we need an alphabet Γ_2 which can be larger than Γ_k. The trade-off is represented by the ratio $\frac{|\Gamma_2|}{|\Gamma_k|}$. By Remark 1, this ratio is proportional to the area k^2 of the k-tiles: $\frac{|\Gamma_2|}{|\Gamma_k|} = \Theta(k^2)$.

Next, we show the unsurprising fact that the family REC constitutes an infinite hierarchy with respect to the size of the local alphabet.

Proposition 2. *For every $\ell \geq 1$, let REC_ℓ be the family of languages recognized by tiling systems with a local alphabet of cardinality at most ℓ. Then, $REC_\ell \subsetneq REC_{\ell+1}$.*

Proof. Let $\ell \geq 1$ and consider a TS $\mathcal{T} = (\{a,b\}, \Gamma, T, \pi)$ accepting the word language $R_\ell = \{a^{\ell-1}b\}^+$ –a word is just a special case of (say) a one-row picture. We claim that $|\Gamma| \geq \ell$. By contradiction, assume that there is a TS recognizing R_ℓ such that $\Gamma = \{1, 2, \ldots, j\}$ for some $j < \ell$. Let $\alpha = i_1 i_2 \ldots i_j, \ldots i_\ell \in L(T)$ (whose projection is $a^{\ell-1}b$), for suitable $i_1, i_2, \ldots, i_j, \ldots, i_\ell \in \Gamma$. Therefore, the tiles of the form $\boxed{\begin{smallmatrix} \# & \# \\ i_h & i_{h+1} \end{smallmatrix}}$, for all $1 \leq h < \ell$ must be in T. Since $j < \ell$, there exist m, n, with $1 \leq m < n \leq \ell$ such that $\alpha = i_1 i_2 \ldots i_m i_{m+1} \ldots i_{n-1} i_n \ldots i_\ell$ with $i_m = i_n$.

Therefore, the picture $\beta = i_1 i_2 \ldots i_m i_{m+1} \ldots i_n i_{m+1} \ldots i_{n-1} i_n \ldots i_\ell$ has the same tiles of α, hence also $\beta \in L(T)$, with $\pi(\beta) = a^{\ell-1+m-n}b$, a contradiction. $\square$

An example illustrates Proposition 2.

Fig. 1. Tilings for Example 1. The obvious projection is: for all $c \in \Gamma_3$ or $c \in \Gamma_2$, $\pi(c) = a$.

Example 1. The language $R \subseteq \{a\}^{++}$ such that for any $p \in R$, $|p|_{col} = 2 \cdot |p|_{row} - 1$, is defined by the TS consisting of the 2-tiles $T_2 \subseteq \Gamma_3^{2,2}$ with $\Gamma_3 = \{b, \searrow, \nearrow\}$ which are in the pre-image (Fig. 1, column 1). If we merge together the letters $\searrow$ and $\nearrow$ by reducing the local alphabet to $\Gamma_2 = \{b, \rightarrow\}$, the corresponding pre-image is shown in column 2; let T_2' be its tiles. But then illegal pictures, e.g. the one having the pre-image in column 3, would be tiled using a subset T_2', hence $\pi(L(T_2')) \supset R$. On the other hand, the smaller alphabet Γ_2 suffices to eliminate the illegal picture in column 3 if, instead of a 2-TS, we use a 3-TS with the 3-tiles occurring in column 2.

3.1   Comma-Free Picture Codes

In later constructions we use picture codes comprising a set of isometric square pictures, that we call code-pictures (the analog of code-words). The codes we use have the property that for any picture overlaid with code-pictures it is impossible to overlay a code-picture in a position where it overlaps other code-pictures. Such property characterizes comma-free codes, and we keep the name for picture codes.

We introduce the notion of picture code by means of a picture morphism, then we define the comma-free codes, we state a known result on the cardinality of codes that cannot overlap, and we finish with the statement that the set of pictures overlaid with a comma-free code is an SLT language.

Definition 4 (code-picture).   *Given two alphabets Γ, Λ and a one-to-one morphism $\varphi : \Gamma^{++} \rightarrow \Lambda^{++}$, the set $X = \varphi(\Gamma) \subseteq \Lambda^{++}$ is called a (uniform) picture code; its elements are called code-pictures. For convenience, the morphism "φ" is denoted as $[\![-]\!]_X : \Gamma^{++} \rightarrow \Lambda^{++}$.*

Let p be a picture of size (r, c); a subpicture $p_{(i,j;\,n,m)}$, such that $1 < i \leq j < r$ and $1 < n \leq m < c$ is called *internal*.

Given a set $X \subseteq \Lambda^{k,k}$, consider $X^{2,2}$, i.e., the set of all pictures p of size $(2k, 2k)$ of the form $(X \oplus X) \ominus (X \oplus X)$.

Definition 5 (comma-free code).   *Let Λ be an alphabet and let $k \geq 2$. A (finite) set $X \subseteq \Lambda^{k,k}$ is a comma-free picture code ("cf code" for short) if, for all pictures $p \in X^{2,2}$, there is no internal subpicture $q \in \Lambda^{k,k}$ of p such that $q \in X$.*

Although the exact cardinality of a cf code $X \subseteq \Lambda^{++}$ is unknown, the following result from [1] states a useful lower bound for a family of binary codes that cannnot overlap. Since the non-overlapping condition is stronger than the comma-free one, we have:

Theorem 2. *For all $k \geq 4$ there exist comma-free codes $X \subseteq \{0,1\}^{k,k}$ of cardinality $|X| \geq \left(2^{k-2} - 1\right)^{k-2} \cdot 2^{k-3}$.*

The next proposition states in 2D a property of 1D cf codes.

Proposition 3. *Let $X \subseteq \Lambda^{k,k}$ be a cf code. The language X^{++} is 2k-SLT.*

Proof. We show that $L\left(B_{2k,2k}\left(X^{++}\right)\right) = X^{++}$ (hence the statement). If $p \in X^{++}$ then of course $B_{2k,2k}\left(p\right) \subseteq B_{2k,2k}\left(X^{++}\right)$. If $p \in L(B_{2k,2k}\left(X^{++}\right))$, then we claim that if a $2k$-tile $q \in B_{2k,2k}\left(X^{++}\right)$ is such that the picture $q_{nw} = q_{(1,1;k,k)} \in X$, then $q \in X^{2,2}$. In fact, to be in $B_{2k,2k}\left(X^{++}\right)$, q must be a subpicture of a picture $z \in X^{++}$, of size (kr, kc), with $z = [x_{i,j}]$, $x_{i,j} \in X$. Since X is comma free, if $q_{nw} \in X$, then q_{nw} must coincide with one of subpictures $x_{i,j}$, else q_{nw} would be an internal subpicture of a $2k$-tile in $X^{2,2}$, against Definition 5. Therefore, $q \in X^{2,2}$. Consider now the following "northwest" $(k+1)$-tile of $\hat{p}$, which, for some $x_{11} \in X$, has the form: $\begin{array}{|cc|} \hline \# & \#^{\ominus k} \\ \#^{\ominus k} & x_{11} \\ \hline \end{array}$. By the above claim, a $2k$-tile having x_{11} in the nw position must be in $X^{2,2}$. Hence, the nw corner of p can only be extended to: $\begin{array}{|ccc|} \hline \# & \#^{\ominus k} & \#^{\ominus k} \\ \#^{\ominus k} & x_{11} & x_{12} \\ \#^{\ominus k} & x_{21} & x_{22} \\ \hline \end{array}$ with $x_{i,j} \in X$ and $\begin{array}{|cc|} \hline x_{11} & x_{12} \\ x_{21} & x_{22} \\ \hline \end{array} \in X^{2,2}$. Repeating this construction by a simple induction, p must be in X^{++}. □

Next, we consider a local language defined by a set of 2-tiles, encoding each symbol using a cf code. The following lemma states that the resulting language is SLT.

Lemma 1. *Let $T \subseteq \Gamma^{2,2}$ be a set of 2-tiles defining a local language $L(T)$ and let $X \subseteq \Lambda^{k,k}$ be a cf code such that $|X| = |\Gamma|$. The language $[\![L(T)]\!]_X$ is $2k$-SLT.*

Proof. Let $\overline{T}$ be the complement of T, i.e., $\overline{T} = \Gamma^{2,2} - T$, which can be interpreted as the set of "forbidden" 2-tiles of $L(T)$. Let $M_{2k} = B_{2k,2k}\left(X^{++}\right) - [\![\overline{T}]\!]_X$. We claim that $L(M_{2k}) = [\![L(T)]\!]_X$, thus proving the thesis.

Let $p \in [\![L(T)]\!]_X \subseteq X^{++}$, hence there exists $q \in \Gamma^{++}$ such that $p = [\![q]\!]_X$. If picture $q = [\gamma_{i,j}]$, $\gamma_{i,j} \in \Gamma$, has size (r, c), with $r, c \geq 1$, then p has size (kr, kc), with $p = [x_{i,j}]$, for $x_{i,j} \in X$ and $x_{i,j} = [\![\gamma_{i,j}]\!]_X$.

By contradiction, assume that $p \notin L(M_{2k})$; hence, there is a $2k$-tile $\rho \in B_{2k,2k}\left(p\right)$ such that $\rho \notin M_{2k}$. Since $p \in X^{++}$, it must be $\rho \in B_{2k,2k}\left(X^{++}\right)$: by definition of M_{2k}, $\rho \in [\![\overline{T}]\!]_X$. Therefore, $\rho = [\![\overline{\theta}]\!]_X$ for some $\overline{\theta} \in \overline{T}$, thus $\rho \in X^{2,2}$. Since X is a cf code, no subpicture in X of ρ can be an internal subpicture of the $2k$-tiles in $X^{2,2}$ of p, hence $\rho = \begin{array}{|cc|} \hline x_{i,j} & x_{i,j+1} \\ x_{i+1,j} & x_{i+1,j+1} \\ \hline \end{array}$ for some i, j. It follows that $\rho = [\![\theta]\!]_X$ for $\theta = \begin{array}{|cc|} \hline \gamma_{i,j} & \gamma_{i,j+1} \\ \gamma_{i+1,j} & \gamma_{i+1,j+1} \\ \hline \end{array} \in T$. Since $[\![\,]\!]_X$ is one-to-one, ρ cannot also be equal to $[\![\overline{\theta}]\!]_X$ for $\overline{\theta} \neq \theta$, a contradiction.

Now, let $p \in L(M_{2k})$. Since, by definition of M_{2k}, $p \in X^{++}$ and, by Proposition 3, X^{++} is $2k$-SLT, we have that p has size (kr, kc), with $p = [x_{i,j}]$, for $x_{i,j} \in X$. Since $[\![\,]\!]_X$ is a bijection from Γ to X, there exists one, and only one, $\gamma_{i,j} \in \Gamma$ such that $x_{i,j} = [\![\gamma_{i,j}]\!]_X$. Therefore, we can define a picture $q = [\gamma_{i,j}]$, with $p = [\![q]\!]_X$, $x_{i,j} = [\![\gamma_{i,j}]\!]_X$. Consider a $2k$-tile $\xi \in M_{2k} \cap X^{2,2}$, denoted by $\xi = \begin{array}{|cc|} \hline x_{i,j} & x_{i,j+1} \\ x_{i+1,j} & x_{i+1,j+1} \\ \hline \end{array}$. Since $\xi \notin [\![\overline{T}]\!]_X$, it must be $\xi \in [\![T]\!]_X$, i.e., there is $\theta \in T$ such that $\xi = [\![\theta]\!]_X$, with $\theta = \begin{array}{|cc|} \hline \gamma_{i,j} & \gamma_{i,j+1} \\ \gamma_{i+1,j} & \gamma_{i+1,j+1} \\ \hline \end{array} \in T$. Therefore, all the tiles in q are in θ, hence $q \in L(T)$. □

4   Main Result

We are ready to present the main result that any recognizable language is the projection of an SLT language having alphabetic ratio two, but we pause a while to show that for some language in REC a ratio smaller than two does not suffice.

Theorem 3. *There exists a tiling recognizable language R over an alphabet Σ such that for every alphabet Γ and SLT language $L \subseteq \Gamma^{++}$, if R is the image of L under a projection, then the alphabetic ratio is $\frac{|\Gamma|}{|\Sigma|} \geq 2$.*

Proof. For a generic letter a, let R_a be the language of all square pictures over $\{a\}$, of size at least $(2, 2)$. It is obvious that R_a can only be recognized by TSs having a local alphabet Γ of cardinality at least 2. In fact, if $|\Gamma| = 1$, then a non-square (rectangular) picture and a square picture can be covered by the same set of 2-tiles.

Let $\Sigma = \{b, c\}$; we prove the thesis for $R = R_b \cup R_c$. If $|\Gamma| < 4$, consider two pictures: $p' \in R_b, p'' \in R_c$. Let $\beta, \gamma \in \Gamma^{++}$ be their respective pre-images. Since p' only includes symbol b, every symbol of β must be projected to b; similarly, every symbol of γ must be projected to c. Since $|\Gamma| < 4$ (e.g. $|\Gamma| = 3$) and the symbols in β must be different from the symbols in γ, one of the two pictures, say, β, must be composed of just one type of symbol (i.e., it is on a unary alphabet), but we already noticed that each R_a requires two local symbols. The generalization to an alphabet Σ of larger cardinality is immediate, by considering $R = \bigcup_{a \in \Sigma} R_a$.   □

The above theorem leaves open the possibility that the alphabetic ratio two may suffice for all recognizable languages. This is indeed the case, as stated and proved next. Let $R \subseteq \Sigma^{++}$ be in REC and let $k \geq 2$. We denote with $R^{(k)} \subseteq (\Sigma \cup \{\$\})^{++}$, where $\$ \notin \Sigma$, the language obtained by concatenating vertically and then horizontally each picture of R with two rectangular pictures in $\{\$\}^{++}$, such that the resulting picture has size (m, n), where both m and n are multiple of k. This "padding" of a picture with $\$$ symbols is formalized next and illustrated in the Appendix.

Definition 6. *Let $R \subseteq \Sigma^{++}$ be in REC and let $k \geq 2$. Let $V_k, H_k \subseteq \{\$\}^{++}$ be the languages such that: $V_k = \{\{\$\}^{n,h} \mid n > 0, h < k\}$ and $H_k = \{\{\$\}^{h,n} \mid n > 0, h < k\}$. Then the padded language over the alphabet $\Sigma_\$ = \Sigma \cup \{\$\}$ is:*

$$R^{(k)} = (R \cup (R \ominus V_k) \cup (R \oplus H_k) \cup ((R \ominus V_k) \oplus H_k)) \cap \left((\Sigma_\$)^{k,k}\right)^{++}. \quad (1)$$

Lemma 2. *For all R in REC and for all $k \geq 2$, the padded language $R^{(k)}$ can be defined by a TS such that its local alphabet has size $|\Gamma_k| < C \cdot k^2$ for some constant C.*

Proof. The languages $V_k, H_k \in$ REC. In fact, V_k (and similarly H_k) can be defined by a TS with a local alphabet $\{\$_i \mid 0 \le i < k\}$, where the index i is used to count up to $k - 1$. We show a few of the tiles:

$$\left\{ \boxed{\begin{smallmatrix} \# & \# \\ \$_0 & \$_0 \end{smallmatrix}}, \boxed{\begin{smallmatrix} \# & \# \\ \# & \$_0 \end{smallmatrix}}, \boxed{\begin{smallmatrix} \# & \# \\ \$_0 & \# \end{smallmatrix}} \right\} \cup \left\{ \boxed{\begin{smallmatrix} \# & \$_i \\ \# & \$_j \end{smallmatrix}}, \boxed{\begin{smallmatrix} \$_i & \# \\ \$_j & \# \end{smallmatrix}}, \boxed{\begin{smallmatrix} \$_i & \$_i \\ \$_j & \$_j \end{smallmatrix}}, \cdots \mid 0 \le i < k - 1, j = i + 1 \right\}$$

Hence, if $R \in$ REC then also $R^{(k)} \in$ REC. We show how to obtain a TS $\mathcal{T}^{(k)}$ for $R^{(k)}$, given a TS $\mathcal{T}$ for R. In the identity (1) we have: in the TSs of V_k, of H_k and of $(\Sigma_\$^{k,k})^{++}$, the local alphabets have size $O(k)$; in the TS defining the union (resp. the intersection) of two REC languages, the local alphabet size is the sum (the product) of the local alphabet sizes of the individual TSs. Therefore, the size of the local alphabet of $\mathcal{T}^{(k)}$ satisfies the statement.   □

Theorem 4. *For any $R \subseteq \Sigma^{++}$ in REC, there exist an SLT language L over an alphabet Λ with $|\Lambda| = 2|\Sigma|$, and a projection $\rho : \Lambda \to \Sigma$ such that $R = \rho(L)$.*

Proof. Let $k \ge 2$ be an integer. Let $R^{(k)}$ be the padded language of Definition 6. We first prove the statement using the REC language $R^{(k)}$ instead of R. Let $\mathcal{T} = (\Sigma_\$, \Gamma, T, \pi)$ be a TS recognizing $R^{(k)}$, i.e., $R^{(k)} = \pi(L(T))$. Consider the set of k-tiles: $B_{k,k}(L(T)) = \{r \in B_{k,k}(q) \mid q \in L(T)\}$. Remark that $L(T) \subseteq (B_{k,k}(L(T)))^{++}$. For any picture $p \in \Gamma^{k,k}$, define the *frame*, denoted by $f(p)$, as the quadruple of words

$$f(p) = (p_n, p_e, p_s, p_w), \quad p_n, p_e, p_s, p_w \in \Gamma^k \tag{2}$$

such that p_n is the subpicture $p_{(1,1;k,1)}$ (north row), p_e is $p_{(k,1:k,k)}$ (east column), and so on for p_s, p_w. (The four words are not independent since any corner of p is shared by two of them.)

For any element $r \in B_{k,k}(L(T))$, consider the pair (γ_r, p_r) defined as follows:

$$\begin{cases} \gamma_r &= f(r) = (n_r, e_r, s_r, w_r) \in \Gamma^{4k} \\ p_r &= \pi(r) \in \Sigma_\$^{k,k}. \end{cases}$$

Introduce a new alphabet $B_k \subseteq \Gamma^{4k} \times \Sigma_\$^{k,k}$ as: $B_k = \{(\gamma_r, p_r) \mid r \in B_{k,k}(L(T))\}$. Let $\pi_k : B_k^{++} \to \Sigma_\$^{++}$ be the morphism defined by associating each element $x = (\gamma, p) \in B_k$ with its second component: $\pi_k(x) = p$ (which is a frame). Denote further by φ the mapping associating each element $x = (\gamma, p) \in B_k$ with its first component: $\varphi(x) = \gamma$. In the sequel, when no confusion can arise, $\varphi(x)$ is simply denoted by (n_x, e_x, s_x, w_x). Moreover, it is convenient to denote by Q_k the set:

$$Q_k = \{\varphi(x) \mid x \in B_k\} \subseteq \Gamma^{4k}; \quad \text{therefore } |Q_k| \le |\Gamma|^{4k}. \tag{3}$$

The definition of the set M of 2-tiles, over the alphabet $B_k \cup \{\#\}$, that we now introduce, translates the adjacency in $L(T)$ of the k-tiles of $B_{(k,k)}(L(T))$ in terms of the elements of B_k. The idea is that this adjacency is determined only by the tiles of T in the *frames* of the adjacent k-tiles. Now, we define the set

$M \subseteq (B_k \cup \{\#\})^{2,2}$ of 2-tiles over the alphabet $B_k \cup \{\#\}$, distinguishing between *internal, border* and *corner* tiles.

The bordered picture of size $(2k, 2k)$ (below), composed of four k-tiles x, y, z, t and with their frames (e.g., n_x, e_x, s_x, w_x) highlighted, may clarify the notation used below.

Internal tiles. Given $x, y, z, t \in B_k$, $\begin{array}{cc} x & y \\ z & t \end{array} \in M$ if the subpictures of size $(2,2)$ identified by the neighboring frames of k-tiles x, y, z, t are in T. This is formalized by requiring that $B_{2,2}\left(s_x \oslash s_y\right) \ominus (n_z \oslash n_t)) \subseteq T$ and that $B_{2,2}\left(e_x \ominus e_y\right) \oslash (w_z \ominus w_t)) \subseteq T$.

Border Tiles.

$\begin{array}{cc} \# & \# \\ x & y \end{array} \in M$ iff $B_{2,2}\left(\#^{2k \oslash} \ominus (n_x \oslash n_y)\right) \in T$; $\begin{array}{cc} \# & x \\ \# & z \end{array} \in M$ iff $B_{2,2}\left(\#^{2k \ominus} \oslash (w_x \ominus w_z)\right) \in T$;

$\begin{array}{cc} z & t \\ \# & \# \end{array} \in M$ iff $B_{2,2}\left((s_z \oslash s_t) \ominus \#^{2k \oslash}\right) \in T$; $\begin{array}{cc} x & \# \\ z & \# \end{array} \in M$ iff $B_{2,2}\left((e_x \ominus e_z) \oslash \#^{2k \ominus}\right) \in T$.

Corner Tiles. As in the above picture, let a be the first symbol of n_x, b the last symbol of n_y, c the first symbol of s_z, and d the last symbol of s_t.

$\begin{array}{cc} \# & \# \\ \# & x \end{array} \in M$ iff $\begin{array}{cc} \# & \# \\ \# & a \end{array} \in T$; $\begin{array}{cc} \# & \# \\ y & \# \end{array} \in M$ iff $\begin{array}{cc} \# & \# \\ b & \# \end{array} \in T$;

$\begin{array}{cc} \# & z \\ \# & \# \end{array} \in M$ iff $\begin{array}{cc} \# & c \\ \# & \# \end{array} \in T$; $\begin{array}{cc} t & \# \\ \# & \# \end{array} \in M$ iff $\begin{array}{cc} d & \# \\ \# & \# \end{array} \in T$.

Let $L(M) \subseteq B_k^{++}$ be the local language defined by the tile set M. From the above construction, one derives that $R = \pi_k(L(M))$.

A comma-Free Picture Code for B_k. Let a cf code $Z \subseteq (\{0,1\} \times \Sigma_\$)^{k,k}$ be the composition of a cf binary code $X \subseteq \{0,1\}^{k,k}$ with the pictures in $\Sigma_\$^{k,k}$:

$$Z = X \otimes \Sigma_\$^{k,k}. \qquad (4)$$

where the operator $\otimes$ merges two pictures into one, symbol by symbol. E.g., if $u = \begin{array}{cc} 0 & 0 \\ 1 & 1 \end{array}$ and $y = \begin{array}{cc} a & b \\ b & a \end{array}$ then $u \otimes y = \begin{array}{cc} \langle 0,a \rangle & \langle 0,b \rangle \\ \langle 1,b \rangle & \langle 1,a \rangle \end{array}$. The operator can be immediately extended to a pair of sets of isometric pictures.

From Theorem 2, there exists a comma-free code $X \subseteq \{0,1\}^{k,k}$ with cardinality $|X| \geq (2^{k-2} - 1)^{k-2} \cdot 2^{k-3} \geq (2^{k-3})^{k-2} \cdot 2^{k-3} = (2^{k-3})^{k-1}$. Hence, $\lg(|X|) \geq (k-1) \cdot (k-3) \in \Theta(k^2)$, while $\lg(|Q_k|) \leq 4k \lg(|\Gamma|)$ as shown in (3).

Since by Lemma 2, $|\Gamma| < C \cdot k^2$ for a constant C, we have $\lg(|Q_k|) \leq 4k \lg C + 8k \lg k \in \Theta(k \lg k)$. Therefore, for a fixed Γ, there exists a sufficiently large integer k and a cf code $X \subseteq \{0,1\}^{k,k}$ such that $|X| = |Q_k|$.

We now encode the elements of Q_k, i.e., we consider the morphism $[\![\;]\!]_X : Q_k \to X$ that associates each element $\gamma \in Q_k$ with a different code-picture $[\![\gamma]\!]_X$.

The cf code Z in Eq. (4) is then defined by morphism $[\![\;]\!]_Z : B_k^{++} \to (\{0,1\} \times \Sigma_\$)^{++}$ associating each $x = (\gamma, p)$ with the code-picture $[\![x]\!]_Z = [\![\gamma]\!]_X \otimes p$.

We set the alphabet Λ of the statement to $\{0,1\} \times \Sigma_\$$. By Lemma 1, the language $[\![L(M)]\!]_Z \subseteq \Lambda^{++}$ is $2k$-SLT. Let M_{2k} denote the set of $2k$-tiles over the alphabet Λ defining the language $[\![L(M)]\!]_Z$. Let $\rho : \Lambda \to \Sigma_\$$ be the projection of each element $(b,a) \in \{0,1\} \times \Sigma_\$$ to its second component a. We prove that $\rho([\![L(M)]\!]_Z) = R^{(k)}$.

If $p \in R^{(k)}$, with p of size (kr, kc) with $r, c \geq 1$, then there exists a picture $q \in L(T)$ such that $\pi(q) = p$. Let $\tilde{q} = [\![q]\!]_Z$. By definition of Z, $\rho(\tilde{q}) = \pi(q) = p$, hence $p = \rho([\![q]\!]_Z) \in \rho([\![L(M)]\!]_Z)$.

If $p \in \rho([\![L(M))]\!]_Z$, with p of size (kr, kc) for some $r, c \geq 1$, then there is $q \in L(M)$ such that $p = \rho([\![q]\!]_Z)$. By definition of ρ and π, we have $\pi(q) = p$, i.e., $p \in R^{(k)}$.

We now sketch the proof of the statement of the theorem for R. We define a set of $2k$-tiles M' over an alphabet Λ', defining a $2k$-slt language $L(M')$ and a projection $\rho' : \Lambda' \to \Sigma$ such that $R = \rho'(L(M'))$. Let $\Lambda_\$ \subseteq \Lambda$ be the set $\{(0,\$), (1,\$)\}$, let Λ' be $\Lambda - \Lambda_\$$. Hence, $|\Lambda'| = 2|\Sigma_\$| - 2 = 2|\Sigma|$. Define the projection ρ' as the restriction of ρ induced by Λ'. The set M' of $2k$-tiles is constructed in two steps:

1. Delete, from the set M_{2k}, the tiles having at least two rows and/or at least two columns containing elements in $\Lambda_\$$;
2. Substitute (in the set obtained after the first step) all the occurrences of the elements in $\Lambda_\$$ with the symbol $\#$.

For instance, in step 1 the $2k$-tile $\boxed{s \begin{smallmatrix} z & z' \\ & \end{smallmatrix}}$ with $s \in (\Lambda')^{2k,2k-2}, z, z' \in \Lambda_\$^{\ominus 2k}$, is deleted; in step 2 the $2k$-tiles: $\boxed{t \begin{smallmatrix} z \\ \end{smallmatrix}}$ and $\boxed{u \begin{smallmatrix} z \\ z'' \end{smallmatrix}}$, with $t \in (\Lambda')^{2k,2k-1}, z \in \Lambda_\$^{\ominus 2k}$, $u \in (\Lambda')^{2k-1,2k-1}$ and $z'' \in \Lambda_\$^{\oplus 2k}$, are respectively replaced by: $\boxed{t \begin{smallmatrix} \# \\ \# \end{smallmatrix}}$, and $\boxed{u \begin{smallmatrix} \# \\ \# & \# \end{smallmatrix}}$.

From the above construction, one can derive: $R = \rho'(L(M'))$. □

The Appendix may help to understand the proofs of Lemma 2 and Theorem 4.

5 Conclusion

Our main result (Theorem 4) can be placed next to the similar ones pertaining to regular word languages (v.s. Sect. 1 and [3]) and to tree languages [4], which says that every regular tree language is the letter-to-letter homomorphic image of a strictly locally testable tree language that uses 2 as alphabetic ratio. Altogether, they give evidence that, for a quite significant sample of formal language families, the same property, that we may call Extended Medvedev's theorem, holds: more explicitly, the alphabetic ratio of two is sufficient and necessary to characterize a language as a morphic image an SLT language. The three cases encompass mathematical objects of quite different kinds: words, pictures and trees. What is common is, of course, the prerequisite that a (non-extended) Medvedev's theorem exists, which is based on a notion of locality, respectively, for words, for rectangular arrays, and for acyclic tree graphs. In the future, it would be interesting to see if any family endowed with the basic Medvedev's theorem also has the extended form with alphabetic ratio two.

Acknowledgements. We thank the anonymous reviewers for their useful suggestions.

A Appendix: Example 1 Continued to Illustrate the Main Theorem

The following example aims to show the entities used in the proof of Theorem 4, though not an exhaustive construction.

The picture sizes in language R (Example 1) are $(r, c) = (r, 2r - 1)$, therefore the language has to be padded according to Definition 6, before applying the construction in the main theorem. In fact, it suffices to concatenate language R with the column $\$^{\ominus r}$, to obtain the language R' over $\Sigma_\$ = \Sigma \cup \{\$\}$ with picture sizes $(r, c) = (r, 2r)$. For simplicity, consider the language $R^{(4)} \subset R'$ having sizes multiple of 4; it is defined by a TS $\mathcal{T}'$ that for brevity we represent by means of the pre-image of $a^{8,15} \oplus \$^{8,1}$ below.

1	a a a a a a a a a a a a a a a	$
	a a a a a a a a a a a a a a a	$
	a a a a a a a a a a a a a a a	$
	a a a a a a a a a a a a a a a	$
	a a a a a a a a a a a a a a a	$
	a a a a a a a a a a a a a a a	$
	a a a a a a a a a a a a a a a	$
8	a a a a a a a a a a a a a a a	$
	1 8 16	

1	1 n n n n n n n n n n n n n	↗	g
	n 2 n n n n n n n n n n n	↗	n g
	n n 3 n n n n n n n n	↗	n n g
	n n n 0 n n n n n n	↗	n n n g
	n n n n 1 n n n n a	↗	n n n n g
	n n n n n 2 n n a	↗	n n n n n g
	n n n n n n 3 n	↗	n n n n n n g
8	n n n n n n n 0	n	n n n n n n g
	1 8 16		

Pre-image

The alphabet is $\Sigma_\$ = \{a, \$\}$ and the local alphabet is $\Gamma' = \{0, 1, 2, 3, g, n, ↗\}$; notice that the symbols $0 \ldots 3$ are used to ensure that the picture size is multiple of four. The image returned by the projection is $\pi'(g) = \$$ and elsewhere a.

Next, we apply the constructions in the proof of Theorem 4. We have to compute the set $B_{4,4}(L(T_4))$, for brevity we list just four elements easily visible in the above pre-image:

$$
\begin{array}{|cccc|}\hline 1 & n & n & n\\ n & 2 & n & n\\ n & n & 3 & n\\ n & n & n & 0\\\hline\end{array}
\quad
\begin{array}{|cccc|}\hline n & n & n & n\\ n & n & n & n\\ n & n & n & n\\ n & n & n & n\\\hline\end{array}
\quad
\begin{array}{|cccc|}\hline n & n & n & g\\ n & n & n & g\\ n & n & n & g\\ n & n & n & g\\\hline\end{array}
\quad
\begin{array}{|cccc|}\hline n & n & n & \nearrow\\ n & n & \nearrow & n\\ n & \nearrow & n & n\\ \nearrow & n & n & n\\\hline\end{array}
$$

Then, we compute the new alphabet $B_4 = \{(\gamma_r, p_r) \mid r \in B_{4,4}(L(T_4))\}$. It comprises, among others, the following elements:

$$
x_1 = \left(
\begin{array}{|cccc|}\hline 1 & n & n & n\\ n & & & n\\ n & & & n\\ n & n & n & 0\\\hline\end{array}
\begin{array}{|cccc|}\hline a & a & a & a\\ a & a & a & a\\ a & a & a & a\\ a & a & a & n\\\hline\end{array}
\right)
\quad
x_2 = \left(
\begin{array}{|cccc|}\hline n & n & n & n\\ n & & & n\\ n & & & n\\ n & n & n & n\\\hline\end{array}
\begin{array}{|cccc|}\hline a & a & a & a\\ a & a & a & a\\ a & a & a & a\\ a & a & a & n\\\hline\end{array}
\right)
\quad
x_3 = \left(
\begin{array}{|cccc|}\hline n & n & n & g\\ n & & & g\\ n & & & g\\ n & n & n & g\\\hline\end{array}
\begin{array}{|cccc|}\hline n & a & a & \$\\ a & a & a & \$\\ a & a & a & \$\\ a & a & a & \$\\\hline\end{array}
\right)
$$

Then, we define the tile set $M \subseteq (B_4 \cup \{\#\})^{2,2}$, classified into internal, border and corner tiles; we show just one internal and one border tile.

$$
\begin{array}{|cc|}\hline x_1 & x_2\\ x_2 & x_1\\\hline\end{array} \in M \text{ since } B_{2,2}\left(\begin{array}{cc} s_{x_1} & s_{x_2}\\ n_{x_2} & n_{x_1}\end{array}\right) = B_{2,2}\left(\begin{array}{|cccccccc|}\hline n\,n\,n\,0\,n\,n\,n\,n\\ n\,n\,n\,n\,1\,n\,n\,n\\\hline\end{array}\right) = \left\{\begin{array}{|cc|}\hline n & n\\ n & n\\\hline\end{array}, \begin{array}{|cc|}\hline n & 0\\ n & n\\\hline\end{array}, \begin{array}{|cc|}\hline 0 & n\\ n & 1\\\hline\end{array}, \begin{array}{|cc|}\hline n & n\\ 1 & n\\\hline\end{array}\right\} \subseteq T_4
$$

$$
\begin{array}{|cc|}\hline \# & \#\\ x_1 & x_2\\\hline\end{array} \in M \text{ since } B_{2,2}\left(\begin{array}{cc} \#^{\textcircled{4}} & \#^{\textcircled{4}}\\ n_{x_1} & n_{x_2}\end{array}\right) = B_{2,2}\left(\begin{array}{|cccccccc|}\hline \#\,\#\,\#\,\#\,\#\,\#\,\#\,\#\\ 1\,n\,n\,n\,n\,n\,n\,n\\\hline\end{array}\right) = \left\{\begin{array}{|cc|}\hline \# & \#\\ 1 & n\\\hline\end{array}, \begin{array}{|cc|}\hline \# & \#\\ n & n\\\hline\end{array}\right\} \subseteq T_4.
$$

Assuming M is completed, we have to choose the cf code $Z \subseteq (\{0,1\} \times \Sigma)^{k,k}$ for encoding all the elements of B_4. (We have not figured out how many they are and it may be that with $k = 4$ the code cardinality for the code family in [1] does not suffice; then a larger value for k will do.)

First, we assign to the second component φ of each elements $x_1, x_2, \ldots \in B_4$ a binary code-picture in $X \subseteq \{0,1\}^{4,4}$. Then we build the code-pictures of Z:

	$\varphi(x)$	$[\![\varphi(x)]\!]_X$	$[\![x]\!]_Z$	
$x_1 =$	$\begin{array}{cccc}1&n&n&n\\ n& & &n\\ n& & &n\\ n&n&n&0\end{array}$	$\begin{array}{cccc}\mathbf{1}&\mathbf{1}&\mathbf{1}&\mathbf{1}\\ 1&0&1&0\\ 0&1&1&1\\ 0&0&0&0\end{array}$	$\begin{array}{cccc}(1,a)&(1,a)&(1,a)&(1,a)\\ (1,a)&(0,a)&(1,a)&(0,a)\\ (0,a)&(1,a)&(1,a)&(1,a)\\ (0,a)&(0,a)&(0,a)&(0,a)\end{array}$	Coding
$x_2 =$	$\begin{array}{cccc}n&n&n&n\\ n& & &n\\ n& & &n\\ n&n&n&n\end{array}$	$\begin{array}{cccc}\mathbf{1}&\mathbf{1}&\mathbf{1}&\mathbf{1}\\ 1&0&0&0\\ 0&1&1&0\\ 0&0&0&0\end{array}$	$\begin{array}{cccc}(1,a)&(1,a)&(1,a)&(1,a)\\ (1,a)&(0,a)&(0,a)&(0,a)\\ (0,a)&(1,a)&(1,a)&(0,a)\\ (0,a)&(0,a)&(0,a)&(0,a)\end{array}$	

(Incidentally, the symbols in bold in column $[\![\varphi(x)]\!]_X$ are fixed in the code family [1].)

The h-SLT language L in the thesis has $h = 2 \cdot 4$ and is defined by such 8-tiles as the following one: $\begin{array}{|cc|}\hline [\![x_1]\!]_Z & [\![x_2]\!]_Z\\ [\![x_2]\!]_Z & [\![x_1]\!]_Z\\\hline\end{array}$.

References

1. Anselmo, M., Giammarresi, D., Madonia, M.: Non-expandable non-overlapping sets of pictures. Theoret. Comput. Sci. **657**, 127–136 (2017)
2. Berstel, J., Perrin, D., Reutenauer, C.: Codes and Automata, volume 129 of Encyclopedia of Mathematics and its Applications. CUP (2009)

3. Crespi-Reghizzi, S., San Pietro, P.: From regular to strictly locally testable languages. Int. J. Found. Comput. Sci. **23**(8), 1711–1728 (2012)
4. Crespi Reghizzi, S., San Pietro, P.: Homomorphic characterization of tree languages based on comma-free encoding. In: Leporati, A., Martín-Vide, C., Shapira, D., Zandron, C. (eds.) LATA 2021. LNCS, vol. 12638, pp. 241–254. Springer, Cham (2021). https://doi.org/10.1007/978-3-030-68195-1_19
5. Giammarresi, D., Restivo, A.: Recognizable picture languages. Int. J. Pattern Recognit. Artif. Intell. **6**(2–3), 241–256 (1992)
6. Giammarresi, D., Restivo, A.: Two-dimensional languages. In: Rozenberg, G., Salomaa, A. (eds.) Handbook of Formal Languages, pp. 215–267. Springer, Heidelberg (1997). https://doi.org/10.1007/978-3-642-59126-6_4
7. Giammarresi, D., Restivo, A., Seibert, S., Thomas, W.: Monadic second-order logic over rectangular pictures and recognizability by tiling systems. Inf. Comput. **125**(1), 32–45 (1996)
8. McNaughton, R., Papert, S.: Counter-Free Automata. MIT Press, Cambridge (1971)
9. Medvedev, Y.T.: On the class of events representable in a finite automaton. In: Moore, E.F. (ed.) Sequential Machines - Selected Papers, pp. 215–227. Addison-Wesley (1964)
10. Eilenberg, S.: Automata, Languages, and Machines, vol. A. Academic Press, Cambridge (1974)

Properties of Graphs Specified
by a Regular Language

Volker Diekert[1], Henning Fernau[2($\boxtimes$)], and Petra Wolf[2]

[1] Formal Methods in Informatics, Universität Stuttgart, Stuttgart, Germany
diekert@fmi.uni-stuttgart.de
[2] Universität Trier, FB 4 – Informatikwissenschaften, Trier, Germany
{fernau,wolfp}@informatik.uni-trier.de

Abstract. Traditionally, graph algorithms get a single graph as input, and then they should decide if this graph satisfies a certain property Φ. What happens if this question is modified in a way that we get a possibly infinite family of graphs as an input, and the question is if there exists one graph satisfying Φ? We approach this question by using formal languages for specifying families of graphs. In particular, we show that certain graph properties can be decided by studying the syntactic monoid of the specification language.

Keywords: Graph properties · Regular languages · Periodic semigroups

1 Introduction

When dealing with algorithms on graphs, a graph is often specified by its adjacency matrix, i.e., a graph comes with a linear order on the vertices, and there are no multiple edges. We follow these conventions in our paper. Moreover, we represent graphs by words from a regular set $\mathbb{G}$ over the binary alphabet $\Sigma = \{a, b\}$. Given $w \in \mathbb{G}$, we denote by $\rho(w)$ the corresponding graph. Hence, every subset $L \subseteq \mathbb{G}$ defines a family of graphs $\rho(L)$. Although our results go beyond regular sets L, the focus and the motivation comes from a situation when L is regular. A typical question could be if some (or all) graphs in $\rho(L)$ satisfy a graph property Φ. For example: "are there some planar graphs in $\rho(L)$?" Solving this type of decision problems was the motivation to study *regular realizability problems* in [1,13] and, independently, calling them int_{Reg}-problems (*intersection non-emptiness with regular languages*) in [6,14,15].

Typical graph properties ignore the linear vertex orders and the direction of edges. For example, consider the property that the number of vertices is even. The linear order helps describe this property in Monadic Second-Order logic, *MSO* for short. As we will see, we encounter only four different classes $\mathcal{C}_1 \subset \cdots \subset \mathcal{C}_4$ of graphs $\rho(L)$.

P. Wolf—Research supported by DFG project FE 560/9-1.

N. Moreira and R. Reis (Eds.): DLT 2021, LNCS 12811, pp. 117–129, 2021.
https://doi.org/10.1007/978-3-030-81508-0_10

1. $\rho(L) \in \mathcal{C}_1$ if and only if the set $\rho(L)$ is finite.
2. $\rho(L) \in \mathcal{C}_2$ implies that $\rho(L)$ has bounded tree-width.
3. $\rho(L) \in \mathcal{C}_3$ implies that every connected finite bipartite graph appears as a connected component of some $G \in \rho(L)$.
4. $\rho(L) \in \mathcal{C}_4$ implies that every connected finite graph appears as a connected component of some $G \in \rho(L)$.

Moreover, if L is regular, then we can compute the smallest ℓ such that $\rho(L) \in \mathcal{C}_\ell$. We use a straightforward encoding of vertices and edges: the i-th vertex u_i of a graph is encoded by $ab^i a$ and the edge (u_i, u_j) is encoded by $ab^i aaab^j a$. Since the syntactic monoid of a regular language is finite, we find some $t, p \in \mathbb{N}$ with $p \geq 1$, *threshold* and *period*, such that for every $n \in \mathbb{N}$ there is some $c \leq t+p-1$ with $b^c \equiv_L b^n$ where $\equiv_L$ denotes the *syntactic equivalence*. The threshold t tells us that $b^c \equiv_L b^n$ implies $n = c$ for all $0 \leq c < t$ and $b^n \equiv_L b^{n+p} \iff n \geq t$. This is the key observation when proving that we have no more than these four classes above. If $L \subseteq \mathbb{G}$ is not regular, then the syntactic monoid M_L is infinite. We find interesting examples where M_L satisfies the *Burnside condition* that all cyclic submonoids of M_L are finite. If so, then there exist $t, p \in \mathbb{N}$ with $p \geq 1$ such that the syntactic properties stated above hold for the powers of the letter b. In this case, we say that L satisfies the (b, t, p)-*torsion property*. This is a strong restriction, as Theorem 1 shows that for every subset $L \subseteq \mathbb{G}$ satisfying the (b, t, p)-torsion property, there exists a regular set $R \subseteq \mathbb{G}$ such that $\rho(L) = \rho(R)$. This is quite an amazing result. Its proof relies on the fact that $\rho(L)$ is determined once we know the Parikh-image $\pi_C(\mathrm{rf}(L)) \subseteq \mathbb{N}^C$, where for $w \in \mathbb{G}$, the *reduced form* $\mathrm{rf}(w)$ is obtained by replacing every b^n by b^c, where c is the smallest $0 \leq c \leq t+p-1$ such that $b^c \equiv_L b^n$. Hence, for deciding whether some graph $G \in \rho(L)$ satisfies a property, we can assume that L is regular. We are interested in decidable properties Φ, only. Thus, we assume that the set $\{G \text{ is a finite graph} \mid G \models \Phi\}$ is decidable.

First consider that $\rho(L)$ is finite. Then, we can compute all graphs in $\rho(L)$ and we can output all $G \in \rho(L)$ satisfying Φ. Finiteness of $\rho(L)$ is actually quite interesting and important. It is a case where a representation of L by a DFA or a regular expression can be used for data compression. The minimal size of a regular expression (or the size of a DFA) for L is never worse than listing all graphs in $\rho(L)$, but it might be exponentially better. For a concrete and illustrative case, we refer to Example 2 for a succinct representation of all so-called *crowns with at most n cusps*. The compression rate becomes even better if we use a context-free grammar which produces a finite set L of words in Σ^*, only.

The second class $\mathcal{C}_2$ implies that $\rho(L)$ has bounded tree-width. In this case, by [2,3,11] we know that given any property Φ which is expressible in MSO, it is decidable whether there is a graph in $\rho(L)$ satisfying Φ. For languages $L \subseteq \mathbb{G}$ satisfying the (b, t, p)-torsion property, we understand when $\rho(L)$ has finite tree-width. Hence, we have Theorem 2: The satisfiability problem for MSO-sentences is decidable for language in the second class. For the other two classes, the picture changes drastically: the First-Order theory (*FO* for short) becomes undecidable [12]. Conversely, we are not aware of any "natural" graph property Φ where the satisfiability problem for Φ is not trivial for $\mathcal{C}_3$ and $\mathcal{C}_4$.

2   Notation and Preliminaries

We let $\mathbb{N} = \{0, 1, 2, \ldots\}$ be the set of natural numbers and $\mathbb{N}_\infty = \mathbb{N} \cup \{\infty\}$. Throughout, if S is a set, then we identify a singleton set $\{x\} \subseteq S$ with the element $x \in S$. The power set of S is identified with 2^S (via characteristic functions). If $E \subseteq X \times Y$ is a relation, then E^{-1} denotes its inverse relation $E^{-1} = \{(y, x) \in Y \times X \mid (x, y) \in E\}$. By id_X, we mean the identity relation $\mathrm{id}_X = \{(x, x) \in X \times X \mid x \in X\}$. Recall that Y^X denotes the set of mappings from a set X to a set Y. If $f : X \to Y$ and $g : Y \to Z$ are mappings, then $gf : X \to Z$ denotes the mapping defined by $gf(x) = g(f(x))$. If convenient, we abbreviate $f([x])$ as $f[x]$. Throughout, Γ denotes a finite alphabet and we fix $\Sigma = \{a, b\}$ with $a \neq b$. Each alphabet is equipped with a linear order on its letters. For Σ, we let $a < b$. The linear order on Γ induces the *short-lex linear order* $\leq_{\mathrm{slex}}$ on Γ^*. That is, for $u, v \in \Gamma^*$, we let $u \leq_{\mathrm{slex}} v$ if either $|u| < |v|$ or $|u| = |v|$, $u = pcu'$, and $v = pdv'$ where $c, d \in \Gamma$ with $c < d$. Here, $|u|$ denotes the length of u. Similarly, $|u|_a$ counts the number of occurrences of letter a in u. A language $L \subseteq \Gamma^*$ is a *code* if $c_1 \cdots c_m = d_1 \cdots d_n \in \Gamma^*$ with $c_i, d_j \in L$ implies $m = n$ and $c_i = d_i$ for all $1 \leq i \leq m$. If M is a monoid, then $u \leq v$ means $v \in MuM$, i.e., u is a *factor* of v. This notation is used for the monoids Γ^* and $\mathbb{N}^\Gamma$. Elements in $\mathbb{N}^\Gamma$ are called *vectors*. For $w \in \Gamma^*$, $\overline{w}$ is the *reversal* of w.

Every subset $R \subseteq \Gamma^*$ has a *syntactic monoid* $M = M_R$, see, e.g., [5]. The elements of M_R are the congruence classes $[u] = \{v \in \Sigma^* \mid v \equiv_R u\}$ w.r.t. the *syntactic congruence* $\equiv_R$. If R is regular, then M_R is finite. Monoids with a single generator are called *cyclic*. Every finite cyclic monoid M is defined by two numbers $t, p \in \mathbb{N}$ with $p \geq 1$ such that M is isomorphic to the quotient monoid $C_{t,p}$ of $(\mathbb{N}, +, 0)$ with the defining relation $t = t + p$. Hence, the carrier set of $C_{t,p}$ equals $\{0, 1, \ldots, t + p - 1\}$. If $t = 0$ and $p = 1$, then $C_{t,p}$ is trivial.

Parikh-Images. If $v, w \in \Gamma^*$, then $|w|_v$ denotes the number how often v appears as a factor in w, i.e., $|w|_v = |\{u \in \Gamma^* \mid \exists s : uvs = w\}|$. If $V \subseteq \Gamma^*$, then the *Parikh-mapping w.r.t.* V is defined by $\pi_V : \Gamma^* \to \mathbb{N}^V$, mapping a word w to its *Parikh-vector* $(|w|_v)_{v \in V} \in \mathbb{N}^V$. The classical case is $V = \Gamma$; then the Parikh-vector becomes $(|w|_a)_{a \in \Gamma}$ and the Parikh-mapping is the canonical homomorphism from the free monoid Γ^* to the free commutative monoid $\mathbb{N}^\Gamma$.

A subset $S \subseteq \mathbb{N}^\Gamma$ is called *positively downward-closed* if, for all $v \in S$, (a) $v(z) \geq 1$ for all $z \in \Gamma$, and (b) $u \leq v$ and $u(z) \geq 1$ for all $z \in \Gamma$ imply $u \in S$. The complement of a positively downward-closed set $S \subseteq \mathbb{N}^\Gamma$ is *upward-closed*, i.e., $u \geq v$ and $v \in S$ imply $u \in S$. An upward-closed set S is determined by its set M_S of minimal elements. By Dickson's Lemma, for every upward-closed subset $S \subseteq \mathbb{N}^\Gamma$, M_S is finite. Hence, every upward-closed subset is semi-linear. As the set of all semi-linear sets in $\mathbb{N}^\Gamma$ is closed under Boolean operations, every positively downward-closed set $S \subseteq \mathbb{N}^\Gamma$ is also semi-linear, a key for Theorem 1.

Retractions and retracts. Let $\rho : X \to Y$ and $\gamma : Y \to X$ be mappings between sets. Then, ρ is called a *retraction* and Y is called a *retract* of X with *section* γ if $\rho(\gamma(y)) = y$ for all $y \in Y$. Then, $\rho^{-1}(y)$ is the *fiber* of $y \in Y$. If $\rho : X \to Y$ is a homomorphism of groups X and Y and $H = \ker(\rho)$ is the kernel, then ρ is a retraction if and only if X is a semi-direct product of H by Y.

3   Graphs

All graphs are assumed to be (at most) countable, given as a pair $G = (V, E)$ where $E \subseteq V \times V$. An *undirected graph* is the special case where $E = E^{-1}$. If $G = (V, E)$ is a directed graph, then G also defines the *undirected graph* $(V, E \cup E^{-1})$; and it defines the *undirected graph without self-loops* $(V, (E \cup E^{-1}) \setminus \mathrm{id}_V)$. A graph without isolated vertices is called an *edge-graph*; hence, specifying the edge set suffices. If $G' = (V', E')$ and $G = (V, E)$ are graphs such that $V' \subseteq V$ and $E' \subseteq E$, then G' is a *subgraph* of graph G and we denote this fact by $G' \leq G$. If $U \subseteq V$ is any subset, then $G[U] = (U, E \cap U \times U)$ denotes the *induced subgraph* of U in G. A *graph morphism* $\varphi : (V', E') \to (V, E)$ is given by a mapping $\varphi : V' \to V$ such that $(u, v) \in E'$ implies $(\varphi(u), \varphi(v)) \in E$. If (V', E') and (V, E) are undirected graphs without self-loops, then $\varphi : (V', E') \to (V, E)$ is a graph morphism when $(\varphi(u), \varphi(v)) \in E \cup \mathrm{id}_V$. If φ is surjective on vertices and edges, i.e., $\varphi(V') = V$ and $\varphi(E') = E$, φ is a *projection*. We consider graphs up to isomorphism, only. Hence, writing $G = G'$ means that G and G' are isomorphic. A graph $F = (V, E)$ is a *retract* of a graph $F' = (V', E')$ if there are morphisms $\varphi : F' \to F$ and $\gamma : F \to F'$ where $\varphi\gamma$ is the identity on vertices and edges of (V, E), i.e., F appears in F' as the induced subgraph $F'[\gamma(V)]$.

In our paper, every word $w \in \Sigma^*$ represents a directed finite graph $\rho(w) = (V(w), E(w))$ with a linear order on vertices as follows.

$$V(w) = \{ ab^m a \in ab^+ a \mid ab^m a \leq w \}$$
$$E(w) = \{ (ab^m a, ab^n a) \in ab^+ a \times ab^+ a \mid ab^m aaab^n a \leq w \}$$

The empty word represents the empty graph: there are no vertices and no edges. We extend ρ to 2^{Σ^*} by $\rho(L) = \{\rho(w) \mid w \in L\}$. Vice versa, if $G = (V, E)$ denotes a finite graph with a linear order on its vertices, then, for $1 \leq i, j \in \mathbb{N}$, the i-th vertex is represented by the factor $ab^i a$, and an edge from the i-th vertex to the j-th vertex is represented by the factor $ab^i aaab^j a$. Thus, vertices are encoded by elements in the set $\mathbb{V} = \{ ab^i a \mid 1 \leq i \in \mathbb{N} \}$ and edges are encoded by elements is the set $\mathbb{E} = \{ ab^i aaab^j a \mid 1 \leq i, j \in \mathbb{N} \}$. Note that $\mathbb{V} \cap \mathbb{E} = \emptyset$ and $\mathbb{V} \cup \mathbb{E}$ is an infinite regular code. Using these conventions, the regular set $\mathbb{G} = (\mathbb{V} \cup \mathbb{E})^*$ as well as its subset $\mathbb{E}^* \mathbb{V}^*$ represents all finite graphs. The set $\mathbb{E}^*$ represents all edge-graphs, i.e., graphs without isolated vertices. Every nonempty finite graph has infinitely many representations. For example, there are uncountably many subsets $L \subseteq (aba)^+ \subseteq \mathbb{V}^+$ and each $\rho(L)$ represents nothing but the one-point graph without self-loop. In order to choose a unique (and minimal) representation for a finite graph $G = (V, E)$, we choose the minimal word $\gamma(G) = u_1 \cdots u_m v_1 \cdots v_n \in \mathbb{G}$ in the short-lex ordering on Σ^* such that $\rho\gamma(G) = G$, $u_k \in \mathbb{E}$ for $1 \leq k \leq m$ and $v_\ell \in \mathbb{V}$ for $1 \leq \ell \leq n$. Each u_k is of the form $ab^i aaab^j a$ representing an edge and each v_ℓ is of the form $ab^i a$ representing an isolated vertex. We call $\gamma(G)$ the *short-lex representation* of G. Since $\gamma(G)$ is minimal w.r.t. $\leq_{\mathrm{slex}}$, we have $m = |E|$ and n is the number of isolated vertices. For a graph without isolated vertices, this means that it is given by its edge list. The set of all $\gamma\rho(\mathbb{G})$ is context-sensitive but not context-free. The *uvwxy-*Theorem does not hold for $\gamma\rho(\mathbb{G})$.

A subset $L \subseteq \mathbb{G}$ is viewed as a description of the set of graphs $\rho(L)$. The mapping $\rho : \rho^{-1}(\mathcal{L}) \to \mathcal{L}$ is a retraction in the sense of Sect. 2, since $\rho\gamma(G) = G$ for any finite graph G. The main results of the paper are: (1) for $L \subseteq \mathbb{G}$ satisfying the b-torsion property, there is a regular language $R \subseteq \mathbb{G}$ with $\rho(L) = \rho(R)$ and (2) for a context-free language satisfying the b-torsion property (e.g., any regular language) $R \subseteq \mathbb{G}$, we have an effective geometric description of $\rho(R)$. The description is obtained as follows. Using the fact that R is regular, in a first step, we find effectively a semi-linear description of $\rho(R)$. In a second step, we compute a finite set of finite graphs. Each member F in that finite family is a retraction of some possibly infinite graph F^{∞}. The description of each $G \in \rho(L)$ is given by selecting some F and the cardinality of every fiber. The precise meaning will become clear later. As a consequence of the description, we are able to show various decidability results. The following example serves as an illustration.

Example 1. In the following, we let $R \subseteq \mathbb{E}^*$ and $t, p \in \mathbb{N}$ with $p \geq 1$, $t > 1$, such that $b^n \equiv_R b^{n+p}$ for all $n \geq t$. Since $t > 1$, we have $[b] = \{b\}$. By a *star*, we denote a graph (V, E) such that there exists a vertex $z \in V$ with the property $E = \{ (z, s) \mid s \in V \setminus \{z\} \}$. Thus, a star has a *center* z and the directed edges are the outgoing *rays* of the star.

Furthermore, we assume that $R \subseteq (abaaab^n (b^p)^* a)^+$ for some fixed $n \geq t$. This implies $t \leq n < t + p$. Let $w \in R$. We have $w \in (abaaab^n (b^p)^* a)^m$ for $m = |w|_a/5$, i.e., $w = (abaaab^{d_1} a) \cdots (abaaab^{d_m} a)$ where $d_i = n + k_i p$ with $k_i \in \mathbb{N}$ for $1 \leq i \leq m$. The set $\{ d_i \mid 1 \leq i \leq m \}$ can have any cardinality s in $\{1, \ldots, m\}$. Therefore, $\rho(w)$ is a single star with at least one ray and at most m rays. If R is finite, then $\mathcal{F} = \rho(R)$ is an effective finite collection of stars with at least one ray and at most r rays where $r = \max \{ |w|_a/5 \mid w \in R \}$.

Claim: $\mathcal{F}$ is infinite if and only if there is some $M \geq |M_R|$ with $(abaaab^n a)^M \in R$. The claim holds if $\sup \{ |w|_a/5 \mid w \in R \} < \infty$, as in this case $\mathcal{F}$ is finite. Thus, let $\sup \{ |w|_a/5 \mid w \in R \} = \infty$. Then, there is some $w \in R$ such that $abaaab^n a$ appears at least $|M_R|$ times as a factor. This implies that there is some $M \geq |M_R|$ such that $(abaaab^n a)^M \in R$. The claim follows. Moreover, if $\mathcal{F}$ is infinite, then $\mathcal{F}$ is the set of all finite stars with at least one ray.

One can show that $S = (abaaab^2 b^* a)^* (aba)$ is locally testable and therefore star-free. Hence, the set of all finite stars is specified by a star-free subset of Σ^*.

We study properties of graphs specified by languages $L \subseteq \mathbb{G}$. If L can be arbitrary, then we can specify uncountably many families of graphs. So, we cannot expect any general decidability results. Hence, we restrict our attention to subsets $L \subseteq \mathbb{G}$ where membership for $\rho(L)$ is decidable. In fact, membership for $\rho(L)$ might be decidable although membership for L is undecidable. By Corollary 1, the following definition yields a sufficient condition for decidability of $\rho(L)$.

Definition 1. *Let $b \in \Gamma$ be a letter. A subset $L \subseteq \Gamma^*$ satisfies the (b, t, p)-torsion property if we have: $b^t \equiv_L b^{t+p}$. It satisfies the b-torsion property if there are $t, p \in \mathbb{N}$ with $p \geq 1$ such that L satisfies the (b, t, p)-torsion property.*

Every regular language $R \subseteq \Gamma^*$ satisfies the b-torsion property because the syntactic monoid M_R is finite. The language $\{wa\overleftarrow{w} \mid w \in \{aba, ab^2a\}^*\}$ is not regular, but it satisfies the b-torsion property for $t = 3$ and $p = 1$. The b-torsion property is exceptional if R is not regular: even deterministic linear context-free one-counter languages do not satisfy this property, in general. Consider $\{ a^n b^n \mid n \in \mathbb{N} \}$. Clearly, $b^k \equiv_R b^m \iff k = m$.

Remark 1. Let $b \in \Gamma$ and $|\Gamma| = m$. Let $L \subseteq \Gamma^*$ with M_L as its syntactic monoid. If all cyclic submonoids of M_L are finite, L satisfies the b-torsion property. In the following, let $1 \leq p \in \mathbb{N}$. Recall that the quotient monoid $\Gamma^* / \{ x^p = 1 \mid x \in \Gamma^* \}$ defines the *free Burnside group* $\mathcal{B}(m, p)$. It is a group because every x has the inverse element x^{p-1} as $p \geq 1$. For p large enough, Adjan showed in the 1970s that $\mathcal{B}(2, p)$ is infinite, answering a question of Burnside from 1902. A group is called *p-periodic* if it is the homomorphic image of some $\mathcal{B}(m, p)$.

Let $\varphi : \Gamma^* \to G$ be a surjective homomorphism to a group G. Then, the *Word Problem* of G denotes the set $\mathrm{WP}(G) = \{ w \in \Gamma^* \mid \varphi(w) = 1 \}$. It is a classical fact that the syntactic monoid of $\mathrm{WP}(G)$ is the group G itself. Kharlampovich constructed in [7] a periodic group $B(2, p)$ where the Word Problem is undecidable. Since the $B(2, p)$ is periodic, the b-torsion property holds trivially. Therefore, as we will see, there exists a regular subset R such that $\rho(\mathrm{WP}(B(2, p))) = \rho(R)$.

For the rest of the paper, if $L \subseteq \Sigma^*$ satisfies the b-torsion property, then the cyclic submonoid of M_L generated by the letter b is isomorphic to $C_{t,p}$. That is, we have $t, p \in \mathbb{N}$ with $p \geq 1$, where $t + p$ is minimal such that $\{ [b^n] \mid n \in \mathbb{N} \} = \{ [b^c] \mid 0 \leq c \leq t + p - 1 \}$. Moreover, we assume that L is specified such that on input $n \in \mathbb{N}$, we can compute the value $0 \leq c \leq t + p - 1$ with $b^n \equiv_L b^c$. This assumption is satisfied if L is regular and specified, say, by some NFA. For $L \subseteq \mathbb{G}$, we have $[ab^c a] = a[b^c]a$ and $[ab^c aaab^d a] = a[b^c]aaa[b^d]a$.

Definition 2. *Let $L \subseteq \mathbb{G}$ satisfy the (b, t, p)-torsion property according to Definition 1. For every $[b^n]$, we define its* reduced form *by* $\mathrm{rf}[b^n] = b^c$ *if* $[b^c] = [b^n]$ *and* $0 \leq c \leq t + p - 1$. *Given $w \in \mathbb{G}$, we define the* reduced form $\mathrm{rf}(w)$ *by replacing every factor $ab^m a \leq w$ by $a\,\mathrm{rf}[b^m]a$. The* saturation $\widehat{w}$ *of w is defined by replacing every factor $ab^m a \leq w$ by the set $a[b^m]a$. Hence, $\mathrm{rf}(w) \in \widehat{w} \subseteq \mathbb{G}$.*

Remark 2. Let $L \subseteq \mathbb{G}$ satisfy the (b, t, p)-torsion property. By possibly decreasing t and/or p, we may assume that for every $1 \leq c \leq t + p - 1$, there is some $w \in L$ such that $ab^c a \leq \mathrm{rf}(w)$. Moreover, we have $[b^c] = \{b^c\}$ if and only if $c < t$.

Lemma 1. *Let $L \subseteq \mathbb{G}$ satisfy the (b, t, p)-torsion property. Then, for every $w \in \mathbb{G}$, $w \in L \iff \widehat{w} \subseteq L \iff \mathrm{rf}(w) \in L$.*

The (b, t, p)-torsion property is trivially satisfied if $L \subseteq \mathbb{G}$ is a finite set, an interesting case motivated by data compression. As mentioned in Sect. 1: if L is finite, then the minimal size of a regular expression for L is never worse than listing all graphs in $\rho(L)$, but it might be exponentially better. This type of data compression with formal language methods is also applied in practice [8,9].

Example 2. Let $G = ([n], E)$ be a connected planar graph with vertices $1, \ldots, n$. Then, for every subset $S \subseteq \{n + 1, \ldots, 2n\}$, we define a graph G_S by $G_S =$

$([n] \cup S, E \cup \{(s, s - n) \mid s \in S\})$. The family $\mathcal{C}_n = \{G_S \mid S \subseteq \{n + 1, \ldots, 2n\}\}$ might contain up to $2^{\Omega(n)}$ connected planar graphs, e.g., if G is a cycle of n nodes. If we embed G in the 2-dimensional sphere where the additional edges are spikes pointing out of the sphere, then G_S can be visualized as a discrete model of a 3-dimensional "crown with at most n cusps". One can write down a $2n$-fold concatenation of finite sets describing a finite set $L_n \subseteq \mathbb{G}$ with $\rho(L_n) = \mathcal{C}_n$. The size of the corresponding regular expression is $\mathcal{O}(n^2)$. This leads to a polynomial-size blueprint potentially producing a family of exponentially many "crowns".

Definition 3. *Let $L \subseteq \mathbb{G}$ satisfy the (b, t, p)-torsion property. We introduce two new finite and disjoint alphabets (depending on L)*

$$A = \{\, \mathrm{rf}(ab^m aaab^n a) \mid m, n \in \mathbb{N}, m, n \geq 1 \,\} \subseteq \mathbb{E},$$
$$B = \{\, \mathrm{rf}(ab^m a) \mid m \in \mathbb{N}, m \geq 1 \,\} \subseteq \mathbb{V}.$$

Note that $A \subseteq BaB$. By C, we denote the union of A and B, which is also a finite alphabet with a linear order between letters given by the following definition:

$$x \leq_C y \iff xy \in AB \vee (xy \in (AA \cup BB) \wedge x \leq_{\mathrm{slex}} y). \tag{1}$$

The linear order $\leq_C$ on C defines a short-lex ordering on C^*. Actually, C is a code. Moreover, if $uxv \in C^+$ with $x \in A$ and $u, v \in \Sigma^*$, then $u, v \in C^*$. The analogue for $y \in B$ does not hold, in general. As C is a code, the inclusion $C \subseteq \Sigma^*$ yields an embedding $h_C : C^+ \to \Sigma^+$. If G is a finite graph, then the minimal element in $\mathbb{H} = h_C^{-1}(\rho^{-1}(G)) \cap A^* B^*$ w.r.t. the short-lex ordering for words in C^* is the same as the minimal element in $h_C(\mathbb{H})$ w.r.t. the ordering $a < b$. We assume henceforth that C only contains factors of words from L.

Lemma 2. *Let L, C, and rf as in Definitions 2 and 3. Let $v \in C^*$ and $w \in L$ such that $\pi_C(v) \leq \pi_C(\mathrm{rf}(w))$. If $\pi_C(v)(z) \geq 1$ for all $z \in C$, then we have $\rho(v) \in \rho(L)$.*

Theorem 1. *Let $L \subseteq \mathbb{G}$ be any language satisfying the b-torsion property. Then, there is a regular set $R \subseteq \mathbb{G}$ such that $\rho(L) = \rho(R)$.*

Corollary 1. *Let $L \subseteq \mathbb{G}$ satisfy the b-torsion property. Then, given a finite graph $G = (V_G, E_G)$ as an input, it is decidable whether $G \in \rho(L)$.*

Corollary 2. *Let $L \subseteq \mathbb{G}$ be context-free satisfying the (b, t, p)-torsion property. Then, we can effectively calculate a regular set $R \subseteq \mathbb{G}$ such that $\rho(R) = \rho(L)$.*

Let $R \subseteq \mathbb{G}$ be regular. Then, it is well-known that there might be a much more concise representation by some context-free language $K \subseteq \mathbb{G}$ such that $\pi_C(K) = \pi_C(R)$ and hence $\rho(K) = \rho(R)$.

By Theorem 1, we know that regular languages suffice to describe all sets $\rho(L)$ where $L \subseteq \mathbb{G}$ satisfies the b-torsion property. Therefore, we restrict ourselves to regular languages. In the following, $R \subseteq \mathbb{G}$ denotes a regular language. Hence, we can calculate numbers $t \geq 0$ and $p \geq 1$ such that R satisfies the (b, t, p)-torsion property. As R is regular, the set $L = h_C^{-1}(R) \cap A^* B^*$ is regular; its *Parikh-image* $\pi_C(L) \subseteq \mathbb{N}^C$ is effectively semi-linear. Thus, for some finite set J:

$$\pi_C(L) = \bigcup_{j \in J} \left(q_j + \sum_{i \in I_j} \mathbb{N} p_i \right), \tag{2}$$

where $q_j, p_i \in \mathbb{N}^C$ are vectors. Splitting $\pi_C(L)$ into more linear sets by making the index set J larger and the sets I_j smaller (if necessary), we can assume without restriction that for all $j \in J$ and $z \in C$ we have $\sum_{i \in I_j} p_i(z) \le q_j(z)$. To see this, let $1 \in I_j$. Then, we have

$$q_j + \sum_{i \in I_j} \mathbb{N} p_i = (q_j + \sum_{i \in I_j \setminus \{1\}} \mathbb{N} p_i) \cup (q_j + p_1 + \sum_{i \in I_j} \mathbb{N} p_i).$$

Splitting L into even more but finitely many cases, we can assume without restriction (for simplifying the notation) that the set J is a singleton. Thus, $\pi_C(L) = q + \sum_{i \in I} \mathbb{N} p_i$ for some $q, p_i \in \mathbb{N}^C$ such that $\sum_{i \in I} p_i(z) \le q(z)$. By possibly reducing A, B, C, we may assume that $q(z) \ge 1$ for all $z \in C$ and $C = A \cup B$. In order to understand the set of graphs in $\rho(R)$, it suffices to understand the set of finite graphs defined by linear sets of the form $S = q + \sum_{i \in I} \mathbb{N} p_i \subseteq \mathbb{N}^C$, where $q(z) \ge 1$ for all $z \in C$ and $\sum_{i \in I} p_i \le q$. For that purpose, we let $r = \sum_{i \in I} p_i \le q$ and we define a function $\alpha : C \to \mathbb{N}_\infty$ as follows.

$$\alpha(z) = \begin{cases} q(z) & \text{if } r(z) = 0 \wedge \exists m \in \mathbb{N} : t \le m \wedge ab^m a \le z \\ \infty & \text{if } r(z) \ge 1 \wedge \exists m \in \mathbb{N} : t \le m \wedge ab^m a \le z \\ 1 & \text{otherwise. That is: } \forall m \in \mathbb{N} : ab^m a \le z \implies m < t. \end{cases} \tag{3}$$

For all $z \in C$, let $L_z \subseteq \Sigma^*$. Then, we write $\prod_{z \in C} L_z = L_{z_1} \cdots L_{z_{|C|}}$, where $z_i \le z_j$ for all $i \le j$ according to the linear order defined in Eq. (1). Observe that $\prod_{z \in C} L_z$ is regular if all L_z are regular. With this notation, we define:

$$R_\alpha = \prod_{z \in C} z^{\alpha(z)} \quad \text{and} \quad L_\alpha = \prod_{z \in C} [z]^{\alpha(z)} \tag{4}$$

Notice that L^∞ is just another notation for L^+ if L is any set of words.

Lemma 3. *The sets R_α, L_α of Eq. (4) are regular with $R_\alpha \subseteq L_\alpha$, $\rho(L_\alpha) = \rho(R)$.*

Now, we define for α a finite family of finite graphs $\mathcal{F}_\alpha$ and then, for each $F \in \mathcal{F}_\alpha$, we define a possibly infinite graph F^∞, using the notion of marked graphs.

Definition 4. *For $z \in C$, let $\alpha'(z) = \alpha(z)$ if $\alpha(z) < \infty$ and $\alpha'(z) = 1$, otherwise. We let $R'_\alpha = \prod_{z \in C} z^{\alpha'(z)}$, and we define $\mathcal{F}_\alpha = \rho(R'_\alpha)$.*

Since R'_α is a finite set of words, $\mathcal{F}_\alpha$ is a finite set of finite graphs. Now, we define the crucial notion of a marked graph, with some vertices and edges marked.

Definition 5. *A marked graph is a tuple $F = (V_F, E_F, \mu)$, where (V_F, E_F) is a finite graph and $\mu \subseteq V_F \cup E_F$ denotes the set of marked vertices and edges. Isolated vertices may appear, but if an isolated vertex is marked, then there is exactly* *one isolated vertex. We also require that whenever an edge (u, v) is marked, then at least one of its endpoints is marked, too. A* marked edge-graph *is a marked graph without isolated vertices.*

In the following, each graph $(V_F, E_F) \in \mathcal{F}_\alpha$ as in Definition 4 defines a marked graph $F = (V_F, E_F, \mu)$ as follows, where μ denotes a marking (as in Definition 5) that we call the *canonical marking*. We begin by marking those vertices and edges $z \in C$ where $\alpha(z) = \infty$. In particular, if $z \in C$ is marked, then $[z] \neq \{z\}$ and $[z]$ is an infinite set. In the second step, we mark also all vertices u which satisfy $[u] \neq \{u\}$ and which appear as an endpoint in some marked edge. Thereafter, every marked edge contains at least one marked endpoint. In the third step, if an isolated vertex is marked, then remove all isolated marked vertices $y \in B$ except one isolated vertex which is marked. In particular, after that procedure, if a marked isolated vertex y appears, then $\alpha(y) = \infty$.

Now, we switch to a more abstract viewpoint. We let $\mathcal{F}$ be any finite family of marked graphs. For each $F = (V_F, E_F, \mu) \in \mathcal{F}$, we define a possibly infinite graph F^∞ where (V_F, E_F) appears as an induced subgraph, and we define a family of finite graphs $\mathcal{G}_F$. We consider finitely many $\mathcal{F}_\alpha$, and then we study $\bigcup \{\mathcal{G}_F \mid (V_F, E_F) \in \mathcal{F}_\alpha\}$, where $F = (V_F, E_F, \mu)$ is the marked graph obtained by the canonical marking procedure above (which might have removed isolated marked vertices). For understanding $\rho(R)$, we need to describe sets $\mathcal{G}_F$ for marked graphs $F = (V_F, E_F, \mu)$. This requires to define F^∞ as follows.

Definition 6. *Let $F = (V_F, E_F, \mu)$ be a marked graph as in Definition 5. Then, the graph $F^\infty = (V_F^\infty, E_F^\infty)$ is defined as follows.*

$$V_F^\infty = V_F \times \{0\} \cup \bigcup_{u \in V_F} \{(u, k) \mid u \text{ is marked } \wedge k \in \mathbb{N}\},$$

$$E_F^\infty = E_F \times \{0\} \cup \{((u, k), (v, \ell)) \in V_F^\infty \times V_F^\infty \mid (u, v) \in E_F \wedge (u, v) \text{ is marked}\},$$

with $E_F \times \{0\} = \{((u, 0), (v, 0)) \mid (u, v) \in E_F\}$. The family $\mathcal{G}_F$ is the set of finite subgraphs of F^∞ containing $(V_F \times \{0\}, E_F \times \{0\})$ as an induced subgraph.

Observe that $F^\infty = F$ if and only if there is no marking, i.e., if $\mu = \emptyset$. We embed F into F^∞ by a graph morphism γ which maps each vertex $u \in V_F$ to the pair $\gamma(u) = (u, 0) \in V_F^\infty$. The projection onto the first component $\varphi(u, k) = (u)$ yields a retraction for every $G \in \mathcal{G}_F$ with retract F. If no isolated vertex is marked, then F^∞ has at most $|V_F|$ isolated vertices, but if there are marked vertices, then for every sufficiently large k, there is some graph in $\mathcal{G}_F$ which has exactly k isolated vertices. In order to understand the graphs in $\mathcal{G}_F$ (which is our goal), it is enough to understand the graphs G satisfying $F \leq G \leq F^\infty$. For $F = F^\infty$, we know everything about that set. Let us hence consider $F \neq F^\infty$. Proposition 1 shows that $\rho(R)$ is rather rich as soon as some $F \in \mathcal{F}_\alpha$ satisfies $F \neq F^\infty$. Confer the next result with the classification $\mathcal{C}_1 \subset \cdots \subset \mathcal{C}_4$ of graphs from Sect. 1.

Proposition 1. *Let $F = (V_F, E_F, \mu)$ be any marked graph.*

1. *If F contains a marked edge (u, v) where v is marked, then every finite star with center $(u, 0)$ appears as an induced subgraph of some $G \in \mathcal{G}_F$.*
2. *Suppose we represent a bipartite graph as a triple (U, V, E) where $U \cap V = \emptyset$ and $E \subseteq U \times V$. Let H be any finite bipartite edge-graph. If F contains a marked edge (u, v) where u and v are marked, then a disjoint union of F and H appears in $\mathcal{G}_F$.*
3. *Let H be any finite graph. If F contains a marked self-loop (u, u), then the disjoint union of F and H belongs to $\mathcal{G}_F$.*
4. *Let F be any marked graph such that one or two vertices are marked. Then, the following holds. A disjoint union of F and any non-bipartite graph appears in $\mathcal{G}_F$ if and only if there is some marked self-loop in F.*

By Schützenberger's classical theorem [10] characterizing star-freeness via finite and aperiodic syntactic monoids, this case distinction entails:

Corollary 3. *Let $L \subseteq \mathbb{G}$ be any language satisfying the b-torsion property. If there is a star-free language R such that $\rho(L) = \rho(R)$, then there is no $F \in \mathcal{F}_\alpha$ such that a disjoint union of F and a triangle appears in $\mathcal{G}_F$.*

4   Graph Properties

Throughout this section, F denotes a marked graph and $\mathcal{G}_F$ denotes the family of graphs defined in Definition 6. A *graph property* is a **decidable** subset $\Phi \subseteq \mathbb{G}$. For a finite graph G, we write $G \models \Phi$ if the short-lex representation $\gamma(F)$ belongs to Φ. Given a word $w \in \mathbb{G}$, we can compute $\gamma\rho(w)$. Hence, we can assume $\rho^{-1}(\rho(\Phi)) = \Phi$. As $\rho(w)$ is realized as a graph with a natural linear order on the vertices, we have $ab^c a \leq ab^d a \iff c \leq d$. We consider properties of undirected finite graphs, only: if $u \in \mathbb{G}$ represents the graph $\rho(u) = (V, E)$, then $\rho(u) \models \Phi$ if and only if $(V, E \cup E^{-1}) \models \Phi$. We focus on the satisfiability problem $\text{Sat}(\mathcal{G}_F, \Phi)$:

– Input: A marked graph F.
– Question: "$\exists G \in \mathcal{G}_F : G \models \Phi$?"

For various well-studied graph properties, $\text{Sat}(\mathcal{G}_F, \Phi)$ is decidable. For example, when Φ states that a graph is planar, or k-colorable, etc. This follows from:

Proposition 2. *Let either $\mathcal{G}_F$ be finite or Φ be any graph property which is closed under taking induced subgraphs (or both). Then, $\text{Sat}(\mathcal{G}_F, \Phi)$ is decidable.*

In many cases, graph properties are expressible either in MSO or even in FO. MSO is a rich and versatile class to define graph properties[1]. Since $w \in \mathbb{G}$ defines graphs with a linear order, we can express in MSO, for example, that the number of vertices is even. We use the following well-known results as black boxes. First, (Trakhtenbrot's Theorem) [12]: given an FO-sentence Φ, it is undecidable whether there exists a graph (resp. bipartite graph) satisfying Φ. Second, given an MSO-sentence Φ and $k \in \mathbb{N}$, it is decidable whether there exists a graph of tree-width at most k satisfying Φ, see, e.g., [2,3,11].

---

[1] For our purposes, we allow quantification over both sets of vertices and sets of edges.

Theorem 2. *Let Φ be an MSO-sentence. Then, $\mathrm{Sat}(\mathcal{G}_F, \Phi)$ is decidable for marked graphs $F = (V_F, E_F, \mu)$ if at most one endpoint of each edge is marked.*

Theorem 3. *Let Φ be an FO-sentence. Then, $\mathrm{Sat}(\mathcal{G}_F, \Phi)$ is undecidable for marked graphs $F = (V_F, E_F, \mu)$ where both endpoints of some edge are marked.*

Some graph properties where the problem $\mathrm{Sat}(\mathcal{G}_F, \Phi)$ is trivially decidable are covered by the next theorem, including the problem whether $\mathcal{G}_F$ contains a non-planar graph, and various parametrized problems like: "Is there some $(V_G, E_G) \in \mathcal{G}_F$ with a clique bigger than $\sqrt{|V_G|}$?".

Theorem 4. *Let F be any marked graph and Φ be a non-trivial graph property such that $G \models \Phi$ if and only if there is a connected component G' of G such that $G' \models \Phi$. Then, the answer to $\mathrm{Sat}(\mathcal{G}_F, \Phi)$ is "Yes" in the following two cases. [3] (a) The property Φ is true for some bipartite edge-graph and there is some marked edge where both endpoints are marked. (b) There is some marked self-loop.*

Example 3 lists a few graph properties which are not covered by the results above, but nevertheless the satisfiability problem is decidable.

Example 3. Let $F = (V_F, E_F, \mu)$ denote a marked graph as input. Then, the following problems are decidable. Is there some $G \in \mathcal{G}_F$ (a) with a Hamiltonian cycle (See [4]), or (b) with a perfect matching, or (c) with a dominating set of size at most $\sqrt{|V_G|}$?

Perfect Matching. Let $V_F = \{x_1, \dots, x_k\}$ and suppose some $G = (V_G, E_G) \in \mathcal{G}_F$ has a perfect matching. We have $V_F \subseteq V_G$. Hence, all $x_i \in V_F$ are matched by vertices $y_i \in V_G$. The induced subgraph $G[V_F \cup \{y_1, \dots, y_k\}]$ has a perfect matching with at most $2|V_F|$ vertices. All such small $G \in \mathcal{G}_F$ can be enumerated.

Dominating Set. If F contains no marked edge, then decide if the property holds for (V_F, E_F). Otherwise, there is a marked edge $(u, v) \in E_F$. Let $V_G = (V_F \times \{0\}) \cup (\{v\} \times \{1, \dots, |V_F|^2\})$ and $E_G = E_F \cup \{((u, 0), (v, i)) \mid 1 \le i \le |V_F|^2\}$. Then, $G = (V_G, E_G) \in \mathcal{G}_F$. Also, V_F is a sufficiently small dominating set of G.

With the results above, we have a meta-theorem for graph properties Φ with a decidable satisfiability problem, covering all cases where we have positive results.

Theorem 5. *Let $r : \mathbb{N} \to \mathbb{N}$ be a non-decreasing computable function and let Φ be a graph property such that, for each marked graph $F = (V_F, E_F, \mu)$, if some graph in $\mathcal{G}_F$ satisfies Φ, then there is a graph $G = (V, E) \in \mathcal{G}_F$ such that $G \models \Phi$ and $|V| \le r(|V_F|)$. Then, given as input a context-free language $L \subseteq \mathbb{G}$ satisfying the (b, t, p)-torsion property, $\mathrm{Sat}(\rho(L), \Phi)$ is decidable.*

5   Conclusion and Open Problems

The starting point of our paper was the following idea: Decide a graph property Φ not for a single instance as in traditional algorithmic graph theory, but generalize this question to a set of graphs specified by a regular language. We chose a natural representation of graphs by words over a binary alphabet Σ, but other choices would work equally well. Next, pick your favorite graph property Φ. For example, Φ says that the number of vertices is a prime number. The property does not look very regular, there is no way to express the property, say, in MSO. Still, given a context-free language $L \subseteq \Sigma^*$ which satisfies the b-torsion property and which encodes sets of graphs, we can answer the question if there exists a graph represented by L and which satisfies Φ. This is a consequence of Theorem 5 and Bertrand's postulate that for all $n \geq 1$, there is a prime between n and $2n$.

Various problems remain open. For instance, given a graph property Φ, we can define $\mathcal{G}(\Phi) = \{G$ is a finite graph $\mid G \models \Phi\}$. Suppose that $\rho^{-1}(\mathcal{G}(\Phi))$ is regular. Given a regular language $R \subseteq \Sigma^*$, can we decide whether $\mathcal{G}(\Phi) \subseteq \rho(R)$? What about the equality $\mathcal{G}(\Phi) = \rho(R)$? We can ask the same two questions if R is context-free. Future research should address complexity issues. For example, given a typical NP-complete graph property Φ and ask how complex it is to decide the satisfiability for $\mathcal{G}_F$ if the input is a marked graph F.

Note: Missing proofs can be found in [4].

References

1. Anderson, T., Loftus, J., Rampersad, N., Santean, N., Shallit, J.: Detecting palindromes, patterns and borders in regular languages. Inf. Comp. **207**, 1096–1118 (2009)
2. Courcelle, B.: The expression of graph properties and graph transformations in Monadic Second-Order Logic. In: Rozenberg, G. (ed.) Handbook of Graph Grammars and Computing by Graph Transformations, Vol. 1: Foundations, pp. 313–400. World Scientific (1997)
3. Courcelle, B., Engelfriet, J.: Graph Structure and Monadic Second-Order Logic -A Language-Theoretic Approach, Encyclopedia of Mathematics and Its Applications, vol. 138. Cambridge University Press, Cambridge (2012)
4. Diekert, V., Fernau, H., Wolf, P.: Properties of graphs specified by a regular language. arXiv eprints arXiv:2105.00436 (2021)
5. Eilenberg, S.: Automata, Languages, and Machines, vol. A. Academic Press, Cambridge (1974)
6. Güler, D., Krebs, A., Lange, K.-J., Wolf, P.: Deciding regular intersection emptiness of complete problems for PSPACE and the polynomial hierarchy. In: Klein, S.T., Martín-Vide, C., Shapira, D. (eds.) LATA 2018. LNCS, vol. 10792, pp. 156–168. Springer, Cham (2018). https://doi.org/10.1007/978-3-319-77313-1_12
7. Kharlampovich, O.: The word problem for the burnside varieties. J. Algebra **173**, 613–621 (1995)
8. Larsson, N.J., Moffat, A.: Off-line dictionary-based compression. Proc. IEEE **88**, 1722–1732 (2000)
9. Lohrey, M., Maneth, S., Mennicke, R.: XML tree structure compression using RePair. Inf. Syst. **38**(8), 1150–1167 (2013)
10. Schützenberger, M.P.: On finite monoids having only trivial subgroups. Inf. Control **8**, 190–194 (1965)
11. Seese, D.: The structure of the models of decidable monadic theories of graphs. Ann. Pure Appl. Logic **53**, 169–195 (1991)

12. Trahtenbrot, B.A.: The impossibility of an algorithm for the decision problem for finite domains. In: Doklady Akademii Nauk SSSR, New Series, vol. 70, pp. 569–572 (1950)
13. Vyalyi, M.N., Rubtsov, A.A.: On regular realizability problems for context-free languages. Probl. Inf. Transm. **51**(4), 349–360 (2015). https://doi.org/10.1134/S0032946015040043
14. Wolf, P.: On the decidability of finding a positive ILP-instance in a regular set of ILP-instances. In: Hospodár, M., Jirásková, G., Konstantinidis, S. (eds.) DCFS 2019. LNCS, vol. 11612, pp. 272–284. Springer, Cham (2019). https://doi.org/10.1007/978-3-030-23247-4_21
15. Wolf, P.: From decidability to undecidability by considering regular sets of instances. In: Cordasco, G., et al. (eds.) ICTCS Proceedings of the CEUR, vol. 2756, pp. 33–46. CEUR-WS.org (2020)

Balanced-By-Construction Regular and ω-Regular Languages

Luc Edixhoven[1,2]([✉]) [iD] and Sung-Shik Jongmans[1,2] [iD]

[1] Open University, Heerlen, The Netherlands
{led,ssj}@ou.nl
[2] Centrum Wiskunde and Informatica (CWI), Amsterdam, The Netherlands

Abstract. $Paren_n$ is the typical generalisation of the Dyck language to multiple types of parentheses. We generalise its notion of balancedness to allow parentheses of different types to freely commute. We show that balanced regular and ω-regular languages can be characterised by syntactic constraints on regular and ω-regular expressions and, using the shuffle on trajectories operator, we define grammars for balanced-by-construction expressions with which one can express every balanced regular and ω-regular language.

Keywords: Dyck language · Shuffle on trajectories · Regular languages

1 Introduction

The Dyck language of balanced parentheses is a textbook example of a context-free language. Its typical generalisation to multiple types of parentheses, $Paren_n$, is central in characterising the class of context-free languages, as shown by the Chomsky-Schützenberger theorem [1]. Many other generalisations of the Dyck language have been studied over the years [2,4,5,8,9].

The notion of balancedness in $Paren_n$ requires parentheses of different types to be properly nested: $[_1 [_2]_2]_1$ is balanced but $[_1 [_2]_1]_2$ is not. In this paper, we consider a more general notion of balancedness, in which parentheses of the same type must be properly nested but parentheses of different types may freely commute. This notion of balancedness is of particular interest in the context of distributed computing, where different components communicate by exchanging messages: if we assign a unique type of parentheses to every communication channel between two participants, and interpret a left parenthesis as a message send event and a right parenthesis as a receive event, then balancedness characterises precisely all sequences of communication with no lost or orphan messages.

Specifically, we are interested in specifying languages that are balanced by construction, which correspond to communication protocols that are free of lost and orphan messages. More precisely, we aim to answer the question: can we define balanced atoms and a set of balancedness-preserving operators with which one can express all balanced languages?

© Springer Nature Switzerland AG 2021
N. Moreira and R. Reis (Eds.): DLT 2021, LNCS 12811, pp. 130–142, 2021.
https://doi.org/10.1007/978-3-030-81508-0_11

Our main result is that we answer this question positively for the classes of regular and ω-regular languages. Our contributions are as follows:

- In Sect. 2 we show how balancedness of regular languages corresponds to syntactic properties of regular expressions.
- In Sect. 3 we show that, by using a parametrised shuffle operator, we can define a grammar of balanced-by-construction expressions with which one can express all balanced regular languages.
- In Sect. 4 we extend these results to ω-regular languages and expressions.

Related work and detailed proofs appear in a technical report [3].

Notation. $\mathbb{N} = \{1, 2, \ldots\}$, $\mathbb{N}_0 = \{0, 1, \ldots\}$ and $\mathbb{Z}$ is the set of integers. Let Σ_n be the alphabet $\{[_1,]_1, \ldots, [_n,]_n\}$. Its size is typically clear from the context, in which case we omit the subscript. We write λ for the empty word. We write Σ^* for the set of finite words over Σ. We write Σ^ω for the set of infinite words $\{w \mid w : \mathbb{N} \to \Sigma\}$ over Σ. We write $\Sigma^\infty = \Sigma^* \cup \Sigma^\omega$. We write $w(i)$ to refer to the symbol at position i in w. We write $w(i, \ldots, j)$ for the substring of w beginning at position i and ending at position j. Let $v, w \in \Sigma^\infty$. Then v is a prefix of w, denoted $v \preceq w$, if $v = w$ or if there exists $v' \in \Sigma^\infty$ such that $vv' = w$. We write $|w|, |w|_\sigma \in \mathbb{N}_0 \cup \{\aleph_0\}$ respectively for the length of w and for the number of occurrences of symbol σ in w. Let $\mathbb{E}$ be the set of all regular expressions over $\bigcup_{n \geq 1} \Sigma_n$. For $e_1, e_2 \in \mathbb{E}$, we write $e_1 \equiv e_2$ iff $L(e_1) = L(e_2)$.

2 Balanced Regular Languages

In this section, we formally define our notion of balancedness and characterise balanced regular languages in terms of regular expressions.

Balancedness. A word $w \in \Sigma^*$ is *i-balanced* if $|w|_{[_i} = |w|_{]_i}$ and if, for all prefixes v of w, $|v|_{[_i} \geq |v|_{]_i}$. It is *balanced* if it is *i*-balanced for all i. We extend this terminology to languages and expressions in the expected way.

Regular Expressions. Using standard algebraic rules, we can rewrite any regular expression representing a non-empty language into an equivalent expression that does not contain $\varnothing$. Therefore, without loss of generality, we may assume that regular expressions do not contain $\varnothing$, unless they are simply $\varnothing$.

To every regular expression e and for every i, we assign a value which we call its *i-balance*, denoted $\nabla(e, i)$. We show that this value corresponds to the number of unmatched left *i*-parentheses in every word of its language (see Lemma 1(i)), if such a number exists. Also, to differentiate between words such as $[_i]_i$ and $]_i[_i$, we assign a second value to regular expressions which we call its *minimum i-balance*, denoted $\nabla^{\min}(e, i)$, which we show to correspond to the smallest *i*-balance among every prefix of every word in its language (see Lemma 1(ii–iii)).

$$\nabla(\lambda, i) = 0 \qquad \nabla(\text{[}_i, i) = 1 \qquad \nabla(\text{]}_i, i) = -1 \qquad \nabla(\text{[}_j, i) = \nabla(\text{]}_j, i) = 0$$

$$\nabla(e_1 + e_2, i) = \nabla(e_1, i) \text{ if } \nabla(e_1, i) = \nabla(e_2, i)$$

$$\nabla(e_1 \cdot e_2, i) = \nabla(e_1, i) + \nabla(e_2, i) \qquad \nabla(e^*, i) = 0 \text{ if } \nabla(e, i) = 0$$

$$\nabla^{\min}(\lambda, i) = \nabla^{\min}(\text{[}_i, i) = 0 \qquad \nabla^{\min}(\text{]}_i, i) = -1 \qquad \nabla^{\min}(\text{[}_j, i) = \nabla^{\min}(\text{]}_j, i) = 0$$

$$\nabla^{\min}(e_1 + e_2, i) = \min(\nabla^{\min}(e_1, i), \nabla^{\min}(e_2, i))$$

$$\nabla^{\min}(e_1 \cdot e_2, i) = \min(\nabla^{\min}(e_1, i), \nabla(e_1, i) + \nabla^{\min}(e_2, i)) \qquad \nabla^{\min}(e^*, i) = \nabla^{\min}(e, i)$$

Fig. 1. The i-balance and minimum i-balance of regular expressions, where $i \neq j$.

Formally, we define partial functions $\nabla, \nabla^{\min} : \mathbb{E} \times \mathbb{N} \mapsto \mathbb{Z}$ as in Fig. 1. Lemma 1 states that $\nabla(e, i)$ and $\nabla^{\min}(e, i)$ have the intended properties we described and Lemma 2 states that if the number of unmatched i-parentheses of words in $L(e)$ is uniquely defined, then both $\nabla(e, i)$ and $\nabla^{\min}(e, i)$ are defined. We note that ∇ is partial. For instance, $\nabla(\text{[}_1 + \lambda, 1)$ and $\nabla(\text{[}_1^*, 1)$ are both undefined since their languages contain [_1 and λ, which have different numbers of unmatched left i-parentheses. As $\nabla^{\min}$ relies on ∇, $\nabla^{\min}$ is partial as well.

Lemma 1. *If $\nabla(e, i)$ and $\nabla^{\min}(e, i)$ are defined, then:*

(i) $|w|_{\text{[}_i} - |w|_{\text{]}_i} = \nabla(e, i)$ *for every* $w \in L(e)$;
(ii) $|v|_{\text{[}_i} - |v|_{\text{]}_i} \geq \nabla^{\min}(e, i)$ *for every prefix* v *of every* $w \in L(e)$; and
(iii) $|v|_{\text{[}_i} - |v|_{\text{]}_i} = \nabla^{\min}(e, i)$ *for some prefix* v *of some* $w \in L(e)$.

Lemma 2. *If $|v|_{\text{[}_i} - |v|_{\text{]}_i} = |w|_{\text{[}_i} - |w|_{\text{]}_i}$ for every $v, w \in L(e)$ and $L(e) \neq \varnothing$, then $\nabla(e, i)$ and $\nabla^{\min}(e, i)$ are defined.*

The proofs are straightforward by structural induction on e. Applying them gives us the following characterisation:

Theorem 1. *Let $e \in \mathbb{E}$. Then e is balanced iff $\nabla(e, i) = \nabla^{\min}(e, i) = 0$ for every i or if $e = \varnothing$.*

3   Balanced-By-Construction Regular Languages

The main contribution of this section is a grammar of balanced-by-construction expressions, $\mathbb{E}^{\sqcup\!\sqcup}$ in Fig. 2, with which one can express all balanced regular languages. It differs from regular expressions in two ways:

- Parentheses can syntactically occur only in ordered pairs instead of separately, so the atoms are all balanced.
- We add a family of operators $\sqcup\!\sqcup_\theta^n(e_1, \ldots, e_n)$, called *shuffle on trajectories*, in order to interleave words of subexpressions.

The shuffle on trajectories operator is a powerful variation of the traditional shuffle operator, which adds a control trajectory (or a set thereof) to restrict the permitted orders of interleaving. This allows for fine-grained control over

$$e ::= \varnothing \mid \lambda \mid [_1 \cdot]_1 \mid [_2 \cdot]_2 \mid \ldots \mid e_1 + e_2 \mid e_1 \cdot e_2 \mid e^* \mid \sqcup\!\sqcup_\theta^1 (e_1) \mid \sqcup\!\sqcup_\theta^2 (e_1, e_2) \mid \ldots$$
$$\theta ::= \varnothing \mid \lambda \mid 1 \mid 2 \mid \ldots \mid \theta_1 + \theta_2 \mid \theta_1 \cdot \theta_1 \mid \theta^*$$

Fig. 2. A grammar $\mathbb{E}^{\sqcup\!\sqcup}$ for expressing balanced regular languages.

orderings when shuffling words or languages. The binary operator was defined—and its properties thoroughly studied—by Mateescu et al. [6]; the slightly later introduced multiary variant [7] is formally defined as follows.

Let $w_1, \ldots, w_n \in \Sigma^*$ and let $t \in \{1, \ldots, n\}^*$ be a *trajectory*. Then:

$$\sqcup\!\sqcup_t^n (w_1, \ldots, w_n) = \begin{cases} \sigma \sqcup\!\sqcup_{t'}^n (w_1, \ldots, w_i', \ldots, w_n) & \text{if } t = it' \wedge w_i = \sigma w_i', \\ \lambda & \text{if } t = w_1 = \ldots = w_n = \lambda. \end{cases}$$

The operator naturally generalises to languages and expressions:

$$\sqcup\!\sqcup_T^n (L_1, \ldots, L_n) = \{\sqcup\!\sqcup_t^n (w_1, \ldots, w_n) \mid t \in T, w_1 \in L_1, \ldots, w_n \in L_n\}.$$
$$L(\sqcup\!\sqcup_\theta^n (e_1, \ldots, e_n)) = \sqcup\!\sqcup_{L(\theta)}^n (L(e_1), \ldots, L(e_n)).$$

As the operator's arity is clear from its operands, we generally omit it. For the trajectories, we allow any regular expression over $\mathbb{N}$.

Note that $\sqcup\!\sqcup_t^n (w_1, \ldots, w_n)$ is defined only if $|t|_i = |w_i|$ for every i. If $|t|_i = |w_i|$, we say that t *fits* w_i. For example, $\sqcup\!\sqcup_{121332}([_1]_1, [_2]_2, [_3]_3) = [_1 [_2]_1 [_3]_3]_2$ and $\sqcup\!\sqcup_{121}([_1]_1, [_2]_2)$ is undefined since 121 does not fit $[_2]_2$. Similarly, $\sqcup\!\sqcup_{12+21}([_1 + [_2]_2,]_1) \equiv [_1]_1 +]_1[_1$, $\sqcup\!\sqcup_{12+22}([_1,]_1) \equiv [_1]_1$ and $\sqcup\!\sqcup_{(12)^*}(([_1]_1)^*, ([_2]_2)^*) \equiv ([_1 [_2]_1]_2)^*$, while $\sqcup\!\sqcup_{12+11}([_1, \lambda) \equiv \sqcup\!\sqcup_{(12)^*}([_1]_1, [_2(]_2 [_2)^*) \equiv \varnothing$ since in both cases no trajectory fits at least one word in every operand. Additionally, we say that T fits L_i if *every* $t \in T$ fits some $w_i \in L_i$ and that θ fits e_i if $L(\theta)$ fits $L(e_i)$.

In the remainder of this section, we show that the grammar $\mathbb{E}^{\sqcup\!\sqcup}$ can express all (completeness) and only (soundness) balanced regular languages.

Soundness. Showing that every expression in $\mathbb{E}^{\sqcup\!\sqcup}$ represents a balanced regular language is straightforward. The base cases all comply and both balanced and regular languages are closed under nondeterministic choice, concatenation and finite repetition. The shuffle on trajectories operator yields an interleaving of its operands: a simple inductive proof will show closure of balanced languages under the operation. Mateescu et al. show that regular languages are closed under binary shuffle on regular trajectory languages by constructing an equivalent finite automaton [6, Theorem 5.1]; their construction can be generalised in a straightforward way to fit the multiary operator, which shows that:

Theorem 2. $\{L(e) \mid e \in \mathbb{E}^{\sqcup\!\sqcup}\} \subseteq \{L \mid L \text{ is a balanced and regular language}\}.$

Completeness. To show that every balanced regular language has a representation in $\mathbb{E}^{\sqcup\!\sqcup}$, we take a balanced regular expression e, rewrite it into a disjunctive normal form $e_1 + \ldots + e_n$ such that all e_i contain no $\varnothing$ or choice operators—unless $e = \varnothing$, but since $\varnothing \in \mathbb{E}^{\sqcup\!\sqcup}$ we do not need to consider that specific case.

$$\bigcirc_i^k = ([_i]_i)^k([_i]_i)^* \qquad\qquad \langle\lambda\rangle_i^k = (\bigcirc_i^k)^* \qquad \bigcirc_i^\omega = ([_i]_i)^\omega$$

$$\oplus_i^k = \bigcirc_i^k[_i \qquad \ominus_i^k =]_i\bigcirc_i^k \qquad \pm_i^k =]_i\bigcirc_i^k[_i \qquad \langle*\rangle_i^k = (\pm_i^k)^* \qquad \pm_i^\omega = (]_i[_i)^\omega$$

Fig. 3. Factors, with $i \in \mathbb{N}, k \in \mathbb{N}_0$; balanced factors in the top row, unbalanced factors in the bottom row. We omit the superscript when it is not relevant. The ω-factors will be used in Sect. 4.

$$(\oplus_i^k, \ominus_i^\ell) \to \bigcirc_i^{k+\ell+1} \qquad (\oplus_i^k, \pm_i^\ell) \to \oplus_i^{k+\ell+1} \qquad\qquad (\pm_i^k, \ominus_i^\ell) \to \ominus_i^{k+\ell+1}$$

$$(\ominus_i^k, \oplus_i^\ell) \to \pm_i^{k+\ell} \qquad (\oplus_i^k, \langle*\rangle_i^\ell) \to \oplus_i^k \qquad\qquad (\langle*\rangle_i^k, \ominus_i^\ell) \to \ominus_i^\ell$$

$$(\pm_i^k, \pm_i^\ell) \to \pm_i^{k+\ell+1} \qquad (\langle*\rangle_i^k, \langle*\rangle_i^\ell) \to \langle*\rangle_i^{\min(k,\ell)} \qquad (\pm_i^k, \langle*\rangle_i^\ell), (\langle*\rangle_i^\ell, \pm_i^k) \to \pm_i^k$$

$$(\oplus_i^k, \pm_i^\omega) \to \bigcirc_i^\omega$$

Fig. 4. Merging common pairs of factors, with $i \in \mathbb{N}$ and $k, \ell \in \mathbb{N}_0$.

We then show that, for every i, $e_i \equiv \sqcup_\theta(e_{i,1}, \ldots, e_{i,m})$ for some $e_{i,1}, \ldots, e_{i,m}$, where every $e_{i,j}$ is essentially of the form $([_k]_k)^*$ for some k.

To do this, we show the more general result that, in fact, any regular expression containing no $\varnothing$ or $+$, and whose every i-balance is defined, can be written as the shuffle of the expressions in Fig. 3, which we call *factors*. Additionally, this can be done in such a way that the number of unbalanced i-factors is limited by the expression's i-balance and minimum i-balance, which implies that if the expression is balanced then it can be written as a shuffle of balanced factors—which is in $\mathbb{E}^\sqcup$. To prove this inductively for the concatenation case, we use that $\sqcup_{\theta_1}(e_1, \ldots, e_n) \cdot \sqcup_{\theta_2}(e_{n+1}, \ldots, e_{n+m}) \equiv \sqcup_{\theta_3}(e_1, \ldots, e_n, e_{n+1}, \ldots, e_{n+m})$ for some θ_3. We then merge certain pairs of factors to retain the correspondence between unbalanced factors and i-balance; for example, $\oplus_i$ and $\ominus_i$ into $\bigcirc_i$.

Lemma 3 justifies this merging operation and specifies the conditions under which it may be applied. We note that in particular these conditions, with the right T, hold for the pairs of factors in Fig. 4. Using this, Lemma 4 justifies the rewriting of regular expressions into shuffles of factors.

Lemma 3 (Merge). *Let $L = \sqcup_T(L_1, \ldots, L_m)$. If*

(a) T fits every L_i,
(b) for every $t \in T$, if $t(i) = m - 1$ and $t(j) = m$ then $i < j$, and
(c) for all $v, w \in L_{m-1}L_m$, if $|v| = |w|$ then $v = w$,

then $L = \sqcup_{T'}(L_1, \ldots, L_{m-1}L_m)$ for some T' such that T' fits $L_1, \ldots, L_{m-1}L_m$.

Proof. Let φ be a homomorphism such that $\varphi(m - 1) = 1$, $\varphi(m) = 2$ and $\varphi(i) = \lambda$ for all other i. Let ψ be a homomorphism such that $\psi(m) = m - 1$ and $\psi(i) = i$ for all other i. We proceed to show that $L = \sqcup_{\psi(T)}(L_1, \ldots, L_{m-1}L_m)$. Since T fits every L_i, $\psi(T)$ also fits $L_1, \ldots, L_{m-1}L_m$. $\square$

Lemma 4 (Rewrite). *Let $\mathsf{pos}_i(e_1, \ldots, e_n)$, $\mathsf{neg}_i(e_1, \ldots, e_n)$, $\mathsf{neut}_i(e_1, \ldots, e_n)$ be the number of $\oplus_i$, $\ominus_i$ and $[\pm_i$ or $\langle*\rangle_i]$ among $e_1, \ldots, e_n$.*

Let $e \in \mathbb{E}$ containing no $+$, whose i-balance is defined for every i. Then there exist θ and factors $e_1, \ldots, e_n$ such that $e \equiv \sqcup\!\sqcup_\theta(e_1, \ldots, e_n)$ and, additionally,

(a) $\mathsf{pos}_i(e_1, \ldots, e_n) - \mathsf{neg}_i(e_1, \ldots, e_n) = \nabla(e, i)$ for every i,
(b) $-\mathsf{neg}_i(e_1, \ldots, e_n) - \mathsf{neut}_i(e_1, \ldots, e_n) = \nabla^{\min}(e, i)$ for every i,
(c) there are not both $\langle\!+\!\rangle_i$ and $\langle\!-\!\rangle_i$ among $e_1, \ldots, e_n$ for some i, and
(d) θ fits every e_i.

Proof. This is a proof by induction on the structure of e.

The base cases λ, $[_i$ and $]_i$ are covered by $\sqcup\!\sqcup^1_\lambda(\langle\!\bigcirc\!\rangle^0_i)$, $\sqcup\!\sqcup^1_1(\langle\!+\!\rangle^0_i)$ and $\sqcup\!\sqcup^1_1(\langle\!-\!\rangle^0_i)$. Since e contains no $+$, this leaves us with two inductive cases:

– Let $e = \hat{e}^*$. The induction hypothesis gives us some $\hat{e}_1, \ldots, \hat{e}_n$ and $\hat{\theta}$ satisfying all conditions for $\hat{e}$. It should be clear that $L((\sqcup\!\sqcup_{\hat\theta}(\hat{e}_1, \ldots, \hat{e}_n))^*) \subseteq L((\sqcup\!\sqcup_{\hat\theta}(\hat{e}^*_1, \ldots, \hat{e}^*_n))^*) \subseteq L(\sqcup\!\sqcup_{\hat\theta^*}(\hat{e}^*_1, \ldots, \hat{e}^*_n))$. Since $\nabla(e, i)$ is defined for all i, $\nabla(\hat{e}, i) = 0$ for all i. It then follows from (a) and (c) that $\hat{e}_1, \ldots, \hat{e}_n$ contain no $\langle\!+\!\rangle_i$ or $\langle\!-\!\rangle_i$, so all $\hat{e}^*_i$ are also factors.
  To prove inclusion in the other direction, we show in two steps that $L(\sqcup\!\sqcup_{\hat\theta^*}(\hat{e}^*_1, \ldots, \hat{e}^*_n)) \subseteq L((\sqcup\!\sqcup_{\hat\theta}(\hat{e}^*_1, \ldots, \hat{e}^*_n))^*) \subseteq L((\sqcup\!\sqcup_{\hat\theta}(\hat{e}_1, \ldots, \hat{e}_n))^*)$.
  The balances, minimum balances and factor counts are unchanged, so (a–c) are satisfied. Finally, since $\hat{\theta}$ fits every $\hat{e}_i$, $\hat{\theta}^*$ fits every $\hat{e}^*_i$, so (d) also holds.
– Let $e = \hat{e}_1 \cdot \hat{e}_2$. The induction hypothesis gives us some $e_{1,1}, \ldots, e_{1,m_1}$ and θ_1 satisfying all conditions for $\hat{e}_1$, and similarly for $\hat{e}_2$. Let φ be a homomorphism such that $\varphi(i) = i + m_1$. Then $e' = \sqcup\!\sqcup_{\theta_1\varphi(\theta_2)}(e_{1,1}, \ldots, e_{1,m_1}, e_{2,1}, \ldots, e_{2,m_2}) \equiv e$ and e' satisfies (d), but not necessarily (a–c). We resolve the latter by merging operands $e_{1,j}, e_{2,k}$ where applicable by Lemma 3. We merge pairs of factors from Fig. 4, taking care to prioritise pairs containing both $\langle\!+\!\rangle_i$ and $\langle\!-\!\rangle_i$ over pairs containing only one of these, and pairs containing only one over pairs containing none. By Lemma 3, the resulting expression is equivalent to e' and satisfies (d). It also satisfies (a–c). □

Since a balanced regular expression has an i-balance and minimum i-balance of 0 for every i (Theorem 1), the following theorem follows directly from Lemma 4.

Theorem 3. $\{L(e) \mid e \in \mathbb{E}^{\sqcup\!\sqcup}\} \supseteq \{L \mid L \text{ is a balanced and regular language}\}$.

As an example, consider $e = [_1([_1]_1 +]_1[_1)(]_1[_1)^*]_1$. We first rewrite e as $[_1[_1]_1(]_1[_1)^*]_1 + [_1]_1[_1(]_1[_1)^*]_1$. We proceed to show how to construct an expression in $\mathbb{E}^{\sqcup\!\sqcup}$ for the first part of the disjunction:

$$
\begin{aligned}
[_1[_1]_1(]_1[_1)^*]_1 &\equiv \underline{\sqcup\!\sqcup_1(\langle\!+\!\rangle^0_1)} \, \sqcup\!\sqcup_1(\langle\!+\!\rangle^0_1) \, \sqcup\!\sqcup_1(\langle\!-\!\rangle^0_1)(\sqcup\!\sqcup_1(\langle\!-\!\rangle^0_1) \, \sqcup\!\sqcup_1(\langle\!+\!\rangle^0_1))^* \, \sqcup\!\sqcup_1(\langle\!-\!\rangle^0_1) \\
&\equiv \underline{\sqcup\!\sqcup_{12}(\langle\!+\!\rangle^0_1, \langle\!+\!\rangle^0_1)} \, \sqcup\!\sqcup_1(\langle\!-\!\rangle^0_1)(\sqcup\!\sqcup_1(\langle\!-\!\rangle^0_1) \, \sqcup\!\sqcup_1(\langle\!+\!\rangle^0_1))^* \, \sqcup\!\sqcup_1(\langle\!-\!\rangle^0_1) \\
&\equiv \underline{\sqcup\!\sqcup_{121}(\langle\!\bigcirc\!\rangle^1_1, \langle\!+\!\rangle^0_1)}(\sqcup\!\sqcup_1(\langle\!-\!\rangle^0_1) \, \sqcup\!\sqcup_1(\langle\!+\!\rangle^0_1))^* \, \sqcup\!\sqcup_1(\langle\!-\!\rangle^0_1) \\
&\equiv \sqcup\!\sqcup_{121}(\langle\!\bigcirc\!\rangle^1_1, \langle\!+\!\rangle^0_1) \underline{(\sqcup\!\sqcup_{11}(\langle\!+\!\rangle^0_1))^*} \, \sqcup\!\sqcup_1(\langle\!-\!\rangle^0_1) \\
&\equiv \sqcup\!\sqcup_{121}(\langle\!\bigcirc\!\rangle^1_1, \langle\!+\!\rangle^0_1) \underline{\sqcup\!\sqcup_{(11)^*}(\langle\!\star\!\rangle^0_1)} \, \sqcup\!\sqcup_1(\langle\!-\!\rangle^0_1) \\
&\equiv \underline{\sqcup\!\sqcup_{121(22)^*}(\langle\!\bigcirc\!\rangle^1_1, \langle\!+\!\rangle^0_1)} \, \sqcup\!\sqcup_1(\langle\!-\!\rangle^0_1) \\
&\equiv \underline{\sqcup\!\sqcup_{121(22)^*2}(\langle\!\bigcirc\!\rangle^1_1, \langle\!\bigcirc\!\rangle^1_1)}.
\end{aligned}
$$

4   Balanced-By-Construction ω-regular Languages

We generalise the notion of balancedness to also include bounded infinite words and ω-languages: a word $w \in \Sigma^\infty$ is i-*balanced* iff $|w|_{[_i} = |w|_{]_i}$, $|v|_{[_i} \geq |v|_{]_i}$ for all *finite* prefixes v of w, and w is bounded, as defined below. A language $L \subseteq \Sigma^\infty$ is i-balanced if all of its words are and if it is bounded. This is extended to balancedness and expressions in the expected way. We note that all finite words and balanced regular languages are bounded by default; boundedness is only a restriction on infinite words and ω-languages.[1]

Boundedness. A word $w \in \Sigma^\infty$ is i-*bounded* by $n \in \mathbb{N}_0$ if $|v|_{[_i} - |v|_{]_i} \leq n$ for all finite prefixes v of w. A language is i-bounded by n if all of its words are. A word or language is *bounded* if it is i-bounded for all i. The *minimal i-bound* of a word or language is the smallest n for which it is i-bounded. We extend these definitions to expressions in the expected way.

We note that by this definition $[_i([_i]_i)^\omega$ is balanced, but $[_i^*([_i]_i)^\omega$ is not since it is not bounded, even though all of its words are.

4.1   Balanced ω-Regular Expressions

We use Ω for the set of all ω-regular expressions. It is defined as follows:

$$\frac{}{\varnothing \in \Omega} \qquad \frac{e \in \mathbb{E} \quad \lambda \notin L(e)}{e^\omega \in \Omega} \qquad \frac{e_1 \in \mathbb{E} \quad e_2 \in \Omega}{e_1 \cdot e_2 \in \Omega} \qquad \frac{e_1, e_2 \in \Omega}{e_1 + e_2 \in \Omega} \qquad (1)$$

As before, we assume without loss of generality that an ω-regular expression e does not contain $\varnothing$, unless $e = \varnothing$, to simplify definitions and proofs.

Our characterisation of balanced ω-regular expressions is a generalisation of that of balanced regular expressions. We note two main complications:

- We need to distinguish between finite and infinite numbers of parentheses: $[_1([_1]_1)^\omega$ is balanced but $[_1([_2]_2)^\omega$ is not. We introduce two predicates for expressions: $\xi(e, i)$ and $\xi^\omega(e, i)$, as defined in Fig. 5. Intuitively, and as shown in Lemma 5, $\xi(e, i)$ iff every word in $L(e)$ contains at least one i-parenthesis, and $\xi^\omega(e, i)$ iff every word in $L(e)$ contains infinitely many.
- Not every subexpression of a balanced ω-regular expression can be assigned a unique i-balance: $(\lambda + [_i)([_i]_i)^\omega$ is balanced, but $(\lambda + [_i)$ has no unique i-balance. Instead, we now assign an upper bound ∇^U and a lower bound ∇^L to an expression's i-balance instead of a single value. These are defined in Fig. 6. The definition of minimum i-balance is unchanged, other than the addition of $\nabla^{\min}(e^\omega, i) = \nabla^{\min}(e, i)$ and the redefinition of $\nabla^{\min}(e_1 \cdot e_2, i) = \min(\nabla^{\min}(e_1, i), \nabla^L(e_1, i) + \nabla^{\min}(e_2, i))$. We note that, for any regular expression $e \in \mathbb{E}$, $\nabla^L(e, i) = \nabla^U(e, i) = \nabla(e, i)$.

---

[1] Our choice for boundedness stems from our interest in communication protocols (Sect. 1), where channels often require buffers of finite size.

$$\overline{\xi(\mathtt{[}_i,i)} \qquad \overline{\xi(\mathtt{]}_i,i)} \qquad \frac{\xi(e_1,i) \vee \xi(e_2,i)}{\xi(e_1 \cdot e_2, i)} \qquad \frac{\xi(e_1,i) \quad \xi(e_2,i)}{\xi(e_1 + e_2, i)} \qquad \frac{\xi(e,i)}{\xi(e^\omega, i)}$$

$$\frac{\xi^\omega(e_2,i)}{\xi^\omega(e_1 \cdot e_2, i)} \qquad \frac{\xi^\omega(e_1,i) \quad \xi^\omega(e_2,i)}{\xi^\omega(e_1 + e_2, i)} \qquad \frac{\xi(e,i)}{\xi^\omega(e^\omega, i)}$$

Fig. 5. The i-occurrence of regular and ω-regular expressions.

$$\nabla^\dagger(\lambda,i) = 0 \qquad \nabla^\dagger(\mathtt{[}_i,i) = 1 \qquad \nabla^\dagger(\mathtt{]}_i,i) = -1 \qquad \nabla^\dagger(\mathtt{[}_j,i) = \nabla^\dagger(\mathtt{]}_j,i) = 0$$

$$\nabla^\dagger(e_1 \cdot e_2, i) = \begin{cases} \nabla^\dagger(e_2, i) & \text{if } \xi^\omega(e_2,i) \\ \nabla^\dagger(e_1,i) + \nabla^\dagger(e_2,i) & \text{otherwise} \end{cases}$$

$$\nabla^\dagger(e^*,i) = \nabla^\dagger(e^\omega,i) = 0 \text{ if } \nabla^\dagger(e,i) = 0$$

$$\nabla^L(e_1 + e_2, i) = \min(\nabla^L(e_1,i), \nabla^L(e_2,i)) \quad \nabla^U(e_1 + e_2, i) = \max(\nabla^U(e_1,i), \nabla^L(e_2,i))$$

Fig. 6. The i-balance bounds of ω-regular expressions, where $i \neq j$ and $\dagger \in \{L, U\}$.

Lemma 5. *Let $e \in \mathbb{E} \cup \Omega$ such that $e \neq \varnothing$. Then:*

(i) $\xi(e,i)$ if and only if $|w|_{\mathtt{[}_i} + |w|_{\mathtt{]}_i} > 0$ for every $w \in L(e)$;
(ii) $\xi^\omega(e,i)$ if and only if $|w|_{\mathtt{[}_i} + |w|_{\mathtt{]}_i} = \aleph_0$ for every $w \in L(e)$.

We extend Lemmas 1 and 2 about properties of i-balance and minimum i-balance to i-balance bounds and ω-regular expressions in Lemmas 6 and 7.

Lemma 6 (cf. Lemma 1). *Let $e \in \mathbb{E} \cup \Omega$. If $\nabla^L(e,i)$, $\nabla^U(e,i)$ and $\nabla^{\min}(e,i)$ are defined, then:*

(i) For every $w \in L(e)$, $|w|_{\mathtt{[}_i}$ and $|w|_{\mathtt{]}_i}$ are either both finite or both infinite;
(ii) For every $w \in L(e)$, if $|w|_{\mathtt{[}_i}, |w|_{\mathtt{]}_i}$ are finite, then $\nabla^L(e,i) \leq |w|_{\mathtt{[}_i} - |w|_{\mathtt{]}_i} \leq \nabla^U(e,i)$;
(iii) If $e \in \mathbb{E}$, then there exist $w_1, w_2 \in L(e)$ such that $|w_1|_{\mathtt{[}_i} - |w_1|_{\mathtt{]}_i} = \nabla^L(e,i)$ and $|w_2|_{\mathtt{[}_i} - |w_2|_{\mathtt{]}_i} = \nabla^U(e,i)$;
(iv) If $\xi^\omega(e,i)$, then $\nabla^L(e,i) = \nabla^U(e,i) = 0$;
(v) $|v|_{\mathtt{[}_i} - |v|_{\mathtt{]}_i} \geq \nabla^{\min}(e,i)$ for every finite prefix v of every $w \in L(e)$;
(vi) $|v|_{\mathtt{[}_i} - |v|_{\mathtt{]}_i} = \nabla^{\min}(e,i)$ for some finite prefix v of some $w \in L(e)$;
(vii) $L(e)$ is i-bounded.

Lemma 7 (cf. Lemma 2). *Let $e \in \mathbb{E} \cup \Omega$. If $e \neq \varnothing$, e is i-bounded and if there exists some n such that $|(|v|_{\mathtt{[}_i} - |v|_{\mathtt{]}_i}) - (|w|_{\mathtt{[}_i} - |w|_{\mathtt{]}_i})| \leq n$ for all $v, w \in L(e)$ with finite i-parenthesis counts, then $\nabla^L(e,i)$, $\nabla^U(e,i)$ and $\nabla^{\min}(e,i)$ are defined.*

The proofs are straightforward by structural induction on e. Applying these lemmas gives us the following characterisation:

Theorem 4. *Let $e \in \mathbb{E} \cup \Omega$. Then e is balanced iff $\nabla^L(e,i) = \nabla^U(e,i) = \nabla^{\min}(e,i) = 0$ for every i or if $e = \varnothing$.*

4.2   Balanced-By-Construction ω-Regular Languages

The grammar in Fig. 2 can be extended with ω as in (1) to obtain an expression grammar $\Omega^{\sqcup\!\!\sqcup}$ for balanced ω-regular languages [3, Appendix B].

Since the inductive definition of the shuffle on trajectories operator does not support words of infinite length, we redefine it as follows. Let $w_1, \ldots, w_n \in \Sigma^\infty$ and let $t \in \{1, \ldots, n\}^\infty$. If t fits $w_1, \ldots, w_n$, i.e., if $|t|_i = |w_i|$ for every i, then $\sqcup\!\!\sqcup_t(w_1, \ldots, w_n) = w(1)w(2) \ldots w(|t|)$ if t has finite length and $w(1)w(2) \ldots$ if t has infinite length, where $w(i) = w_j(k)$ for $j = t(i)$ and $k = |t(1, \ldots, i)|_j$. As before, this naturally extends to languages and expressions.

Soundness. Balanced languages being closed under shuffle follows immediately from its definition. To show that $\sqcup\!\!\sqcup_T(L_1, \ldots, L_n)$ is ω-regular if T is ω-regular and all L_i are either regular or ω-regular, we can further generalise the construction used by Mateescu et al. [6] to build a Muller automaton for the resulting language. Recall that a Muller automaton differs from a finite automaton only in its acceptance criterion: instead of a single set of final states it has a set of sets of final states F, and it accepts all infinite words for which the set of states that are visited infinitely often is an element of F.

The construction of the new Muller automaton is analogous to the construction of a finite automaton for a shuffle of regular languages and differs only in the construction of F. Let Q be the set of states of our new Muller automaton. Let F_i be the acceptance criterion of the automaton for L_i, whether a finite automaton or a Muller automaton. If L_i is regular, then without loss of generality we may assume that no state in F_i has any outgoing transition. Furthermore, since ω-regular languages are closed under intersection and the language of all trajectories containing infinitely many i is ω-regular for every i, we may also assume without loss of generality that T only contains trajectories with infinitely many occurrences of every i.

We define F as the cross product of all the F_i: F is the set of sets of states such that, if L_i is ω-regular then the projection of these states on i is an element of F_i, and if L_i is regular then the projection of these states on i is a single state in F_i. Formally: if $\varphi_i((q_t, q_1, \ldots, q_n)) = q_i$ and $\varphi_i(S) = \{\varphi_i(q) \mid q \in S\}$, then $F = \{S \mid S \subseteq Q \wedge (\varphi_i(S) \in F_i \vee (\varphi_i(S) \subseteq F_i \wedge |\varphi_i(S)| = 1))\}$. The automaton for T forces that every Muller automaton for some L_i takes infinitely many steps. By our assumption that the final states of finite automata have no outgoing transitions, all finite automata only take a finite number of steps. It follows that our constructed Muller automaton accepts the language of $\sqcup\!\!\sqcup_T(L_1, \ldots, L_n)$, which then is ω-regular. In other words:

Theorem 5. $\{L(e) \mid e \in \Omega^{\sqcup\!\!\sqcup}\} \subseteq \{L \mid L \text{ is a balanced } \omega\text{-regular language}\}$.

Completeness. Our approach to showing that every balanced ω-regular expression has an equivalent expression in $\Omega^{\sqcup\!\!\sqcup}$ mirrors that of Sect. 3: we first rewrite an expression into a disjunctive normal form and then recursively construct an expression in $\Omega^{\sqcup\!\!\sqcup}$ for every term of the disjunction by merging pairs of factors.

Let $e \neq \varnothing$ be a balanced ω-regular expression. Without loss of generality, we may assume that $e = e_1 e_2^\omega + \ldots + e_{2m-1} e_{2m}^\omega$, where every e_i is a regular expression containing no $+$. Otherwise, we can rewrite it as such. We show how to construct an expression in $\Omega^{\sqcup\!\sqcup}$ for $e_1 e_2^\omega$.

Since $\nabla^L(e,i) = \nabla^U(e,i) = \nabla^{\min}(e,i) = 0$ by Theorem 4, it follows that $\nabla^{\min}(e_1,i) = \nabla^L(e_2,i) = \nabla^U(e_2,i) = 0$. Then, by Lemma 4, we can write e_1 as a shuffle of $\bigcirc_i, \langle\!\wedge\!\rangle_i, \langle+\rangle_i$ and e_2 as a shuffle of $\bigcirc_i, \langle\!\wedge\!\rangle_i, \langle\pm\rangle_i, \langle *\rangle_i$. The idea is to: (a) rewrite e_2^ω in terms of $\bigcirc_i, \langle\!\wedge\!\rangle_i, \bigcirc_i^\omega, \langle\pm\rangle_i^\omega$ and then; (b) merge every $\langle+\rangle_i$ in e_1 with a $\langle\pm\rangle_i^\omega$ in e_2^ω into $\bigcirc_i^\omega$, using Lemma 3. We run into two complications:

- In step (a), e_2^ω may not necessarily be expressible as a single shuffle of factors: if $e_2 = [_1]_1([_2]_2)^*$, then e_2^ω contains both words with finite and infinite numbers of $[_2,]_2$. The latter requires a factor $\bigcirc_2^\omega$, while the former requires its absence. To remedy this, we write e_2^ω as a *disjunction* of shuffles of factors; one for every combination of finite and infinite versions of $\bigcirc_i, \langle\!\wedge\!\rangle_i$. This is further detailed in Lemma 8.
- In step (b), the number of $\langle\pm\rangle_i^\omega$ in a term of e_2^ω may not necessarily match the number of $\langle+\rangle_i$ in e_1: if $e_1 = [_1$ and $e_2 = [_1]_1$, then e_1 contains one $\langle+\rangle_1$ and e_2 contains one factor $\bigcirc_1$. To solve this, we use two observations:
  - We can apply Lemma 3 to split a $\bigcirc_i$ into $\langle+\rangle_i$ and $\langle-\rangle_i$.
  - $e_2^\omega \equiv (e_2 \cdot e_2)^\omega$, so we can essentially multiply the factors in e_2.
  Thus, we can always split a $\bigcirc_i$ into $\langle+\rangle_i$ and $\langle-\rangle_i$, then create copies of them and merge them back into one $\bigcirc_i$ and one $\langle\pm\rangle_i$. Since we can merge all other factors with their own copy, this effectively adds one $\langle\pm\rangle_i$. Now that we have at least one, we can create more: we create a copy of every factor, then merge every factor with its own copy except for some number of $\langle\pm\rangle_i$. This is further detailed in Lemma 9.

Lemma 8. *Let $e = \sqcup\!\sqcup_\theta(e_1, \ldots, e_n) \in \mathbb{E}^{\sqcup\!\sqcup}$ be a shuffle of factors $\bigcirc_i, \langle\!\wedge\!\rangle_i, \langle\pm\rangle_i$ such that θ fits every e_j and contains no $+$. Then $e^\omega \equiv \hat{e}_1 + \ldots + \hat{e}_m$, where $\hat{e}_k = \sqcup\!\sqcup_{\theta_k}(e_{k,1}, \ldots, e_{k,n})$ is a shuffle of factors $\bigcirc_i, \langle\!\wedge\!\rangle_i, \bigcirc_i^\omega, \langle\pm\rangle_i^\omega$ for every k such that the number of $\langle\pm\rangle_i$ in e is the same as the number of $\langle\pm\rangle_i^\omega$ in $\hat{e}_k$ for every i, and θ_k fits every $e_{k,j}$.*

Proof. Let $\varphi : \mathbb{E} \mapsto 2^{\mathbb{E}\cup\Omega}$ such that $\varphi(\bigcirc_i^k) = \{\bigcirc_i^k, \bigcirc_i^\omega\}$, $\varphi(\langle\!\wedge\!\rangle_i^k) = \{\langle\!\wedge\!\rangle_i^k, \bigcirc_i^\omega\}$ and $\varphi(\langle\pm\rangle_i^k) = \{\langle\pm\rangle_i^\omega\}$. We can then show that $e^\omega \equiv \hat{e}_1 + \ldots + \hat{e}_m$, where $\{\hat{e}_1, \ldots, \hat{e}_m\} = \{\sqcup\!\sqcup_{\theta^\omega}(e_1', \ldots, e_n') \mid e_1' \in \varphi(e_1), \ldots, e_n' \in \varphi(e_n)\}$.

Moreover, since φ maps $\langle\pm\rangle_i$ to $\langle\pm\rangle_i^\omega$, the number of factors $\langle\pm\rangle_i^\omega$ in every $\hat{e}_k$ matches the number of factors $\langle\pm\rangle_i$ in e. However, if $\hat{e}_k = \sqcup\!\sqcup_{\theta^\omega}(e_1', \ldots, e_n')$, then θ^ω may not necessarily fit every e_j': if e_j' is one of $\bigcirc_i, \langle\!\wedge\!\rangle_i$, then there are $t \in L(\theta^\omega)$ with infinitely many j, while every word in $L(e_j')$ is finite. Instead of θ^ω, we can use the trajectory $\theta^* \cdot \psi(\theta)^\omega$, where ψ is a homomorphism such that $\psi(j) = \lambda$ if e_j' is one of $\bigcirc_i, \langle\!\wedge\!\rangle_i$ and $\psi(j) = j$ otherwise. This covers exactly the part of θ^ω that fits every e_j'. $\qquad\square$

Lemma 9. *Let $\sqcup\!\sqcup_\theta(e_1, \ldots, e_n) \equiv e \in \mathbb{E}$ be a shuffle of factors $\bigcirc_i, \langle\!\wedge\!\rangle_i, \langle\pm\rangle_i, \langle *\rangle_i$ such that θ fits every e_j and contains no $+$, and $\xi(e,i)$. If there are ℓ factors*

$\langle\pm\rangle_i, \langle *\rangle_i$ among $e_1, \ldots, e_n$, then for every $k \geq \ell$ (such that $k > 0$), there exists some shuffle of factors $\hat{e} = \amalg_{\hat\theta}(\hat e_1, \ldots, \hat e_m)$ such that $e^\omega \equiv \hat e^\omega$, $\hat e$ contains k factors $\langle\pm\rangle_i$ and no $\langle *\rangle_i$ and $\hat\theta$ fits every $\hat e_j$.

Proof. This proof consists of three steps. First, we need to make sure that we have at least one $\langle\pm\rangle_i$. Second, we replace any remaining factors $\langle *\rangle_i$ with $\langle\pm\rangle_i$. Third, we create additional copies of $\langle\pm\rangle_i$ as needed.

1. Suppose that there are no $\langle\pm\rangle_i$ among $e_1, \ldots, e_n$. Then our first step consists of creating one. Since $\xi(e, i)$ and θ contains no $+$, there exists some $e_j \in \{\langle\bigcirc\rangle_i, \langle\lambda\rangle_i, \langle *\rangle_i\}$ such that $|t|_j > 0$ for every $t \in L(\theta)$. Without loss of generality, we may assume that $j = n$.
   If $e_n = \langle *\rangle_i^k$, since $|t|_n > 0$ for every t then $e \equiv \amalg_\theta(e_1, \ldots, \langle\pm\rangle_i^k)$ and we can proceed with step 2. Otherwise, if $e_n = \langle\lambda\rangle_i^k$, then $e \equiv \amalg_\theta(e_1, \ldots, \langle\bigcirc\rangle_i^k)$ and if $e_n = \langle\bigcirc\rangle_i^0$, then $e \equiv \amalg_\theta(e_1, \ldots, \langle\bigcirc\rangle_i^1)$. Going forward, we may thus assume that $e_n = \langle\bigcirc\rangle_i^k$ with $k \geq 1$. Since $|t|_n > 0$ for every $t \in L(\theta)$ and θ contains no $+$, it follows that $\theta = \theta_1 \cdot \theta_2$ such that both θ_1 and θ_2 only contain trajectories with odd numbers of n. We can then apply the proof of Lemma 3 to show that $e \equiv \amalg_{\theta_3}(e_1, \ldots, e_{n-1}, \langle +\rangle_i^{k_1}, \langle -\rangle_i^{k_2})$ for some θ_3, k_1, k_2. If $e_1, \ldots, e_{n-1}$ contain a $\langle *\rangle_i$, then without loss of generality we may assume that $e_{n-1} = \langle *\rangle_i^{k_3}$. We may assume that there exists some $t \in L(\theta)$ such that $|\theta|_{n-1} = 0$; otherwise we would have selected this factor as e_n earlier in this step and then proceeded with step 2. It follows that all trajectories in θ_1 and θ_2, and therefore in θ_3, contain even numbers of n. Then, in the same way that we split $\langle\bigcirc\rangle_i^k$ into $\langle +\rangle_i^{k_1}$ and $\langle -\rangle_i^{k_2}$ before, we can show that $e \equiv \amalg_{\theta_4}(e_1, \ldots, e_{n-2}, \langle *\rangle_i^{k_4}, \langle *\rangle_i^{k_5}, \langle +\rangle_i^{k_1}, \langle -\rangle_i^{k_2})$ for some θ_4, k_4, k_5. As seen in Fig. 4, we can then merge $\langle *\rangle_i^{k_4}$ with $\langle -\rangle_i^{k_2}$ and $\langle *\rangle_i^{k_5}$ with $\langle +\rangle_i^{k_1}$ to obtain $e \equiv \amalg_{\theta_5}(e_1, \ldots, e_{n-2}, \langle +\rangle_i^{k_1}, \langle -\rangle_i^{k_2})$ for some θ_5. This takes care of the special case where $k = \ell > 0$ but there are no factors $\langle\pm\rangle_i$. We may thus assume without loss of generality that $e \equiv \amalg_{\theta_6}(e_1, \ldots, \langle +\rangle_i^{k_1}, \langle -\rangle_i^{k_2})$ for some θ_6. Since we still lack a $\langle\pm\rangle_i$, we use that $e^\omega \equiv (e \cdot e)^\omega$ to construct $e' = \amalg_{\theta_6}(e_1, \ldots, \langle +\rangle_i^{k_1}, \langle -\rangle_i^{k_2}) \cdot \amalg_{\theta_6}(e_1, \ldots, \langle +\rangle_i^{k_1}, \langle -\rangle_i^{k_2}) \equiv \amalg_{\theta_7}(e_1, \ldots, \langle +\rangle_i^{k_1}, \langle -\rangle_i^{k_2}, e_1, \ldots, \langle +\rangle_i^{k_1}, \langle -\rangle_i^{k_2})$ for some θ_7. We can then merge the first $\langle +\rangle_i^{k_1}$ with the second $\langle -\rangle_i^{k_2}$ into $\langle\bigcirc\rangle_i^{k_1+k_2+1}$ and merge the second $\langle +\rangle_i^{k_1}$ with the first $\langle -\rangle_i^{k_2}$ into $\langle\pm\rangle_i^{k_1+k_2}$. We can merge every other factor with its own copy, which gives us $e' \equiv \amalg_{\theta_8}(e'_1, \ldots, \langle\bigcirc\rangle_i^{k_1+k_2+1}, \langle\pm\rangle_1^{k_1+k_2})$ and $e'^\omega \equiv e^\omega$.

2. Now that we have at least one $\langle\pm\rangle_i$, we can reuse methods applied in the first step to replace any remaining $\langle *\rangle_i$: create a copy of every factor using $e^\omega \equiv (e \cdot e)^\omega$, then merge the two copies of $\langle *\rangle_i$ with the copies of some $\langle\pm\rangle_i$ as in Fig. 4. By merging every other factor with its own copy, we effectively replace one $\langle *\rangle_i$ with one $\langle\pm\rangle_i$. We repeat this step until there are no $\langle *\rangle_i$ left.

3. Finally, by copying every factor and then merging every factor with its own copy except for a number of $\langle\pm\rangle_i$, we can create any additional number of $\langle\pm\rangle_i$, until we have some $\hat e = \amalg_{\hat\theta}(\hat e_1, \ldots, \hat e_m)$ with k $\langle\pm\rangle_i$. Since every

rewriting step preserves equivalence of the ω-closures and the fitting of the trajectories, it follows that $\hat{e}^\omega \equiv e^\omega$ and that $\hat{\theta}$ fits every $\hat{e}_j$. $\square$

Summarising, given $e_1 \cdot e_2^\omega$, by applying Lemmas 9 and 8 we can rewrite e_1 as a shuffle of factors $\langle\rangle_i, \langle\lambda\rangle_i, \langle+\rangle_i$, and e_2^ω as a disjunction of shuffles of factors $\langle\rangle_i, \langle\lambda\rangle_i, \langle\rangle_i^\omega, \langle\pm\rangle_i^\omega$, such that the number of $\langle\pm\rangle_i^\omega$ in every term of the disjunction equals the number of $\langle+\rangle_i$ in e_1. By applying the laws of distributivity, we can then rewrite $e_1 \cdot e_2^\omega$ as a disjunction of concatenations of shuffles. Since the numbers of $\langle+\rangle_i$ and $\langle\pm\rangle_i^\omega$ match in every term of this disjunction, we can apply Lemma 3 to merge every pair into $\langle\rangle_i^\omega$. Since all factors are now balanced, every balanced ω-regular language has a corresponding expression in $\Omega^{\sqcup\!\sqcup}$:

Theorem 6. $\{L(e) \mid e \in \Omega^{\sqcup\!\sqcup}\} \supseteq \{L \mid L \text{ is a balanced } \omega\text{-regular language}\}.$

As an example, we show how to build an expression in $\Omega^{\sqcup\!\sqcup}$ for $e = \texttt{[}_1(\texttt{[}_1\texttt{]}_1)_1)^\omega$.

$$
\begin{aligned}
\texttt{[}_1(\texttt{[}_1\texttt{]}_1)_1)^\omega &\equiv \sqcup\!\sqcup_1(\langle+\rangle_1^0)(\sqcup\!\sqcup_{11}(\langle\rangle_1^1))^\omega \\
&\equiv \sqcup\!\sqcup_1(\langle+\rangle_1^0)(\underline{\sqcup\!\sqcup_1(\langle+\rangle_1^0)} \sqcup\!\sqcup_1 (\langle-\rangle_1^0))^\omega \\
&\equiv \sqcup\!\sqcup_1(\langle+\rangle_1^0)(\sqcup\!\sqcup_1(\langle+\rangle_1^0)\underline{\sqcup\!\sqcup_1(\langle-\rangle_1^0)} \sqcup\!\sqcup_1 (\langle+\rangle_1^0) \sqcup\!\sqcup_1 (\langle-\rangle_1^0))^\omega \\
&\equiv \sqcup\!\sqcup_1(\langle+\rangle_1^0)(\sqcup\!\sqcup_1(\langle+\rangle_1^0) \sqcup\!\sqcup_{11} (\langle+\rangle_1^0) \sqcup\!\sqcup_1 (\langle-\rangle_1^0))^\omega \\
&\equiv \sqcup\!\sqcup_1(\langle+\rangle_1^0)(\sqcup\!\sqcup_{1221}(\langle\rangle_1^1, \langle+\rangle_1^0))^\omega \\
&\equiv \underline{\sqcup\!\sqcup_1(\langle+\rangle_1^0)} \sqcup\!\sqcup_{(1221)^\omega} (\langle\rangle_1^\omega, \langle+\rangle_1^\omega) \\
&\equiv \sqcup\!\sqcup_{1(2112)^\omega} (\langle\rangle_1^\omega, \langle\rangle_1^\omega).
\end{aligned}
$$

References

1. Chomsky, N., Schützenberger, M.: The algebraic theory of context-free languages. In: Computer Programming and Formal Systems, Studies in Logic and the Foundations of Mathematics, vol. 26, pp. 118–161. Elsevier (1959)
2. Duchon, P.: On the enumeration and generation of generalized Dyck words. Discret. Math. **225**(1–3), 121–135 (2000). https://doi.org/10.1016/S0012-365X(00)00150-3
3. Edixhoven, L., Jongmans, S.S.: Balanced-by-construction regular and ω-regular languages (technical report). Tech. Rep. OUNL-CS-2021-1, Open University of the Netherlands (2021)
4. Labelle, J., Yeh, Y.: Generalized Dyck paths. Discret. Math. **82**(1), 1–6 (1990). https://doi.org/10.1016/0012-365X(90)90039-K
5. Liebehenschel, J.: Lexicographical generation of a generalized Dyck language. SIAM J. Comput. **32**(4), 880–903 (2003). https://doi.org/10.1137/S0097539701394493
6. Mateescu, A., Rozenberg, G., Salomaa, A.: Shuffle on trajectories: syntactic constraints. Theor. Comput. Sci. **197**(1–2), 1–56 (1998). https://doi.org/10.1016/S0304-3975(97)00163-1
7. Mateescu, A., Salomaa, K., Yu, S.: On fairness of many-dimensional trajectories. J. Autom. Lang. Comb. **5**(2), 145–157 (2000). https://doi.org/10.25596/jalc-2000-145

8. Moortgat, M.: A note on multidimensional Dyck languages. In: Casadio, C., Coecke, B., Moortgat, M., Scott, P. (eds.) Categories and Types in Logic, Language, and Physics. LNCS, vol. 8222, pp. 279–296. Springer, Heidelberg (2014). https://doi. org/10.1007/978-3-642-54789-8_16

9. Prodinger, H.: On a generalization of the Dyck-language over a two letter alphabet. Discret. Math. **28**(3), 269–276 (1979). https://doi.org/10.1016/0012-365X(79)90134-1

Weighted Prefix Normal Words:
Mind the Gap

Yannik Eikmeier, Pamela Fleischmann$^{(\boxtimes)}$, Mitja Kulczynski,
and Dirk Nowotka

Kiel University, Kiel, Germany
stu204329@mail.uni-kiel.de, {fpa,mku,dn}@informatik.uni-kiel.de

Abstract. A prefix normal word is a binary word whose prefixes contain
at least as many 1s as any of its factors of the same length. Introduced by
Fici and Lipták in 2011, the notion of prefix normality has been, thus far,
only defined for words over the binary alphabet. In this work we investigate a generalisation for finite words over arbitrary finite alphabets,
namely weighted prefix normality. We prove that weighted prefix normality is more expressive than binary prefix normality. Furthermore, we
investigate the existence of a weighted prefix normal form, since weighted
prefix normality comes with several new peculiarities that did not already
occur in the binary case. We characterise these issues and finally present
a standard technique to obtain a generalised prefix normal form for all
words over arbitrary, finite alphabets.

1 Introduction

Complexity measures of words are a central topic of investigation when dealing with properties of sequences, e.g., factor complexity [2,4,6,26], binomial
complexity [19,22,23,25], cyclic complexity [12]. Characterising the maximum
density of a particular letter in the set of factors of a given length, hence considering an abelian setting, falls into that category (see for instance [5,13,24] and
the references therein). Such characterisations inevitably prompt the search for
and investigation of normal forms representing words with equivalent measures.
Prefix normality is the concept considered in this paper and was first introduced
by Fici and Lipták in 2011 [17] as a property describing the distribution of a
designated letter within a binary word. A word over the binary alphabet $\{0, 1\}$ is
prefix normal if every prefix contains at least as many 1s as any of its factors of
the same length. For example, the word 1101001 is prefix normal. Thus, prefixes
of prefix normal words give an upper bound for the amount of 1s any other factor
of the word may contain. For a given binary word w the *maximum-1s function*
maps n to the maximum amount of 1s, a length-n factor of w can have. Burcsi et
al. [11] show that there exists exactly one prefix normal word (the prefix normal
form) in the set of all binary words that have an identical maximum-1s function,
e.g., the prefix normal form of 1001101 is 1101001.

P. Fleischmann—Supported by DFG grant 437493335.

© Springer Nature Switzerland AG 2021
N. Moreira and R. Reis (Eds.): DLT 2021, LNCS 12811, pp. 143–154, 2021.
https://doi.org/10.1007/978-3-030-81508-0_12

From an application point of view this complexity measure is directly connected to the *Binary Jumbled Pattern Matching Problem (BJPM)* (see e.g., [1,7,9] and for the general JPM, see e.g., [21]). The BJPM problem is to determine whether a given finite binary word has factors containing given amounts of 1s and 0s. In [17] prefix normal forms were used to construct an index for the BJPM problem in $O(n)$ time where n is the given word's length. The fastest known algorithm for this problem has a runtime of $O(n^{1.864})$ (see [14]). Balister and Gerke [3] showed that the number of length-n prefix normal words is $2^{n-\Theta(\log^2(n))}$, and the class of a given prefix normal word contains at most $2^{n-O(\sqrt{n\log(n)})}$ elements. In more theoretical settings, the language of binary prefix normal words has also been extended to infinite binary words [16]. Prefix normality has been shown to be connected to other fields of research within combinatorics on words, e.g., Lyndon words [17] and bubble languages [10]. Furthermore, efforts have been made to recursively construct prefix normal words, via the notions of extension critical words (collapsing words) and prefix normal palindromes [10,15,18]. The goal therein was to learn more about the number of words with the same prefix normal form and the number of prefix normal palindromes. Very recently in [8] a Gray code for prefix normal words in amortized polylogarithmic time per word was generated. Four sequences related to prefix normal words can be found in the OEIS [20]: A194850 (number of prefix normal words of length n), A238109 (list of prefix normal words over the binary alphabet), A238110 (maximum number of binary words of length n having the same prefix normal form), and A308465 (number of prefix normal palindromes of length n).

Our Contribution. In this work, we investigate a generalisation of prefix normality for finite words over arbitrary finite alphabets. We define a *weight measure*, which is a morphic function assigning a weight (an element from an arbitrary but a priori chosen monoid) to every letter of an arbitrary finite alphabet. Based on those weights we can again compare factors and prefixes of words over this alphabet w.r.t. their weight. A word is *prefix normal w.r.t. a weight measure* if no factor has a higher weight than that of the prefix of the same length. Note that for some weight measures not every word has a unique prefix normal form. We prove basic properties of weight measures and weighted prefix normality and give a characterisation of weight measures for which every word has a prefix normal form. Finally, we define a standard weight measure which only depends on the alphabetic order of the letters and a unique *weighted prefix normal form* that does not depend on the choice of a weight measure.

Structure of the Paper. In Sect. 2, we define the basic terminology. Following that, in Sect. 3, we prove that weighted prefix normality is a proper generalisation of the binary case and present our results on the existence of a weighted prefix normal form. Finally, in Sect. 4, we present our main theorem on the standard weight measure, as well as the weighted prefix normal form.

2   Preliminaries

Let $\mathbb{N}$ denote the positive natural numbers $\{1, 2, 3, \dots\}$, $\mathbb{Z}$ the integer numbers, and $\mathbb{P} \subset \mathbb{N}$ the set of prime numbers. Set $\mathbb{N}_0 := \mathbb{N} \cup \{0\}$. For $i, j \in \mathbb{N}$, we define the interval $[i, j] := \{n \in \mathbb{N} \mid i \leq n \leq j\}$ and for $n \in \mathbb{N}$, we define $[n] := [1, n]$ and $[n]_0 := [0, n]$. For two monoids A and B with operations $*$ and $\circ$ respectively, a function $\mu : A \to B$ is a *morphism* if $\mu(x * y) = \mu(x) \circ \mu(y)$ holds for all $x, y \in A$. Note that if the domain A is a free monoid over some set S, a morphism from $A \to B$ is sufficiently defined by giving a mapping from S to B.

An *alphabet* Σ is a finite set of letters. A *word* is a finite sequence of letters from a given alphabet. Let Σ^* denote the set of all finite words over Σ, i.e., the free monoid over Σ. Let ε denote the *empty word* and set $\Sigma^+ := \Sigma^* \backslash \{\varepsilon\}$ as the free semigroup over Σ. We denote the length of a word $w \in \Sigma^*$ by $|w|$, i.e., the number of letters in w. Thus $|\varepsilon| = 0$ holds. Let w be a word of length $n \in \mathbb{N}$. Let $w[i]$ denote the ith letter of w for $i \in [|w|]$, and set $w[i \dots j] = w[i] \cdots w[j]$ for $i, j \in [|w|]$ and $i \leq j$. Let $w[i \dots j] = \varepsilon$ if $i > j$. The number of occurrences of a letter $\mathsf{a} \in \Sigma$ in w is denoted by $|w|_{\mathsf{a}} = |\{i \in [|w|] \mid w[i] = \mathsf{a}\}|$. We say $x \in \Sigma^*$ is a *factor* of w if there exist $u, v \in \Sigma^*$ with $w = uxv$. In this case u is called a *prefix* of w. We denote the set of w's factors (prefixes resp.) by $\text{Fact}(w)$ ($\text{Pref}(w)$ resp.) and $\text{Fact}_i(w)$ ($\text{Pref}_i(w)$ resp.) denotes the set of factors (prefixes) of length $i \in [|w|]$. Given a total order $<$ over Σ let $<_{\text{lex}}$ denote the extension of $<$ to a lexicographic order over Σ^*. Fixing a strictly totally ordered alphabet $\Sigma = \{\mathsf{a}_1, \mathsf{a}_2, \dots, \mathsf{a}_n\}$ with $\mathsf{a}_i < \mathsf{a}_j$ for $1 \leq i < j \leq n$, the *Parikh vector* of a word is defined by $p : \Sigma^* \to \mathbb{N}^n : w \mapsto (|w|_{\mathsf{a}_1}, |w|_{\mathsf{a}_2}, \dots, |w|_{\mathsf{a}_n})$. For a function f set $f(A) = \{f(a) \mid a \in A\}$ for $A \subseteq \text{dom}(f)$.

Before we define the weight measures and weighted prefix normality we recall the definition for binary prefix normality as introduced by Fici and Lipták in [17].

Definition 1. *([17]) Given $w \in \{0, 1\}^*$ the* maximum-ones function f_w *and the* prefix-ones function p_w *are respectively defined by* $f_w : [|w|]_0 \to \mathbb{N}_0$, $i \mapsto \max(|\text{Fact}_i(w)|_1)$ *and* $p_w : [|w|]_0 \to \mathbb{N}_0$, $i \mapsto |\text{Pref}_i(w)|_1$. *The word w is called* prefix normal *if $f_w = p_w$ holds.*

Our generalisation of binary prefix normality is based on *weight measures*, i.e., we apply weights represented by elements from a strictly totally ordered, cancellative monoid A to every letter of the alphabet. In the following we denote the neutral element of an arbitrary monoid A by $\mathbb{1}_A$, its operation by $\circ_A$, and its total order by $<_A$ (in the case of existence).

Definition 2. *Let A be a totally ordered and cancellative monoid. A morphism $\mu : \Sigma^* \to A$ is a* weight measure *over the alphabet Σ w.r.t. A if $\mu(vw) = \mu(wv)$ and $\mu(w) <_A \mu(wv)$ hold for all words $w \in \Sigma^*$ and $v \in \Sigma^+$. We refer to the second property as the* increasing *property. We say the weights of the letters of Σ are the* base weights *of μ, so $\mu(\Sigma)$ is the set of all* base weights.

Remark 3. Note that if there exists a weight measure μ w.r.t. the monoid A then $|A|$ is infinite, $\circ_A$ is commutative on $\mu(\Sigma^*)$, and $\mu(\varepsilon) = \mathbb{1}_A$ holds. Moreover, the increasing property of weight measures ensures that only the neutral element ε of Σ^* is mapped to the neutral element $\mathbb{1}_A$. Hence, we will see that our factor- and prefix-weight functions are strictly monotonically increasing, in contrast to the functions defined in [17]. However, if we allow letters from Σ to be also assigned the neutral weight $\mathbb{1}_A$, we get the known results for binary alphabets.

Remark 4. Note that a weight measure μ can be defined for any alphabet Σ in two steps: choose some infinite commutative monoid with a total and strict order and assign a base weight that is greater than the neutral element to each letter in Σ. Since μ is a morphism, the weight of a word $w \in \Sigma^*$ is well defined.

In the following definition we introduce seven (for us the most intuitive) special types of weight measures.

Definition 5. *A weight measure μ over the alphabet Σ w.r.t. the monoid A is*

⋄ injective *if μ is injective on Σ,*
⋄ alphabetically ordered *if $\mu(\mathsf{a}) \leq_A \mu(\mathsf{b})$ holds for all $\mathsf{a}, \mathsf{b} \in \Sigma$ with $\mathsf{a} \leq \mathsf{b}$ for a total order $\leq$ on Σ,*
⋄ binary *if $|\mu(\Sigma)| = 2$ holds, and* non-binary *if $|\mu(\Sigma)| > 2$,*
⋄ natural *if A is $\mathbb{N}_0$ or $\mathbb{N}$ with $<_A$ being the usual order $<$ on integers,*
⋄ a sum weight measure *if it is natural and the operation on A is $+$,*
⋄ a product weight measure *if it is natural and the operation on A is $*$,*
⋄ prime *if it is a product weight measure and $\mu(\Sigma) \subseteq \mathbb{P}$ holds.*

Consider, for instance, the alphabet $\Sigma = \{\mathsf{a}, \mathsf{b}, \mathsf{c}\}$. The weight measure μ over Σ with $\mu(\mathsf{a}) = 1$, $\mu(\mathsf{b}) = 2$, and $\mu(\mathsf{c}) = 3$ is *non-binary*, *natural*, and with the monoid $(\mathbb{N}_0, +)$ it is a *sum weight measure*. It cannot be a *product weight measure* with $(\mathbb{N}, *)$ since then $\mu(\mathsf{a}) = 1$ would violate the increasing property. However, the weight measure ν over Σ w.r.t. $(\mathbb{N}, *)$ with $\nu(\mathsf{a}) = 2$, $\nu(\mathsf{b}) = 3$, and $\nu(\mathsf{c}) = 5$ is not only a *product weight measure*, but also a *prime weight measure*.

Remark 6. For the binary alphabet $\Sigma = \{0, 1\}$ a sum weight measure μ with $\mu(w) = |w|_1$ for all $w \in \Sigma^*$ cannot exist since we would have $\mu(0) = 0 = \mu(\varepsilon)$ which is a contradiction to the increasing property. Later on we are going to circumvent this problem by setting $\mu(w) = |w|_1 + |w|$ for all $w \in \Sigma^*$ when implementing binary prefix normality via the usage of weight measures. Alternatively, we may relax the increasing property and allow $\mu(0) = 0$; this results exactly in the same properties as discussed in [17].

We now define the analogues to the maximum-ones and prefix-ones functions.

Definition 7. *Let $w \in \Sigma^*$ and μ be a weight measure over the alphabet Σ w.r.t. the monoid A. Define the* factor-weight function $f_{w,\mu}$ *and* prefix-weight function $p_{w,\mu}$ *respectively by* $f_{w,\mu} : [\![w]\!]_0 \to A$, $i \mapsto \max(\mu(\mathrm{Fact}_i(w)))$ *and* $p_{w,\mu} : [\![w]\!]_0 \to A$, $i \mapsto \mu(\mathrm{Pref}_i(w))$.

For instance, let μ be a sum weight measure with the base weights $\mu(\mathsf{a}) = 1$, $\mu(\mathsf{n}) = 2$, $\mu(\mathsf{b}) = 3$ for the alphabet $\Sigma = \{\mathsf{a}, \mathsf{n}, \mathsf{b}\}$.

Now consider the words banana and nanaba. Table 1 shows the mappings of their prefix- and factor-weight functions. The factor-weight function of nanaba is realised by the factors b, ab, nab, anab, nanab, nanaba.

i	1 2 3 4 5 6
$p_{\text{nanaba},\mu}(i)$	2 3 5 6 9 10
$f_{\text{nanaba},\mu}(i)$	3 4 6 7 9 10
$p_{\text{banana},\mu}(i)$, $f_{\text{banana},\mu}(i)$	3 4 6 7 9 10

Table 1. Comparing banana's and nanaba's prefix- and factor-weights.

Finally, we define a generalised approach for prefix normality, namely the *weighted prefix normality* for a given weight measure μ. As in the binary case, for a prefix normal word the factor-weight function and the prefix-weight function have to be identical.

Definition 8. *Let $w \in \Sigma^*$ and let μ be a weight measure over Σ. We say w is μ-prefix normal (or weighted prefix normal w.r.t. μ) if $p_{w,\mu} = f_{w,\mu}$ holds.*

In the example above we see $p_{\text{banana},\mu} = f_{\text{banana},\mu}$ holds and hence banana is prefix normal w.r.t. μ. On the other hand we have $p_{\text{nanaba},\mu}(1) = 2 < 3 = f_{\text{nanaba},\mu}(1)$ and therefore nanaba is not prefix normal w.r.t. μ.

3 Weighted Prefix Normal Words and Weighted Prefix Normal Form

In this section we show that *weighted prefix normality* is a proper generalisation of binary prefix normality and further investigate the weighted prefix normal form. By examining special properties of weight measures, we intend to guide the reader from the general approach to a characterisation of special weight measures for which every word has a weighted prefix normal equivalent, namely *injective and gapfree weight measures*. Before we define the analogue to the prefix-equivalence for factor weights, we show that weighted prefix normality is more general and more expressive than binary prefix normality, i.e., every statement on binary prefix normality can be expressed by weighted prefix normality but not vice versa.

Proposition 9. *Binary prefix normality is expressible by weighted prefix normality, i.e., there exists a weight measure μ such that μ-prefix normality is equivalent to binary prefix normality.*

With the binary sum weight measure μ over $\Sigma = \{0,1\}$ where $\mu(1) = 2$ and $\mu(0) = 1$, we can transform any statement on binary prefix normality into an analogue in the weighted setting. For example, for $w = 11001101$ we have $f_w(4) = 3$ and $p_w(4) = 2$ (so w is not prefix normal) and in the weighted setting we have $f_{w,\mu}(4) = 7 = f_w(4) + 4$ and $p_{w,\mu}(4) = 6 = p_w(4) + 4$; or in general $f_w(i) = f_{w,\mu}(i) - i$ holds for all $w \in \Sigma^*$ and $i \in [|w|]$. Therefore, w is μ-prefix normal if and only if it is prefix normal.

Definition 10. *Let μ be a weight measure over Σ. Two words $w, w' \in \Sigma^*$ are factor-weight equivalent w.r.t. μ (denoted by $w \sim_\mu w'$) if $f_{w,\mu} = f_{w',\mu}$ holds. We denote the equivalence classes by $[w]_{\sim_\mu} := \{w' \in \Sigma^* \mid w \sim_\mu w'\}$.*

In the following we highlight three peculiarities about the factor-weight equivalence that do not occur in the binary case: the existence of factor-weight equivalent words with *different Parikh vectors*, the existence of *multiple* words that are weighted prefix normal and factor-weight equivalent, and the *absence* of a factor-weight equivalent word that is weighted prefix normal. The words banana and nanaba over $\Sigma = \{a, n, b\}$ with the weight measure $\mu(a) = 1$, $\mu(n) = 2$, and $\mu(b) = 3$ are factor-weight equivalent. The complete equivalence class is given by $[banana]_{\sim_{\mu}} = \{ananab, anaban, abanan, nanaba, nabana, banana\}$. Note that all words in the class have the same Parikh vector but only banana is μ-prefix normal. If we were to add c to Σ and expand μ by $\mu(c) = \mu(n) = 2$ then $[banana]_{\sim_{\mu}}$ contains all words previously in it, but also those where some ns are substituted by c. So $[banana]_{\sim_{\mu}}$ contains four μ-prefix normal words, namely banana, bacana, banaca, and bacaca. Lastly, consider the sum weight measure ν over the alphabet $\Sigma = \{a, n, x\}$ with the base weights $\nu(a) = 1$, $\nu(n) = 2$, $\nu(x) = 4$. Now $[xaxn]_{\sim_{\nu}}$ only contains xaxn and its reverse nxax. Interestingly none of the two words are ν-prefix normal, witnessed by $f_{xaxn,\nu} = f_{nxax,\nu} = (4, 6, 9, 11)$, $p_{xaxn,\nu} = (4, 5, 9, 11)$, and $p_{nxax,\nu} = (2, 6, 7, 11)$ (the functions are written as sequences for brevity). In order for a weighted prefix normal word to exist in the class, a letter with weight $f_{xaxn,\nu}(3) - f_{xaxn,\nu}(2) = 9 - 6 = 3$ is missing. For example with such a letter b in Σ with $\nu(b) = 3$ the word xnbn is ν-prefix normal and in $[xaxn]_{\sim_{\nu}}$. These examples show that factor-weight equivalence classes can contain words with different Parikh vectors, multiple prefix normal words, and even no prefix normal words at all. We now investigate the question which weight measures lead to such peculiar equivalence classes and characterise the equivalence classes that contain a single weighted prefix normal word, a *normal form*, as it always exists for the binary case (see [17]).

Definition 11. *For $w \in \Sigma^*$ and a weight measure μ over Σ we define the μ-prefix normal subset of the factor-weight equivalence class of w by $\mathcal{P}_{\mu}(w) := \{v \in [w]_{\sim_{\mu}} \mid p_{v,\mu} = f_{v,\mu}\}$.*

In the example above, multiple prefix normal words in a single class are a direct result of ambiguous base weights, i.e., non-injective weight measure: all letters with the same weights are interchangeable in any word with no effect on the weight of that word; thus there exist multiple prefix normal words for such a word. By choosing an injective weight measure we can avoid this behaviour. However, the problematic case where some equivalence classes contain no prefix normal words at all, still remains. We give a characterisation of special, referred to as *gapfree*, weight measures and show that they guarantee the existence of a prefix normal word in every equivalence class of the factor-weight equivalence. Before we prove the claims just stated, we formally define the previous observations of *gaps*.

Definition 12. *A weight measure μ over the alphabet Σ w.r.t. the monoid A is gapfree if for all words $w \in \Sigma^*$ and all $i \in [\|w\|]$ there exists $a \in \Sigma$ such that $f_{w,\mu}(i) = f_{w,\mu}(i - 1) \circ_A \mu(a)$ holds. Otherwise, if for any word $w \in \Sigma^*$ and*

$i \in [\|w\|]$ there exists no $\mathsf{a} \in \Sigma$ such that $f_{w,\mu}(i) = f_{w,\mu}(i-1) \circ_A \mu(\mathsf{a})$ holds, we say μ is gapful and has a gap over the word w at the index i.

Consider, for example, the sum weight measure over $\Sigma = \{\mathsf{a}, \mathsf{b}, \mathsf{c}\}$ with $\mu(\mathsf{a}) = 2$, $\mu(\mathsf{b}) = 4$, and $\mu(\mathsf{c}) = 6$. We show that μ is gapfree by proving the existence of letters in Σ with weight $x_i = f_{w,\mu}(i) - f_{w,\mu}(i-1) \in \mathbb{N}$ for all $w \in \Sigma^*$ and $i \in [\|w\|]$. Since the factor-weight function is defined as a maximum, we get $x_i \leq \mu(\mathsf{c}) = 6$. On the other hand $x_i \geq \mu(\mathsf{a}) = 2$ because the factor-weight function is strictly increasing. Since all the base weights $\mu(\Sigma) = \{2, 4, 6\}$ are even, the same is true for $f_{w,\mu}(i)$ and $f_{w,\mu}(i-1)$. Thus, x_i has to be even as well. This implies $x_i \in \{2, 4, 6\} = \mu(\Sigma)$. Hence, there exist letters in Σ with the appropriate weight to fill every possible gap, i.e., μ is gapfree. As a counter example, the sum weight measure ν over Σ with $\nu(\mathsf{a}) = 1$, $\nu(\mathsf{b}) = 3$, and $\nu(\mathsf{c}) = 4$ is gapful. Consider the word $w = \mathsf{bcac}$ then ν has a gap over w at the index 3 since $f_{w,\nu}(3) = 9$ (witnessed by the factor cac) and $f_{w,\nu}(2) = 7$ (witnessed by the factor bc) and there is no letter with weight 2.

Coming back to the original question of multiple prefix normal words, the following theorem characterises exactly when an equivalence class contains zero, exactly one, or more than one weighted prefix normal word.

Theorem 13. *Let μ be a weight measure over Σ. Then*
- there exists $w \in \Sigma^*$ such that $|\mathcal{P}_\mu(w)| = 0$ iff μ is gapful,
- there exists $w \in \Sigma^*$ such that $|\mathcal{P}_\mu(w)| > 1$ iff μ is not injective, and
- for all $w \in \Sigma^*$ we have $|\mathcal{P}_\mu(w)| = 1$ iff μ gapfree and injective.

Definition 14. *Let μ be a gapfree and injective weight measure over Σ and let $w \in \Sigma^*$. Then $|\mathcal{P}_\mu(w)| = 1$ and its element is the μ-prefix normal form of w.*

Again with the alphabet $\Sigma = \{\mathsf{a}, \mathsf{n}, \mathsf{b}, \mathsf{x}\}$ and the sum weight measure μ over Σ with base weights $\mu(\mathsf{a}) = 1$, $\mu(\mathsf{n}) = 2$, $\mu(\mathsf{b}) = 3$, and $\mu(\mathsf{x}) = 4$ we have $\mathcal{P}_\mu(\mathsf{nanaba}) = \{\mathsf{banana}\}$ and $\mathcal{P}_\mu(\mathsf{xaxn}) = \{\mathsf{xnbn}\}$. So banana is the μ-prefix normal form of nanaba and xnbn is the μ-prefix normal form of xaxn. Additionally, note xaxn is an example of a word such that its Parikh vector is different from that of its prefix normal form.

Remark 15. Let μ be a gapfree and injective weight measure over the alphabet Σ w.r.t. the monoid A and $w \in \Sigma^*$. Then the μ-prefix normal form w' of w can be constructed inductively: $w'[1] = \mathsf{a}$ if $f_{w,\mu}(1) = \mu(\mathsf{a})$ and for all $i \in [\|w\|]$, $i > 1$ set $w'[i] = \mathsf{a} \in \Sigma$ if $f_{w,\mu}(i) = f_{w,\mu}(i-1) \circ_A \mu(\mathsf{a})$. In contrast, for a weight measure that is gapfree but *not* injective this inductive construction can be used to non-deterministically construct all prefix normal words within the factor-weight equivalence class of a word.

4   Gapfree Weight Measures

In this section we investigate the behaviour of gapfree weight measures in more detail. In order to present a natural and gapfree *standard weight measure* for ordered alphabets that is *equivalent* to every other injective, alphabetically ordered, and gapfree weight measure (over arbitrary monoids), and thus works as a representative, we give an alternative condition for gapfree weight measures; which we refer to as weight measures with *stepped based weights*.

First of all, by their definition we can infer that every binary weight measure is gapfree. Consequently we consider non-binary weight measures for the rest of this section.

Lemma 16. *All binary weight measures are gapfree.*

Remark 17. By Lemma 16, we see that when modelling binary prefix normality by means of weighted prefix normality we automatically have the existence of a unique binary prefix normal form as expected.

In the last section we saw that we have exactly one weighted prefix normal form in a factor-weight equivalence class if and only if the weight measure is injective and gapfree. We now give an alternative condition under which a weight measure is gapfree, which in most cases is easier to check. Later we will also see that this condition is part of a characterisation for gapfree weight measures.

Definition 18. *Let A be a strictly totally ordered monoid. A step function is a right action of an element $s \in A$ (the* step*) on A, i.e., $\sigma_s : A \to A; a \mapsto a \circ_A s$. The weight measure μ over Σ w.r.t the monoid A is said to have* stepped base weights *if there exists a step function σ_s for some $s \in A$ such that $\mu(\Sigma) = \{\sigma_s^i(\min(\mu(\Sigma))) \mid i \in [0, |\mu(\Sigma)| - 1]\}$ holds.*

In the previous example for $\Sigma = \{\mathsf{a}, \mathsf{b}, \mathsf{c}\}$, the gapfree sum weight measure μ over Σ with $\mu(\mathsf{a}) = 2$, $\mu(\mathsf{b}) = 4$, and $\mu(\mathsf{c}) = 6$ has stepped base weights with the step of 2. In contrast, the gapful sum weight measure ν over Σ with $\nu(\mathsf{a}) = 1$, $\nu(\mathsf{b}) = 3$, and $\nu(\mathsf{c}) = 4$ does not, because $\nu(\mathsf{b}) - \nu(\mathsf{a}) = 2$ but $\nu(\mathsf{c}) - \nu(\mathsf{b}) = 1$. In general, stepped base weights imply *gapfreeness* but not vice versa.

Proposition 19. *All weight measures with stepped base weights are gapfree.*

For further investigations of gapfree weight measures we define an equivalence on weight measures based on their behaviour on words of the same length.

Definition 20. *Let μ_A and μ_B be weight measures over the same alphabet Σ w.r.t. the monoids A and B. We say that μ_A and μ_B are equivalent if for all words $v, w \in \Sigma^n$, for all $n \in \mathbb{N}$, we have $\mu_A(v) <_A \mu_A(w)$ iff $\mu_B(v) <_B \mu_B(w)$.*

The reasoning behind such an equivalence of weight measures lies in the fact that using different but equivalent weight measures does not change their relative behaviour. Most notably, Definition 20 and the totality of the orders imply $\mu_A(v) = \mu_A(w)$ iff $\mu_B(v) = \mu_B(w)$ and therefore, the prefix normal form remains.

For instance, considering again the alphabet $\Sigma = \{\mathsf{a}, \mathsf{b}, \mathsf{c}\}$ and the gapfree sum weight measure μ over Σ with $\mu(\mathsf{a}) = 2$, $\mu(\mathsf{b}) = 4$, and $\mu(\mathsf{c}) = 6$ as well as the product weight measure ν over Σ with $\nu(\mathsf{a}) = 2$, $\nu(\mathsf{b}) = 6$, and $\nu(\mathsf{c}) = 18$. Then μ and ν are equivalent since they both are alphabetically ordered and $2 + 3^{\frac{\mu(w)}{2} - 1} = \nu(w)$ holds for all $w \in \Sigma^*$. Therefore, since μ is gapfree so is ν, and for instance $\mathcal{P}_\mu(\mathsf{bcac}) = \{\mathsf{cbbb}\} = \mathcal{P}_\nu(\mathsf{bcac})$ holds.

Proposition 21. *If μ and ν are equivalent weight measures, the prefix normal form of any word is the same w.r.t. equivalent weight measures, i.e., $\mathcal{P}_\mu(w) = \mathcal{P}_\nu(w)$ holds for all $w \in \Sigma^*$.*

Before we present the generalised weight measure, we prove three auxiliary lemmata and give the definition of the standard weight measure.

Lemma 22. *For any two equivalent weight measures, if one of them is gapfree, injective, or alphabetically ordered then so is the other.*

Finally, we define the *standard weight measure* as an injective gapfree weight measure that is innate to any strictly totally ordered alphabet.

Definition 23. *Let $\Sigma = \{a_1, a_2, \ldots, a_n\}$ be a strictly totally ordered alphabet, where $n \in \mathbb{N}$. We define the* standard weight measure μ_Σ *as the alphabetically ordered sum weight measure over Σ with base weights $\mu_\Sigma(a_i) = i$ for all $i \in [n]$.*

For instance, considering again the alphabet $\Sigma = \{a, b, c\}$ with the usual order, the standard weight measure μ_Σ has the base weights $\mu_\Sigma(a) = 1$, $\mu_\Sigma(a) = 2$, and $\mu_\Sigma(a) = 3$. And in the following, we will see that indeed μ_Σ is equivalent to both μ and ν from the previous example.

Lemma 24. *The standard weight measure is gapfree, injective, and alphabetically ordered.*

The definition of the equivalence on weight measures raises the question whether the standard weight measure is suitable as a representative for all gapfree, injective, and alphabetically ordered weight measures. If there were other equivalence classes of such weight measures then the standard weight measure would merely represent *one* of many choices. To answer this question we first present a peculiar property every gapfree weight measure has and then present our main theorem on the equivalence class of the standard weight measure.

Lemma 25. *Let μ be an injective and alphabetically ordered weight measure over Σ w.r.t. the monoid A. Let Σ be strictly totally ordered by $<_\Sigma$ and let $\Sigma = \{a_1, \ldots, a_n\}$ with $n \in \mathbb{N}_{>2}$ and $a_1 <_\Sigma a_2 <_\Sigma \cdots <_\Sigma a_n$. If μ has no gap over any word of the form cacb where $a <_\Sigma b <_\Sigma c \in \Sigma$ then $\mu(a_i a_{i+x}) = \mu(a_{i+y} a_{i+x-y})$ holds for all $i, x, y \in \mathbb{N}$ with $y < x$ and $i + x \leq n$.*

Theorem 26. *Let μ be a non-binary, injective, and alphabetically ordered weight measure over the alphabet Σ which is strictly ordered by $<_\Sigma$. The following statements are equivalent:*
1. *μ is gapfree.*
2. *μ has no gap over any word of the form cacb where $a <_\Sigma b <_\Sigma c \in \Sigma$.*
3. *μ is equivalent to the standard weight measure μ_Σ.*

Note, with (1. ⇔ 2.) in the above we know that any gapful weight measure
over $\Sigma = \{a, b, c\}$ already has a gap over bcac.
For instance, consider the sum weight measure
μ over Σ with $\mu(a) = 1$, $\mu(b) = 2$, and
$\mu(c) = 4$. We see that μ is gapful, since it has
a gap over the word $w = $ ccabccb at index 5,
witnessed by the factor-weight function $f_{w,\mu} =$
$(4, 8, 10, 12, 15, 19, 21)$ and the fact that there is
no letter with weight $15 - 12 = 3$. We visualise
this gap in Fig. 1. However, we already have a gap

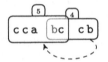

Fig. 1. Visualisation of the factor-weight function's gap for $w = $ ccabccb.

within the even shorter word bcac at index 3, witnessed by $f_{\text{bcac},\mu} = (4, 6, 9, 11)$.

On the other hand, with (1. ⇔ 3.) in Theorem 26 we immediately see there
only exists *one* equivalence class of gapfree, injective, and alphabetically ordered
weight measures w.r.t. the same alphabet, justifying our choice of μ_Σ as the standard weight measure. Also, since by transitivity all gapfree, injective, and alphabetically ordered weight measures w.r.t. to the same alphabet are equivalent,
they therefore yield the same prefix normal form (by Proposition 21). In other
words, assuming a strictly totally ordered alphabet, every word has exactly one
weighted prefix normal form that is independent of any chosen gapfree, injective,
and alphabetically ordered weight measure over the same alphabet. With that
in mind, paralleling the work presented by Fici and Lipták in [17], we introduce
the weighted prefix normal form of a word $w \in \Sigma^*$.

Definition 27. *Let Σ be a strictly totally ordered alphabet and let $w \in \Sigma^*$. We say the μ_Σ-prefix normal form is the weighted prefix normal form of w or simply the prefix normal form of w.*

For instance, consider the strictly totally ordered alphabet $\Sigma = \{a, b, c\}$, with
the standard weight measure μ_Σ such that $\mu_\Sigma(a) = 1, \mu_\Sigma(b) = 2, \mu_\Sigma(c) = 3$.
The weighted prefix normal form of bcac is cbbb, since $\mathcal{P}_{\mu_\Sigma}(\text{bcac}) = \{\text{cbbb}\}$
holds as seen in previous examples. With Theorem 26 the same also holds for
any other gapfree, injective, and alphabetically ordered weight measure.

Remark 28. By Theorem 26 we immediately see that the gapfree property of a
weight measure is decidable. Since any gapful weight measure already has a gap
over a word of length four using three letters, one can check whether a weight
measure is gapfree in the following way: test for all $\binom{|\Sigma|}{3}$ possible enumerations
of three letters $a <_\Sigma b <_\Sigma c$ whether there exist $x \in \Sigma$ with $\mu(bx) = \mu(ac)$. We
obtain a running time of $\mathcal{O}(|\Sigma|^4)$.

5   Conclusions

In this work we presented the generalisation of prefix normality on binary alphabets as introduced by [17] to arbitrary alphabets by applying weights to the
letters and comparing the weight of a factor with the weight of the prefix of the
same length.

Since one of the main properties of binary prefix normality, namely the existence of a unique prefix normal form, does not hold for weighted prefix normality with arbitrary weight measures, we investigated necessary restrictions to obtain a unique prefix normal form even in the generalised setting. Here, it is worth noting that we did not only generalise the size of the alphabet but also the weights are rather general: they belong to any (totally ordered) monoid. This is of interest because some peculiarities do not occur if $\mathbb{N}$ or $\mathbb{N}_0$ are chosen. In Sect. 3 we proved that there always exists a unique prefix normal form if the weight measure is gapfree and injective. In Sect. 4 we further demonstrated that all gapfree weight measures over the same alphabet are equivalent and therefore every word has the same weighted prefix normal form w.r.t. each of them. Which led to the definition of the standard weight measure and ultimately to a unique prefix normal form in the generalised setting that exists independent of chosen weight measures. Additionally, we showed that *gapfreeness* as a property of weight measures is decidable and can easily be checked in time $\mathcal{O}(|\Sigma|^4)$.

However, the exact behaviour of the weighted prefix normal form, or generally factor-weight equivalent words, especially regarding changes in their Parikh vectors, remains an open problem. Moreover, a reconnection of weighted prefix normality to the initial problem of indexed jumbled pattern matching would be of some interest and might prove useful when investigating pattern matching problems w.r.t. a non-binary alphabet.

Finally, we like to mention that an easier, but weaker, approach to work with prefix normality on arbitrary alphabets can be achieved by considering a subset X of Σ: each letter a in a word is treated like a 1 if a $\in X$ and 0 otherwise, which can also be expressed by weighted prefix normality.

References

1. Amir, A., Chan, T.M., Lewenstein, M., Lewenstein, N.: On hardness of jumbled indexing. In: Esparza, J., Fraigniaud, P., Husfeldt, T., Koutsoupias, E. (eds.) ICALP 2014. LNCS, vol. 8572, pp. 114–125. Springer, Heidelberg (2014). https://doi.org/10.1007/978-3-662-43948-7_10
2. Baláži, P., Masáková, Z., Pelantová, E.: Factor versus palindromic complexity of uniformly recurrent infinite words. Theor. Comput. Sci. **380**(3), 266–275 (2007)
3. Balister, P., Gerke, S.: The asymptotic number of prefix normal words. Theor. Comput. Sci. **784**, 75–80 (2019)
4. Bernat, J., Masáková, Z., Pelantová, E.: On a class of infinite words with affine factor complexity. Theor. Comput. Sci. **389**(1–2), 12–25 (2007)
5. Blanchet-Sadri, F., Seita, D., Wise, D.: Computing abelian complexity of binary uniform morphic words. Theor. Comput. Sci. **640**, 41–51 (2016)
6. Bucci, M., De Luca, A., Gien, A., Zamboni, L.Q.: A connection between palindromic and factor complexity using return words. Adv. Appl. Math. **42**(1), 60–74 (2009)
7. Burcsi, P., Cicalese, F., Fici, G., Lipták, Z.: Algorithms for jumbled pattern matching in strings. Int. J. Found. Comput. Sci. **23**(02), 357–374 (2012)
8. Burcsi, P., Fici, G., Lipták, Z., Raman, R., Sawada, J.: Generating a gray code for prefix normal words in amortized polylogarithmic time per word. Theoret. Comput. Sci. **842**, 86–99 (2020)

9. Burcsi, P., Fici, G., Lipták, Z., Ruskey, F., Sawada, J.: Normal, abby normal, prefix normal. In: Ferro, A., Luccio, F., Widmayer, P. (eds.) International Conference on Fun with Algorithms, pp. 74–88. Springer, Cham (2014). https://doi.org/10.1007/978-3-319-07890-8_7

10. Burcsi, P., Fici, G., Lipták, Z., Ruskey, F., Sawada, J.: On combinatorial generation of prefix normal words. In: Kulikov, A.S., Kuznetsov, S.O., Pevzner, P. (eds.) CPM 2014. LNCS, vol. 8486, pp. 60–69. Springer, Cham (2014). https://doi.org/10.1007/978-3-319-07566-2_7

11. Burcsi, P., Fici, G., Lipták, Z., Ruskey, F., Sawada, J.: On prefix normal words and prefix normal forms. Theor. Comput. Sci. **659**, 1–13 (2017)

12. Cassaigne, J., Fici, G., Sciortino, M., Zamboni, L.Q.: Cyclic complexity of words. J. Comb. Theor. Ser. A, 145, 36–56 (2017)

13. Cassaigne, J., Karhumäki, J., Saarela, A.: On growth and fluctuation of k-abelian complexity. In: Beklemishev, L.D., Musatov, D.V. (eds.) CSR 2015. LNCS, vol. 9139, pp. 109–122. Springer, Cham (2015). https://doi.org/10.1007/978-3-319-20297-6_8

14. Chan, T.M., Lewenstein, M.: Clustered integer 3SUM via additive combinatorics. In: Proceedings of the Forty-Seventh Annual ACM Symposium on Theory of Computing, pp. 31–40 (2015)

15. Cicalese, F., Lipták, Z., Rossi, M.: Bubble-flip–a new generation algorithm for prefix normal words. Theor. Comput. Sci. **743**, 38–52 (2018)

16. Cicalese, F., Lipták, Z., Rossi, M.: On infinite prefix normal words. Theor. Comput. Sci. **859**, 134–148 (2021)

17. Fici, G., Lipták, Z.: On prefix normal words. In: Mauri, G., Leporati, A. (eds.) DLT 2011. LNCS, vol. 6795, pp. 228–238. Springer, Heidelberg (2011). https://doi.org/10.1007/978-3-642-22321-1_20

18. Fleischmann, P., Kulczynski, M., Nowotka, D., Poulsen, D.B.: On collapsing prefix normal words. In: Leporati, A., Martín-Vide, C., Shapira, D., Zandron, C. (eds.) LATA 2020. LNCS, vol. 12038, pp. 412–424. Springer, Cham (2020). https://doi.org/10.1007/978-3-030-40608-0_29

19. Freydenberger, D.D., Gawrychowski, P., Karhumäki, J., Manea, F., Rytter, W.: Testing k-binomial equivalence (2015). arXiv preprint arXiv:1509.00622

20. OEIS Foundation Inc., The On-Line encyclopedia of integer sequences (2021). http://oeis.org/

21. Kociumaka, T., Radoszewski, J., Rytter, W.: Efficient indexes for jumbled pattern matching with constant-sized alphabet. In: Bodlaender, H.L., Italiano, G.F. (eds.) ESA 2013. LNCS, vol. 8125, pp. 625–636. Springer, Heidelberg (2013). https://doi.org/10.1007/978-3-642-40450-4_53

22. Lejeune, M., Leroy, J., Rigo, M.: Computing the k-binomial complexity of the Thue-Morse word. J. Comb. Theor. Ser. A **176**, 105284 (2020)

23. Leroy, J., Rigo, M., Stipulanti, M.: Generalized pascal triangle for binomial coefficients of words. Adv. Appl. Math. **80**, 24–47 (2016)

24. Richomme, G., Saari, K., Zamboni, L.Q.: Abelian complexity of minimal subshifts. J. London Math. Soc. **83**(1), 79–95 (2011)

25. Rigo, M., Salimov, P.: Another generalization of abelian equivalence: binomial complexity of infinite words. Theor. Comput. Sci. **601**, 47–57 (2015)

26. Shallit, J., Shur, A.: Subword complexity and power avoidance. Theor. Comput. Sci. **792**, 96–116 (2019). Special issue in honor of the 70th birthday of Prof. Wojciech Rytter

Two-Way Non-uniform Finite Automata

Fabian Frei[1], Juraj Hromkovič[1], Richard Královič[1], and Rastislav Královič[2(✉)]

[1] ETH, Zürich, Switzerland
{fabian.frei,juraj.hromkovic,richard.kralovic}@inf.ethz.ch
[2] Comenius University in Bratislava, Bratislava, Slovakia
kralovic@dcs.fmph.uniba.sk

Abstract. We consider two-tape automata where one tape contains the input word w, and the other contains an *advice string* $\alpha(|w|)$ for some function $\alpha : \mathbb{N} \to \Sigma^*$. Such an automaton recognizes a language L if there is an advice function for which every word on the input tape is correctly classified. This model has been introduced by Küçük with the aim to model non-uniform computation on finite automata. So far, most of the results concerned automata whose tapes are both 1-way. First, we show that making even one of the tapes 2-way increases the model's power. Then we turn our attention to the case of both tapes being 2-way, which can also be viewed as a restricted version of the non-uniform families of automata used by Ibarra and Ravikumar to define the class NUDSPACE. We show this restriction to be not very significant since, e.g., $\mathscr{L}(^{2r}_{2A}\text{DFA/poly})$, i.e., languages recognized by automata with 2-way input and advice tape with polynomial advice equals $\text{NUDSPACE}(O(\log(n)))$. Hence, we can show that many interesting problems concerning the state complexity of families of automata carry over to the problems concerning advice size of non-uniform automata. In particular, the question whether there can be a more than polynomial gap in advice between determinism and non-determinism is of great interest: e.g., the existence of a language that can be recognized by some 2-way NFA with some k heads on the advice tape and with polynomial (resp. logarithmic) advice, while a corresponding 2-head DFA would need exponential (resp. polynomial) advice, would imply $\text{L} \neq \text{NL}$ (resp. $\text{LL} \neq \text{NLL}$). We show that for advice of size $(\log n)^{o(1)}$ there is no gap between determinism and non-determinism. In general, we can show that the gap is not more than exponential.

1 Non-uniformity in Finite Automata

Uniformity, i.e., the property that a single, finitely described device is used to process inputs of infinitely many lengths is a central notion in the theory of computational models. Some models, like Turing machines, are inherently uniform, others, like circuits, are inherently non-uniform, and uniformity greatly

R. Královič—The research has been supported by the grant 1/0601/20 of the Slovak Scientific Grant Agency VEGA.

© Springer Nature Switzerland AG 2021
N. Moreira and R. Reis (Eds.): DLT 2021, LNCS 12811, pp. 155–166, 2021.
https://doi.org/10.1007/978-3-030-81508-0_13

influences both the power of the model, and the techniques that can be employed for its analysis. To investigate the role of uniformity, non-uniform versions of uniform models, and vice versa, have been extensively studied. A general way to define a non-uniform version of a uniform model is as follows: Instead of a machine M that recognizes a language $\mathcal{L}(M)$, one considers a family $\{M_n\}_{n \geq 0}$ of machines such that M_n recognizes the corresponding slice, i.e., $\mathcal{L}(M_n) \cap \Sigma^n = \mathcal{L}(M) \cap \Sigma^n$. Following Karp and Lipton's seminal paper [10], a non-uniform version of Turing machines, known as *oracle* machines, have become the standard. An oracle machine working with an *advice* function $f : \mathbb{N} \to \Sigma^*$ is a Turing machine that works on a tape on which the input word x is prefixed by the string $f(|x|)$. Since Turing machines are powerful enough to include the universal machine, the two definitions are obviously equivalent, but for weaker models, a Karp-Lipton-like definition should be weaker.

In this paper we focus on the non-uniform versions of finite automata since finite automata are considered the most basic computational devices whose understanding should be conducive to insight into more powerful models. When considering their non-uniform version based on families of automata, it is to be noted that since all slices $L \cap \Sigma^n$ are finite languages, a family of finite automata can recognize any language. Ibarra and Ravikumar [7] considered the state complexity of a family of 2-way automata to investigate sub-logarithmic non-uniform space complexity. Also closely related is the so called *minicomplexity*, a term coined by Kapoutsis [8] to describe the theory of state complexity of finite automata.

On the side of Karp-Lipton-like definitions, several models have been considered: Damm and Holzer [1] considered a direct analogue of oracle Turing machines with the advice word prefixed to the input. To overcome the bottleneck that only finite information can be carried between the advice string and the input word, the model introduced by Tadaki et al. [12] considers the advice written on a separate track. In this paper we adopt the model introduced by Küçük [11] where the advice string is written on a separate tape, allowing the automaton to simultaneously read different positions from the input and the advice words. A similar model has been proposed by Freivalds [5] with the additional property that an advice string that is valid for input words of length n must be also valid for all shorter words.

The model we consider has been investigated in a series of papers [2,3,11] for deterministic, non-deterministic, and randomized automata with 1-way input. However, results for 2-way automata have been scarce, and in this paper we provide more results about them. Our motivation for this is two-fold.

First, the non-uniform model behaves very differently from the uniform one in the sense that versions of automata that have the same expressive power in the uniform setting can exhibit significant differences in the non-uniform setting. E.g., there are languages that can be recognized by a 1-way non-deterministic automaton with a very little advice but cannot be recognized by a 1-way deterministic automaton, regardless of the amount of the advice [2]. We are trying to understand how the expressive power of the non-uniform model depends on the type of the automaton used. In this respect the 2-way automata are a natural choice to study.

Second, 2-way non-uniform automata can be viewed as a restricted version of non-uniform space complexity. In a relationship similar to that of an oracle machine to a family of Turing machines, in a non-uniform automaton the non-uniformity is restricted only to the contents of the advice tape. Of course, unlike Turing machines, finite automata are expected to become weaker with such a restriction. However, we show that for 2-way automata, this is not always true, as $\mathscr{L}(^{2\tau}_{2A}\text{DFA}/\text{poly}) = \mathsf{NUDSPACE}(\log)$, i.e., deterministic automata with 2-way input and 2-way advice of polynomial size recognize exactly the languages with logarithmic non-uniform space complexity (Corollary 1). This means that proving results about 2-way non-uniform automata could have consequences in complexity theory.

2   Model

We consider two-tape automata with one input tape and one advice tape, both containing words with delimiters on both ends. For an input word x, the advice tape contains an advice word $\alpha(|x|)$ (a 'best-case' advice that depends only on the length of the input).

For a formal definition we use the model of multi-tape automata; see, e. g., [4]. A non-deterministic finite two-tape automaton (NFA, for short) is a tuple $A = (Q, \Sigma_1, \Sigma_2, \delta, q_0, F)$, where Q is a finite set of states, Σ_1, Σ_2 are the finite alphabets of the two tapes, q_0 is the initial state, $F \subseteq Q$ is the set of accepting states, and the transition function is $\delta : Q \times (\Sigma_1 \cup \{\triangleright, \triangleleft\}) \times (\Sigma_2 \cup \{\triangleright, \triangleleft\}) \mapsto 2^{OUT}$, where $OUT = Q \times \{\rightarrow, \leftarrow, \perp\} \times \{\rightarrow, \leftarrow, \perp\}$. The meaning is the usual one: The transition is based on the current state of the automaton, and the symbols or end-delimiters scanned by both heads. The transition results in an action that changes the state, and possibly moves each of the heads independently to the following or preceding symbol. The automaton A accepts a word $(w_1, w_2) \in \Sigma_1^* \times \Sigma_2^*$ if there is an accepting computation of A starting from $(q_0, \triangleright w_1 \triangleleft, \triangleright w_2 \triangleleft)$. If $|\delta(q, a, b)| = 1$ for all $q \in Q$, $a \in \Sigma_1 \cup \{\triangleright, \triangleleft\}$, and $b \in \Sigma_2 \cup \{\triangleright, \triangleleft\}$, then the automaton is called deterministic (DFA).

For any automaton A, the recognized language is denoted by $\mathscr{L}(A)$. The symbol $\mathcal{X}$ denotes any class of considered automata: DFA or NFA. The non-uniformity is modeled according to [2,11], and the class of languages recognized by automata of type $\mathcal{X}$ with advice of size $f(n)$ is denoted by $\mathscr{L}(\mathcal{X})/f(n)$:

Definition 1. *Let $\mathcal{X}$ be a class of automata. Let $\alpha : \mathbb{N} \mapsto \Sigma_2^*$ be a function such that $\forall n, |\alpha(n)| = f(n)$. Let $\Sigma_1^{*\alpha} = \{(w, \alpha(n)) \mid w \in \Sigma_1^*, n = |w|\} \subseteq (\Sigma_1^* \times \Sigma_2^*)$. For a language $L \subseteq \Sigma_1^*$, let $L_\alpha = \{(w, \alpha(n)) \mid w \in L, n = |w|\} \subseteq (\Sigma_1^* \times \Sigma_2^*)$. Then a language L is recognized by an $\mathcal{X}$ automaton A with advice α if each word $(w_1, w_2) \in L_\alpha$ is accepted, and each word $(w_1, w_2) \in \Sigma_1^{*\alpha} - L_\alpha$ is not accepted. The class of recognized languages is*

$$\mathscr{L}(\mathcal{X})/f(n) := \{L \subseteq \Sigma_1^* \mid some\ A \in \mathcal{X}\ recognizes\ L\ with\ advice\ of\ length\ f(n)\}.$$

We write $\mathscr{L}(\mathcal{X})/*$ if the size of the advice is unlimited, and $\mathscr{L}(\mathcal{X})/\text{poly}$ if it is at most polynomial in the input length.

For $i, j \in \{1, 2\}$, we denote by $_{jA}^{iI}\text{DFA}$ (resp. $_{jA}^{iI}\text{NFA}$) the deterministic (resp. non-deterministic) automaton with i-way input tape and j-way advice tape. We always consider one input head. For $k > 1$ advice heads we write $_{jA}^{iI}\text{DFA}(k)$ (resp. $_{jA}^{iI}\text{NFA}(k)$).

We use the standard complexity classes. Following [8], we denote LL (resp. NLL) the counterpart of L (resp. NL) for space $O(\log\log n)$. For non-uniform complexity we follow the definition by Ibarra and Ravikumar (compare [7]):

Definition 2. *A language L has non-uniform space complexity $s(n)$ if there exists a collection $\{M_n\}_{n \geq 1}$ of 2-way DFAs such that M_n has at most $2^{s(n)}$ states, and $\mathscr{L}(M_n) \cap \Sigma^n = L \cap \Sigma^n$. The set of languages with non-uniform space complexity $s(n)$ is denoted* NUDSPACE$(s(n))$.

Note that the original definition aimed at asymptotic complexity, so instead of $2^{s(n)}$ states it required $2^{O(s(n))}$ states. For our purposes, we need to be slightly more precise. Closely connected to non-uniform space complexity is *minicomplexity*, a term coined by Kapoutsis [8] for the theory of state complexity of finite automata. A problem is formalized as a family of languages $\{L_p\}_{p \geq 1}$ parameterized by a parameter p. The problem is solved with state complexity $s(p)$ by a family of automata $\{M_p\}_{p \geq 1}$ such that $\mathscr{L}(M_i) = L_i$, and M_i has at most $s(p)$ states. The distinction of non-uniform space complexity is that the languages in the considered family are all finite languages parameterized by the length of the words in the respective language, whereas in minicomplexity the languages may be arbitrary. However, several minicomplexity results concern families of languages with bounded size. E.g., a notable result is

Theorem 1 ([8,9]).   SHORTTWL$\in$ 2D $\iff$ L/poly $\supseteq$ NL.

Here, SHORTTWL is a family of languages where the ith language TWL$_i$ contains the (binary-encoded) instances of 2-way liveness of height i and length at most polynomial in i (so it is a finite language). One can pad the words of TWL$_i$ to have a distinct common length, so Definition 2 can be used.

3   Previous Work

The model we use has been studied in a series of papers [2,3,11]. The main focus has been on deterministic, non-deterministic, and randomized automata with 1-way input and 1-way advice. Generally, increasing the advice size up to polynomial size (resp. $n2^n$) for deterministic and randomized (resp. non-deterministic) automata increases the power, larger advice does not help. Also, one cannot in general trade determinism or randomization for larger advice. With enough advice, the automata can usually recognize all languages; notable exceptions are 1-way DFAs and 1-way PFAs. Here we present a selection of known facts that are relevant for this paper:

$$[11] \quad \mathscr{L}(^{1r}_{1A}\mathrm{DFA}(2))/n2^n = \mathscr{L}(^{2r}_{1A}\mathrm{DFA})/n2^n = \mathsf{ALL} \tag{1}$$

$$[11] \quad \forall k : \ \mathscr{L}(^{1r}_{1A}\mathrm{DFA})/n^k \subsetneq \mathscr{L}(^{1r}_{1A}\mathrm{DFA})/n^{k+1} \tag{2}$$

$$[3,11] \quad \mathscr{L}(^{1r}_{1A}\mathrm{DFA})/* \subsetneq \mathscr{L}(^{2r}_{1A}\mathrm{DFA})/O(n^2) \tag{3}$$

$$\text{because } \{ww\} \in \mathscr{L}(^{2r}_{1A}\mathrm{DFA})/O(n^2) - \mathscr{L}(^{1r}_{1A}\mathrm{DFA})/*.$$

$$[2] \quad \mathscr{L}(^{1r}_{1A}\mathrm{NFA})/n2^n = \mathsf{ALL} \tag{4}$$

$$[3] \quad \mathscr{L}(^{1r}_{1A}\mathrm{DFA})/poly = \mathscr{L}(^{1r}_{1A}\mathrm{DFA})/* \tag{5}$$

$$[2] \quad \forall f(n) \in \omega(1) : \ \mathscr{L}(^{1r}_{1A}\mathrm{NFA})/o(f(n)) \not\subseteq \mathscr{L}(^{1r}_{1A}\mathrm{DFA})/* \tag{6}$$

$$[2] \quad \text{Let } g(n) \le n2^{\frac{n}{2}}, \text{ and } f(n)\log(f(n)) = o(g(n)).$$
$$\text{Then } \mathscr{L}(^{1r}_{1A}\mathrm{NFA})/g(n) - \mathscr{L}(^{1r}_{2A}\mathrm{NFA})/f(n) \ne \emptyset. \tag{7}$$

$$[2] \quad \text{Let } f(n) \le n, \text{ and } g(n) = o(f(n)).$$
$$\text{Then } \mathscr{L}(^{1r}_{1A}\mathrm{DFA})/f(n) \not\subseteq \mathscr{L}(^{1r}_{1A}\mathrm{NFA})/g(n). \tag{8}$$

In particular, if both input and advice are 1-way, we know (6) that an arbitrarily slowly growing advice is sufficient for $^{1r}_{1A}$NFAs to recognize languages that are not in $\mathscr{L}(^{1r}_{1A}\mathrm{DFA})/*$. On the other hand, (8) for sub-linear advice even a slight increase of the advice gives $^{1r}_{1A}$DFA s power outside that of $^{1r}_{1A}$NFAs.

4 The Power of Two-Way Advice

In this section we study how the 2-way tapes (input and/or advice) affect the power of automata. It has been known that 2-way input increases the power of DFAs significantly: $^{2r}_{1A}$DFAs can, with enough advice, recognize all languages (1), but the language $\{ww\} \in \mathscr{L}(^{2r}_{1A}\mathrm{DFA}/O(n^2))$ cannot be recognized by $^{1r}_{1A}$DFAs with any advice (3).

We ask how much power 2-way advice can add. For 1-way input, bigger advice cannot be fully compensated by making the advice 2-way (7). On the other hand, we show now that even arbitrarily small non-constant 2-way advice is sufficient, even for a DFA with 1-way input, to recognize languages for which even an NFA with 2-way input needs linear 1-way advice.

Theorem 2. *Let $s(n)$ be any growing function. Then there is a language L such that $L \in \mathscr{L}(^{1r}_{2A}\mathrm{DFA})/s(n)$ but $L \notin \mathscr{L}(^{2r}_{1A}\mathrm{NFA})/o(n)$.*

Proof. Without loss of generality suppose that $s(n) = o(n)$. Consider the following language L: For each n, L contains a single word of length n, namely the prefix of length n of the sequence $0^{s(n)}1^{s(n)}0^{s(n)}\cdots$. Suppose that L is recognized by a $^{2r}_{1A}$NFA automaton A with r states, working with advice of size $o(n)$. Let Δ be a suitable constant (depending only on r) specified later. Fix a sufficiently large n, and consider the single word $w \in L$ of length n. Partition w into n/Δ blocks of size Δ, and disregard all blocks that contain both 0 and 1. Since there are at most $n/s(n) = o(n)$ blocks containing both 0 and 1 overall, we end up regarding $\Omega(n)$ blocks. Now consider a shortest accepting computation ξ of A on w. Each position i on the input tape may be visited many times in this computation; call a position i *clean*, if the advice head is never moved during any of the visits. Since the advice tape is 1-way and the advice size is $o(n)$, there are $\Omega(n)$ blocks containing clean positions exclusively. Consider any such clean block B. Call *window* any maximal subsequence of ξ that moves the head within B. For each window, we call the *interface* the tuple consisting of the following: the letter on the advice tape, the incoming direction of the input head (i.e., whether the block is entered from left or from right), the state when entering B, the outgoing direction of the input head, and the state when leaving B. Overall, there are $8r^2$ interfaces. We can easily alter ξ in such a way that in each block A's behavior is identical for all windows with the same interface. Now consider an arbitrary position $i \in \{1, \ldots, \Delta\}$ within B. In each window, there is a crossing sequence of states at position i, and there are at most $c := r^{O(r)}$ distinct crossing sequences. Since the crossing sequence depends only on the interface of the window, the position i can be described by its *characteristic*, which is an $8r^2$-tuple of crossing sequences (one for each interface). Choosing a $\Delta > c^{8r^2}$ ensures that there are two positions i_B and j_B within each clean block B with the same characteristics. The interval in the input word between these positions can be cut out or duplicated without affecting the outcome of the computation. However, care must be taken, since altering the length of the input word alters the advice as well. However, for a clean block B there are only Δ possibilities for the length of the interval between i_B and j_B. Since Δ is constant, for large enough n there are two clean blocks B and B' with $j_B - i_B = j_{B'} - i_{B'}$. Cutting out one interval and duplicating the other produces a word not in L with an accepting computation.

Finally, it is trivial to see how L can be recognized using 2-way advice of size $s(n)$, so the theorem follows. $\qquad\square$

5 Relation to Non-uniform Space Complexity

As we discussed in the introduction, 2-way non-uniform automata can be seen as a restricted model of non-uniform space complexity. On the one hand, any language has non-uniform space complexity at most $O(n)$, and also any language over a binary alphabet can be recognized by a $^{2r}_{2A}$DFA with advice $O(n2^n)$. On the other hand, clearly $\mathsf{NUDSPACE}(O(1)) = \mathscr{L}(^{2r}_{2A}\mathrm{DFA}/O(1))$. We are interested in the relation to non-uniform space complexity for the intermediate values.

Lemma 1. *Languages from $\mathscr{L}(^{2r}_{2A}\mathrm{DFA}(k))/s(n)$ can be recognized by a family of DFAs with $O(s(n)^k)$ states, i. e., have non-uniform space complexity at most $k \log s(n) + O(1)$.*

Proof. Suppose there is a 2-way DFA A with advice of size $s(n)$, with k heads on the advice tape. Fix n. We construct a 2-way 1-head DFA A' recognizing the same slice of n-letter words. The states of A' will consist of tuples $\langle c_1, c_2, \ldots, c_k, q \rangle$ where the c_i's represent positions of A's advice heads and q is A's state. For each letter a, the transition from $\langle c_1, c_2, \ldots, c_k, q \rangle$ is constructed based on the values of the advice (which is fixed for fixed n) on the corresponding positions. $\qquad\square$

Lemma 2. *Let L be a language with non-uniform space complexity $s(n)$. Then*

$$L \in \mathscr{L}(_{2A}^{2r}\mathrm{DFA}(2))/O(s(n)2^{s(n)}).$$

Proof. Since the non-uniform space complexity of L is $s(n)$, there is, for each n, an automaton M_n with $2^{s(n)}$ states that recognizes the corresponding slice of L. We construct an automaton A with two heads on the advice tape working with advice in such a way that for each n the advice contains a description of M_n such that A is able to simulate it.

The advice tape is divided into *blocks*, each block describing one state of M_n. The blocks are separated by delimiters. Each block starts with a *header* encoding the number of the current state in binary, and then contains two *actions*, one for each letter of the alphabet. An action consists of a binary encoding of the number of the new state, and constant-sized information about the movement of the input head.

In the simulation, A keeps the input head on the input position of M_n, and the first advice head on the beginning of the block corresponding to the current state of M_n. Based on the input letter, A finds the corresponding action block and moves the input head appropriately. It then uses the second advice head to scan through all blocks on the advice tape and locate the one that matches the new block specified by the current action. Technically, each block can encode the three parts (the header and the two actions) in space $O(s(n))$ using a self-delimited encoding. For the size of the advice tape note that there are $2^{s(n)}$ blocks (equal to the number of states). □

The observations by Ibarra and Ravikumar [7] directly yield a hierarchy result for $_{2A}^{2r}\mathrm{DFA}$: Let f be any increasing function such that $f(n) \le n/2$. Consider the language $L_f = \{ww0^i \mid |w| = f(n),\ i = n - 2f(n)\}$. Following the arguments by Ibarra and Ravikumar [7] one can observe that L_f cannot be recognized by a family of automata with $o(f(n)/\log(f(n)))$ states. Following Lemma 1 $L_f \notin \mathscr{L}(_{2A}^{2r}\mathrm{DFA})/(o(f(n)/\log(f(n))))$. On the other hand, it is easy to see that $L_f \in \mathscr{L}(_{2A}^{2r}\mathrm{DFA})/f(n)$.

Note that there is still a gap between the simulations: E.g., for $_{2A}^{2r}\mathrm{DFA}(2)$, advice of size $s(n)$ yields a family with $s(n)^2$ states, but a family with $s(n)^2$ states yields advice of size $O(s(n)^2 \log s(n))$. However, the two lemmas are sufficient to translate several questions from minicomplexity into the language of non-uniform automata. E.g., if one shows that the version of the 2-way liveness language from Theorem 1 requires more than polynomial advice for $_{2A}^{2r}\mathrm{DFA}(2)$, from Lemma 2 one can conclude that $\mathsf{L/poly} \not\supseteq \mathsf{NL}$.

The previous result needed 2 advice heads in order to maintain the counters. For short advice, however, the input head can be used as one counter, so we can save one head at the expense of larger advice:

Lemma 3. *Let L be a language with space complexity $s(n) \le k \log n$ for some k. Then $L \in \mathscr{L}(_{2A}^{2r}\mathrm{DFA})/O(n^{2k+1})$.*

Proof. The proof goes the same way as the previous one, only this time the advice tape contains a block for each pair of state and input position; so there are altogether $n2^{s(n)}$ blocks. The blocks are arranged in such a way that the blocks for a given input position form a consecutive sequence. Each block contains a unary counter storing the current input position, and two actions. An action consists of a unary counter indicating how many blocks the head should move. Due to the ordering of the blocks, each action can move the current block only among $2 \cdot 2^{s(n)}$ neighboring blocks; the input head can move at most by one. Hence, we get $n + 4 \cdot 2^{s(n)}$ for the length of a block. Overall, the size of the advice is $O(n2^{s(n)}(n + 2^{s(n)})) = O(n^{2k+1})$ since $s(n) \leq k \log n$.

During the simulation, A uses the input head to store the counter from the action; note that the input tape is long enough for that. Then it recovers the input head using the counter in the target block.   □

Lemma 3 together with Lemma 1 give the following

Corollary 1. *We have* $\mathscr{L}(^{2r}_{2A}\mathrm{DFA}/\mathrm{poly}) = \mathsf{NUDSPACE}(O(\log(n)))$.

6   Determinism Vs Non-determinism

The relation between determinism and non-determinism is a central question in many computational models. For 1-way non-uniform automata the situation is easier, since the deterministic automata are less expressive than their non-deterministic counterparts. Even arbitrarily small non-constant advice makes non-determinism stronger than determinism with unlimited advice (6).

In this section we consider 2-way automata. In this case, both deterministic and non-deterministic automata can recognize all languages, so the central question is the increase in the advice size between non-determinism and determinism. First, we show that for advice of size $(\log n)^{O(1)}$ there is no difference between determinism and non-determinism, basically due to the fact that $\mathsf{NSPACE}(o(\log \log n)) = \mathsf{REG}$. Note, however, that no such threshold is in the $\mathsf{NUDSPACE}$ class where the hierarchy continues all the way down to $O(1)$ [7].

Definition 3. *Let A be a (deterministic or non-deterministic) automaton working with advice of size $s(n) \leq n$. Consider an input word $x = x_1, \ldots, x_n$. First, pad the word by some special blank symbol so that the new length n' is divisible by $s(n)$. Let the advice for length n be $a_1 a_2 \cdots a_{s(n)}$. We call* extended word x *the word $ext(x) = x_1 a_1 x_2 a_2 \cdots x_{s(n)} a_{s(n)} x_{s(n)+1} a_1 x_{s(n)+2} a_2 \cdots x_{n'} a_{s(n)}$. Note that $2n \leq |ext(x)| \leq 2(n + s(n))$.*

We shall interpret $ext(x)$ as a two-track word (of length between n and $n + s(n)$) where consecutive copies of the advice string are placed on top of the input word:

a_1	a_2	a_3	a_4	a_5	a_1	a_2	a_3	a_4	a_5	a_1	a_2	a_3	a_4	a_5	a_1	a_2	a_3	a_4	a_5
x_1	x_2	x_3	x_4	x_5	x_6	x_7	x_8	x_9	x_{10}	x_{11}	x_{12}	x_{13}	x_{14}	x_{15}	x_{16}	x_{17}	B	B	B

Two-track version of $ext(x)$ where $x = x_1 \cdots x_{17}$ and the advice for $n = 17$ is $a_1 \cdots a_5$.

We use the standard definition of promise problems as a pair $(\mathsf{YES}, \mathsf{NO})$ of sets of positive and negative instances. We can also assume that the advice is self-delimited, i. e., a Turing machine can determine the value $s(n)$ for $ext(x)$ in space $\log(s(n))$.

Lemma 4. *Let A be a $_{2_A}^{2_T}\mathrm{NFA}(k)$ working with advice of size $s(n)$ and recognizing some language L. Then there is an $\mathsf{NSPACE}(\log s(n))$ Turing machine recognizing the promise problem $(\{ext(x) \mid x \in L\}, \{ext(x) \mid x \notin L\})$.*

Proof. Consider the following non-deterministic Turing machine M_A that will, on a two-track word $ext(x)$ simulate the computation of A on x. M_A will keep A's state in internal memory, and will use k counters $c_1, \ldots, c_k$, each storing an integer up to $s(n)$, to represent the positions of A's advice heads. Specifically, the counter c_i stores the distance from the current input head position (on $ext(x)$) to a position where the upper track contains the same letter as read by the ith advice head of A on x.

M_A works in rounds. At the beginning of each round, M_A fetches the advice symbols read by the respective heads using the counters $c_1, \ldots, c_k$, and returns the head to the current input position. This can be done with the use of an extra auxiliary counter. M_A then non-deterministically chooses a transition of A, updates the counters $c_1, \ldots, c_k$, the internal state, and moves the input head. The counter updates are done in modulo $s(n)$, which can be done because M_A can recover the value of $s(n)$ from the self-delimited advice.   □

Theorem 3. *Let s be any non-decreasing function such that $s(n) = (\log n)^{o(1)}$. Then for any fixed $k \geq 1$, we have $\mathscr{L}(_{2_A}^{2_T}\mathrm{NFA}(k))/s(n) = \mathscr{L}(_{2_A}^{1_T}\mathrm{DFA})/s(n)$.*

Proof. The "$\supseteq$" is trivial. For the other direction, consider a $_{2_A}^{2_T}\mathrm{NFA}(k)$ automaton A recognizing some language L with some advice α of size $s(n)$. From Lemma 4 it follows that there is an $\mathsf{NSPACE}(\log s(n))$ Turing machine M_A accepting all words $ext(x)$ for $x \in L$, and rejecting all words $ext(x)$ for $x \notin L$. However, since the space of M_A is $O(\log s(n)) = o(\log \log n)$, due to [6] it recognizes some regular language. Hence, there is a 1-way DFA A' such that $ext(x) \in \mathscr{L}(A')$ for all $x \in L$ and $ext(x) \notin \mathscr{L}(A')$ for all $x \notin L$.

Finally, a $_{2_A}^{1_T}\mathrm{DFA}$ B with advice α can simulate A' on words $ext(x)$ by supplementing A' with a virtual tape containing $ext(x)$: B starts by serving the symbols from input and advice tape in an alternating order, when the advice head reaches the end, B rewinds it and starts from the beginning.   □

We have seen that for small advice, there is no difference between determinism and non-determinism. For larger advices, however, the question becomes more difficult since we have:

Theorem 4. *If $\mathsf{DSPACE}(\log s(n)) = \mathsf{NSPACE}(\log s(n))$, then for any fixed $k \geq 1$ it holds that $\mathscr{L}(_{2_A}^{2_T}\mathrm{NFA}(k))/s(n) \subseteq \mathscr{L}(_{2_A}^{2_T}\mathrm{DFA}(2))/poly(s(n))$.*

Proof. Let $L \in \mathscr{L}(_{2_A}^{2_T}\mathrm{NFA}(k))/s(n)$ be given. Following Lemma 4 there is an $\mathsf{NSPACE}(\log s(n))$ Turing machine – whose exact space depends on k; it is at least $(k + 1) \log s(n)$ – accepting all words $ext(x)$ for $x \in L$, and rejecting all words $ext(x)$ for $x \notin L$. From the theorem's hypothesis it follows that there exist an equivalent DSPACE$(\log s(n))$ machine M_A. (Note that since the definition of DSPACE involves asymptotic notation, we are not able to determine the exact degree of the polynomial in the statement of the theorem.)

We shall simulate M_A on a $_{2A}^{2T}$DFA(2) with advice. The advice tape will consists of blocks; there is one block for each combination of the possible content of the working tape of M_A, the position of the working head, and the input position (on the two-track word $ext(x)$) modulo $s(n)$. Hence, if M_A has a working tape of size $m = O(\log s(n))$, there are $N = 2^m m s(n)$ blocks. Each block starts by a binary encoding of its number, the letter read by the working head, the advice letter on the upper track – which is fully determined by the position of the input head modulo $s(n)$ –, and a block number representing the action of M_A for each possible input letter.

The $_{2A}^{2T}$DFA(2) machine keeps the position of the input head (on the word x) the same as the position of M_A's input head (on the two-track word $ext(x)$), and the first advice head is located at the beginning of the corresponding block. The second advice head is used to navigate to the appropriate block.

The length of a block is $O(\log N)$, so the overall length of the advice is $O(N \log N) = O(2^m m s(n)(m + \log m + \log s(n))) = poly(s(n))$.   □

This means, for example, that the existence of a language that can be recognized by an NFA with some k advice heads with polynomial (resp. logarithmic) advice, while a corresponding 2-head DFA would need exponential (resp. polynomial) advice, would imply L $\neq$ NL (resp. LL $\neq$ NLL).

Again, for short advices we can save one head in the simulation by using the input head as a counter:

Theorem 5. *Let $s(n) = n^{o(1)}$. If* DSPACE$(\log s(n))$ = NSPACE$(\log s(n))$, *then for any fixed $k \geq 1$ it holds that* $\mathscr{L}(_{2A}^{2T}\text{NFA}(k))/s(n) \subseteq \mathscr{L}(_{2A}^{2T}\text{DFA})/n^2 poly(s(n))$.

Proof. The proof goes the same way as in the previous theorem, only this time there will be one block for each combination of the content of the working tape, the position of the working head, and the input position (not modulo $s(n)$), so that overall there are $N = nm2^m$ blocks (where $m \leq c \log s(n)$ for some c is the space of the DSPACE machine M_A). A block does not contain its binary number but contains a unary encoding of the input head position. Also, the pointers in the actions in each block are encoded in unary. The blocks are sorted according to the input position, so each action requires to navigate to a block in the neighborhood of $m2^m$ from the current block. That means that the unary counters in the block are of length at most $m2^m \leq c \log s(n) s(n)^c \leq c'n$ for some c' since $s(n) = n^{o(1)}$. Hence, it is possible to navigate using the input head.

The overall length of the advice is $O(Nm2^m) = n^2 poly(s(n))$.   □

This means that, for example, the existence of a language that can be recognized with logarithmic advice by some NFA with k heads but would require more than $n^2 polylog(n)$ advice for a 1-head DFA, would imply LL $\neq$ NLL.

As the previous discussion shows, we would like to know if there can be a superpolynomial gap in advice between determinism and non-determinism of automata with 2-way advice and input. We can prove that the gap cannot be more that exponential:

Theorem 6. *For each fixed k, and each $s(n)$ it holds that*

$$\mathscr{L}(_{2_A}^{2_I}\text{NFA}(k))/s(n) \subseteq \mathscr{L}(_{2_A}^{2_I}\text{DFA}(2))/2^{O(s(n)^{2k})}.$$

Proof (sketch). Let $\text{DSPACE}(f(n))/s(n)$ be the class of Turing machines with working tape of size $O(f(n))$ and advice tape of size $s(n)$. Conceptually, the proof can be split in two steps.

First show that $\mathscr{L}(_{2_A}^{2_I}\text{NFA}(k))/s(n) \subseteq \text{DSPACE}(s(n)^{2k})/s(n)$. This can be done by observing that a configuration of the $_{2_A}^{2_I}\text{NFA}(k)$ when reading the ith input is described by the state and the positions of the k advice heads. The Turing machine can use the same advice as the $_{2_A}^{2_I}\text{NFA}(k)$ and in space $O(s(n)^{2k})$ perform a construction similar to the known 2NFA→1DFA crossing-sequence-based transformation.

Next, prove $\text{DSPACE}(f(n))/s(n) \subseteq \mathscr{L}(_{2_A}^{2_I}\text{DFA}(2))/s(n)\log(s(n))2^{O(f(n))}$. To see this, note that for a given position on the input tape, the configuration of the Turing machine is described by the content of the working tape and the position on the advice tape. The advice of the $_{2_A}^{2_I}\text{DFA}(2)$ consists of $s(n)2^{f(n)}$ blocks, each of length $O(f(n) + \log(s(n)))$, each block containing the content of the working tape (including the head position and the state), a binary encoding of the position on the advice tape, and the letter on the advice tape of the Turing machine. The automaton maintains the input head on the same position as the Turing machine, uses one advice head to keep track of the current configuration, and the other head to scan for the appropriate transition. Since the machine is deterministic, this can be done with one head. □

7   Conclusion and Further Research

Since majority of the results about the non-uniform automata targeted the 1-way tapes, we were interested to see what happens if the tapes are allowed to be 2-way. It was known that making the input tape 2-way increases the expressive power. We showed that also making the advice tape 2-way yields a more powerful model. A more detailed analysis could follow to show the relationship among the advice sizes. E.g., we know that $\mathscr{L}(_{1_A}^{1_I}\text{DFA})/n2^n = \text{ALL} \supsetneq \mathscr{L}(_{1_A}^{1_I}\text{DFA})/*$, but what can be said about $\mathscr{L}(_{1_A}^{2_I}\text{DFA})/\text{poly}$? Is it possible to extend Theorem 2 to address languages from $\mathscr{L}(_{1_A}^{2_I}\text{NFA})/\Omega(n)$?

Further, we examined the connection between minicomplexity (resp. non-uniform space complexity) and non-uniform automata (e. g., Corollary 1), essentially showing that restricting the non-uniformity to the content of the advice tape (instead of having an arbitrary transition function) is not a fundamental change. This is especially true if the automaton is allowed several advice heads, but even automata with one advice head are rich enough to pose questions with direct consequences to important complexity-theoretic open problems (e. g. Theorem 5 and relation to LL vs NLL).

The main question for the 2-way automata seems to be the gap between determinism and non-determinism. For advice $(\log n)^{o(1)}$ there is no difference between determinism and non-determinism, and in general the gap is at most exponential. Showing a superpolynomial gap for $^{2r}_{2_A}\text{DFA}(2)$ would have huge consequences, but a more modest result may be feasible, e. g., along the lines of

Conjecture 1. There is a language $L \in \mathscr{L}(^{2r}_{2_A}\text{NFA})/O(\log n)$ such that $L \notin \mathscr{L}(^{2r}_{2_A}\text{DFA})/o(n/\log n)$.

References

1. Damm, C., Holzer, M.: Automata that take advice. In: Wiedermann, J., Hájek, P. (eds.) MFCS 1995. LNCS, vol. 969, pp. 149–158. Springer, Heidelberg (1995). https://doi.org/10.1007/3-540-60246-1_121

2. Duriš, P., Korbaš, R., Královič, R., Královič, R.: Determinism and nondeterminism in finite automata with advice. In: Böckenhauer, H.-J., Komm, D., Unger, W. (eds.) Adventures Between Lower Bounds and Higher Altitudes. LNCS, vol. 11011, pp. 3–16. Springer, Cham (2018). https://doi.org/10.1007/978-3-319-98355-4_1

3. Ďuriš, P., Královič, R., Královič, R., Pardubská, D., Pašen, M., Rossmanith, P.: Randomization in non-uniform finite automata. In: Esparza, J., Král', D. (eds.) 45th International Symposium on Mathematical Foundations of Computer Science, MFCS 2020, 24–28 August 2020, Prague, Czech Republic. LIPIcs, vol. 170, pp. 30:1–30:13. Schloss Dagstuhl - Leibniz-Zentrum für Informatik (2020)

4. Fischer, P.C., Rosenberg, A.L.: Multitape one-way nonwriting automata. J. Comput. Syst. Sci. **2**(1), 88–101 (1968)

5. Freivalds, R.: Amount of nonconstructivity in deterministic finite automata. Theor. Comput. Sci. **411**(38–39), 3436–3443 (2010)

6. Hopcroft, J.E., Ullman, J.D.: Some results on tape-bounded Turing machines. J. ACM **16**(1), 168–177 (1969)

7. Ibarra, O.H., Ravikumar, B.: Sublogarithmic-space Turing machines, nonuniform space complexity, and closure properties. Math. Syst. Theory **21**(1), 1–17 (1988)

8. Kapoutsis, C.A.: Minicomplexity. J. Autom. Lang. Comb. **17**(2–4), 205–224 (2012)

9. Kapoutsis, C.A.: Two-way automata versus logarithmic space. Theory Comput. Syst. **55**(2), 421–447 (2014)

10. Karp, R.M., Lipton, R.J.: Turing machines that take advice. Enseignement Mathématique **28**(2), 191–209 (1982)

11. Küçük, U., Say, A.C.C., Yakaryilmaz, A.: Finite automata with advice tapes. Int. J. Found. Comput. Sci. **25**(8), 987–1000 (2014)

12. Tadaki, K., Yamakami, T., Lin, J.C.H.: Theory of one-tape linear-time Turing machines. Theor. Comput. Sci. **411**(1), 22–43 (2010)

Integer Weighted Automata
on Infinite Words

Vesa Halava[1] , Tero Harju[1] , Reino Niskanen[2($\boxtimes$)] , and Igor Potapov[2]

[1] Department of Mathematics and Statistics, University of Turku, Turku, Finland
{`vesa.halava,harju`}`@utu.fi`
[2] Department of Computer Science, University of Liverpool, Liverpool, UK
{`reino.niskanen,potapov`}`@liverpool.ac.uk`

Abstract. In this paper we combine two classical generalisations of finite automata (weighted automata and automata on infinite words) into a model of integer weighted automata on infinite words and study the universality and the emptiness problems under zero weight acceptance. We show that the universality problem is undecidable for three-state automata by a direct reduction from the *infinite Post correspondence problem*. We also consider other more general acceptance conditions as well as their complements with respect to the universality and the emptiness problems. Additionally, we build a universal integer weighted automaton where the automaton is fixed and the word problem is undecidable.

1   Introduction

Weighted automata have been extensively studied in recent years [1,6,12] and have a wide range of applications, such as speech-recognition [17] and image compression [4]. In weighted automata models a quantitative value (weight) is added to each transition of a finite automaton allowing to enrich the computational model with extra semantics. For example, these weights could be associated with the consumption of resources, time needed for the execution or the probability of the execution. Depending on the semantics (how these weights are used), the acceptance conditions could be defined in various ways, significantly changing the complexity of the weighted automata model.

The acceptance conditions could be defined using various aggregation functions for deterministic or non-deterministic automata that combine weights either on a single path or a set of equivalent paths. For example for weighted automata over tropical semirings, i.e., $(\mathbb{Z} \cup \{\infty\}, \min, +, \infty, 0)$, where a weight of a word is calculated using the semiring product (i.e., $+$) and the acceptance can be defined using the semiring sum (i.e., min) – a word is accepted if its value using the semiring sum is at most ν. In [3], the acceptance of infinite words was based on the property that, in the corresponding computation path, a label with the maximal weight is appearing infinitely often in analogy to Büchi automaton.

© Springer Nature Switzerland AG 2021
N. Moreira and R. Reis (Eds.): DLT 2021, LNCS 12811, pp. 167–179, 2021.
https://doi.org/10.1007/978-3-030-81508-0_14

The automata on infinite words have been often motivated for modeling concurrent and communicating systems [20] and more recently infinite words have been used to simulate various processes in computational games [10,16].

In this paper we combine these two fundamental extensions by considering weighted automata on infinite words. The model we consider has weights from the additive group of integers $\mathbb{Z}$ with the zero element 0 and the weights are summed along the path. This model can be seen as a blind one-counter automaton operating on infinite words. Under the zero acceptance condition an infinite word w is accepted if there exists a path in the automaton reading w reaching a final state with weight 0 on a finite prefix of w. First we consider two classical decision problems for integer weighted automata on infinite words – the emptiness (checking whether some word is accepted) and the universality problems (checking whether all words are accepted). In contrast to other acceptance conditions with decidable emptiness and universality problems [3], we show that for the zero acceptance, while the emptiness problem is decidable, the universality problem is undecidable.

In this paper we improve the result of [10], where it was shown that the universality problem is undecidable for automata with five states. We prove that the problem remains undecidable for a very minimalistic automaton with only three states. The undecidability result is based on the reductions from the undecidability of the infinite Post correspondence problem (ω PCP) and the state reduction is achieved by proving more restricted form of the ω PCP than in [9]. The idea of proving the undecidability of the universality problem is to construct an automaton that verifies whether a given word is not a solution of a given instance of the infinite Post correspondence problem. This is done by storing the difference of lengths of images in the counter until automaton reaches a symbol that we try to show is different in the images under the morphisms. We store this symbol and let the second morphism catch up after which we verify that the symbols were indeed different. This proof is presented in Sect. 3.

In Sect. 4, we investigate variants of zero acceptance in the sense of expanding the condition from the existence of a zero on a path to existence of a weight in a given set. We also modify the acceptance to consider all paths rather than an existence of an accepting path. We call this strong acceptance. This leads to new variants of universality and emptiness problems with emptiness problem being undecidable for strong acceptance for co-zero acceptance.

Finally, in Sect. 5 we consider a variant of the automaton where all transitions are fixed and the weight given as an input determines whether a word is accepted or not. This automaton can be seen as *universal* in the same sense as a universal Turing machine. For this universal automaton it is undecidable whether a given word with an initial integer weight is accepted.

2   Notation and Definitions

An *infinite word* w over a finite alphabet A is an infinite sequence of letters $w = a_0 a_1 a_2 a_3 \cdots$ where $a_i \in A$ is a letter for each $i = 0, 1, 2, \ldots$. We denote the set of all infinite words over A by A^ω. The monoid of all finite words over A is denoted by A^*. The empty word is denoted by ε. A word $u \in A^*$ is a *prefix* of $v \in A^*$, denoted by $u \leq v$, if $v = uw$ for some $w \in A^*$. If u and w are both nonempty, then the prefix u is called *proper*, denoted by $u < v$. A *prefix* of an infinite word $w \in A^\omega$ is a finite word $p \in A^*$ such that $w = pw'$ where $w' \in A^\omega$. This is also denoted by $p \leq w$. The length of a finite word w is denoted by $|w|$. The length of ε is 0. For a word w, we denote by $w(i)$ the ith letter of w, i.e., $w = w(1)w(2)\cdots$. The number of letters a in a word w is denoted by $|w|_a$. The set dA^ω denotes all infinite words starting with d, i.e., $\{dw \mid w \in A^\omega\}$.

Consider a finite (integer) weighted automaton $\mathcal{A} = (Q, A, \sigma, q_0, F, \mathbb{Z})$ with the set of states Q, the finite alphabet A, the set of transitions $\sigma \subseteq Q \times A \times Q \times \mathbb{Z}$, the initial state q_0, the set of final states $F \subseteq Q$, and the additive group of integers $\mathbb{Z}$. We write the transitions in the form $t = \langle q, a, p, z \rangle \in \sigma$.

A *configuration* of $\mathcal{A}$ is any triple $(q, u, z) \in Q \times A^* \times \mathbb{Z}$ and it is said to *yield* a configuration $(p, ua, z_1 + z_2)$ if there is a transition $\langle q, a, p, z_2 \rangle \in \sigma$.

Let $\pi = t_1 t_2 t_3 \cdots$ be an infinite path of transitions of $\mathcal{A}$ where $t_i = \langle q_{j_i}, a_{k_i}, q_{j_{i+1}}, z_i \rangle$ for $i > 0$ and $q_{j_0} = q_0$. We call such path π a *computation path*. Denote by $\mathcal{R}(\pi)$ the set of all reachable configurations following a path π. That is, for $\pi = \langle q_0, a_{k_0}, q_{j_1}, z_0 \rangle \langle q_{j_1}, a_{k_1}, q_{j_2}, z_1 \rangle \langle q_{j_2}, a_{k_2}, q_{j_3}, z_2 \rangle \cdots$ the set of reachable configurations is $\mathcal{R}(\pi) = \{(q_0, \varepsilon, 0), (q_{j_1}, a_{k_0}, z_0), (q_{j_2}, a_{k_0}a_{k_1}, z_0 + z_1), (q_{j_3}, a_{k_0}a_{k_1}a_{k_2}, z_0 + z_1 + z_2), \ldots\}$. Further, we denote path π by π_w if $w = a_{k_0}a_{k_1}a_{k_2}\cdots$. Let $c = (q, u, z) \in \mathcal{R}(\pi)$ for some computation path π. The *weight* of the configuration c is $\gamma(c) = z$. We say that the configuration c *reaches* state q. If computation path π reading w is fixed, by the *weight of prefix* $\gamma(p)$ we denote the weight of configuration $(q, p, z) \in \mathcal{R}(\pi)$ where $w = pu$ for some $u \in \mathcal{A}^\omega$.

We are ready to define an acceptance condition. An infinite word $w \in A^\omega$ is accepted by $\mathcal{A}$ if there exists an infinite path π such that at least one configuration c in $\mathcal{R}(\pi)$ reaches a final state and has weight $\gamma(c) = 0$. The language *accepted by* $\mathcal{A}$ is $L(\mathcal{A}) = \{w \in A^\omega \mid \exists \pi_w \in \sigma^\omega \; \exists (q, u, 0) \in \mathcal{R}(\pi_w) \colon q \in F\}$. We call this *zero acceptance*. We discuss other acceptance conditions in Sect. 4.

The *universality problem* for weighted automata over infinite words is a problem to decide whether the language accepted by a weighted automaton $\mathcal{A}$ is the set of all infinite words. In other words, whether or not $L(\mathcal{A}) = A^\omega$. The problem of *non-universality* is the complement of the universality problem, that is, whether or not $L(\mathcal{A}) \neq A^\omega$ or, for zero acceptance, whether there exists $w \in A^\omega$ such that for every computation path π reading w and every configuration $c \in \mathcal{R}(\pi)$, $\gamma(c) \neq 0$ holds.

An *instance* of the *Post correspondence problem* (PCP, for short) consists of two morphisms $g, h : A^* \to B^*$ where A and B are alphabets. A nonempty word $w \in A^*$ is a solution of an instance (g, h) if it satisfies $g(w) = h(w)$. It is well known that it is undecidable whether or not an instance of the PCP has a solution. The problem remains undecidable for A with $|A| \geq 5$; see [15]. The cardinality of the domain alphabet A is said to be the *size* of the instance.

The *infinite Post correspondence problem*, $\omega\,$PCP, is a natural extension of the PCP. An infinite word w is a *solution* of an instance (g, h) of the $\omega\,$PCP if for every finite prefix p of w either $h(p) < g(p)$ or $g(p) < h(p)$ holds. In the $\omega\,$PCP it is asked whether or not a given instance has a solution or not. Note that in our formulation prefixes have to be proper. It was proven in [9] that the problem is undecidable for domain alphabets A with $|A| \geq 9$ and in [5] it was improved to $|A| \geq 8$. A more general formulation of the $\omega\,$PCP was used in both proofs, namely the prefixes did not have to be proper. However, both constructions rule out non-proper prefixes; see [5,9] for details.

3   Universality Problem for Zero Acceptance

In this section we improve the result of [10], where it was shown that the universality problem is undecidable for automata with five states. We prove that the problem remains undecidable for automata with three states. The tighter bound relies on deriving new properties about the $\omega\,$PCP instance. In the proof of undecidability of the universality problem for weighted automata, for each instance (g, h) of the $\omega\,$PCP, we need to construct a weighted automaton $\mathcal{A}$ such that $L(\mathcal{A}) \neq A^{\omega}$ if and only if the instance (g, h) has an infinite solution.

Theorem 1. *It is undecidable whether or not* $L(\mathcal{A}) = A^{\omega}$ *holds for 3-state integer weighted automaton* $\mathcal{A}$ *over its alphabet* A.

Let us first focus on constructing the instance of the $\omega\,$PCP. In [10], a weighted automaton was constructed from an arbitrary instance of the $\omega\,$PCP. We reiterate the construction of an instance of the $\omega\,$PCP found in [9], highlighting the properties that simplify the construction of the automaton.

The $\omega\,$PCP was shown to be undecidable for instances of size 9 in [9]. The proof uses a reduction from the termination problem of the semi-Thue systems proved to be undecidable for the 3-rule semi-Thue systems from [13]. We shall now present the construction from [9].

Let $T = (\{a, b\}, R)$ be an n-rule semi-Thue system with the undecidable termination problem, and let the rules in T be $t_i = (u_i, v_i)$ for $i = 1, 2, \ldots, n$. Let u be the input word.

The domain alphabet of our instance of the $\omega\,$PCP is $A = \{a_1, a_2, b_1, b_2, d, \#\} \cup R$, where d is for the beginning and synchronisation and $\#$ is a special separator of the words in a derivation. Note that the rules in R are considered as letters in the alphabet. Define two special morphisms for $x \in A^+$. Morphisms ℓ_x and r_x are called the *desynchronising* morphisms, and defined by $\ell_x(a) = xa$ and $r_x(a) = ax$ for each letter a.

In [9] the following construction was given for a semi-Thue system T and an input word u: Define the morphisms $g, h \colon A^* \to \{a, b, d, \#\}^*$ by (recall that for $t_i \in R$, we denoted $t_i = (u_i, v_i)$)

$$h(a_1) = dad, \qquad g(a_1) = add,$$
$$h(b_1) = dbd, \qquad g(b_1) = bdd,$$
$$h(a_2) = dda, \qquad g(a_2) = add,$$
$$h(b_2) = ddb, \qquad g(b_2) = bdd, \qquad (1)$$
$$h(t_i) = d^{-1}\ell_{dd}(v_i), \ g(t_i) = r_{dd}(u_i), \ \text{for } t_i \in R,$$
$$h(d) = \ell_{dd}(u)dd\#d, \ g(d) = dd,$$
$$h(\#) = dd\#d, \qquad g(\#) = \#dd.$$

Note, that $d^{-1}\ell_{dd}(\cdot)$ means that the image starts with a single d. In the special case, where $v_i = \varepsilon$, we define $h(t_i) = d$.

It was proved in [9] that the following property holds:

Property 1. Let (g, h) be an ω PCP defined in (1). Each infinite solution of (g, h) is of the form

$$dw_1\#w_2\#w_3\# \cdots , \quad \text{where } w_j = x_j t_{i_j} y_j \qquad (2)$$

for some $t_{i_j} \in R$, $x_j \in \{a_1, b_1\}^*$ and $y_j \in \{a_2, b_2\}^*$ for all j.

Indeed, the image $g(w)$ is always of the form $r_{d^2}(v)$, and therefore, by the form of h, between two separators $\#$ there must occur exactly one letter $t \in R$. Also, the separator $\#$ must be followed by words in $\{a_1, b_1\}^*$ before the next occurrence of a letter $t \in R$. By the form of $h(t)$ the following words before the next separator must be in $\{a_2, b_2\}^*$. The form (2) follows when we observe that there must be infinitely many separators $\#$ in each infinite solution. Indeed, all solutions begin with a d, and there is one occurrence of $\#$ in $h(d)$ and no occurrences of $\#$ in $g(d)$. Later each occurrences of $\#$ is produced from $\#$ by both g and h. Therefore there are infinitely many letters $\#$ in each infinite solution.

Property 2. Let (g, h) be as in (1). In a solution, the image under g cannot be longer than the image under h.

Property 3. Let (g, h) be as in (1). In a word w beginning with the letter d, the first position where $h(w)$ and $g(w)$ differ (called the *error*) is reached in $h(w)$ at least one letter (of w) earlier than it is reached in $g(w)$.

The two properties are illustrated in Fig. 1. In the next theorem, we restate and sharpen the result of [9] by improving the undecidability claim of the ω PCP.

Theorem 2. *Let (g, h) be an instance of the ω PCP defined as in (1) that satisfies Properties 1, 2, 3. It is undecidable whether a solution to (g, h) exists.*

Next, we construct the weighted automaton based on the undecidable instance of the ω PCP of Theorem 2. This will allow us to prove Theorem 1.

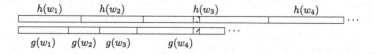

Fig. 1. An illustration of a solution candidate to the instance of the ω PCP satisfying Properties 2 and 3. Here, ▧ represent the first letter of $h(w_1 w_2 w_3 w_4 \cdots)$ that is compared to a letter of $g(w_1 w_2 w_3 w_4 \cdots)$ which is represented by ▨.

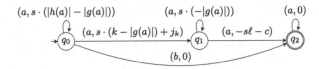

Fig. 2. The weighted automaton $\mathcal{A}$. In the figure $a \in A$ and $b \in A \setminus \{d\}$.

Let (g, h) be a fixed instance of the ω PCP as defined in (1). Then $g, h \colon A^* \to B^*$ where $A = \{a_1, \ldots, a_m\}$ and $B = \{b_1, \ldots, b_{s-1}\}$. We construct a weighted automaton $\mathcal{A} = (Q, A, \sigma, q_0, F, \mathbb{Z})$, where $Q = \{q_0, q_1, q_2\}$ and $F = \{q_2\}$, corresponding to the instance (g, h) such that an infinite word $w \in A^\omega$ is accepted by $\mathcal{A}$ iff for some finite prefix p of w, $g(p) \not\preceq h(p)$. Moreover, by Property 3, such p exists for all infinite words except for the solutions of the instance (g, h). We call the verification that $g(p) \not\preceq h(p)$, for a prefix p, the *error checking*.

Let us begin with the transitions of $\mathcal{A}$. The automaton is depicted in Fig. 2. Recall that the cardinality of the alphabet B is $s - 1$. First for each $a \in A$, let $\langle q_0, a, q_0, s(|h(a)| - |g(a)|) \rangle$, $\langle q_1, a, q_1, s(-|g(a)|) \rangle$, $\langle q_2, a, q_2, 0 \rangle$ be in σ and for all $b \in A \setminus \{d\}$, let $\langle q_0, b, q_2, 0 \rangle \in \sigma$. For the error checking we need the following transitions for all letters $a \in A$: Let $h(a) = b_{j_1} b_{j_2} \cdots b_{j_{n_1}}$, where $b_{j_k} \in B$, for each index $1 \le k \le n_1$. Then let, for each $k = 1, \ldots, n_1$,

$$\langle q_0, a, q_1, s(k - |g(a)|) + j_k \rangle \in \sigma \tag{3}$$

Let $g(a) = b_{i_1} b_{i_2} \cdots b_{i_{n_2}}$, where $b_{i_\ell} \in B$, for each index $1 \le \ell \le n_2$. For each $\ell = 1, \ldots, n_2$ and letter $b_c \in B$ such that $b_{i_\ell} \ne b_c$, let

$$\langle q_1, a, q_2, -s\ell - c \rangle \in \sigma. \tag{4}$$

We call the transitions in (3) *error guessing transitions* and in (4) *error verifying transitions*. The next lemma shows a key property about words accepted by $\mathcal{A}$. The proof relies on analysis of weights along computation paths.

Lemma 1. *A word $w \in A^\omega$ is accepted by $\mathcal{A}$ if and only if w is not a solution of the instance (g, h) of the ω PCP as defined in (1).*

We are ready to prove the main theorem. By Lemma 1, a word $w \in A^\omega$ is accepted by the above constructed integer weighted automaton $\mathcal{A}$ iff w is not a solution of a given instance (g, h) of the ω PCP. By Theorem 2, it is undecidable whether or not the instance (g, h) has a solution or not. This proves Theorem 1.

Note that the number of the letters in the alphabet A in Theorem 1 is small. Indeed, $|A| = 9$ by the construction in (1). The number of transitions on the other hand is huge. The number of error guessing and verifying transitions is dependent on the lengths of the images. One of the rules consists of encoding of all the rules of the 83-rule semi-Thue system with an undecidable termination problem. Its image is several hundreds of thousands letters long.

Next, we consider the universality problem for automata, where all states are final. That is, we consider an acceptance condition, where a word is accepted based solely on weight. Formally, $\mathcal{L}(\mathcal{A}) = \{w \in A^\omega \mid \exists \pi_w \in \sigma^\omega \; \exists (q, u, 0) \in \mathcal{R}(\pi_w)\}$. Relaxing the state reachability condition on the previously defined automaton leads to new accepting paths. For example, an infinite word starting with a_1 is accepted in the state q_0 since $|h(a_1)| - |g(a_1)| = 0$. On the other hand this word can also be accepted in q_2 with transition $\langle q_0, a_1, q_2, 0 \rangle$. So we need to show that no new words are accepted in states q_0 and q_1.

Corollary 1. *It is undecidable whether or not $\mathcal{L}(\mathcal{A}) = A^\omega$ holds for 3-state integer weighted automaton $\mathcal{A}$ over its alphabet A.*

It is also natural to consider the emptiness problem for weighted automata. That is, whether for a given weighted automaton $\mathcal{A}$, $L(\mathcal{A}) = \emptyset$. In contrast to the result of Theorem 1, the emptiness problem is decidable.

Theorem 3. *It is decidable whether or not $L(\mathcal{A}) = \emptyset$ holds for integer weighted automaton $\mathcal{A}$ over its alphabet A.*

Proof. Let $\mathcal{A}$ be a weighted automaton on infinite words. Consider it as a weighted automaton on finite words, $\mathcal{B}$, defined in [8]. Clearly $L(\mathcal{A}) = \emptyset$ if and only if $L(\mathcal{B}) = \emptyset$. Indeed, an infinite word w is accepted by $\mathcal{A}$ if and only if there is a finite prefix u of w with $\gamma(u) = 0$. This u is accepted by $\mathcal{B}$. On the other hand, if some finite word u is accepted by $\mathcal{B}$ then an infinite word starting with u is accepted by $\mathcal{A}$. In [7] it was shown that languages defined by weighted automata on finite words are context-free languages. It is well-known that emptiness is decidable for context-free languages. $\qquad\square$

Corollary 1 (follows from Theorem *1*)

1. *For weighted automata $\mathcal{A}$ and $\mathcal{B}$ the following problems are undecidable:*
   (i) *Language equality: Whether $L(\mathcal{A}) = L(\mathcal{B})$.*
   (ii) *Language inclusion: Whether $L(\mathcal{B}) \subset L(\mathcal{A})$.*
   (iii) *Language union: Whether $L(\mathcal{A}) \cup L(\mathcal{B}) = A^\omega$.*
   (iv) *Language regularity: Whether $L(\mathcal{A})$ is recognised by a Büchi automaton.*
2. *It is undecidable whether $L(\mathcal{A}) = L(\mathcal{A}')$ for two weighted automata $\mathcal{A}, \mathcal{A}'$ such that there exists a bijective mapping from edges of $\mathcal{A}$ to edges of $\mathcal{A}'$.*

4   Different Acceptance Conditions

We will examine another non-deterministic acceptance that we call *strong acceptance*. It is informally defined as "a word is accepted iff every path in the machine according to this word satisfies property φ". We will use notation $\mathbb{Z}\text{-WA}(\exists\, \varphi)$ for integer weighted finite automata on infinite words with acceptance condition φ. Analogously, $\mathbb{Z}\text{-WA}(\forall\, \varphi)$ denotes the strong acceptance.

In [10], integer weighted automata on infinite words were introduced and it was proven that the universality problem is undecidable for *zero acceptance*. In this section, we investigate other acceptance properties and their effect on the decidability of language theoretic problems. The two problems we study are

Table 1. Different acceptances and acceptance conditions. Note that $S \subseteq \mathbb{Z}$.

Acceptance ($\exists$):	$w \in L(A) \iff \exists \pi_w \in \sigma^\omega \; \varphi(\pi_w)$
Strong acceptance ($\forall$):	$w \in L(A) \iff \forall \pi_w \in \sigma^\omega \; \varphi(\pi_w)$
Zero acceptance (Z):	$\varphi(\pi_w) = \exists (q, u, z) \in \mathcal{R}(\pi_w) \; (q \in F \wedge z = 0)$
Co-zero acceptance ($\neg$Z):	$\varphi(\pi_w) = \forall (q, u, z) \in \mathcal{R}(\pi_w) \; (q \notin F \vee z \neq 0)$
Set acceptance (S):	$\varphi(\pi_w) = \exists (q, u, z) \in \mathcal{R}(\pi_w) \; (q \in F \wedge z \in S)$
Co-set acceptance ($\neg$S):	$\varphi(\pi_w) = \forall (q, u, z) \in \mathcal{R}(\pi_w) \; (q \notin F \vee z \notin S)$

the universality and the emptiness problems. In the universality problem we are asked whether every word is accepted and in the emptiness problem whether at least one infinite word is accepted. That is, we are interested in the universality and the emptiness problems for $\mathbb{Z}$-WA($\exists \varphi$) and $\mathbb{Z}$-WA($\forall \varphi$) for various φ. We present different acceptances and acceptance conditions in Table 1.

Let us discuss these acceptance properties next. In the already mentioned zero acceptance, word w is accepted iff on a computation path reading w there is an intermediate configuration where the state is final and the weight is zero. We denote this property by Z. The complementary property, co-zero acceptance, is defined in the obvious way. That is, word w is accepted iff on a computation path reading w, all configurations are either not in a final state or do not have weight zero. This property is denoted by $\neg$Z.

It is straightforward to see that since the universality problem is undecidable for $\mathbb{Z}$-WA($\exists$Z) proven in [10] and Theorem 1, the emptiness problem is undecidable for $\mathbb{Z}$-WA($\forall \neg$Z). Indeed, the universality and the emptiness problems are complementary and so are zero acceptance and strong co-zero acceptance. We next show the decidability of the other combinations. That is, that the emptiness problem is decidable for $\mathbb{Z}$-WA($\exists$Z), $\mathbb{Z}$-WA($\exists \neg$Z), $\mathbb{Z}$-WA($\forall$Z), $\mathbb{Z}$-WA($\forall \neg$Z) and that the universality problem is decidable for $\mathbb{Z}$-WA($\exists \neg$Z), $\mathbb{Z}$-WA($\forall$Z), $\mathbb{Z}$-WA($\forall \neg$Z).

Theorem 4. *Let A be a $\mathbb{Z}$-WA($\exists \neg$Z) or $\mathbb{Z}$-WA($\forall$Z). It is decidable whether $L(A) = \emptyset$ holds.*

Proof. Let us consider $\mathbb{Z}$-WA($\exists \neg$Z) as the proof for the other class is analogous. Let A be a $\mathbb{Z}$-WA($\exists \neg$Z). Now the question can be restated as

$$\exists w \in A^\omega \; \exists \pi_w \in \sigma^\omega \; \forall (q, u, z) \in \mathcal{R}(\pi_w)(q \notin F \vee z \neq 0).$$

As we are interested in an existence of such path, we can ignore the letters. Indeed, if we find a path, there is a corresponding word that is accepted and hence $L(A)$ is not empty. That is, A can be considered as a $\mathbb{Z}$-VASS for which the reachability relation is effectively semi-linear [2]. Hence, the property can be expressed a sentence in Presburger arithmetics, which is a decidable logic. $\square$

Corollary 2. *Let A be a $\mathbb{Z}$-WA($\forall \neg$Z), $\mathbb{Z}$-WA($\forall$Z) or $\mathbb{Z}$-WA($\exists \neg$Z). It is decidable whether $L(A) = A^\omega$ holds, where A is over alphabet A.*

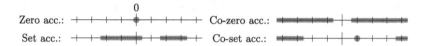

Fig. 3. An illustration of different acceptance conditions. In red are weights that are to be reached in an accepting path.

Proof. The universality problem for $\mathbb{Z}\text{-WA}(\forall\,\neg Z)$ is dual to the emptiness problem for $\mathbb{Z}\text{-WA}(\exists\,Z)$, which is decidable by Theorem 3. Analogously, the universality problems for $\mathbb{Z}\text{-WA}(\forall\,Z)$ and $\mathbb{Z}\text{-WA}(\exists\,\neg Z)$ are dual to the emptiness problems for $\mathbb{Z}\text{-WA}(\exists\,\neg Z)$ and $\mathbb{Z}\text{-WA}(\forall\,Z)$, respectively, which are decidable.   □

In both zero acceptance and co-zero acceptance, integer 0 seems to play an important role. This is not true. One can alter some of the transitions to have acceptance for any fixed integer. For example, by introducing a new initial state q_0' and transitions $\langle q_0', a, q, z + 1\rangle$ for every transition $\langle q_0, a, q, z\rangle \in \sigma$. Furthermore, one can multiply all the weights in the transitions by some constant N to ensure that in the interval $\{0, \ldots, N-1\}$ only 0 is actually reachable. This leads to an acceptance condition for intervals with the same decidability statuses. Note that due to the construction, no weights $1k, \ldots, (N-1)k$ are reachable for any integer k. This leads us to an observation that we can consider finite or infinite sets and retain the decidability statuses. For example, multiplying all the weights in the transitions by an even N, we can specify an acceptance condition where "a word is accepted iff upon reaching a final state, weight is either in interval $\{0, \ldots, \frac{N}{2} - 1\}$ or interval $\{\frac{N}{2} + 1, N - 1\}$". Let us call this acceptance condition *set acceptance*. Figure 3 illustrates the differences between zero, co-zero, set and co-set acceptances with respect to weights that are reached on accepting paths.

Let $S \subseteq \mathbb{Z}$. In set acceptance, a word w is accepted iff on a computation path reading w there is an intermediate configuration where the state is final and the weight is in S. For the dual co-set acceptance, a word w is accepted iff on a computation path reading w all intermediate configurations are either not in a final state or the weight is not in S.

It is straightforward to see that the undecidability of the universality problem follows from the undecidability of the universality problem for zero acceptance. Likewise, the emptiness problem is decidable due to the decidability of the emptiness problem for zero acceptance. The other decidability results for variants of set acceptance can be proven *mutatis mutandis*. This is summarised in Table 2 where the decidability statuses of the universality and the emptiness problems for the different acceptance conditions.

Corollary 3. *The universality problem is decidable for $\mathbb{Z}\text{-WA}(\exists\,\neg S)$, $\mathbb{Z}\text{-WA}(\forall\,S)$ and $\mathbb{Z}\text{-WA}(\forall\,\neg S)$ and undecidable for $\mathbb{Z}\text{-WA}(\exists\,S)$. The emptiness problem is decidable for $\mathbb{Z}\text{-WA}(\exists\,S)$, $\mathbb{Z}\text{-WA}(\exists\,\neg S)$ and $\mathbb{Z}\text{-WA}(\forall\,S)$ and undecidable for $\mathbb{Z}\text{-WA}(\forall\,\neg S)$.*

It is worth highlighting that the construction of [10] constructs a weighted automaton that non-deterministically checks for error in a ω PCP solution

Table 2. Decidability status of the universality and emptiness problems under different acceptances The result in blue implies other undecidability results.

Acceptance	Universality	Emptiness
Zero	Undecid.	Decid.
Co-zero	Decid.	Decid.
Set	Undecid.	Decid.
Co-set	Decid.	Decid.

Strong acc.	Universality	Emptiness
Zero	Decid.	Decid.
Co-zero	Decid.	Undecid.
Set	Decid.	Decid.
Co-set	Decid.	Undecid.

candidate. It is possible to construct an automaton with strong co-set acceptance for which the emptiness problem is undecidable and the automaton verifies that the input word is a solution to the ω PCP instance. The automaton relies on the properties of both strong and co-set acceptance with two intervals to be avoided.

5   A Universal Weighted Automaton

In this section we consider a universal weighted automaton. The goal is to construct a universal weighted automaton similar to a universal machine which has fixed rules and can simulate any machine that is given as an input. It is well-known that there exists a universal Turing machine [18] and a universal 2-counter machine [14]. A less well-known fact is that there is also a universal semi-Thue system [19]. In [11], the authors constructed a universal semi-Thue system where the rewriting rules are fixed and the initial word is an encoding of the system to be simulated.

From the details of the ω PCP construction presented in (1), it is evident that only one of the pairs is not fixed and depends on the input to the given semi-Thue system. Namely, d contains the initial word of the semi-Thue system. Note, that d has to be the first letter of a solution.

We construct a weighted automaton with fixed state structure and transitions. The automaton is constructed using the same idea as in Sect. 3. Namely, that all words but a solution to the ω PCP are accepted. Unlike the previous definition, where the initial weight was 0, in the universal weighted automaton, there is an additional initial weight. This weight is used to store the information on the input word of the semi-Thue system. Note that due to our approach of storing only partial information about the images of the morphisms in the weight, we do not actually need to know what the input is.

From the previous remark in our weighted automaton only transitions corresponding to the letter d are not fixed. We use the fact that d has to be the first letter by fixing weight for d to be 0 and having the input, i.e., the initial weight, depend on d. There are two cases that can happen when reading d with the weighted automaton. Either the error is in the image of d or not. If there is no error in the image of d, then the difference of lengths of the images is given as an input. If there is an error, then its position and letter are given. That is, the input of our universal weighted automaton is an integer

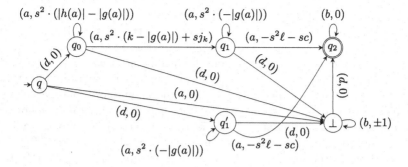

Fig. 4. The universal weighted automaton $\mathcal{U}$. In the figure $a \in A \setminus \{d\}$ and $b \in A$.

$zs^2 + js + j$ where $z \in \mathbb{N}$, $j \in \{0, \ldots, s-1\}$ and $s = |B| + 1$. This integer is either $(|h(d)| - |g(d)|)s^2 + 0s + 0$ corresponding to the case when there are no errors in the image of d or $(k - |g(a)|)s^2 + j_k s + j_k$ corresponding to the case where k is the position of the error in d and j_k is the error. For these two cases, we have two paths in the automaton. In the first path the automaton of Sect. 3 has all the weights multiplied by s. In the second path the error verifying part of the automaton is used with weights multiplied by s and error verifying transitions have weights $-\ell s^2 - cs - c$ instead of $-\ell s - c$ as in the original automaton (Fig. 4).

The universal automaton is $\mathcal{U} = (\{q, q_0, q_1, q_2, q_1', \perp\}, A, \sigma, q, \{q_2\}, \mathbb{Z})$. The states q_0, q_1, q_2 correspond to the first path with transitions for each $a \in A \setminus \{d\}$ and $b \in A$, $\langle q_0, a, q_0, s^2(|h(a)| - |g(a)|) \rangle$, $\langle q_1, a, q_1, s^2(-|g(a)|) \rangle$, $\langle q_2, b, q_2, 0 \rangle$ are in σ. For the error checking we need the following transitions for all letters $a \in A \setminus \{d\}$: Let $h(a) = b_{j_1} b_{j_2} \cdots b_{j_{n_1}}$ where $b_{j_k} \in B$, for each index $1 \le k \le n_1$. Then let, for each $k = 1, \ldots, n_1$, $\langle q_0, a, q_1, s^2(k - |g(a)|) + s j_k \rangle \in \sigma$. Let $g(a) = b_{i_1} b_{i_2} \cdots b_{i_{n_2}}$ where $b_{i_\ell} \in B$, for each index $1 \le \ell \le n_2$. For each $\ell = 1, \ldots, n_2$ and letter $b_c \in B$ such that $b_{i_\ell} \ne b_c \in B$, let $\langle q_1, a, q_2, -s^2\ell - sc \rangle \in \sigma$.

The state q_1' corresponds to the second path with transitions, for each $a \in A \setminus \{d\}$, $\langle q_1', a, q_1', s^2(-|g(a)|) \rangle$ are in σ. For the error verification we need the following transitions for all letters $a \in A \setminus \{d\}$. Let $g(a) = b_{i_1} b_{i_2} \cdots b_{i_{n_2}}$ where $b_{i_\ell} \in B$, for each index $1 \le \ell \le n_2$. For each $\ell = 1, \ldots, n_2$ and letter $b_c \in B$ such that $b_{i_\ell} \ne b_c \in B$, let $\langle q_1', a, q_2, -s^2\ell - sc - c \rangle \in \sigma$.

Finally, transitions $\langle q, d, q_0, 0 \rangle, \langle q, d, q_1', 0 \rangle$ to pick a path, transitions $\langle q, a, \perp, 0 \rangle$, for each $a \in A \setminus d$, for words not starting with d, transitions $\langle p, d, \perp, 0 \rangle$ where $p \in \{q_0, q_1, q_1'\}$, for words that have letter d, transitions $\langle \perp, b, \perp, \pm 1 \rangle, \langle \perp, b, q_2, 0 \rangle$ for $b \in A$ and finally $\langle q_2, d, q_2, 0 \rangle$.

Let the set of inputs corresponding to the letter d be $\alpha(d)$, defined as the union of $\{(|h(d)| - |g(d)|)s^2\}$ and $\{is^2 + js + j \mid i = |g(d)|, |g(d)| + 1, \ldots, |h(d)|$ and $b_j = h(d)(i) \in B\}$. Now a word $dw \in A^\omega$ is accepted by $\mathcal{U}$ if and only if for a computation path π of dw there exists a prefix $p \le \pi$ that reaches q_2 with weight 0. That is, $\gamma(p) + \beta = 0$ where $\beta \in \alpha(d)$.

Next, we show that an input defines the path that needs to be chosen. Assume first that the input is $zs^2 + j_k s + j_k$ and the first transition is $\langle q, d, q_0, 0 \rangle$. Now the automaton is in state q_0 with weight $zs^2 + j_k s + j_k$ but none of the weights on this path modify the coefficient of s^0 (unless letter d is read) and thus the weight is nonzero in state q_2. Assume then that the input is $zs^2 + 0s + 0$ and the first transition is $\langle q, d, q_1', 0 \rangle$. The path reaching q_2 (without visiting $\bot$) has $xs^2 - cs - c$ for some $x \in \mathbb{Z}$ and $c \in \{1, \ldots, s-1\}$ which is nonzero. That is for input $zs^2 + j_k s + j_k$ the upper path has to be chosen and for input zs^2 the lower path has to be chosen. It is clear that after that the computation follows the corresponding computation of $\mathcal{A}$. If the input is 0, then the only path ending in q_2 with weight 0 goes through $\bot$, that is, it is not a solution to the ω PCP.

From the construction, it is evident that only a solution to the ω PCP instance does not have a path that ends in q_2 with weight 0. Note that in $\mathcal{U}$ all transitions are fixed as, regardless of $h(d)$ and $g(d)$, the transitions are always $\langle p, d, p', 0 \rangle$ or $\langle \bot, d, \bot, \pm 1 \rangle$. Let $w \in A^\omega$ and $\beta \in \mathbb{Z}$. If w is accepted by $\mathcal{U}$ with input β, we denote it by $(w, \beta) \in L(\mathcal{U})$. From the previous consideration we get:

Theorem 5. *Let $w \in A^\omega$ and $\beta \in \mathbb{Z}$. It is undecidable whether $(w, \beta) \in L(\mathcal{U})$, where $\mathcal{U}$ is a fixed weighted automaton on infinite words under zero acceptance.*

References

1. Almagor, S., Boker, U., Kupferman, O.: What's decidable about weighted automata? Inf. Comput. (2020). https://doi.org/10.1016/j.ic.2020.104651
2. Blondin, M., Haase, C., Mazowiecki, F.: Affine extensions of integer vector addition systems with states. In: Proceedings of CONCUR 2018. LIPIcs, vol. 118, pp. 14:1–14:17 (2018). https://doi.org/10.4230/lipics.concur.2018.14
3. Chatterjee, K., Doyen, L., Henzinger, T.A.: Quantitative languages. ACM Trans. Comput. Log. **11**, 4 (2010). https://doi.org/10.1145/1805950.1805953
4. Culik, K., Kari, J.: Image compression using weighted finite automata. Comput. Graph. **17**(3), 305–313 (1993). https://doi.org/10.1016/0097-8493(93)90079-O
5. Dong, J., Liu, Q.: Undecidability of infinite Post correspondence problem for instances of size 8. ITA **46**(3), 451–457 (2012). https://doi.org/10.1051/ita/2012015
6. Droste, M., Kuich, W., Vogler, H.: Handbook of Weighted Automata. Springer, Heidelberg (2009). https://doi.org/10.1007/978-3-642-01492-5
7. Halava, V.: Finite Substitutions and Integer Weighted Finite Automata. Licentiate thesis, University of Turku, Turku, Finland (1998)
8. Halava, V., Harju, T.: Undecidability in integer weighted finite automata. Fundam. Inform. **38**(1–2), 189–200 (1999). https://doi.org/10.3233/FI-1999-381215
9. Halava, V., Harju, T.: Undecidability of infinite post correspondence problem for instances of size 9. RAIRO - ITA **40**(4), 551–557 (2006)
10. Halava, V., Harju, T., Niskanen, R., Potapov, I.: Weighted automata on infinite words in the context of Attacker-Defender games. Inf. Comput. **255**, 27–44 (2017)
11. Halava, V., Matiyasevich, Y., Niskanen, R.: Small Semi-Thue system universal with respect to the termination problem. Fundam. Inform. **154**(1–4), 177–184 (2017)
12. Kiefer, S., Murawski, A., Ouaknine, J., Wachter, B., Worrell, J.: On the complexity of equivalence and minimisation for Q-weighted automata. LMCS **9**(1) (2013)
13. Matiyasevich, Y., Sénizergues, G.: Decision problems for Semi-Thue systems with a few rules. Theor. Comput. Sci. **330**(1), 145–169 (2005)

14. Minsky, M.L.: Computation: Finite and Infinite Machines. Prentice-Hall, Inc. (1967)
15. Neary, T.: Undecidability in binary tag systems and the Post correspondence problem for five pairs of words. In: STACS 2015. LIPIcs, vol. 30, pp. 649–661 (2015)
16. Niskanen, R., Potapov, I., Reichert, J.: On decidability and complexity of low-dimensional robot games. J. Comput. Syst. Sci. **107**, 124–141 (2020)
17. Roche, E., Schabes, Y.: Speech recognition by composition of weighted finite automata. In: Finite-State Language Processing, pp. 431–454. MIT Press (1997)
18. Rogozhin, Y.: Small universal Turing machines. Theor. Comput. Sci. **168**(2), 215–240 (1996). https://doi.org/10.1016/S0304-3975(96)00077-1
19. Sénizergues, G.: Some undecidable termination problems for Semi-Thue systems. Theor. Comput. Sci. **142**(2), 257–276 (1995)
20. Thomas, W.: Automata on infinite objects. In: Handbook of Theoretical Computer Science, Volume B: Formal Models and Sematics, pp. 133–192. MIT Press (1990)

Deciding FO² Alternation for Automata over Finite and Infinite Words

Viktor Henriksson[1] and Manfred Kufleitner[2]([⊠])

[1] Loughborough University, Loughborough, UK
b.v.d.henriksson@lboro.ac.uk
[2] University of Stuttgart, Stuttgart, Germany
kufleitner@fmi.uni-stuttgart.de

Abstract. We consider two-variable first-order logic FO² and its quantifier alternation hierarchies over both finite and infinite words. Our main results are forbidden patterns for deterministic automata (finite words) and for Carton-Michel automata (infinite words). In order to give concise patterns, we allow the use of subwords on paths in finite graphs. This concept is formalized as subword patterns. Deciding the presence or absence of such a pattern in a given automaton is in **NL**. In particular, this leads to **NL** algorithms for deciding the levels of the FO² quantifier alternation hierarchies. This applies to both full and half levels, each over finite and infinite words. Moreover, we show that these problems are **NL**-hard and, hence, **NL**-complete.

1 Introduction

Many interesting varieties of finite monoids can be defined by a finite set of identities of ω-terms, i.e., terms with a formal idempotent power denoted by ω (not to be confused with the ordinal ω in ω-words). By Eilenberg's Variety Theorem [7], every variety of finite monoids corresponds to a unique variety for regular languages. In particular, identities of ω-terms can be used for describing classes of regular languages. If $L \subseteq A^*$ is given by a homomorphism $\varphi : A^* \to M$ to a finite monoid together with an accepting set $P \subseteq M$ such that $L = \varphi^{-1}(P)$, then one can check in nondeterministic logarithmic space **NL** whether L satisfies a fixed identity of ω-terms; see e.g. [26, Theorem 2.19] or [8]. If L is given by a (deterministic or nondeterministic) finite automaton, then this algorithm yields a **PSPACE**-algorithm for deciding whether L satisfies the identity (by applying the **NL** algorithm to the transition monoid of the automaton; in the case of nondeterministic automata, this monoid can be represented by Boolean matrices). Since universality of nondeterministic automata is **PSPACE**-complete [14], there is no hope for more efficient algorithms if L is given by a nondeterministic automaton.

The star-free languages can be defined by a very short identity of ω-terms [23]. In 1985, Stern showed that deciding whether a given deterministic automaton accepts a star-free language is **coNP**-hard, leaving open whether it was in fact **PSPACE**-complete [25]. This was later given an affirmative answer by Cho and

© Springer Nature Switzerland AG 2021
N. Moreira and R. Reis (Eds.): DLT 2021, LNCS 12811, pp. 180–191, 2021.
https://doi.org/10.1007/978-3-030-81508-0_15

Huynh [3]. For other important varieties, the situation is very different. In the same paper, Stern gave polynomial time algorithms for deciding membership of the $\mathcal{J}$-trivial (also referred to as piecewise testable) languages and languages of dot-depth one [25] when the languages are given by deterministic finite automata. The exact complexity for these problems was again given by Cho and Huynh, showing that they are **NL**-complete [3].

Forbidden patterns are a common approach for efficiently solving the membership problem. Stern's polynomial time algorithms build on pattern characterizations [24]. Characterizations of $\mathcal{R}$ and $\mathcal{L}$-trivial languages using forbidden patterns were given by Cohen et al. [4], and Schmitz et al. used the approach for characterizing the first levels of the Straubing-Thérien hierarchy [10,22].

The pattern approach usually relies on the DFA of a language. Since deterministic Büchi automata cannot express all ω-regular languages, this has inhibited the adaptation of the pattern approach in the study of ω-regular languages. In 2003, Carton and Michel introduced a type of automata [2], (originally called complete unambigous Büchi automata, but nowadays known as Carton-Michel automata) which they showed to be expressively complete for ω-regular languages. These automata associate every word to a unique path, making it an ideal candidate for using patterns in the context of ω-regular languages. Preugschat and Wilke [21] pioneered this approach by giving characterizations of fragments of temporal logic relying partly on patterns. Their method involved separating the finite behaviour of the language from the infinite behaviour; the finite behaviour was then characterized using patterns, while the infinite behaviour was characterized using conditions on loop languages.

The variety of languages definable in FO^2, i.e., first order logic with only two variables, is well studied. Thérien and Wilke [27] showed that this variety was the collection of languages whose syntactic monoid was in **DA**. In particular, this established an equivalence between FO^2 and $\Sigma_2 \cap \Pi_2$ over finite words.

One can consider the quantifier alternation hierarchy inside FO^2. Due to the restriction on the number of variables, one needs to consider parse trees rather than translating formulae into prenex normal form. Over finite words, Weis and Immerman gave a combinatorial characterization of the join levels of this hierarchy [28]; algebraic characterizations were given by Weil and the second author [17] and independently by Krebs and Straubing [15]. The half-levels were characterized by Fleischer, Kufleitner and Lauser [9].

For ω-regular languages, algebraic characterizations often utilize Arnold's congruence. However, not every interesting class of languages can be characterized directly using this congruence; see e.g. [18]. On the other hand, combining algebraic properties with topology has proven a fruitful alternative in some cases where algebra alone is not enough; see e.g. [6,12,16]. In particular, this approach was used in yet unpublished work by Boussidan and the second author for the characterization of the join levels of the alternation hierarchies, and by the authors for the characterization of the half-levels [11].

In this contribution, we devote Sect. 3 to the development of a formalism for *subword patterns*: patterns where we can not only use identical words as labels of different paths, but also subwords. Patterns taking subwords into account were used, e.g. in [22]. Our formalism is a variation of that of Klíma and Polák [13], but considering automata instead of ordered semiautomata. For DFAs, this difference is superficial since the relevant semi-DFA can be obtained via minimization. Minimizing a Carton-Michel automaton (based on the reverse deterministic transition relation) does not necessarily produce a Carton-Michel automaton. For patterns which do not take final states into account, such as those used in [21], this is not a problem. However, this contribution contains patterns for which it matters.

In Sect. 4, we use the mentioned formalism to give DFA patterns for the algebraic varieties used in the characterizations of the quantifier alternation hierarchies inside FO^2. In Sect. 5, we extend this approach to Carton-Michel automata. This is done by separating the finite and infinite behaviours of the languages. The finite behaviour can be characterized by a pattern just as in the DFA-case. For varieties $\mathbf{J}_1 \subseteq \mathbf{V} \subseteq \mathbf{DA}$ the infinite behaviour of the recognized languages is completely determined by the imaginary alphabets (see [6]). A single fixed pattern is sufficient for all such varieties. Finally, we give patterns for open sets in the Cantor and alphabetic topology.

2   Preliminaries

We assume familiarity with standard concepts from the theory of regular and ω-regular languages and its connections to monoids and logic. For an introduction, we refer the reader to [20] for regular and [18] for ω-regular languages.

For a word $u \in A^*$, we denote by $u^\omega = uuu\cdots$ the infinite iteration of u. Let $\mathcal{A} = (Q, A, \cdot, i, F)$ be a (partial semi-)DFA. For $j \in Q$, $u \in A^*$, we write $j \cdot u$ for the value of the transition function at (j, u).

We introduce *Carton-Michel automata*, a particular type of Büchi automata. Let $\mathcal{A} = (Q, A, \circ, I, F)$ be a Büchi automaton. A *run* of $\mathcal{A}$ is an infinite path in $\mathcal{A}$. Each such run is *labeled* by an infinite word by reading the letters corresponding to each edge of the path. A run is *final* if it visits a final state infinitely often. The run is *accepting* if it is final and starts at an initial state. A word is *accepted* by $\mathcal{A}$ if it labels some accepting run, and the language *accepted* by $\mathcal{A}$, denoted $L(\mathcal{A})$, is the collection of all such words.

If following the edges backwards determines a function $\circ : Q \times A \to Q$, we say that $\mathcal{A}$ is *reverse deterministic*. A *Carton-Michel automaton* is a reverse deterministic Büchi automaton where every infinite word has a unique final run. Here we use the definition from [21] which differs slightly from the original definition by Carton and Michel [2]. The definitions coincide for automata which are *trim*, i.e., where every state is part of some final run.

For a DFA $\mathcal{A} = (Q, A, \cdot, i, F)$, we say that $j \leq_{\mathcal{A}} k$ if $j \cdot u \in F$ implies $k \cdot u \in F$ for all $u \in A^*$. We say that $i \equiv_{\mathcal{A}} j$ if $i \leq_{\mathcal{A}} j$ and $j \leq_{\mathcal{A}} i$. We use the same notation for reverse DFAs and Carton-Michel automata; we say $j \leq_{\mathcal{A}} k$ if $u \circ j \in I$ implies $u \circ k \in I$, and $j \equiv_{\mathcal{A}} k$ if $j \leq_{\mathcal{A}} k$ and $k \leq_{\mathcal{A}} j$.

The *Cantor topology* $\mathcal{O}_{cantor}$ is generated by the base $\{uA^\omega\}_{u\in A^*}$, and the *alphabetic topology* $\mathcal{O}_{alph}$ is generated by $\{uB^\omega\}_{u\in A^*, B\subseteq A}$. We denote by $\mathbb{B}(\mathcal{T})$ the Boolean closure of a topology.

Unless specified otherwise, we use the following notation: suppose $\mathbf{V}$ is a variety of (ordered) monoids; then $\mathcal{V}$ is the (positive) variety of languages whose syntactic monoids are in $\mathbf{V}$. The following varieties are of particular importance throughout this contribution:

- $\mathbf{DA} = [\![((yx)^\omega y(yx)^\omega = (xy)^\omega]\!]$
- $\mathbf{R} = [\![(yx)^\omega y = (yx)^\omega]\!]$, $\mathbf{L} = [\![y(xy)^\omega = (xy)^\omega]\!]$
- $\mathbf{J}_1 = [\![z^2 = z, xy = yx]\!]$, $\mathbf{J}^+ = [\![1 \leq z]\!]$

Here, ω is a formal symbol, corresponding to the idempotent power of a given monoid, and is thus unrelated to the ω denoting infinite iterations. The meaning of the symbol will be clear from context.

One way to generate new varieties from known ones is by using the Malcev product. Generally, Malcev products are defined using relational morphisms. However, for certain varieties, a more direct approach using the relations $\sim_{\mathbf{K}}$ and $\sim_{\mathbf{D}}$ is sufficient. This approach was refined in [11] to define a chain of varieties of ordered monoids. Let $s, t \in M$, then:

- $s \sim_{\mathbf{K}} t$ if for all idempotent elements e, we have $es, et <_{\mathcal{J}} e$ or $es = et$,
- $s \sim_{\mathbf{D}} t$ if for all idempotent elements f, we have $sf, tf <_{\mathcal{J}} f$ or $sf = tf$,
- $s \preceq_{\mathbf{KD}} t$ if for all $p, q \in M$: $p \mathrel{\mathcal{R}} ptq$ implies $p \mathrel{\mathcal{R}} psq$, $ptq \mathrel{\mathcal{L}} q$ implies $psq \mathrel{\mathcal{L}} q$, and $p \mathrel{\mathcal{R}} pt \wedge tq \mathrel{\mathcal{L}} q$ implies $psq \leq ptq$.

Given a variety $\mathbf{V}$, we have $M \in \mathbf{K} \text{\textcircled{m}} \mathbf{V}$ if $M/\sim_{\mathbf{K}} \in \mathbf{V}$, we have $M \in \mathbf{D} \text{\textcircled{m}} \mathbf{V}$ if $M/\sim_{\mathbf{D}} \in \mathbf{V}$ and $M \in \mathbf{V}_{\mathbf{KD}}$ if $M/\preceq_{\mathbf{KD}} \in \mathbf{V}$. Here $M/\preceq_{\mathbf{KD}}$ denotes the monoid consisting of the equivalence classes of the conjugacy induced by $\preceq_{\mathbf{KD}}$ and the order induced by the same relation. Let:

- $\mathbf{R}_1 = \mathbf{L}_1 = \mathbf{R} \cap \mathbf{L}$, $\mathbf{R}_{m+1} = \mathbf{K} \text{\textcircled{m}} \mathbf{L}_m$, $\mathbf{L}_{m+1} = \mathbf{D} \text{\textcircled{m}} \mathbf{R}_m$
- $\mathbf{Si}_1 = \mathbf{J}^+$, $\mathbf{Si}_{m+1} = (\mathbf{Si}_m)_{\mathbf{KD}}$

It is well known that $\mathbf{R}_2 = \mathbf{R}$ and $\mathbf{L}_2 = \mathbf{L}$ (see e.g. [19]).

Table 1. Decidability criteria for a language L with syntactic monoid M

	Finite words	Infinite words
Σ_1^2	$M \in \mathbf{Si}_1$	$M \in \mathbf{Si}_1$
		$L \in \mathcal{O}_{cantor}$
FO_1^2	$M \in \mathbf{R} \cap \mathbf{L}$	$M \in \mathbf{R} \cap \mathbf{L}$
		$L \in \mathbb{B}(\mathcal{O}_{cantor})$
Σ_2^2	$M \in \mathbf{Si}_2$	$M \in \mathbf{Si}_2$
		$L \in \mathcal{O}_{alph}$
$\mathrm{FO}_m^2, m \geq 2$	$M \in \mathbf{R}_{m+1} \cap \mathbf{L}_{m+1}$	
$\Sigma_m^2, m \geq 3$	$M \in \mathbf{Si}_m$	

Let $A = \{a_1, \ldots, a_n\}$ be an alphabet. We consider the fragment FO^2 of first order logic over the signature $(\leq, a_1, \ldots, a_n)$ where we only allow the use (and reuse) of two different variables. This fragment can be restricted further, by considering the number of allowed alternations. Consider the syntax

$$\varphi_0 ::= \top \mid \bot \mid \lambda(x) = a \mid x = y \mid x < y \mid \neg\varphi_0 \mid \varphi_0 \vee \varphi_0 \mid \varphi_0 \wedge \varphi_0$$

$$\varphi_m ::= \varphi_{m-1} \mid \neg\varphi_{m-1} \mid \varphi_m \vee \varphi_m \mid \varphi_m \wedge \varphi_m \mid \exists x \varphi_m \mid \exists y \varphi_m$$

where $a \in A$, and x and y are variables. The fragment Σ_m^2 consists of all formulae φ_m, the fragment Π_m^2 of all negations of formulae in Σ_m^2 and the fragment FO_m^2 of the Boolean combinations of formulae in Σ_m^2.

Each of these logical fragments defines a language variety. These varieties have decidability characterizations for both finite words [9,17] and infinite words [1,11]. These criteria are presented in Table 1.

3   Subword-Patterns

In this section, we introduce subword-patterns. Our formalism is inspired by that of Klíma and Polák [13], with two main differences; we work with DFAs instead of ordered semi-DFAs, and we allow our patterns to take subwords into account.

In **DA**, there is semantic equivalence between being a subword of and a factor of sufficiently long words. Thus, the patterns introduced in Sect. 4 can be rewritten to equivalent patterns which do not rely on subwords. However, the patterns obtained in this way are less readable than their equivalent subword patterns, arguably giving less insight into the actual behaviour of the varieties in consideration.

For the definition of subword patterns, we rely on homomorphism of semi-DFAs. The following definition is standard, and gives a way to define homomorphisms between semi-DFAs which originally had different alphabets.

Definition 1. *Let $\mathcal{A} = (Q, A, \cdot)$ be a semi-DFA, and let $h : B^* \to A^*$ be a homomorphism. The h-renaming of $\mathcal{A}$ is the semi-DFA $\mathcal{A}^h = (Q, B, \cdot^h)$ where $i \cdot^h b = i \cdot h(b)$.*

We give the formal definition of a subword-pattern. Intuitively, we can think of the edges of the pattern as paths in a given automaton and the relation $\preceq$ as being the subword relation which we impose on the words labeling these paths.

Definition 2. *Let X be a finite set with a partial order $\preceq$. A type 1 subword-pattern $\mathcal{P} = (\mathcal{S}, j \neq k)$ or type 2 subword-pattern $\mathcal{P} = (\mathcal{S}, j \not\preceq k)$ consists of a finite partial semiautomaton $\mathcal{S} = (V, X, \cdot)$ and two states $j, k \in V$. If $\mathcal{P} = (\mathcal{S}, j \neq k)$, we say that $\mathcal{P}$ is present in an automaton $\mathcal{A}$ if there exists a homomorphism $h : X^* \to A^*$ where $x \preceq y$ implies that $h(x)$ is a subword of $h(y)$ and a semiautomata homomorphism $g : \mathcal{S} \to \mathcal{A}^h$ such that $g(j) \neq_{\mathcal{A}} g(k)$ and for all $\ell \in V$, the state $g(\ell)$ is reachable from the initial state of $\mathcal{A}$. Analogously, we say that $\mathcal{P} = (\mathcal{S}, j \not\preceq k)$ is present if there exist h and g such that*

$g(j) \not\leq_{\mathcal{A}} g(k)$. *Since the type of the pattern is clear from the notation, we usually do not reference its type.*

We say that a pattern is rooted *if there is some state $r \in V$ such that every i satisfies $i = r \cdot x$ for some $x \in X^*$. Finally, two patterns $\mathcal{P}_1$, $\mathcal{P}_2$ are* equivalent *if for all $\mathcal{A}$, the pattern $\mathcal{P}_1$ is present in $\mathcal{A}$ if and only if $\mathcal{P}_2$ is.*

Let us consider the following example. Let $X = \{x, A_x\}$ with $A_x \preceq x$ and let $\mathcal{P}_{\mathbf{DA}} = (\mathcal{S}, j \neq k)$ where $\mathcal{S}$ is

This pattern is present in an automaton $\mathcal{A}$, if there are two cycles starting at different states, but labeled by the same word, as well as a path between them labeled by a word which is a subword of the aforementioned one. It can be shown that this pattern is present in a DFA if and only if the syntactic monoid of the accepted language is not in **DA**.

Since we later consider Carton-Michel automata, we also need to consider patterns for reverse DFAs. This adaptation is trivial: we reverse the direction of transversal in the underlying graph of $\mathcal{P}$, turning it into a partial reverse semi-DFA. Instead of requiring that $g(\ell)$ is reachable from the initial state, we require that $g(\ell)$ is reachable from some cycle containing a final state. In particular, if $\mathcal{P}$ is a subword-pattern, then $\overline{\mathcal{P}}$ is the same pattern with all edges reversed. All of the following results are valid also for patterns in reverse DFAs.

In general, the presence of patterns is a feature of the particular automata, and not the language (cf. [13, Example 3.4]). We are interested in patterns which are indeed a feature of the language rather than the particular automata, and thus we make the following definition. It is essentially the same as the H-invariant configurations of Klíma and Polák [13].

Definition 3. *A (subword-)pattern is a* language pattern *if for all $\mathcal{A}, \mathcal{A}'$ such that $L(\mathcal{A}) = L(\mathcal{A}')$, we have $\mathcal{P}$ present in $\mathcal{A}$ if and only if it is present in $\mathcal{A}'$.*

Definition 4. *Let $\mathbf{P}$ be a collection of language patterns. Then $\langle \mathbf{P} \rangle$ is the set of languages $L(\mathcal{A})$ such that $\mathcal{A}$ does not have any of the patterns $\mathcal{P} \in \mathbf{P}$. For a finite set of patterns $\{\mathcal{P}_1, \ldots, \mathcal{P}_n\}$, we use the notation $\langle \mathcal{P}_1, \ldots, \mathcal{P}_n \rangle$ rather than $\langle \{\mathcal{P}_1, \ldots, \mathcal{P}_n\} \rangle$.*

Definition 5. *Let $\mathcal{S} = (V, X, \circ)$ be a partial semiautomaton, and $\mathcal{P} = (\mathcal{S}, j \leq k)$ a subword-pattern. Then $\mathcal{P}$ is* simple *if it is a tree after removing all self-loops.*
Let $\mathcal{L} = \{x \in X \mid \ell \circ x = \ell \text{ for some } \ell \in V\}$ and let

$$\mathcal{K} = \{(x, y) \in X \times \mathcal{L} \mid \ell \neq \ell \circ x = \ell \circ xy \text{ for some } \ell \in V\}.$$

That is, $\mathcal{L}$ is the collection of variables which occur as some loop in $\mathcal{S}$, and $\mathcal{K}$ is the collection of all pairs (x, y) occurring together with $\ell \neq \ell'$ as follows:

$$\text{(1)}$$

The pattern $\mathcal{P}$ is balanced *if*

(i) *for every $y \in \mathcal{L}$, there exists $x \in X$ such that $(x, y) \in \mathcal{K}$,*

(ii) *for all $(x, y) \in \mathcal{K}$, if $(x, y') \in \mathcal{K}$ then $y' = y$,*

(iii) *for all $(x, y) \in \mathcal{K}$, if $\ell \circ x$ is defined, then $\ell \circ xy = \ell \circ x$ and if $\ell \circ y = \ell$, then there exists $\ell' \neq \ell$ such that $\ell' \circ x = \ell$. In other words, whenever x or y occurs in $\mathcal{S}$, then it occurrs together with the other variable as in (1),*

(iv) *for all $y \in \mathcal{L}$, if $y \preceq z$, then $z \in \mathcal{L}$,*

(v) *for all $(x, y) \in \mathcal{K}$, if $x \preceq z$ for $x \neq z$ then $y \preceq z$.*

If $\preceq$ is the identity, then conditions (iv) and (v) are trivial, and the definition reduces to that in [13].

Proposition 1. *A simple and balanced subword-pattern is a language pattern.*

As an example, consider the pattern $\mathcal{P}_{\mathbf{DA}}$. Then $(A_x, x) \in \mathcal{K}$. However, x occurrs as a loop at j while there is no edge labeled by A_x ending at j. Thus $\mathcal{P}_{\mathbf{DA}}$ is not balanced. However, we get an equivalent balanced pattern $\mathcal{P}'_{\mathbf{DA}}$:

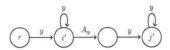

We note that finding a pattern is in **NL** (cf. [3, 10]).

Proposition 2. *Let $\mathcal{A}$ be a DFA or a Carton-Michel automata. Checking the presence of a pattern $\mathcal{P}$ in $\mathcal{A}$ is in **NL** in the size of $\mathcal{A}$.*

Proposition 3. *Let P be a nontrivial property of regular (resp. ω-regular) languages containing the empty language and such that whenever $L \in P$, then $Lu^{-1} \in P$ (resp. $u^{-1}L \in P$). Given a DFA (resp. Carton-Michel automata) $\mathcal{A}$, deciding such a property is **NL**-hard in the size of $\mathcal{A}$.*

4   Hierarchies of Subword-Patterns

In this section, we show how to use patterns which characterize a variety $\mathbf{V} \subseteq \mathbf{DA}$ to create new patterns characterizing $\mathbf{K} \Ⓜ\mathbf{V}$, $\mathbf{D} \ⓂY \mathbf{V}$ and $\mathbf{V}_{\mathbf{KD}}$. Patterns characterizing $\mathbf{R}_m$, $\mathbf{L}_m$ and $\mathbf{Si}_m$ becomes an immediate corollary. We also give these patterns explicitly.

Given a pattern $\mathcal{P}$, we construct patterns $\mathcal{P}_k$, $\mathcal{P}_d$ and $\mathcal{P}_{kd}$. These are obtained by appending new states either at the root of $\mathcal{P}$ as in (2) below (for $\mathcal{P}_k$), at the two states which were compared in $\mathcal{P}$ as in (3) below (for $\mathcal{P}_d$), or both (for $\mathcal{P}_{kd}$).

When appending states as in (3), we compare j' and k' in the new pattern. The variables e and f are new, and defined to satisfy $x \preceq e, f$ for all variables x of the original pattern $\mathcal{P}$. Formally, we have the following definition.

Definition 6. *Let $\mathcal{P} = (\mathcal{S}, j \neq k)$ be a rooted pattern where $\mathcal{S} = (V, X, \circ)$ with the root r. Let $X_k = X \cup \{e\}$ where $x \prec e$ for all $x \in X$, and let $V_k = V \cup \{r'\}$. Let $\mathcal{S}_k = (V_k, X_k, \circ_k)$ where $r' \circ_k e = r$, $r \circ_k e = r$ and $\ell \circ_k x = \ell \circ x$ for all $\ell \in V$, $x \in X$ for which $\ell \circ x$ is defined. We define $\mathcal{P}_k = (\mathcal{S}_k, j \neq k)$.*

Next, let $X_d = X \cup \{f\}$, $V_d = V \cup \{j', k'\}$ and let $j \circ_d f = j'$, $k \circ_d f = k'$, $j' \circ_d f = j'$, $k' \circ_d f = k'$ and $\ell \circ_d x = \ell \circ x$ for all $\ell \in V$, $x \in X$ for which $\ell \circ x$ is defined. Then $\mathcal{S}_d = (V_d, X_d, \circ_d)$ and $\mathcal{P}_d = (\mathcal{S}_d, j' \neq k')$.

Finally, let $X_{kd} = X \cup \{e, f\}$ where $x \prec e$, $x \prec f$ for all $x \in X$, and let $V_{kd} = V \cup \{r', i', j'\}$. We define $r' \circ_{kd} e = r$, $r \circ_{kd} e = r$, $j \circ_{kd} f = j'$, $k \circ_{kd} f = k'$, $j' \circ_{kd} f = j'$, $k' \circ_{kd} f = k'$ and $\ell \circ_{kd} x = \ell \circ x$ for all $\ell \in V$, $x \in X$ for which $\ell \circ x$ is defined. Then $\mathcal{S}_{kd} = (V_{kd}, X_{kd}, \circ_{kd})$ and $\mathcal{P}_{kd} = (\mathcal{S}_{kd}, j' \neq k')$.

We make analogous definitions for type 2 patterns $\mathcal{P} = (\mathcal{S}, j \not\leq k)$.

As an example, we consider the simple and balanced pattern $\mathcal{P}'_{\mathbf{DA}}$. Let y and A_y as in $\mathcal{P}'_{\mathbf{DA}}$. The pattern $(\mathcal{P}'_{\mathbf{DA}})_{kd}$ is given by

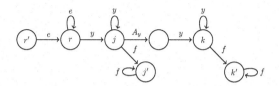

It is straightforward to show that $(\mathcal{P}_{\mathbf{DA}})_{kd}$ is in fact equivalent to $\mathcal{P}_{\mathbf{DA}}$.

If $\mathcal{P}$ is simple and balanced, then $\mathcal{P}_k$, $\mathcal{P}_d$ and $\mathcal{P}_{kd}$ are all simple and balanced. The constructions also preserve another property. We want to consider patterns where the alphabet of one path is a subset of the other (for type 2 patterns), or where they are the same (for type 1 patterns).

Definition 7. *Let $\mathcal{P} = (\mathcal{S}, j \not\leq k)$ be a pattern such that whenever x is on the path from r to j, then there exists y on the path from r to k such that $x \preceq y$. We say that $\mathcal{P}$ is one-alphabeted. If $\mathcal{P} = (\mathcal{S}, j \neq k)$, then it is one-alphabeted if both the above holds and for every x on a path from r to k, there is y on the path from r to j such that $x \preceq y$.*

The following theorem shows how, for some collections of patterns, these constructions can be used to obtain pattern characterizations for Malcev products and varieties constructed using the $\preceq_{\mathbf{KD}}$-relation. For a collection $\mathbf{P}$ of patterns, we let $\mathbf{P}_k = \{\mathcal{P}_k \mid \mathcal{P} \in \mathbf{P}\}$, and similarly for $\mathbf{P}_d$ and $\mathbf{P}_{kd}$.

Theorem 1. *Let $\mathbf{P}$ be a collection of simple, balanced and one-alphabeted patterns with $\mathcal{P}'_{\mathbf{DA}} \in \mathbf{P}$. Suppose $\mathcal{V} = \langle \mathbf{P} \rangle$. If all patterns in $\mathbf{P}$ are type 1, then*

(i) the language variety corresponding to $\mathbf{K} \circledM \mathbf{V}$ is $\langle \mathbf{P}_k \rangle$,
(ii) the language variety corresponding to $\mathbf{D} \circledM \mathbf{V}$ is $\langle \mathbf{P}_d \rangle$,

and for $\mathbf{P}$ containing any combination of type 1 and type 2 patterns, we have

(iii) the language variety corresponding to $\mathbf{V}_{\mathbf{KD}}$ is $\langle \mathbf{P}_{kd} \rangle$.

The explicit patterns for $\mathbf{R}_m$, $\mathbf{L}_m$ and $\mathbf{Si}_m$ all build on the same class of directed graphs. However, the orderings of the variables are different.

Definition 8. *For $m \geq 1$, we define the following sets of variables:*

- $X_m = \{x, e_1, \ldots, e_{\lfloor m/2 \rfloor}, f_1, \ldots, f_{\lfloor (m-1)/2 \rfloor}\}$ *with* $x \preceq e_i \preceq f_i \preceq e_{i+1}$,
- $Y_m = \{x, e_1, \ldots, e_{\lfloor (m-1)/2 \rfloor}, f_1, \ldots, f_{\lfloor m/2 \rfloor}\}$ *with* $x \preceq f_i \preceq e_i \preceq f_{i+1}$,
- $Z_m = \{x, e_1, \ldots, e_{m-1}, f_1, \ldots, f_{m-1}\}$ *with* $x \preceq y$ *for all* $y \in Z_m$ *and* $z_i \preceq z_{i+1}$ *for* $z_i \in \{e_i, f_i\}$, $z_{i+1} \in \{e_{i+1}, f_{i+1}\}$.

Let $\mathcal{S}_m^X$ (resp. $\mathcal{S}_m^Y$, $\mathcal{S}_m^Z$) have the following structure, where $x, e_i, f_{i'} \in X_m$ (resp. in Y_m, Z_m) and ℓ and ℓ' are chosen to match the maximal e_i and $f_{i'}$ respectively.

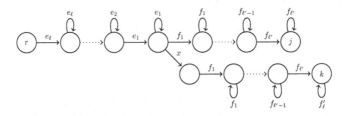

Then

- $\mathcal{P}_m^{\mathbf{R}} = \left(\mathcal{S}_m^X, j \neq k\right)$ *for even* $m \geq 2$, $\mathcal{P}_m^{\mathbf{R}} = \left(\mathcal{S}_m^Y, j \neq k\right)$ *for odd* $m \geq 3$,
- $\mathcal{P}_m^{\mathbf{L}} = \left(\mathcal{S}_m^Y, j \neq k\right)$ *for even* $m \geq 2$, $\mathcal{P}_m^{\mathbf{L}} = \left(\mathcal{S}_m^X, j \neq k\right)$ *for odd* $m \geq 3$,
- $\mathcal{P}_m^{\mathbf{Si}} = \left(\mathcal{S}_m^Z, j \not\preceq k\right)$ *for* $m \geq 1$.

Although Theorem 1 requires the presence of the pattern $\mathcal{P}_{\mathbf{DA}}'$, it need not be a part of the explicit characterization; the non-presence of either of the patterns $\mathcal{P}_m^{\mathbf{R}}$ or $\mathcal{P}_m^{\mathbf{L}}$ implies the non-presence of $\mathcal{P}_{\mathbf{DA}}'$.

Corollary 1. *Let $\mathcal{A}$ be a DFA, and let M be the syntactic monoid of $L(\mathcal{A})$. Then the following holds:*

(i) $M \in \mathbf{R}_m$ if and only if the pattern $\mathcal{P}_m^{\mathbf{R}}$ is not present in $\mathcal{A}$,
(ii) $M \in \mathbf{L}_m$ if and only if the pattern $\mathcal{P}_m^{\mathbf{L}}$ is not present in $\mathcal{A}$,
(iii) $M \in \mathbf{Si}_m$ if and only if neither $\mathcal{P}_m^{\mathbf{Si}}$ nor $\mathcal{P}_{\mathbf{DA}}$ is present in $\mathcal{A}$.

5   Patterns for Carton-Michel Automata

In this section, we introduce results on patterns for Carton-Michel automata. The characterizations, inspired by Table 1, are for the levels $\mathbf{R}_m$, $\mathbf{L}_m$ and $\mathbf{Si}_m$, as well as the Cantor and alphabetic topologies.

Our main approach is to separate the finite and infinite behaviour of the language. On the algebra side, we formalize this via the introduction of the fin-syntactic and inf-syntactic monoids. The former identifies words which behaves the same with respect to finite prefixes of the language, and the latter identifies words which behaves the same with respect to infinitely iterated words.

Definition 9. *Let $L \subseteq A^\omega$ be a language and let $u, v \in A^*$. We say that $u \leq_{fin} v$ if for all $x, y, z \in A^*$,*

$$xuyz^\omega \in L \Rightarrow xvyz^\omega \in L.$$

We define the fin-syntactic morphism *to be the natural projection $\pi : A^* \to A^*/\leq_{fin}$ and the codomain is called the* fin-syntactic monoid. *We define the inf-syntactic morphism and monoid analogously using $\leq_{inf}$ defined by $u \leq_{inf} v$ if for all $x, y \in A^*$, we have*

$$x(uy)^\omega \in L \Rightarrow x(vy)^\omega \in L.$$

It is clear that the syntactic semigroup is in some variety $\mathbf{V}$ if and only if both the fin-syntactic monoid and inf-syntactic semigroup are in $\mathbf{V}$. Furthermore, it can be shown that if $\mathcal{P}$ is some pattern characterizing $\mathbf{V}$ over reverse-DFAs, then the fin-syntactic monoid is in $\mathbf{V}$ if and only if $\mathcal{A}$ does not have the pattern $\mathcal{P}$.

Thus, the main difficult step in the generalization from (reverse-)DFAs to Carton-Michel automata is dealing with the infinite behaviour (i.e., the inf-syntactic morphism). For varieties $\mathbf{J}_1 \subseteq \mathbf{V} \subseteq \mathbf{DA}$, this requires only a pattern for the infinite behaviour of $\mathbf{DA}$; the syntactic monoid is in $\mathbf{V}$ if and only if the fin-syntactic monoid is in $\mathbf{V}$ and the inf-syntactic monoid is in $\mathbf{DA}$.

We use a modified version of subword-patterns. The witness h is now required to be a homomorphism of semigroups $h : X^+ \to A^+$. Furthermore, edges can be required to be *final*, meaning that at least one state on the path in the image of the edge is a final state. This problem is still in **NL**. Since $\mathbf{Si}_1 \not\subseteq \mathbf{J}_1$, we also need a special characterization for its inf-syntactic monoid.

Proposition 4. *Let $\mathcal{A}$ be a Carton-Michel automaton, and let M_{inf} be the inf-syntactic monoid of $L(\mathcal{A})$. Let $\mathcal{S}_{si}$ and $\mathcal{S}_{da}$ be the following partial semiautomata:*

where $A_z \preceq z$ and for each pattern the black bold edge as well as at least one of the gray bold edges are final edges. We then have the following characterizations:

(i) *$M_{inf} \in \mathbf{Si}_1$ if and only if $\mathcal{P}^{\mathbf{Si}}_{1\text{-}inf} = (\mathcal{S}_{si}, j \not\leq k)$ is not present in $\mathcal{A}$,*

(ii) *suppose $\overline{\mathcal{P}}_{\mathbf{DA}}$ is not in $\mathcal{A}$, then $M_{inf} \in \mathbf{DA}$ if and only if $\mathcal{P}_{\mathbf{DA}\text{-}inf} = (\mathcal{S}_{da}, j \neq k)$ is not present in $\mathcal{A}$.*

Theorem 2. *Let $\mathcal{A}$ be a Carton-Michel automaton, and let M be the syntactic monoid of $L(\mathcal{A})$. Then for $m \geq 2$:*

(i) *$M \in \mathbf{Si}_1$ if and only if neither $\overline{\mathcal{P}}^{\mathbf{Si}}_1$ nor $\mathcal{P}^{\mathbf{Si}}_{1\text{-}inf}$ is present in $\mathcal{A}$,*

(ii) *$M \in \mathbf{Si}_m$ if and only if neither $\overline{\mathcal{P}}^{\mathbf{Si}}_m$, $\overline{\mathcal{P}}_{\mathbf{DA}}$ nor $\mathcal{P}_{\mathbf{DA}\text{-}inf}$ is present in $\mathcal{A}$,*

(iii) *$M \in \mathbf{R}_m \cap \mathbf{L}_m$ if and only if neither $\overline{\mathcal{P}}^{\mathbf{R}}_m$, $\overline{\mathcal{P}}^{\mathbf{L}}_m$ nor $\mathcal{P}_{\mathbf{DA}\text{-}inf}$ is present in $\mathcal{A}$.*

We provide patterns for the Cantor and alphabetic topology. One can obtain patterns for being closed in the respective topology by switching j and k, and for being clopen (i.e., both open and closed) by replacing the inequality by an equality. The latter is of particular importance; for $\mathcal{A}$ in which $\overline{\mathcal{P}}_{\mathbf{DA}}$ is not present, being in $\mathbb{B}(\mathcal{O}_{cantor})$ is equivalent to being clopen in the alphabetic topology.

Proposition 5. *Let $\mathcal{A}$ be a Carton-Michel automaton, and let $\mathcal{S}_c$ and $\mathcal{S}_a$ be the partial semiautomata defined below:*

Where for $\mathcal{S}_a$, we have $A_z, B_z \preceq z$. Then

(i) $L(\mathcal{A}) \in \mathcal{O}_{cantor}$ if and only if $\mathcal{P}_{cantor} = (\mathcal{S}_c, j \not\leq k)$ is not present in $\mathcal{A}$,
(ii) $L(\mathcal{A}) \in \mathcal{O}_{alph}$ if and only if $\mathcal{P}_{alph} = (\mathcal{S}_a, j \not\leq k)$ is not present in $\mathcal{A}$,
(iii) $L(\mathcal{A})$ is clopen in the alphabetic topology if and only if $\mathcal{P}_{alph\text{-}clopen} = (\mathcal{S}_a, k \neq j)$ is not present in $\mathcal{A}$.

To conclude this contribution, we note some optimizations. It can be shown that nonexistence of $\overline{\mathcal{P}}_1^{\mathbf{Si}}$ and $\mathcal{P}_{cantor}$ implies nonexistence of $\mathcal{P}_{1\text{-}inf}^{\mathbf{Si}}$. Similarly, the non-existence of $\mathcal{P}_{alph}$ and $\overline{\mathcal{P}}_{\mathbf{DA}}$ implies the non-existence of $\mathcal{P}_{\mathbf{DA}\text{-}inf}$. Thus, in checking the conditions for Σ_1^2, Σ_2^2 and FO_1^2 of Table 1, one need not consider the patterns $\mathcal{P}_{1\text{-}inf}^{\mathbf{Si}}$ and $\mathcal{P}_{\mathbf{DA}\text{-}inf}$.

Conclusion

For all full and half levels of the FO^2 quantifier alternation hierarchy, we give automata characterizations in terms of forbidden subword patterns. These results rely on algebraic and topological characterizations of the FO^2 levels (see Table 1). For finite words, we consider DFAs (Corollary 1) and for infinite words, our patterns apply to Carton-Michel automata (Theorem 2 and Proposition 5). For every fixed level, these patterns yield an **NL**-algorithm to decide whether a given automaton accepts a language at this level (Proposition 2); this problem is sometimes called the membership problem for the respective level. Together with a more general **NL**-hardness result (Proposition 3), this shows that the membership problem is **NL**-complete for every level of the FO^2 quantifier alternation hierarchy for both finite and infinite words.

References

1. Boussidan, A., Kufleitner, M.: FO^2 quantifier alternation over infinite words (2018). Unpublished manuscript
2. Carton, O., Michel, M.: Unambiguous Büchi automata. Theoret. Comput. Sci. **297**(1–3), 37–81 (2003)

3. Cho, S., Huỳnh, D.T.: Finite-automaton aperiodicity is PSPACE-complete. Theoret. Comput. Sci. **88**(1), 99–116 (1991)
4. Cohen, J., Perrin, D., Pin, J.É.: On the expressive power of temporal logic. J. Comput. System Sci. **46**(3), 271–294 (1993)
5. Diekert, V., Gastin, P., Kufleitner, M.: A survey on small fragments of first-order logic over finite words. Internat. J. Found. Comput. Sci. **19**(3), 513–548 (2008)
6. Diekert, V., Kufleitner, M.: Fragments of first-order logic over infinite words. Theory Comput. Syst. **48**(3), 486–516 (2011)
7. Eilenberg, S.: Automata, Languages, and Machines, vol. B. Academic Press (1976)
8. Fleischer, L.: Efficient membership testing for pseudovarieties of finite semigroups. arXiv:1805.00650 (2018)
9. Fleischer, L., Kufleitner, M., Lauser, A.: The half-levels of the FO2 alternation hierarchy. Theory Comput. Syst. **61**(2), 352–370 (2017)
10. Glaßer, C., Schmitz, H.: Languages of dot-depth 3/2. Theory Comput. Syst. **42**(2), 256–286 (2008)
11. Henriksson, V., Kufleitner, M.: Nesting negations in FO^2 over infinite words. arXiv:2012.01309 (2020)
12. Kallas, J., Kufleitner, M., Lauser, A.: First-order fragments with successor over infinite words. In: Proceedings STACS 2011, LIPIcs, vol. 9, pp. 356–367. Dagstuhl Publishing (2011)
13. Klíma, O., Polák, L.: Forbidden patterns for ordered automata. J. Autom. Lang. Comb. **25**(2–3), 141–169 (2020)
14. Kozen, D.: Lower bounds for natural proof systems. In: FOCS 1977, Proceedings, pp. 254–266, Providence, Rhode Island. IEEE Computer Society Press (1977)
15. Krebs, A., Straubing, H.: An effective characterization of the alternation hierarchy in two-variable logic. ACM Trans. Comput. Log. **18**(4), 30:1–22 (2017)
16. Kufleitner, M., Walter, T.: Level two of the quantifier alternation hierarchy over infinite words. Theory Comput. Syst. **62**(3), 467–480 (2018)
17. Kufleitner, M., Weil, P.: The FO^2 alternation hierarchy is decidable. In: Proceedings CSL 2012, LIPIcs, vol. 16, pp. 426–439. Dagstuhl Publishing (2012)
18. Perrin, D., Pin, J.-É.: Infinite Words. Elsevier (2004)
19. Pin, J.É.: Varieties of Formal Languages. Foundations of Computer Science, North Oxford Academic (1986)
20. Pin, J.-É.: Mathematical foundations of automata theory (2020). https://www.irif.fr/~jep/PDF/MPRI/MPRI.pdf
21. Preugschat, S., Wilke, T.: Effective characterizations of simple fragments of temporal logic using Carton-Michel automata. Log. Methods Comput. Sci. **9**(2:08), 1–22 (2013)
22. Schmitz, H., Wagner, K.W.: The Boolean Hierarchy over Level 1/2 of the Straubing-Thérien Hierarchy. arXiv:cs/9809118 (1998)
23. Schützenberger, M.P.: Sur le produit de concaténation non ambigu. Semigroup Forum **13**(1), 47–75 (1976)
24. Stern, J.: Characterizations of some classes of regular events. Theoret. Comput. Sci. **35**(1), 17–42 (1985)
25. Stern, J.: Complexity of some problems from the theory of automata. Inform. Control **66**(3), 163–176 (1985)
26. Straubing, H., Weil, P.: Varieties. arXiv:1502.03951 (2015)
27. Thérien, D., Wilke, T.: Over words, two variables are as powerful as one quantifier alternation. In: Proceedings STOC 1998, pp. 234–240. ACM Press (1998)
28. Weis, P., Immerman, N.: Structure theorem and strict alternation hierarchy for FO^2 on words. Log. Methods Comput. Sci. **5**(3:3), 1–23 (2009)

State Complexity of Projection
on Languages Recognized by Permutation
Automata and Commuting Letters

Stefan Hoffmann$^{(\boxtimes)}$ (iD)

Informatikwissenschaften, FB IV, Universität Trier,
Universitätsring 15, 54296 Trier, Germany
hoffmanns@informatik.uni-trier.de

Abstract. The projected language of a general deterministic automaton with n states is recognizable by a deterministic automaton with $2^{n-1} + 2^{n-m} - 1$ states, where m denotes the number of states incident to unobservable non-loop transitions, and this bound is best possible. Here, we derive the tight bound $2^{n-\lceil \frac{m}{2} \rceil} - 1$ for permutation automata. For a state-partition automaton with n states (also called automata with the observer property) the projected language is recognizable with n states. Up to now, these, and finite languages projected onto unary languages, were the only classes of automata known to possess this property. We show that this is also true for commutative automata and we find commutative automata that are not state-partition automata.

Keywords: State complexity · Finite automata · Projection ·
Permutation automata · State-partition automata · Commutative
automata

1 Introduction

The state complexity of a regularity-preserving operation is the minimal number of states needed in a recognizing automaton for the result of this operation, dependent on the size of the input automaton. The study of the state complexity was initiated in [18] and systematically started in [33]. As the number of states of a recognizing automaton could be interpreted as the memory required to describe the recognized language and is directly related to the runtime of algorithms employing regular languages, obtaining state complexity bounds is a natural question with applications in verification, natural language processing or software engineering [7,15,21,25,30].

Here, in terms of state complexity, we are concerned with deterministic automata only. There were also investigations using nondeterministic automata [8]. However, deterministic automata have better algorithmic properties: (1) equality could be done in almost linear time [10], (2) the minimal automaton is unique up to isomorphism [11] and (3) there is an $O(n \log n)$-time minimization algorithm [9]. Contrary, for nondeterministic automata, equality testing is

© Springer Nature Switzerland AG 2021
N. Moreira and R. Reis (Eds.): DLT 2021, LNCS 12811, pp. 192–203, 2021.
https://doi.org/10.1007/978-3-030-81508-0_16

PSPACE-complete [27], minimal automata are not unique and minimization is a PSPACE-complete problem [8].

The state complexity of the projection operation was investigated in [13,31]. In [31], the tight upper bound $3 \cdot 2^{n-2} - 1$ was shown, and in [13] the refined, and tight, bound $2^{n-1} + 2^{n-m} - 1$ was shown, where m is related to the number of unobservable transitions for the projection operator.

The projection operator has applications in engineering, verification, fault diagnosis and supervisory control [5,16,17,32], as it corresponds to the observable behavior, a simplified or a restricted view of a modeled system. However, as, in general, the resulting automaton could be exponentially large, in practical applications only those projections that avoid this blow-up are interesting. Motivated by this, in [14] state-partition automata for a projection were introduced, a class of automata for which the projection is recognizable with n states, if the input automaton has n states.

Permutation automata were introduced in [29] and by McNaugthon [19] in connection with the star-height problem. The languages recognized by permutation automata are called (pure-)group languages [19,23,24]. However, one could argue that, if not viewed as language recognizing devices, but as mere state-transition systems, sometimes also just called semi-automata, permutation automata were around under the disguise of finite permutation groups, i.e., subgroups of the group of all permutation on a finite set, since the beginning of the 19th century, starting with the work of Galois, Lagrange, Jordan and others [3,22]. However, certainly, the viewpoint was different.

Languages recognized by permutation automata are not describable by first-order formulae using only the order relation [20] and commutative regular languages correspond to threshold and modulo counting of letters [24]. The languages recognized by certain permutation automata, for example whose transformation monoids are solvable or supersoluble groups, were described in [4,6,28]. Investigation of the state complexity of common operations on permutation automata was initiated on last years edition of this conference [12].

Here, we investigate the projection operator on permutation automata. We give a better tight bound for permutation automata, also parameterized by the number of unobservable transitions, that, however, also grows exponentially. We give sufficient conditions, related to normal subgroups, to yield a state-partition permutation automaton for a given projection. Then, we investigate projections for commuting letters, this in particular encompasses commutative languages and automata. We show that if we delete commuting letters by a projection operator, then we also just need n states for an n-state input automaton for the projected language. In particular this applies to commutative automata. We find commutative automata that are not state-partition automata for a given projection. This is in particular interesting, as in [13], it was noted that up to then, only state-partition automata and automata describing finite language with a unary projected language were known to have the property that we only need n states for the projected languages.

Lastly, we derive that the projection operator preserves every variety of commutative languages. This includes, for example, the commutative aperiodic, the commutative group languages or the commutative piecewise-testable languages.

2   General Notions

By Σ we denote a finite set of symbols, also called an *alphabet*. By Σ^* we denote the set of all *words* over Σ, i.e., finite sequences with the concatenation operation. The *empty word* is denoted by ε. A *language* L is a subset $L \subseteq \Sigma^*$. Languages using only a single symbol are called *unary languages*.

If X is a set, by $\mathcal{P}(X) = \{Y \mid Y \subseteq X\}$ we denote the *power set* of X.

If x is a non-negative real number, by $\lceil x \rceil$ we denote the smallest natural number greater or equal to x and by $\lfloor x \rfloor$ the largest natural number smaller or equal to x.

Let $\Gamma \subseteq \Sigma$. The homomorphism $\pi_\Gamma : \Sigma^* \to \Gamma^*$ given by $\pi_\Gamma(x) = x$ for $x \in \Gamma$ and $\pi_\Gamma(x) = \varepsilon$ for $x \in \Sigma \backslash \Gamma$ is called a *projection (for Γ)*. If $p, q \in Q$, $x \in \Sigma$, then a transition $\delta(p, x) = q$ is said to be *unobservable* with respect to the projection π_Γ if $x \in \Sigma \backslash \Gamma$, i.e., $\pi_\Gamma(x) = \varepsilon$. Here, only non-loop unobservable transitions are of interest, i.e., those such that $p \neq q$.

A *(partial) deterministic finite automaton (DFA)* is denoted by a quintuple $\mathcal{A} = (Q, \Sigma, \delta, q_0, F)$, where Q is a *finite set of states*, Σ the *input alphabet*, $\delta : Q \times \Sigma \to Q$ is a *partial transition function*, q_0 the *start state* and $F \subseteq Q$ the set of *final states*. The DFA is said to be *complete* if δ is a total function. In the usual way, the transition function δ can be extended to a function $\hat{\delta} : Q \times \Sigma^* \to Q$ by setting, for $q \in Q$, $u \in \Sigma^*$ and $a \in \Sigma$, $\hat{\delta}(q, \varepsilon) = q$ and $\hat{\delta}(q, ua) = \delta(\hat{\delta}(q, u), a)$. In the following, we drop the distinction between δ and $\hat{\delta}$ and denote both functions simply by δ.

For $S \subseteq Q$ and $u \in \Sigma^*$, we set $\delta(S, u) = \{\delta(s, u) \mid s \in S \text{ and } \delta(s, u) \text{ is defined}\}$.

The language *recognized* by $\mathcal{A}$ is $L(\mathcal{A}) = \{u \in \Sigma^* \mid \delta(q_0, u) \in F\}$. A language $L \subseteq \Sigma^*$ is called *regular*, if there exists an automaton $\mathcal{A}$ such that $L = L(\mathcal{A})$.

For $u \in \Sigma^*$, we write $\delta(p, u) = \delta(q, u)$ if both are defined and the results are equal or both are undefined.

We say that q is *reachable* from p (in $\mathcal{A}$) if there exists a word $u \in \Sigma^*$ such that $\delta(p, u) = q$. The DFA $\mathcal{A}$ is called *initially connected*, if every state is reachable from the start state.

The DFA $\mathcal{A} = (Q, \Sigma, \delta, q_0, F)$ is called *commutative*, if, for each $a, b \in \Sigma$ and $q \in Q$, we have $\delta(q, ab) = \delta(q, ba)$.

Let $\mathcal{A} = (Q, \Sigma, \delta, q_0, F)$ be a complete DFA. For a word $u \in \Sigma^*$, the *transition function (in $\mathcal{A}$) associated to u* is the function $\delta_u : Q \to Q$ given by $\delta_u(q) = \delta(q, u)$ for $q \in Q$. The *transformation monoid* is $\mathcal{T}_\mathcal{A} = \{\delta_u \mid u \in \Sigma^*\}$. Note that we defined the transformation monoid only for complete DFAs, as this is the only context where we need this notion here.

To denote transitions in permutation DFAs, we use a *cycle notation* also used in [2,12]. More formally, $(q_1, \ldots, q_k)$ denotes the cyclic permutation mapping q_i to q_{i+1} for $i \in \{1, \ldots, k-1\}$ and q_k to q_1. For example, $a = (1, 2)(3, 4, 5)$ means the letter a swaps the states 1 and 2, cyclically permutes the states $3, 4$ and 5 in the indicated order and fixes all other states.

A *variety (of formal languages)* $\mathcal{V}$ [6,23,24] associates, to each alphabet Σ, a class of recognizable languages $\mathcal{V}(\Sigma^*)$ over Σ such that (1) $\mathcal{V}(\Sigma^*)$ is a boolean algebra, (2) if $\varphi : \Sigma^* \to \Gamma^*$ is a homomorphism, then $L \in \mathcal{V}(\Gamma^*)$ implies $\varphi^{-1}(L) \in$

$\mathcal{V}(\Sigma^*)$ and (3) if $L \in \mathcal{V}(\Sigma^*)$ and $x \in \Sigma$, then $\{u \in \Sigma^* \mid xu \in L\}$ and $\{u \in \Sigma^* \mid ux \in L\}$ are in $\mathcal{V}(\Sigma^*)$.

3 Orbit Sets, Projected Languages and Permutation Automata

First, we introduce the orbit set of a set of states for a subalphabet. An orbit set collects those states that are reachable from a given set of states by only using words from a given subalphabet. This is also called *unobservable reach* in [5].

Definition 1. *Let* $\mathcal{A} = (Q, \Sigma, \delta, q_0, F)$ *be a DFA. Suppose* $\Sigma' \subseteq \Sigma$ *and* $S \subseteq Q$. *The* Σ'-*orbit of* S *is the set*

$$\mathrm{Orb}_{\Sigma'}(S) = \{\delta(q, u) \mid \delta(q, u) \text{ is defined, } q \in S \text{ and } u \in \Sigma'^*\}.$$

Also, for $q \in Q$, *we set* $\mathrm{Orb}_{\Sigma'}(q) = \mathrm{Orb}_{\Sigma'}(\{q\})$.

Let $\mathcal{A} = (Q, \Sigma, \delta, q_0, F)$ be a DFA and $\Gamma \subseteq \Sigma$. Set $\Delta = \Sigma \backslash \Gamma$. Next, we define the *projection automaton* of $\mathcal{A}$ for Γ as $\mathcal{R}_{\mathcal{A}}^{\Gamma} = (\mathcal{P}(Q), \Gamma, \mu, \mathrm{Orb}_{\Delta}(q_0), E)$ with, for $S \subseteq Q$ and $x \in \Gamma$, the transition function

$$\mu(S, x) = \mathrm{Orb}_{\Delta}(\delta(S, x)) \tag{1}$$

and $E = \{T \subseteq Q \mid T \cap F \neq \varnothing\}$. In general, $\mathcal{R}_{\mathcal{A}}^{\Gamma}$ is not initially connected. However, non-reachable states could be omitted. Actually, by the definition of the start state and transition function, we can restrict the state set to subsets of the form $\mathrm{Orb}_{\Delta}(S)$ for $\varnothing \neq S \subseteq Q$.

Theorem 2. *Let* $\mathcal{A}$ *be a DFA and* $\Gamma \subseteq \Sigma$. *Then,* $\pi_{\Gamma}(L(\mathcal{A})) = L(\mathcal{R}_{\mathcal{A}}^{\Gamma})$.

We do not introduce ε-NFAs formally here, but only refer to the literature [11]. However, we note in passing that, usually, an automaton for a projected language of a regular language is constructed by replacing the letters to be deleted by ε-transitions and then determinizing the resulting ε-NFA [11,13]. Our construction is a more direct formulation of these steps, where the orbit sets are used in place of the ε-closure computations.

In [13,14], an automaton was called a *state-partition automaton* with respect to a projection π_{Γ} (or, for short, a state-partition automaton for Γ), if the states of the resulting automaton from the above procedure, after discarding non-reachable subsets, form a partition of the original state set. Hence, in our terminology, an automaton $\mathcal{A}$ is a state partition automaton if the reachable states of $\mathcal{R}_{\mathcal{A}}^{\Gamma}$ form a partition of the states of $\mathcal{A}$.

A *permutation automaton* (or *permutation DFA*) is a DFA $\mathcal{A} = (Q, \Sigma, \delta, q_0, F)$ such that every letter permutes the state set, i.e., the function $\delta_x : Q \rightarrow Q$ given by $\delta_x(q) = \delta(q, x)$ is a permutation, or bijection, of Q for every $x \in \Sigma$. The languages recognized by permutation automata are called *group languages*. Note that permutation DFAs are complete DFAs.

The *identity transformation (on Q)* is the permutation id : $Q \to Q$ given by id$(q) = q$ for each $q \in Q$.

Next, we take a closer look at the orbit sets for permutation automata. But first, a general property of permutation automata.

Lemma 3. *Let $\mathcal{A} = (Q, \Sigma, \delta, q_0, F)$ be a permutation automaton and $\Sigma' \subseteq \Sigma^*$. Then, for every $u \in \Sigma'^*$ there exists $u' \in \Sigma'^*$ such that $\delta(q, uu') = q$ for each $q \in Q$, i.e., the word uu' represents the identity transformation on Q.*

With the previous lemma, we can show that the orbit sets for permutation automata partition the state set. This property is crucial to derive our state complexity bound for projection, as it vastly reduces the possible subsets that are reachable in $\mathcal{R}_{\mathcal{A}}^{\Gamma}$, namely only unions of orbit sets.

Lemma 4. *Let $\mathcal{A} = (Q, \Sigma, \delta, q_0, F)$ be a permutation automaton. Suppose $\Sigma' \subseteq \Sigma$. Then, the sets $\mathrm{Orb}_{\Sigma'}(q)$, $q \in Q$, partition Q and for every $S \subseteq Q$, $\mathrm{Orb}_{\Sigma'}(S) = \bigcup_{q \in S} \mathrm{Orb}_{\Sigma'}(q)$.*

4   Projection on Permutation Automata

Here, we state a tight upper bound for the number of states of the projection of a language recognized by a permutation automaton.

Our bound is parameterized by the number of states of the input automaton and by the number of non-loop unobservable transitions. More specifically, we consider the number of states that are incident with non-loop unobservable transitions. Hence, we disregard unobservable multi-transitions and do not take the direction into account, i.e., counting multiple transitions resulting from multiple letters between the same states only once and do not take their direction into account. This is the same usage of this parameter as in [14] for the general case.

Theorem 5. *Let $\mathcal{A} = (Q, \Sigma, \delta, q_0, F)$ be a permutation DFA and $\Gamma \subseteq \Sigma$. Set $m = |\{ p, q \in Q \mid p \neq q$ and $q \in \delta(p, \Sigma \backslash \Gamma) \}|$. Then, if $m > 0$, the projected language $\pi_\Gamma(L)$ is recognizable by a DFA with at most $2^{|Q| - \lceil \frac{m}{2} \rceil} - 1$ states and if $m = 0$, the projected language is recognizable by a DFA with at most $|Q|$ states.*

Proof. Set $\Delta = \Sigma \backslash \Gamma$, $S = \{p, q \in Q \mid p \neq q$ and $q \in \delta(p, \Delta)\}$ and $T = \{p \in Q \mid \forall x \in \Delta : \delta(p, x) = p\}$. Then, as $\mathcal{A}$ is a permutation automaton, Q is the disjoint union of S and T and

$$q \in T \Leftrightarrow \mathrm{Orb}_{\Delta}(q) = \{q\} \text{ and } q \in S \Leftrightarrow |\mathrm{Orb}_{\Delta}(q)| \geqslant 2. \qquad (2)$$

Set $\mathcal{B} = \mathcal{R}_{\mathcal{A}}^{\Gamma}$. If $m = 0$, then $Q = T$ and every $a \in \Delta$ induces a self-loop at every state. In this case, it is clear that we can simply leave out all the transitions labeled with letters from Δ and the resulting permutation automaton recognizes $\pi_\Gamma(L(\mathcal{A}))$. More formally, in the definition of $\mathcal{B}$, in this case, the starting state is $\{q_0\}$ and as $\mathcal{A}$ is deterministic we have $|\delta(R, x)| \leqslant |R|$ for every $R \subseteq Q$. So, as the empty set is never reachable for permutation DFAs, only the singleton sets $\{q\}$ are reachable in $\mathcal{B}$.

Now, suppose $m = |S| > 0$, which implies $m \geqslant 2$.

<u>Claim:</u> Let $m > 0$. Then, in $\mathcal{B}$ at most $2^{|Q|-\lceil\frac{m}{2}\rceil} - 1$ states are reachable from the start state.

Proof of the Claim: With the assumption $m > 0$, there exists $q \in Q$ such that $|\mathrm{Orb}_\Delta(q)| > 1$. By Equation (2) and Lemma 4, we have at most $|T| + \left\lfloor\frac{|S|}{2}\right\rfloor$ many Δ-orbits, where the maximum number of Δ-orbits is reached if every Δ-orbit of a state from S has size exactly two if $|S|$ is even or every such orbit has size two, except one that has size three, if $|S|$ is odd. By Lemma 4, the sets $\mathrm{Orb}_\Delta(\{q\})$, $q \in Q$, partition the state set and, for every $R \subseteq Q$, we have $\bigcup_{q\in R}\mathrm{Orb}_a(q) = \mathrm{Orb}_a(R)$. So, by Equation (1), every set reachable is a union of Δ-orbits, i.e., every such set corresponds uniquely to a subset of Δ-orbits for a single state. Finally, note that, as $\mathcal{A}$ is a permutation automaton, and hence complete, we have $\delta(R,x) \neq \varnothing$ for every non-empty $R \subseteq Q$, which also gives that in $\mathcal{B}$ the empty set is not reachable. So, in total, we find that at most

$$2^{|T|+\left\lfloor\frac{|S|}{2}\right\rfloor} - 1 = 2^{|Q|-m+\lfloor\frac{m}{2}\rfloor} - 1 = 2^{|Q|-\lceil\frac{m}{2}\rceil} - 1$$

subsets of states are reachable. *[End, Proof of the Claim]*

So, we have shown the upper bound.   □

Next, we show that the bound stated in the previous theorem is actually tight for permutation automata.

Theorem 6. *Let $n, m > 0$ be such that $0 < 2m + 1 < n$, $\Sigma = \{a, b, c, d, e, f, g\}$ and $\Gamma = \{b, c, d, e, f, g\}$. Then, there exists a permutation automaton $\mathcal{A} = (Q, \Sigma, \delta, q_0, F)$ with $2m$ states incident to non-loop unobservable transitions for π_Γ, i.e.,*

$$2m = |\{\ p, q \in Q \mid p \neq q \text{ and } q \in \delta(p, \Sigma\backslash\Gamma)\}|,$$

such that every DFA for $\pi_\Gamma(L(\mathcal{A}))$ needs at least $2^{n-m} - 1$ states.

Proof (sketch). See Fig. 1 for a permutation automaton giving the lower bound. The automaton has n states, and the letters act the following way:

$$a = (1,2)(3,4)\cdots(2m-1,2m),$$
$$b = (2m+1,2m+2), \qquad c = (2m+1,2m+2,\ldots,n),$$
$$d = (1,3)(2,4), \qquad\qquad e = (1,3,\ldots,2m-1)(2,4,\ldots,2m),$$
$$f = (1,n), \qquad\qquad\qquad g = (1,n)(2,n-1).$$

With $\Delta = \{a\}$, the Δ-orbits are $\{1,2\}, \{3,4\},\ldots,\{2m-1,2m\}, \{2m+1\},\ldots,\{n\}$. The letters b, c are chosen such that every permutation of the states $\{2m+1,\ldots,n\}$ could be written as a word over them, and the letters d and e such that every permutation on the Δ-orbits $\{1,2\},\ldots,\{2m-1,2m\}$ could be written as a word over them. The letters f and g help to map between these Δ-orbits in such a way that every non-empty union of Δ-orbits is reachable, and all these Δ-orbits give distinguishable states. By mapping onto the two element Δ-orbits and back, we can enlarge the sets that are reachable.   □

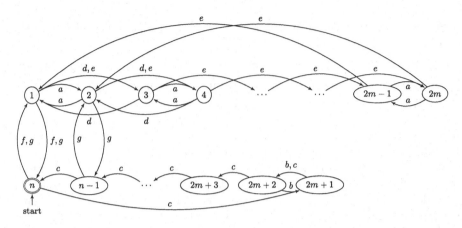

Fig. 1. All transitions not shown, for example for the letter b at the state n, correspond to self-loops, as permutation automata are complete. Then, the permutation automaton shown reaches the upper bound stated in Theorem 5 for the projection $\pi_\Gamma : \{a,b,c,d,e,f,g\}^* \to \Gamma^*$ with $\Gamma = \{b,c,d,e,f,g\}$.

Remark 1. Note that if $\mathcal{A} = (Q, \Sigma, \delta, q_0, F)$ is initially connected and has the property that from every state $q \in Q$ a final state is reachable, then also $\mathcal{R}_\mathcal{A}^\Gamma$ has this property. As permutation DFAs are complete by definition, this implies that the tight bound stated in Theorem 5 remains the same if we would additionally demand the resulting DFA for the projection to be complete.

We used an alphabet of size seven to match the bound. So, the question arises if we can reach the bound using a smaller alphabet. I do not know the answer yet, but by using a result from [13, Theorem 6] that every projection onto a unary language needs less than $\exp((1 + o(1))\sqrt{n \ln(n)})$ states, we can deduce that we need at least a ternary alphabet to reach the bound stated in Theorem 5. For the bound stated in Theorem 5 is lowest possible, apart from the trivial case $m = 0$, if $m = n$. Then, the bound is $2^{\lceil n/2 \rceil} - 1$. However, asymptotically, this grows way faster than $\exp((1 + o(1))\sqrt{n \ln(n)})$, in fact, the ratio of both expressions could be arbitrarily large.

Proposition 7. *Each permutation automaton $\mathcal{A}$ such that $\pi_\Gamma(L(\mathcal{A}))$ for a nonempty and proper subalphabet $\Gamma \subsetneq \Sigma$ attains the bound stated in Theorem 5 with $m > 0$ must be over an alphabet with at least three letters and $|\Gamma| \geqslant 2$.*

5   State-Partition Automata and Normal Subgroups

First, we derive a sufficient condition for a permutation automaton to be a state-partition automaton for a projection. Then, we introduce normal subgroups and show that if the letters generate a normal subgroup, this condition is fulfilled.

Proposition 8. *Let $\mathcal{A} = (Q, \Sigma, \delta, q_0, F)$ be a permutation automaton and $\Gamma \subseteq \Sigma$. Set $\Delta = \Sigma \backslash \Gamma$. Then, $\mathcal{A}$ is a state-partition automaton for π_Γ if the Δ-orbits of the form $\mathrm{Orb}_\Delta(q)$ are permuted, i.e., for each $x \in \Sigma$ and $q \in Q$, we have $\delta(\mathrm{Orb}_\Delta(q), x) = \mathrm{Orb}_\Delta(\delta(q, x))$.*

With Lemma 4, if the orbits for some $\Delta \subseteq \Sigma$ are permuted, then, for each $q \in Q$ and $x \in \Sigma$, $\delta(\mathrm{Orb}_\Delta(q), x) = \mathrm{Orb}_\Delta(q)$ or $\delta(\mathrm{Orb}_\Delta(q), x) \cap \mathrm{Orb}_\Delta(q) = \varnothing$.

Remark 2. The following example shows that $\mathcal{A}$ being a state-partition automaton for Γ does not imply that the sets $\mathrm{Orb}_\Delta(q)$ are permuted. Let $\mathcal{A} = (\{1, 2, 3, 4, 5, 6, 7, 8\}, \{a, b\}, \delta, 1, \{1\})$ with the transitions $a = (1, 2, 3, 4)(5, 6)(7, 8)$ and $b = (1, 5)(2, 6)(3, 7)(4, 8)$. Then, for $\Gamma = \{b\}$ the automaton is a state-partition automaton, as the reachable states in $\mathcal{R}_{\mathcal{A}}^{\Gamma}$ are $\{1, 2, 3, 4\}$ and $\{5, 6, 7, 8\}$, but the a-orbits are $\{1, 2, 3, 4\}$, $\{5, 6\}$ and $\{7, 8\}$.

Recall that $\mathcal{T}_{\mathcal{A}}$ denotes the transformation semigroup of $\mathcal{A}$. A subgroup of $\mathcal{T}_{\mathcal{A}}$, if $\mathcal{A}$ is a finite permutation automaton, is a subset containing the identity transformation and closed under function composition. As we are only concerned with finite automata, this also implies closure under inverse functions.

Next, we show that when the symbols deleted by a projection generate a normal subgroup, then the automaton is a state-partition automaton for this projection.

Normal subgroups are ubiquitous [3, 26] in abstract group theory as well as in permutation group theory. We give a definition for subgroups of $\mathcal{T}_{\mathcal{A}}$, when $\mathcal{A}$ is a permutation automaton, using our notation. We refer to more specialized literature for other definitions and more motivation [3, 26].

Definition 9. *Let $\mathcal{A} = (Q, \Sigma, \delta, q_0, F)$ be a permutation automaton. Then, a subgroup N of $\mathcal{T}_{\mathcal{A}}$ is called* normal, *if, for each $\delta_u, \delta_v \in \mathcal{T}_{\mathcal{A}}$ ($u, v \in \Sigma^*$),*

$$(\exists \delta_w \in N : \delta_u = \delta_{wv}) \Leftrightarrow (\exists \delta_{w'} \in N : \delta_u = \delta_{vw'}).$$

If a set of letters generates a normal subgroup, then the orbits of these letters are permuted by the other letters. As they are invariant under the letters themselves that generate these orbits, every word over Σ permutes these orbits. This is the statement of the next lemma.

Lemma 10. *Let $\mathcal{A} = (Q, \Sigma, \delta, q_0, F)$ be a permutation automaton and $\Sigma' \subseteq \Sigma$ be such that $N = \{\delta_u : Q \to Q \mid u \in \Sigma'^*\}$ is a normal subgroup of $\mathcal{T}_{\mathcal{A}}$. Then, for each $x \in \Sigma$ and $q \in Q$, we have $\delta(\mathrm{Orb}_{\Sigma'}(q), x) = \mathrm{Orb}_{\Sigma'}(\delta(q, x))$.*

So, combining Proposition 8 and Lemma 10.

Theorem 11. *Let $\Gamma \subseteq \Sigma$, $\Delta = \Sigma \backslash \Gamma$ and $\mathcal{A} = (Q, \Sigma, \delta, q_0, F)$ be a permutation automaton. Set $N = \{\delta_u : Q \to Q \mid u \in \Delta^*\}$, the subgroup in $\mathcal{T}_{\mathcal{A}}$ generated by Δ. If N is normal in $\mathcal{T}_{\mathcal{A}}$, then $\mathcal{A}$ is a state-partition automaton for π_Γ. Hence, in this case, $\pi_\Gamma(L(\mathcal{A}))$ is recognizable by an automaton with at most $|Q|$ states.*

6   Commuting Letters

Let $\mathcal{A} = (Q, \Sigma, \delta, q_0, F)$ be a DFA. We say that two letters $a, b \in \Sigma$ *commute* *(in $\mathcal{A}$)*, if $\delta(q, ab) = \delta(q, ba)$ for each $q \in Q$. Hence, an automaton $\mathcal{A}$ is commutative precisely if all letters commute pairwise.

Here, we investigate commuting letters with respect to the projection operation. Our first lemma states that if we can partition the alphabet of an n-state DFA into two subalphabets of letters such that each letter in the first set commutes with each letter in the second set, then for a projection onto one subalphabet, the projected language is recognizable by an n-state automaton. By this result, the projected language of every n-state commutative automaton is recognizable by an n-state automaton. We construct commutative automata that are not state-partition automata. Hence, we have new examples of automata whose projected languages are recognizable by automata with no more states than the original automaton, but which are not state-partition automata. Lastly, by investigating the proofs, we can show, with not much more effort, that varieties of commutative languages are closed under projections.

Lemma 12. *Suppose $\mathcal{A} = (Q, \Sigma, \delta, q_0, F)$ is an arbitrary DFA. Let $\Gamma \subseteq \Sigma$ be such that, for each $a \in \Sigma \backslash \Gamma$, $b \in \Gamma$ and $q \in Q$, we have $\delta(q, ab) = \delta(q, ba)$. Then, $\pi_\Gamma(L)$ is recognizable by a DFA with at most $|Q|$ states.*

Proof. Intuitively, we take the input automaton and leave out all unobservable transitions and make a state accepting if, in the input automaton, we can go from this state to a final state by a word formed out of the deleted letters.

Let $\mathcal{B} = (Q, \Gamma, \delta_{|\Gamma}, q_0, E)$ be the DFA with $\delta_{|\Gamma}(q, x) = \delta(q, x)$, the same start state q_0 and $E = \{p \in Q \mid \exists q \in F\ \exists u \in (\Sigma \backslash \Gamma)^* : \delta(p, u) = q\}$. Then, $L(\mathcal{B}) = \pi_\Gamma(L(\mathcal{A}))$.

If $\delta_{|\Gamma}(q_0, u) \in E$, then there exists $v \in (\Sigma \backslash \Gamma)^*$ such that $\delta(q_0, uv) \in F$. So, $uv \in L(\mathcal{A})$ and $u = \pi_\Gamma(uv)$.

Conversely, suppose $u = \pi_\Gamma(v)$ for some $v \in L(\mathcal{A})$. By assumption, as we can successively push all letters in $\Sigma \backslash \Gamma$ to the end, we have $\delta(q_0, v) = \delta(q_0, \pi_\Gamma(v)\pi_{\Sigma \backslash \Gamma}(v))$. So, $\delta(q_0, \pi_\Gamma(v)\pi_{\Sigma \backslash \Gamma}(v)) \in F$, which yields $\delta_{|\Gamma}(q_0, \pi_\Gamma(v)) \in E$, hence $u \in L(\mathcal{B})$. $\square$

So, with Lemma 12, we get the next result.

Theorem 13. *Let $\mathcal{A} = (Q, \Sigma, \delta, q_0, F)$ be a DFA such that $L(\mathcal{A})$ is commutative. If $\Gamma \subseteq \Sigma$, then $\pi_\Gamma(L(\mathcal{A}))$ is recognizable by a DFA with at most $|Q|$ states.*

The definition of normality could be seen as a generalization of commutativity. Hence, with Theorem 11, we can deduce the next statement.

Proposition 14. *Let $\mathcal{A} = (Q, \Sigma, \delta, q_0, F)$ be a commutative permutation automaton and $\Gamma \subseteq \Sigma$. Then, $\mathcal{A}$ is a state-partition automaton for π_Γ.*

However, there exist commutative automata that are not state-partition automata, as shown by Example 1.

Example 1. Let $\mathcal{A} = (\{q_\varepsilon, q_a, q_b\}, \{a, b\}, \delta, q_\varepsilon, \{q_\varepsilon, q_b\})$ with

$$\delta(q_x, y) = \begin{cases} q_a \text{ if } x = \varepsilon, y = a; \\ q_b \text{ if } x = \varepsilon, y = b; \\ q_b \text{ if } x = a, y = b; \\ q_x \text{ otherwise.} \end{cases}$$

Then, $L(\mathcal{A}) = \{u \in \{a, b\}^* \mid |u|_a = 0 \text{ or } |u|_b > 0\}$. However, we see that $\text{Orb}_{\{b\}}(q_\varepsilon) = \{q_\varepsilon, q_b\}$, $\text{Orb}_{\{b\}}(q_b) = \{q_b\}$ and $\text{Orb}_{\{b\}}(q_a) = \{q_a, q_b\}$. Hence, $\mathcal{A}$ is not a state-partition automaton for the projection $\pi_{\{a\}} : \{a, b\}^* \rightarrow \{a\}^*$. Also, it is not a state-partition automaton for the projection onto $\{b\}^*$.

The proofs of Lemma 12 and Theorem 13 also show that the projected language of a commutative permutation automaton is recognizable by a permutation automaton, i.e., a group language. On the other hand, in the general case, Example 2 below gives a permutation automaton whose projected language is not a group language. Also, most properties defined in terms of automata are preserved by projection in the commutative case. For example the property of being aperiodic [6,23,24]. We give a more general statement next, showing that many classes from the literature [6,23,24] are closed under projection when restricted to commutative languages.

Theorem 15. *Let Σ be an alphabet and $\Gamma \subseteq \Sigma$. Suppose $\mathcal{V}$ is a variety of commutative languages. If $L \in \mathcal{V}(\Sigma^*)$, then $\pi_\Gamma(L) \in \mathcal{V}(\Gamma^*)$. In particular, the variety of commutative languages is closed under projection.*

Hence, for example commutative locally-testable, piecewise-testable, star-free or group languages are preserved under every projection operator, as these classes form varieties [23].

Remark 3. In [13] it was stated that languages satisfying the observer property, i.e., that are given by a state-partition automaton for a given projection operator, and the finite languages projected onto unary finite languages were the only known languages for which we can recognize the projected language with at most the number of states as the original language. Note that Theorem 13 provides genuinely new instances for which this holds true, see Example 1.

Example 2. Also, for projections, consider the group language given by the permutation automaton $\mathcal{A} = (\{a, b\}, \{0, 1, 2\}, \delta, 0, \{2\})$ with $a = (0, 1)$ and $b = (0, 1, 2)$. Then, $\pi_{\{b\}}(L(\mathcal{A})) = bb^*$, which is not a group language. For example, b is the projection of $ab \in L(\mathcal{A})$, or bbb the projection of $abbab \in L(\mathcal{A})$.

7 Conclusion

We have continued the investigation of the state complexity of operations on permutation automata, initiated in [12], and the investigation of the projection operation [13,31]. We improved the general bound to the tight bound $2^{n-\lceil \frac{m}{2} \rceil} - 1$

in this case. Note that the general bound $2^{n-1} + 2^{n-m} - 1$ for the projection is only achieved for automata with precisely $m - 1$ non-loop unobservable transitions [13]. However, if we have more such unobservable transitions, then it was also shown in [13] that we have the better tight bound $2^{n-2} + 2^{n-3} + 2^{n-m} - 1$. For our lower bound stated in Theorem 6 in the case of permutation automata, we have precisely the same number of non-loop unobservable transitions as states incident with them. Lastly, note that the condition in Proposition 8 could be easily checked. Likewise, checking if a subset of letters Δ generate a normal subgroup could also be checked efficiently using results from [1].

Acknowledgement. I sincerely thank the anonymous reviewers for careful reading and detailed feedback that helped me in finding better formulations or fixing typos. Also, Sect. 5 was restructured after this feedback and the cycle notation was pointed out to me by one reviewer.

References

1. Babai, L., Luks, E.M., Seress, Á.: Permutation groups in NC. In: Aho, A.V. (ed.) STOC 1987, pp. 409–420. ACM (1987)
2. Brzozowski, J.A., Sinnamon, C.: Complexity of proper prefix-convex regular languages. Theor. Comput. Sci. **787**, 2–13 (2019)
3. Cameron, P.J.: Permutation Groups. London Mathematical Society Student Texts. Cambridge University Press, Cambridge (1999)
4. Carton, O., Pin, J., Soler-Escrivà, X.: Languages recognized by finite supersoluble groups. J. Autom. Lang. Comb. **14**(2), 149–161 (2009)
5. Cassandras, C.G., Lafortune, S.: Introduction to Discrete Event Systems, 2nd edn. Springer, Boston (2008). https://doi.org/10.1007/978-0-387-68612-7
6. Eilenberg, S.: Automata, Languages, and Machines, vol. B. Academic Press Inc., Orlando (1976)
7. Gao, Y., Moreira, N., Reis, R., Yu, S.: A survey on operational state complexity. J. Autom. Lang. Comb. **21**(4), 251–310 (2017)
8. Holzer, M., Kutrib, M.: Nondeterministic finite automata - recent results on the descriptional and computational complexity. Int. J. Found. Comput. Sci. **20**(4), 563–580 (2009)
9. Hopcroft, J.: An $n \log n$ algorithm for minimizing states in a finite automaton. In: Theory of Machines and Computations (Proceedings International Symposium, Technion, Haifa, 1971), pp. 189–196. Academic Press, New York (1971)
10. Hopcroft, J., Karp, R.: A linear algorithm for testing equivalence of finite automata, technical Report 71-114, University of California (1971)
11. Hopcroft, J.E., Ullman, J.D.: Introduction to Automata Theory, Languages, and Computation. Addison-Wesley Publishing Company (1979)
12. Hospodár, M., Mlynárčik, P.: Operations on permutation automata. In: Jonoska, N., Savchuk, D. (eds.) DLT 2020. LNCS, vol. 12086, pp. 122–136. Springer, Cham (2020). https://doi.org/10.1007/978-3-030-48516-0_10
13. Jirásková, G., Masopust, T.: On a structural property in the state complexity of projected regular languages. Theor. Comput. Sci. **449**, 93–105 (2012)
14. Jirásková, G., Masopust, T.: On properties and state complexity of deterministic state-partition automata. In: Baeten, J.C.M., Ball, T., de Boer, F.S. (eds.) TCS 2012. LNCS, vol. 7604, pp. 164–178. Springer, Heidelberg (2012). https://doi.org/10.1007/978-3-642-33475-7_12

15. Kohavi, Z., Jha, N.K.: Switching and Finite Automata Theory, 3 edn. Cambridge University Press (2009)
16. Komenda, J., Masopust, T., van Schuppen, J.H.: Supervisory control synthesis of discrete-event systems using a coordination scheme. Autom. **48**(2), 247–254 (2012)
17. Komenda, J., Masopust, T., van Schuppen, J.H.: Coordination control of distributed discrete-event systems. In: Seatzu, C., Silva, M., van Schuppen, J.H. (eds.) Control of Discrete-Event Systems, LNCIS, vol. 433, pp. 147–167. Springer, London (2013). https://doi.org/10.1007/978-1-4471-4276-8_8
18. Maslov, A.N.: Estimates of the number of states of finite automata. Dokl. Akad. Nauk SSSR **194**(6), 1266–1268 (1970)
19. McNaughton, R.: The loop complexity of pure-group events. Inf. Control **11**(1/2), 167–176 (1967)
20. McNaughton, R., Papert, S.A.: Counter-Free Automata (M.I.T. Research Monograph No. 65). The MIT Press (1971)
21. Mihov, S., Schulz, K.U.: Finite-state techniques: automata, transducers and Bimachines. In: Cambridge Tracts in Theoretical Computer Science. Cambridge University Press (2019)
22. Neumann, P.M.: The Mathematical Writings of Évariste Galois. European Mathematical Society, Heritage of European Mathematics (2011)
23. Pin, J.: Varieties Of Formal Languages. Plenum Publishing Co. (1986)
24. Pin, J.-E.: Syntactic Semigroups. In: Rozenberg, G., Salomaa, A. (eds.) Handbook of Formal Languages, pp. 679–746. Springer, Heidelberg (1997). https://doi.org/10.1007/978-3-642-59136-5_10
25. Roche, E., Schabes, Y. (eds.): Finite-State Language Processing. MIT Press (1997)
26. Rotman, J.: An Introduction to the Theory of Groups. Springer, New York (1995). https://doi.org/10.1007/978-1-4612-4176-8
27. Stockmeyer, L.J., Meyer, A.R.: Word problems requiring exponential time (preliminary report). In: STOC, pp. 1–9. ACM (1973)
28. Thérien, D.: Languages of nilpotent and solvable groups (extended abstract). In: Maurer, H.A. (ed.) ICALP 1979. LNCS, vol. 71, pp. 616–632. Springer, Heidelberg (1979). https://doi.org/10.1007/3-540-09510-1_49
29. Thierrin, G.: Permutation automata. Math. Syst. Theory **2**(1), 83–90 (1968)
30. Wang, J. (ed.): Handbook of Finite State Based Models and Applications. Chapman and Hall/CRC (2012)
31. Wong, K.: On the complexity of projections of discrete-event systems. In: Proceedings of WODES 1998, Cagliari, Italy, pp. 201–206 (1998)
32. Wonham, W.M., Cai, K.: Supervisory Control of Discrete-Event Systems. CCE, Springer, Cham (2019). https://doi.org/10.1007/978-3-319-77452-7
33. Yu, S., Zhuang, Q., Salomaa, K.: The state complexities of some basic operations on regular languages. Theoret. Comput. Sci. **125**(2), 315–328 (1994)

Constrained Synchronization and Subset Synchronization Problems for Weakly Acyclic Automata

Stefan Hoffmann[✉] [iD]

Informatikwissenschaften, FB IV, Universität Trier,
Universitätsring 15, 54296 Trier, Germany
hoffmanns@informatik.uni-trier.de

Abstract. We investigate the constrained synchronization problem for weakly acyclic, or partially ordered, input automata. We show that, for input automata of this type, the problem is always in NP. Furthermore, we give a full classification of the realizable complexities for constraint automata with at most two states and over a ternary alphabet. We find that most constrained problems that are PSPACE-complete in general become NP-complete. However, there also exist constrained problems that are PSPACE-complete in the general setting but become polynomial time solvable when considered for weakly acyclic input automata. We also investigate two problems related to subset synchronization, namely if there exists a word mapping all states into a given target subset of states, and if there exists a word mapping one subset into another. Both problems are PSPACE-complete in general, but in our setting the former is polynomial time solvable and the latter is NP-complete.

Keywords: Automata theory · Constrained synchronization ·
Computational complexity · Weakly acyclic automata · Subset synchronization

1 Introduction

A deterministic semi-automaton is synchronizing if it admits a reset word, i.e., a word which leads to a definite state, regardless of the starting state. This notion has a wide range of applications, from software testing, circuit synthesis, communication engineering and the like, see [28,30]. The famous Černý conjecture [7] states that a minimal length synchronizing word, for an n-state automaton, has length at most $(n-1)^2$. We refer to the mentioned survey articles [28,30] for details[1].

Due to its importance, the notion of synchronization has undergone a range of generalizations and variations for other automata models. In some generalizations, related to partial automata [22], only certain paths, or input words, are allowed (namely those for which the input automaton is defined).

---

[1] A new and updated survey article (in Russian) is currently in preparation by Mikhail V. Volkov [29].

© Springer Nature Switzerland AG 2021
N. Moreira and R. Reis (Eds.): DLT 2021, LNCS 12811, pp. 204–216, 2021.
https://doi.org/10.1007/978-3-030-81508-0_17

In [15] the notion of constrained synchronization was introduced in connection with a reduction procedure for synchronizing automata. The paper [13] introduced the computational problem of constrained synchronization. In this problem, we search for a synchronizing word coming from a specific subset of allowed input sequences. For further motivation and applications we refer to the aforementioned paper [13]. In this paper, a complete analysis of the complexity landscape when the constraint language is given by small partial automata with up to two states and an at most ternary alphabet was done. It is natural to extend this result to other language classes, or even to give a complete classification of all the complexity classes that could arise. For commutative regular constraint languages, a full classification of the realizable complexities was given in [16]. In [17], it was shown that for polycyclic constraint languages, the problem is always in NP.

Let us mention that restricting the solution space by a regular language has also been applied in other areas, for example to topological sorting [1], solving word equations [9,10], constraint programming [23], or shortest path problems [24]. The road coloring problem asks for a labeling of a given graph such that a synchronizing automaton results. A closely related problem to our problem of constrained synchronization is to restrict the possible labeling(s), and this problem was investigated in [32].

In [13] it was shown that we can realize PSPACE-complete, NP-complete or polynomial time solvable constrained problems by appropriately choosing a constraint language. Investigating the reductions from [13], we see that most reductions yield automata with a sink state, which then must be the unique synchronizing state. Hence, we can conclude that we can realize these complexities with this type of input automaton.

Contrary, for example, unary automata are synchronizing only if they admit no non-trivial cycle, i.e., only a single self-loop. In this case, we can easily decide synchronizability for any constraint language in polynomial time. Hence, for these simple types of automata, the complexity drops considerably. So, a natural question is, if we restrict the class of input automata, what complexities are realizable?

Here, we will investigate this question for the class of weakly acyclic input automata. These are automata such that the transition relation induces a partial order on the state sets. We will show that for this class, the constrained synchronization problem is always in NP. Then, in the spirit of the work [13], we will give a full classification of the complexity landscape for constraint automata with up to three states and a ternary alphabet. Compared with the classification result from [13], we find that most problems that are PSPACE-complete in general will become NP-complete. However, a few, in general PSPACE-complete, cases become polynomial time solvable for weakly acyclic input automata.

Related synchronization problems for weakly acyclic automata were previously investigated in [27]. For example, in [27], it was shown that the problem to decide if a given subset of states could be mapped to a single state, a problem

PSPACE-complete for general automata [2, 25], is NP-complete for weakly acyclic automata.

Furthermore, we investigate two problems related to subset synchronization, namely the problem if we can map the whole state set into a given target set by some word, and if we can map any given starting set into another target set. Both problems are PSPACE-complete in general [2, 3, 17, 21, 25, 28]. However, for weakly acyclic automata the former becomes polynomial time solvable, as we will show here, and the latter becomes NP-complete.

Similar subset synchronization problems, for general, strongly connected and synchronizing automata, were investigated in [2].

Weakly acyclic automata are also known as partially ordered automata [6], or acyclic automata [19]. As shown in [6], the languages recognized by weakly acyclic automata are precisely the languages recognized by $\mathcal{R}$-trivial monoids.

2   Preliminaries

By Σ we denote a finite set of symbols, also called an *alphabet*. By Σ^* we denote the set of all *words* over Σ, i.e., finite sequences with the concatenation operation. The *empty word* is denoted by ε. A *language* L is a subset $L \subseteq \Sigma^*$.

A *partial deterministic finite automaton (PDFA)* is denoted by a quintuple $\mathcal{A} = (\Sigma, Q, \delta, q_0, F)$, where Q is a *finite set of states*, Σ the *input alphabet*, $\delta : Q \times \Sigma \to Q$ is a *partial transition function*, q_0 the *start state* and $F \subseteq Q$ the set of *final states*. An automaton $\mathcal{A} = (\Sigma, Q, \delta, q_0, F)$ is called *complete*, if δ is a total function, i.e., $\delta(q, x)$ is defined for any $q \in Q$ and $x \in \Sigma$.

In the usual way, the transition function δ can be extended to a function $\hat{\delta} : Q \times \Sigma^* \to Q$ by setting, for $q \in Q$, $u \in \Sigma^*$ and $x \in \Sigma$, $\hat{\delta}(q, \varepsilon) = q$ and $\hat{\delta}(q, ux) = \delta(\hat{\delta}(q, u), x)$. In the following, we will drop the distinction between δ and $\hat{\delta}$ and will denote both functions simply by δ.

For $S \subseteq Q$ and $u \in \Sigma^*$, we set $\delta(S, u) = \{\delta(s, u) \mid s \in S$ and $\delta(s, u)$ is defined$\}$ and $\delta^{-1}(S, u) = \{q \in Q \mid \delta(q, u)$ is defined and $\delta(q, u) \in S\}$. For $q \in Q$ and $u \in \Sigma^*$, we set $\delta^{-1}(q, u) = \delta^{-1}(\{q\}, u)$.

The language *recognized* by $\mathcal{A}$ is $L(\mathcal{A}) = \{u \in \Sigma^* \mid \delta(q_0, u) \in F\}$.

We say that $q \in Q$ is *reachable* from $p \in Q$ (in $\mathcal{A}$) if there exists a word $u \in \Sigma^*$ such that $\delta(p, u) = q$.

For $\mathcal{A} = (\Sigma, Q, \delta, q_0, F)$ and $\Gamma \subseteq \Sigma$, by $\mathcal{A}_{|\Gamma} = (\Gamma, Q, \delta_{|\Gamma}, q_0, F)$ we denote the automaton $\mathcal{A}$ *restricted to the subalphabet* Γ, i.e., $\delta_{|\Gamma} : Q \times \Gamma \to Q$ with $\delta_{|\Gamma}(q, x) = \delta(q, x)$ for $q \in Q$ and $x \in \Gamma$.

We say a letter $x \in \Sigma$ induces a *self-loop* at a state $q \in Q$, if $\delta(q, x) = q$.

A state $s \in Q$ is called a *sink state*, if every letter induces a self-loop at it, i.e., $\delta(q, x) = q$ for any $x \in \Sigma$.

An automaton $\mathcal{A} = (\Sigma, Q, \delta, q_0, F)$ is called *weakly acyclic*, if it is complete and for any $q \in Q$ and $u \in \Sigma^* \setminus \{\varepsilon\}$, if $\delta(q, u) = q$, then $\delta(q, x) = q$ for any letter x

appearing in u, i.e., the simple[2] cycles are self-loops. Equivalently, the reachability relation is a partial order. Here, we say a state q is larger than another state p, if q is reachable from p in $\mathcal{A}$. A state in a weakly acyclic automaton is called *maximal*, if it is maximal with respect to this partial order. Note that here, we require weakly acyclic automata to be complete. This is in concordance with [27]. However, partially ordered automata are sometimes allowed to be partial in the literature [20]. Equivalently, an automaton is weakly acyclic if and only if there exists an ordering $q_1, \ldots, q_n$ of its states such that if $\delta(q_i, x) = q_j$ for some letter $x \in \Sigma$, then $i \leqslant j$, i.e., we can *topologically sort* the states.

A *semi-automaton* $\mathcal{A} = (\Sigma, Q, \delta)$ is a finite complete automaton without a specified start state and with no specified set of final states. Every notion defined for complete automata that does not explicitly use the start state and the set of final states is also defined in the same way for semi-automata. For example, being weakly acyclic. When the context is clear, we call both finite automata and semi-automata simply *automata*.

A complete automaton $\mathcal{A}$ is called *synchronizing* if there exists a word $w \in \Sigma^*$ with $|\delta(Q, w)| = 1$. In this case, we call w a *synchronizing word* for $\mathcal{A}$. We call a state $q \in Q$ with $\delta(Q, w) = \{q\}$ for some synchronizing word $w \in \Sigma^*$ a *synchronizing state*.

For a fixed PDFA $\mathcal{B} = (\Sigma, P, \mu, p_0, F)$, we define the *constrained synchronization problem*:

Definition 1. $L(\mathcal{B})$-CONSTR-SYNC
Input: *Deterministic semi-automaton* $\mathcal{A} = (\Sigma, Q, \delta)$.
Question: *Is there a synchronizing word w for $\mathcal{A}$ with $w \in L(\mathcal{B})$?*

The automaton $\mathcal{B}$ will be called the *constraint automaton*. If an automaton $\mathcal{A}$ is a yes-instance of $L(\mathcal{B})$-CONSTR-SYNC we call $\mathcal{A}$ *synchronizing with respect to $\mathcal{B}$*. Occasionally, we do not specify $\mathcal{B}$ and rather talk about L-CONSTR-SYNC. The unrestricted synchronization problem, i.e., Σ^*-CONSTR-SYNC in our notation, is in P [30]. We are going to investigate this problem for weakly acyclic input automata only.

Definition 2. $L(\mathcal{B})$-WAA-CONSTR-SYNC
Input: *Weakly acyclic semi-automaton* $\mathcal{A} = (\Sigma, Q, \delta)$.
Question: *Is there a synchronizing word w for $\mathcal{A}$ with $w \in L(\mathcal{B})$?*

We assume the reader to have some basic knowledge in computational complexity theory and formal language theory, as contained, e.g., in [18]. For instance, we make use of regular expressions to describe languages. And we make use of complexity classes like P, NP, or PSPACE. The following was shown in [13].

Theorem 3 ([13]). *Let $\mathcal{B} = (\Sigma, P, \mu, p_0, F)$ be a PDFA. If $|P| \leqslant 1$ or $|P| = 2$ and $|\Sigma| \leqslant 2$, then $L(\mathcal{B})$-CONSTR-SYNC $\in$ P. For $|P| = 2$ with $|\Sigma| = 3$, up to*

---

[2] A cycle is simple if it only involves distinct states [27].

symmetry by renaming of the letters, $L(\mathcal{B})$-CONSTR-SYNC *is* PSPACE-*complete precisely in the following cases for* $L(\mathcal{B})$:

$$
\begin{array}{llll}
a(b+c)^* & (a+b+c)(a+b)^* & (a+b)(a+c)^* & (a+b)^*c \\
(a+b)^*ca^* & (a+b)^*c(a+b)^* & (a+b)^*cc^* & a^*b(a+c)^* \\
a^*(b+c)(a+b)^* & a^*b(b+c)^* & (a+b)^*c(b+c)^* & a^*(b+c)(b+c)^*
\end{array}
$$

and polynomial time solvable in all other cases.

In weakly acyclic automata, maximal states, sink states and synchronizing states are related as stated in the next lemmata.

Lemma 4. *In a weakly acyclic automaton[3] a state is maximal if and only if it is a sink state.*

Lemma 5. *Let* $\mathcal{A} = (\Sigma, Q, \delta)$ *be a weakly acyclic automaton. If* $\mathcal{A}$ *is synchronizing, then the synchronizing state must be a unique sink state in* $\mathcal{A}$ *that is reachable from every other state and, conversely, such a state is a synchronizing state.*

With Lemma 5, we can test if a given weakly acyclic automaton is synchronizing. First, check every state if it is a sink state. If we have found a unique sink state, then do a breadth-first search from this sink state by traversing the transitions in the reverse direction. This gives a better algorithm than the general algorithm, which runs in time $O(|\Sigma||Q|^2)$, see [30].

Corollary 6. *For weakly acyclic automata we can decide in time* $O(|\Sigma||Q|+|Q|)$ *if it is synchronizing.*

3   Constrained Synchronization of Weakly Acyclic Automata

In general, for any constraint automaton, the constrained synchronization problem is always in PSPACE, see [13]. Here, we show that for weakly acyclic input automata, the constrained synchronization problem is always in NP. First, we establish a bound on the size of a shortest synchronizing word, which directly yields containment in NP as we have a polynomially bounded certificate which could be verified in polynomial time.

Proposition 7. *Let* $\mathcal{A}$ *be a weakly acyclic automaton with* n *states and* $\mathcal{B} = (\Sigma, P, \mu, p_0, F)$ *be a fixed PDFA. Then, a shortest synchronizing word* $w \in L(\mathcal{B})$ *for* $\mathcal{A}$ *has length at most* $|P|\binom{n}{2}$.

---

[3] Recall that here, weakly acyclic automata are always complete. For partial automata such that the reachability relation is a partial order, this does not have to be true.

Proof. Let $q_1, \ldots, q_n$ be a topological sorting of the states of $\mathcal{A}$. We represent the situation after reading a word $u \in \Sigma^*$, i.e., the set $\delta(Q, u)$, by a tuple $(i_1, \ldots, i_n) \in \{1, \ldots, n\}^n$, where i_j is the index of $\delta(q_j, u)$ in the topological sorting, i.e., $\delta(q_j, u) = q_{i_j}$. Then, $u \in \Sigma^*$ is synchronizing if and only if the corresponding tuple is $(n, \ldots, n)$. The starting tuple is $(1, \ldots, n)$. For $(i_1, \ldots, i_n), (j_1, \ldots, j_n) \in \{1, \ldots, n\}^n$ we write $(i_1, \ldots, i_n) < (j_1, \ldots, j_n)$ if, for all $r \in \{1, \ldots, n\}$, we have $i_r \leqslant j_r$ and there exists at least one $s \in \{1, \ldots, n\}$ such that $i_s < j_s$.

Let $w = x_1 \cdots x_m \in L(\mathcal{B})$ with $x_i \in \Sigma$ for $i \in \{1, \ldots, m\}$. Then, set $S_i = \delta(Q, x_1 \cdots x_i)$ and $S_0 = Q$. Suppose $S_{i+|P|} = S_i$ for some $i \in \{0, 1, \ldots, n\}$. Then, as $\mathcal{A}$ is weakly acyclic[4], for the word $u = x_{i+1} \cdots x_{i+|P|}$ we have $\delta(q, u) = q$ for any $q \in S_i$ and, as it has length $|P|$, it induces a loop in the constraint automaton $\mathcal{B}$. So, we can replace this factor of w by a shorter word $v \in \Sigma^*$ of length less than $|P|$ that yields the same result, i.e., $S_{i+|P|} = \delta(Q, x_1 \cdots x_i v)$ and $x_1 \cdots x_i v x_{i+|P|+1} \cdots x_n \in L(\mathcal{B})$.

Now, suppose $w = x_1 \cdots x_m \in L(\mathcal{B})$ is a shortest synchronizing word for $\mathcal{A}$. By the previous paragraph, we can suppose $S_{i+|P|} \neq S_i$ for any $i \in \{1, \ldots, n\}$. As $\mathcal{A}$ is weakly acyclic, and we can only move forward in the topological sorting, if $\delta(Q, u) \neq \delta(Q, uv)$, then for the tuple $(i_1, \ldots, i_n)$ corresponding to $\delta(Q, u)$ and for the tuple $(j_1, \ldots, j_n)$ for $\delta(Q, uv)$ we have $(i_1, \ldots, i_n) < (j_1, \ldots, j_n)$. Note that we have equality if and only if $\delta(Q, u) = \delta(Q, uv)$. As we start with $(1, \ldots, n)$ and want to reach $(n, \ldots, n)$, we have to increase at least $n - 1$ times the first entry, $n - 2$ times the second and so on. Now, by the previous reasoning, every $|P|$ symbols we can suppose we increase some component. Combining these observations yields that a shortest synchronizing word has length at most

$$|P| \cdot ((n-1) + (n-2) + \ldots + 1) = |P| \cdot \binom{n}{2}.$$

This finishes the proof.   □

With Proposition 7 we can conclude that for weakly acyclic input automata, the constrained synchronization problem is always in NP.

Theorem 8. *For weakly acyclic input automata and an arbitrary constraint automaton, the constrained synchronization problem is in* NP.

4   Subset Synchronization Problems

Here, we will investigate the following problems from [2, 3, 17, 21, 25, 28, 31] for weakly acyclic input automata.

Definition 9. SYNC-FROM-SUBSET
Input: $A = (\Sigma, Q, \delta)$ and $S \subseteq Q$.
Question: Is there a word w with $|\delta(S, w)| = 1$?

Definition 10. SYNC-INTO-SUBSET
Input: $A = (\Sigma, Q, \delta)$ and $S \subseteq Q$.
Question: Is there a word w with $\delta(Q, w) \subseteq S$?

---

[4] More generally, it is also easy to see that in weakly acyclic automata, no word can induce a non-trivial permutation of a subset of states.

Definition 11. SETTRANSPORTER
Input: $\mathcal{A} = (\Sigma, Q, \delta)$ and two subsets $S, T \subseteq Q$.
Question: Is there a word $w \in \Sigma^*$ such that $\delta(S, w) \subseteq T$?

These problems are PSPACE-complete in general [2,3,25,28] for at least
binary alphabets. In [27] it was shown that SYNC-FROM-SUBSET is NP-complete
for weakly acyclic input automata. Interestingly, for weakly acyclic input
automata, the complexity of SYNC-INTO-SUBSET drops considerably. Namely,
we could solve the problem in polynomial time. Hence, the ability to have transitions that go backward seems to be essential to get hardness above polynomial
time solvability for this problem.

Theorem 12. The problem SYNC-INTO-SUBSET is polynomial time solvable for
weakly acyclic input automata. More generally[5], given $S, T \subseteq Q$ such that S
contains all maximal states reachable from S, the existence of a word $w \in \Sigma^*$
such that $\delta(S, w) \subseteq T$ could be decided in polynomial time.

Not surprisingly, as SYNC-FROM-SUBSET is NP-complete [27] for at least
binary alphabets, SETTRANSPORTER is NP-complete for at least binary alphabets.

Theorem 13. SETTRANSPORTER is NP-complete for weakly acyclic input
automata when the alphabet is fixed but contains at least two distinct letters.

Proof. For containment in NP, suppose $(\mathcal{A}, S, T)$ with $\mathcal{A} = (\Sigma, Q, \delta)$, $S, T \subseteq Q$,
is an instance of SETTRANSPORTER with $\mathcal{A}$ being weakly acyclic. Let $a, b \notin \Sigma$ be
two new symbols and $s_f \notin Q$ a new state. We can suppose S, T are non-empty,
for otherwise, if $S = \varnothing$ we have a trivial solution and if S is non-empty and
$T = \varnothing$ we have no solution at all. Then, construct $\mathcal{A}' = (\Sigma \cup \{a, b\}, Q \cup \{s_f\}, \delta')$
with, for $q \in Q$ and $x \in \Sigma \cup \{a, b\}$,

$$
\delta'(q, x) = \begin{cases}
\delta(q, x) & \text{if } x \in \Sigma; \\
s_f & \text{if } x = a \text{ and } q \notin S; \\
s_f & \text{if } x = b \text{ and } q \in T; \\
q & \text{otherwise.}
\end{cases}
$$

and $\delta'(s_f, x) = s_f$ for any $x \in \Sigma \cup \{a, b\}$. Note that $\delta'(Q \cup \{s_f\}, a) = S \cup \{s_f\}$,
$\delta'(q, b) = s_f$ for $q \in Q$ if and only if $q \in T$ and that $\mathcal{A}'$ is weakly acyclic as
we have only added self-loops or transitions going into the sink state s_f. Then,
there exists $w \in \Sigma^*$ such that $\delta(S, w) \subseteq T$ in $\mathcal{A}$ if and only if $\delta'(Q, awb) = \{s_f\}$
in $\mathcal{A}'$. So, we have reduced the original problem to the problem to decide if $\mathcal{A}'$
has a synchronizing word for the constraint language $a\Sigma^*b$. By Theorem 8, the
last problem is in NP.

For NP-hardness, we can use the same reduction as used in [27, Theorem 4]
to show NP-hardness of SYNC-FROM-SUBSET with the same set S but setting
$T = \{f\}$, where f is the sink state used in the reduction from [27]. □

---

[5] This more general formulation was pointed out by an anonymous referee.

In [17], it was shown that SETTRANSPORTER is NP-complete for general unary automata. For unary weakly acyclic automata, the problem is in P.

Proposition 14. *If $|\Sigma| = 1$, then* SETTRANSPORTER *is in P for weakly acyclic input automata.*

5   Constraint Automata with Two States and at Most Three Letters

Here, we give a complete classification of the complexity landscape of the constraint synchronization problem with weakly acyclic automata as input automata and when the constraint is given by an at most two state PDFA over an at most ternary alphabet.

For our NP-hardness result, we adapt a construction due to Eppstein and Rystsov [11,26] which uses the NP-complete SAT problem [8].

SAT
Input: *A set X of n boolean variables and a set C of m clauses;*
Question: *Does there exist an assignment of values to the variables in X such that all clauses in C are satisfied?*

First, we single out those constraint languages that give NP-hard problems.

Proposition 15. *For the following constraint languages, the constrained synchronization problem for weakly acyclic automata is* NP-*hard:*

$$
\begin{array}{lll}
a(b+c)^* & (a+b+c)(a+b)^* & (a+b)(a+c)^* \\
(a+b)^*c(a+b)^* & a^*b(a+c)^* & a^*(b+c)(a+b)^* \\
a^*b(b+c)^* & (a+b)^*c(b+c)^* & a^*(b+c)(b+c)^*.
\end{array}
$$

Proof (Sketch). We only sketch the case $L(\mathcal{B}) = (a+b)^*c(b+c)^*$, the other cases could be handled similarly. We adapt a reduction by Eppstein and Rystsov [11, 26] to show NP-hardness for the decision variant of the problem of a shortest synchronizing word. Given a SAT instance with variables $X = \{x_1, \ldots, x_n\}$ and clauses $C = \{c_1, \ldots, c_m\}$, we construct a weakly acyclic automaton $\mathcal{A} = (\Sigma, Q, \delta)$ over the alphabet $\{a, b, c\}$ with states $q_{i,j}$ for $1 \leqslant i \leqslant m$ and $0 \leqslant j \leqslant n+1$, plus a sink state q_f. Then δ is defined, for $i \in \{1, \ldots, m\}$ and $j \in \{1, \ldots, n\}$, as

$$
\delta(q_{i,j}, b) = \begin{cases} q_{i,j+1} & \text{if } \overline{x}_j \in c_i \vee \{x_j, \overline{x}_j\} \cap c_i = \varnothing; \\ q_f & \text{if } x_j \in c_i; \end{cases}
$$

and, symmetrically,

$$
\delta(q_{i,j}, c) = \begin{cases} q_{i,j+1} & \text{if } x_j \in c_i \vee \{x_j, \overline{x}_j\} \cap c_i = \varnothing; \\ q_f & \text{if } \overline{x}_j \in c_i. \end{cases}
$$

Furthermore, for $i \in \{1, \ldots, m\}$ and $j \in \{0, \ldots, n+1\}$,

$$
\delta(q_{i,j}, a) = \begin{cases} q_{i,j} & \text{if } j \in \{0, 1\}; \\ q_f & \text{if } j \notin \{0, 1\}. \end{cases}
$$

Lastly, for $i \in \{1, \ldots, m\}$, we set $\delta(q_{i,n+1}, b) = \delta(q_{i,n+1}, c) = q_{i,n+1}$, $\delta(q_{i,0}, b) = \delta(q_{i,0}, a) = q_{i,0}$, $\delta(q_{i,0}, c) = q_{i,1}$ and $q_f = \delta(q_f, a) = \delta(q_f, b) = \delta(q_f, c)$. Note that $\{q_{1,1}, \ldots, q_{m,1}\} \subseteq \delta(Q, uc)$ for any $u \in \{a, b\}^*$ and, for $v \in \{b, c\}^*$, $\delta(q_{i,1}, v) = q_f$ if and only if some symbol in v at a position smaller or equal than n branches out of the strand $q_{i,1}, \cdots, q_{i,n}$, which means v could be identified with a satisfying assignment for the clause c_i. Conversely, if we have a satisfying assignment, construct a word $v = v_1 \cdots v_n \in \{b, c\}^*$ by setting $v_i = b$ if the i-th variable is set to one, and $v_i = c$ otherwise. Then, $\delta(Q, acv) = \{q_f\}$. So, we can show that $\mathcal{A}$ has a synchronizing word in $L(\mathcal{B})$ if and only if there exists a satisfying assignment for all clauses in C. □

In the next two propositions, we handle those cases from the list given in Theorem 3 that do not appear in Proposition 15. It will turn out that for these cases, the complexity drops from PSPACE-completeness to polynomial time solvable.

Proposition 16. *We have* $((a + b)^* c)$-WAA-CONSTR-SYNC $\in$ P

Proof (Sketch). By Lemma 5, if $\mathcal{A}$ is synchronizable, it must possess a unique synchronizing sink state s_f. In that case, set $T = \delta^{-1}(s_f, c)$. Then, we have a synchronizing word in $(a + b)^* c$ if and only if there exists a word $w \in (a + b)^*$ such that $\delta_{|\{a,b\}}(Q, w) \subseteq T$ in $\mathcal{A}_{|\{a,b\}} = (\Sigma, Q, \delta_{|\{a,b\}})$. The latter problem is in P by Theorem 12. □

Proposition 17. *We have* $((a + b)^* c a^*)$-WAA-CONSTR-SYNC $\in$ P *and* $((a + b)^* c c^*)$-WAA-CONSTR-SYNC $\in$ P.

Proof (sketch). By Lemma 5, the automaton $\mathcal{A}$ could only be synchronizing if it has a unique sink state s_f. In this case, set $S_i = \delta^{-1}(s_f, a^i)$ and $n = |Q|$. We have $S_i = S_n$ for any $i \geq n$. Then, for each $i \in \{0, \ldots, n\}$, set $T_i = \delta^{-1}(S_i, c)$ and decide, which could be done in polynomial time by Theorem 12, if there exists a word $w \in \{a, b\}^*$ in $A_{|\{a,b\}} = (\{a, b\}, Q, \delta_{|\{a,b\}})$ such that $\delta_{|\{a,b\}}(Q, w) \subseteq T_i$, which is equivalent to $\delta(Q, wca^i) = \{s_f\}$. □

Combining the results of this section, we can give a precise classification of the complexity landscape for the problem with weakly acyclic input automata and when the constraint automaton[6] has at most two states over a ternary alphabet.

Theorem 18. *Let* $\mathcal{B} = (\Sigma, P, \mu, p_0, F)$ *be a PDFA. If* $|P| \leq 1$ *or* $|P| = 2$ *and* $|\Sigma| \leq 2$, *then* $L(\mathcal{B})$-WAA-CONSTR-SYNC $\in$ P. *For* $|P| = 2$ *with* $|\Sigma| = 3$, *up to symmetry by renaming of the letters,* $L(\mathcal{B})$-WAA-CONSTR-SYNC *is* NP-complete *precisely for the cases listed in Proposition 15 and in* P *otherwise.*

---

[6] Recall that the constraint automaton is a partial automaton, whereas the input (semi-)automaton is always complete.

6   Relation to Automata with TTSPL Automaton Graphs

In [4,5] the decision problem related to minimal synchronizing words was investigated for TTSPL automata. These are automata whose automaton graph, i.e., the multigraph resulting after forgetting about the labels, is a TTSPL graph, i.e., a two-terminal series-parallel graph with a start and sink node and where self-loops are allowed.

In the context of automata theory, such automata were originally studied in connection with the size of resulting regular expressions, i.e., motivated by questions on the descriptional complexity of formal languages [14].

Many problems for series-parallel graphs are computationally easy [12], which partly motivated the aforementioned studies [4,5]. However, from a fixed parameter complexity perspective, for most parameters, synchronization problems remain hard on the corresponding automata class [4,5].

We will not give all the definitions, but refer the interested reader to the aforementioned papers. We only mention in passing that TTSPL automata form a proper subclass of the weakly acyclic automata. Also, by employing a similar construction as used in [4, Proposition 4.1], i.e., introducing two additional letters, an additional starting state and some auxiliary states to realize several paths from the start state by a tree-like structure to the starting states of the paths corresponding to the clauses in the reduction, we can alter the reduction from Proposition 15 to yield a TTSPL graph. However, we can even do better and note that for the reductions used in Proposition 15, we do not need additional letters, but can realize the branching from the additional starting state with two existing letters and use a third letter to map the additional states to the sink state. The resulting automaton is a TTSPL automaton, for example the transitions going directly to the sink state arise out of parallel compositions. Hence, we can even state the following.

Theorem 19. *For the constrained synchronization problem restricted to input automata whose automaton graph is a TTSPL graph, we have the same classification result for small constraint PDFAs as stated in Theorem 18. In particular, we can realize NP-complete constrained problems.*

7   Conclusion

We have investigated the complexity of the constrained synchronization problem for weakly acyclic input automata. We noticed that in this setting, the problem is always in NP. In the general setting, it was possible to have PSPACE-complete constrained problems, whereas this is no longer possibly in our setting. We have investigated the complexities for small constrained automata in the same way as done in the general case in [13]. We found out that certain problems that are PSPACE-complete in general become NP-complete, whereas others that are PSPACE-complete even become polynomial time solvable. A similar phenomenon was observed for certain subset synchronization problems that are all PSPACE-complete in general.

It is natural to continue this investigation for other classes of automata, to find out what properties are exactly needed to realize PSPACE-complete problems or for what other classes we only have NP-complete constrained problems, or what are the minimum requirements on the input automata to realize NP-complete problems.

Also, a complete classification of all possible realizable complexities, a problem orginally posed in [13], is still open. Hence, as a first step it would be interesting to know if for our restricted problem only the complexities P and NP-complete arise, or if we can realize a constrained problem equivalent to some NP-intermediate candidate problem.

Acknowledgement. I thank the anonymous reviewers for noticing some issues in the proofs of Theorem 13 and Proposition 15 that have been fixed. Also, I thank them for pointing out typos and some unclear formulations.

References

1. Amarilli, A., Paperman, C.: Topological sorting with regular constraints. In: Chatzigiannakis, I., Kaklamanis, C., Marx, D., Sannella, D. (eds.) ICALP 2018, July 9–13, 2018, Prague, Czech Republic. LIPIcs, vol. 107, pp. 115:1–115:14. Schloss Dagstuhl - Leibniz-Zentrum für Informatik (2018)
2. Berlinkov, M.V., Ferens, R., Szykula, M.: Preimage problems for deterministic finite automata. J. Comput. Syst. Sci. **115**, 214–234 (2021)
3. Blondin, M., Krebs, A., McKenzie, P.: The complexity of intersecting finite automata having few final states. Comput. Complex. **25**(4), 775–814 (2014). https://doi.org/10.1007/s00037-014-0089-9
4. Bruchertseifer, J., Fernau, H.: Synchronizing series-parallel automata with loops. In: Freund, R., Holzer, M., Sempere, J.M. (eds.) NCMA 2019, Valencia, Spain, July 2–3, 2019, pp. 63–78. Österreichische Computer Gesellschaft (2019)
5. Bruchertseifer, J., Fernau, H.: Synchronizing words and monoid factorization: a parameterized perspective. In: Chen, J., Feng, Q., Xu, J. (eds.) TAMC 2020. LNCS, vol. 12337, pp. 352–364. Springer, Cham (2020). https://doi.org/10.1007/978-3-030-59267-7_30
6. Brzozowski, J.A., Fich, F.E.: Languages of R-trivial monoids. J. Comput. Syst. Sci. **20**(1), 32–49 (1980)
7. Černý, J.: Poznámka k homogénnym experimentom s konečnými automatmi. Matematicko-fyzikálny časopis **14**(3), 208–216 (1964)
8. Cook, S.A.: The complexity of theorem proving procedures. In: Proceedings of the Third Annual ACM Symposium, pp. 151–158. ACM, New York (1971)
9. Diekert, V.: Makanin's algorithm for solving word equations with regular constraints. Report, Fakultät Informatik, Universität Stuttgart (March 1998)
10. Diekert, V., Gutiérrez, C., Hagenah, C.: The existential theory of equations with rational constraints in free groups is PSPACE-complete. Inf. Comput. **202**(2), 105–140 (2005)
11. Eppstein, D.: Reset sequences for monotonic automata. SIAM J. Comput. **19**(3), 500–510 (1990)
12. Eppstein, D.: Parallel recognition of series-parallel graphs. Inf. Comput. **98**(1), 41–55 (1992)

13. Fernau, H., Gusev, V.V., Hoffmann, S., Holzer, M., Volkov, M.V., Wolf, P.: Computational complexity of synchronization under regular constraints. In: Rossmanith, P., Heggernes, P., Katoen, J. (eds.) MFCS 2019, August 26–30, 2019, Aachen, Germany. LIPIcs, vol. 138, pp. 63:1–63:14. Schloss Dagstuhl - Leibniz-Zentrum für Informatik (2019)
14. Gulan, S.: Series parallel digraphs with loops - graphs encoded by regular expression. Theory Comput. Syst. **53**(2), 126–158 (2013)
15. Gusev, V.V.: Synchronizing automata of bounded rank. In: Moreira, N., Reis, R. (eds.) CIAA 2012. LNCS, vol. 7381, pp. 171–179. Springer, Heidelberg (2012). https://doi.org/10.1007/978-3-642-31606-7_15
16. Hoffmann, S.: Computational complexity of synchronization under regular commutative constraints. In: Kim, D., Uma, R.N., Cai, Z., Lee, D.H. (eds.) COCOON 2020. LNCS, vol. 12273, pp. 460–471. Springer, Cham (2020). https://doi.org/10.1007/978-3-030-58150-3_37
17. Hoffmann, S.: On a class of constrained synchronization problems in NP. In: Cordasco, G., Gargano, L., Rescigno, A.A. (eds.) Proceedings of the 21st Italian Conference on Theoretical Computer Science, Ischia, Italy, September 14–16, 2020. CEUR Workshop Proceedings, vol. 2756, pp. 145–157. CEUR-WS.org (2020)
18. Hopcroft, J.E., Ullman, J.D.: Introduction to Automata Theory, Languages, and Computation. Addison-Wesley Publishing Company (1979)
19. Jirásková, G., Masopust, T.: On the state and computational complexity of the reverse of acyclic minimal DFAs. In: Moreira, N., Reis, R. (eds.) CIAA 2012. LNCS, vol. 7381, pp. 229–239. Springer, Heidelberg (2012). https://doi.org/10.1007/978-3-642-31606-7_20
20. Krötzsch, M., Masopust, T., Thomazo, M.: Complexity of universality and related problems for partially ordered NFAs. Inf. Comput. **255**, 177–192 (2017)
21. Luks, E.M., McKenzie, P.: Parallel algorithms for solvable permutation groups. J. Comput. Syst. Sci. **37**(1), 39–62 (1988)
22. Martyugin, P.V.: Synchronization of automata with one undefined or ambiguous transition. In: Moreira, N., Reis, R. (eds.) CIAA 2012. LNCS, vol. 7381, pp. 278–288. Springer, Heidelberg (2012). https://doi.org/10.1007/978-3-642-31606-7_24
23. Pesant, G.: A regular language membership constraint for finite sequences of variables. In: Wallace, M. (ed.) CP 2004. LNCS, vol. 3258, pp. 482–495. Springer, Heidelberg (2004). https://doi.org/10.1007/978-3-540-30201-8_36
24. Romeuf, J.: Shortest path under rational constraint. Inf. Process. Lett. **28**(5), 245–248 (1988)
25. Rystsov, I.K.: Polynomial complete problems in automata theory. Inf. Process. Lett. **16**(3), 147–151 (1983)
26. Rystsov, I.K.: On minimizing the length of synchronizing words for finite automata. In: Theory of Designing of Computing Systems, pp. 75–82. Institute of Cybernetics of Ukrainian Academic Science (1980). (in Russian)
27. Ryzhikov, A.: Synchronization problems in automata without non-trivial cycles. Theor. Comput. Sci. **787**, 77–88 (2019)
28. Sandberg, S.: 1 homing and synchronizing sequences. In: Broy, M., Jonsson, B., Katoen, J.-P., Leucker, M., Pretschner, A. (eds.) Model-Based Testing of Reactive Systems. LNCS, vol. 3472, pp. 5–33. Springer, Heidelberg (2005). https://doi.org/10.1007/11498490_2
29. Volkov, M.V.: Synchronizing finite automata. I. (in Russian, submitted)
30. Volkov, M.V.: Synchronizing automata and the Černý conjecture. In: Martín-Vide, C., Otto, F., Fernau, H. (eds.) LATA 2008. LNCS, vol. 5196, pp. 11–27. Springer, Heidelberg (2008). https://doi.org/10.1007/978-3-540-88282-4_4

31. Vorel, V.: Subset synchronization and careful synchronization of binary finite automata. Int. J. Found. Comput. Sci. **27**(5), 557–578 (2016)
32. Vorel, V., Roman, A.: Complexity of road coloring with prescribed reset words. J. Comput. Syst. Sci. **104**, 342–358 (2019)

Lyndon Words Formalized in Isabelle/HOL

Štěpán Holub[1] and Štěpán Starosta[2(✉)]

[1] Charles University, Prague, Czech Republic
[2] Czech Technical University in Prague, Prague, Czech Republic
stepan.starosta@fit.cvut.cz

Abstract. We present a formalization of Lyndon words and basic relevant results in Isabelle/HOL. We give a short review of Isabelle/HOL and focus on challenges that arise in this formalization. The presented formalization is based on an ongoing larger project of formalization of combinatorics on words.

Keywords: Isabelle/HOL · Lyndon word · Lyndon factorization · Combinatorics on words

1 Introduction

Lyndon words, named after Roger Lyndon [17], are defined as words which are the least elements in their conjugacy class with respect to a lexicographic order induced by a total order on the letters. For instance, consider the word aab. Its conjugacy class contains all the cyclic rotations, that is aab, aba, and baa. If $a < b$, then aab is a Lyndon word since it is the smallest of the 3 words. If $b < a$, then baa is Lyndon. They were originally conceived to construct bases in free Lie algebras [17] and found many applications later on; for instance, they may serve to construct de Bruijn sequence [7] and to characterize maximum runs in words [2]. They are also object of numerous generalizations [4,5,18].

In this article, we are concerned with a formalization of Lyndon words. Since the first computer-assisted proof of the four-color theorem in 1970s, the field of mathematics formalization, machine-verified proofs and automated reasoning has grown considerably. Let us name some prominent available general proof systems such as Mizar, HOL-Light, Coq, Lean and Isabelle. We refer the reader to the survey [15] for a more detailed overview of the state of mathematics formalization, and to [3] for a starting point on the state of automated reasoning. The advancement may be also tracked on the formalization state of 100 prominent theorems in various provers [24].

Topics related to combinatorics on words are formalized in various systems such as the Coq package Coq-Combi by Hivert [9], which formalizes specific results of combinatorics on words results to prove other results such as the Littlewood–Richardson rule, or related packages Coq-free-groups, formalizing

© Springer Nature Switzerland AG 2021
N. Moreira and R. Reis (Eds.): DLT 2021, LNCS 12811, pp. 217–228, 2021.
https://doi.org/10.1007/978-3-030-81508-0_18

elements of the free group theory, or general concepts of the free monoids and free groups in the Lean Mathematical Library. From the viewpoint of formal languages, many tools and results are available; for instance, the Isabelle's Archive of Formal Proofs [1] contains a category "Automata and formal languages" with a few dozen of reusable formalizations. However, to our knowledge, none build on the elementary concepts of combinatorics on words and formalize Lyndon words. The first author's previous formalization attempt (in the automated theorem prover Prover9) at such a general task is described in [11], while the presented formalization is a part of the current project of formalization of basics of combinatorics on words and various results [10] in the proof assistant Isabelle/HOL. This project intends to create a library of formalized results with three objectives:

1. verified basic facts that can become a standard starting point for further formalization;
2. verified classical results, such as the presented formalization of Lyndon words, with polished, human-readable and possibly more straightforward proofs;
3. allowing to push boundaries of the current research in areas where a sheer complexity of the topic may be the most important barrier for further advances.

One of the main motivations for this project is that proofs, or some of their parts, in combinatorics on words are somewhat regularly tedious and repetitive. It is desirable to outsource these tasks to a computer.

The proof assistant of choice, Isabelle/HOL [14,21], is an open-source project with a lively community and a vast collection of formalized results available in the already mentioned Archive of Formal Proofs [1]. Isabelle's main interface language which allows to write structured proofs is Isar. One of Isar's objective is to provide human-readable proofs, see [19] or the code examples below.

In Sect. 2, we give a short overview of the formalization of basic elements of combinatorics on words of our project [10]. We describe relevant parts of the two basic auxiliary theories (a *theory* is the main structural unit in Isabelle). In Sect. 3, we describe the formalization of Lyndon words and point out the challenges: formalization of the underlying total order and selecting the "good" definitions in order to obtain smooth polished proofs. We conclude by the formalization of the minimal relation needed for a word to be Lyndon, as a counterpart of the usual strong requirement of having an alphabet with a total order.

2   Combinatorics on Words in Isabelle/HOL

We start by the description of related concepts from the theory CoWBasic of [10], the cornerstone of further formalization. We use, in this article and in the formalization, the notation familiarly used in combinatorics on words. Concatenation is denoted by ·, and is often omitted in the article (contrary to the machine-readable code, of course). The length of a word w is denoted $|w|$.

Let us first mention that Isabelle/HOL's logic framework is a typed one, similar to a system of functional programming languages. Here, type theory serves as an alternative to classical set theory [23]. Each term given in this logic framework is linked to a type which defines its basic structure and restrictions.

A (finite) word is formalized as a list, which is a basic type provided with the main distribution of Isabelle/HOL (in the theory Main). This choice allows to build on many available tools, while it is fully general to formalize free monoids, since the elements of a free monoid will eventually be represented as lists of generators. The characteristic property of a free monoid, the presence of a length function (compatible with concatenation) and equidivisibility

$$xy = uv, |x| \leq |u| \quad \text{implies} \quad \exists t, xt = u \wedge tv = y,$$

is already present in the Main theory distributed along with Isabelle/HOL.

A variable of list type is denoted in Isabelle/HOL as 'a list, where 'a is a type variable, that is, a variable of type 'a list represents a finite word over the alphabet given by the type 'a. For instance, the term

```
term "[0,1,0]::nat list"
```

represents the word 010 over natural integers formalized by the type nat. The keyword **term** checks validity and prints a valid Isabelle term.

The Main theory provides many lemmas and definitions related to lists which are relevant to combinatorics on words. Let us exhibit basic elements of Isabelle/HOL and its interface on some tools from Main related to Lyndon words. The first is the definition of the mapping rotate which stems from rotate1:

```
primrec rotate1 :: "'a list ⇒ 'a list" where
    "rotate1 ε = ε" |
    "rotate1 (a # w) = w · [a]"

definition rotate :: "nat ⇒ 'a list ⇒ 'a list" where
    "rotate n = rotate1 ^^ n"
```

The mapping rotate1 is defined as a primitively recursive mapping of type 'a list ⇒ 'a list, which is a mapping taking one argument of type 'a list and returning again a value of type 'a list. The definition has two rules. The first rule defines rotate1 on the empty word ε, while the second rule defines it on a # w, which stands for prepending the letter a to the word w. Altogether, rotate1 takes away the first letter of a word and appends it (as the word [a] of length one) at its end, and leaves the empty word untouched. As these two rules cover the two constructors of the type list (the empty word and #), the mapping is correctly defined for all lists. In fact, all mappings in Isabelle/HOL are total.

The mapping rotate is defined as the n-fold composition of rotate1, producing for instance rotate 2 [a,b,c] = [c,a,b].

Let us illustrate theorem-proving in Isabelle/HOL and its interface language Isar on two elementary lemmas on rotate:

```
lemma rotate_add: "rotate (m+n) = rotate m o rotate n"
  by (simp add:rotate_def funpow_add)
```

```
lemma rotate_rotate: "rotate m (rotate n w) = rotate (m+n) w"
  by (simp add:rotate_add)
```

The first theorem, introduced by the keyword **lemma**, is named `rotate_add`, and claims that rotating by n and then by m is the same as rotating by $m + n$. The term `rotate n` represents the rotation of a word by n, i.e., is the mapping of type `'a list ⇒ 'a list`, and the claim `rotate_add` in fact states equality of such mappings. The keyword **by** starts a terminal backward proof using the method `simp`, which is one of the most direct proof methods using elementary simplifications. Here, besides the standard armoury of simp's simplification rules, two facts, i.e., proven named claims, are needed: `rotate_def` and `funpow_add`. While the first is in fact the definition of `rotate` stated above (named automatically), the second is an elementary lemma on n-fold composition `^^`:

```
lemma funpow_add: "f ^^ (m + n) = f ^^ m o f ^^ n"
  by (induct m) simp_all
```

The proof is done by induction on m, and all the induction steps are proven again by the simplifier simp.

The next component is the existing theory HOL-Library. Sublist, which provides relevant tools such as the predicates `prefix` and `strict_prefix`:

```
definition prefix :: "'a list ⇒ 'a list ⇒ bool"
  where "prefix p w ⟷ (∃s. w = p · s)"
```

```
definition strict_prefix :: "'a list ⇒ 'a list ⇒ bool"
  where "strict_prefix p w ⟷ prefix p w ∧ p ≠ w"
```

The CoWBasic theory adopts a shorthand notation for these definitions: $p \leq_p w$ stands for `prefix p w`, $p <_p w$ stands for `strict_prefix p w`, and similarly, we introduce nonempty prefix predicate, denoted $p \leq_{np} w$. Suffixes have an analogous notation: $\leq_s, <_s, \leq_{ns}$.

Let us now introduce some relevant elements from the CoWBasic theory that shall be used later, starting with left and right quotient:

```
definition left_quotient:: "'a list ⇒ 'a list ⇒ 'a list"
  ("(_⁻¹>)(_)")
  where "left_quotient u v = (THE z. u · z = v)"
```

```
definition right_quotient :: "'a list ⇒ 'a list ⇒ 'a list"
  ("(_)(<⁻¹_)")
  where "right_quotient u v = rev ((rev v)⁻¹>(rev u))"
```

The definition of left quotient stems from the usual definition: if u is a prefix of v, then *the* word z with the property $uz = v$ is the left quotient of u and v. The definite description *the* is formalized by the syntax THE, introduced in Isabelle/HOL's basis of Higher-Order Logic. Compared to the usual definition, the assumption u is a prefix of v is not present. If it is not satisfied, i.e., u is not a prefix of v, then nothing can be shown about left_quotient u v. An alternative shorthand notation $u^{-1}>v$ is introduced by the definition as well. Special characters such as $^{-1}$ (represented in the source file as \<inverse>) can be input conveniently in the default integrated development environment Isabelle/jEdit, present in Isabelle distribution, in a very similar way to the usual typesetting in LaTeX.[1]

The definition of right quotient is not using THE, but is based on the definition of the left quotient using the reversal/mirror mapping rev, which reverses the order of the elements in the list, i.e., reads the word backwards. This choice here is made in order to fully exploit the symmetry induced by rev (for details on this symmetry see [22]).

Primitivity is defined as follows:

definition primitive :: "'a list ⇒ bool"
  where "primitive u = (∀ r k. r@k = u ⟶ k = 1)"

The term $r@k$ stands for the k-th power of the word r. Finally, the predicates for a word having a border and being bordered are defined as

definition border :: "'a list ⇒ 'a list ⇒ bool" ("_ ≤b _")
  where "border x w = (x ≤p w ∧ x ≤s w ∧ x ≠ w ∧ x ≠ ε)"

definition bordered :: "'a list ⇒ bool"
  where "bordered w = (∃b. b ≤b w)"

3 Lyndon Words Formalized

Let $\mathcal{A}$ be an alphabet. Recall that the lexicographic order of words from $\mathcal{A}^+$ is induced by a total order of $\mathcal{A}$ as follows: for nonempty words $u, v \in \mathcal{A}^+$ we have that $u <_{\text{lex}} v$ if $u <_p v$ or

$$u = pau', v = pbv' \quad \text{with} \quad a, b \in \mathcal{A}, \quad a < b, \quad p, u', v' \in \mathcal{A}^*.$$

A word w is a *Lyndon word* if it is a primitive word and it is the least in its conjugacy class with respect to the lexicographic order $<_{\text{lex}}$.

While the definition is quite simple, there are several variants how to formalize it since the underlying orders may be specified in various manners. We describe our approach in the next subsection. Section 3.2 covers the formalization of selected claims on Lyndon words, notably Lyndon factorization. Section 3.3 concludes this section with the description of a characterization of Lyndon words based on a minimal partial order o that needs to be specified for a word to be Lyndon with respect to o. The description focuses on unveiling specific choices that were made in the formalization, notably those that lead to a version which differs from the usual template.

---

[1] More advice for beginners is available in the README of [10].

3.1   Specifying the Order and Lyndon Word Definition

Before specifying the order, let us be explicit on how the formalization deals with the specification of the alphabet. The alphabet is implicitly given by the type variable 'a in 'a list. This implies that the alphabet is the whole type. The main advantage is that there is no need for any additional assumptions specifying the omnipresent alphabet in all the claims that concern some words.

A total order on a type may be defined in a number of ways using existing tools in Isabelle/HOL. For instance, a possible approach is its definition using a predicate or by specifying the relation as a set, and then use the existing list tools to produce a lexicographic order in a similar manner. This approach leaves the order as a parameter that needs to be repeated as an assumption, or can be fixed using a **locale**, Isabelle's mechanism to avoid repetition of global assumptions. After trials of numerous variants, our choice is a more implicit approach using so-called *sorts*, which is an Isabelle's way to control polymorphism of types without breaking the logical structure [20]. The existing class representing a total order is called linorder in Isabelle/HOL, and by wrapping the code as

context linorder
begin
⋮
end

one declares that the type 'a is equipped with a total order, also called a linear order. Within this context, the lexicographic order is introduced in the same manner. We first define the relevant predicates:

definition Lyndon_less :: "'a list ⇒ 'a list ⇒ bool" ("<lex")
    where "Lyndon_less xs ys ≡ ord_class.lexordp xs ys"

definition Lyndon_le :: "'a list ⇒ 'a list ⇒ bool" ("≤lex")
    where "Lyndon_le xs ys ≡ ord_class.lexordp_eq xs ys"

These are based on the lexicographic order integrated with Isabelle's class ord, representing a partial order:

context ord
begin

inductive lexordp :: "'a list ⇒ 'a list ⇒ bool"
where
    Nil: "lexordp ε (y # ys)"
| Cons: "x < y ⟹ lexordp (x # xs) (y # ys)"
| Cons_eq:
    "⟦ ¬ x < y; ¬ y < x; lexordp xs ys ⟧ ⟹ lexordp (x # xs) (y # ys)"
end

This inductive predicate has 3 constructor rules and is in fact slightly more general that the required lexicographic order since it is induced by a partial order.

The last step is to declare that the predicates `Lyndon_less` and `Lyndon_le` satisfy the assumptions of the `linorder` class, and make all the facts of the `linorder` class available for lists. This is done by the following command:

```
interpretation rlex: linorder "(≤lex)" "(<lex)"
using lexordp_linorder Lyndon_less_def Lyndon_le_def by
presburger
```

The command **interpretation** requires a proof of the claim that ≤lex and <lex are indeed a linorder. The proof here starts by the keyword **using**, which states additional facts that are needed for the proof: the definitions introduced above and the fact `lexordp_linorder`, which states that the lexicographic order induced on a total order is indeed total. The keyword **by** invokes a terminal proof method. Once shown, **interpretation** makes all the claims of linorder available for ≤lex and <lex under qualified names such as rlex.lexordp˙linorder.

At this point, the underlying lexicographic order is set up, and we may proceed with a definition of a Lyndon word:

```
definition Lyndon :: "'a list ⇒ bool" where
"Lyndon w = (w ≠ ε ∧ (∀n. 0 < n ∧ n < |w| ⟶ w <lex rotate n
w))"
```

Since <lex is used in the definition, primitivity of the word is not required but shown as a property in the following lemma where we exhibit a structured isar proof:

```
lemma Lyndon_prim: assumes "Lyndon w"
  shows "primitive w"
proof-
    have "0 < n ⟹ n < |w| ⟹ rotate n w ≠ w" for n
      using Lyndon_less_def LyndonD[OF ⟨Lyndon w⟩, of n]
rlex.less_irrefl[of w] by argo
    thus ?thesis
      using no_rotate_prim[OF LyndonD_nemp[OF ⟨Lyndon w⟩]] by
blast
qed
```

The command **proof-** starts the proof of the preceding claim. The keyword **have** introduces an intermediate claim, followed by its proof, and **thus** uses this claim to show the actual goal of the whole proof hidden under the variable ?thesis.

With a slightly more elaborate proofs using the auxiliary combinatorics on words theories, we prove elementary properties of Lyndon words such as

```
theorem Lyndon_unbordered: assumes "Lyndon w"
  shows "¬ bordered w"
```

```
lemma conjug_Lyndon_ex: assumes "primitive w"
  obtains n where "Lyndon (rotate n w)"
```

```
theorem Lyndon_suf_char: assumes "w ≠ ε"
  shows "Lyndon w ⟷ (∀s. s ≤ns w ∧ s ≠ w ⟶ w <lex s)"
```

Let us now focus on more elaborate elements of the formalization that differ from human proofs written in mathematical prose (the latter being usually called "paper proofs" in this context).

3.2   Formal Proofs Concerning Lyndon Words

A proof in mathematical prose typically contains commonly accepted informal arguments or omitted steps that must be settled by the formalization. Obviously, these include "Obviously", "One can show", and "The proof is left to the reader". It includes also "without loss of generality" or "by symmetry" (see [8]). But it also includes some primary school arithmetic manipulations, as these are usually based on a multitude of trivial elementary facts which need to be specified and made available to the proof assistant.

Let us illustrate this on the following lemma from Duval [6, Lemma 2.3].

Lemma 1. *The product $u \cdot v$ of two Lyndon words u and v is a Lyndon word if and only if $u <_{\text{lex}} v$.*

While one direction follows easily from the characterization by suffixes (displayed above as `Lyndon_suf_char`), the other direction is left to the reader, i.e., no proof is given. A short paper proof might go as follows:

Proof. If $v = uv'$, then since v is a Lyndon word, we have $v <_{\text{lex}} v'$. It follows that $uv <_{\text{lex}} uv' = v$. If u is not a prefix of v, then since $u <_{\text{lex}} v$ we have $uv <_{\text{lex}} v$. Let z be a strict suffix of uv. If $uv = uv'z$, then $uv <_{\text{lex}} v <_{\text{lex}} z$. If $z = z'v$, then $u <_{\text{lex}} z'$, thus $uv <_{\text{lex}} z'v$, i.e., uv is smaller than any its strict suffix, and therefore is a Lyndon word.

This direction is formalized in this form:

```
theorem Lyndon_concat: assumes "Lyndon u" and "Lyndon v"
  and  "u <lex v"  shows "Lyndon (u·v)"
```

Its proof is some 40 lines long, containing a case analysis and steps which are based on simple arithmetic, still hidden in the presented paper proof.

Let us now focus on the formulation of Lyndon's result as given in [16, Theorem 5.1.5]:

Theorem 1. *Any nonempty word w may be written uniquely as a nonincreasing product of Lyndon words:*

$$w = \ell_1 \ell_2 \cdots \ell_n \quad \text{with } \ell_i \text{ Lyndon and } \ell_{i+1} \leq_{\text{lex}} \ell_i.$$

This factorization is often referred to as Lyndon factorization. A 1-to-1 formalization of this classical result turned out to be unsuitable since it is not constructive. In general, finding a suitable characteristic properties and equipping the proof assistant with suitable lemmas is very helpful to obtain a good mixture between what is obvious for a human reader and what is required for a machine verification. Therefore, our chosen definition is a constructive one:

definition longest_Lyndon_suffix::"'a list ⇒ 'a list" ("LynSuf")
  where "longest_Lyndon_suffix w = (drop (LEAST i. (Lyndon (drop i w))) w)"

function Lyndon_fac::"'a list ⇒ 'a list list" ("LynFac")
  where "Lyndon_fac w = (if w ≠ ε then ((Lyndon_fac (w $^{<-1}$(LynSuf w))) · [LynSuf w]) else ε)"

The first definition is a constructive definition of the longest Lyndon suffix, abbreviated as LynSuf. It relies upon drop which is used to drop first i letters from the beginning of a word w (altogether as drop i w). In the definition, i is the least such that drop i w is a Lyndon word. Note that the definition of LynSuf w is correct for a nonempty word w (since a word of length one is Lyndon by definition). For the empty word, nothing can be shown about LynSuf ε since LEAST internally relies on the definite descriptor THE. This is reflected in the definition of Lyndon_fac which is introduced by the keyword **function** and it requires a proof that the definition is correct (which is not the case in the case of **definition** which may be seen rather as a form of syntactic abbreviation). Notably, the termination of this function needs to be shown. The recursive definition of LynFac finds the Lyndon factorization by repeatedly finding the longest Lyndon suffix of the word to be decomposed. As it needs to be total, by the design choice we have that LynFac ε = ε.

An advantage of **function** over **definition** is that Isabelle automatically produces a number of facts related to the function. Let us reveal one of those facts that will allow us to easily prove claims using a structural induction. It is stored under the name Lyndon_fac.induct and reads

"(⋀w. (w ≠ ε ⟹ P (w$^{<-1}$LynSuf w)) ⟹ P w) ⟹ P v"

In other words, if for all nonempty word w we have that P (w$^{<-1}$LynSuf w) implies P w, then P v holds for any word v and any predicate P. The induction hypothesis here says that the fact that the claim P holds for the previous step in the Lyndon factorization implies that it holds for the Lyndon factorization. This fact may be used as an induction rule and eases and clarifies proofs of elementary facts that need to be shown next, for instance:

lemma Lyndon_fac_set: "z ∈ set (Lyndon_fac w) ⟹ Lyndon z"
proof(induction w rule: Lyndon_fac.induct)
  case (1 w)
  then show "Lyndon z"
  proof (cases "w = ε")

```
  assume "w ≠ ε"
  have "Lyndon_fac w = (Lyndon_fac (w <⁻¹(LynSuf w) )) ·
[LynSuf w]" using Lyndon_fac_simp[OF ⟨w ≠ ε⟩].
    from set_ConsD[OF "1.prems"(1)[unfolded rotate1.simps(2)[of
"LynSuf w" "Lyndon_fac (w <⁻¹(LynSuf w) )", folded this,
symmetric], unfolded set_rotate1]]
    have "z = LynSuf w ∨ z ∈ set (Lyndon_fac (w <⁻¹(LynSuf w)
))".
  thus "Lyndon z"
    using "1.IH"[OF ⟨w ≠ ε⟩] longest_Lyndon_suf_Lyndon[OF ⟨w ≠
ε⟩] by blast
  next
    assume "w = ε"
    thus "Lyndon z"
      using "1.prems"
      unfolding Lyndon_fac_emp[folded ⟨w = ε⟩] list.set(1)
empty_iff by blast
  qed
qed
```

We do not comment further on the proof and leave the reader to assess its understandability.

Besides the exhibited fact that LynFac w is composed of Lyndon words, we show that it is indeed a factorization of the word w, and that if we take any starting segment $\ell_1\ell_2\cdots\ell_q$ of LynFac $w = [\ell_1, \ell_2, \ldots, \ell_n]$, we obtain $[\ell_1, \ell_2, \ldots, \ell_q] =$ LynFac $\ell_1\ell_2\cdots\ell_q$. These preparatory facts are now completed with the definition of a nonincreasing sequence of Lyndon words:

```
definition Lyndon_mono :: "'a list list ⇒ bool" where
  "Lyndon_mono ws ≡ (∀ u ∈ set ws. Lyndon u) ∧ (rlex.sorted
(rev ws))"
```

Which is used to formalize the claim of Theorem 1 as follows:

```
theorem Lyndon_mono_fac_iff: "Lyndon_mono ws ⟷ ws = LynFac
(concat ws)"
```

```
theorem Lyndon_mono_unique: assumes "Lyndon_mono ws" and
"Lyndon_mono zs" and "concat ws = concat zs"
  shows "ws = zs"
```

The mapping concat retrieves the word from its factorization, for instance, concat $[\ell_1, \ell_2] = \ell_1 \cdot \ell_2$.

3.3   Using the Minimal Relation

In contrast to a somewhat implicit specification of the total orders involved, we add an explicit specification of the minimal relation required for a word w to be a Lyndon word in the spirit of a more general construction in [4]. This relation, as a subset of $\mathcal{A} \times \mathcal{A}$, is constructed as an inductive set:

```
inductive_set rotate_rel :: "'a list ⇒ ('a × 'a) set" for w
  where   "0 < n ⟹ n < |w| ⟹ (mismatch_pair w (rotate n w))
  ∈ rotate_rel w",
```

where `mismatch_pair u v` returns the pair of letters of u and v where they first differ, i.e., it returns (a, b) with $a \neq b$, pa a prefix of u and pb a prefix of v. If no such pair is found, the inductive definition produces the empty set, i.e., for a letter a, `rotate_rel` a^k equals the empty set.

Its minimality is proven as follows (in the context of the class linorder):

```
lemma rotate_rel_iff: assumes "w ≠ ε"
  shows  "Lyndon w ⟷ rotate_rel w ⊆ {(x,y). x < y}"
```

It is a noteworthy fact that the implication starting from the minimal relation requires to extend the minimal partial order to a total order. This is provided by the entry [25] in the Archive of Formal Proofs [1], which formalizes the Szpilrajn extension theorem stating that every partial order can be extended to a total order. This is an example of an advanced set-theoretic claim that is usually and rather implicitly taken for granted in paper proofs. One of the merits (or annoyances) of a formalization is that such steps become explicit and have to be dealt with.

4   Final Remark

The presented formalization of Lyndon words (and parts of the auxiliary cornerstone theories) is the result of an iterative development process of formalization of elements of combinatorics on words [10]. The current version is in fact a result of several optimizations based on our usage experience. We thus consider it to be a suitable as basis for a further formalization of more elaborate results, for instance, universal Lyndon words [4]. A release version is available in the Archive of Formal Proofs [12,13].

Acknowledgements. The authors acknowledge support by the Czech Science Foundation grant GAČR 20-20621S.

References

1. Archive of Formal Proofs. https://www.isa-afp.org/topics.html
2. Bannai, H., Tomohiro, I., Inenaga, S., Nakashima, Y., Takeda, M., Tsuruta, K.: A new characterization of maximal repetitions by Lyndon trees. In: Proceedings of the Twenty-Sixth Annual ACM-SIAM Symposium on Discrete Algorithms. Society for Industrial and Applied Mathematics (December 2015)
3. Blanchette, J.C., Kaliszyk, C., Paulson, L.C., Urban, J.: Hammering towards QED. J. Form. Reason. **9**(1), 101–148 (2016)
4. Carpi, A., Fici, G., Holub, Š., Opršal, J., Sciortino, M.: Universal Lyndon words. In: Csuhaj-Varjú, E., Dietzfelbinger, M., Ésik, Z. (eds.) MFCS 2014. LNCS, vol. 8634, pp. 135–146. Springer, Heidelberg (2014). https://doi.org/10.1007/978-3-662-44522-8_12

5. Dolce, F., Restivo, A., Reutenauer, C.: On generalized Lyndon words. Theor. Comput. Sci. **777**, 232–242 (2019)
6. Duval, J.P.: Génération d'une section des classes de conjugaison et arbre des mots de Lyndon de longueur bornée. Theor. Comput. Sci. **60**(3), 255–283 (1988)
7. Fredricksen, H., Maiorana, J.: Necklaces of beads in k colors and k-ary de Bruijn sequences. Discret. Math. **23**(3), 207–210 (1978)
8. Harrison, J.: Without loss of generality. In: Berghofer, S., Nipkow, T., Urban, C., Wenzel, M. (eds.) TPHOLs 2009. LNCS, vol. 5674, pp. 43–59. Springer, Heidelberg (2009). https://doi.org/10.1007/978-3-642-03359-9_3
9. Hivert, F., et al.: Coq-Combi (2021). https://github.com/hivert/Coq-Combi
10. Holub, Š., Starosta, Š., et al.: Combinatorics on words formalized (2021). https://gitlab.com/formalcow/combinatorics-on-words-formalized
11. Holub, Š., Veroff, R.: Formalizing a fragment of combinatorics on words. In: Kari, J., Manea, F., Petre, I. (eds.) CiE 2017. LNCS, vol. 10307, pp. 24–31. Springer, Cham (2017). https://doi.org/10.1007/978-3-319-58741-7_3
12. Holub, Š., Raška, M., Starosta, Š.: Combinatorics on words basics. Archive of Formal Proofs (May 2021). https://isa-afp.org/entries/Combinatorics_Words.html. Formal proof development
13. Holub, Š., Starosta, Š.: Lyndon words. Archive of Formal Proofs (May 2021). https://isa-afp.org/entries/Combinatorics_Words_Lyndon.html. Formal proof development
14. Isabelle generic proof assistant. https://isabelle.in.tum.de/
15. Kaliszyk, C., Rabe, F.: A survey of languages for formalizing mathematics. In: Benzmüller, C., Miller, B. (eds.) CICM 2020. LNCS (LNAI), vol. 12236, pp. 138–156. Springer, Cham (2020). https://doi.org/10.1007/978-3-030-53518-6_9
16. Lothaire, M.: Combinatorics on Words. Cambridge Mathematical Library. Cambridge University Press, Cambridge (1997)
17. Lyndon, R.C.: On Burnside's problem. Trans. Am. Math. Soc. **77**(2), 202–215 (1954)
18. Marcus, S., Sokol, D.: 2D Lyndon words and applications. Algorithmica **77**(1), 116–133 (2015)
19. Nikpow, T.: A tutorial introduction to structured Isar proofs. https://courses.grainger.illinois.edu/cs576/sp2015/doc/isar-overview.pdf
20. Nipkow, T., Prehofer, C.: Type reconstruction for type classes. J. Funct. Program. **5**(2), 201–224 (1995)
21. Nipkow, T., Wenzel, M., Paulson, L.C. (eds.): 9. Advanced Simplification, Recursion, and Induction. Isabelle/HOL. LNCS, vol. 2283, pp. 175–193. Springer, Heidelberg (2002). https://doi.org/10.1007/3-540-45949-9_9
22. Raška, M., Starosta, Š.: Producing symmetrical facts for lists induced by the list reversal mapping in Isabelle/HOL. http://arxiv.org/abs/2104.11622 (2021)
23. Thompson, S.: Type Theory and Functional Programming. Addison-Wesley, Boston (1991). https://www.cs.kent.ac.uk/people/staff/sjt/TTFP
24. Wiedijk, F.: Formalizing 100 theorems. https://www.cs.ru.nl/~freek/100/
25. Zeller, P.: Szpilrajn extension theorem. Archive of Formal Proofs (July 2019). https://isa-afp.org/entries/Szpilrajn.html. Formal proof development

The Range of State Complexities of Languages Resulting from the Cascade Product—The General Case (Extended Abstract)

Markus Holzer$^{(\boxtimes)}$ and Christian Rauch

Institut für Informatik, Universität Giessen, Arndtstr. 2, 35392 Giessen, Germany
{holzer,christian.rauch}@informatik.uni-giessen.de

Abstract. We continue our investigation on the descriptional complexity of the cascade product of finite state devices started in [M. HOLZER, C. RAUCH: The Range of State Complexities of Languages Resulting from the Cascade Product—The Unary Case (Extended Abstract). Proc. CIAA, 2021]. Here we study the general case, that is, cascade products of reset, permutation-reset, permutation, and finite automata in general, where the left operand automaton has an alphabet of size at least two. In all cases, except for the cascade product of two permutation automata, it is shown that the whole range of state complexities, namely the interval $[1, nm]$, where n is the state complexity of the left operand and m that of the right one, is reachable. The cascade product of two permutation automata produces a lot of non-reachable numbers—numbers of this kind are called magic in the relevant literature—even for arbitrary alphabet sizes. These results are in sharp contrast to the unary case.

1 Introduction

The Krohn-Rhodes Theorem [2] states that any finite automaton can be decomposed into (several) simple "automata prime factors." Here simple means permutation-reset automata, that is, devices where each letter induces either a permutation or a constant function on the state set. The decomposition operation is that of the cascade product, which shares similarity with the direct product of automata. Although the descriptional complexity of the Krohn-Rhodes Theorem is well understood [11,12], the one-time application of the cascade product operation still lacks a descriptional complexity investigation until recently. In [6] the descriptional complexity of the cascade product, where the left operand is a unary automaton, is studied in detail. There a complete picture on the reachable state complexities for the cascade product of reset (RFA), permutation (PFA), permutation-reset (PRFA), and finite automata in general (DFA) is drawn. It

N. Moreira and R. Reis (Eds.): DLT 2021, LNCS 12811, pp. 229–241, 2021.
https://doi.org/10.1007/978-3-030-81508-0_19

turned out, that in the majority of the cases—in 7 out of 12 cases[1]—studied in [6], state complexities were identified that cannot be reached by the application of a single cascade operation on a minimal unary n- and a minimal m-state finite automaton of a certain kind. This research falls into the line of operation problems on finite state devices, see, e.g., [3,4,7,8,10], and their descriptional complexity. Adapting the notion of [9] on the determinization of nondeterministic finite automata, state numbers that cannot be reached by a binary operation on two state devices of a particular size are called "magic." For instance, for a minimal unary n-state PFA A and a minimal m-state PFA B the minimal automaton accepting the language $L(A \circ B)$, where $\circ$ refers to the cascade product, can only have α states with α in

$$\{1\} \cup \{\, nx \mid 1 \leq x \leq m \,\} \cup \{\, tx \mid 1 \leq x < m \,\},$$

where t is a non-trivial divisor of n, that is, a divisor that is neither 1 nor n. All other numbers in the interval $[1, nm]$ are called magic. Interestingly, one can show that $nm - 1$ is magic in all cases, where numbers exist that cannot be reached by the cascade operation problem where at least one automaton is not a RFA. It is worth mentioning, that the existence of these magic numbers does not contradict the Krohn-Rhodes decomposition theorem.

Here we continue the research started in [6] by considering the descriptional complexity of the cascade product of automata with input alphabets of size at least two. Compared to the unary case the situation on the existence of magic numbers completely changes for automata with larger input alphabet sizes. In almost all cases—in 15 out of 16 cases[2]—no magic numbers exist and thus the whole interval $[1, nm]$ can be obtained. For the case of the cascade product of two PFAs we identify numerous magic numbers. In fact, for large n with a lot of non-trivial divisors, and small m a legion of magic numbers exist. For instance, for $n = 10 = 2 \cdot 5$ and $m = 3$ at least the numbers (in increasing order) 3, 7, 9, 11, 13, 17, 19, 21, 23, 27, and 29 are magic. Except for a precise characterization of the reachable state sizes for the cascade product of two PFAs in general, we solve the magic number problem for the cascade product completely.

2 Preliminaries

We recall some definitions on finite automata as contained in [5]. A *deterministic finite automaton* (DFA) is a quintuple $A = (Q, \Sigma, \cdot, q_0, F)$, where Q is the finite set of *states*, Σ is the finite set of *input symbols*, $q_0 \in Q$ is the *initial state*, $F \subseteq Q$ is the set of *accepting states*, and the *transition function* $\cdot$ maps $Q \times \Sigma$ to Q. The *language accepted* by the DFA A is defined as $L(A) = \{\, w \in \Sigma^* \mid q_0 \cdot w \in F \,\}$, where the

---

[1] There are three types of automata for the left operand of the cascade product, namely unary reset, unary permutation(-reset), and unary finite automata in general and four types of automata for the right operand, that are reset, permutation, permutation-reset, and finite state device without restrictions.

[2] For automata with input alphabet of size at least two we have four types of left operands instead of three as in the unary case. This leads to $4 \cdot 4 = 16$ cases.

transition function is recursively extended to a mapping $Q \times \Sigma^* \to Q$ in the usual way. Obviously, every letter $a \in \Sigma$ induces a mapping from the state set Q to Q by $q \mapsto \delta(q, a)$, for every $q \in Q$. A DFA is *unary* if the input alphabet Σ is a singleton set, that is, $\Sigma = \{a\}$, for some input symbol a. Moreover, a DFA is said to be a *permutation-reset* automaton (PRFA) if every input letter induces either a permutation or a constant mapping on the state set. If every letter of the automaton induces only permutations on the state set, then we simply speak of a *permutation automaton* (PFA). Finally, a DFA is said to be a *reset* automaton (RFA) if every letter induces either the identity or a constant mapping on the state set. The class of reset, permutation, permutation-reset, and deterministic automata in general are referred to as **RFA**, **PFA**, **PRFA**, and **FA**, respectively. It is obvious that inclusions $X\mathbf{FA} \subseteq \mathbf{PRFA} \subseteq \mathbf{FA}$, where $X \in \{\mathbf{P}, \mathbf{R}\}$, holds. Moreover, it is not hard to see that the classes **RFA** and **PFA** are incomparable.

The cascade product [2] is originally introduced for semi-automata, which are automata with no initial nor final states. For our needs we enrich the cascade product with initial and final states and follow for the definition of the final states the lines of [1]. The *cascade product* of two DFAs $A = (Q_A, \Sigma, \cdot_A, q_{0,A}, F_A)$ and $B = (Q_B, Q_A \times \Sigma, \cdot_B, q_{0,B}, F_B)$, denoted by $A \circ B$, is defined as the automaton

$$A \circ B = (Q_A \times Q_B, \Sigma, \cdot, (q_{0,A}, q_{0,B}), F_A \times F_B),$$

where the transition function is given by

$$(q, p) \cdot a = (q \cdot_A a, p \cdot_B (q, a)),$$

for $q \in Q_A$, $p \in Q_B$, and $a \in \Sigma$. We say that A is the *first automaton* and B the *second automaton* in the cascade product $A \circ B$. A schematic drawing of the cascade product is given in Fig. 2. It is obvious that the cascade product of two DFAs generalizes the direct product. In order to explain the notation we give an example.

Example 1. Consider the PRFA $A = (\{q_0, q_1, q_2\}, \{a, b\}, \cdot_A, q_0, \{q_0, q_2\})$, where

$$q_0 \cdot_A a = q_1, \qquad\qquad q_1 \cdot_A a = q_0, \qquad\qquad q_2 \cdot_A a = q_2,$$
$$q_0 \cdot_A b = q_2, \qquad\qquad q_1 \cdot_A b = q_2, \qquad\qquad q_2 \cdot_A b = q_2.$$

Then assume that m is an arbitrary integer greater than or equal three and let

$$B = (\{p_0, p_1, \ldots, p_{m-1}\}, \{q_0, q_1, q_2\} \times \{a, b\}, \cdot_B, p_0, \{p_1\}),$$

be the PFA, where

$$p_i \cdot_B (q_j, b) = p_{i+1 \bmod m}, \qquad \text{for } 0 \le j \le 1 \text{ and } 0 \le i \le m - 1,$$
$$p_i \cdot_B (q_2, a) = p_{i+1 \bmod 3}, \qquad \text{for } 0 \le i \le 2,$$

and all other not explicitly stated transitions are self-loops. The automata A and B, for $m = 3$, are depicted in Fig. 1 on the top and lower right, respectively. It is easy to see that both automata are minimal.

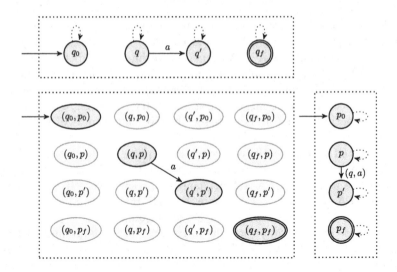

Fig. 1. Schematic drawing of the cascade product of the DFAs A and B. The automaton A is depicted on top and the automaton B on the right. The automaton AB is shown in the middle, where only the transition of the state (q; p) is displayed. Note that self-loops will be only drawn by dotted loops without letters.

By construction the cascade product of A and B is given by

$$A \circ B = (\{q_0, q_1, q_2\} \times \{p_0, p_1, \dots, p_{m-1}\}, \{a, b\}, \cdot, (q_0, p_0), \{q_0, q_2\} \times \{p_1\}),$$

where the transitions of the initially reachable states

$$(q_0, p_0), (q_1, p_0), (q_2, p_0), (q_2, p_1), (q_2, p_2),$$

can be deduced from Fig. 1, too, on the lower left. Although the drawing is only for automaton B with three states, the initially reachable part of $A \circ B$ remains the same for larger B's as defined. Observe, that $A \circ B$ is not a PRFA and it is not minimal. By inspection the only equivalent states in $A \circ B$ are (q_0, p_0) and (q_1, p_0). Hence, the minimal DFA accepting $L(A \circ B)$ has $\alpha = 4$ states. □

The following result is immediate by the lower bound results on the operational complexity of the intersection operation on finite automata [8].

Theorem 1. *Let A be a n-state and B a m-state DFA. Then $n \cdot m$ states are sufficient and necessary in the worst case for any DFA accepting $L(A \circ B)$. The lower bound even holds for automata with binary input alphabet.*

When considering the descriptional complexity of the cascade product, we limit ourselves to the case where the involved automata are non-trivial, i.e., they have more than one state. This is due to the fact that if the second automaton in the operation under consideration is a singleton device, then the cascade product accepts either the empty set or the same language as the involved other device.

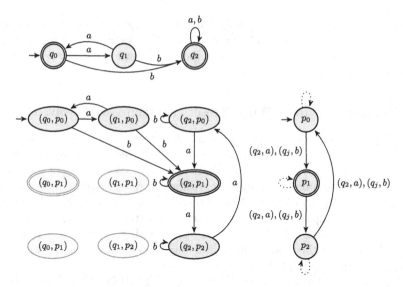

Fig. 2. The example automata A and B on the top and lower right, respectively. For a better representability not all transitions of an automaton are shown. In particular, this is the case for automaton AB, where only the transitions of the initially reachable states are shown. The cascade product AB is depicted on the lower left. Additionally the index j is a placeholder for numbers 0 and 1. Note that as before self-loops will be only depicted by dotted loops without letters.

If the first automaton is a singleton device, then the cascade product accepts either the empty language or the language L that is the image of the language that the second automaton accepts under the homomorphism $(q, a) \mapsto a$, for the letters a of the first automaton, where q is the state of the first automaton. Therefore, only 1-, n-, or m-state automata, for $n, m \geq 1$, appear as results of a cascade product with a trivial automaton. Thus, in the following we only consider non-trivial automata.

3   Results

We assume the reader to be familiar with the results on the cascade product of unary automata, as contained in the forerunner paper [6]. In the following we prove results for the general case, that is, if the input alphabet of the left operand automaton in the cascade product is at least two. Since we are dealing with permutation automata very often, we find the following result on the minimality of PFAs quite useful. The following statement was already shown in [6].

Lemma 1. *Let A be a PFA with a sole accepting state with all states reachable from the initial state. Then A is minimal. Minimality is preserved even if the initial state is changed to any other state.*

Our investigation is started with cascade products, where reset automata are involved. Observe, that all our results on the cascade product of binary automata remain valid for arbitrary alphabets of at least two letters, since adding duplicitous letters does not change the complexity.

3.1   Cascade Products Where Reset Automata are Involved

The magic number problem in the binary input alphabet case of the cascade product, where at least one reset automaton is involved, is already almost completely solved in [6]. It is easy to see that (minimal) reset automata form a very limited class of automata, because every minimal reset automaton has at most two states. For the cascade product of two RFAs A and B it was shown in [6] that if A has an input alphabet of at least two letters, then the minimal DFA accepting the language $L(A \circ B)$ has α states with $1 \leq \alpha \leq 4$, which is the maximal range for this case. This is different from the unary case, where only the values from the set $\{1, 2, 3\}$ can be reached.

Next consider the cascade product of RFAs with PFAs, where we show that no magic numbers exist. The upper bound on the size of the minimal automaton equivalent to the cascade product of a non-trivial minimal reset automaton with a minimal m-state permutation automaton is $2m$. In the unary case this bound cannot be reached, since only the interval $[1, m + 1]$ is obtained [6].

Theorem 2. *Let $m \geq 1$. Then for every α with $1 \leq \alpha \leq 2m$, there exists a non-trivial minimal RFA A and minimal m-state PFA B such that the minimal DFA for the language $L(A \circ B)$ has α states.*

Proof (Sketch). By the above mentioned result in the unary case it remains to show that the integers within the interval $[m + 2, 2m]$ are reachable. So let $\alpha = m + \ell$, for $2 \leq \ell \leq m$.

Define the RFA $A = (\{q_0, q_1\}, \{a, b\}, \cdot_A, q_0, \{q_1\})$, where the transition function is defined as

$$q_0 \cdot_A a = q_1, \qquad\qquad q_1 \cdot_A a = q_1$$
$$q_0 \cdot_A b = q_0, \qquad\qquad q_1 \cdot_A b = q_1.$$

It is easy to see that this automaton is minimal. Next let the PFA B be

$$B = (\{p_0, p_1, \ldots, p_{m-1}\}, \{q_0, q_1\} \times \{a, b\}, \cdot_B, p_0, \{p_0\}),$$

where

$$p_i \cdot_B (q_0, a) = p_{i+1 \bmod m}, \qquad\qquad \text{for } 0 \leq i \leq m - 1,$$
$$p_i \cdot_B (q_0, b) = p_{i+1 \bmod \ell}, \qquad\qquad \text{for } 0 \leq i \leq \ell - 1,$$
$$p_i \cdot_B (q_0, b) = p_i, \qquad\qquad\qquad \text{for } \ell \leq i \leq m - 1,$$

and

$$p_i \cdot_B (q_1, a) = p_{i+1 \bmod m}, \qquad\qquad \text{for } 0 \leq i \leq m - 1,$$
$$p_i \cdot_B (q_1, b) = p_i, \qquad\qquad \text{for } 0 \leq i \leq m - 1.$$

This completes the descriptions of the automaton B. By Lemma 1 the automaton B is minimal.

Next we show that the set of initially reachable states of the cascade product $A \circ B$ can be partitioned into the union $E_a \cup E_b$, where

$$E_a = \{ (q_0, p_0) \cdot a^i \mid i \geq 1 \} \quad \text{and} \quad E_b = \{ (q_0, p_0) \cdot b^i \mid i \geq 0 \}.$$

Here $\cdot$ refers to the transition function of $A \circ B$; see Fig. 3. A close inspection reveals that $E_a = \{q_1\} \times \{p_0, p_1, \ldots, p_{m-1}\}$ and $E_b = \{q_0\} \times \{p_0, p_1, \ldots, p_{\ell-1}\}$. Finally, it remains to prove that the states in $E_a \cup E_b$ are pairwise inequivalent. The tedious details are left to the interested reader. Then the stated claim follows, because the number of states in $E_a \cup E_b$ is $\ell + m$, which by construction is equal to α. □

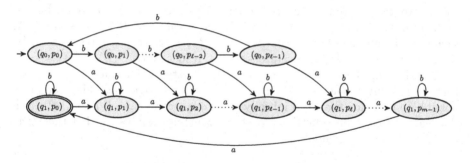

Fig. 3. The initially reachable part of the automaton $A \circ B$.

In the remainder of this section we discuss the cases where the right operand of the cascade product is an RFA. For the cascade product of a unary minimal n-state PFA with an RFA it was shown in [6] that the maximal possible interval $[1, 2n]$ can be reached, and therefore no magic numbers exist. This result generalizes to unary PRFAs and DFAs and moreover to the non-unary case. This is summarized in the following theorem.

Theorem 3. *Let $n \geq 1$. Then for every α with $1 \leq \alpha \leq 2n$, there exists a n-state PFA (PRFA, or DFA, respectively) A and a non-trivial RFA B such that the minimal DFA for the language $L(A \circ B)$ has α states.*

This settles all cases where RFAs are involved in the cascade product of two automata. In summary, in all cases no magic numbers exist, whenever the input alphabet of the first automaton contains at least two alphabet symbols.

3.2 Cascade Products of Two Permutation Automata

In [6] it was shown for the cascade product of two permutation automata in the unary case that all numbers which are relatively prime to the number of states of the first device are magic numbers. We show that this also holds in the general setting, i.e., for input alphabets of arbitrary size. Before we prove this, we recall a structural result on the cascade product of two PFAs from [6].

Theorem 4. *Let A and B be minimal n- and m-state PFAs, respectively. Then there is an x with $1 \leq x \leq m$ such that for every state q in A the number of initially reachable states in $A \circ B$ that have q as their first component is exactly x. As a direct consequence the initially reachable part of $A \circ B$ has exactly nx states. Moreover, the minimal deterministic finite automata that accepts $L(A \circ B)$ has α states, where α is a divisor of the quantity of initially reachable states of $A \circ B$.*

Now we are ready to prove the above mentioned result on the existence of magic numbers in the general case.

Lemma 2. *Let $n, m \geq 2$. For every α in $[2, nm]$ that is coprime to n, there does not exist a minimal n-state PFA A and a minimal m-state PFA B such that the minimal DFA for the language $L(A \circ B)$ has α states.*

Proof. We give a proof by contradiction. So we assume that α is an integer in $[2, nm]$, which is coprime to n, and A is a n-state and B is a m-state PFA, such that the minimal DFA accepting $L(A \circ B)$ has exactly α states. Let Q_A be the state set of A and Q_B the state set of B, respectively.

By Theorem 4 we know, that there are nx states, for some $1 \leq x \leq m$, that are initially reachable in $A \circ B$, and that α must divide nx. Therefore, it is possible to partition the set of initially reachable states of $A \circ B$ into α sets such that each set contains exactly nx/α states which are equivalent. Let these sets be $T_0, T_1, \ldots, T_{\alpha-1}$. Define

$$S_i := \{\, q \in Q_A \mid \text{there exists } p \in Q_B \text{ such that } (q, p) \in T_i \,\}.$$

Because $A \circ B$ is a PFA, for every pair of states there exists a word which maps one of those states onto the other. Since every word acts directly on the first component of a state we find that $|(\{q\} \times Q_B) \cap T_i|$ is equal for every state q of A for which S_i is not empty. Since it makes the further considerations a lot easier we fix q as an arbitrary state of A. Again, by Theorem 4 we know, that for every state q of A there are x states (with first component q) initially reachable in $A \circ B$. Thus, we obtain for a set T_i, which contains a state that has q as its first component

$$|\{(\{q\} \times Q_B) \cap T_i \neq \emptyset \mid 0 \leq i \leq \alpha - 1\}| \cdot |(\{q\} \times Q_B) \cap T_i| = x,$$

and $|(\{q\} \times Q_B) \cap T_i| \cdot |Q_A \cap S_i| = |T_i| = n\frac{x}{\alpha}$. By inserting the first equation into the second we obtain

$$|(\{q\} \times Q_B) \cap T_i| \cdot |Q_A \cap S_i|$$
$$= n \cdot \frac{|\{(\{q\} \times Q_B) \cap T_i \neq \emptyset \mid 0 \leq i \leq \alpha - 1\}| \cdot |(\{q\} \times Q_B) \cap T_i|}{\alpha}.$$

Dividing by $|(\{q\} \times Q_B) \cap T_i|$ gives us

$$|Q_A \cap S_i| = n \cdot \frac{|\{ (\{q\} \times Q_B) \cap T_i \neq \emptyset \mid 0 \leq i \leq \alpha - 1\}|}{\alpha}.$$

Since $|Q_A \cap S_i|$ is an integer and the numbers n and α are coprime we obtain that $|\{ (\{q\} \times Q_B) \cap T_i \neq \emptyset \mid 0 \leq i \leq \alpha - 1\}|$ is divisible by α. This in turn implies that it is equal to α, since it is upward limited by α. Therefore, for every set T_i, for $0 \leq i \leq \alpha - 1$, there exists a state which has q as its first component. Because α is at least two, there must be an initially reachable accepting state in $A \circ B$. Thus, there exists an i with $0 \leq i \leq \alpha - 1$, such that T_i contains only (equivalent) accepting states. In conclusion that means that q must be accepting. Since state q was arbitrarily chosen this implies that every state of A must be accepting, which is a contradiction to the fact that A is minimal. □

3.3 Cascade Products with Permutation and Permutation-Reset Automata and Beyond

Next we investigate the descriptional complexity of the cascade product of a permutation and a permutation-reset device. For the first case, where the first automaton of the cascade product is a PFA no magic numbers exist. This is in contrast to the unary case [6].

Theorem 5. *Let $n, m \geq 2$. Then for every α with $1 \leq \alpha \leq nm$, there exists a minimal binary n-state PFA A and a minimal m-state PRFA B such that the minimal DFA accepting the language $L(A \circ B)$ has exactly α states.*

Proof (Sketch). In [6] it was shown that in the unary case the numbers $[1, 2n]$ are reachable. Thus, we may assume that $\alpha > 2n$. One can show that every number α in the interval $[n, nm]$ can be written in the form $\alpha = km + n - k + \ell$, for integers $0 \leq k \leq n - 1$ and $0 \leq \ell \leq m - 1$. In order to simplify the constructions to come, we want to exclude the case $\ell = m - 1$. In case α has a representation as above with $\ell = m - 1$, we may rewrite it to $\alpha = km + n - k + (m - 1) = (k + 1)m + n - (k + 1)$, as long as $k < n - 1$. For $k = n - 1$, the value of α is equal to nm, which can be reached by a result in [6] already in the unary case. In summary, α belongs now to the interval $[2n + 1, nm - 1]$ and can be written as above with $0 \leq k \leq n - 1$ and $0 \leq \ell < m - 1$.

Let $A = (\{q_0, q_1, \ldots, q_{n-1}\}, \{a, b\}, \cdot_A, q_0, F_A)$, with

$$
\begin{aligned}
q_i \cdot_A a &= q_{i+1 \bmod n}, & &\text{for } 0 \leq i \leq n - 1, \\
q_i \cdot_A b &= q_i, & &\text{for } 0 \leq i \leq n - k - 2, \\
q_i \cdot_A b &= q_{i+1}, & &\text{for } n - k - 1 \leq i \leq n - 3, \\
q_{n-2} \cdot_A b &= q_{n-k-1}, \\
q_{n-1} \cdot_A b &= q_{n-1},
\end{aligned}
$$

where all non-specified transitions are self-loops as usual, and $F_A = \{q_{n-1}\}$, if $n = 2$ and $k = 0$, $F_A = \{q_{n-2}\}$, if $n = 2$ and $k > 0$, and $F_A = \{q_{n-2}, q_{n-1}\}$, otherwise. That A is minimal follows for $n = 2$ by Lemma 1. In case $n > 2$ the minimality of the device A is seen because the states q_{n-2} and q_{n-1} are distinguishable by applying the word a and for every other state pair there exists a bijection which maps at least one of them into $\{q_{n-2}, q_{n-1}\}$.

Next let the PRFA B be

$$B = (\{p_0, p_1, \ldots, p_{m-1}\}, \{q_0, q_1, \ldots, q_{n-1}\} \times \{a, b\}, \cdot_B, p_0, \{p_0\}),$$

where

$$p_i \cdot_B (q_{n-2}, a) = \begin{cases} p_{i+1 \bmod m}, & \text{for } 0 \leq i \leq m-1 \text{ and } k = 0, \\ p_i, & \text{for } 0 \leq i \leq m-1 \text{ and } k > 0, \end{cases}$$

$$p_i \cdot_B (q_{n-2}, b) = \begin{cases} p_i, & \text{for } 0 \leq i \leq m-1 \text{ and } k = 0, \\ p_{i+1 \bmod m}, & \text{for } 0 \leq i \leq m-1 \text{ and } k > 0, \end{cases}$$

$$p_i \cdot_B (q_{n-1}, a) = \begin{cases} p_i, & \text{for } 0 \leq i \leq m-1, n = 2 \text{ and } k > 0, \\ p_0, & \text{for } 0 \leq i \leq m-1, n > 2 \text{ or } k = 0, \end{cases}$$

and

$$p_i \cdot_B (q_{n-1}, b) = p_{i+1 \bmod \ell+1}, \quad \text{for } 0 \leq i \leq \ell,$$

and all non-specified transitions are self-loops. The given construction ensures that all states in B are reachable (by the sole letter (q_{n-2}, a), if $k = 0$, and by the letter (q_{n-2}, b), otherwise). Thus, Lemma 1 shows that the automaton is minimal in all cases.

For the analysis of the cascade automaton $A \circ B$ we similarly proceed as in the proof of Theorem 2. First one shows that the following three sets

$$E_{a \leq n-k-2} = \{ (q_0, p_0) \cdot a^j \mid 0 \leq j \leq n-k-2 \},$$

$$E_{a^{n-k-1}b^*} = \begin{cases} \{ (q_0, p_0) \cdot a^{n-k-1}b^i \mid i \geq 0 \} & \text{if } k > 0, \\ \emptyset & \text{otherwise,} \end{cases}$$

and

$$E_{a^{n-1}b^*} = \{ (q_0, p_0) \cdot a^{n-1}b^i \mid i \geq 0 \},$$

where $\cdot$ refers to the transition function of $A \circ B$, form the initially reachable states of $A \circ B$. To this end one distinguishes two cases depending on n with appropriate subcases on k; the sets under consideration, e.g., for the case $n > 2$ and $k > 0$ are depicted in Fig. 4. In all the considered cases it turns out that $A \circ B$ has α initially reachable states. Minimality of the automaton $A \circ B$ is shown by proving that the states in $E_{a \leq n-k-2} \cup E_{a^{n-k-1}b^*} \cup E_{a^{n-1}b^*}$ are pairwise inequivalent. The cumbersome details are left to the reader. Then this proves the stated claim. □

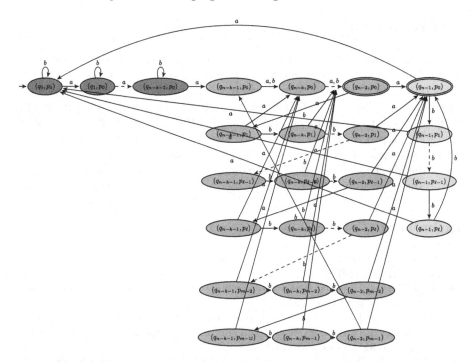

Fig. 4. The initially reachable states of $A \circ B$ in the case $n > 2$ and $k > 0$. The states of $E_{a \leq n-k-2}$, $E_{a^{n-k-1}b^*}$, and $E_{a^{n-1}b^*}$ are coloured dark gray, gray, and light gray, respectively.

Obviously this theorem implies that the minimal DFA accepting $L(A \circ B)$ for a n-state device A and a m-state device B can have every number of states in the integer interval $[1, nm]$ in the following cases:

- A is a binary PFA and B is an arbitrary DFA,
- A is a binary PRFA and B is a PRFA,
- A is an arbitrary binary DFA and B is a PRFA, and
- A is an arbitrary binary DFA and B is an arbitrary DFA,

where both automata are always assumed to be minimal.

So it only remains to study the cascade product of an n-state PRFA A and an m-state PFA B. Recall that in the unary case magic numbers exist in this case [6].

Theorem 6. *Let $n, m \geq 2$. Then for every α with $1 \leq \alpha \leq nm$, there exists a minimal binary n-state PRFA A and a minimal m-state PFA B such that the minimal DFA accepting the language $L(A \circ B)$ has exactly α states.*

Obviously, this statement generalizes to the remaining missing cases.

4   Conclusions

We continued our research on the magic number problem for the cascade product on finite automata of certain types. Compared to the unary case, which was studied in [6], where in almost all cases magic numbers were identified, here the situation is completely the other way around. In all cases, except one (Lemma 2), we do not find magic numbers. In fact, only for the cascade product of two minimal PFAs, a precise answer to the reachable states sizes are missing. Moreover, since the cascade product as introduced here uses final states, it also remains to study the effect on the descriptional complexity of the choice of final states in the product automaton.

References

1. Ae, T.: Direct or cascade product of pushdown automata. J. Comput. Syst. Sci. **14**(2), 257–263 (1977)
2. Arbib, M.A.: Algebraic Theory of Machines, Languages, and Semigroups. Academic Press, Cambridge (1968)
3. Čevorová, K.: Kleene star on unary regular languages. In: Jurgensen, H., Reis, R. (eds.) DCFS 2013. LNCS, vol. 8031, pp. 277–288. Springer, Heidelberg (2013). https://doi.org/10.1007/978-3-642-39310-5_26
4. Čevorová, K., Jirásková, G., Krajňáková, I.: On the square of regular languages. In: Holzer, M., Kutrib, M. (eds.) CIAA 2014. LNCS, vol. 8587, pp. 136–147. Springer, Cham (2014). https://doi.org/10.1007/978-3-319-08846-4_10
5. Harrison, M.A.: Introduction to Formal Language Theory. Addison-Wesley, Boston (1978)
6. Holzer, M., Rauch, C.: The range of state complexities of languages resulting from the cascade product—the unary case (extended abstract). In: Maneth, S. (eds.) Implementation and Application of Automata. CIAA 2021. Lecture Notes in Computer Science, vol. 12803. Springer, Cham (2021). https://doi.org/10.1007/978-3-030-79121-6_8
7. Holzer, M., Hospodár, M.: The range of state complexities of languages resulting from the cut operation. In: Martín-Vide, C., Okhotin, A., Shapira, D. (eds.) LATA 2019. LNCS, vol. 11417, pp. 190–202. Springer, Cham (2019). https://doi.org/10.1007/978-3-030-13435-8_14
8. Hricko, M., Jirásková, G., Szabari, A.: Union and intersection of regular languages and descriptional complexity. In: Mereghetti, C., Palano, B., Pighizzini, G., Wotschke, D. (eds.) Proceedings of the 7th Workshop on Descriptional Complexity of Formal Systems, pp. 170–181. Universita degli Studi di Milano, Como (2005)
9. Iwama, K., Kambayashi, Y., Takaki, K.: Tight bounds on the number of states of DFAs that are equivalent to n-state NFAs. Theor. Comput. Sci. **237**(1–2), 485–494 (2000)
10. Jirásková, G.: Magic numbers and ternary alphabet. Internat. J. Found. Comput. Sci. **22**(2), 331–344 (2011)

11. Maler, O.: On the Krohn-Rhodes cascaded decomposition theorem. In: Manna, Z., Peled, D.A. (eds.) Time for Verification. LNCS, vol. 6200, pp. 260–278. Springer, Heidelberg (2010). https://doi.org/10.1007/978-3-642-13754-9_12
12. Maler, O., Pnueli, A.: Tight bounds on the complexity of cascaded decomposition of automata. In: Proceedings of the 31st Annual Symposium on Foundations of Computer Science, pp. 672–682. IEEE Computer Society Press, St. Louis (1990)

Second-Order Finite Automata: Expressive Power and Simple Proofs Using Automatic Structures

Dietrich Kuske$^{(\boxtimes)}$

Technische Universität Ilmenau, Ilmenau, Germany
dietrich.kuske@tu-ilmenau.de

Abstract. Second-order finite automata, introduced recently by Andrade de Melo and de Oliveira Oliveira, represent classes of languages. Since their semantics is defined by a synchronized rational relation, they can be studied using the theory of automatic structures. We exploit this connection to uniformly reprove and strengthen known and new results regarding closure and decidability properties concerning these automata. We then proceed to characterize their expressive power in terms of automatic classes of languages studied by Jain, Luo, and Stephan.

Keywords: Classes of languages · Automatic classes

1 Introduction

Andrade de Melo and de Oliveira Oliveira [1] propose a mechanism to represent possibly infinite classes of regular languages by a single finite automaton $\mathcal{A}$. The idea is to start with an alphabet of simple automata that can make only one step. A word W over this alphabet is understood as a concatenation of such small automata, and therefore as an automaton $\mathcal{A}_W$. Consequently, the "second-order finite automaton" $\mathcal{A}$ describes a class of languages: the class of languages accepted by these finite automata $\mathcal{A}_W$ for W accepted by $\mathcal{A}$. We call such a class "full-length regular". The central result in [1] is an effective canonisation procedure for second-order finite automata. Then, the authors derive effective closure and decidability results for the collection of all full-length regular classes.

Recall that at the basis of the definition of second-order finite automata and their language class lies the interpretation of a word W from $L(\mathcal{A})$ as an automaton $\mathcal{A}_W$. We consider the natural binary relation of all pairs (W, w) where the NFA $\mathcal{A}_W$ accepts the word w. Since this relation is synchronized rational (a basic observation not made explicte in [1]), we can use automatic structures [4,7,9] as a tool to reason about second-order finite automata – and this is the core of the current paper's first part. This approach gives a uniform and simple way

- to build several normalized second-order finite automata (e.g., saturated),
- to uniformly prove closure properties (e.g., intersection and difference) shown in [1] and to improve them partly, and

© Springer Nature Switzerland AG 2021
N. Moreira and R. Reis (Eds.): DLT 2021, LNCS 12811, pp. 242–254, 2021.
https://doi.org/10.1007/978-3-030-81508-0_20

– to prove decidability of inclusion, equality, and disjointness uniformly (the results are known from [1]).

We demonstrate that it also allows to prove new closure properties (e.g., the class of differences of languages from two classes) and new decidabilities (e.g., whether the intervals of languages in a full-length regular class, ordered by inclusion, are of bounded size). In a nutshell, all these results hold since they amount to the evaluation of some formula (from an appropriate and proper extension of first-order logic) in some automatic structure.

The second part of this paper is devoted to the expressiveness of second-order finite automata. The definition of full-length regular classes of languages via a rational relation is very similar to that of automatic classes of languages from [8] (that studies the learnability of such classes). Fernau (discussion at "Computer Science in Russia 2020") conjectured the two concepts to be closely related; this paper's second part details and confirms his conjecture. At this point, it is only important that an automatic class is given by a regular language and a synchronized rational relation. We show that a class of languages is full-length regular iff it is automatic with a length-preserving synchronized rational relation.

This characterization allows us to reduce the isomorphism problem for automatic equivalence structures to that of full-length regular classes ordered by inclusion. As a consequence, this latter problem is undecidable.

A limitation of full-length regular classes is that all languages in such a class are sets of words of equal length. In this paper, we extend the definition from [1] to regular and to ω-regular classes (that can contain arbitrary finite and regular languages, resp.). We actually prove the above mentioned closure and decidability results for regular classes, but the proofs can be transfered to full-length regular and partly to ω-regular classes of languages. We also present characterisations of these classes in terms of automatic classes.

In summary, we investigate classes of languages presented by finite automata and we demonstrate that the established theory of automatic structures can be useful in this study.

2   Second-Order Finite Automata and Regular Classes of Languages

For an alphabet Σ, let Σ^*, Σ^+, and Σ^ω denote the set of finite, finite nonempty, and ω-words, resp. A language $L \subseteq \Sigma^*$ is *single-length* if all its words have the same length. A relation $R \subseteq \Gamma^* \times \Sigma^*$ is *length-reducing* (*length-increasing*, *length-preserving*, resp.) if $(u, v) \in R$ implies $|u| \geq |v|$ ($|u| \leq |v|$, $|u| = |v|$, resp.).

Definition. Let A and B be sets, $W \in A$, $L \subseteq A$, and $R \subseteq A \times B$ a relation. Then we set $W^R = \{w \in B \mid (W, w) \in R\}$ and $L^R = \{W^R \mid W \in L\}$.

Intuitively, we consider the relation R as a function $R \colon A \to \mathcal{P}(B)$. Then W^R is the image of W under this mapping and L^R is the class of images of elements of the set L. We apply these constructions mainly for $A = \Gamma^+$ and $B = \Sigma^+$.

Definition. Let Σ be some alphabet and S be some finite set. A (Σ, S)-*block* is a tuple $B = (I, T, F)$ where $I, F \subseteq S$ and $T \subseteq S \times \Sigma \times S$; $\mathcal{B}(\Sigma, S)$ denotes the set of all (Σ, S)-blocks.

A block is an NFA over the alphabet Σ with set of states S. We will consider sequences of such blocks as a single NFA and run a word by chosing a transition from the ith block for its ith letter. We found it convenient to think of a block as consisting of two copies of the set of *locations* S where the *transition* $(s_1, a, s_2) \in T$ connects the location s_1 from the first copy to the location s_2 from the second copy. The *initial locations* $\iota \in I$ are considered as elements of the first copy, the *final locations* $f \in F$ as belonging to the second copy.

Definition. An NFA over $\mathcal{B}(\Sigma, S)$ is called *second-order* or *SO automaton over* Σ *and* S.

For an NFA $M = (Q, \Gamma, I, \Delta, F)$ (with sets of initial states I, of transitions $\Delta \subseteq Q \times \Gamma \times Q$, and of final states F) over Γ, we write $L^+(M) \subseteq \Gamma^+$ for the set of nonempty words accepted by M.

We will define the second-order language of the SO automaton $\mathcal{A}$ which will be a class of languages over Σ. To this aim, we need the following relation.

Definition. The relation $\mathrm{Acc}_{\Sigma, S}$ consists of all pairs $(B_1 B_2 \cdots B_m, c_1 c_2 \cdots c_n)$ with $m \geq n \geq 1$, $B_i = (I_i, T_i, F_i) \in \mathcal{B}(\Sigma, S)$ for all $i \in [m]$, and $c_i \in \Sigma$ for all $i \in [n]$ such that there exist locations $s_1, s_2, \ldots, s_{n+1} \in S$ with

(1) $s_1 \in I_1$, (2) $(s_i, c_i, s_{i+1}) \in T_i$ for all $i \in [n]$, and (3) $s_{n+1} \in F_n$.

Intuitively, we understand the word W as an NFA over Σ. Its state space consists of $m+1$ layers of the set of locations S. The transitions from B_i connect the locations from layer i to those of layer $i+1$. The initial states of the NFA are the initial states of B_1 in the first layer, the final states are those of B_i in layer $i+1$ (for any $i \in [m]$). Then $(W, w) \in \mathrm{Acc}_{\Sigma, S}$ iff the word $w \in \Sigma^+$ is accepted by the NFA described by the word $W \in \mathcal{B}(\Sigma, S)^+$.

Definition. Let $\mathcal{A}$ be an SO automaton over Σ and S. Then the *second-order language of* $\mathcal{A}$ is the class $\mathcal{L}_2(\mathcal{A}) = L^+(\mathcal{A})^{\mathrm{Acc}_{\Sigma, S}} = \{W^{\mathrm{Acc}_{\Sigma, S}} \mid W \in L^+(\mathcal{A})\}$.

By the definition, $L^+(\mathcal{A})$ is a language over $\mathcal{B}(\Sigma, S)$, but $\mathcal{L}_2(\mathcal{A})$ is a class of ε-free languages over Σ, i.e., a subset of $\mathcal{P}(\Sigma^+)$.

Definition. A class of languages $\mathcal{C} \subseteq \mathcal{P}(\Sigma^+)$ is *regular* if there exists an SO automaton $\mathcal{A}$ over Σ and some finite set of locations S such that $\mathcal{C} = \mathcal{L}_2(\mathcal{A})$.

Since $\mathrm{Acc}_{\Sigma, S}$ is length-reducing, the class $\mathcal{L}_2(\mathcal{A})$ consists of finite languages, only. Hence regular classes of languages are classes of finite languages.

In [1], the authors consider words W only where all words in $W^{\mathrm{Acc}_{\Sigma, S}}$ are of length $|W|$. We capture this by the following concept.

Definition. A word over $\mathcal{B}(\Sigma, S)$ is *full-length* if at most its last block has a non-empty set of accepting states. An SO automaton $\mathcal{A}$ is *full-length* iff all words from $L^+(\mathcal{A})$ are full-length. A class $\mathcal{C}$ of languages is *full-length regular* if there exists a full-length SO automaton $\mathcal{A}$ with $\mathcal{C} = \mathcal{L}_2(\mathcal{A})$.

To overcome the limitation to classes of finite languages, we will now consider infinite words $\alpha \in \mathcal{B}(\Sigma, S)^\omega$ and understand them as "infinite NFAs" M over Σ that can accept some infinite language (of finite words).

Definition. The binary relation $\mathrm{Acc}^\omega_{\Sigma, S}$ consists of all pairs $(B_1 B_2 \cdots, w)$ with $B_i \in \mathcal{B}(\Sigma, S)$ for all $i \geq 1$ and $w \in \Sigma^+$ such that $(B_1 B_2 \cdots B_{|w|}, w) \in \mathrm{Acc}_{\Sigma, S}$.

Example 2.1. Let $M = (S, \Sigma, I, \Delta, F)$ be some NFA over Σ. We consider it as block $B = (I, \Delta, F) \in \mathcal{B}(\Sigma, S)$ and set $\alpha = B^\omega$. Then $\alpha^{\mathrm{Acc}^\omega_{\Sigma, s}} = L^+(M)$. Hence, all regular languages $K \subseteq \Sigma^+$ are of the form $\alpha^{\mathrm{Acc}^\omega_{\Sigma, s}}$ for some ω-word α.

Definition. A Büchi-automaton over $\mathcal{B}(\Sigma, S)$ is called an *SO Büchi-automaton* over Σ and S. Let $\mathcal{A}$ be an SO Büchi-automaton over Σ and S. Then the *second-order language of* $\mathcal{A}$ is the class $\mathcal{L}^\omega_2(\mathcal{A}) = \left\{ \alpha^{\mathrm{Acc}^\omega_{\Sigma, s}} \mid \alpha \in L^\omega(\mathcal{A}) \right\} \subseteq \mathcal{P}(\Sigma^+)$. A class $\mathcal{C} \subseteq \mathcal{P}(\Sigma^+)$ of languages is ω-*regular* if there exists an SO Büchi-automaton $\mathcal{A}$ over Σ and some finite set of locations S such that $\mathcal{C} = \mathcal{L}^\omega_2(\mathcal{A})$.

Note that, for any block $B \in \mathcal{B}(\Sigma, S)$, the ω-language $\{B^\omega\}$ is ω-regular. Hence, in view of Example 2.1, any class $\{K\}$ with $K \subseteq \Sigma^+$ regular is ω-regular.

Example 2.2. For $c \in \Sigma$, consider the block $B_c = (\{s\}, \{(s, c, s)\}, \{s\})$ and let $L = \{B_c \mid c \in \Sigma\}^\omega$. For any $\alpha \in \Sigma^\omega$, the ω-regular class $L^{\mathrm{Acc}^\omega_{\Sigma, s}}$ contains the language of all prefixes of α, i.e., is uncountable and contains non-regular languages.

3 Closure Properties and Special Representations of Regular Classes of Languages

From the canonisation result in [1], the authors infer closure properties of the collection of all full-length regular classes of languages. This section is devoted to alternative proofs and strengthenings (e.g., by providing much smaller automata) of these results. For notational simplicity, we only give our proofs for the collection of all regular classes, the results as well as the proofs all carry over to full-length regular classes and to ω-regular classes (if not stated otherwise). Since the main tool in our proofs are automatic structures, we first sketch their definition and their relation to SO automata.

3.1 Automatic Structures

Basically, automatic structures are relational structures whose universe and relations can be accepted by finite automata. This is rather straightforward for the universe and unary relations: they have to form regular languages. Relations of larger arity are required to be synchronized rational [6], i.e., accepted by a synchronous multi-head automaton.

Definition ([7,9]). A relational structure $S = (U, (R_i)_{i \in [k]})$ with $R_i \subseteq U^{n_i}$ for $i \in [k]$ is *automatic* if there is an alphabet Σ such that $U \subseteq \Sigma^*$ is regular and R_i is synchronized rational for all $i \in [k]$.

For the current paper, the following is the most interesting example.

Theorem 3.1. *The relation* $\mathrm{Acc}_{\Sigma,S}$ *is effectively synchronized rational.*

Consequently, given SO automata $\mathcal{A}_i$ *over* Σ_i *and* S_i *(for* $i \in [n]$*), the following structure* $S((\mathcal{A}_i)_{i \in [n]})$ *is effectively automatic:*

- *Its universe is* $\bigcup_{i \in [n]} (\mathcal{B}(\Sigma_i, S_i)^+ \cup \Sigma_i^+)$.
- *Its relations are* $\mathcal{B}(\Sigma_i, S_i)^+$, Σ_i^+, $L^+(\mathcal{A}_i)$, *and* $\mathrm{Acc}_{\Sigma_i, S_i}$ *for* $i \in [n]$.

The proofs in this section are all based on relations in this structure that are defined by logical formulas. As an example, consider the formula

$$\forall w \colon \Big((W_1, w) \in \mathrm{Acc}_{\Sigma, S_1} \leftrightarrow \big((W_2, w) \in \mathrm{Acc}_{\Sigma, S_2} \wedge (W_3, w) \notin \mathrm{Acc}_{\Sigma, S_3} \big) \Big)$$

with three free variables W_1, W_2, and W_3. In $S(\mathcal{A}_1, \mathcal{A}_2, \mathcal{A}_3)$, it expresses that

$$W_1^{\mathrm{Acc}_{\Sigma, S_1}} = W_2^{\mathrm{Acc}_{\Sigma, S_2}} \setminus W_3^{\mathrm{Acc}_{\Sigma, S_3}}$$

holds. We will therefore allow to write such Boolean combinations in formulas.

Furthermore, our formulas allow not only the classical first-order quantifiers $\exists$ and $\forall$, but also the following:

- *infinity quantifier* $\exists^\infty$ [3]: For instance, $\forall x \neg \exists^\infty y \colon E(x, y)$ holds in a directed graph iff the graph has finite out-degree.
- *boundedness quantifer* B [11]: For instance, the number of paths of length two between any two nodes of a possibly infinite directed graph is uniformly bounded iff the directed graph satisfies $\mathsf{B}(x_1, x_2; y) \colon (E(x_1, y) \wedge E(y, x_2))$.
- *Ramsey quantifier* H [14]: Let $k \in \mathbb{N}$ and let $\overline{x_i}$ be mutually disjoint k-tuples of variables (for $1 \leq i \leq n$). The formula $\mathsf{H}(\overline{x_1}, \dots, \overline{x_n}) \colon \varphi(\overline{x_1}, \dots, \overline{x_n})$ holds in a structure S if there exists an infinite k-ary relation R such that any n tuples from R satisfy φ. For instance, with $k = 2$, the formula $\mathsf{H}(\overline{x_1}, \overline{x_2}) \colon E(\overline{x_1}) \wedge E(\overline{x_2}) \wedge (\overline{x_1} = \overline{x_2} \vee \{x_{1,1}, x_{1,2}\} \cap \{x_{2,1}, x_{2,2}\} = \emptyset)$ expresses of a graph that it contains infinitely many mutually disjoint edges.

We denote the extension of first-order logic by these quantifiers by FO^+.

Theorem 3.2 ([3,9,11,14]). *Let* $S = (U, (R_i)_{i \in [n]})$ *be an automatic structure and* $\varphi(x_1, \dots, x_n)$ *a formula from* FO^+. *Then the relation* $\varphi^S = \{\overline{u} \in U^n \mid S \models \varphi(\overline{u})\}$ *of all witnesses for* φ *in* S *is effectively synchronized rational (uniformly in the automatic structure* S *given by a tuple of finite automata).*

The proof of this theorem proceeds by induction on the construction of the formula φ. Standard constructions on NFAs allow to handle Boolean operations and classical quantification. The infinity quantifier can be reduced to existential quantification (using the synchronized rational relation $|u| \leq |v|$) [3]. For the boundedness quantifier, one resorts to [15]; the Ramsey quantifier requires new automata constructions [14].

Blumensath and Grädel [3,4] introduced the more general notion of an ω-automatic structure that is based on Büchi-automata instead of NFAs. The relation $\mathrm{Acc}^{\omega}_{\Sigma,S}$ is synchronized ω-rational such that Theorem 3.1 also holds: for SO Büchi-automata $\mathcal{A}_i$, the analogous structure is ω-automatic.

Theorem 3.2 holds for ω-automatic structures and for the extension of first-order logic with the quantifiers $\exists^{\aleph_0}$ and $\exists^{>\aleph_0}$ [4,13], but not for the quantifier $\mathcal{H}$ [10]; the status of the quantifier $\Game$ is not known. Consequently, whenever the following proofs use at most the existential and the cardinality quantifiers, they carry over to the case of ω-regular classes of languages.

3.2 Special Representations of Regular Classes

Let $\mathcal{A}$ be some SO automaton and let, intuitively, $\mathcal{N}$ denote the class of NFAs represented by words $W \in L^+(\mathcal{A})$. We show that every regular class $\mathcal{C}$ of languages can be represented by some SO automaton such that $\mathcal{N}$ is a class of deterministic finite automata. Alternatively, we can require $\mathcal{N}$ to consist of all NFAs that accept some language from $\mathcal{C}$ and can be represented by some word over $\mathcal{B}(\Sigma, S)$. In the other extreme, we can require that every language from $\mathcal{C}$ is accepted by only one NFA from $\mathcal{N}$.

A block $B = (I, T, F) \in \mathcal{B}(\Sigma, S)$ is *deterministic*, i.e., belongs to $\det\mathcal{B}(\Sigma, S)$, if $|I| = 1$ and, for every $s \in S$ and $a \in \Sigma$, there is precisely one location $s' \in S$ with $(s, a, s') \in T$. Then any word from $\det\mathcal{B}(\Sigma, S)^+$ describes a DFA.

Theorem 3.3 (cf. [1, Theorem 4(4)]). *From an SO automaton $\mathcal{A}$ over Σ and S, one can construct an SO automaton $\mathcal{A}'$ over Σ and $\mathcal{P}(S)$ such that $\mathcal{L}_2(\mathcal{A}) = \mathcal{L}_2(\mathcal{A}')$ and $L^+(\mathcal{A}') \subseteq \det\mathcal{B}(\Sigma, \mathcal{P}(S))^+$.*

Proof. We extend the universe of the automatic structure $\mathcal{S}(\mathcal{A})$ by the set $\det\mathcal{B}(\Sigma, \mathcal{P}(S))^+$ and consider this set as an additional unary relation.

Now consider the following formula $\varphi(W')$ with free variable W':

$$W' \in \det\mathcal{B}(\Sigma, \mathcal{P}(S))^+ \land \exists W \in L^+(\mathcal{A}): W^{\mathrm{Acc}_{\Sigma,S}} = W'^{\mathrm{Acc}_{\Sigma,\mathcal{P}(S)}}$$

It expresses that W' describes a DFA that accepts some language from $\mathcal{L}_2(\mathcal{A})$.

Since the structure $\mathcal{S}$ is effectively automatic, the set L_φ of words W' satisfying this formula is effectively regular, i.e., we can construct an NFA $\mathcal{A}'$ over $\det\mathcal{B}(\Sigma, \mathcal{P}(S))$ with $L^+(\mathcal{A}') = L_\varphi$. Then $L_\varphi^{\mathrm{Acc}_{\Sigma,\mathcal{P}(S)}} \subseteq \mathcal{L}_2(\mathcal{A})$ by the construction of the language L_φ. For the converse inclusion, one shows that any word W over $\mathcal{B}(\Sigma, S)$ has a word $W' \in \det\mathcal{B}(\Sigma, \mathcal{P}(S))^+$ with $W^{\mathrm{Acc}_{\Sigma,S}} = W'^{\mathrm{Acc}_{\Sigma,\mathcal{P}(S)}}$. The idea is to first apply the powerset construction to all blocks from W and then concatenate the resulting deterministic blocks to obtain W'. $\quad\square$

Any word $W \in \mathcal{B}(\Sigma, S)^+$ (considered as NFA) has infinitely many equivalent words over $\mathcal{B}(\Sigma, S)$, e.g., all those from $W (S, T, \emptyset)^*$ (where T is an arbitrary set of transitions). Consequently, any language in the regular class of languages $\mathcal{L}_2(\mathcal{A})$ can have more than one representing word in $L^+(\mathcal{A})$. But this number of representing words can be controlled:

Theorem 3.4. *From an SO automaton $\mathcal{A}$ over Σ and S, one can construct SO automata $\mathcal{A}_{\min}$ and $\mathcal{A}_{\max}$ over Σ and S with $\mathcal{L}_2(\mathcal{A}) = \mathcal{L}_2(\mathcal{A}_{\min}) = \mathcal{L}_2(\mathcal{A}_{\max})$ such that the following hold:*

(1) Any word $W \in \mathcal{B}(\Sigma, S)^+$ with $W^{\mathrm{Acc}_{\Sigma,S}} \in \mathcal{L}_2(\mathcal{A})$ belongs to $L^+(\mathcal{A}_{\max})$.
(2) For any language $K \in \mathcal{L}_2(\mathcal{A})$, there exists a unique word $W \in L^+(\mathcal{A}_{\min})$ with $K = W^{\mathrm{Acc}_{\Sigma,S}}$.

Proof. Let $\sqsubseteq$ be a length-lexicographic order on the set $\mathcal{B}(\Sigma, S)^+$. The extension of the structure $\mathcal{S}(\mathcal{A})$ from Theorem 3.1 with $\sqsubseteq$ is automatic. The following formula $\varphi_{\max}(W)$ with free variable W expresses $W^{\mathrm{Acc}_{\Sigma,S}} \in \mathcal{L}_2(\mathcal{A})$:

$$W \in \mathcal{B}(\Sigma, S)^+ \wedge \exists W' \in L^+(\mathcal{A}) : W^{\mathrm{Acc}_{\Sigma,S}} = W'^{\mathrm{Acc}_{\Sigma,S}}$$

Similarly, the formula $\varphi_{\min}(W)$

$$\varphi_{\max}(W) \wedge \forall W' \in \mathcal{B}(\Sigma, S)^+ : \left(W^{\mathrm{Acc}_{\Sigma,S}} = W'^{\mathrm{Acc}_{\Sigma,S}} \rightarrow W \sqsubseteq W' \right)$$

expresses $W^{\mathrm{Acc}_{\Sigma,S}} \in \mathcal{L}_2(\mathcal{A})$ and that it is the length-lexicographically minimal representative of this language. In both cases, we can continue as in the proof of Theorem 3.3. $\square$

Remark. Since no synchronized rational well-order exists on the set $\mathcal{B}(\Sigma, S)^{\omega}$ [5], the above construction of $\mathcal{A}_{\min}$ does not transfer to SO Büchi-automata.

3.3   Decidable Properties of Regular Classes

Since emptiness of regular languages is decidable, it follows from Theorem 3.2 that the FO^+-theory of every automatic structure is decidable (even if the automatic structure is part of the input). This classical result immediately gives the following from [1].

Theorem 3.5 ([1, Theorem 4(6,7)]). *For SO automata $\mathcal{A}_1$ and $\mathcal{A}_2$, inclusion and disjointness of $\mathcal{L}_2(\mathcal{A}_1)$ and $\mathcal{L}_2(\mathcal{A}_2)$ are decidable.*

Let $\mathcal{A}$ be an SO automaton. Then, by Theorem 3.4, we can construct an "unambiguous" SO automaton $\mathcal{A}_{\min}$ with $\mathcal{L}_2(\mathcal{A}) = \mathcal{L}_2(\mathcal{A}_{\min})$. Consequently, the class $\mathcal{L}_2(\mathcal{A})$ is finite iff $\mathcal{A}_{\min}$ accepts a finite language. Since this is decidable, we obtain that finiteness of $\mathcal{L}_2(\mathcal{A})$ is decidable for any SO automaton $\mathcal{A}$.

Apart from this, we can also decide further properties of the class $\mathcal{L}_2(\mathcal{A})$:

Theorem 3.6. *The following problems are decidable:*
input: an SO automaton $\mathcal{A}$ over Σ and S
question 1: Do all words over Σ belong to some language from $\mathcal{L}_2(\mathcal{A})$?
question 2: Do all $w \in \Sigma^+$ belong to only finitely many languages from $\mathcal{L}_2(\mathcal{A})$?
question 3: Do all $w \in \Sigma^+$ belong to a bounded number of languages from $\mathcal{L}_2(\mathcal{A})$?
question 4: Are the languages from $\mathcal{L}_2(\mathcal{A})$ of bounded size?

Proof. By Theorem 3.4, we can assume $\mathcal{A}$ to be "unambiguous". The formulas

1. $\forall w \in \Sigma^+ \, \exists W \in L^+(\mathcal{A}) \colon (W, w) \in \mathrm{Acc}_{\Sigma, S}$
2. $\neg\exists w \in \Sigma^+ \, \exists^\infty W \in L^+(\mathcal{A}) \colon (W, w) \in \mathrm{Acc}_{\Sigma, S}$
3. $\exists (w, W) \colon (W, w) \in \mathrm{Acc}_{\Sigma, S} \wedge W \in L^+(\mathcal{A})$
4. $\exists (W, w) \colon (W, w) \in \mathrm{Acc}_{\Sigma, S} \wedge W \in L^+(\mathcal{A})$

express the four properties such that the claims follow from Theorem 3.2.   □

3.4   Closure Properties of the Collection of Regular Classes

We now strengthen some results from [1] that concern Boolean combinations of regular classes of languages. The corresponding constructions in [1] increase the number of locations exponentially. Our proofs are analogous to the proof of Theorem 3.3.

Theorem 3.7 (cf. [1, Theorem 4(1–3)]). *From SO automata $\mathcal{A}_i$ over Σ_i and S_i (for $i \in \{1, 2\}$), one can construct SO automata $\mathcal{A}_1'$ over $\Sigma_1 \cup \Sigma_2$ and $S_1 \cup S_2$ and $\mathcal{A}_2'$, $\mathcal{A}_3'$ over Σ_1 and S_1 such that $\mathcal{L}_2(\mathcal{A}_1') = \mathcal{L}_2(\mathcal{A}_1) \cup \mathcal{L}_2(\mathcal{A}_2)$, $\mathcal{L}_2(\mathcal{A}_2') = \mathcal{L}_2(\mathcal{A}_1) \cap \mathcal{L}_2(\mathcal{A}_2)$, and $\mathcal{L}_2(\mathcal{A}_3') = \mathcal{L}_2(\mathcal{A}_1) \backslash \mathcal{L}_2(\mathcal{A}_2)$.*

So far, we considered, e.g., the intersection of two regular classes $\mathcal{C}_1$ and $\mathcal{C}_2$ of languages. Now, we will, e.g., consider the class of all intersections of languages in $\mathcal{C}_1$ and $\mathcal{C}_2$.

Theorem 3.8. *From SO automata $\mathcal{A}_i$ over Σ_i and S_i (for $i \in [2]$), one can construct SO automata $\mathcal{A}_i'$ such that*

1. $\mathcal{L}_2(\mathcal{A}_1') = \{ K_1 \cup K_2 \mid K_i \in \mathcal{L}_2(\mathcal{A}_i) \}$ *and $\mathcal{A}_1'$ is over $\Sigma_1 \cup \Sigma_2$ and $S_1 \uplus S_2$,*
2. $\mathcal{L}_2(\mathcal{A}_2') = \{ K_1 \cap K_2 \mid K_i \in \mathcal{L}_2(\mathcal{A}_i) \}$ *and $\mathcal{A}_2'$ is over $\Sigma_1 \cup \Sigma_2$ and $S_1 \times S_2$,*
3. $\mathcal{L}_2(\mathcal{A}_3') = \{ K_1 \backslash K_2 \mid K_i \in \mathcal{L}_2(\mathcal{A}_i) \}$ *and $\mathcal{A}_3'$ is over Σ_1 and $S_1 \times \mathcal{P}(S_2)$.*

Proof. One first proceeds analogously to the proof of Theorem 3.3. In the final step, one adapts the corresponding constructions for union, intersection, and difference of NFAs to blocks.   □

Note that, for any regular class of languages $\mathcal{L}_2(\mathcal{A})$, the union $\bigcup_{L \in \mathcal{L}_2(\mathcal{A})} L$ is regular since it is the image of the regular language $L^+(\mathcal{A})$ under the rational relation $\mathrm{Acc}_{\Sigma, S}$. Using automatic structures, we can show that also the *limit inferior* and the *limit superior* is effectively regular since both these languages can be defined (using the quantifier $\exists^\infty$) in the automatic structure $\mathcal{S}(\mathcal{A}_{\min})$ from Theorem 3.1 (where $\mathcal{A}_{\min}$ is the "unambiguous" automaton from Theorem 3.4).

Theorem 3.9. *From an SO automaton $\mathcal{A}$ over Σ and S, one can construct NFAs accepting the languages*

$$\liminf \mathcal{L}_2(\mathcal{A}) = \bigcup_{\substack{\mathcal{C} \subseteq \mathcal{L}_2(\mathcal{A}) \\ \text{finite}}} \bigcap_{K \in \mathcal{L}_2(\mathcal{A}) \backslash \mathcal{C}} K \text{ and } \limsup \mathcal{L}_2(\mathcal{A}) = \bigcap_{\substack{\mathcal{C} \subseteq \mathcal{L}_2(\mathcal{A}) \\ \text{finite}}} \bigcup_{K \in \mathcal{L}_2(\mathcal{A}) \backslash \mathcal{C}} K.$$

4   Expressiveness of Second-Order Finite Automata

In this section, we determine what classes of languages can be described by SO automata, i.e., are regular. We obtain a close relation to so-called automatic classes of languages as defined by Jain *et al.* in [8].

Definition. A class of languages $\mathcal{C} \subseteq \mathcal{P}(\Sigma^+)$ is *automatic* if there are a regular language $L \subseteq \Gamma^+$ over some alphabet Γ and a synchronized rational relation $R \subseteq \Gamma^+ \times \Sigma^+$ with $\mathcal{C} = L^R$.

Example (from [8]). For any alphabet Σ, the following classes $\mathcal{C} \subseteq \mathcal{P}(\Sigma^+)$ are automatic:

- The class of finite languages with at most k elements (for any $k \in \mathbb{N}$).
- The class of all finite and cofinite subsets of $\{a\}^+$.
- The class of all intervals of $(\Sigma^+, \leq)$ where $\leq$ is the lexicographic order.
- Let U be the universe of any automatic structure $\mathcal{S}$ and let $\varphi(x,y)$ be any formula from FO$^+$. For $w \in U$, $\mathcal{S}^{\varphi(x,w)} \subseteq U$ is a language. The class of all these languages $\mathcal{S}^{\varphi(x,w)}$ with $w \in U$ is automatic.

4.1   Regular and Automatic Classes of Languages

From the very definition, we obtain that every regular class $\mathcal{C}$ of languages is effectively automatic and contains only finite languages.

For the converse implication, one first shows that automatic classes of finite languages can be represented by length-reducing rational relations:

Lemma 4.1. *Let $L \subseteq \Gamma^+$ be regular and $R \subseteq \Gamma^+ \times \Sigma^+$ be a synchronized rational relation with W^R finite for all $W \in L$. There effectively exist an alphabet Γ', a regular language $L' \subseteq \Gamma'^+$, and a synchronized rational and length-reducing relation $R' \subseteq \Gamma'^+ \times \Sigma^+$ such that $L'^{R'} = \mathcal{C} \backslash \{\emptyset\}$.*

If R is length-increasing and all languages in L^R are single-length, then R' can be chosen length-preserving.

Proof. The relation R' consists of all pairs $(W \$^n, w)$ with $(W, w) \in R$ such that $|W| + n$ is the maximal length of words from $W^R \cup \{W\}$.   □

Then one proves that, indeed, any length-reducing synchronized rational relation R gives rise to a regular class of languages:

Proposition 4.2. *Let $L \subseteq \Gamma^+$ be regular and $R \subseteq \Gamma^+ \times \Sigma^+$ be length-reducing and synchronized rational. Then L^R is, effectively, a regular class of languages.*

Proof. One starts with a synchronous 2-head automaton M accepting R. For any input letter $A \in \Gamma$, one restricts the behavior of M to its output behavior when A is input. In addition, depending on the remaining input word V, one defines a state to be accepting if, from that state, M can read V with empty output. This defines a block $B_{A,V} \in \mathcal{B}(\Sigma, S)$ as well as a sequence of blocks for every input word W. One then obtains an automaton $\mathcal{A}$ that accepts the set of block sequences for all valid input words. Then $L^R = \mathcal{L}_2(\mathcal{A})$.   □

The following theorem summarises the work reported in this section.

Theorem 4.3. *The following are effectively equivalent for any class C of ε-free languages:*

(a) C is a regular class of languages.
(b) C is an automatic class of finite languages.
(c) $C = L^R$ for some regular language L and some length-reducing synchronized rational relation R.

4.2   Regular and Automatic Classes of Single-Length Languages

In this section, we want to characterise, similarly to Theorem 4.3, the full-length regular classes of languages, i.e., the language classes considered in [1].

Theorem 4.4. *The following are effectively equivalent for any class C of ε-free languages:*

(a) C is a full-length regular class of languages.
(b) C is a regular class of single-length languages.
(c) C is an automatic class of single-length languages.
(d) $C = L^R$ for some regular language L and some length-preserving synchronized rational relation R.

The implication (a) $\Rightarrow$ (b) is clear by the definition of full-length words, the implication (b) $\Rightarrow$ (c) is an immediate consequence of Theorem 4.3. The implication (d) $\Rightarrow$ (a) can be shown as Proposition 4.2. For the remaining implication (c) $\Rightarrow$ (d), one first splits R into its length-increasing and its length-reducing parts $R_<$ and $R_>$. Since L^R is a class of single-length languages, it equals $L^{R_\leq} \cup L^{R_\geq}$. The final claim of Lemma 4.1 allows to replace $R_\leq$ by some length-preserving relation. For the length-reducing part $R_\geq$, one then proves a slightly weaker fact:

Lemma 4.5. *Let $L \subseteq \Gamma^+$ be regular and $R \subseteq \Gamma^+ \times \Sigma^+$ be synchronized rational and length-reducing such that L^R is a class of single-length languages. Then there exist, effectively, $k \in \mathbb{N}$, regular languages $L_1, \ldots, L_k \subseteq \Gamma^+$, and synchronized rational length-preserving relations $R_1, \ldots, R_k \subseteq \Gamma^+ \times \Sigma^+$ with $\bigcup_{1 \leq i \leq k} L_i^{R_i} = L^R \backslash \{\emptyset\}$.*

Proof. Since L is regular, we can assume $R \subseteq L \times \Sigma^+$. Let M be some synchronous 2-head automaton accepting R. For a set X of states, we define relations $R_X, S_X \subseteq \Gamma^* \times \Sigma^*$ as follows: R_X is the set of pairs (W_1, w_1) of nonempty words of equal length such that (W_1, w_1) allows to reach (from some initial state) *some* state in X. Further, S_X is the set of pairs (W_2, w_2) such that X *equals* the set of states that allow to reach some accepting state via (W_2, w_2).

The crucial point is that for $(W_1, w) \in R_X$ and $(W_2, \varepsilon) \in S_X$, one has $\emptyset \neq W_1^{R_X} = (W_1 W_2)^R$ and $W_1 W_2 \in L$. It can be infered that $L^R \setminus \{\emptyset\}$ is the union of the classes $\mathrm{proj}_1(R_X)^{R_X}$ for X such that $S_X \cap (\Gamma^* \times \{\varepsilon\}) \neq \emptyset$. $\qquad\square$

It follows that any automatic class of single-length languages is the union of finitely many classes L^R with L regular and R length-preserving. Considering copies of the languages L over mutually disjoint alphabets allows to infer the missing implication (c) $\Rightarrow$ (d) in Theorem 4.4

4.3 ω-regular and Automatic Classes of Languages

An ω-regular class of languages is always *countable* and consists of *regular languages*, only. By Example 2.2, both these properties may fail for automatic classes. The main result of this section states that these are the two only (and equivalent) reasons for an ω-regular class not to be automatic.

Theorem 4.6. *The following are effectively equivalent for any class $\mathcal{C}$ of ε-free languages:*

(a) $\mathcal{C}$ is an ω-regular class of regular languages.
(b) $\mathcal{C}$ is a countable ω-regular class of languages.
(c) $\mathcal{C}$ is an automatic class of languages.

The implication (a) $\Rightarrow$ (b) is trivial since there are only countably many regular languages. The proof of the implication (c) $\Rightarrow$ (a) is based on the idea of Example 2.1. For the implication (b) $\Rightarrow$ (c), one considers the ω-automatic structure $(\mathcal{B}(\Sigma, S)^\omega \cup \Sigma^+, L^\omega(\mathcal{A}), \mathcal{B}(\Sigma, S)^\omega, \mathrm{Acc}_{\Sigma, S}^\omega)$. Identifying pairs of ω-words over $\mathcal{B}(\Sigma, S)$ that represent the same language over Σ gives rise to a countable quotient that is ω-automatic [2] and therefore automatically representable [3]. This automatic structure then allows to prove that the class is automatic.

5   Regular Classes of Languages, Ordered by Inclusion

In this final section, we consider regular classes $\mathcal{L}_2(\mathcal{A})$ of languages under inclusion, i.e., the structure $(\mathcal{L}_2(\mathcal{A}), \subseteq)$. Note that the universe of $(\mathcal{L}_2(\mathcal{A}), \subseteq)$ is not a language, but a class of languages. Hence this structure cannot be automatic. The first result shows that $(\mathcal{L}_2(\mathcal{A}), \subseteq)$ is effectively isomorphic to some automatic structure, i.e., is *automatically representable*.

Lemma 5.1. *Let $\mathcal{A}$ be some SO automaton over Σ and S. Then $(\mathcal{L}_2(\mathcal{A}), \subseteq)$ is effectively automatically representable.*

Now we have, again, the theory of automatic structures at our disposal. In particular, Theorem 3.2 allows to infer the following decidabilities.

Theorem 5.2. *The following problems are decidable:*
input: an SO automaton $\mathcal{A}$

question 1: Is $(\mathcal{L}_2(\mathcal{A}), \subseteq)$ a lattice?
question 2: Does $(\mathcal{L}_2(\mathcal{A}), \subseteq)$ contain some infinite antichain or some infinite chain, resp.?
question 3: Are intervals in $(\mathcal{L}_2(\mathcal{A}), \subseteq)$ of bounded finite size?

By Lemma 5.1, regular classes of languages (ordered by inclusion) can be understood as automatic partial order. By the theorems from Sect. 4, one can conversely understand automatic partial orders as regular classes of languages. This allows to infer results concerning the isomorphism problem from [12].

Theorem 5.3. *There exist partial orders $\mathcal{P}_1$ and $\mathcal{P}_2$ such that the set of*

1. SO automata $\mathcal{A}$ with $\mathcal{P}_1 \cong (\mathcal{L}_2(\mathcal{A}), \subseteq)$ is Σ_1^1-hard and
2. full-length SO automata $\mathcal{A}$ with $\mathcal{P}_2 \cong (\mathcal{L}_2(\mathcal{A}), \subseteq)$ is Π_1^0-hard.

In particular, the isomorphism problem for structures $(\mathcal{L}_2(\mathcal{A}), \subseteq)$ is (highly) undecidable.

References

1. de Melo, A.A., de Oliveira Oliveira, M.: Second-order finite automata. In: Fernau, H. (ed.) CSR 2020. LNCS, vol. 12159, pp. 46–63. Springer, Cham (2020). https://doi.org/10.1007/978-3-030-50026-9_4
2. Bárány, V., Kaiser, Ł., Rubin, S.: Cardinality and counting quantifiers on omega-automatic structures. In: STACS 2008, pp. 385–396. IFIB Schloss Dagstuhl (2008)
3. Blumensath, A.: Automatic structures. Diplomarbeit, RWTH Aachen (1999)
4. Blumensath, A., Grädel, E.: Automatic structures. In: LICS 2000, pp. 51–62. IEEE Computer Society Press (2000)
5. Carayol, A., Löding, C.: MSO on the infinite binary tree: choice and order. In: Duparc, J., Henzinger, T.A. (eds.) CSL 2007. LNCS, vol. 4646, pp. 161–176. Springer, Heidelberg (2007). https://doi.org/10.1007/978-3-540-74915-8_15
6. Frougny, C., Sakarovitch, J.: Synchronized rational relations of finite and infinite words. Theor. Comput. Sci. **108**, 45–82 (1993)
7. Hodgson, B.: On direct products of automaton decidable theories. Theor. Comput. Sci. **19**, 331–335 (1982)
8. Jain, S., Luo, Q., Stephan, F.: Learnability of automatic classes. J. Comput. Syst. Sci. **78**(6), 1910–1927 (2012)
9. Khoussainov, B., Nerode, A.: Automatic presentations of structures. In: Leivant, D. (ed.) LCC 1994. LNCS, vol. 960, pp. 367–392. Springer, Heidelberg (1995). https://doi.org/10.1007/3-540-60178-3_93
10. Kuske, D.: Is Ramsey's theorem ω-automatic? In: STACS 2010, vol. 5, pp. 537–548. Leibniz International Proceedings in Informatics (LIPIcs), Schloss Dagstuhl-Leibniz-Zentrum für Informatik (2010)
11. Kuske, D.: Where automatic structures benefit from weighted automata. In: Kuich, W., Rahonis, G. (eds.) Algebraic Foundations in Computer Science. LNCS, vol. 7020, pp. 257–271. Springer, Heidelberg (2011). https://doi.org/10.1007/978-3-642-24897-9_12

12. Kuske, D., Liu, J., Lohrey, M.: The isomorphism problem on classes of automatic structures with transitive relations. Trans. AMS **365**, 5103–5151 (2013)
13. Kuske, D., Lohrey, M.: First-order and counting theories of ω-automatic structures. In: Aceto, L., Ingólfsdóttir, A. (eds.) FoSSaCS 2006. LNCS, vol. 3921, pp. 322–336. Springer, Heidelberg (2006). https://doi.org/10.1007/11690634_22
14. Rubin, S.: Automata presenting structures: a survey of the finite string case. Bull. Symb. Logic **14**, 169–209 (2008)
15. Weber, A.: On the valuedness of finite transducers. Acta Informatica **27**, 749–780 (1990)

Reversible Top-Down Syntax Analysis

Martin Kutrib[1]([✉])[iD] and Uwe Meyer[2][iD]

[1] Institut für Informatik, Universität Giessen, Arndtstr. 2, 35392 Giessen, Germany
`kutrib@informatik.uni-giessen.de`
[2] Technische Hochschule Mittelhessen, Wiesenstr. 14, 35390 Giessen, Germany
`uwe.meyer@mni.thm.de`

Abstract. Top-down syntax analysis can be based on $LL(k)$ grammars. The canonical acceptors for $LL(k)$ languages are deterministic stateless pushdown automata with input lookahead of size k. We investigate the computational capacity of reversible computations of such automata. A pushdown automaton with lookahead k is said to be reversible if its predecessor configurations can uniquely be computed by a pushdown automaton with backward input lookahead (lookback) of size k. It is shown that we cannot trade a lookahead for states or vice versa. The impact of having states or a lookahead depends on the language. While reversible pushdown automata with states accept all regular languages, we are going to prove that there are regular languages that cannot be accepted reversibly without states, even in case of an arbitrarily large lookahead. This completes the comparison of reversible with ordinary pushdown automata in our setting. Finally, it turns out that there are problems which can be solved by reversible deterministic stateless pushdown automata with lookahead of size $k + 1$, but not by any reversible deterministic stateless pushdown automaton with lookahead of size k. So, an infinite and tight hierarchy of language families dependent on the size of the lookahead is shown.

1 Introduction

The theory of top-down syntax analysis originates in [15] and [6], where $LL(k)$ grammars were introduced. Properties of the induced language families as well as constructive properties of the grammars themselves are derived in [18]. In this seminal work also canonical acceptors for $LL(k)$ languages were considered. These canonical acceptors are essentially deterministic stateless pushdown automata with input lookahead of size k. On the one hand, any $LL(k)$ language is accepted by such a device. On the other hand, there are languages that are not $LL(k)$ for any $k \geq 1$, but that are accepted by some deterministic stateless pushdown automata with input lookahead of size 2. An example is the deterministic context-free language $\{\, a^n b^n \mid n \geq 1 \,\} \cup \{\, a^n c^n \mid n \geq 1 \,\}$ [18]. So, these canonical acceptors capture a wider class of languages than $LL(k)$ grammars while keeping most of their neat properties [18,19]. Moreover, $LL(k)$ grammars are a popular means to describe the syntax of most programming languages and corresponding parsers are often used in compilers.

© Springer Nature Switzerland AG 2021
N. Moreira and R. Reis (Eds.): DLT 2021, LNCS 12811, pp. 255–266, 2021.
https://doi.org/10.1007/978-3-030-81508-0_21

Another line of research investigates (logical) reversibility of automata models. The observation that loss of information results in heat dissipation [14] strongly suggests to study computations without loss of information. First studies of reversibility computations have been done for the massively parallel model of cellular automata since the sixties of the last century. Nowadays it is known from [16] that every, possibly irreversible, one-dimensional cellular automaton can always be simulated by a reversible one-dimensional cellular automaton in a constructive way. In [2] reversible Turing machines have been considered. Again, a fundamental result is that every Turing machine can be made reversible. These two types of devices received a lot of attention in connection with reversibility. Valuable surveys with further references to literature are, for example, [5] for cellular automata and [17], where one may find a summary of results on reversible Turing machines, reversible cellular automata, and other reversible models such as logic gates, logic circuits, or logic elements with memory (see also [7,9,10,12] for further investigations). In particular, reversible pushdown automata with states and without lookahead have been studied [11]. In contrast to Turing machines it turned out that the family of languages accepted by reversible pushdown automata or reversible finite automata are proper subsets of the general families. Also reversible finite automata as well as reversible pushdown automata with states and lookahead have been considered [1,13].

Here we focus on the essence of both lines of research described. So, we are interested in reversible deterministic stateless pushdown automata with lookahead. That is, we study reversible top-down syntax analysis. The first steps in this direction are done with respect to the computational capacity of reversible canonical acceptors for $LL(k)$ languages. To this end, we compare the induced families of languages with respect to the impact of states or a lookahead, with respect to the impact of reversibility, and with respect to the impact of the lookahead size on the computational capacity.

The rest of this paper is organized as follows. In the next section we define the underlying model of reversible deterministic stateless pushdown automata and provide an illustrative example of their way of processing languages. Section 3 is devoted to exploring the computational capacity by comparing it to the capacity of related models. In general, an ordinary deterministic pushdown automaton can use states to compensate for a lookahead. So, a lookahead does not increase the computational capacity of ordinary pushdown automata. In Subsect. 3.1 it is shown that the situation is different in our setting. It is shown that there are languages for which a lookahead is better than states. Conversely, it is proved that there are languages for which states are better than a lookahead of arbitrary size. In Subsect. 3.2, deterministic stateless pushdown automata with lookahead are compared with their reversible variant. To this end, it is shown that there are regular languages that cannot be accepted by any reversible deterministic stateless pushdown automata with arbitrary lookahead. So, adding the requirement to work reversibly strictly weakens the computational capacity of our automata. Finally, in Sect. 4, the impact of the lookahead size on the computational capacity of reversible deterministic stateless pushdown automata is studied. It is shown that there exists an infinite and tight hierarchy of language families dependent on the size of the lookahead. The relations between the language families are summarized in Fig. 2.

2   Preliminaries and Definitions

Let Σ^* denote the *set of all words* over the finite alphabet Σ. The *empty word* is denoted by λ, and $\Sigma^+ = \Sigma^* \setminus \{\lambda\}$. The set of words of length at most $k \geq 0$ is denoted by $\Sigma^{\leq k}$. The reversal of a word w is denoted by w^R and for the length of w we write $|w|$. For $k \geq 0$, we denote by $\mathrm{prf}_k(w)$ the longest prefix of w which has length at most k and analogously by $\mathrm{suf}_k(w)$ the longest suffix of w which has length at most k. Set inclusion is denoted by $\subseteq$, and strict set inclusion by $\subset$.

Now we turn to defining stateless pushdown automata with lookahead on the input. These are deterministic pushdown automata with a sole state. Since a single state is useless, such automata are called *stateless*. On the other hand, a lookahead window of a fixed size k is attached to the pushdown automata that allows to see the next k input symbols in advance. (For reversible computation steps these are the next k input symbols to the left of the current input position.) General deterministic pushdown automata that are not allowed to perform λ-steps are weaker than DPDA that may move on λ input [3]. However, in [11] it has been shown that every reversible pushdown automaton can be simulated by a *realtime* reversible pushdown automaton, that is, without λ-steps. This realtime reversible machine can effectively be constructed from the given one. Therefore, in order to simplify matters, we do not allow λ-steps from the outset.

A *deterministic   stateless   pushdown   automaton   with   lookahead k* ((k)-DSPDA) is a system $M = \langle \Sigma, \Gamma, \delta, k, \bot, I, G \rangle$, where Σ is the finite set of *input symbols*, Γ is the finite set of *pushdown symbols*, $k \geq 1$ is the *size of the input window, that is, the lookahead*, $\bot \notin \Gamma$ is the so-called *empty-pushdown symbol*, $I \in \Gamma \cup \{\lambda\}$ is the *initial pushdown symbol*, $G \subseteq \Gamma \cup \{\bot\}$ is the set of *accepting pushdown symbols*, and $\delta \colon \Sigma \Sigma^{\leq k-1} \times (\Gamma \cup \{\bot\}) \to \Gamma^*$ is the (possibly partial) *transition function*.

A *configuration* of a (k)-DSPDA is a triple (u, v, γ), where $u \in \Sigma^*$ is the part of the input to the left of the input head, $v \in \Sigma^*$ the part of the input to the right of the input head, thus, $\mathrm{prf}_k(v)$ appears in the input window, and $\gamma \in \Gamma^*$ is the current content of the pushdown store, the leftmost symbol of γ being the top symbol. On input w the initial configuration is defined to be (λ, w, I).

For a configuration $(u, v, Z\gamma)$ with $u \in \Sigma^*$, $v \in \Sigma^+$, $Z \in \Gamma$, and $\gamma \in \Gamma^*$, we call $(u\,\mathrm{prf}_1(v), \mathrm{suf}_{|v|-1}(v), \beta\gamma)$ its *successor configuration* if and only if $\delta(\mathrm{prf}_k(v), Z) = \beta$. The successor configuration of (u, v, λ) is $(u\,\mathrm{prf}_1(v), \mathrm{suf}_{|v|-1}(v), \beta)$ if and only if $\delta(\mathrm{prf}_k(v), \bot) = \beta$. Such a step from a configuration to its successor configuration is denoted by $\vdash$. The reflexive transitive closure of $\vdash$ is denoted by $\vdash^*$.

So, whenever the pushdown store is empty, the successor configuration is computed by the transition function with the special empty-pushdown symbol $\bot$.

Note that there are no successor configurations if $v = \lambda$.

The *language accepted* by a (k)-DSPDA M is

$$L(M) = \{\, w \in \Sigma^* \mid (\lambda, w, I) \vdash^* (w, \lambda, \gamma),$$
$$\text{where } \gamma \in (G \setminus \{\bot\})\Gamma^* \text{ or } \gamma = \lambda \text{ if } \bot \in G \,\}.$$

In general, the family of all languages that are accepted by some type of automaton X is denoted by $\mathscr{L}(X)$.

Now we turn to reversible (k)-DSPDAs. Reversibility is meant with respect to the possibility of stepping the computation back and forth. To this end, a configuration must have a unique predecessor for all computations that lead to the current configuration along the symbols seen in the input window and are consistent with the symbols at the top of the stack. For reverse computation steps the head of the input tape is always moved to the *left* (see Fig. 1). A (k)-DSPDA is said to be *reversible* (REV(k)-DSPDA) if and only if there exists a reverse (k)-DSPDA with reverse transition function $\delta^\leftarrow\colon \Sigma\Sigma^{\leq k-1} \times (\Gamma \cup \{\bot\}) \to \Gamma^*$ inducing a relation $\vdash^\leftarrow$ from one configuration to the next, so that

$$(u', v', \gamma') \vdash^\leftarrow (u, v, \gamma) \text{ if and only if}$$

(i) $(u, v, \gamma) \vdash (u', v', \gamma')$,
(ii) if $|u'| \geq k$, then $(\mathrm{prf}_{|u'|-k}(u'), \mathrm{suf}_k(u')v', \hat{\gamma}') \vdash^* (u, v, \gamma) \vdash (u', v', \gamma')$ for all
$\hat{\gamma}' \in \Gamma^*$ such that $(\mathrm{prf}_{|u'|-k}(u'), \mathrm{suf}_k(u')v', \hat{\gamma}') \vdash^* (u', v', \gamma')$, and
(iii) if $1 \leq |u'| < k$, then $(\lambda, u'v', I) \vdash^* (u, v, \gamma) \vdash (u', v', \gamma')$.

Condition (i) means that (u, v, γ) is a predecessor configuration of (u', v', γ') in forward computations. Conditions (ii) and (iii) ensure that (u, v, γ) is unique for all computations that lead to (u', v', γ') along the symbols seen in the input window and are consistent with the symbols at the top of the stack. Condition (ii) applies if there are at least k symbols in the input window for the backward

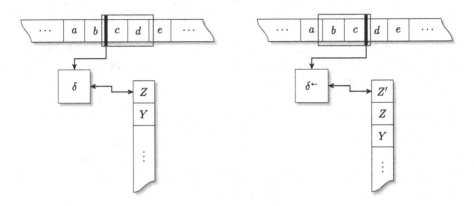

Fig. 1. Successive configurations of a reversible stateless pushdown automaton with lookahead of size two, where $\delta(cd, Z) = Z'Z$ (left to right) and $\delta^\leftarrow(bc, Z') = \lambda$ (right to left).

step, while Condition (iii) applies in the case the the input window is close to the beginning of the input. More precisely, Condition (ii) says that there may be more than one configurations that lead to (u', v', γ') in forward computations along the last k input symbols. However, all these configurations must evolve to the unique predecessor configuration (u, v, γ) after having processed $k - 1$ input symbols. In this case, (u, v, γ) is the unique direct predecessor of (u', v', γ') in forward computations. Since the REV(k)-DSPDA can see the last k input symbols in a backward step, $\delta^\leftarrow$ can compute (u, v, γ) from (u', v', γ'). Similarly, for Condition (iii).

Let M be a REV(k)-DSPDA. In any step, $\delta^\leftarrow$ can decrease the height of the pushdown store by at most one. Therefore, δ may increase the height of the pushdown store by at most one, too. Furthermore, when $\delta^\leftarrow$ pops a symbol this operation simply reveals the next-to-top symbol. Therefore, when δ increases the height of the pushdown store, it must do so by leaving the previous top-of-stack symbol intact. Thus for a REV(k)-DSPDA there are only three possible operations on the pushdown store: popping the top of the pushdown, replacing the topmost symbol with another symbol, or pushing one new symbol on the top of the pushdown store. Otherwise, the reverse transition function cannot be defined.

To clarify our notion we continue with an example.

Example 1. The context-free Dyck language of words of well-balanced parentheses D_n is defined over the alphabet $\Sigma_n = \{a_1, b_1, a_2, b_2, \ldots, a_n, b_n\}$ of $n \geq 1$ pairs of parentheses. Here, a_i is an opening and b_i is the matching closing parenthesis. The language D_n is defined through the context-free grammar with sole nonterminal X and productions

$$\{(X \to \lambda), (X \to a_1 X b_1 X), (X \to a_2 X b_2 X), \ldots, (X \to a_n X b_n X)\}.$$

It is accepted by the REV(1)-DSPDA $M = \langle \Sigma_n, \Gamma, \delta, 1, \bot, \lambda, \{\bot\} \rangle$, where $\Gamma = \{A_1, A_2, \ldots, A_n\}$ and the transition functions δ and $\delta^\leftarrow$ are as follows, for $1 \leq i, j \leq n$:

Transition function δ	Reverse transition function $\delta^\leftarrow$
(1) $\delta(a_i, \bot) = A_i$	(4) $\delta^\leftarrow(a_i, A_i) = \lambda$
(2) $\delta(a_i, A_j) = A_i A_j$	(5) $\delta^\leftarrow(b_i, \bot) = A_i$
(3) $\delta(b_i, A_i) = \lambda$	(6) $\delta^\leftarrow(b_i, A_j) = A_i A_j$

The idea of the forward computations is straightforward: Whenever an opening parenthesis appears in the input, it is pushed onto the pushdown store (Transitions 1 and 2). If a closing parenthesis is read that matches the opening parenthesis on the top of the pushdown then the opening parenthesis is popped (Transition 3). In any other cases the computation halts and, since the input is not read entirely, rejects. If the input belongs to D_n, it can be processed entirely by M such that the pushdown gets empty at the end of the computation. So, M accepts D_n.

For the construction of δ^- that is applied to backward computations we have to consider all combinations of input symbol and top-of-pushdown symbol. Let the last input symbol read in the forward computation be a_i and A_i be on top of the pushdown. Since in the last forward step on a_i the A_i must have been pushed, it is popped by δ^- (Transition 4). There is no other predecessor configuration leading to a_i and A_i. If, on the other hand, the top-of-pushdown symbol is A_j, for $i \neq j$, then there is no predecessor configuration leading to a_i and A_j. Therefore, the reverse transition function δ^- can safely be undefined. Similarly, if the pushdown store is empty.

Now let the last input symbol read in the forward computation be b_i. On any non-blocking forward step on b_i the topmost pushdown symbol A_i must have been popped. So, in a reverse step it is pushed again (Transitions 5 and 6). Altogether, we conclude that M is reversible.   ∎

3 Computational Capacity

Here we first turn to explore the computational capacity of deterministic state-less pushdown automaton with lookahead. The relations between the language families are summarized in Fig. 2.

3.1 Lookahead Versus States

Reversible classical pushdown automata with states but without lookahead (REV-DPDA) have been investigated in [11], where it is shown that their corresponding language family lies properly in between the regular and the deterministic context-free languages.

In general, a deterministic pushdown automaton can use states to compensate for a lookahead. Basically, it simply reads the symbols that appear in a lookahead window successively and stores them as part of the current state. Then it can simulate a transition and so on. So, a lookahead does not increase the computational capacity of classical pushdown automata. Here we next consider the situation for reversible pushdown automata and show that it is different. First we obtain that there are languages for which a lookahead is better than states. Clearly, a lookahead of size one is not a true lookahead.

The proof of the next lemma uses the language $L_{ab} = \{\, a^n b^n \mid n \geq 0 \,\}$ as witness. It is not accepted by any REV-DPDA [11].

Lemma 2. *There is a language accepted by some REV(2)-DSPDA that cannot be accepted by any REV-DPDA.*

Now we know that there are languages for which a lookahead is better than states. Does this hold in general? The answer is no, which means that there are languages for which states are better than a lookahead of arbitrary size.

Lemma 3. *There is a language accepted by some REV-DPDA that cannot be accepted by any REV(k)-DSPDA, for $k \geq 1$.*

Proof. We use the language $L_{\mathrm{umi}} = \{\, a^n \# a^n \mid n \geq 0 \,\}$ as witness. It is accepted by some REV-DPDA [11].

Assume in contrast to the assertion that, for $k \geq 1$, L_{umi} is accepted by some REV(k)-DSPDA $M = \langle \Sigma, \Gamma, \delta, k, \bot, I, G \rangle$ and let n be large enough. During the computation of M on input prefixes a^+ such that only a's appear in the input window no content of the pushdown store may appear twice: If

$$(\lambda, a^n \# a^n, I) \vdash^* (a^{p_1}, a^{n-p_1} \# a^n, \gamma_1) \vdash^+ (a^{p_1+p_2}, a^{n-p_1-p_2} \# a^n, \gamma_1)$$

is the beginning of an accepting computation, then so is

$$(\lambda, a^{n-p_2} \# a^n, I) \vdash^* (a^{p_1}, a^{n-p_1-p_2} \# a^n, \gamma_1),$$

but $a^{n-p_2} \# a^n$ does not belong to L_{umi}. This implies that each height of the pushdown store may appear only finitely often and, thus, that the height increases arbitrarily. So, M runs into a loop while processing a's, that is, for any fixed number h, some h topmost pushdown symbols α appear again and again. To render the loop more precisely, let $(a^{n-x}, a^x \# a^n, \alpha\gamma)$ be a configuration of the loop. Then there is a successor configuration with the same topmost pushdown symbols $(a^{n-x+y}, a^{x-y} \# a^n, \alpha\beta)$. We may choose α so that during the computation starting in $(a^{n-x}, a^x \# a^n, \alpha\gamma)$ no symbol of γ is touched, that is, $\alpha\beta = \alpha\gamma'\gamma$. Therefore, the computation continues as

$$(a^{n-x+y}, a^{x-y} \# a^n, \alpha\gamma'\gamma) \vdash^+ (a^{n-x+2y}, a^{x-2y} \# a^n, \alpha\gamma'\gamma'\gamma).$$

Now we turn to the input suffixes. While M processes the input suffixes a^+, no content of the pushdown store may appear twice: If

$$(a^n \#, a^n, \gamma_2) \vdash^* (a^n \# a^{q_1}, a^{n-q_1}, \gamma_3) \vdash^+ (a^n \# a^{q_1+q_2}, a^{n-q_1-q_2}, \gamma_3)$$

results in an accepting computation, then so does

$$(a^n \#, a^{n-q_2}, \gamma_2) \vdash^* (a^n \# a^{q_1}, a^{n-q_1-q_2}, \gamma_3),$$

but $a^n \# a^{n-q_2}$ does not belong to L_{umi}. This implies that each height of the pushdown store appears only finitely often. Moreover, in any accepting computation the pushdown store has to be decreased until some symbol of γ appears. Otherwise, we could increase the number of a's in the prefix by y to drive M through an additional loop. The resulting computation would also be accepting but the input does not belong to L_{umi}. Together we conclude that M runs into a loop that decreases the height of the pushdown store while processing the a's of the suffix, and that there are only finitely many possible contents of the pushdown store at the end of accepting computations.

Let us now consider an accepting computation on input $a^n \# a^n$ where, again, n is large enough. There must be integers $x_1, y_1, x_2, y_2 \geq 1$ and $\kappa \in G\Gamma^*$ such that

$$(\lambda, a^n \# a^n, I) \vdash^+ (a^{n-x_1}, a^{x_1} \# a^n, \alpha\gamma) \vdash^+ (a^{n-x_1+y_1}, a^{x_1-y_1} \# a^n, \alpha\gamma'\gamma) \vdash^+$$
$$(a^n \# a^{x_2}, a^{n-x_2}, \alpha\gamma'\gamma) \vdash^+ (a^n \# a^{x_2+y_2}, a^{n-x_2-y_2}, \gamma'\gamma) \vdash^+ (a^n \# a^n, \lambda, \kappa).$$

However this implies that on input factor a^{y_1} the α on the top of the pushdown store is replace by a longer word $\alpha\gamma'$ and, at the same time, on input factor a^{y_2} the α on the top of the pushdown store is popped. Since α has been chosen such that during its processing (with input symbols a) none of the subjacent symbols is touched, we obtain a contradiction. □

Lemma 2 and Lemma 3 show the following incomparability, which means that the impact of lookaheads and states on the computational capacity of reversible pushdown automata depends on the language in question.

Theorem 4. *For any $k \geq 2$, the language families $\mathscr{L}(REV(k)\text{-}DSPDA)$ and $\mathscr{L}(REV\text{-}DPDA)$ are incomparable.*

3.2   Reversibility Versus Irreversibility

This subsection is devoted to comparing deterministic stateless pushdown automata with lookahead with their reversible variant. Does the additional property to be reversible decrease the computational capacity? If yes, can we regain the capacity by increasing the lookahead? We will get answers to these question by comparing reversible deterministic stateless pushdown automata with lookahead with classical deterministic finite automata, that is, for all $k \geq 1$, the families $\mathscr{L}(REV(k)\text{-}DSPDA)$ and REG.

In [11] it is shown that any regular language is accepted by some REV-DPDA. Basically, the idea is to store the history of a DFA computation on the pushdown store. However, in order to obtain a reversible pushdown automaton this construction requires states.

For all $n \geq 2$, we define the language $L'_n = \{\, a^{m \cdot n} \mid m \geq 2 \,\}$, define a regular substitution by $s(a) = \#^* a \#^*$, and consider the language $L_n = s(L'_n)$. It consists of all words from L'_n with an arbitrary number of # symbols around each and between each two symbols a. Clearly, $s(L)$ is regular.

Theorem 5. *For all $n \geq 2$ and $k \geq 1$, the language L_n is not accepted by any REV(k)-DSPDA.*

Proof. Assume in contrast to the assertion that, for some $n \geq 2$ and $k \geq 1$, language L_n is accepted by some REV(k)-DSPDA $M = \langle \{a, \#\}, \Gamma, \delta, k, \bot, I, G \rangle$. We consider input words of the form $(\#^k a)^+ \#^k$.

First we assume further that the height of the pushdown store does not exceed some constant $h \geq 0$ for all computations on these words. Then a reversible DFA M' accepting L'_n can be constructed as follows. Essentially, M' on input a^i simulates the computation of M on input $(\#^k a)^i \#^k$. To this end, the state set Q of M' is set to $\Gamma^{\leq h}$ such that M' simulates the pushdown content in its states. The initial state of M' is defined to be I. Now the transition function $\delta' \colon Q \times \{a\} \to Q$ of M' is defined as $\delta'(\beta, a) = \gamma$ if and only if $(\lambda, \#^k a \#^k, \beta) \vdash^+ (\#^k a, \#^k, \gamma)$. Finally, the set of accepting states of M' is defined to be the set of states γ_+ of M' such that M accepts the suffix $\#^k$ when γ_+ is initially put into the pushdown store. So, it is

$$\{\, \gamma_+ \mid (\lambda, \#^k, \gamma_+) \vdash^+ (\#^k, \lambda, \gamma) \text{ where } \gamma \in (G \setminus \{\bot\})\Gamma^* \text{ or } \gamma = \lambda \text{ if } \bot \in G \,\}.$$

By construction, if M accepts some input $(\#^k a)^i \#^k$ then M' accepts a^i and vice versa. Therefore, M' accepts the language L'_n. Moreover, M' is a reversible DFA. Since its input alphabet is unary, this means that each state has at most one predecessor state. This can be seen as follows: the current state of M' gives the entire pushdown content of M. Moreover, if $\delta'(\beta, a) = \gamma$ then $(\lambda, \#^k a \#^k, \beta) \vdash^+ (\#^k a, \#^k, \gamma)$. Since M is reversible, we derive

$$(\#^k a, \#^k, \gamma)(\vdash^{\leftarrow})^+(\lambda, \#^k a \#^k, \beta) \text{ and } (\#^k a \#^k a, \#^k, \gamma)(\vdash^{\leftarrow})^+(\#^k a, \#^k a \#^k, \beta)$$

dependent on whether M goes back to the beginning of the input or not. This implies $\delta'^{\leftarrow}(\gamma, a) = \beta$.

However, it is well known that language L'_n is not accepted by any reversible DFA (with lookahead 1) [1,8]. This is a contradiction to our assumption that the height of the pushdown store of M does not exceed some constant for all computations on the words $(\#^k a)^+ \#^k$.

Since M is deterministic, we conclude that, for any constant $h \geq 0$, there are infinitely many $m \geq 2$ such that the height of the pushdown store of M exceeds h in the computations on the words $(\#^k a)^{m \cdot n} \#^k$.

During the computation up to the k last symbols on a word $(\#^k a)^{m \cdot n} \#^k$ with m large enough, the lookahead window contents $\#^k$, $\#^{k-1}a$, $\#^{k-2}a\#,\ldots$, $a\#^{k-1}$ appear cyclically. For each of these window contents we consider the associated action on the pushdown store. To this end, let w be a possible window content.

If $\delta(w, Z) = XZ$ is a push move, then $\delta(w, Z') = XZ'$, for all $Z' \in \Gamma \cup \{\bot\}$, that is, the push move is independent of the topmost pushdown symbol. The reason is that M is reversible and, thus, $\delta^{\leftarrow}(w', X) = \lambda$ is the corresponding backward step, for all appropriate backward window contents w'. So, if we construct a configuration such that below the X there is some pushdown store symbol Z' then after popping the X in a backward step a configuration with Z' at the top of the pushdown store is reached. This implies that the forward step that reaches the constructed configuration again has to push X on top of Z'.

If $\delta(w, Z) = \lambda$ is a pop move, then $\delta(w, Z')$ is undefined, for all $Z' \in \Gamma \cup \{\bot\}$. This is obvious for $Z' = \bot$. Since M is reversible, we can construct a configuration such that below the Z there is some pushdown store symbol $X \in \Gamma \cup \{\bot\}$. Then after popping the Z in a forward step a configuration with X at the top of the pushdown store is reached. This implies that the backward step that reaches the constructed configuration again has to push Z on top of any X. So, no transition $\delta(w, Z')$ with $Z' \neq Z$, whether it is a pop, push, or top move, can be reversed.

If $\delta(w, Z) = X$ is a top move, then $\delta(w, Z')$ with $Z' \neq Z$ is undefined or a top move, for all $Z' \in \Gamma \cup \{\bot\}$. This is obvious for $Z' = \bot$ as shown above for pop and push moves.

So, any of the window contents that appear cyclically is associated either with a top, pop, or push operation. Additionally, we know that the height of the pushdown is increasing. We derive that in a cycle there are more push than pop operations. Moreover, for any prefix of a cycle there are no more pop than push operations, since M cannot pop from the empty pushdown. Additionally, for any window content of the cycle associated with a push operation, the symbol pushed is always the same. We conclude that at latest after the second cycle the content of pushdown store grows cyclically.

Therefore, there is some m large enough and the beginning of an accepting computation

$$(\lambda, (\#^k a)^{m \cdot n} \#^k, I) \vdash^+ ((\#^k a)^2, (\#^k a)^{m \cdot n - 2} \#^k, \gamma) \vdash^+$$
$$((\#^k a)^3, (\#^k a)^{m \cdot n - 3} \#^k, \alpha \gamma) \vdash^+ ((\#^k a)^{m \cdot n}, \#^k \alpha \alpha \cdots \alpha \gamma).$$

But then there is the beginning of an accepting computation

$$(\lambda, (\#^k a)^3 \#^k, I) \vdash^+ ((\#^k a)^2, \#^k a \#^k, \gamma) \vdash^+ ((\#^k a)^3, \#^k, \alpha \gamma).$$

However, the length $|(\#^k a)^3 \#^k| = 3(k+1)+k$ of the accepted word is shorter than the shortest word of the form $(\#^k a)^+ \#^k$ in L_n. This has the length $2n(k+1)+k \geq 4(k+1)+k$. So, we obtain a contradiction to the assumption that M accepts L_n. $\square$

So, in contrast to the family of languages accepted by reversible pushdown automata with states but without lookahead, the family of regular languages is not included in the family $\mathscr{L}(\mathrm{REV}(k)\text{-DSPDA})$. To separate the computational capacities of reversible from general (k)-DSPDAs it remains to be shown that the latter accept all regular languages.

Theorem 6. *Any regular language is accepted by some (1)-DSPDA.*

It turned out that the family of regular languages is too wide to obtain a lower bound for the computational capacity of REV(k)-DSPDAs. However, the family of reversible regular languages is well suited, where a reversible regular language is a language accepted by some reversible deterministic DFA [4,8]. Though the technique to store the history of a DFA computation on the pushdown store [11] does not work here, a simulation of a DFA can maintain the current state at the top of the pushdown. Updating the state cannot be done by pushing the successor state but by changing the symbol at the top of the pushdown.

Theorem 7. *Any language accepted by some reversible DFA is accepted by some REV(1)-DSPDA.*

4 Impact of the Lookahead Size

In this section we consider the impact of the lookahead size on the computational capacity of reversible deterministic stateless pushdown automata. In fact, it is shown that there exists an infinite and tight hierarchy of language families dependent on the size of the lookahead. To this end, we consider deterministic linear context-free languages as witnesses. For any integer $k \geq 1$, let the deterministic linear context-free language L_k be defined as $\{\lambda\} \cup \{ a^n b^m c^n \mid n \geq 1, m \geq k \}$.

Lemma 8. *For any integer $k \geq 1$, the language L_{2k} can be accepted by some $REV(k+1)$-DSPDA.*

Lemma 9. *For any integer $k \geq 1$, the language L_{2k} cannot be accepted by any $REV(k)$-DSPDA.*

Lemma 8 and Lemma 9 reveal that the size of the lookahead matters.

Theorem 10. *For any integer $k \geq 1$, the family $\mathscr{L}(REV(k)\text{-}DSPDA)$ is properly included in the family $\mathscr{L}(REV(k+1)\text{-}DSPDA)$.*

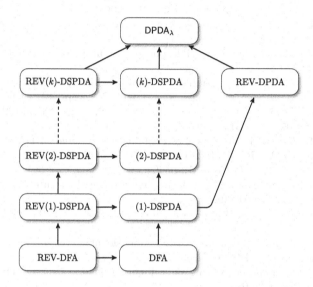

Fig. 2. Relations between the language families, where an arrow denotes a proper inclusion and a dashed arrow indicates an infinite hierarchy. All families which are not linked by a path are mutually incomparable. The family of languages accepted by realtime deterministic pushdown automata is denoted by DPDA$_\lambda$.

References

1. Angluin, D.: Inference of reversible languages. J. ACM **29**, 741–765 (1982)
2. Bennett, C.H.: Logical reversibility of computation. IBM J. Res. Dev. **17**, 525–532 (1973)
3. Harrison, M.A.: Introduction to Formal Language Theory. Addison-Wesley, Reading (1978)
4. Holzer, M., Jakobi, S., Kutrib, M.: Minimal reversible deterministic finite automata. Int. J. Found. Comput. Sci. **29**, 251–270 (2018)

5. Kari, J.: Reversible cellular automata. In: De Felice, C., Restivo, A. (eds.) DLT 2005. LNCS, vol. 3572, pp. 57–68. Springer, Heidelberg (2005). https://doi.org/10.1007/11505877_5
6. Knuth, D.E.: Top-down syntax analysis. Acta Inform. 1, 79–110 (1971)
7. Kutrib, M.: Aspects of reversibility for classical automata. In: Calude, C.S., Freivalds, G.R., Iwama, K. (eds.) Computing with New Resources. LNCS, vol. 8808, pp. 83–98. Springer (2014)
8. Kutrib, M.: Reversible and irreversible computations of deterministic finite-state devices. In: Italiano, G.F., Pighizzini, G., Sannella, D.T. (eds.) MFCS 2015. LNCS, vol. 9234, pp. 38–52. Springer, Heidelberg (2015). https://doi.org/10.1007/978-3-662-48057-1_3
9. Kutrib, M., Malcher, A.: Fast reversible language recognition using cellular automata. Inform. Comput. 206, 1142–1151 (2008)
10. Kutrib, M., Malcher, A.: Real-time reversible iterative arrays. Theor. Comput. Sci. 411, 812–822 (2010)
11. Kutrib, M., Malcher, A.: Reversible pushdown automata. J. Comput. Syst. Sci. 78, 1814–1827 (2012)
12. Kutrib, M., Malcher, A., Wendlandt, M.: Real-time reversible one-way cellular automata. In: Isokawa, T., Imai, K., Matsui, N., Peper, F., Umeo, H. (eds.) AUTOMATA 2014. LNCS, vol. 8996, pp. 56–69. Springer, Cham (2015). https://doi.org/10.1007/978-3-319-18812-6_5
13. Kutrib, M., Worsch, T.: Degrees of reversibility for DFA and DPDA. In: Yamashita, S., Minato, S. (eds.) RC 2014. LNCS, vol. 8507, pp. 40–53. Springer, Cham (2014). https://doi.org/10.1007/978-3-319-08494-7_4
14. Landauer, R.: Irreversibility and heat generation in the computing process. IBM J. Res. Dev. 5, 183–191 (1961)
15. Lewis II, P.M., Stearns, R.E.: Syntax-directed transduction. J. ACM 15, 465–488 (1968)
16. Morita, K.: Reversible simulation of one-dimensional irreversible cellular automata. Theor. Comput. Sci. 148, 157–163 (1995)
17. Morita, K.: Reversible computing and cellular automata - a survey. Theor. Comput. Sci. 395, 101–131 (2008)
18. Rosenkrantz, D.J., Stearns, R.E.: Properties of deterministic top-down grammars. Inform. Control 17, 226–256 (1970)
19. Sippu, S., Soisalon-Soininen, E.: On LL(k) parsing. Inform. Control 53, 141–164 (1982)

Symmetry Groups of Infinite Words

Sergey Luchinin[1]($\boxtimes$) and Svetlana Puzynina[1,2]

[1] Saint Petersburg State University, Saint Petersburg, Russia
[2] Sobolev Institute of Mathematics, Novosibirsk, Russia

Abstract. In this paper we introduce a new notion of a symmetry group of an infinite word. Given a subgroup G_n of the symmetric group S_n, it acts on the set of finite words of length n by permutation. For each n, a symmetry group of an infinite word w is a subgroup G_n of the symmetric group S_n such that $g(v)$ is a factor of w for each permutation $g \in G_n$ and each factor v of w. We study general properties of symmetry groups of infinite words and characterize symmetry groups of several families of infinite words. We show that symmetry groups of Sturmian words and more generally Arnoux-Rauzy words are of order two for large enough n; on the other hand, symmetry groups of certain Toeplitz words have exponential growth.

Keywords: Infinite words · Symmetry groups · Arnoux-Rauzy words · Toeplitz words

1 Introduction

In this paper we introduce and study a new notion of a symmetry group of an infinite word. This group is related to certain algebraic and combinatorial properties of the language of factors of an infinite word, and is defined as follows. A permutation of order n acts on a word of length n in a natural way by permuting its letters. For every integer n, the symmetry group of order n of an infinite word w is defined as the set of permutations of order n that map every factor of w to a factor of w. It is easy to verify that this set indeed forms a subgroup of a symmetric group of order n. So, we associate with an infinite word a sequence $(G_n)_{n \geq 1}$ of subgroups of S_n characterizing symmetries of the language of factors of the infinite word. A related concept of group complexity of infinite words has been studied in [4].

We investigate general properties of symmetry groups of infinite words. We show that any subgroup of the symmetry group is a group of symmetries of some infinite word. However, the conditions for a sequence $(G_n)_{n \geq 1}$ to be a sequence of symmetry groups of an infinite word seem to be quite restrictive. We provide a series of conditions of this kind: for example, $(G_n)_{n \geq 1}$ cannot contain certain cycles and transpositions infinitely often, unless the word contains all words as its factors and $G_n = S_n$ for each n.

Supported by Russian Foundation of Basic Research (grant 20-01-00488).

N. Moreira and R. Reis (Eds.): DLT 2021, LNCS 12811, pp. 267–278, 2021.
https://doi.org/10.1007/978-3-030-81508-0_22

The symmetry groups of certain infinite words and classes of infinite words are studied. In particular, we characterize the symmetry groups of Sturmian words [6, Chapter 2] and more generally Arnoux-Rauzy words [5]. Sturmian words can be defined as infinite aperiodic words which have $n + 1$ distinct factors for each length n. They admit various characterizations in combinatorial, algebraic and arithmetical form. Their most natural generalization to non-binary alphabet, Arnoux-Rauzy words, share most of the structural properties of Sturmian words. We show that for Sturmian words and more generally Arnoux-Rauzy words the symmetry groups are small: they are of order 2 for sufficiently large n. The same situation holds for the Thue-Morse word [8].

Another family of words considered in the paper, Toeplitz words, can be defined iteratively as follows. Take an infinite periodic word w on the alphabet $\Sigma \cup \{?\}$, where ? corresponds to a hole. Fill the holes iteratively by substituting the word itself into the remaining holes. In the limit, all holes are filled and an infinite word is defined. The most studied Toeplitz words are the paperfolding word [2], giving rise to the famous fractal curve, and the period-doubling word [7]. We obtain recurrent formulas for the symmetry groups of these words, showing that contrary to Arnoux-Rauzy and the Thue-Morse words, their symmetry groups are large; more precisely, they have exponential growth order.

The paper is organized as follows. In Sect. 2, we fix some notation and introduce the notion of a symmetry group. We prove that the symmetry group of an infinite word is indeed a group, and show that any permutation group is a symmetry group of some word. In Sect. 3, we provide a series of conditions on the sequence $(G_n)_{n \geq 1}$ implying that the language of the underlying word contains all finite words. In Sects. 4, 5 and 6, we describe symmetry groups of Arnoux-Rauzy words, the period-doubling word, the Thue-Morse word and the paperfolding word. In Sect. 7, we study symmetry groups of a subclass of Toeplitz words. We finish with some open problems.

2   Preliminaries

An *alphabet* Σ is a finite set of letters. A *word* on Σ is a finite or infinite sequence of letters from Σ, i.e., $u = u_1 u_2 \cdots$, where $u_i \in \Sigma$. We let Σ^* denote the set of finite words on Σ. The *length* of the finite word $u = u_1 \cdots u_n$ is the number of its letters: $|u| = n$. An empty word is denoted by ε, and we set $|\varepsilon| = 0$. We let u^R denote the *reversed word* u: $u^R = u_n u_{n-1} \cdots u_1$.

A finite word $u = u_1 \cdots u_n$ is a *factor* of a finite or infinite word w if there exists $i \in \mathbb{N}$ such that $u = w_i \cdots w_{i+n-1}$. We let $F(w)$ denote the set of factors of w and $F_n(w)$ the set of its factors of length n. A factor u of a finite or infinite word w is said to be *left special* (resp., *right special*) in w if there exists at least two distinct letters a, b such that au and bu (resp., ua, ub) are factors of w. An infinite word is called *recurrent* if each of its factors occurs infinitely often. An infinite word w is called *universal* over an alphabet Σ if $F(w) = \Sigma^*$.

Let S_n be a group of permutations on n elements. We use the following notation: $[m_1, m_2, \ldots, m_n] = \begin{pmatrix} 1 & 2 & \ldots & n \\ m_1 & m_2 & \ldots & m_n \end{pmatrix}$. This should be distinguished from the notation $(m_1 m_2 \ldots m_k)$, which means the cycle where the element m_i takes the place of m_{i+1} for each i. We say that a cycle is *independent* in a permutation $g \in S_n$ if it is one of the cycles in the decomposition of g into disjoint cycles.

Let $u = u_1 u_2 \ldots u_n$ be a word of length n, and $g \in S_n$ be a permutation on n elements. Then the permutation g acts on the word u in the following way: $g(u) = u_{g^{-1}(1)} u_{g^{-1}(2)} \cdots u_{g^{-1}(n)}$.

Definition 1. *The symmetry group $G_n(w)$ of an infinite word w of order n is defined as follows:*

$$G_n(w) = \{\pi \in S_n \mid \pi(x) \in F_n(w) \text{ for all } x \in F_n(w)\}.$$

In what follows when it is clear for which word this symmetric group is considered, we omit the argument and write G_n for brevity.

Proposition 1. *Let w be an infinite word, then $G_n(w)$ is a subgroup of S_n.*

Proof. For the proof it is enough to check the three properties of the group:

1. Let $g, h \in G_n$, then $hg \in G_n$. Indeed, let x be a factor of w. By definition G_n, we have that $g(x)$ is a factor of w. So $h(g(x)) = hg(x)$ is a factor of w.
2. Let $e \in S_n$ be the identity permutation. Then $e \in G_n$. For each finite word x, we have $e(x) = x$. So if x is a factor of w, then $e(x)$ is a factor of w.
3. For $g \in G_n$, we have $g^{-1} \in G_n$. Since the group S_n is finite, there is an integer k that $g^k = 1$. Then $g^{k-1} = g^{-1}$ and from item 1 we know that $g^{k-1}(x)$ is a factor of w. Thus $g^{-1}(x)$ is a factor of w.

Example 1. The symmetry group G_n of a universal word is S_n for each n. Indeed, for each $g \in S_n$ and each $v \in \Sigma^n$ we have $g(v) \in F_n(w)$, since all finite words are factors. In particular, this holds for $|\Sigma| = 1$: $g(a^n) = a^n$ is a factor of $a^\mathbb{N}$.

Proposition 2. *For each n and each subgroup $G \leq S_n$, there exists an infinite word w with symmetry group $G_n(w) = G$.*

Proof. We build w on an $(n+1)$-letter alphabet $\{a_1, a_2, \ldots, a_{n+1}\}$ as follows. Set $v_i = g_i(a_1 a_2 \ldots a_n)$ for each $g_i \in G$, $u = a_{n+1}^n$, and $w_1, w_2, \ldots, w_j$ are all possible words of length n that contain the letter a_{n+1}. Then w is defined by

$$w = u \, v_1 \, u \, v_2 \, u \, \cdots \, u \, v_i \, u \, w_1 \, u \, w_2 \, u \, \cdots u \, w_j \, u \, u \, u \, \cdots .$$

Let x be a factor of w of length n and $g \in S_n$. Let $g \in G$. If x contains a_{n+1}, then $g(x)$ contains a_{n+1}, thus $g(x)$ is a factor of w. If $x = g_i(a_1 a_2 \ldots a_n), g_i \in G$, then $gg_i \in G$ and $g(x) = gg_i(a_1 a_2 \ldots a_n)$ is a factor of w. So if $g \in G$, then $g \in G_n$. If $g \notin G$, then $g(a_1 a_2 \ldots a_n)$ is not a factor of w. So $G_n = G$.

Remark 1. In the previous proposition the size of the alphabet depends on n and the subgroup $G < S_n$, since for some pairs $(|\Sigma|, G)$ words on Σ with $G_n(w) = G$ do not exist.

For example, on a unary alphabet we always have $G_n = S_n$. For a binary alphabet, the group $G \leq S_3$ generated by the cycle $g = (123)$ cannot be a symmetry group of a binary infinite word w. Indeed, using the fact that for each $x \in F_3(w)$ we have $g(x), g^2(x) \in F_3(w)$, we can show that for any $h \in S_3$ we have $h(x) \in F_3(w)$. For $x = 000$ or $x = 111$ the statement is clear. If $x = 001$, then w contains the factors 010 and 100, which means that $h(x)$ is also a factor. Similarly if $x = 110$.

3   Sequences of Symmetry Groups

As we showed in the previous section, each subgroup of S_n is a symmetry group of some infinite word. However, there are lots of restrictions on the structure of the sequence $(G_n(w))_{n \geq 1}$ of symmetry groups. For example, we have the following:

Proposition 3. *If for each n a symmetry group $G_n(w)$ of a word w contains the cycle $(12 \ldots n)$, then w is universal. In particular, $G_n(w) = S_n$ for each n.*

Proof. First notice that each letter of the word occurs in it infinitely many times. Indeed, suppose that a letter a occurs for the last time at some position i. Then for $n > i$ the cycle $(12 \ldots n)$ maps the prefix of length n of w to a factor with a at position $i + 1$. Any occurrence of this factor in w gives an occurrence of a at a position greater than i.

To prove the universality, we show that each factor of w is left special and that it can be extended by any letter. Take any factor v and consider any occurrence of v in a word; denote its position by i, and consider an occurrence j of any letter a, such that $j > i + |v|$. Now applying the cycle $(1 \ldots j - i + 1)$ to the factor $w_i \cdots w_j$ gives a word with the prefix av. Hence each factor of w is left special and can be extended by any letter, thus w is universal.

More generally, the following holds:

Proposition 4. *Let w be a recurrent infinite word. If for each m there exist $n \geq m$ and $i \leq n - m$ such that $G_n(w)$ has an element σ that contains an independent cycle $((i+1)(i+2)\ldots(i+m))$, then w is universal.*

Proof. We will prove that in fact for each m the group $G_m(w)$ contains the cycle $(1 \ldots m)$. Indeed, given m, consider any factor $v \in F(w)$ of length m and any its occurrence $l > i$, where i is as in the statement. Now since G_n contains a permutation σ that contains an independent cycle $((i+1)(i+2)\ldots(i+m))$, we apply this permutation to the factor $w_{l-i+1} \cdots w_{l-i+n}$. The word $\sigma(w_{l-i+1} \cdots w_{l-i+n})$ is factor of w, and it contains $v_2 \cdots v_m v_1$ at position i. Hence $G_m(w)$ contains the cycle $(1 \ldots m)$, and by Proposition 3 the word w is universal.

Remark 2. For non-recurrent words there exist counterexamples, e.g., symmetry groups of $a^5 b^\infty$ contain cycles $((i+1)\ldots(i+m))$ for $i \geq 5$, although the word is not universal. It contains a universal tail though, and actually this is the general case: an infinite word with this property has a universal tail on $\Sigma' \subseteq \Sigma$.

Let n, m be integers with $n \geq m$, and $\sigma \in S_n$ a cycle of length m: $\sigma = (j_1 j_2 \ldots j_m)$, i.e., j_k are pairwise distinct. We say that σ is *arithmetical* if there exists an integer $l \geq 2$ such that all j_k are congruent modulo l: $j_1 \equiv j_2 \equiv \ldots \equiv j_m$ (mod l). For example, (137) is arithmetical with $l = 2$, while (134) is not.

Proposition 5. *Let w be a recurrent infinite word, and $\sigma = (j_1 j_2 \ldots j_m)$ a cycle of length m which is not arithmetical. If there exist increasing sequences of integers $(n_k)_{k \geq 1}$ and $(i_k)_{k \geq 1}$ such that there exists $\beta_{n_k} \in G_{n_k}(w)$ with $\beta(i_k + j_1) = i_k + j_2$, $\beta(i_k + j_2) = i_k + j_3$, $\ldots$, $\beta(i_k + j_m) = i_k + j_1$, and $\beta(l) = l$ for each $l = 1, \ldots, i_k + \min\limits_{1 \leq l \leq m} j_l - 1$, then the word w is universal.*

Proof. As in Proposition 3, we will prove that each factor is right special and can be extended in all possible ways. Without loss of generality assume that $j_1 = \min\limits_{1 \leq k \leq m} j_k = 1$.

Consider a factor v of w. Choose k with $i_k > |v|$, and consider a position i of v in w with $i + |v| \geq i_k$. Now consider a factor $u = w_{i+|v|-i_k} \cdots w_{i+|v|-i_k+n_k-1}$. If a letter a occurs at one of the positions $i + |v| + j_l - 1$ for some $l = 1, \ldots, m$, then applying $(m - l)$ times β_{n_k} to u, we obtain va as a prefix of $\beta_{n_k}^{m-l}(u)$.

If a letter a does not occur at one of the positions $i + |v| + j_l - 1$ for some $l = 1, \ldots, m$, then consider some its occurrence at a position $j \geq i + |v| + \max\limits_{1 \leq l \leq m} j_l$. The idea is that we are going to move this a to the left to the position $i + |v| + \max\limits_{1 \leq l \leq m} j_l - 1$ using permutations β_{n_k} at different positions and keeping v untouched. Now we order j_l in increasing order and we let $d_1, \ldots, d_{m-1}$ denote the distances between consecutive i_l in this order, so that the sets $\{j_1, j_2, \ldots, j_m\}$ and $\{j_1, j_1 + d_1, j_1 + d_1 + d_2, \ldots, j_1 + d_1 + \ldots + d_{m-1}\}$ coincide. Since the cycle σ is not arithmetical, we have that d_l's are relatively prime: $(d_1, \ldots, d_{m-1}) = 1$.

First notice that for each l we can move the letter a by d_l to the right or to the left, keeping v untouched. We let s and t denote indices such that $d_l = j_s - j_t$. To move it to the right, we can apply $\beta_{n_k}^{t-s}$ to $(w_{j-i_k-j_t-1} \cdots w_{j-i_k-j_t-1+n_k})$. Here we must take k big enough to have $j - i_k - j_t < i$ to keep v untouched. If $j - i_k - j_t < 0$, then we can either consider a later occurrence of $w_i \cdots w_j$ in the word, or extend it to the left to biinfinite word keeping its set of factors (we can do it since w is recurrent). Moving a by d_l to the left is symmetric.

Since d_l's are relatively prime, there exist $s_1, \ldots, s_{m-1} \in \mathbb{Z}$ such that $s_1 d_1 + \ldots + s_{m-1} d_{m-1} = -1$. Now applying the procedure from the previous paragraph first for l's for which s_l's are positive, s_l times for d_l, then for l's for which s_l's are negative. This way we moved the letter a to the left by 1. We now repeat the procedure until a is at the position $i + |v| + \max\limits_{1 \leq l \leq m} j_l - 1$, reducing to the above case when a occurs at of the positions $i + |v| + j_l - 1$.

As an example, the above proposition gives the following corollary:

Corollary 1. *If for infinitely many n the symmetry group $G_n(w)$ contains a transposition $(i(i + 1))$, then w is universal.*

Proof. For the proof, we take in Proposition 4 σ to be a transposition (12), and we apply the proposition either as stated, or in reversed form.

Remark 3. Most results of this section can be slightly generalized, for example, for shifts, or reversed statements from right to left, or for subpermutations of a bit more general form. Also, they can be adapted to arithmetic progressions $kN + i$, so that each arithmetic subword $w_i w_{i+k} \cdots$ is universal (probably with smaller alphabets on some progressions). For example, Proposition 3 can be reformulated as follows: Let w be a recurrent infinite word and k be an integer. If for each n the symmetry group $G_n(w)$ of the word w contains the cycle $(1(1 + k)(1 + 2k)\ldots)$, then each of the arithmetical subwords $w_{i+k} w_{i+2k} w_{i+3k} \cdots$, $1 \le i \le k$, is universal over an alphabet $\Sigma_i \subseteq \Sigma$.

4 The Symmetry Groups of Arnoux-Rauzy Words

In this section, we show that starting from some length symmetry groups of Arnoux-Rauzy words contain only two elements, identity and mirror image.

Definition 2. *An infinite word w on an alphabet Σ is called an Arnoux-Rauzy word if the following conditions hold:*

- *if a finite word u is a factor of w, then u^R is a factor of w*
- *w has exactly one left special factor (or, equivalently, right special factor) of each length. Moreover, each special factor extends in exactly $|\Sigma|$ ways.*

We denote the left special factor of length n by U_n^l and the right one by U_n^r. It follows from the definition that $U_n^r = (U_n^l)^R$.

Definition 3. *[5] The palindromic right-closure $w^{(+)}$ of a finite word w is the (unique) shortest palindrome having w as a prefix. That is, $w^{(+)} = wv^{-1}w^R$, where v is the longest palindromic suffix of w. The iterated palindromic closure function, denoted by Pal, is defined recursively as follows. Set $Pal(\varepsilon) = \varepsilon$, and for any word w and letter x define $Pal(wx) = (Pal(w)x)^{(+)}$.*

Theorem 1. *[5] A word w is an Arnoux-Rauzy word if and only if there exists an infinite word v with each letter occurring in it infinitely many times such that w has the same set of factors as the limit of iterated palindromic closures of prefixes of the word v.*

Let w be an Arnoux-Rauzy word with the language of the palindromic closure of v. Let v begin with t identical letters; then we denote the number t by $A(w)$.

Theorem 2. *Let w be an Arnoux-Rauzy word and $t = A(w)$. Then for $n \ge 4t+2$ the symmetry group of w is*

$$G_n = \{[1, 2, \ldots, n - 1, n], [n, n - 1, \ldots, 2, 1]\}.$$

Proof. From the definition of Arnoux-Rauzy words it follows that $\{[1, 2, \ldots, n - 1, n], [n, n - 1, \ldots, 2, 1]\} \subset G_n$. It remains to prove that any other permutation cannot belong to G_n. Let be $\sigma \in G_n$. We first show that $\sigma(n) = 1$ or $\sigma(n) = n$ for $n \geq 2t + 1$. Suppose that $\sigma(n) = k$, for some $1 < k < n$.

We let a denote the letter which is the special factor of length 1. Suppose first that $k < n - t$. Then consider all possible factors $U_{n-1}^r x$, where x is any letter. Then applying σ to all such factors, for some $u \in F_{k-1}(w)$, $v \in F_{n-k}(w)$ and any $x \in \Sigma$, we get $|\Sigma|$ factors of the form uxv, which differ from each other only at position k. Since a is the only left and right special factor of length 1, then the letter preceding x and the letter following x is a. So, we get factors of the form $u'axav'$, where x is any letter. Suppose that v starts with a^r and then there is another letter $b \neq a$. Then we get the factors $u'axa^r bv''$. Now if we take $x = a$, we see that the factor a^{r+1} can continue to the right with the letters a and b, and the factor $a^r b$ can continue to the left with any letter (x can be any letter). So we get at least two special factors, which is impossible. Thus we showed that the word v can only consist of the letters a. But v is longer than t ($|v| = n - k > t$), so this is impossible (w cannot contain more than t consecutive letters a). If $k \geq n - t$, then we apply the same line of reasoning for the word u. This is possible, because $n \geq 2t + 1$, so $k > t$ and $|u| \geq t$.

So, we have $\sigma(n) = 1$ or $\sigma(n) = n$. Similarly we show that $\sigma(1) = 1$ or $\sigma(1) = n$.

Suppose that $\sigma(n) = n$, then $\sigma(1) = 1$. Then for similar reasons we get that $\sigma(2) = 2, \sigma(3) = 3, \ldots, \sigma(n - 2t - 1) = n - 2t - 1$. Indeed, let $U = u_1 \cdots u_n$ be a factor of w. Then $V = u_2 u_3 \cdots u_n$ is a factor of w. This means that $\sigma'(V)$ is factor of w, where σ' is the restriction of σ to the word V. So, $\sigma' \in G_{n-1}$. It follows that $\sigma'(n - 1) = n - 1$ and $\sigma'(1) = 1$ or $\sigma'(n - 1) = 1$ and $\sigma'(1) = n - 1$, because $n - 1 \geq 2t + 1$. Since $\sigma(n) = n$, we have $\sigma'(n-1) = n-1$, so $\sigma'(1) = 1$ and $\sigma(2) = 2$. In the same way step by step we get that $\sigma(k) = k$ for all $k \leq n - 2t - 1$. Similarly, we can show that $\sigma(k) = k$ for any $k \geq 2t + 1$. Since $n \geq 4t + 2$, we get that $\sigma(k) = k$ for any $1 \leq k \leq n$. So $\sigma = \mathrm{Id} = [1, 2, \ldots, n]$.

If $\sigma(1) = n$, $\sigma(n) = 1$, then we can prove that $\sigma(k) = n - k$ in a similar way. So, in this case we prove that $\sigma = [n, n - 1, \ldots, 2, 1]$. The theorem is proved.

Since Sturmian words are binary Arnoux-Rauzy words, we have

Corollary 2. *Let w be a Sturmian word and k be the length of the longest block of the more frequent letter in w. Then*

$$G_n = \{[1, 2, \ldots, n - 1, n], [n, n - 1, \ldots, 2, 1]\} \quad \text{for any} \quad n > 4k + 2.$$

5   Symmetry Group of the Period-Doubling Word

In this section we characterize symmetry groups of the period-doubling word and show that the size of the group grows exponentially.

Definition 4. *The period-doubling word $w = 0100010101000100 \cdots$ is a binary word defined as follows: $w_i \equiv k \pmod 2$, where $i = 2^k l$ and l is odd.*

In other words, w_i is equal to the maximal exponent of 2 dividing i, modulo 2.

Theorem 3. *For $n \geq 4$ the symmetry group G_n of the period-doubling word satisfies the following recurrence relations:*

$$G_n = \begin{cases} G_{n/2} \times G_{n/2} \times S_2, & \text{if } n \text{ is even,} \\ G_{(n-1)/2} \times G_{(n+1)/2}, & \text{if } n \text{ is odd,} \end{cases}$$

and $G_1 = S_1$, $G_2 = S_2$, $G_3 = \{[1,2,3],[3,2,1]\}$.

For the proof, we need the following lemma:

Lemma 1. *Let $g \in S_n$. Suppose that there are two positions c and d of the same parity such that $g(c)$ is even and $g(d)$ is odd. Then $g \notin G_n$.*

Proof. Note that for any $u \in F(w)$ either on even positions of u or on odd positions of u we have only 0's, since $w_{2k+1} = 0$ for any k. Next, each factor of length at least 4 contains an occurrence of 1, because there is a number that is not a multiple of 4 among two consecutive even numbers.

We set $d - c = 2k$; then there is an integer s such that $w_s = w_{s+2k} = 1$, which is equivalent to the fact that the maximal exponent of 2 in s and $s + 2k$ is odd. Indeed, if k is odd, then we can take $s = 2^{2m+1}$ for some $m \in \mathbb{N}$. Then the maximal exponent of 2 in s and $s+2k$ is equal to $2m+1$ and 1, respectively. If k is even, then we can take $s = 2m$, where m is odd, since the maximal exponent of 2 in s and $s + 2k$ is equal to 1. Then we get that there is a factor u which has $w_s = w_{s+d-c} = 1$ at positions c and d, because s can be chosen sufficiently large. But then $g(u)$ has even and odd positions that have 1, which is impossible. It follows that $g(u)$ is not a factor of w, so $g \notin G_n$. The lemma is proved.

Proof of Theorem 3. It is easy to see that $G_1 = S_1, G_2 = S_2, G_3 = \{[1,2,3],[3,2,1]\}$. Consider $n \geq 4$. Lemma 1 implies that if n is odd, then g does not change the parity of positions. If n is even, then g either does not change the parity of positions, or changes the parity of all positions (the latter is impossible for an odd n since there are more odd positions).

Let $n = 2l + 1$ be odd, then $g \in S_n$ permutes odd positions as a permutation $h \in S_{l+1}$ and even positions as a permutation $p \in S_l$. Let $u = w_{m+1}w_{m+2}\ldots w_{m+n}$ be a factor of length n.

If m is even, then u has 0 at odd positions, and hence $g(u)$ also has 0 at odd positions. There is an occurrence of 1 in any factor of length $n \geq 4$, so $g(u)$ occurs at an odd position: $g(u) = w_{r+1}w_{r+2}\cdots w_{r+n}$, where r is even. Then $p(w_{m+2}w_{m+4}\cdots w_{m+n-1}) = w_{r+2}w_{r+4}\cdots w_{r+n-1}$. The definition of the period-doubling word implies that $w_k = 1 - w_{2k}$. It follows that $p(w_{\frac{m+2}{2}}w_{\frac{m+4}{2}}\cdots w_{\frac{m+n-1}{2}}) = w_{\frac{r+2}{2}}w_{\frac{r+4}{2}}\cdots w_{\frac{r+n-1}{2}}$ for any even m. This means that $p \in G_l$, because otherwise we can pick m such that $p(w_{\frac{m+2}{2}}w_{\frac{m+4}{2}}\ldots w_{\frac{m+n-1}{2}})$ is not a factor of w. These arguments also imply that if $p \in G_l$, then $g(u)$ is a factor, because there is a factor of $p(w_{\frac{m+2}{2}}w_{\frac{m+4}{2}}\cdots w_{\frac{m+n-1}{2}}) = w_{\frac{r+2}{2}}w_{\frac{r+4}{2}}\cdots w_{\frac{r+n-1}{2}}$ and hence $g(w_{m+1}w_{m+2}w_{m+3}\cdots w_{m+n}) = g(0w_{m+2}0w_{m+4}\cdots) = 0w_{r+2}0w_{r+4}\cdots = w_{r+1}w_{r+2}\cdots w_{r+n}$. Then $p \in G_l$. If m is odd, in a similar way we get that $h \in G_{l+1}$. And the arguments above imply that if $p \in G_l$ and $h \in G_{l+1}$, then $g \in G_{2l+1}$.

As a result, we get for odd $n = 2l + 1$ that g acts on even positions as a permutation from G_l and on odd positions as a permutation from G_{l+1}.

Now let $n = 2l$ be even, and first consider the case when the permutation $g \in G_{2l}$ does not change the parity of positions. Similarly to the case of odd n, we get that g acts on even positions as a permutation p from G_l and on odd positions as a permutation h from G_l. Now consider the case when g changes the parity of all positions. For a factor $u = w_{m+1}w_{m+2}\cdots w_{m+n}$, its image occurs at some position $r + 1$: $g(u) = w_{r+1}w_{r+2}\cdots w_{r+n}$. Then $h(w_{m+1}w_{m+3}\cdots w_{m+n-1}) = w_{r+2}w_{r+4}\cdots w_{r+n}$ and $p(w_{m+2}w_{m+4}\ldots w_{m+n}) = w_{r+1}w_{r+3}\cdots w_{r+n-1}$. If u has 0 at odd positions, then $g(u)$ has 0 in even positions, which means that similarly to the previous case we can get that $p \in G_l$ and $h \in G_l$. The arguments above also imply that if $p \in G_l$ and $h \in G_{l+1}$, then $g \in G_{2l+1}$.

Summing up, we proved that permutations from G_{2n+1} act as G_n at even positions and as G_{n+1} at odd ones independently, so that $G_{2n+1} = G_n \times G_{n+1}$. Permutations from G_{2n} act as G_n at even and odd positions independently, plus we can trade places even and odd positions. Therefore, the permutations from G_{2n} form the group $G_n \times G_n \times S_2$. The theorem is proved.

Corollary 3. *The size of the symmetry group of the period-doubling word satisfies the following lower bound: $|G_n| > 2^{\frac{n}{3}}$. In particular, $|G_{2^n}| = 2^{2^n-1}$.*

Proof. First we prove by induction that $|G_n| > 2^{\frac{n}{3}}$. For small n we check directly that it holds. Then $|G_{2n+1}| = |G_n| \cdot |G_{n+1}| > 2^{\frac{n}{3}+\frac{n+1}{3}} = 2^{\frac{2n+1}{3}}$ and $|G_{2n}| = 2|G_n| \cdot |G_n| > 2^{2\frac{n}{3}+1} = 2^{\frac{2n}{3}+1}$.

Now we prove that $|G_{2^n}| = 2^{2^n-1}$. Obviously, $|G_2| = 2$. Then $|G_{2^{n+1}}| = 2|G_{2^n}| \cdot |G_{2^n}| = 2 \cdot 2^{2^n-1} \cdot 2^{2^n-1} = 2^{2^{n-1}}$.

6 Symmetry Groups of the Thue-Morse Word and the Paperfolding Word

In this section we describe the symmetry groups of the Thue-Morse and the paperfolding words. The proofs are omitted due to space constraints.

Definition 5. *The Thue-Morse word is the infinite word $w = a_1a_2\cdots$, where a_n is the number of 1's in the binary expansion of n.*

Theorem 4. *The symmetry group of the Thue-Morse word is expressed as follows:*

$$G_n = \begin{cases} S_n, & \text{if } n \le 3, \\ \{[1,2,3,4],[4,3,2,1],[1,3,2,4]\}, & \text{if } n = 4, \\ \{[1,2,3,4,5],[5,4,3,2,1],[2,1,3,5,4]\}, & \text{if } n = 5, \\ \{[1,2,3,4,5,6],[6,5,4,3,2,1],[6,2,4,3,5,1]\}, & \text{if } n = 6, \\ \{[1,2,\ldots,n-1,n],[n,n-1,\ldots,2,1]\}, & \text{if } n > 6. \end{cases}$$

Definition 6. *The paperfolding word* $w = 110110011100100\cdots$ *is defined as follows:* $w_i = 1$ *if* $\frac{i}{2^m} \equiv 1 \pmod 4$, *where* m *is the maximal exponent of 2 dividing* i, *and 0 otherwise.*

We say that a permutation g is *of type 1* if g keeps the parity of each position. A permutation g is *of type 2* if it changes the parity of each position.

Theorem 5. *Let* w *be the paperfolding word. We let* G_k^1 *and* G_k^2 *denote all permutations in* G_k *of types 1 and 2, respectively. Then the symmetry group of* w *is* $G_n = G_n^1$ *for odd* n *and* $G_n = G_n^1 \cup G_n^2$ *for even* n, *and the following recurrent formula holds:*

$$G_n = \begin{cases} G_{[\frac{n}{2}]}^1 \times G_{[\frac{n+1}{2}]}^1 \cup G_{[\frac{n}{2}]}^2 \times G_{[\frac{n+1}{2}]}^2, & \text{if } n \text{ is odd,} \\ G_{[\frac{n}{2}]} \times G_{[\frac{n}{2}]}, & \text{if } n \text{ is even.} \end{cases}$$

Corollary 4. *For* $n \geq 3$, *we have* $|G_n| > 2^{\frac{n}{5}}$.

7 Symmetry Groups of Toeplitz Words

In this section we characterize symmetry groups of a subclass of Toeplitz words and show that symmetry groups of Toeplitz words are quite diverse.

Definition 7. *Let* $?$ *be a letter not in* Σ. *For a word* $u \in \Sigma(\Sigma \cup \{?\})^*$, *let*

$$T_0(u) = ?^\omega, \quad T_{i+1}(u) = F_u(T_i(u)),$$

where $F_u(w)$, *defined for any* $w \in (\Sigma \cup \{?\})^\omega$, *is the word obtained from* u^ω *by replacing the sequence of all occurrences of* $?$ *by* w. *Clearly,*

$$T(u) = \lim_{i \to \infty} T_i(u) \in \Sigma^\omega$$

is well defined, and it is referred to as the Toeplitz word *determined by the pattern* u.

Example 2. The paperfolding and the period-doubling words are Toeplitz words determined by patterns $1?0?$ and $010?$, respectively.

Let u be a pattern with one space (or symbol $?$), $|u| = k \geq 4$ and all letters of u distinct. Let w be the Toeplitz word determined by u, and G_n be the symmetry group of w. We divide the positions of w into k groups of positions congruent modulo k. On one of these groups there are spaces in the word $T_1(u)$; we let T_{space} denote this group. The positions of any factor of w are also divided into k corresponding groups. We first prove two lemmas concerning these groups.

Lemma 2. *Any* $\sigma \in G_n$ *translates positions from the same group to positions from the same group (probably distinct from the initial group).*

Proof. Assume the converse. Let A be a group whose positions move to the positions of different groups B and C. Then consider any factor v_x of the word w of length n in which the letter x stands at each position from the group A. Then $v' = \sigma(v)$ is a factor of w. So the word v' has the letter x at some positions of the groups B and C. Then for any occurrence of v' in w, one of the groups B and C of v' corresponds to T_{space} in $T_1(u)$.

Since $|u| \geq 4$, we can choose three words v_x, v_y, v_z in which all positions of A are filled with three distinct letters x, y, and z, respectively. Then for at least two of the three factors $\sigma(v_x), \sigma(v_y)$ and $\sigma(v_z)$, the group T_{space} corresponds to either B or C; say in $\sigma(v_x)$ and $\sigma(v_y)$ the group B corresponds to T_{space}. Hence only one letter can correspond to the group C in w. But in the words $\sigma(v_x)$ and $\sigma(v_y)$ the positions at the group C have the letters x and y. A contradiction.

Lemma 3. *Any $\sigma \in G_n$ acts on the groups as a cyclic shift or as the identity permutation.*

Proof. Lemma 2 implies that groups are not split. Since all the letters in u are distinct, the distance between any two groups does not change. This means that the order of the groups remains the same. Also note that if n is not divisible by k, then the groups are not of the same size. Then $\sigma \in G_n$ acts on the groups as the identity permutation.

Theorem 6. *Let $n = ak + b$, where $0 \leq b \leq k - 1$. Then*

$$G_n = \begin{cases} G_{a+1}^b \times G_a^{k-b}, & \text{if } b \neq 0, \\ G_a^k \times \mathbb{Z}/k\mathbb{Z}, & \text{if } b = 0. \end{cases}$$

Proof. Let v be a factor of length n. Then u has b groups with $a+1$ positions and $k-b$ groups with a positions; we let $A_1, \ldots, A_k$ denote these groups. Suppose first that n is not divisible by k. Then from the previous lemmas we get that $\sigma \in G_n$ translates the group A_i to itself for each i. Let $\pi_1, \ldots, \pi_k$ be restrictions of σ to the groups $A_1, \ldots, A_k$, respectively. Then $\pi_i \in G_a$ or $\pi_i \in G_{a+1}$, depending on the size of A_i. Indeed, consider any factor v for which the group A_i corresponds to T_{space}. Let v' be the word consisting of the letters of the word v located at the positions from A_i. From the definition of Toeplitz words, it follows that the scattered subword at positions T_{space} in the word w is w. This means that v' can be any factor of w of corresponding length. Since $\sigma(v)$ translates positions from A_i to positions from A_i, which corresponds to T_{space}, the word v' is translated to the word $\pi_i(v')$, which is located at positions T_{space} of the factor $\sigma(v)$. Then $\pi_i(v')$ is a factor of w. So $\pi_i \in G_a$ or $\pi_i \in G_{a+1}$.

Let us prove that if all permutations π_i are from G_a or G_{a+1}, then $\sigma \in G_n$. Consider any factor v of w. Let A_i be the group corresponding to T_{space} and v' be the word consisting of the letters of the word v located at positions from A_i. Since $\pi_i \in G_a$ (or G_{a+1}), we have that $\pi_i(v')$ is a factor of w. So we can find the word $\pi_i(v')$ at the positions T_{space} of w. Then it follows that $\sigma(v)$ is a factor of w. So in this case we get that $G_n = G_{a+1}^b \times G_a^{k-b}$, because the factor of length n has b groups with $a + 1$ positions and $k - b$ groups with a positions.

If $b = 0$, then a shift can be applied to the permutation σ, and there are k possible shifts. So, in this case we have $G_n = G_a^k \times \mathbb{Z}/k\mathbb{Z}$. The theorem is proved.

Corollary 5. *Consider the function* $f(n) = |G_n(w)|$. *Let* $n = ak + b$, *where* $0 \le b \le k - 1$. *Then*

$$f(ak + b) = \begin{cases} f(a)^{k-b} f(a+1)^b & \text{if } b \ne 0, \\ f(a)^k k & \text{if } b = 0. \end{cases}$$

Remark 4. The corollary shows that $f(n) = |G_n|$ can fluctuate. For example, by induction one can show that if $n = ak + b$, $b \ne 0$ and a does not contain 0 and $k - 1$ in the k-ary expansion, then $f(n) = 1$. For $n = k^s$ we have $f(n) = k^{\frac{k^s - 1}{k - 1}}$.

If there is more than one space in u, the groups can behave differently. Contrary to the paperfolding word, for which the symmetry groups are large, the following words have trivial groups:

Proposition 6. *The symmetry groups of* $T(1??23)$ *and* $T(12??34)$ *are equal to* Id *for each* n.

8   Conclusions and Open Problems

In this paper, we introduced and studied a new notion of symmetry groups of infinite words. We remark that all the words considered in the paper have similar properties: linear complexity, rich combinatorial structure, all of them except for Arnoux-Rauzy words are automatic, but their symmetry groups are completely different. It would be interesting to understand in general what properties of a word make its symmetry group large. An interesting direction of future research is generalising results from Sect. 3, answering the following question: Which infinite sequences $(G_n)_{n \ge 1}$, $G_n \le S_n$ are symmetry groups of infinite words?

References

1. Allouche, J.-P., Shallit, J.: Automatic Sequences: Theory, Applications, Generalizations. Cambridge University Press, Cambridge (2003)
2. Allouche, J.-P.: The number of factors in a paperfolding sequence. Bull. Austral. Math. Sot. **46**, 23–32 (1992)
3. Cassaigne, J., Karhumäki, J.: Toeplitz words, generalized periodicity and periodically iterated morphisms. Eur. J. Comb. **18**, 497–510 (1997)
4. Charlier, É., Puzynina, S., Zamboni, L.Q.: On a group theoretic generalization of the Morse-Hedlund theorem. Proc. Amer. Math. Soc. **145**(8), 3381–3394 (2017)
5. Glen, A., Justin, J.: Episturmian words: a survey. RAIRO - Theoret. Inf. Appl. **43**, 402–433 (2009)
6. Lothaire, M.: Algebraic Combinatorics on Words. Cambridge University Press, Cambridge (2002)
7. Madil, B., Rampersad, N.: The abelian complexity of the paperfolding word. Discrete Math. **313**(7), 831–838 (2013)
8. Thue, A.: Über die gegenseitige Lage gleicher Teile gewisser Zeichenreihen. Norske vid. Selsk. Skr. Mat. Nat. Kl. 1, 1–67 (1912)

Bounded Languages Described by GF(2)-grammars

Vladislav Makarov$^{(\boxtimes)}$

St. Petersburg State University, 7/9 Universitetskaya nab.,
Saint Petersburg 199034, Russia

Abstract. GF(2)-grammars are a recently introduced grammar family that has some unusual algebraic properties and is closely connected to the family of unambiguous grammars. By using the method of formal power series, we establish strong conditions that are necessary for subsets of $a_1^* a_2^* \cdots a_k^*$ to be described by some GF(2)-grammar. By further applying the established results, we settle the long-standing open question of proving the inherent ambiguity of the language $\{\, a^n b^m c^\ell \mid n \neq m \text{ or } m \neq \ell \,\}$, as well as give a new, purely algebraic, proof of the inherent ambiguity of the language $\{\, a^n b^m c^\ell \mid n = m \text{ or } m = \ell \,\}$.

Keywords: Formal grammars · Finite fields · Bounded languages · Unambiguous grammars · Inherent ambiguity

1 Introduction

GF(2)-grammars, recently introduced by Bakinova et al. [3], and further studied by Makarov and Okhotin [10], are a variant of ordinary context-free grammars (or just *ordinary grammars*, as I will call them later in the text) in which the disjunction is replaced by exclusive OR, whereas the classical concatenation is replaced by a new operation called GF(2)-concatenation: $K \odot L$ is the set of all strings with an odd number of partitions into a concatenation of a string in K and a string in L.

There are several reasons for studying GF(2)-grammars. Firstly, they are a class of grammars with better algebraic properties, compared to ordinary grammars and similar grammar families, because the underlying boolean semiring logic is replaced by the logic of the field with two elements. As we will see later in the paper, that makes GF(2)-grammars lend themselves very well to algebraic manipulations.

Secondly, GF(2)-grammars provide a new way of looking at unambiguous grammars. For example, instead of proving that some language is inherently ambiguous, one can prove that no GF(2)-grammar describes it. While the latter condition is, strictly speaking, stronger, it may turn out to be easier to prove,

V. Makarov—Supported by Russian Science Foundation, project 18-11-00100.

N. Moreira and R. Reis (Eds.): DLT 2021, LNCS 12811, pp. 279–290, 2021.
https://doi.org/10.1007/978-3-030-81508-0_23

because the family of languages defined by GF(2)-grammars has good algebraic properties and is closed under symmetric difference.

Finally, GF(2)-grammars generalise the notion of parity nondeterminism to grammars. Recall that the most common types of nondeterminism that are considered in complexity theory are classical nondeterminism, which corresponds to the *existence* of an accepting computation, unambiguous nondeterminism, which corresponds to the existence of a *unique* accepting computation and parity nondeterminism, which corresponds to the *number of accepting computations being odd*.

In a similar way, classical and parity nondeterminism can be seen as two different generalisations of unambiguous nondeterminism: if the number of accepting computations is in the set $\{0, 1\}$, then it is positive (classical case) if and only if it is odd (parity case); the same is not true for larger numbers, of course.

The main result of this paper is Theorem 15, which establishes a strong necessary conditions on subsets of $a_1^* a_2^* \cdots a_k^*$ that are described by GF(2)-grammars. Theorem 14, a special case of Theorem 15, implies that there are no GF(2)-grammars for the languages $L_1 := \{ a^n b^m c^\ell \mid n = m \text{ or } m = \ell \}$ and $L_2 := \{ a^n b^m c^\ell \mid n \neq m \text{ or } m \neq \ell \}$.

As a consequence, both languages are inherently ambiguous. For L_1, all previously known arguments establishing its inherent ambiguity were combinatorial, mainly based on Ogden's lemma.

Proving inherent ambiguity of L_2 was a long-standing open question due to Autebert et al. [2, p. 375]. There is an interesting detail here: back in 1966, Ginsburg and Ullian fully characterised bounded languages described by unambiguous grammars in terms of semi-linear sets [9, Theorems 5.1 and 6.1]. However, most natural ways to apply this characterisation suffer from the same limitation: they mainly rely on words that *are not* in the language and much less on the words that *are*. Hence, "dense" languages like L_2 leave them with almost nothing to work with. Moreover, L_2 has an algebraic generating function, meaning that analytic methods cannot tackle it either. In fact, Flajolet [6], in his seminal work on analytic methods for proving grammar ambiguity, refers to inherent ambiguity of L_2 as to a still open question (see page 286).

2   Basics

We will use some algebraic notions very often in the text. The intended "theoretical minimum" is being familiar with concepts of rings, fields, polynomials, rational functions, formal power series and linear algebra over fields.

Let us recall the definition and the basic properties of GF(2)-grammars first. This section is completely based on already published work: the original paper about GF(2)-operations by Bakinova et al. [3] and the paper about basic properties of GF(2)-grammars by Makarov and Okhotin [10]. Hence, proofs are omitted.

GF(2)-grammars are built upon GF(2)-operations [3]: symmetric difference and a new operation called GF(2)-concatenation:

$$K \odot L = \{ w \mid \text{number of partitions } w = uv, \text{ with } u \in K \text{ and } v \in L, \text{ is odd} \}$$

Syntactically, GF(2)-grammars do not differ from ordinary grammars. However, in the right-hand sides of the rules, the normal concatenation is replaced with GF(2)-concatenation, whereas multiple rules for the same nonterminal correspond to symmetric difference of given conditions, instead of their disjunction.

Definition 1 ([3]). *A GF(2)-grammar is a quadruple $G = (\Sigma, N, R, S)$, where:*

- Σ *is the alphabet of the language;*
- N *is the set of nonterminal symbols;*
- *every rule in R is of the form $A \to X_1 \odot \cdots \odot X_\ell$, with $\ell \geqslant 0$ and $X_1, \ldots, X_\ell \in \Sigma \cup N$, which represents all strings that have an odd number of partitions into $w_1 \cdots w_\ell$, with each w_i representable as X_i;*
- $S \in N$ *is the initial symbol.*

The grammar must satisfy the following condition. Let $\widehat{G} = (\Sigma, N, \widehat{R}, S)$ be the corresponding ordinary grammar, with $\widehat{R} = \{ A \to X_1 \cdots X_\ell \mid A \to X_1 \odot \cdots \odot X_\ell \in R \}$. It is assumed that, for every string $w \in \Sigma^*$, the number of parse trees of w in $\widehat{G}$ is finite; if this is not the case, then G is considered ill-formed.

Then, for each $A \in N$, the language $L_G(A)$ is defined as the set of all strings with an odd number of parse trees from A in $\widehat{G}$.

Remark 2. There are several ways to get an ill-formed GF(2)-grammar. The most common one is caused by ε-s in derivations causing the number of parse trees for some words to be infinite. However, each well-formed GF(2)-grammar has an equivalent GF(2)-grammar in Chomsky normal form [3, Theorem 5]. Chomsky normal form has the very convenient property that all strings have a finite number of parse trees.

Remark 3. Every unambiguous grammar can be seen as a GF(2)-grammar that defines the same language.

Theorem A ([3]). *Let $G = (\Sigma, N, R, S)$ be a GF(2)-grammar. Then the substitution $A = L_G(A)$ for all $A \in N$ is a solution of the following system of language equations.*

$$ A = \bigoplus_{A \to X_1 \odot \cdots \odot X_\ell \in R} X_1 \odot \cdots \odot X_\ell \qquad (A \in N) $$

Multiple rules for the same nonterminal symbol can be denoted by separating the alternatives with the "sum modulo two" symbol ($\oplus$), as in the following example.

Example 4 ([3]). The following GF(2)-grammar defines the language $\{ a^\ell b^m c^n \mid \ell = m$ or $m = n$, but not both $\}$.

$$S \to A \oplus C \qquad\qquad A \to (a \odot A) \oplus B$$
$$B \to (b \odot B \odot c) \oplus \varepsilon \qquad\qquad C \to (C \odot c) \oplus D$$
$$D \to (a \odot D \odot b) \oplus \varepsilon$$

Indeed, each string $a^\ell b^m c^n$ with $\ell = m$ or with $m = n$ has one or two parse trees, and there are two canceling out parse trees exactly when $\ell = m = n$.

Example 5 ([3]). The following grammar describes the language $\{\, a^{2^n} \mid n \geqslant 0 \,\}$:

$$S \rightarrow (S \odot S) \oplus a.$$

By Theorem A, the language S satisfies equation $S = (S \odot S) \oplus a$. The main idea behind this grammar is that the GF(2)-square over a unary alphabet doubles the length of each string: $L \odot L = \{\, a^{2\ell} \mid a^{\ell} \in L \,\}$. The grammar iterates this doubling to produce all powers of two.

As the previous example illustrates, GF(2)-grammars can describe non-regular unary languages, unlike ordinary grammars. We will need the classification of unary languages describable by GF(2)-grammars in the following Sections.

Definition 6. *A set of natural numbers $S \subseteq \mathbb{N}$ is called q-automatic [1] if there exists a deterministic finite automaton over the alphabet $\Sigma_q = \{0, 1, \ldots, q-1\}$ recognizing base-q representations of these numbers.*

Definition 7. *Similarly, a language L over a unary alphabet is 2-automatic if and only if the corresponding set $\{\, |w| \mid w \in L \,\}$ is 2-automatic.*

Let $\mathbb{F}_q[t_1, t_2, \ldots, t_k]$ denote the ring of polynomials in variables $t_1, t_2, \ldots, t_k$ over the q-element field GF(q), and let $\mathbb{F}_q[[t_1, t_2, \ldots, t_k]]$ denote the ring of formal power series in the same variables over the same field.

Definition 8. *A formal power series $f \in \mathbb{F}_q[[t]]$ is said to be algebraic if there exists a non-zero polynomial P with coefficients from $\mathbb{F}_q[t]$, such that $P(f) = 0$.*

Theorem B (Christol's theorem for GF(2) [5]). *Formal power series $f = \sum_{n=0}^{\infty} f_n t^n \in \mathbb{F}_2[[t]]$ is algebraic if and only if the set $\{\, n \in \mathbb{N}_0 \mid f_n = 1 \,\}$ is 2-automatic.*

Theorem C (GF(2) grammars pver unary alphabets [10]). *For a unary alphabet, the class of all 2-automatic languages coincides with the class of languages described by GF(2)-grammars.*

3   Subsets of a^*b^*

Suppose that some GF(2)-grammar over the alphabet $\Sigma = \{a, b\}$ generates a language that is a subset of a^*b^*. What does the resulting language look like?

It is convenient to associate subsets of a^*b^* with (commutative) formal power series in two variables a and b over the field $\mathbb{F}_2$. This correspondence is similar to the correspondence between languages over a unary alphabet with GF(2)-operations $(\odot, \oplus)$ and formal power series in one variable with multiplication and addition [10].

Formally speaking, for every set $S \subset \mathbb{N}_0^2$, the language $\{\, a^n b^m \mid (n, m) \in S \,\} \subset a^*b^*$ corresponds to the formal power series $\sum_{(n,m) \in S} a^n b^m$ in variables a and b. Let asSeries: $2^{a^*b^*} \rightarrow \mathbb{F}_2[[a, b]]$ denote this correspondence. Then asSeries($K \oplus$

$L) = \mathrm{asSeries}(K) + \mathrm{asSeries}(L)$, so symmetric difference of languages corresponds to addition of power series.

On the other hand, multiplication of formal power series does not *always* correspond to the GF(2)-concatenation of languages. Indeed, GF(2)-concatenation of subsets of a^*b^* does not have to be a subset of a^*b^*. However, the correspondence does hold in the following important special case.

Lemma 9. *If $K \subset a^*$ and $L \subset a^*b^*$, then $\mathrm{asSeries}(K \odot L) = \mathrm{asSeries}(K) \cdot \mathrm{asSeries}(L)$. The same claim holds when $K \subset a^*b^*$ and $L \subset b^*$.*

Proof (a sketch). Follows from definitions.

Let $\mathcal{A}$ denote the set of all algebraic power series from $\mathbb{F}_2[[a]]$. By Christol's theorem [5], $\mathcal{A}$ corresponds to the set of all 2-automatic languages over $\{a\}$. Similarly, let $\mathcal{B}$ denote the set of all algebraic power series from $\mathbb{F}_2[[b]]$.

Let $\mathbb{F}_2[a, b]$ denote the set of all polynomials in variables a and b by $\mathrm{poly}(a, b)$ and the set $\mathbb{F}_2(a, b)$ of all rational functions in variables a and b by $\mathrm{rat}(a, b)$. It should be mentioned that $\mathrm{poly}(a, b)$ is a subset of $\mathbb{F}_2[[a, b]]$, but $\mathrm{rat}(a, b)$ is not. Indeed, $\frac{1}{a} \in \mathrm{rat}(a, b)$, but $\frac{1}{a} \notin \mathbb{F}_2[[a, b]]$. The following statement is true: $\mathrm{rat}(a, b) \subset \mathbb{F}_2((a, b))$, where $\mathbb{F}_2((a, b))$ denotes the set of all *Laurent series* in variables a and b. Here, rational functions and Laurent series are defined as the fractions of polynomials and formal power series respectively (with equality, addition and multiplication defined in the usual way).

Definition 10. *Let $R_{a,b}$ denote the set of all Laurent series that can be represented as $\frac{\sum_{i=1}^{n} A_i B_i}{p}$, where n is a nonnegative integer, $A_i \in \mathcal{A}$ and $B_i \in \mathcal{B}$ for all i from 1 to n, and $p \in \mathrm{poly}(a, b)$, $p \neq 0$.*

It is not hard to see that $R_{a,b}$ is a commutative ring. However, a stronger statement is true:

Lemma 11. $R_{a,b}$ *is a field.*

Proof (outline). $R_{a,b}$ is the result of adjoining the elements of $\mathcal{A} \cup \mathcal{B}$, which are all algebraic over $\mathrm{rat}(a, b)$, to $\mathrm{rat}(a, b)$. It is known that the result of adjoining an arbitrary set of algebraic elements to a field is still a field.

4   The Main Result for Subsets of a^*b^*

Let us establish our main result about subsets of a^*b^*.

Theorem 12. *Assume that a language $K \subset a^*b^*$ is described by a GF(2)-grammar. Then the corresponding power series $\mathrm{asSeries}(K)$ is in the set $R_{a,b}$.*

Proof. Without loss of generality, the GF(2)-grammar G that describes K is in Chomsky normal form [3, Theorem 5]. Moreover, we can assume that K does not contain the empty string.

The language a^*b^* is accepted by the following DFA M: M has two states q_a and q_b, both accepting, and its transition function is $\delta(q_a, a) = q_a, \delta(q_a, b) = q_b, \delta(q_b, b) = q_b$.

Let us formally intersect the GF(2)-grammar G with the regular language a^*b^*, recognised by the automaton M (the construction of intersection of an ordinary grammar with regular expression by Bar-Hillel et al. [4] can be easily adapted to the case of GF(2)-grammars [10, Section 6]). The language described by the GF(2)-grammar will not change, because it already was a subset of a^*b^* before.

The grammar itself changes considerably, however. Every nonterminal C of the original GF(2)-grammar splits into three nonterminals: $C_{a \to a}$, $C_{a \to b}$ and $C_{b \to b}$. These nonterminals will satisfy the following conditions: $L(C_{a \to a}) = L(C) \cap a^*$, $L(C_{b \to b}) = L(C) \cap b^*$ and $L(C_{a \to b}) = L(C) \cap (a^*b^+)$. Also, a new starting nonterminal S' appears.

Moreover, every "normal" rule $C \to DE$ splits into four rules: $C_{a \to a} \to D_{a \to a}E_{a \to a}$, $C_{a \to b} \to D_{a \to a}E_{a \to b}$, $C_{a \to b} \to D_{a \to b}E_{b \to b}$ and $C_{b \to b} \to D_{b \to b}E_{b \to b}$.

The following happens with "final" rules: $C \to b$ turns into two rules $C_{a \to b} \to b$ and $C_{b \to b} \to b$, and $C \to a$ turns into one rule $C_{a \to a} \to a$. Finally, two more rules appear: $S' \to S_{a \to a}$ and $S' \to S_{a \to b}$.

For each nonterminal C of G, the languages $L(C_{a \to a})$ and $L(C_{b \to b})$ are 2-automatic languages over the unary alphabets $\{a\}$ and $\{b\}$ respectively. Indeed, every parse tree of $C_{a \to a}$ contains only nonterminals of type $a \to a$. Therefore, only the symbol a can occur as a *terminal* in the parse tree. So, $L(C_{a \to a})$ is described by some GF(2)-grammar over the alphabet $\{a\}$, and is therefore 2-automatic by Theorem C. Similarly, $L(C_{b \to b})$ is 2-automatic.

By Theorem A, the languages $L(C_{a \to b})$ for each nonterminal $C_{a \to b}$ of the new grammar satisfy the following system of language equations (System (1)).

Here, for each nonterminal C, the summation is over all rules $C \to DE$ of the original GF(2)-grammar. Also, end($C_{a \to b}$) denotes either $\{b\}$ or $\varnothing$, depending on whether or not there is a rule $C_{a \to b} \to b$ in the new GF(2)-grammar.

$$L(C_{a \to b}) = \text{end}(C_{a \to b}) \oplus \bigoplus_{(C \to DE) \in R} (L(D_{a \to a}) \odot L(E_{a \to b})) \oplus (L(D_{a \to b}) \odot L(E_{b \to b}))$$

$$(1)$$

It is easy to see that all GF(2)-concatenations on the right-hand sides satisfy the conditions of Lemma 9. For brevity, let Center(C), Left(C), Right(C) and final(C) denote asSeries($L(C_{a \to b})$), asSeries($L(C_{a \to a})$), asSeries($L(C_{b \to b})$) and asSeries(end($C_{a \to b}$)) respectively. Therefore, the algebraic equivalent of System (1) also holds:

$$\text{Center}(C) = \text{final}(C) + \sum_{(C \to DE) \in R} \text{Left}(D)\,\text{Center}(E) + \text{Center}(D)\,\text{Right}(E).$$

$$(2)$$

Let us look at this system as a system of $\mathbb{F}_2[[a, b]]$-linear equations over variables Center(C) = asSeries($L(C_{a \to b})$) for every nonterminal C of the original GF(2)-grammar.

We will consider final(C), Left(C) and Right(C) to be the coefficients of the system. While we do not know their *exact* values, the following is known: final(C) is 0 or b, Left$(C) \in \mathcal{A}$ as a formal power series that corresponds to a 2-automatic language over the alphabet $\{a\}$ and, similarly, Right$(C) \in \mathcal{B}$. That means that all coefficients of the system lie in $\mathcal{A} \cup \mathcal{B}$ and, therefore, in $R_{a,b}$. The latter is a field by Lemma 11.

Let n denote the number of nonterminals in the original GF(2)-grammar, (so there are n nonterminals of type $a \to b$ in the new GF(2)-grammar), a column vector of values Center(C) by x and a column vector of values final(C) in the same order by f. Let us fix the numeration of nonterminals C of the old GF(2)-grammar. After that, we can use them as "indices" of rows and columns of matrices.

Let I be the identity matrix of dimension $n \times n$, A be the $n \times n$ matrix with the sum of Left(D) over all rules $C \to DE$ of the original grammar standing on the intersection of C-th row and E-th column:

$$A_{C,E} := \sum_{(C \to DE) \in R} \text{Left}(D). \tag{3}$$

Similarly, let B be the $n \times n$ matrix with

$$B_{C,D} := \sum_{(C \to DE) \in R} \text{Right}(E). \tag{4}$$

Then the equation System (2) can be rewritten as $x = f + (A + B)x$ in matrix form. In other words, $(A + B + I)x = f$. Consider a homomorphism $h \colon \mathbb{F}_2[[a, b]] \to \mathbb{F}_2$ that maps power series to their constant terms (coefficients in $a^0 b^0$). Then $h(\det(A + B + I)) = \det(h(A + B + I)) = \det(h(A) + h(B) + h(I))$, where h is extended to the $n \times n$ matrices with components from $\mathbb{F}_2[[a, b]]$ in the natural way (replace each component of the matrix by its constant term). Because the new GF(2)-grammar for K is also in Chomsky normal form, all languages $L(C_{a \to a})$ and $L(C_{b \to b})$ do not contain the empty word. Therefore, all series Left$(C) = \text{asSeries}(L(C_{a \to a}))$ and Right$(C) = \text{asSeries}(L(C_{b \to b}))$ have zero constant terms. Hence, $h(A) = h(B) = \mathbf{0}$, where by $\mathbf{0}$ I mean the zero $n \times n$ matrix. On the other hand, $h(I) = I$. Hence, $h(\det(A + B + I)) = \det(h(A) + h(B) + h(I)) = \det(I) = 1$. Therefore, $\det(A + B + I) \neq 0$, because $h(0) = 0$.

Hence, the System (2) has exactly one solution within the field $\mathbb{F}_2((a, b))$ — the actual values of Center(C). Moreover, we know that all coefficients of the system lie in the field $R_{a,b} \subset \mathbb{F}_2((a, b))$. Therefore, all components of the unique solution also lie within the field $R_{a,b}$. Hence, asSeries$(K) = \text{asSeries}(L(S')) = \text{asSeries}(L(S_{a \to a})) + \text{asSeries}(L(S_{a \to b}))$ also lies in $R_{a,b}$.

5   Subsets of $a^* b^* c^*$

The language $\{\, a^n b^n c^n \mid n \geqslant 0 \,\}$ is, probably, the most famous example of a simple language that is not described by any ordinary grammar. Intuitively, it is not described by a GF(2)-grammar as well.

There is a natural one-to-one correspondence between subsets of $a^*b^*c^*$ and formal power series in variables a, b and c over field $\mathbb{F}_2$. Indeed, for every set $S \subset \mathbb{N}_0^3$, we can identify the language $\{ a^n b^m c^k \mid (n, m, k) \in S \} \subset a^*b^*c^*$ with the formal power series $\sum_{(n,m,k)\in S} a^n b^m c^k$. Let $\mathrm{asSeries}\colon 2^{a^*b^*c^*} \to \mathbb{F}_2[[a, b, c]]$ denote this correspondence. Then $\mathrm{asSeries}(L \oplus K) = \mathrm{asSeries}(L) + \mathrm{asSeries}(K)$. In other words, the symmetric difference of languages corresponds to the sum of formal power series.

Similarly to Lemma 9, $\mathrm{asSeries}(K \odot L) = \mathrm{asSeries}(K) \cdot \mathrm{asSeries}(L)$ in the following important special cases: when K is a subset of a^*, when K is a subset of a^*b^* and L is a subset of b^*c^*, and, finally, when L is a subset of c^*. Indeed, in each of these three cases, symbols "are in the correct order": if $u \in K$ and $v \in L$, then $uv \in a^*b^*c^*$.

Of course, nothing like this is true in the general case: if $K = \{b\}$ and $L = \{abc\}$, then $K \odot L = \{babc\}$ is not even a subset of $a^*b^*c^*$.

Denote the set of algebraic power series in variable c by $\mathcal{C}$, the set of polynomials in variables a and c by $\mathrm{poly}(a, c)$, et cetera.

Similarly to Definition 10, define $R_{a,c} \subset \mathbb{F}_2((a, c))$ and $R_{b,c} \subset \mathbb{F}_2((b, c))$. Finally, denote by $R_{a,b,c}$ the set of all Laurent series that can be represented as

$$\frac{\sum_{i=1}^{n} A_i B_i C_i}{p_{a,b} \cdot p_{a,c} \cdot p_{b,c}},$$

where n is a nonnegative integer, $A_i \in \mathcal{A}$, $B_i \in \mathcal{B}$, $C_i \in \mathcal{C}$ for all i from 1 to n, and $p_{a,b}$, $p_{a,c}$ $p_{b,c}$ are non-zero elements of $\mathrm{poly}(a, b)$, $\mathrm{poly}(a, c)$, $\mathrm{poly}(b, c)$.

Lemma 13. $R_{a,b,c}$ *is a subring of* $\mathbb{F}_2((a, b, c))$. *Moreover,* $R_{a,b}$, $R_{a,c}$ *and* $R_{b,c}$ *are subsets of* $R_{a,b,c}$.

Proof (a sketch). It is easy to see that $R_{a,b,c}$ is closed under addition and multiplication. Setting $C_1 = C_2 = \cdots = C_n = p_{a,c} = p_{b,c} = 1$ yields $R_{a,b} \subset R_{a,b,c}$. $\square$

6   The Main Result

Unlike $R_{a,b}$, $R_{a,b,c}$ *is not* a field (in fact, Theorem 16 tells us that $(1 + abc)^{-1} \notin R_{a,b,c}$), so a bit more involved argument will be necessary for the proof of the following theorem:

Theorem 14. *Suppose that* $K \subset a^*b^*c^*$ *is described by a GF(2)-grammar. Then the corresponding formal power series* $\mathrm{asSeries}(K)$ *is in the set* $R_{a,b,c}$.

Proof. The proof is mostly the same as the proof of Theorem 12. Let us focus on the differences. As before, we can assume that K does not contain the empty word.

In the same manner, we formally intersect our GF(2)-grammar in Chomsky's normal form with the language $a^*b^*c^*$. Now, all nonterminals C of the original GF(2)-grammar split into *six* nonterminals: $C_{a\to a}, C_{a\to b}, C_{a\to c}, C_{b\to b} C_{b\to c}$ and

$C_{c \to c}$. However, their meanings stay the same: for example, $L(C_{a \to b}) = L(C) \cap (a^* b^+)$ and $L(C_{a \to c}) = L(C) \cap (a^* b^* c^+)$.

However, only the "central" nonterminals $C_{a \to c}$ are important, similarly to the nonterminals of the type $a \to b$ in the proof of Theorem 12. Why? Before, we had some a priori knowledge about the languages $L(C_{a \to a})$ and $L(C_{b \to b})$ from Christol's theorem. But now, because of Theorem 12, we have a priori knowledge about the languages $L(C_{a \to b})$ and $L(C_{b \to c})$ as well, because they are subsets of $a^* b^*$ and $b^* c^*$ respectively. In a sense, we used Theorem C as a stepping stone towards the proof of Theorem 12, and now we can use Theorem 12 as a stepping stone towards the proof of Theorem 14.

Let $end(C)$ denote the language $\left(\bigoplus_{(C \to DE) \in R} L(D_{a \to b}) \odot L(E_{b \to c}) \right) \oplus T_C$,

where T_C is either $\{c\}$ or $\varnothing$, depending on whether or not there is a "final" rule $C_{a \to c} \to c$ in the new GF(2)-grammar.

This means that we again can express the values asSeries($L(C_{a \to c})$) as a solution to a system of linear equations with *relatively simple* coefficients (denote asSeries($L(C_{a \to c})$) by Center(C), asSeries($L(C_{a \to a})$) by Left(C), asSeries($L(C_{c \to c})$) by Right(C) and asSeries($end(C)$) by final(C)):

$$\text{Center}(C) = \text{final}(C) + \sum_{(C \to DE) \in R} \text{Left}(D)\,\text{Center}(E) + \text{Center}(D)\,\text{Right}(E) \quad (5)$$

Here, the summation is over all rules $C \to DE$ of the original GF(2)-grammar. Similarly to the proof of Theorem 12, this system can be rewritten as $(A + B + I)x = f$, where x and f are column-vectors of Center(C) and final(C) respectively, while the matrices A and B are defined as follows:

$$A_{C,E} := \sum_{(C \to DE) \in R} \text{Left}(D),$$

$$B_{C,E} := \sum_{(C \to DE) \in R} \text{Right}(E).$$

Again, this system has a unique solution, because we can prove that $\det(A + B + I) \neq 0$ in the same way as before. Because $\det(A + B + I) \neq 0$, then, by Cramer's formula, each component of the solution, Center(S), in particular, can be represented in the following form:

$$\frac{\det(A + B + I, \text{but one of the columns was replaced by } f)}{\det(A + B + I)}.$$

The numerator of the above fraction is the determinant of some matrix, all whose components are in the ring $R_{a,b,c}$ by Lemma 13. The denominator, on the other hand lies in the field $R_{a,c}$, because all components of $A + B + I$ lie in $\mathcal{A} \cup \mathcal{C} \subset R_{a,c}$. Because $R_{a,c}$ is a field, the inverse of the denominator also lies in $R_{a,c}$. Hence, Center(S) is a product of an element of $R_{a,b,c}$ and an element of $R_{a,c}$. Hence, Center(S) $\in R_{a,b,c}$. Therefore, asSeries(K) = asSeries($L(S')$) = asSeries($L(S_{a \to a})$) + asSeries($L(S_{a \to b})$) + Center(S) also lies in the set.

Consider the case of larger alphabets. Let $\mathcal{A}_i$ be the set of all algebraic formal power series in variable a_i. Similarly to $R_{a,b,c}$, let $R_{a_1,a_2,\ldots,a_k}$ denote the set of all Laurent series that can be represented as $\dfrac{\sum_{i=1}^{n} A_{i,1} A_{i,2} \cdots A_{i,k}}{\prod\limits_{1 \leqslant i < j \leqslant n} p_{i,j}}$, for some $n \geqslant 0$,

$p_{i,j} \in \mathrm{poly}(a_i, a_j)$ and $A_{i,j} \in \mathcal{A}_j$.

Theorem 15. *If a language $K \subset a_1^* a_2^* \cdots a_k^*$ is described by a GF(2)-grammar, then the corresponding power series* asSeries(K) *is in the set $R_{a_1,a_2,\ldots,a_k}$.*

Proof (a sketch). Induction over k. The induction step is analogous to the way we used Theorem 12 in the proof of Theorem 14.

7   The Language $\{\, a^n b^n c^n \mid n \geqslant 0 \,\}$ and Its Relatives

In this subsection, we will use our recently obtained knowledge to prove that there is no GF(2)-grammar for the language $\{\, a^n b^n c^n \mid n \geqslant 0 \,\}$. It will almost immediately follow that there are no GF(2)-grammars for the languages $\{\, a^n b^m c^\ell \mid n = m \text{ or } m = \ell \,\}$ and $\{\, a^n b^m c^\ell \mid n \neq m \text{ or } m \neq \ell \,\}$ either.

Consider the formal power series asSeries$(\{\, a^n b^n c^n \mid n \geqslant 0 \,\}) = \sum\limits_{n=0}^{+\infty} a^n b^n c^n$.

For brevity, let f denote these series. Then $f = (1 + abc)^{-1}$.

It sounds intuitive that $(1 + abc)^{-1}$ "depends" on a, b and c in a way that the $R_{a,b,c}$ cannot capture; series in $R_{a,b,c}$ should "split" nicely into functions that depend only on two variables out of three. Now, let us establish that $f \notin R_{a,b,c}$ formally.

Theorem 16. *The language $\{\, a^n b^n c^n \mid n \geqslant 0 \,\}$ is not described by a GF(2)-grammar.*

Proof. Indeed, suppose that the language is described by a GF(2) grammar. Then, by Theorem 14,

$$f = \left(\sum_{i=1}^{n} A_i B_i C_i \right) /(pqr), \tag{6}$$

where $A_i \in \mathcal{A}, B_i \in \mathcal{B}, C_i \in \mathcal{C}$ for every i from 1 to n and, also, $p \in \mathrm{poly}(a,b)$, $q \in \mathrm{poly}(a,c)$ and $r \in \mathrm{poly}(b,c)$. Let us rewrite Equation (6) as $pqrf = \sum\limits_{i=1}^{n} A_i B_i C_i$ with an additional condition that none of p, q and r is zero: otherwise the denominator of the right-hand side of Equation (6) is zero.

For every formal power series of three variables a, b and c, we can define its *trace*: such subset of $\mathbb{N}_0^3$, that a triple (x, y, z) is in this subset if and only if the coefficient of the series in $a^x b^y c^z$ is one. Traces of equal power series coincide.

What do the traces of left-hand and right-hand sides of the equation $pqrf = \sum\limits_{i=1}^{n} A_i B_i C_i$ look like? Intuitively, the trace of the left-hand side should be near the diagonal $x = y = z$ in its entirety, because $pqrf$ is a polynomial pqr, multiplied by $f = \sum_{i=0}^{+\infty} a^i b^i c^i$. On the other hand, one can prove that the trace of the right-hand side is a finite union of disjoint sets of type $X \times Y \times Z$.

The formalisation of the above argument leads to the following lemma (proof omitted due to space limitations):

Lemma 17. *If traces of $\sum_{i=1}^{n} A_i B_i C_i$ and $pqrf$ coincide, then both are finite sets.*

Because $pqrf = \sum_{i=1}^{n} A_i B_i C_i$, the trace of $pqrf$ is finite by Lemma 17. In other words, $pqrf$ is a polynomial. Recall that $f = (1 + abc)^{-1}$, so $\frac{pqr}{1+abc}$ is a polynomial. Because the product of three polynomials p, q and r is divisible by an irreducible (and, therefore, prime) element $1 + abc$ of factorial ring $\mathbb{F}_2[a, b, c]$, one of them is also divisible by $1 + abc$. But this is impossible, because each of polynomials p, q and r is non-zero (here we used that condition, at last) and does not depend on one of the variables.

Therefore, there is no GF(2)-grammar for the language $\{\, a^n b^n c^n \mid n \geqslant 0 \,\}$.

Corollary 18. *The language $\{\, a^n b^m c^\ell \mid n = m \text{ or } m = \ell \,\}$ is not described by a GF(2)-grammar.*

Proof. Suppose that $\{\, a^n b^m c^\ell \mid n = m \text{ or } m = \ell \,\}$ is described by a GF(2)-grammar. Then $\{\, a^n b^n c^n \mid n \geqslant 0 \,\}$ also is, as symmetric difference of $\{\, a^n b^m c^\ell \mid n = m \text{ or } m = \ell \,\}$ and $\{\, a^n b^m c^\ell \mid n = m \text{ or } m = \ell, \text{ but not both} \,\}$. The latter language is described by a GF(2)-grammar, as Example 4 shows. Contradiction.

Corollary 19. *The language $\{\, a^n b^m c^\ell \mid n \neq m \text{ or } m \neq \ell \,\}$ is not described by a GF(2)-grammar.*

Proof. Otherwise $\{\, a^n b^n c^n \mid n \geqslant 0 \,\} = (a^* b^* c^*) \oplus \{\, a^n b^m c^\ell \mid n \neq m \text{ or } m \neq \ell \,\}$ would be described by a GF(2)-grammar as well.

We have just proven that the language $\{\, a^n b^m c^\ell \mid n = m \text{ or } m = \ell \,\}$ is not described by a GF(2)-grammar. Hence, it is inherently ambiguous. Previous proofs of its inherent ambiguity were purely combinatorial, mainly based on Ogden's lemma, while our approach is mostly algebraic.

More importantly, we proved that the language $\{\, a^n b^m c^\ell \mid n \neq m \text{ or } m \neq \ell \,\}$ is not described by a GF(2)-grammar, therefore inherently ambiguous. Inherent ambiguity of this language was a long-standing open question [2, p. 375].

8   Concluding Remarks

Firstly, note that it took us roughly the same effort to prove the inherent ambiguity of $\{\, a^n b^m c^\ell \mid n = m \text{ or } m = \ell \,\}$ and $\{\, a^n b^m c^\ell \mid n \neq m \text{ or } m \neq \ell \,\}$, despite the former being a textbook example of inherently ambiguous language and the latter not being known to be inherently ambiguous before.

Secondly, it *would be* possible to modify the argument in Subsect. 7 of this paper to use only Ginsburg's and Ullian's result instead of Theorem 14. However, I do not know how to discover such a proof without using algebraic intuition that comes from the proof that uses GF(2)-grammars.

Thirdly, the proofs of Theorems 12 and 14 start similarly to the reasoning Ginsburg and Spanier used to characterise bounded languages described by ordinary grammars [7,8], but diverge after taking some steps. This is not surprising; ordinary grammars have good monotonicity properties (a word needs only one parse tree to be in the language), but bad algebraic properties (solving systems of language equations is much harder than solving systems of linear equations). In GF(2)-grammars, it is the other way around: there are no good monotonicity properties, but algebraic properties are quite remarkable.

Finally, I want to thank Alexander Okhotin and anonymous reviewers from MFCS 2020, STACS 2021, ICALP 2021 and DLT 2021 conferences for numerous suggestions that made this paper look like it looks today.

References

1. Allouche, J.P., Shallit, J.: Automatic Sequences: Theory, Applications. Generalizations. Cambridge University Press (2003). https://doi.org/10.1017/CBO9780511546563
2. Autebert, J.M., Beauquier, J., Boasson, L., Nivat, M.: Quelques problèmes ouverts en théorie des langages algébriques. RAIRO - Theoretical Informatics and Applications - Informatique Théorique et Applications **13**(4), 363–378 (1979)
3. Bakinova, E., Basharin, A., Batmanov, I., Lyubort, K., Okhotin, A., Sazhneva, E.: Formal languages over GF(2). Information and Computation, p. 104672 (2020)
4. Bar-Hillel, Y., Perles, M., Shamir, E.: On formal properties of simple phrase-structure grammars. Zeitschrift für Phonetik, Sprachwissenschaft und Kommunikationsforschung **14**, 143–177 (1961)
5. Christol, G.: Ensembles presque periodiques k-reconnaissables. Theoret. Comput. Sci. **9**(1), 141–145 (1979). https://doi.org/10.1016/0304-3975(79)90011-2
6. Flajolet, P.: Analytic models and ambiguity of context-free languages. Theoret. Comput. Sci. **49**(2), 283–309 (1987). https://doi.org/10.1016/0304-3975(87)90011-9
7. Ginsburg, S., Spanier, E.: Bounded ALGOL-like languages. Trans. Am. Math. Soc. **113**, 333 (1964)
8. Ginsburg, S., Spanier, E.: Semigroups, Presburger formulas, and languages. Pacific Jo. Math. **16**, 285–296 (1966)
9. Ginsburg, S., Ullian, J.: Ambiguity in context free languages. J. ACM **13**, 62–89 (1966)
10. Makarov, V., Okhotin, A.: On the Expressive Power of GF(2)-Grammars. In: Catania, B., Královič, R., Nawrocki, J., Pighizzini, G. (eds.) SOFSEM 2019. LNCS, vol. 11376, pp. 310–323. Springer, Cham (2019). https://doi.org/10.1007/978-3-030-10801-4_25

Definability Results for Top-Down Tree Transducers

Sebastian Maneth[1], Helmut Seidl[2], and Martin Vu[1]($\boxtimes$)

[1] Universität Bremen, Bremen, Germany
{maneth,martin.vu}@uni-bremen.de
[2] TU München, Munich, Germany
seidl@in.tum.de

Abstract. We prove that for a given deterministic top-down transducer with look-ahead it is decidable whether or not its translation is definable (1) by a linear top-down tree transducer or (2) by a tree homomorphism. We present algorithms that construct equivalent such transducers if they exist.

1 Introduction

Tree transducers are fundamental devices that were invented in the 1970's in the context of compilers and mathematical linguistics. Since then they have been applied in a huge variety of contexts. The perhaps most basic type of tree transducer is the top-down tree transducer [13,14] (for short *transducer*). Even though top-down tree transducers are very well studied, some fundamental problems about them have remained open. For instance, given a (deterministic) such transducer, is it decidable whether or not its translation can be realized by a linear transducer? In this paper we show that indeed this problem is decidable, and that in the affirmative case such a linear transducer can be constructed.

In general, it is advantageous to know whether a translation belongs to a smaller class, i.e., can be realized by some restricted model with more properties and/or better resource utilization. The corresponding decision problems for transducers, though, are rarely studied and mostly non-trivial. One recent breakthrough is the decidability of one-way string transducers within (functional) two-way string transducers [1]. Even more recently, it has been proven that look-ahead removal for linear deterministic top-down tree transducers is decidable [10]. In our case, one extra advantage of linear transducers (over non-linear ones) is that linear transducers effectively preserve the regular tree languages—implying that forward type checking (where a type is a regular tree language) can be decided in polynomial time. For non-linear transducers on the other hand, type checking is DEXPTIME-complete [9,12].

The idea of our proof uses the canonical earliest normal form for top-down tree transducers [5] (to be precise, our proof even works for transducers with look-ahead for which a canonical earliest normal form is presented in [6]). A given canonical earliest transducer M produces its output at least as early as

© Springer Nature Switzerland AG 2021
N. Moreira and R. Reis (Eds.): DLT 2021, LNCS 12811, pp. 291–303, 2021.
https://doi.org/10.1007/978-3-030-81508-0_24

any equivalent linear transducer. From this we can deduce that if M is equivalent to some linear transducer, then it has two special properties:

1. M is *lowest common ancestor conform* (*lca-conform*) and
2. M is *zero output twinned*.

Lca-conformity means that if the transducer copies (i.e., processes an input subtree more than once), then the output subtree rooted at the lowest common ancestor of all these processing states may not depend on any other input subtree. Zero output twinned means that in a loop of two states that process the same input path, no output whatsoever may be produced. These properties are decidable in polynomial time and if they hold, an equivalent linear transducer can be constructed.

In our second result we prove that for a transducer (with regular look-ahead) it is decidable whether or not it is equivalent to a *tree homomorphism*, and that in the affirmative case such a homomorphism can be constructed. In order to obtain this result, we prove that whenever a transducer T is equivalent to a homomorphism, then any subtree of a certain height of any partial output of T is either ground, or effectively identical to the axiom of T. This property can again be checked in polynomial time, and if it holds a corresponding homomorphism can be effectively constructed.

For simplicity and better readability we consider total transducers (without look-ahead) in our first result though we remark that the result can be extended to partial transducers with look-ahead. All proofs for partial transducers with look-ahead are technical variations of the proofs for the total case and can be found in the extended version of this paper [11]. Note that our results also work for given bottom-up tree transducers, because they can be simulated by transducers with look-ahead [3].

2   Preliminaries

For $k \in \mathbb{N}$, we denote by $[k]$ the set $\{1, \ldots, k\}$. Let $\Sigma = \{e_1^{k_1}, \ldots, e_n^{k_n}\}$ be a *ranked alphabet*, where $e_j^{k_j}$ means that the symbol e_j has *rank* k_j. By Σ_k we denote the set of all symbols of Σ which have rank k. The set T_Σ of *trees over* Σ consists of all strings of the form $a(t_1, \ldots, t_k)$, where $a \in \Sigma_k$, $k \geq 0$, and $t_1, \ldots, t_k \in T_\Sigma$. We denote by $[a_i \leftarrow t_i \mid i \in [n]]$ the *substitution* that replaces each leaf labeled a_i by the tree t_i (where the a_i are distinct symbols of rank zero and the t_i are trees). The set $V(t)$ of nodes consists of λ (the root node) and strings $i.u$, where i is a positive integer and u is a node. E.g. for the tree $t = f(a, f(a, b))$ we have $V(t) = \{\lambda, 1, 2, 2.1, 2.2\}$. For $v \in V(t)$, $t[v]$ is the label of v, t/v is the subtree of t rooted at v, and $t[v \leftarrow t']$ is obtained from t by replacing t/v by t'. The *size* of a tree t, denoted by $|t|$, is its number of nodes, i.e., $|t| = |V(t)|$.

We fix the *set X of variables* as $X = \{x_1, x_2, x_3 \ldots\}$ and let $X_k = \{x_1, \ldots, x_k\}$. Let A, B be sets. We let $A(B) = \{a(b) \mid a \in A, b \in B\}$ and $T_\Sigma[S] = T_{\Sigma'}$ where Σ' is obtained from Σ by $\Sigma_0' = \Sigma_0 \cup S$. The set of *patterns* $T_\Sigma\{X_k\}$ is T_Σ plus all trees in $T_\Sigma[X_k]$ that contain each $x \in X_k$ exactly once, and in-order of the tree, e.g., $f(a, x_1, f(x_2, x_3))$ is a pattern. We say that a tree $t \in T_\Sigma[X_k]$, $k \geq 0$, is a *prefix* of t' if there are suitable trees $t_1, \ldots, t_k$ such that $t[t_1, \ldots, t_k] = t'$, where $t[t_1, \ldots, t_k]$ denotes the tree $t[x_i \leftarrow t_i \mid x_i \in X_k]$. By definition, any tree t is a prefix of itself. For trees t_1, t_2, $t_1 \sqcup t_2$ denotes the *maximal* pattern that is a prefix of t_1 and t_2. E.g. $f(a, g(a)) \sqcup f(b, b) = f(x_1, x_2)$ and $g(g(b)) \sqcup g(a) = g(x_1)$.

2.1 Transducers

A *deterministic total top-down tree transducer* T (or *transducer* for short) is a tuple $T = (Q, \Sigma, \Delta, R, A)$ where

- Q is a finite set of *states*,
- Σ and Δ are the ranked *input* and *output* alphabets, respectively, disjoint with Q,
- R is the *set of rules*,

and $A \in T_\Delta[Q(X_1)]$ is the *axiom*. For every $q \in Q$ and $a \in \Sigma_k$, $k \geq 0$, the set R contains exactly one rule of the form $q(a(x_1, \ldots, x_k)) \to t$, where $t \in T_\Delta[Q(X_k)]$ is also denoted by $\mathrm{rhs}_T(q, a)$. The *size* $|T|$ of T is $\sum_{q \in Q, \sigma \in \Sigma} |\mathrm{rhs}_T(q, a)| + |A|$. We say that T is *linear* if in the axiom and in each right-hand side, every variable occurs at most once. A transducer h with $|Q| = 1$ and axiom of the form $q(x_1)$ is called a *homomorphism*. As h has only one state, we write $h(a)$ instead of $\mathrm{rhs}(q, a)$. For $q \in Q$, we denote by $[\![q]\!]$ the function from $T_\Sigma[X]$ to $T_\Delta[Q(X)]$ defined as follows:

- $[\![q]\!](s) = \mathrm{rhs}(q, a)[q(x_i) \leftarrow [\![q]\!](s_i) \mid q \in Q, i \in [k]]$ for $s = a(s_1, \ldots, s_k)$, $a \in \Sigma_k$, and $s_1, \ldots, s_k \in T_\Sigma[X]$
- $[\![q]\!](x) = q(x)$ for $x \in X$.

We define the function $[\![T]\!] : T_\Sigma[X] \to T_\Delta[Q(X)]$ by $[\![T]\!](s) = A[q(x_1) \leftarrow [\![q]\!](s) \mid q \in Q]$, where $s \in T_\Sigma[X]$. For simplicity we also write $T(s)$ instead of $[\![T]\!](s)$. Two transducers T_1 and T_2 are *equivalent* if the functions $[\![T_1]\!], [\![T_2]\!]$ restricted to ground input trees are equal.

Example 1. Let $\Sigma = \{a^1, e^0\}$ and $\Delta = \{f^2, e^0\}$. Consider the transducers $T = (Q, \Sigma, \Delta, R, A)$ where $Q = \{q\}$, $A = f(q(x_1), q(x_1))$ and R consists of the rules

$$q(a(x_1)) \to f(q(x_1), q(x_1)) \text{ and } q(e) \to e,$$

and $T' = (Q', \Sigma, \Delta, R', A')$ where $Q' = \{q'\}$, $A' = q'(x_1)$ and R' consists of

$$q'(a(x_1)) \to f(q'(x_1), q'(x_1)) \text{ and } q'(e) \to f(e, e).$$

Clearly, it can be verified that both transducers are equivalent, i.e., both transducers transform a monadic input tree of height n with nodes labeled by a and e to a full binary tree of height $n + 1$ with nodes labeled by f and e. Additionally, we remark that T' is a homomorphism.

We say that a transducer T is *earliest* if $\bigsqcup\{[\![q]\!](s) \mid s \in T_\Sigma\} = x_1$ holds for all $q \in Q$. Informally this means that for each state $q \in Q$ there are input trees $s_1, s_2 \in T_\Sigma$ such that $[\![q]\!](s_1)$ and $[\![q]\!](s_2)$ have different root symbols. We call T *canonical earliest* if T is earliest and for distinct states q_1, q_2 it holds that a ground tree s exists such that $[\![q_1]\!](s) \neq [\![q_2]\!](s)$.

Consider the transducers in Example 1. Clearly, T' is not canonical earliest as for all input trees s' the root symbol of $[\![q']\!](s')$ is f. The transducer T on the other hand is canonical earliest as the root symbol of $[\![q]\!](e)$ is e while for all $s \neq e$ the root symbol of $[\![q]\!](s)$ is f. We remark that canonicity of T is obvious as T has only one state.

Proposition 1 *[5, Theorem 16]. For every transducer T an equivalent canonical earliest transducer T' can be constructed in polynomial time.*

Intuitively, any transducer T' that is equivalent to a canonical earliest transducer T cannot generate "more" output than T on the same input. Therefore the following holds.

Lemma 1. *Let T and T' be equivalent transducers. Let T be canonical earliest. Let $s \in T_\Sigma[X]$. Then $V(T'(s)) \subseteq V(T(s))$ and if $T'(s)[v] = d \in \Delta$ then $T(s)[v] = d$ for all $v \in V(T'(s))$.*

3   From Transducers to Linear Transducers

In the following let T be a transducer with the same tuple as defined in Sect. 2.1 that is canonical earliest. We show that it is decidable in polynomial time whether or not there is a linear transducer T' equivalent to T and if so how to construct such a linear transducer.

Before we introduce properties which any canonical earliest transducer that is equivalent to some linear transducer must have, consider the following definitions. We call a non-ground tree $c \in T_\Sigma\{X_1\}$ a *context*. Let s be an arbitrary tree. For better readability we simply write cs instead of $c[x_1 \leftarrow s]$. Let v_1 and v_2 be distinct nodes with labels $q_1(x_1)$ and $q_2(x_1)$, respectively, that occur in $T(c)$, where $q_1, q_2 \in Q$. Then we say that q_1 and q_2 *occur pairwise in* T.

Next we show a transducer for which no equivalent linear transducer exists.

Example 2. Let T_0 be a canonical earliest transducer with axiom $f(q_1(x_1), q_2(x_1))$ and the following rules.

$$q_1(a(x_1)) \rightarrow g(q_1(x_1)) \quad q_2(a(x_1)) \rightarrow q_2(x_1)$$
$$q_1(e) \quad\quad \rightarrow e \quad\quad\quad\quad q_2(e) \quad\quad \rightarrow e$$
$$q_1(e') \quad\quad \rightarrow e' \quad\quad\quad\quad q_2(e') \quad\quad \rightarrow e'$$

Clearly, $T_0(a^n(x_1)) = f(g^n(q_1(x_1)), q_2(x_1))$ for all $n \in \mathbb{N}$. Assume that a linear transducer T' equivalent to T_0 exists. Clearly $T'(a^n(x_1))$ cannot be of the form $f(t_1, t_2)$, where t_1 and t_2 are some trees as otherwise either t_1 or t_2 must be ground due to the linearity of T'. This contradicts Lemma 1 as T_0 is canonical earliest. Hence, $T'(a^n(x_1)) = q'_n(x_1)$ holds for all $n \in \mathbb{N}$ where q'_n is some state. Thus, for all $k \in \mathbb{N}$ a "partial" input tree s exists such that the height difference of $T_0(s)$ and $T'(s)$ is greater than k. It is well known that the height difference of the trees generated by equivalent transducer on the same partial input tree is bounded [9]. Hence, T' cannot exist.

The reason why no linear transducer that is equivalent to the transducer T_0 in Example 2 exists, is because q_1 and q_2 occur pairwise and $[\![q_1]\!](a(x_1))$ and $[\![q_2]\!](a(x_1))$ are "loops of which at least one generates output". This leads us to our first property, which we call *zero output twinned*.

Let c be a context and q_1 and q_2 be pairwise occurring states. We write $(q_1, q_2)\vdash^c(q'_1, q'_2)$ if a node with label $q'_i(x_1)$ occurs in $[\![q_i]\!](c)$ for $i = 1, 2$ and either q_1 or q_2 *generate output on input* c, i.e., either $[\![q_1]\!](c) \neq q'_1(x_1)$ or $[\![q_2]\!](c) \neq q'_2(x_1)$ holds.

Definition 1. *Let q_1 and q_2 be pairwise occurring states of T. We say that T is zero output twinned if no context $c \neq x_1$ exists such that $(q_1, q_2)\vdash^c(q_1, q_2)$ holds.*

In other words, T is zero output twinned if there exists no context c such that $[\![q_1]\!](c)$ and $[\![q_2]\!](c)$ are loops and at least one of those loops generates output.

Lemma 2. *If T is equivalent to a linear transducer, then T is zero output twinned. It can be decided in time polynomial in $|T|$ whether or not T is zero output twinned.*

Consider the following transducer. Though this transducer is zero output twinned no equivalent linear transducer exists.

Example 3. Let $\Sigma = \{a^2, e^0\}$ and $\Delta = \{f^3, e_0^0, e_1^0, e_2^0, e_3^0\}$. Consider the canonical earliest transducer $T_0 = (Q, \Sigma, \Delta, R, A)$. Let $A = q_0(x_1)$ be the axiom of T_0 and

$$q_0(a(x_1, x_2)) \to f(q_1(x_1), q_2(x_2), q_3(x_1)) \quad q_0(e) \to e_0$$
$$q_i(a(x_1, x_2)) \to f(e_i, e_i, e_i) \qquad\qquad q_i(e) \to e_i,$$

where $i = 1, 2, 3$, be the rules of T_0. Clearly, it holds that $T_0(a(x_1, x_2)) = f(q_1(x_1), q_2(x_2), q_3(x_1))$. Note that as no loops occur in T_0, T_0 is zero output twinned. Assume that a linear transducer T' equivalent to T_0 exists. Analogously to Example 2, Lemma 1 and the linearity of T' yield that either $T'(a(x_1, x_2)) = q'(x_1)$ or $T'(a(x_1, x_2)) = q'(x_2)$ where q' is some state.

W.l.o.g. consider the former case. Let s_1, s_2 be distinct trees. Then $[\![q']\!](s_1) = T'(a(s_1, s_2)) = T_0(a(s_1, s_2)) = f([\![q_1]\!](s_1), [\![q_2]\!](s_2), [\![q_3]\!](s_1))$, which means that the tree generated by q_2 cannot depend on its input s_2. This contradicts the earliest property of T_0. Hence, T' cannot exist.

In the following we show that the situation described in Example 3 occurs if the transducer does not have the following property which we call *lowest common ancestor conform*.

First, we introduce some terminology. Let v, v' be nodes. Recall that by definition nodes are strings. Then v is an *ancestor* v' if v is a prefix of v'.

Furthermore, by the *lowest common ancestor* of nodes $v_1, \ldots, v_n$ we refer to the longest common prefix of those nodes. Let $s \in T_\Sigma\{X_k\}$. For $1 \le i \le k$, we denote by $\nu_T(s, x_i)$ the lowest common ancestor of all leaves of $T(s)$ that have labels of the form $q(x_i)$ where $q \in Q$. If T and s are clear from context we just write $\nu(x_i)$.

Definition 2. *The transducer T is called* lowest common ancestor conform (lca-conform *for short) if for an arbitrary input tree $s \in T_\Sigma\{X_k\}$, $k \in \mathbb{N}$, the output tree $T(s)$ is lca-conform. An output tree $T(s)$ is lca-conform if for all x_i such that $\nu_T(s, x_i)$ is defined, no leaf with label of the form $q(x_j)$, $j \ne i$, occurs in $T(s)/\nu_T(s, x_i)$.*

For instance, T_0 in Example 3 is not lca-conform because $\nu_{T_0}(a(x_1, x_2), x_1)$ is the root of $T_0(a(x_1, x_2)) = f(q_1(x_1), q_2(x_2), q_3(x_1))$ and this tree obviously contains $q_2(x_2)$. On the other hand, the transducer in Example 2 is lca-conform because its input trees are monadic.

Lemma 3. *If T is equivalent to a linear transducer, then T is lca-conform. It can be decided in time polynomial in $|T|$ whether or not T is lca-conform.*

Proof. We prove that T is lca-conform if T is equivalent to a linear transducer T'. For the second part of our statement we refer to [11].

Let $s \in T_\Sigma\{X_k\}$. Let v be a node such that $T'(s)[v] = q'(x_i)$ where q' is some state and $1 \le i \le k$. First, we show that the subtree $T(s)/v$ contains no leaves that have labels of the form $q(x_j)$ with $i \ne j$. Note that due to Lemma 1, $T(s)/v$ is defined.

Assume to the contrary that $T(s)/v$ contains some node labeled $q(x_j)$, i.e., $T(s)[\hat{v}] = q(x_j)$ for some descendant $\hat{v}$ of v. Consider the trees $T'(s[x_i \leftarrow s'])$ and $T(s[x_i \leftarrow s'])$ where s' is some ground tree. Clearly $T(s[x_i \leftarrow s'])[\hat{v}] = q(x_j)$ and hence $T(s[x_i \leftarrow s'])/v$ is not ground. However $T'(s[x_i \leftarrow s'])/v = [\![q']\!](s')$ is ground. This contradicts Lemma 1. Thus we deduce that for all $v \in V(T'(s))$ if $T'(s)/v = q'(x_i)$ then only leaves with labels in Δ or with labels of the form $q(x_i)$, $q \in Q$, occur in $T(s)/v$ (*).

We now show that if leaves with label of the form $q(x_i)$ occur in $T(s)$ then v is an ancestor node of all those leaves. Assume to the contrary that some leaf $\tilde{v}$ with label of the form $q(x_i)$ occurs in $T(s)$ that is not a descendant of v. Due to Lemma 1 it is clear that either $\tilde{v} \notin V(T'(s))$ or $T'(s)[\tilde{v}]$ is not labeled by a symbol in Δ. In both cases, some ancestor of $\tilde{v}$ must have label of the form $q'(x_j)$ in $T'(s)$ otherwise T and T' cannot be equivalent. Note that by definition any node is an ancestor of itself. As $\tilde{v}$ is not a descendant of v, $T'(s)[v] = q'(x_i)$ and T' is linear, we conclude that $x_i \ne x_j$ which contradicts (*). Thus, we conclude that v is a common ancestor of all leaves with label of the form $q(x_i)$ in $T(s)$.

As $T(s)/v$ does not contain leaves that have label of the form $q(x_i)$ neither does $T(s)/\nu(x_i)$ as v is an ancestor of $\nu(x_i)$. Hence, $T(s)$ is lca-conform. $\square$

The next lemma is used to show that the following construction terminates.

Lemma 4. *Let T be lca-conform and zero output twinned. Let c be a context. Then $height(T(c)/\nu(x_1)) \leq (|Q|^2 + 1)\eta$, where $\eta = max\{height(rhs(q,a)) \mid q \in Q, a \in \Sigma\}$.*

3.1   Constructing a Linear Transducer

Subsequently, we give a construction which yields a linear transducer T' equivalent to a given canonical earliest transducer T if T is zero output twinned and lca-conform.

Assume in the following that the axiom A of T is not ground (the case that A is ground is trivial). By Lemma 1 the output of T is "ahead" of the output of any equivalent transducer on the same input tree. Therefore, the basic idea is the same as in [6] and [10]: we store the "aheadness" of T compared to T' in the states of T'. The states of T' are of the form $\langle t \rangle$, where t is a tree in $T_\Delta[Q] \setminus T_\Delta$ that has a height bounded according to Lemma 4. Furthermore, we demand that the root of t is the lowest common ancestor of all leaves of t labeled by symbols in Q. For such a state $\langle t \rangle$ we write $t[\leftarrow x]$ instead of $t[q \leftarrow q(x) \mid q \in Q]$ for better readability.

We define T' inductively. We define its axiom as $A' = c\langle t_0 \rangle(x_1)$, where c is a context and $t_0 \in T_\Delta[Q]$ such that $ct_0[\leftarrow x_1] = A$. Note that $t_0[\leftarrow x_1]$ is the subtree of A rooted at the lowest common ancestor of all nodes with labels of the form $q(x_1)$. We now define the rules of T'. Let $\langle t \rangle$ be a state of T' where $t = p[x_i \leftarrow q_i \mid q_i \in Q, i \in [n]]$ and $p \in T_\Delta[X_n]$. Let $a \in \Sigma_k$ with $k \geq 0$. Then, we define $\langle t \rangle(a(x_1, \ldots x_k)) \rightarrow p'[x_j \leftarrow \langle t_j \rangle(x_j) \mid j \in [k]]$ where $p' \in T_\Delta[X_k]$ such that

$$p'[x_j \leftarrow t_j[\leftarrow x_j] \mid j \in [k]] = p[x_i \leftarrow \text{rhs}(q_i, a) \mid i \in [n]]$$

and $t_j[\leftarrow x_j]$ is the subtree of $p[x_i \leftarrow \text{rhs}(q_i, a) \mid i \in [n]]$ rooted at the lowest common ancestor of all nodes with labels of the form $q(x_j)$. In the following we show that states of T' indeed store the "aheadness" of T compared to T'.

Lemma 5. *Assume that in our construction some state $\langle t \rangle$ has been defined at some point. Then a context c exists such that $T(c)/\nu(x_1) = t[\leftarrow x_1]$.*

Lemmas 4 and 5 yield that the height of any tree t such that $\langle t \rangle$ is a state of T' is bounded. Thus, our construction terminates. In [11] we further show that our construction is well defined (even for partial transducers with regular look-ahead) and that the transducer of our construction is indeed equivalent to the given transducer.

The construction and Lemmas 2 and 3 yield the following theorems.

Theorem 1. *Let T be a canonical earliest transducer. An equivalent linear transducer T' exists if and only if T is zero output twinned and lca-conform.*

Theorem 2. *Let T be a transducer. It is decidable in polynomial time whether or not an equivalent linear transducer T' exists, and if so T' can be effectively constructed.*

Using the results of [10] we show in [11] that our problem is decidable even for *partial transducer with regular look-ahead*.

Theorem 3. *Let M be a transducer with regular look-ahead. It is decidable whether an equivalent linear transducer T exists and if so, T can be effectively constructed.*

A transducer is *partial* if rhs, seen as a function is partial. We remark that while it can be decided in polynomial time whether or not for a given total transducer an equivalent linear transducer exists, the time complexity is double-exponential if the transducer is partial. This is because the canonical earliest normal can be constructed with that complexity [5]; the same holds in the presence of regular-look ahead.

Though for a given total transducer it is decidable in polynomial time whether or not an equivalent linear transducer exists, the linear transducer of our construction may be exponentially larger than the given transducer.

Example 4. Let $\Sigma = \{a^1, e^0\}$ and $\Delta = \{f^2, e,^0\}$. Let $T = (Q, \Sigma, \Delta, R, A)$ where $Q = \{q_0, \dots, q_9\}$, $A = q_0(x_1)$ and

$$q_i(a(x_1)) \rightarrow f(q_{i+1}(x_1), q_{i+1}(x_1)) \quad q_i(e) \rightarrow e$$
$$q_9(a(x_1)) \rightarrow f(e, e) \quad\quad\quad\quad q_9(e) \rightarrow e$$

where $i = 0, \dots, 8$ be the rules of R. The transducer T transforms a monadic tree $a^n e$ into a full binary tree of the same height if $n < 10$ and into a full binary tree of height 10 if $n \geq 10$. Clearly, T is canonical earliest. Furthermore, T is zero output twined as there are no loops and lca-conform as its input trees are monadic. We denote by t_j, $j = 0, \dots, 9$, the full binary tree of height j whose leaves are labeled by q_j and whose remaining nodes are labeled by f. The linear transducer our construction yields is $T' = (Q', \Sigma, \Delta, R', A')$ where $Q' = \{\langle t_j \rangle \mid j = 1, \dots, 9\}$, $A' = \langle t_0 \rangle(x_1) = \langle q_0 \rangle(x_1)$ and

$$\langle t_i \rangle(a(x_1)) \rightarrow \langle t_{i+1} \rangle(x_1) \quad\quad \langle t_i \rangle(e) \rightarrow t_i[q_i \leftarrow e]$$
$$\langle t_9 \rangle(a(x_1)) \rightarrow t_9[q_9 \leftarrow f(e, e)] \quad \langle t_9 \rangle(e) \rightarrow t_9[q_9 \leftarrow e]$$

where $i = 0, \dots, 8$ are the rules of R'. Informally, T' must delay its output until the leaf is read or until T' has verified that its input tree has height at least 10 due to its linearity. The argument is analogous to Example 2. Clearly, T' is exponentially larger than T as rhs($\langle t_9 \rangle, a$) alone has size 2^{10}.

4   When is a Transducer Equivalent to a Homomorphism?

In this section we address the question whether or not a given (total) transducer is equivalent to some homomorphism. In the following let T be a canonical earliest total transducer with the same tuple as defined in Sect. 2.1. If we consider the task of deciding whether or not a homomorphism h equivalent to T exists, then it is tempting to believe that h is equivalent to T iff the canonical earliest normal form of T has only one state. Interestingly, this is not the case.

Example 5. Let $\Sigma = \{a^1, e^0\}$ and T_1 be defined with the axiom $f(q_1(x_1), q_2(x_1))$ and the rules

$$q_1(a(x_1))) \rightarrow f(q_1(x_1), q_2(x_1)) \quad q_2(a(x_1))) \rightarrow f(q_1(x_1), q_2(x_1))$$
$$q_1(e) \quad \rightarrow a \qquad\qquad\quad q_2(e) \quad \rightarrow b$$

Clearly T_1 is canonical earliest and equivalent to the homomorphism h with

$$h(a(x_1)) = f(h(x_1), h(x_1)) \quad h(e) = f(a, b)$$

This is rather surprising when considering *string transducers*, i.e., transducers restricted to monadic trees. It is known that canonical earliest string transducers are state-minimal, i.e., there is no equivalent string transducer with fewer states [8, Section 2.1.2] [2, Section 5]. Hence, the decision problem for string transducer corresponds to determining the equivalent canonical earliest string transducer.

While the general case is more complicated than expected (see Example 5), the decision problem is simple if the axiom of T is of the form $q_0(x_1)$.

Lemma 6. *Let T be a canonical earliest transducer with axiom $q_0(x_1)$. Whether or not an equivalent homomorphism h exists is decidable in linear time.*

Proof. If T has only one state, then T is by definition a homomorphism. If, on the other hand, T has more than one state, then there is no homomorphism equivalent to T. Assume to the contrary that there is a homomorphism h equivalent to T. Due to the equivalence of h and T, $h(s) = T(s) = [\![q_0]\!](s)$ holds for all $s \in T_\Sigma$. As T is earliest, there are trees $s_1, s_2 \in T_\Sigma$ such that $h(s_1) = [\![q_0]\!](s_1)$ and $h(s_2) = [\![q_0]\!](s_2)$ have different root symbols. Hence, h is earliest too. As h has only a single state it is obvious that h is a canonical earliest transducer. The existence of h contradicts the canonicity of T according to Theorem 15 of [5]. Clearly the number of states of T can be determined in linear time.   □

Subsequently, we therefore assume that the axiom of T is not of the form $q_0(x_1)$. Furthermore, we assume that the axiom is not ground as this case is trivial. Let $t_1 \in T_\Sigma[Q(X)]$ and $t_2 \in T_\Sigma[Q(X)]$. Denote by X_{t_1} and X_{t_2} the elements of X that occur in t_1 and t_2, respectively. We write $t_1 \simeq t_2$ if there is a bijection f from X_{t_1} to X_{t_2}, such that $t_2 = t_1[q(a) \leftarrow q(f(a)) \mid q \in Q, a \in X_{t_1}]$. We say that a tree $t \in T_\Sigma[Q(X)]$ is *subtree conform* to $t' \in T_\Sigma[Q(X)]$ if either (1) t is ground or, (2) $t \simeq t'$, or (3) $t = a[t_1, \ldots, t_k]$, $a \in \Sigma_k$, and t_i is subtree conform to t' for all $i \in [k]$.

Example 6. Consider the trees $t_1 = f(q_1(a_1), q_2(a_2))$, $t_2 = f(q_1(b_1), q_2(b_1))$, and $t_3 = f(q_1(a_3), q_2(a_3))$. Clearly $t_1 \not\simeq t_2$ as there is no suitable bijection, but $t_3 \simeq t_2$ holds. The tree $t = d(e, g(f(q_1(a_1), q_2(a_1))), f(q_1(a_2), q_2(a_2)))$ is subtree conform to t_2. While $t \not\simeq t_2$, its subtree e is ground, its subtree $g(f(q_1(a_1), q_2(a_1))$ is subtree conform to t_2 and for its last subtree, $f(q_1(x_2), q_2(x_2)) \simeq t_2$ holds.

Let T be an arbitrary canonical earliest transducer with the axiom A. In the following, we show that T is equivalent to a homomorphism h if and only if $T(a(x_1, \ldots, x_k))$ is subtree conform to A for all $a \in \Sigma$. Consider Example 5. The transducer T_1 is equivalent to the homomorphism h_1 and $T_1(a(x_1))$ and $T_1(e)$ are subtree conform to $f(q_1(x_1), q_2(x_1))$.

Lemma 7. *Let T be a canonical earliest transducer and A be the axiom of T. If T is equivalent to a homomorphism h, then $T(a(x_1, \ldots, x_k))$ is subtree conform to A for all $a \in \Sigma$.*

Lemma 8. *Let T be a transducer and A be its axiom. If $T(a(x_1, \ldots, x_k))$ is subtree conform to A for all $a \in \Sigma$, then T is equivalent to a homomorphism.*

Proof. We construct the homomorphism h as follows. Let $a \in \Sigma_k$, $k \geq 0$. If $T(a(x_1, \ldots, x_k))$ is ground, then we define $h(a(x_1, \ldots, x_k)) = T(a(x_1, \ldots, x_k))$. Otherwise, our premise yields $T(a(x_1, \ldots, x_k)) = t[x_j \leftarrow A(j) \mid j \in [k]]$ for a suitable $t \in T_\Delta[X_k]$ where $A(j) = A[q(x_1) \leftarrow q(x_j) \mid q \in Q]$. Then we define $h(a(x_1, \ldots, x_k)) = t[x_j \leftarrow h(x_j) \mid j \in [k]]$. We prove the equality of h and T in [11]. □

A homomorphism equivalent to a given transducer T exists, if and only if $T(a(x_1, \ldots, x_k))$ is subtree conform to A for all $a \in \Sigma$ due to Lemmas 7 and 8. In [11] we show that subtree conformity to A is decidable in polynomial time and that an equivalent homomrphism can be constructed in polynomial time in the affirmative case. Hence the following theorem holds.

Theorem 4. *The question whether a canonical earliest transducer is equivalent to a homomorphism is decidable in polynomial time. In the affirmative case, such a homomorphism can be constructed in polynomial time.*

Transducers with Regular Look-Ahead and Homomorphisms

We now consider partial transducers with regular look-ahead (or *la-transducers* for short). Such devices consist of a partial transducer and a *bottom-up tree automaton*, called the *look-ahead automaton* (or *la-automaton* for short). Informally, an la-transducer processes its input in two phases: First each input node is annotated by the active states of the bottom-up automaton at its children, i.e., an input node v labeled by $a \in \Sigma_k$ is relabeled by $\langle a, l_1, \ldots, l_k \rangle$ where l_i is the state the look ahead automaton arrives in when processing the i-th subtree of v. Using the information the relabeled nodes provide about their subtrees, the transducer then processes the relabeled tree.

The basic idea for answering the question whether there is an equivalent homomorphism for an arbitrary partial transducer M with regular look-ahead is as follows. Let Σ be the input alphabet of M. If M is equivalent to a homomorphism, a subset Σ' of Σ exists such that M is total if restricted to $T_{\Sigma'}$, i.e., $M(s)$ is defined for all $s \in T_{\Sigma'}$, and undefined for all trees in $T_\Sigma \setminus T_{\Sigma'}$. Let M' be M restricted to $T_{\Sigma'}$. Assume that a homomorphism h equivalent to M' exists, then there exists a transducer T equivalent to M'. (This is because h is by definition a transducer.) As M' is obviously total, we apply the decision procedure in [6] to determine whether T exists and to construct the transducer T as described in [6]—if affirmative. As T is total, we can determine the homomorphism h equivalent to T (and hence M') as described before. Clearly, a homomorphism equivalent to M can be obtained from h. For details on how to determine M' and proofs we refer to [11].

In [6] it is shown that for every total la-transducer one can construct an equivalent canonical earliest la-transducer. Thus, in the following assume that M' is canonical earliest. Note that in order to use the decision in [6] to construct a transducer T equivalent to M' we require a *difference bound* for M'. A difference bound is a natural number dif such that dif is an upper bound on the height of the *difference trees* of M'. Difference trees are defined as follows. Consider some context c over Σ and states l_1, l_2 of the la-automaton of M'. Intuitively, when processing cs, $s \in T_\Sigma$, T cannot make use of any annotations and hence does not know whether l_1 or l_2 would be reached by the la-automaton when processing s. Therefore, when processing c, T can at most generate the largest common prefix t of $M'(cl_1)$ and $M'(cl_2)$, where for $i = 1, 2$, $M'(cl_i)$ denotes output of M' when processing c with the information that its la-automaton reaches l_i when processing s. We formally prove this statement in [11]. Let v be a node such that $t[v] = x_1$, then $M'(cl_1)/v$ and $M'(cl_2)/v$ are called *difference trees* of M'. Intuitively, to simulate M', T has to store difference trees in its states, which means that if M' and T are equivalent, then only finitely many difference trees can exist. This in turn means that the height of all difference trees must be bounded. In the following we show that the difference bound of M' can be determined if M' is equivalent to a homomorphism h.

Lemma 9. *Let $l_1, \ldots, l_n$ be states of the la-automaton and $s_1, \ldots, s_n$ be trees of minimal height that reach these states. Let $i \in [n]$ such that $height(M'(s_i)) \geq height(M'(s_j))$, $j \neq i$, then, $height(M'(s_i))$ is a difference bound of M'.*

Using Lemma 9 we can easily determine dif $\in \mathbb{N}$ such that dif is an upper bound on the height of the difference trees of M' if a homomorphism equivalent to M' exists. Using dif we can apply Algorithm 44 of [6] to determine whether there is a transducer equivalent to M'. If Algorithm 44 of [6] yields "no" then obviously there cannot be a homomorphism equivalent to M'. If on the other hand Algorithm 44 yields a transducer T, then we have to test whether T and M' are truly equivalent. Equivalence of T and M' is decidable [9, Theorem 2]. We must test this equivalence because our input for Algorithm 44 of [6] may yield *false positives*. This occurs if there is no homomorphism equivalent to M' as in this case the difference bound obtained via Lemma 9 is potentially wrong which may cause Algorithm 44 to generate a transducer T that is not equivalent to M'. If our test yields that M' and T are not equivalent, then we output "no".

Otherwise we can determine whether there is a homomorphism h equivalent to T as described in the previous subsection.

Theorem 5. *It is decidable whether there is a homomorphism equivalent to a given la-transducer.*

5   Conclusions

We have proved that for a deterministic top-down tree transducer M with look-ahead, it is decidable whether or not its translation can be realized by a linear transducer (without look-ahead). We have further shown that for such a transducer M it is decidable whether or not its translation is realizable by a one-state transducer (called a tree homomorphism). In both cases, equivalent transducers in the respective subclass can be constructed if affirmative.

One may wonder whether our results can be generalized to larger classes of given transducers. It can easily be generalized to nondeterministic top-down tree transducers: first decide if the transducer is functional [7] and if so, construct an equivalent deterministic top-down tree transducer with look-ahead [4]. Note that the result of Engelfriet [4] shows that for any composition of nondeterministic top-down and bottom-up transducers that is functional, an equivalent deterministic top-down tree transducer with look-ahead can be constructed. This raises the question, whether or not for a composition of nondeterministic transducers, functionality is decidable. To the best of our knowledge, this is an open problem.

In future work, it would be nice to extend our result of deciding homomorphisms within deterministic top-down tree transducers, to the case that for a given k one decides whether an equivalent top-down tree transducer with k states exists (and if so construct such a transducer). This would offer a state-minimization method.

References

1. Baschenis, F., Gauwin, O., Muscholl, A., Puppis, G.: One-way definability of two-way word transducers. Log. Methods Comput. Sci. **14**(4) (2018)
2. Choffrut, C.: Minimizing subsequential transducers: a survey. Theor. Comput. Sci. **292**(1), 131–143 (2003)
3. Engelfriet, J.: Top-down tree transducers with regular look-ahead. Math. Syst. Theory **10**, 289–303 (1977)
4. Engelfriet, J.: On tree transducers for partial functions. Inf. Process. Lett. **7**(4), 170–172 (1978)
5. Engelfriet, J., Maneth, S., Seidl, H.: Deciding equivalence of top-down XML transformations in polynomial time. J. Comput. Syst. Sci. **75**(5), 271–286 (2009)
6. Engelfriet, J., Maneth, S., Seidl, H.: Look-ahead removal for total deterministic top-down tree transducers. Theor. Comput. Sci. **616**, 18–58 (2016)
7. Ésik, Z.: Decidability results concerning tree transducers I. Acta Cybern. **5**(1), 1–20 (1980)
8. Lhote, N.: Definability and synthesis of transductions. (Définissabilité et synthèse de transductions). Ph.D. thesis, University of Bordeaux, France (2018)
9. Maneth, S.: A survey on decidable equivalence problems for tree transducers. Int. J. Found. Comput. Sci. **26**(8), 1069–1100 (2015)

10. Maneth, S., Seidl, H.: When is a bottom-up deterministic tree translation top-down deterministic? In: ICALP, pp. 134:1–134:18 (2020)
11. Maneth, S., Seidl, H., Vu, M.: Definability results for top-down tree transducers (2021). https://arxiv.org/abs/2105.14860/
12. Perst, T., Seidl, H.: Macro forest transducers. Inf. Process. Lett. **89**(3), 141–149 (2004)
13. Rounds, W.C.: Mappings and grammars on trees. Math. Syst. Theory **4**(3), 257–287 (1970)
14. Thatcher, J.W.: Generalized sequential machine maps. J. Comput. Syst. Sci. **4**(4), 339–367 (1970)

The Hardest LL(k) Language

Mikhail Mrykhin$^{(\boxtimes)}$ and Alexander Okhotin

Department of Mathematics and Computer Science, St. Petersburg State University,
7/9 Universitetskaya nab., Saint Petersburg 199034, Russia
alexander.okhotin@spbu.ru

Abstract. This paper establishes an analogue of Greibach's hardest language theorem ("The hardest context-free language", *SIAM J. Comp.*, 1973) for the subfamily of LL languages. The first result is that there is a language L_0 defined by an LL(1) grammar in the Greibach normal form, to which every language L defined by an LL(1) grammar in the Greibach normal form can be reduced by a homomorphism, that is, $w \in L$ if and only if $h(w) \in L_0$. Then it is shown that this statement does not hold for LL(k) languages. The second hardest language theorem is then established in the following form: there is a language L_0 defined by an LL(1) grammar in the Greibach normal form, such that, for every language L defined by an LL(k) grammar, there exists a homomorphism h, for which $w \in L$ if and only if $h(w\$) \in L_0$, where $\$$ is a new symbol.

1 Introduction

Much of the computational complexity theory is centered around complete problems in complexity classes, which are as hard to decide as any problem from that class. The same notion is adapted for the complexity of parsing algorithms: some families of formal grammars have a *hardest language*, that is, a language defined by a grammar from some family, such that the problem of parsing every language from the family can be reduced to parsing for that single "hardest" grammar. The first and the most famous result of this kind is Greibach's [4] "hardest context-free language": this language is defined by a fixed grammar G_0 over an alphabet Σ_0, and for every grammar G over some alphabet Σ, there is a homomorphism $h_G \colon \Sigma^* \to \Sigma_0^*$, such that one can parse w in G by parsing $h_G(w)$ in G_0. Thus, the parsing complexity of context-free languages equals the complexity of parsing a single language, $L(G_0)$.

On the other hand, for one of the two most important families of languages with linear-time parsing, the *LR(k) languages*, Greibach [5] proved that there is no hardest language in this family, in the sense given above.

The existence of hardest languages under homomorphic reductions has been investigated for some further families of formal grammars. For the subclass of *linear grammars*, Boasson and Nivat [2] proved that there is no hardest language. For generalizations of ordinary ("context-free") grammars with Boolean

This work was supported by the Russian Science Foundation, project 18-11-00100.

N. Moreira and R. Reis (Eds.): DLT 2021, LNCS 12811, pp. 304–315, 2021.
https://doi.org/10.1007/978-3-030-81508-0_25

operations—*conjunctive grammars* [10,12] and *Boolean grammars* [11]—hardest languages do exist [13]. On the other hand, no hardest languages are possible for the intermediate family of *linear conjunctive languages* [9].

A few results of this kind are known for several families of automata. Čulík and Maurer [3] proved that there is no hardest regular language. For one-counter automata, non-existence of hardest languages was established by Autebert [1]. Recently, the authors constructed a hardest language for linear-time cellular automata [9].

This paper investigates the existence of hardest languages for the other classical language family parsable in linear time besides the LR(k) languages: *the LL(k) languages*, which are recognized by top-down parsers with a k-symbol lookahead. This family is not closed under inverse homomorphisms, see Lehtinen and Okhotin [8]. This example is revisited in Sect. 2 and modified to show the non-closure already for the lowest family in the hierarchy: the LL(1) grammars in Greibach normal form (these are "simple grammars" of Korenjak and Hopcroft [6]). This does not affect possible existence of hardest languages, but if they do exist, then their inverse homomorphic images would include languages beyond LL(k).

Indeed, in spite of this non-closure, there is a hardest language theorem: the first result of this paper, presented in Sect. 3, is that LL(1) grammars in the Greibach normal form have a hardest language with respect to reductions by homomorphisms. It is natural to try extending this result to the entire LL(k) hierarchy. An apparent obstacle is presented in Sect. 4: it is proved that already for the family of LL(1) languages, there is no hardest language under the strict definition of Greibach, that is, with respect to reductions by homomorphisms. This obstacle leads to a small modification of the definition of hardest languages: as shown in Sect. 5, if a single end-marker is appended to the input, then a hardest LL(k) language does exist.

2   LL Grammars

This paper is concerned with the ordinary kind of formal grammars, called "context-free" in the literature, and here referred to as simply *grammars*.

Definition 1. *A grammar is a quadruple $G = (\Sigma, N, R, S)$, where Σ is a finite alphabet; N is a finite set of nonterminal symbols; R is a finite set of rules, each of the form $A \to \alpha$, where $A \in N$ and $\alpha \in (\Sigma \cup N)^*$; and $S \in N$ is the initial nonterminal.*

The language generated by a grammar is defined in terms of *parse trees*, in which every internal node has an associated rule $A \to X_1 \ldots X_\ell \in R$, so that the node is labelled with A and has ℓ ordered children labelled with $X_1, \ldots, X_\ell$.

Definition 2. *Let $G = (\Sigma, N, R, S)$ be a grammar. The language defined by a nonterminal symbol A, denoted by $L_G(A)$, is the set of such all strings $w \in \Sigma^*$, that there exists a parse tree with A as a root and with the leaves forming the string w. The language defined by the grammar is $L(G) = L_G(S)$.*

For every string $w \in \Sigma^*$, let $\text{First}_k(w)$ denote the first k symbols of w, or the entire string w, if $|w| < k$.

Definition 3. *Let* $G = (\Sigma, N, R, S)$ *be a grammar. Consider a parse tree according to* G, *and a subtree therein. It is said that a string* $v \in \Sigma^*$ *follows this subtree, if the leaves of the tree to the right of this subtree form the string* v.

A string v *is said to* follow *a nonterminal* $A \in N$, *if there exists a tree with an* A-*subtree followed by* v. *The set of all such strings is denoted by* Follow(A).

$$\text{Follow}(A) = \{ v \mid v \in \Sigma^*, v \text{ follows } A \}$$

The *LL(k) grammars* are grammars, for which the membership of a given input string w in the language is recognized by a left-to-right parser of the following kind. The parser's configurations are pairs of the form (u, η), where $u \in \Sigma^*$ is an unread suffix of the input string, and the parser's stack contains the symbols $\eta \in (\Sigma \cup N)^*$. The parser has to determine whether the remaining suffix v of the input string uv is in $L_G(\eta)$, and accordingly attempts to parse v according to η. In a configuration $(u, A\eta)$, the parser sees only A and the first k symbols of u, and based on these data, it should deterministically select a rule $A \to \alpha$ and enter the configuration $(u, \alpha\eta)$. In a configuration $(au, a\eta)$, the next configuration is (u, η). In all other cases, an error is reported. The configuration $(\varepsilon, \varepsilon)$ is accepting.

A grammar is said to be LL(k), if the choice of a rule is always deterministic, that is, there exists the following function that determines the parser's actions.

Definition 4. *A grammar* $G = (\Sigma, N, R, S)$ *is said to be LL(k), if there exists a partial function* $T \colon N \times \Sigma^{\leqslant k} \to R$, *satisfying the following condition: whenever a parse tree has a subtree with root* $A \in N$, *and the rule applied to* A *is* $A \to \alpha$, *and the tree is followed by a string* v, *the table entry* $T(A, \text{First}_k(v))$ *must contain* $A \to \alpha$.

A language L is said to be an *LL(k) language* if it is defined by some LL(k) grammar.

Definition 5. *A grammar* $G = (\Sigma, N, R, S)$ *is said to be in the Greibach normal form if every rule is of the form* $A \to a\alpha$, *with* $a \in \Sigma$ *and* $\alpha \in (\Sigma \cup N)^*$. *Additionally, a rule* $S \to \varepsilon$ *is possible, as long as* S *does not occur on the right-hand sides of any rules.*

The LL(k) languages form a strict hierarchy with respect to k [7], and the Greibach normal form requirement costs one level in the hierarchy.

Theorem 1 (Rosenkrantz and Stearns [14]). *A language is defined by an LL(k) grammar if and only if it is defined by an LL(k + 1) grammar in the Greibach normal form.*

In view of this theorem, it is natural to extend the hierarchy by one level below: a language L defined by an LL(1) grammar in the Greibach normal form shall be called an *LL(0) language*. Such languages were first studied by Korenjak and Hopcroft [6], who called them "simple deterministic languages".

The family of LL(k) languages is not closed under inverse homomorphisms, this was proved by Lehtinen and Okhotin [8, Ex. 4] by constructing an LL(1) grammar G and a homomorphism h, for which $h^{-1}(L(G))$ is not defined by any LL(k) grammar. It is not difficult to modify this example to obtain an LL(0) language with the same property (to be presented in the full version of this paper).

3   The Hardest LL(0) Language

Theorem 2. *There exists such an LL(0) language L_0 over the alphabet $\Sigma_0 = \{a, b, c, \#\}$, that for every LL(0) language L over any alphabet Σ, there is such a homomorphism $h\colon \Sigma \to \Sigma_0^*$, that $L = h^{-1}(L_0)$ if $\varepsilon \notin L$, and $L = h^{-1}(L_0 \cup \{\varepsilon\})$ if $\varepsilon \in L$.*

It is convenient to begin with the construction of homomorphisms, and describe the language L_0 later.

Let L be defined by an LL(1) grammar $G = (\Sigma, N, R, X_1)$ in the Greibach normal form. Assume that the nonterminals of G are numbered as $X_1, \ldots, X_n$, and each rule is of the form $X_i \to sX_{j_1} \ldots X_{j_\ell}$, with $s \in \Sigma$, $\ell \geqslant 0$ and $i, j_1, \ldots, j_\ell \in \{1, \ldots, n\}$, For each $X_i \in N$ and $s \in \Sigma$, there is at most one such rule by the LL(1) condition, and it is convenient to assume that there is always exactly one rule. If a rule is missing, one can use a technical rule $X_i \to sX_{n+1}$, where X_{n+1} is a special "failure" nonterminal, with the following rules.

$$X_{n+1} \to aX_{n+1} \qquad\qquad (a \in \Sigma)$$

In the proposed encoding, the image $h(s)$ of a symbol s lists all rules beginning with s, for $X_1, X_2, \ldots, X_n$, in this exact order. The rules for the failure nonterminal are not listed. The encoding uses the alphabet $\Sigma_0 = \{a, b, c, \#\}$, in which the symbols have the following meaning.

- Symbols a are used to represent a reference to a nonterminal X_i as a^i.
- The symbol c represents *concatenation*. A rule $X_i \to sX_{j_1} \ldots X_{j_\ell}$ has the following encoding.

$$\rho(X_i \to sX_{j_1} \ldots X_{j_\ell}) = a^{j_\ell}c \ldots a^{j_1}c$$

In particular, a rule $X_i \to s$ is encoded as the empty string.
The encoding of X_i is given implicitly by the position of $\rho(X_i \to sX_{j_1} \ldots X_{j_\ell})$ within the image $h(s)$.
- A single symbol b is written in front of the definition of each X_i. Then, within each image $h(s)$, one can always find the definition of X_i after the first i instances of b.
- The separator symbol $\#$ concludes the image of every symbol.

Altogether, the image $h(s)$ of a symbol $s \in \Sigma$ lists the encodings of all rules $T(X_i, s)$, for each nonterminal symbol from X_1 to X_n.

$$h(s) = \left(\prod_{i=1}^{n} b\rho(T(X_i, s)) \right) \#$$

Example 1. Let $\Sigma = \{s, t\}$ and consider a grammar $G = (\Sigma, \{X, Y, Z\}, R, X)$, with the following rules.

$$X \to sXY \mid t$$
$$Y \to sYZ \mid t$$
$$Z \to s$$

This grammar defines all strings of the form $s^n t w_1 \ldots w_n$, where $n \geqslant 0$ and $w_1, \ldots, w_n \in \{ s^m t s^m \mid m \geqslant 0 \}$. A parse tree of the string $stst$ (that is, stw_1, with $w_1 = sts$) is given in Fig. 1.

Let the nonterminals in G be numbered as $X = X_1$, $Y = X_2$ and $Z = X_3$. Each of them has a rule beginning with s, and the image of s lists the encodings of these three rules.

$$h(s) = b \underbrace{a^2 cac}_{\rho(X \to sXY)} \; b \underbrace{a^3 ca^2 c}_{\rho(Y \to sYZ)} \; b \underbrace{}_{\rho(Z \to s)} \#$$

The encoding of the rule for Z is the empty string. For the other symbol t, the rules for X and for Y are listed as usual; as there is no rule for Z, it is replaced by an encoding of a non-existent rule $Z \to tX_4$.

$$h(t) = b \underbrace{}_{\rho(X \to t)} \; b \underbrace{}_{\rho(Y \to t)} \; b \underbrace{a^4 c}_{\text{no rule}} \#$$

The string $stst$ accordingly has the following image.

$$h_G(stst) = ba^2 cacba^3 ca^2 cb \# bbba^4 c \# ba^2 cacba^3 ca^2 cb \# bbba^4 c \# ba^2 cacba^3 ca^2 cb \#$$

Using the encoding h_G, the membership of a string w in $L(G)$ can be tested by analyzing $h_G(w)$. For the grammar and the string in Example 1, this is illustrated in Fig. 1.

To establish the theorem, it should be proved that this analysis of $h_G(w)$ can be carried out by an LL(1) grammar G_0 in the Greibach normal form, which defines a string $h_G(w)$ if and only if $w \in L(G)$. For strings not of the form $h_G(w)$, it is irrelevant whether G_0 defines them or not.

The desired grammar G_0 uses 5 nonterminal symbols: $N_0 = \{S_0, A, F, B, C\}$. The nonterminal symbol A is used to define strings of the form $\rho(r)x \# h(w)$, where $\rho(r)x\#$ is a suffix of an image $h(s)$ of some symbol $s \in \Sigma$, which begins with an encoded rule r of the grammar G, and $w \in \Sigma^*$ is a string defined by the

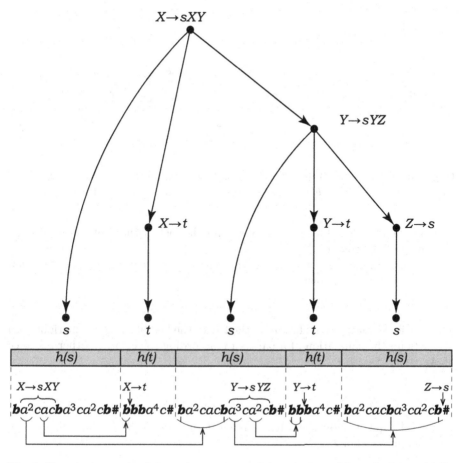

Fig. 1. How a parse tree of the string $w = ststs$ is reconstructed from its image $h(w)$.

rule r in G. To achieve this, the rules for A in G_0 attempt to parse the string $\rho(r)x\#h(w)$ to find out whether w can be parsed according to the rule r in G.

This is done by invoking A on two substrings of $\rho(r)x\#h(w)$, as illustrated in Fig. 2. Let the rule r be $X_i \to sX_{j_1} \ldots X_{j_\ell}$, encoded as $\rho(r) = a^{j_\ell}c \ldots a^{j_1}c$. The nonterminal symbol A should check that w is representable as a concatenation $w = uv$, where $u \in L_G(X_{j_1}) \cdot \ldots \cdot L_G(X_{j_{\ell-1}})$ and $v \in L_G(X_{j_\ell})$. The condition on u is checked by using the same nonterminal A on the substring $a^{j_{\ell-1}}c \ldots a^{j_1}cx\#h(u)$. In order to check the condition on v, one should locate the rule for X_{j_ℓ} in the image of the first symbol of v, and apply another instance of A to check whether v is defined by that rule.

The rule for X_{j_ℓ} is located in the image of v's first symbol as follows. By the definition of h, the rule for a nonterminal symbol X_j is always put in the j-th position in the image, and is preceded by exactly j instances of b. Thus, it is sufficient to match every a in the prefix a^{j_ℓ} with a block of symbols ending with

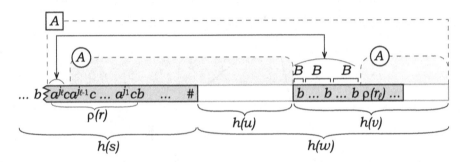

Fig. 2. How the symbol A decodes a parse of w by a rule $r = X_i \to sX_{j_1} \ldots X_{j_\ell}$ from an encoded string $\rho(r)x\#h(w)$, invoking two instances of A on its substrings.

b in the image of the first symbol of v, and the last of these blocks marks the beginning of the rule for X_{j_ℓ}.

In the grammar G_0, a block ending with a b is defined by a nonterminal symbol B using the following rules.

$$B \to aB \mid cB \mid b$$

The rule for A matches the first a on the left to the last block B on the right, and also sets up the simulation of a parse of v according to X_{j_ℓ} by another instance of A.

$$A \to aFBA$$

Every subsequent a on the left is matched to a block B on the right by the nonterminal symbol F.

$$F \to aFB$$

Once the prefix a^{j_ℓ} is exhausted, F invokes one more instance of A to parse u as a concatenation $L_G(X_1) \cdot \ldots \cdot L_G(j_{\ell-1})$.

$$F \to cA$$

This implements the parsing illustrated in Fig. 2. Once all nonterminal symbols on the right-hand side of the rule r are dealt in this way, it remains for the nonterminal A to skip the rest of the image $h(s)$ using the following rules.

$$A \to bC \mid \#$$
$$C \to aC \mid bC \mid cC \mid \#$$

It remains to define the rule for the initial symbol S_0. All it has to do is to skip the first b in the image of the first input symbol, and invoke the parsing of the entire string by the rule for X_1, written in the image right after the first b.

$$S_0 \to bA$$

The correctness statement for this construction reads as follows.

Lemma 1. *Let $G = (\Sigma, N, R, X_1)$ be an LL(1) grammar in the Greibach normal form with no empty rule, let $N = \{X_1, \ldots, X_{|N|}\}$, and let $h_G = h : \Sigma^* \to \Sigma_0^*$ be the homomorphism defined above. Let $G_0 = (\Sigma_0, N_0, R_0, S_0)$ be the grammar defined above. Then, a string $a^{i_\ell}c \ldots a^{i_1}cx\#h(w)$, with $x \in b\{a, b, c\}^* \cup \{\varepsilon\}$, $\ell > 0$, $i_1, \ldots, i_\ell > 0$, $w \in \Sigma^*$, is in $L_{G_0}(A)$ if and only if $i_1, \ldots, i_\ell \leqslant |N|$ and w is in $L_G(X_{i_1}) \cdot \ldots \cdot L_G(X_{i_\ell})$.*

From this, it is not hard to infer that a string $w \in \Sigma^*$ is in $L(G)$ if and only if $h(w)$ is in $L(G_0)$. This completes the proof of Theorem 2.

4   Non-existence Under Standard Definitions

So, the family of LL(0) languages contains a hardest language with respect to reductions by homomorphisms. It turns out that a similar result for LL(1) languages does not hold.

Theorem 3. *There does not exist any "hardest" LL(k) language L_0 over any alphabet Σ_0, such that for every LL(1) language $L \subseteq \Sigma^+$ there would be a homomorphism $h \colon \Sigma^* \to \Sigma_0^*$, such that $w \in L$ if and only if $h(w) \in L_0$.*

The proof is by contradiction: suppose there is such a hardest language, defined by an LL(k) grammar G_0. Then, a large alphabet Σ of size dependent on G_0 is constructed, and it is proved that the LL(1) language $\Sigma \cup \{aa \mid a \in \Sigma\}$ is not an inverse homomorphic image of $L(G_0)$. This is so, because an LL(k) parser reading $h(a)$ would need to push a sufficiently large encoding of a to the stack in order to match it against the second $h(a)$; and if the string ends abruptly, it notices that only k symbols in advance, which is too late to pop all the symbols stored in the stack.

5   Hardest Language for LL(k) Grammars

Theorem 4. *There exists such an LL(0) language L_0 over the alphabet $\Sigma_0 = \{a, b, c, d, e, @, \#, \$, \%\}$, that for every LL($k$) language L over any alphabet Σ, there is such a homomorphism $h \colon (\Sigma \cup \{\bot\}) \to \Sigma_0^*$, that $L\bot = h^{-1}(L_0)$.*

The construction starts similarly to the pure LL(0) case: let L be defined by an LL(k) grammar $G = (\Sigma, N, R, X_1)$ in the Greibach normal form, with $N = \{X_1, \ldots, X_n\}$, and with all rules of the form $X_i \to sX_{j_1} \ldots X_{j_k}$. Let $T \colon N \times \Sigma^{\leqslant k} \to R$ be the LL(k) table for G, which is a total function. For convenience, let X_{n+1} be an extra "failure" nonterminal, and assume that $T(X_i, p)$ always starts with the first symbol of p (unless $p = \varepsilon$, in which case it has to start with any terminal symbol as long as the rule $X_i \to \varepsilon$ is not present in G).

Whereas a parser for G can see the first k symbols of the input in the beginning of its computation, for the "hardest" parser, initially the images of all

312   M. Mrykhin and A. Okhotin

symbols but the first one cannot yet be seen. The idea behind the construction is to delay the simulation of any rules and use the time reading the first $k-1$ symbol images to store these symbols in a queue. Once the queue is filled with $k-1$ symbols and the image of the k-th symbol is processed, the "hardest" parser can determine the rule that would be used at the beginning of the original string.

The question is, how to implement this buffer of non-constant size in a fixed grammar G_0? Let $m = |\Sigma^{<k}|$ be the number of lookahead strings, and let them be enumerated as $\Sigma^{<k} = \{p_0 = \varepsilon, \ldots, p_{m-1}\}$. Each lookahead string p_j is encoded in symbol images in unary notation as d^j. The image $h(s)$ of a symbol $s \in \Sigma$ encodes, in particular, the operation of the queue by listing all pairs (j, j') with $p_j s = t p_{j'}$, where t is a single symbol that is pushed out of the queue. Then the "hardest" grammar can manipulate a queue with no prior bounds on its length and alphabet size.

There is another question: what would the "hardest" parser do when it reaches the end of the input with a buffer full of symbols? This was the problem investigated in Sect. 4. For a parser to handle this, some extra symbols are appended to the image of the string: this is the image $h(\bot)$ of the end-marker.

The images of the symbols in the new construction use all the symbols from the LL(0) case in the same way, and also adds a few more symbols necessary to manipulate the queue.

- Symbols d are used as d^j to represent a reference to a lookahead p_j that would be seen by the original parser $k-1$ positions before (bar the symbol which is being consumed by the parser; it is added at the next step, pushing the oldest symbol out of the other end of the queue).
- For every possible contents of the queue, all rules applied with this lookahead are grouped together, and a single symbol e is written in front of the block of rules for each lookahead. Then, within each image $h(s)$, one can always find the block corresponding to p_j after the first j instances of e.
- Following each rule, the new contents of the queue are encoded, and the symbol @ separates each rule from the following lookahead. The block of rules corresponding to a single lookahead string is encoded differently in the case of an underfull queue, when the next symbol is appended and no rules are applied, and of a full queue, when a rule is applied, and then the oldest symbol is discarded and a new one is appended.

$$\pi(p) = \begin{cases} bac@d^j, & p = p_j \in \Sigma^{<k} \\ \prod_{1 \leqslant j \leqslant n} \left(b\rho(T(X_i, p))@d^j \right), & p = tp_j \in \Sigma^k, \, t \in \Sigma \end{cases}$$

- The separator symbol $ is used in the image $h(\bot)$ of the end-marker in order to simulate the last $k-1$ steps of the original parser, and the final end-marker % concludes the parsing process.

Altogether, the image $h(s)$ of a symbol $s \in \Sigma$ lists the rule blocks for all possible lookahead strings.

$$h(s) = \pi(s)\left(\prod_{j=1}^{m-1} e\pi(p_j s) \right)\#$$

The final $k-1$ symbols are handled by the image $h(\bot)$ of the end-marker, which is split into $k-1$ "pseudo-images", each structured similarly to an image of a regular symbol, and consuming at most one symbol from the remaining queue. Define the final rule block of a lookahead string $p \in \Sigma^{<k}$ as follows:

$$\pi'(p) = \begin{cases} \prod_{1 \leqslant i \leqslant n} \left(b\rho(T(X_i, p))@d^j \right), & p = tp_j, t \in \Sigma \\ b\rho(T(S, \varepsilon))@, & p = \varepsilon \end{cases}$$

The pseudo-image is defined analogously to the image of a regular symbol.

$$h(\bot_1) = \pi'(\varepsilon) \Big(\prod_{j=1}^{m-1} e\pi'(p_j) \Big) \$,$$

Pseudo-images are then concatenated into the desired image $h(\bot) = h(\bot_1)^{k-1}\%$ of the end-marker.

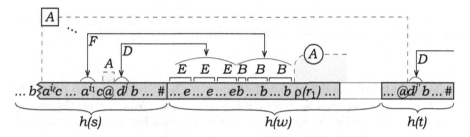

Fig. 3. How the symbol A decodes a parse of $\mathrm{First}_{|p_j wt|-(k-1)}(p_j wt)$ by a rule $r = X_i \to sX_{j_1} \ldots X_{j_\ell}$ from an encoded string $\rho(r)@d^j x\#h(w)y@$, using D to locate the block corresponding to the lookahead p_j.

To process the newly added lookahead blocks, the grammar has to be modified. Specifically, a new nonterminal D is added, which matches the lookahead encoding d^j in each symbol with symbols e in the next symbol, thus locating the correct block of rules, see Fig. 3.

The rules for A and for F, again, match symbols a on the left to blocks B on the right, and A also sets up the simulation of a parse of X_{j_ℓ} by another instance of A.

$$A \to aFBA$$
$$F \to aFB$$
$$B \to aB \mid cB \mid @B \mid dB \mid b$$

Once the prefix a^{j_ℓ} is exhausted, F invokes one more instance of A to recursively parse the concatenation $L_G(X_1) \cdot \ldots \cdot L_G(j_{\ell-1})$. This is where the key modification takes place: F also invokes a new nonterminal D, which ensures that the parser is always looking at rules in the blocks of correct lookahead strings.

$$F \to cAD$$

This is done similarly to the matching of nonterminal indices. This time, each symbol d in a unary encoding of a lookahead string in $h(s)$ it matched to a block in the image of the next symbol, represented by E.

$$D \to dDE$$
$$E \to aE \mid bE \mid cE \mid @E \mid dE \mid e$$

Once the matching of all consecutive d's is complete, the innermost D skips the rest of $h(s)$.

$$D \to bC \mid eC \mid \# \mid \$$$
$$C \to aC \mid bC \mid cC \mid dC \mid eC \mid @C \mid \# \mid \$$$

In this construction, A leaves all symbols d right after the rule along with the rest of $h(s)$ to D to process, and this point is marked by a symbol $@$.

$$A \to @$$

This concludes the modifications illustrated in Fig. 3. It remains to define the rule for the initial symbol S_0. It still has to skip the first b and invoke the parsing of the entire string by the rule for X_1, but now it also has to consume the part of $h(\bot)$ that is left behind because of A ending early.

$$S_0 \to bAU$$
$$U \to bT \mid eT \mid \$T$$
$$T \to aT \mid bT \mid cT \mid dT \mid eT \mid @T \mid \$T \mid \%$$

The correctness of the construction is proved in a lemma analogous to Lemma 1. The following lemma presents an abridged correctness statement referring to computations on the images of proper input symbols. Once the string itself runs out, the parsing continues inside $h(\bot_1)$ due to the processing delay, and there are two further cases stated similarly.

Lemma 2. *Let $G = (\Sigma, N, R, X_1)$ be a grammar in the Greibach normal form, with $N = \{X_1, \ldots, X_{|N|}\}$, let $h_G = h : (\Sigma \cup \{\bot_1\})^* \to \Sigma_0^*$ be the homomorphism defined above and $G_0 = (\Sigma_0, N_0, R_0, S_0)$ be the grammar defined above. Then a string $a^{i_\ell} c \ldots a^{i_1} c @ d^j x \# h(w) y @$, where $x \in \{b, e\}\{a, b, c, d, e, @\}^* \cup \{\varepsilon\}$, $\ell > 0$, $i_1, \ldots, i_\ell > 0$, $|p_j| = k - 1$, $w \in \Sigma^*$, and $y@$ is a prefix of $h(t)$, with $t \in \Sigma$, lies in $L_{G_0}(A)$ if and only if $i_1, \ldots, i_\ell \leqslant |N|$, the string $\mathrm{First}_{|p_j wt| - (k-1)}(p_j wt)$ is in $L_G(X_{i_1}) \cdot \ldots \cdot L_G(X_{i_\ell})$ and y contains exactly j' instances of e, followed by exactly i' instances of b, where $p_{j'} = \mathrm{Last}_{k-1}(p_j w)$ and $X_{i'}$ is the last nonterminal in the left-to-right derivation of $\mathrm{First}_{|p_j wt| - (k-1)}(p_j wt)$ in the aforementioned form.*

6   Conclusions

It has been proved that the LL(0) languages have a hardest language in the strict sense of Greibach, whereas a hardest language for the entire LL(k) hierarchy exists under a slightly relaxed definition. This raises a question on the existence of hardest languages under the relaxed definition for language families known not to contain hardest languages in the sense of Greibach.

Both results in this paper apply to language families not closed under inverse homomorphisms. The inverse homomorphisms closure of the hardest LL(0) language already contains a language outside of the LL hierarchy. It would be interesting to study this closure: are there any LR languages that it does not contain?

References

1. Autebert, J.: Non-principalité du cylindre des langages à compteur. Math. Syst. Theory **11**, 157–167 (1977)
2. Boasson, L., Nivat, M.: Le cylindre des langages linéaires. Math. Syst. Theory **11**, 147–155 (1977)
3. Culik, K. II, Maurer, H.A.: On simple representations of language families. RAIRO Theor. Informatics Appl. **13**(3), 241–250 (1979)
4. Greibach, S.A.: The hardest context-free language. SIAM J. Comput. **2**(4), 304–310 (1973)
5. Greibach, S.A.: Jump PDA's and hierarchies of deterministic context-free languages. SIAM J. Comput. **3**(2), 111–127 (1974)
6. Korenjak, A.J., Hopcroft, J.E.: Simple deterministic languages. In: 7th Annual Symposium on Switching and Automata Theory, Berkeley, California, USA, 23–25 October 1966, pp. 36–46. IEEE Computer Society (1966)
7. Kurki-Suonio, R.: Notes on top-down languages. BIT Numer. Math. **9**(3), 225–238 (1969)
8. Lehtinen, T., Okhotin, A.: Homomorphisms preserving deterministic context-free languages. Int. J. Found. Comput. Sci. **24**(7), 1049–1066 (2013)
9. Mrykhin, M., Okhotin, A.: On hardest languages for one-dimensional cellular automata. In: Leporati, A., Martín-Vide, C., Shapira, D., Zandron, C. (eds.) LATA 2021. LNCS, vol. 12638, pp. 118–130. Springer, Cham (2021). https://doi.org/10.1007/978-3-030-68195-1_10
10. Okhotin, A.: Conjunctive grammars. J. Autom. Lang. Comb. **6**(4), 519–535 (2001)
11. Okhotin, A.: Boolean grammars. Inf. Comput. **194**(1), 19–48 (2004)
12. Okhotin, A.: A tale of conjunctive grammars. In: Hoshi, M., Seki, S. (eds.) DLT 2018. LNCS, vol. 11088, pp. 36–59. Springer, Cham (2018). https://doi.org/10.1007/978-3-319-98654-8_4
13. Okhotin, A.: Hardest languages for conjunctive and Boolean grammars. Inf. Comput. **266**, 1–18 (2019)
14. Rosenkrantz, D.J., Stearns, R.E.: Properties of deterministic top-down grammars. Inf. Control. **17**(3), 226–256 (1970)

Upper Bounds on Distinct Maximal (Sub-)Repetitions in Compressed Strings

Julian Pape-Lange$^{(\boxtimes)}$ [iD]

Technische Universität Chemnitz, StraßE der Nationen 62, 09111 Chemnitz, Germany
julian.pape-lange@informatik.tu-chemnitz.de

Abstract. For $\delta \in \mathbb{R}^+$, maximal δ-repetitions (δ-subrepetitions) are fractional powers with exponent of at least $2+\delta$ (and $1+\delta$, respectively) which are non-extendable with respect to their minimum period.

In this paper, we prove that the number of distinct (unpositioned) maximal δ-repetitions in a string S with z LZ77-factors is bounded from above by $z \left\lfloor 3 + \frac{6}{\delta} \right\rfloor \cdot \left\lceil \log_{1+\frac{\delta}{4}}(|S|) \right\rceil$.

Also, the number of distinct (unpositioned) maximal q-th power-free δ-subrepetitions in a string S with z LZ77-factors is bounded from above by $z \left\lfloor 3 + \frac{4}{\delta} \right\rfloor \cdot \left\lceil \log_{1+\frac{\delta}{2q}}(|S|) \right\rceil$.

We further prove that for fixed δ and q, both upper bounds are asymptotically tight.

Keywords: Maximal repetitions · Maximal subrepetitions · Combinatorics on words · Compressed strings

1 Introduction

For a positive real number δ, a δ-repetition of a string S is a substring of the form P^q with $q \geq 2 + \delta$. Similarly, a δ-subrepetition of a string S is a substring of the form P^q with $q \geq 1+\delta$. These repetitions (subrepetitions) are maximal if there is an occurrence of the repetitions (subrepetitions) in the underlying string which cannot be extended in any direction without increasing the minimum period.

These repetitive patterns have a wide variety of applications from DNA analysis [8] over the analysis of Greek literature [17] to the analysis of musical scores [4]. Maximal repetitions on the one hand provide succinct information about more basic patterns like the powers in a string [5] and on the other hand give rise to more elaborate patterns like two-dimensional maximal repetitions [1].

It may seem arbitrary to discriminate between repetitions and subrepetitions based on whether the exponent is at least 2. However, while the repetitions yield a compact representation of the squares in the underlying string, the subrepetitions which are not repetitions may be squarefree and therefore provide no additional information about the squares. Furthermore, in repetitions each character has at least one copy which is given by the minimum period. On the contrary,

© Springer Nature Switzerland AG 2021
N. Moreira and R. Reis (Eds.): DLT 2021, LNCS 12811, pp. 316–327, 2021.
https://doi.org/10.1007/978-3-030-81508-0_26

subrepetitions with exponent less than 2 have the form $PP'P$ such that the minimum period does not necessarily provide copies of the characters in P'.

When Kolpakov and Kucherov proved in 1999 [13] that the number of positioned maximal repetitions is linear with regard to the length of the underlying string, the natural next question was: Does the upper bound for the positioned maximal subrepetitions with exponent greater than or equal to some constant c lead to another justification for the distinction between repetitions and subrepetitions?

Crochemore and Ilie state this question in [6] more precisely: For which δ is the number of positioned δ-repetitions bounded by the length of the underlying string? And for which δ is the number of positioned δ-subrepetitions still linear with respect to the length of the underlying string?

Both questions have subsequently been answered for uncompressed strings and it seems that the exponent 2 is not special with respect to the upper bounds. Bannai et al. present in [2] an elegant proof that the number of positioned repetitions is bounded by the length of the string. Holub improves this result in [11] and show that the number of positioned repetitions in binary strings is at most $\frac{183}{193}$ times the length of the string.

With regard to the linearity of positioned subrepetitions, Kolpakov et al. show in [14] that for all $\delta > 0$, the number of positioned maximal δ-subrepetitions is in $\mathcal{O}\left(\frac{n}{\delta^2}\right)$. This upper bound was improved independently by Crochemore et al. in [7] and Gawrychowski et al. in [10] who prove that even $\mathcal{O}\left(\frac{n}{\delta}\right)$ is an upper bound for the number of positioned maximal δ-subrepetitions.

We consider strings that have small compressed sizes with respect to the (self-referential) LZ77 compression. However, given the relationship of LZ77 to other strong compression schemes like grammar-compression (as proven simultaneously by Rytter in [18] and by Charikar et al. in [3]) and the run-length encoded Burrows-Wheeler transform (as proven independently by Kempa and Kociumaka in [12] and by Pape-Lange in [16]).

We should expect that there are few maximal (sub-)repetitions which are distinct as factors of the string but instead these factors have many occurrences. Therefore, in the compressed case, it is more natural to consider distinct unpositioned maximal (sub-)repetitions than to consider all different positioned maximal (sub-)repetitions. Also, since it doesn't significantly increases the size of the upper bounds, we will consider extended maximal δ-(sub-)repetitions which do not only include the δ-(sub-)repetition itself but also the first character in both directions which breaks the periodicity.

This approach has already led to Pape-Lange's non-trivial upper bounds for distinct maximal repeats in [15] and a special subset of maximal pairs in [16].

However, we cannot expect a polynomial bound which is only dependent on the number of LZ77-factors and the logarithm of the length of the string for all maximal repetitions with exponent greater than or equal to 2. Figure 1 shows the string $(ab)^n a(ab)^n a$. While this string can be factored in the 4 LZ77-factors $a \cdot b \cdot (ab)^{n-1} a \cdot (ab)^n a$, the number of maximal repetitions is linear with respect to

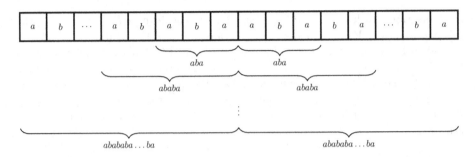

Fig. 1. The string $(ab)^n a(ab)^n a$ with its n distinct maximal repetitions with exponent 2.

the length of the string. Yet, if we only allow maximal repetitions with exponents greater than or equal to $2 + \delta$, there is an upper bound.

Theorem 1. *Let $\delta > 0$ be a real number.*

A string S with z LZ77-factors contains at most $z \lfloor 3 + \frac{6}{\delta} \rfloor \cdot \lfloor \log_{1+\frac{\delta}{4}}(|S|) \rfloor$ distinct unpositioned extended maximal δ-repetitions.

Surprisingly, if we limit the maximal power in the maximal subrepetitions, we obtain a similar upper bound for the maximal δ-subrepetitions.

Theorem 2. *Let $\delta > 0$ be a real number and q be a natural number.*

A string S with z LZ77-factors contains at most $z \lfloor 3 + \frac{4}{\delta} \rfloor \lfloor \log_{1+\frac{\delta}{2q}}(|S|) \rfloor$ distinct unpositioned extended q-th power-free maximal δ-subrepetitions.

Also, both of these theorems are asymptotically tight for fixed δ and q.

2   Preliminaries

A *string* of *length* $|S|$ is a concatenation $S = S[1]S[2]\ldots S[|S|]$ of *characters* of an *alphabet* Σ. We define $S[0] = \$$ and $S[|S| + 1] = \$$ with $\$ \notin \Sigma$. The *substring* $S[i..j]$ with $0 \le i \le j \le |S| + 1$ is the concatenation $S[i]S[i + 1]\ldots S[j]$. If $i > j$ holds, the substring $S[i..j]$ is the empty string. If $i = 1$ holds, the substring $S[i..j]$ is a *prefix* of S.

In this paper, (sub-)strings can be different in two ways. We say that two substrings $S[i..j]$ and $S[i'..j']$ are *different* (as positioned substring) if the starting positions i and i' or the ending positions j and j' differ. On the other hand, we say that two (sub-)strings $S[i..j]$ and $S[i'..j']$ are *distinct* (as factors or individual strings) if they have a different length or for some index k their k-th characters $(S[i..j])[k]$ and $(S[i'..j'])[k]$ are different.

For a string P and a rational number q with $q|P| \in \mathbb{N}_{\ge 0}$, the *$q$-th power* of P, denoted by P^q, is defined by the concatenation $PP\ldots PP[1..q|P| \mod |P|]$ of $\lfloor q \rfloor$ copies of P and the prefix of P with length $(q - \lfloor q \rfloor)|P|$. If q is a natural number and $q \ge 2$ holds, the q-th power is an *integer power*.

For $q \in \mathbb{N}$, a string S is q-th *power-free* if it has no non-empty substring of the form P^q.

A string S has a *period* $p > 0$ if all characters in S with distance p are equal. If S has a period p, the string S is p-*periodic*. The *minimum period* of S is the minimum of all periods of S. Note that S can be written as P^q such that P is a prefix of S, the length $|P|$ is the minimum period of S and $q = \frac{|S|}{|P|}$. With this notation, the prefix P cannot be an integer power.

We use the well-known periodicity lemma by Fine and Wilf from [9] to show that sufficiently long strings with two given periods also have their greatest common divisor as period.

Theorem 3 (Periodicity Lemma). *Let p_1 and p_2 be two positive natural numbers and S a p_1-periodic and p_2-periodic string with a length of at least $p_1 + p_2 - \gcd(p_1, p_2)$.*

Then S is $\gcd(p_1, p_2)$-periodic.

A substring $S[i..j]$ of S is a δ-*subrepetition*, if it is at least $1 + \delta$ times as long as its minimum period. If it is at least $2 + \delta$ times as long as its minimum period, it is a δ-*repetition*. A δ-(sub-)repetition P is maximal if it has an occurrence $S[i..j] = P$ such that both its left-extension $S[i - 1..j]$ or its right-extension $S[i..j + 1]$ have a greater minimum period, i.e. the minimum period neither extends to the left nor to the right. The *extended maximal δ-(sub-)repetition* of a positioned maximal δ-(sub-)repetition $S[i..j]$ is the substring $S[i - 1..j + 1]$.

The (self-referential) *LZ77-decomposition* of a string S is the factorization $S = F_1 F_2 \ldots F_z$ into *LZ77-factors* F_i such that each factor is either

- a single character which does not occur in $F_1 F_2 \ldots F_{i-1}$ or
- the longest prefix of $S[|F_1 F_2 \ldots F_{i-1}| + 1..|S|]$ which has an occurrence starting with one of the first $|F_1 F_2 \ldots F_{i-1}|$ characters in S.

By definition of the LZ77-decomposition, no first occurrence of a substring of length greater than 1 can be contained in a single LZ77-factor. Each extended maximal (sub-)repetition contains at least three characters. Therefore, we get the following corollary.

Corollary 1. *Let S be a string and let $F_1 F_2 \ldots F_z F_{z+1} = S\$$ be the LZ77-decomposition of $S\$$. Then each extended maximal (sub-)repetition of S has an occurrence in $\$S\$$ which contains the indices $s_i - 1$ and s_i for some starting index $s_i = 1 + |F_1 F_2 \ldots F_{i-1}|$ of an LZ77-factor F_i with $i > 1$.*

Note that we have to add another LZ77-factor to account for the appended \$. For example, in the string $S = a \cdot b \cdot bbbb \cdot abbb$, the substring bbb is a maximal 1-repetition because its occurrence $S[8..10]$ is not extendable. However, the substring bbb is fully contained in the fourth LZ77-factor.

On the other hand, we do not have to add another LZ77-factor for the prepended \$ and we can ignore the first LZ77-factor, because the first LZ77-factor F_1 always is a single character. Therefore, each maximal δ-(sub-)repetition which is also a prefix contains both the first character of the second LZ77-factor as well as the character before.

Corollary 1 allows us to obtain an upper bound for the number of distinct, unpositioned factors which are extended maximal δ-(sub-)repetitions from an upper bound for the number of different occurrences of extended maximal δ-(sub-)repetition which cross LZ77-factors.

3   Upper Bound for Maximal δ-Repetitions

In this section, we will prove the following upper bound for the number of distinct extended maximal δ-repetitions in a string S with z LZ77-factors which was stated in the introduction:

Theorem 1. *Let $\delta > 0$ be a real number.*

A string S with z LZ77-factors contains at most $z \left\lfloor 3 + \frac{6}{\delta} \right\rfloor \cdot \left\lceil \log_{1+\frac{\delta}{4}}(|S|) \right\rceil$ distinct unpositioned extended maximal δ-repetitions.

In order to prove this theorem, we will first locally count the different positioned extended maximal δ-repetitions around the boundaries of the LZ77-factors and then use Corollary 1 to show that the total number of distinct unpositioned extended maximal δ-repetitions is at most z times this local upper bound.

Theorem 4. *Let S be a string and $1 \leq t \leq |S| + 1$ be the index of a character of $S\$$.*

Then there are at most $\left\lfloor 3 + \frac{6}{\delta} \right\rfloor \cdot \left\lceil \log_{1+\frac{\delta}{4}}(|S|) \right\rceil$ different positioned extended maximal δ-repetitions $S[s_k..e_k]$ which contain the indices $t - 1$ and t.

The main idea of the proof is to use the pigeonhole principle in order to show that if more of these maximal δ-repetitions existed, there would be two of these repetitions which are neighbors in the following sense which is similar to the definition of neighboring runs introduced by Rytter in [19]:

There would be a real number L such that the minimum periods of the two δ-repetitions are in the interval $\left[L, \left(1 + \frac{\delta}{4}\right) L\right)$ and such that the intersection of these two δ-repetitions contains at least $\left(2 + \frac{\delta}{2}\right) L$ characters.

However, with the periodicity lemma we can show that maximal δ-repetitions cannot be that close together.

Lemma 1. *Let S be a string. Let $S[s_1..e_1]$ and $S[s_2..e_2]$ be different positioned maximal δ-repetitions of S with minimum periods p_1 and p_2, respectively. Let further L be a real number.*

Then at least one of the two periods p_1 and p_2 is not contained in the interval $\left[L, \left(1 + \frac{\delta}{4}\right) L\right)$ or the intersection contains less than $\left(2 + \frac{\delta}{2}\right) L$ characters.

Proof. Assume that neither of the two statements hold, i.e. the negations of both statements hold. Therefore, both $L \leq p_1, p_2 < \left(1 + \frac{\delta}{4}\right) L$ holds and the intersection of $S[s_1..e_1]$ and $S[s_2..e_2]$ contains at least $\left(2 + \frac{\delta}{2}\right) L - 1$ characters.

Since $p_1 + p_2 - \gcd(p_1, p_2) \leq p_1 + p_2 - 1 \leq \left(2 + \frac{\delta}{2}\right) L - 1$ holds, the intersection of the two maximal δ-repetitions is $\gcd(p_1, p_2)$-periodic. Furthermore, because

p_1 and p_2 are minimal, no substring of $S[s_1..e_1]$ of length p_1 and no substring $S[s_2..e_2]$ of length p_2 can be an integer power. Hence $p_1 = \gcd(p_1, p_2) = p_2$ holds.

However, since the intersection contains more than p_1 characters and the equation $p_1 = p_2$ holds, both $S[s_1..e_1]$ and $S[s_2..e_2]$ are the p_1-periodic extensions of this intersection and are therefore equal.

This however contradicts the prerequisite that the two maximal δ-repetitions are different and thereby concludes the proof.

Proof (Proof of Theorem 4). By contradiction:

Assume that there are $\lfloor 3 + \frac{6}{\delta} \rfloor \cdot \lfloor \log_{1+\frac{\delta}{4}}(|S|) \rfloor + 1$ different positioned extended maximal δ-repetitions $S[s_k..e_k]$ which contain the indices $t - 1$ and t.

Let p_k be the minimum period of the maximal δ-repetition $S[s_k..e_k]$ and let $q_k \geq 2 + \delta$ be the corresponding exponent. By construction, the inequality

$$p_k(2 + \delta) \leq p_k q_k \leq s_k + p_k q_k - 1 = e_k \leq |S|$$

holds. Hence, the inequality $1 \leq p_k \leq \frac{|S|}{2+\delta}$ holds as well.

Taking the logarithm on this inequality yields

$$0 = \log_{1+\frac{\delta}{4}}(1) \leq \log_{1+\frac{\delta}{4}}(p_k)$$

$$\leq \log_{1+\frac{\delta}{4}}\left(\frac{|S|}{2+\delta}\right) = \log_{1+\frac{\delta}{4}}(|S|) - \log_{1+\frac{\delta}{4}}(2 + \delta)$$

$$< \left\lceil \log_{1+\frac{\delta}{4}}(|S|) \right\rceil - 1$$

We sort the δ-repetitions with regard to the values $\log_{1+\frac{\delta}{4}}(p_k)$ into the intervals

$$[n, n + 1) \text{ with } n \in \left\{0, 1, 2, \ldots, \left\lceil \log_{1+\frac{\delta}{4}}(|S|) \right\rceil - 2 \right\}.$$

Since $\lceil x \rceil - 1 \leq \lfloor x \rfloor$ holds, this implies that we sort the $\lfloor 3 + \frac{6}{\delta} \rfloor \cdot \lfloor \log_{1+\frac{\delta}{4}}(|S|) \rfloor + 1$ δ-repetitions into at most $\lfloor \log_{1+\frac{\delta}{4}}(|S|) \rfloor$ sets.

Using the pigeonhole principle therefore shows that there is a natural number $L' \geq 0$ such that for

$$\left\lceil \left(\left\lfloor 3 + \frac{6}{\delta} \right\rfloor \cdot \left\lfloor \log_{1+\frac{\delta}{4}}(|S|) \right\rfloor + 1 \right) \frac{1}{\left\lfloor \log_{1+\frac{\delta}{4}}(|S|) \right\rfloor} \right\rceil$$

$$= \left\lfloor 3 + \frac{6}{\delta} \right\rfloor + \left\lceil \frac{1}{\left\lfloor \log_{1+\frac{\delta}{4}}(|S|) \right\rfloor} \right\rceil$$

$$= \left\lfloor 3 + \frac{6}{\delta} \right\rfloor + 1$$

of the maximal δ-repetitions the inequality $L' \leq \log_{1+\frac{\delta}{4}}(p_k) < L' + 1$ holds.

Exponentiating this inequality yields that there is a real number $L = \left(1 + \frac{\delta}{4}\right)^{L'} \geq 1$ such that $L \leq p_k < \left(1 + \frac{\delta}{4}\right) L$ holds for these $\lfloor 3 + \frac{6}{\delta} \rfloor + 1$ maximal δ-repetitions.

Since for each of these maximal δ-repetitions both $S[s_k..s_k + \lfloor(2+\delta)L\rfloor - 1]$ and $S[s_k..t-1]$ are prefixes of $S[s_k..e_k]$, we define

$$s_k' := \begin{cases} t - \lfloor(2+\delta)L\rfloor & \text{if } s_k < t - \lfloor(2+\delta)L\rfloor \\ s_k & \text{if } s_k \geq t - \lfloor(2+\delta)L\rfloor \end{cases}$$

and obtain the p_k-periodic substrings $S[s_k'..s_k' + \lfloor(2+\delta)L\rfloor - 1]$. Furthermore, all s_k' of the remaining $\lfloor 3+\frac{6}{\delta}\rfloor + 1$ maximal δ-repetitions are in the interval $[t - \lfloor(2+\delta)L\rfloor ..t]$.

Dividing this interval into $\lfloor 3 + \frac{6}{\delta}\rfloor$ subintervals of length

$$\frac{\lfloor(2+\delta)L\rfloor + 1}{\lfloor 3 + \frac{6}{\delta}\rfloor} < \frac{(2+\delta)L + 1}{2 + \frac{6}{\delta}} \leq \frac{(3+\delta)L}{(3+\delta)\frac{2}{\delta}} = \frac{\delta}{2}L,$$

we can use the pigeonhole principle again to show that there are at least

$$\left\lceil \left(\left\lfloor 3 + \frac{6}{\delta}\right\rfloor + 1\right) \frac{1}{\lfloor 3 + \frac{6}{\delta}\rfloor} \right\rceil = \left\lceil \frac{1}{\lfloor 3 + \frac{6}{\delta}\rfloor} \right\rceil + 1 = 2$$

maximal δ-repetitions $S[s_i..e_i]$ and $S[s_j..e_j]$ such that $|s_i' - s_j'| < \frac{\delta}{2}L$ and $s_i' \geq s_j'$ hold.

The intersection of these two maximal δ-repetitions contains the substring $S[s_i'..s_j' + \lfloor(2+\delta)L\rfloor - 1]$ and therefore has a length of at least

$$s_j' + \lfloor(2+\delta)L\rfloor - 1 - s_i' + 1 \geq \lfloor(2+\delta)L\rfloor - |s_i' - s_j'|$$

$$> \lfloor(2+\delta)L\rfloor - \frac{\delta}{2}L \geq \left(2 + \frac{\delta}{2}\right)L - 1$$

characters.

However, such two maximal δ-repetitions are a contradiction to Lemma 1. Hence, there are at most $\lfloor 3 + \frac{6}{\delta}\rfloor \cdot \left\lfloor \log_{1+\frac{\delta}{4}}(|S|)\right\rfloor$ different positioned extended maximal δ-repetitions $S[s_k..e_k]$ which contain the indices $t-1$ and t.

Corollary 1 and Theorem 4 then prove Theorem 1.

4   Upper Bound for Maximal δ-Subrepetitions

In this section we will show that with the additional information of the highest power in the string, we can also give a nontrivial upper bound for the number of distinct extended maximal δ-subrepetitions in a string S with z LZ77-factors. More formally, in this section we will prove the following theorem which was stated in the introduction:

Theorem 2. *Let $\delta > 0$ be a real number and q be a natural number.*

A string S with z LZ77-factors contains at most $z \lfloor 3 + \frac{4}{\delta}\rfloor \cdot \left\lfloor \log_{1+\frac{\delta}{2q}}(|S|)\right\rfloor$ distinct unpositioned extended q-th power-free maximal δ-subrepetitions.

As in the last section, we will first prove the local version of this theorem.

Theorem 5. *Let S be a string and $1 \leq t \leq |S| + 1$ be the index of a character of $S\$$. Let further q be a natural number.*

Then there are at most $\left\lfloor 3 + \frac{4}{\delta} \right\rfloor \cdot \left\lceil \log_{1+\frac{\delta}{2q}}(|S|) \right\rceil$ different positioned extended q-th power-free maximal δ-subrepetitions $S[s_k..e_k]$ which contain the indices $t-1$ and t.

Similarly to the last section, we will again use the pigeonhole principle in order to show that if more of these maximal δ-subrepetitions existed, two of them would be neighbors. However, for $\delta \leq 2$, the intersections will necessarily be shorter than two times the larger minimum period. Therefore, we will also require that the minimum periods are more similar than the minimum periods in the last section.

More formally, we will construct two maximal δ-subrepetitions whose minimum periods are in the interval $\left[L, \left(1 + \frac{\delta}{2q}\right)L\right)$ for some real number L and whose intersection contains at least $\left(1 + \frac{\delta}{2}\right)L$ characters.

However, if we allow subrepetitions with an exponent of 2 or less, this does not lead to a contradiction yet. Figure 1 shows a string with only 4 LZ77-factors and linearly many maximal repetitions which are all nested squares. Furthermore, the number of pairs of these maximal repetitions such that both the minimum periods and the starting indices differ by only 2 is also linear.

Instead, we will show that the neighboring maximal δ-subrepetitions only occur if we allow highly periodic substrings in these subrepetitions.

Lemma 2. *Let S be a string and let $S[s_1..e_1]$ and $S[s_2..e_2]$ be different positioned maximal δ-subrepetitions of S with minimum periods p_1 and p_2, respectively. Let further L be a real number and q be a positive natural number such that both periods p_1 and p_2 are contained in the interval $\left[L, \left(1 + \frac{\delta}{2q}\right)L\right)$ and such that the intersection of the two maximal δ-subrepetitions contains at least $\left(1 + \frac{\delta}{2}\right)L$ characters.*

Then the intersection of $S[s_1..e_1]$ and $S[s_2..e_2]$ contains a q-th power.

Proof. Define $s_{\max} := \max(s_1, s_2)$ and $e_{\min} = \min(e_1, e_2)$. Then, the intersection of $S[s_1..e_1]$ and $S[s_2..e_2]$ is given by $S[s_{\max}..e_{\min}]$.

Since the intersection of $S[s_1..e_1]$ and $S[s_2..e_2]$ contains more than p_1 characters and more than p_2 characters, the maximal δ-subrepetitions can be defined by this intersection as a substring and the period alone. Therefore, the periods p_1 and p_2 are different.

Let n be a natural number in the interval $\left\{0, 1, 2, \ldots, \left\lfloor \frac{q\delta - \delta}{2q} L \right\rfloor - 1\right\}$. The following inequality shows that the indices $s_{\max} + n$, $s_{\max} + n + \max(p_1, p_2)$ and $s_{\max} + n + \max(p_1, p_2) - \min(p_1, p_2)$ are contained in the intersection and hence, using the two periodicities, correspond to equal characters.

$$s_{\max} \leq s_{\max} + n$$
$$< s_{\max} + n + \max(p_1, p_2) - \min(p_1, p_2)$$
$$< s_{\max} + n + \max(p_1, p_2)$$
$$\leq s_{\max} + \left\lfloor \frac{q\delta - \delta}{2q} L \right\rfloor - 1 + \left\lfloor \left(1 + \frac{\delta}{2q}\right) L \right\rfloor$$
$$\leq s_{\max} + \left(\frac{q\delta - \delta}{2q} + 1 + \frac{\delta}{2q}\right) L - 1$$
$$\leq s_{\max} + \left(1 + \frac{\delta}{2}\right) L - 1$$
$$\leq e_{\min}$$

This implies that the first $\left\lfloor \frac{q\delta - \delta}{2q} L \right\rfloor + \max(p_1, p_2) - \min(p_1, p_2)$ characters of the intersection $S[s_{\max}..e_{\min}]$ are $(\max(p_1, p_2) - \min(p_1, p_2))$-periodic. Since both p_1 and p_2 are natural numbers in the interval $\left[L, \left(1 + \frac{\delta}{2q}\right) L\right)$, this difference $\max(p_1, p_2) - \min(p_1, p_2)$ is bounded from above by $\left\lfloor \frac{\delta}{2q} L \right\rfloor$.

Therefore, the first $\left\lfloor \frac{q\delta - \delta}{2q} L \right\rfloor + \max(p_1, p_2) - \min(p_1, p_2)$ characters of the intersection $S[s_{\max}..e_{\min}]$ are a power with exponent of at least

$$\frac{\left\lfloor \frac{q\delta - \delta}{2q} L \right\rfloor + \max(p_1, p_2) - \min(p_1, p_2)}{\max(p_1, p_2) - \min(p_1, p_2)} = \frac{\left\lfloor \frac{q\delta - \delta}{2q} L \right\rfloor}{\max(p_1, p_2) - \min(p_1, p_2)} + 1$$
$$\geq \frac{\left\lfloor \frac{(q-1)\delta}{2q} L \right\rfloor}{\left\lfloor \frac{\delta}{2q} L \right\rfloor} + 1$$
$$\geq \frac{\lfloor q - 1 \rfloor \left\lfloor \frac{\delta}{2q} L \right\rfloor}{\left\lfloor \frac{\delta}{2q} L \right\rfloor} + 1$$
$$= (q - 1) + 1$$
$$= q.$$

Hence, the intersection of $S[s_1..e_1]$ and $S[s_2..e_2]$ contains a q-th power.

The proof of Theorem 5 follows the same idea as the proof of Theorem 4 with the only exception that the contradiction is derived from Lemma 2 instead of Lemma 1. Also, in order to derive the contradiction, the maximal δ-subrepetitions have to be much closer together.

5 Tightness

In this section, we prove that for fixed δ and $q \leq \lceil \delta + 3 \rceil$ the upper bounds of Theorem 1 and Theorem 2 are, up to a constant factor, tight.

Theorem 6. *Let δ be a positive real number. For all positive integers z and c with $2\log_2(z) \leq c \leq z$, there is a string S*

- *with $\log_2(|S|) \in \Theta(c)$,*
- *with $\Theta(z)$ LZ77-factors,*
- *with $\Theta(cz)$ maximal δ-repetitions and*
- *without $\lceil \delta + 3 \rceil$-th powers.*

Note that this theorem proves the asymptotic tightness of both Theorem 1 and Theorem 2, since it fixes both δ and the maximal power so that both upper bounds simplify to

$$\#(\text{extended maximal } \delta\text{-(sub-)repetitions})$$
$$\in \mathcal{O}\left(\#(\text{LZ77-factors}) \cdot \log(\text{string length})\right)$$

Proof (Proof of Theorem 6). Define the power $q = \lceil \delta + 2 \rceil$ and the string

$$R = \left(\left(\ldots\left(\left(\sigma_1^q \sigma_2\right)^q \sigma_3\right)^q \ldots\right)^q \sigma_c\right)^q.$$

The string R consists of c different characters and c exponentiations. Therefore, it is easy to see that it decomposes into $2c$ LZ77-factors. Furthermore, the string R does not contain $(q+1)$-th powers and its length is bounded by $q^c \leq |R| < (q+1)^c$. Lastly, the string R contains the c distinct maximal δ-repetitions σ_1^q, $\left(\sigma_1^q \sigma_2\right)^q$, $\left(\left(\sigma_1^q \sigma_2\right)^q \sigma_3\right)^q$, ..., $\left(\left(\ldots\left(\left(\sigma_1^q \sigma_2\right)^q \sigma_3\right)^q \ldots\right)^q \sigma_c\right)^q$. Note that all of these maximal δ-repetitions are prefixes of R.

Define

$$S = \$_0 R[1..|R|]\$_1 R[2..|R|]\$_2 R[3..|R|]\$_3 \ldots R[z..|R|]\$_z.$$

Clearly, the string S does not contain any $(q+1) = \lceil \delta + 3 \rceil$-th powers.

Now, consider $R[s..|R|]$ for $1 < s \leq z$. For each $c' \geq \log_2(z) > \log_q(z)$, the maximal δ-repetition $\left(\left(\ldots\left(\left(\sigma_1^q \sigma_2\right)^q \sigma_3\right)^q \ldots\right)^q \sigma_{c'}\right)^q$ in R has a corresponding maximal δ-repetition in $R[s..|R|]$ which is obtained by removing the first $s-1$ characters from R. This implies that $R[s..|R|]$ has at least $c - \log(z)$ distinct maximal δ-repetitions. Since $2\log(z) \leq c$ holds, this proves that there are at least $\frac{c}{2}$ maximal δ-repetitions. Furthermore, all these described maximal δ-repetitions on all these substrings are distinct.

The separators $\$_i$ make sure that none of the maximal repetitions leaks into another copy of R. Therefore, the string S contains at least $n\frac{c}{2} \in \Theta(cz)$ maximal δ-repetitions. Since each separator needs one LZ77-factor, each copy of R, except for the first one, also needs exactly one LZ77-factor. Therefore, the string S decomposes into $2c + (z+1) + (z-1) \in \Theta(z)$ LZ77-factors. The length $|S|$ of the string S is equal to $z|R| - \frac{(z-1)z}{2} + z + 1$ and thereby bounded by

$$zq^c - \frac{(z-1)z}{2} + z + 1 \leq z|R| - \frac{(z-1)z}{2} + z + 1 \leq z(q+1)^c - \frac{(z-1)z}{2} + z + 1.$$

Since q only depends on the constant δ, this implies that $\log_2(|S|) \in \Theta(c)$.

This concludes the proof and thereby shows that Theorem 1 and Theorem 2 are asymptotically tight for fixed δ.

6   Conclusion

This paper proved that the number of distinct maximal δ-repetitions in compressed strings is bounded by a polynomial only dependent on the number of LZ77-factors, the logarithm of the string length and δ. If we further restrict the exponent of the highest power, we can extend this upper bound to maximal δ-subrepetitions.

While Theorem 6 only shows the tightness for unbounded alphabets, we can use the binary representation $\mathrm{bin}(i)$ of the number i with exactly $\lceil \log z \rceil$ bits in order to represent the $c_i := 20\,\mathrm{bin}(i)2$ and $\$_i := 21\,\mathrm{bin}(i)2$ on a ternary alphabet. Furthermore, we can represent the ternary numbers 0, 1 and 2 with 00, 01 and 11, respectively. It can be shown that Theorem 6 still holds under this binary representation.

Since $\log(1 + x)$ is approximately x for small values of x, for small δ and large q these upper bounds are $\mathcal{O}\left(\frac{z \log(|S|)}{\delta^2}\right)$ for the maximal δ-repetitions and $\mathcal{O}\left(\frac{qz \log(|S|)}{\delta^2}\right)$ for the maximal δ-subrepetitions.

In the uncompressed case, the upper bound for the number of maximal δ-subrepetitions had divisor of δ^2 as well [14], which could be improved to δ [7,10]. Therefore, it might be possible to improve this divisor in the compressed upper bounds as well.

Furthermore, while this paper uses the LZ77-decomposition because of its widespread use, we only use its property described in Corollary 1 for the upper bounds. Therefore, both of these bounds translate, up to a constant factor, to upper bounds using the slightly stronger notion of the string attractor.

References

1. Amir, A., Landau, G.M., Marcus, S., Sokol, D.: Two-dimensional maximal repetitions. Theor. Comput. Sci. **812**, 49–61 (2020). http://www.sciencedirect.com/science/article/pii/S0304397519304323, in memoriam Danny Breslauer (1968–2017)
2. Bannai, H., Inenaga, I.T.S., Nakashima, Y., Takeda, M., Tsuruta, K.: The "runs" theorem. SIAM J. Comput. **46**(5), 1501–1514 (2017). https://doi.org/10.1137/15M1011032
3. Charikar, M., Lehman, E., Liu, D., Panigrahy, R., Prabhakaran, M., Sahai, A., Shelat, A.: The smallest grammar problem. IEEE Trans. Inf. Theory **51**(7), 2554–2576 (2005). https://doi.org/10.1109/TIT.2005.850116
4. Crawford, T.: String matching techniques for musical similarity and melodic recognition. Comput. Musicology **11**, 73–100 (1998). https://ci.nii.ac.jp/naid/10012595883/en/
5. Crochemore, M., Iliopoulos, C., Kubica, M., Radoszewski, J., Rytter, W., Waleń, T.: Extracting powers and periods in a word from its runs structure. Theor. Comput. Sci. **521**, 29–41 (2014). http://www.sciencedirect.com/science/article/pii/S0304397513008621
6. Crochemore, M., Ilie, L.: Maximal repetitions in strings. J. Comput. Syst. Sci. **74**(5), 796–807 (2008). http://www.sciencedirect.com/science/article/pii/S0022000007001420

7. Crochemore, M., Kolpakov, R., Kucherov, G.: Optimal bounds for computing α-gapped repeats. In: Dediu, A.H., Janoušek, J., Martín-Vide, C., Truthe, B. (eds.) Language and Automata Theory and Applications, pp. 245–255. Springer International Publishing, Cham (2016)

8. Doi, K., et al.: Rapid detection of expanded short tandem repeats in personal genomics using hybrid sequencing. Bioinformatics **30**(6), 815–822 (2013). https://doi.org/10.1093/bioinformatics/btt647

9. Fine, N.J., Wilf, H.S.: Uniqueness theorems for periodic functions. Proc. Am. Math. Soc. **16**(1), 109–114 (1965). http://www.jstor.org/stable/2034009

10. Gawrychowski, P., Inenaga, I.T.S., Köppl, D., Manea, F.: Efficiently finding all maximal alpha-gapped repeats. In: Ollinger, N., Vollmer, H. (eds.) 33rd Symposium on Theoretical Aspects of Computer Science (STACS 2016). Leibniz International Proceedings in Informatics (LIPIcs), vol. 47, pp. 39:1–39:14. Schloss Dagstuhl-Leibniz-Zentrum fuer Informatik, Dagstuhl, Germany (2016). https://doi.org/10.4230/LIPIcs.STACS.2016.39

11. Holub, S.: Prefix frequency of lost positions. Theor. Comput. Sci. **684**, 43–52 (2017). https://www.sciencedirect.com/science/article/pii/S0304397517301020, combinatorics on Words

12. Kempa, D., Kociumaka, T.: Resolution of the burrows-wheeler transform conjecture. In: 2020 IEEE 61st Annual Symposium on Foundations of Computer Science (FOCS), pp. 1002–1013 (2020). https://doi.org/10.1109/FOCS46700.2020.00097

13. Kolpakov, R., Kucherov, G.: Finding maximal repetitions in a word in linear time. In: 40th Annual Symposium on Foundations of Computer Science (Cat. No. 99CB37039), pp. 596–604 (1999). https://doi.org/10.1109/SFFCS.1999.814634

14. Kolpakov, R., Kucherov, G., Ochem, P.: On maximal repetitions of arbitrary exponent. Inf. Process. Lett. **110**(7), 252–256 (2010). http://www.sciencedirect.com/science/article/pii/S0020019010000220

15. Pape-Lange, J.: On Maximal Repeats in Compressed Strings. In: Pisanti, N., Pissis, S.P. (eds.) 30th Annual Symposium on Combinatorial Pattern Matching (CPM 2019). Leibniz International Proceedings in Informatics (LIPIcs), vol. 128, pp. 18:1–18:13. Schloss Dagstuhl-Leibniz-Zentrum fuer Informatik, Dagstuhl, Germany (2019). http://drops.dagstuhl.de/opus/volltexte/2019/10489

16. Pape-Lange, J.: On extensions of maximal repeats in compressed strings. In: Gørtz, I.L., Weimann, O. (eds.) 31st Annual Symposium on Combinatorial Pattern Matching, CPM 2020, 17–19 June 2020, Copenhagen, Denmark. LIPIcs, vol. 161, pp. 27:1–27:13. Schloss Dagstuhl - Leibniz-Zentrum für Informatik (2020). https://drops.dagstuhl.de/opus/volltexte/2020/12152

17. Pickering, P.E.: Verbal repetition in "prometheus" and greek tragedy generally. Bull. Inst. Class. Stud. **44**, 81–101 (2000). http://www.jstor.org/stable/43646626

18. Rytter, W.: Application of Lempel-Ziv factorization to the approximation of grammar-based compression. Theor. Comput. Sci. **302**(1–3), 211–222 (2003). https://doi.org/10.1016/S0304-3975-02-00777-6

19. Rytter, W.: The number of runs in a string: improved analysis of the linear upper bound. In: Durand, B., Thomas, W. (eds.) STACS 2006. LNCS, vol. 3884, pp. 184–195. Springer, Heidelberg (2006). https://doi.org/10.1007/11672142_14

Branching Frequency and Markov Entropy of Repetition-Free Languages

Elena A. Petrova(iD) and Arseny M. Shur(✉)(iD)

Ural Federal University, Ekaterinburg, Russia
{elena.petrova,arseny.shur}@urfu.ru

Abstract. We define a new quantitative measure for an arbitrary facto-rial language: the entropy of a random walk in the prefix tree associated with the language; we call it Markov entropy. We relate Markov entropy to the growth rate of the language and the parameters of branching of its prefix tree. We show how to compute Markov entropy for a regu-lar language. Finally, we develop a framework for experimental study of Markov entropy by modelling random walks and present the results of experiments with power-free and Abelian-power-free languages.

Keywords: Power-free language · Abelian-power-free language · Markov entropy · Prefix tree · Random walk

1 Introduction

Formal languages closed under taking factors of their elements (factorial lan-guages) are natural and popular objects in combinatorics. Factorial languages include sets of factors of infinite words, sets of words avoiding patterns or rep-etitions, sets of minimal terms in algebraic structures, sets of palindromic rich words and many other examples. One of the main combinatorial parameters of factorial languages is their asymptotic growth. Usually, "asymptotic growth" means asymptotic behaviour of the function $C_L(n)$ giving the number of length-n words in the language L. (In algebra, the function that counts words of length *at most* n is more popular.)

In this paper we propose a different parameter of asymptotic growth, based on representation of factorial languages as *prefix trees*, which are diagrams of the prefix order on words. Given such an infinite directed tree, one can view each word as a walk starting at the root. We consider *random walks*, in which the next node is chosen uniformly at random among the children of the current node, and define their *entropy* to measure the expected uncertainty of a single step. As a random walk is a Markov chain, we call this parameter the Markov entropy of a language. This parameter was earlier considered for a particular subclass of regular languages in the context of antidictionary data compression

Supported by the Ministry of Science and Higher Education of the Russian Federation (Ural Mathematical Center project No. 075-02-2021-1387).

N. Moreira and R. Reis (Eds.): DLT 2021, LNCS 12811, pp. 328–341, 2021.
https://doi.org/10.1007/978-3-030-81508-0_27

[4]. However, it seems that more general cases were not analysed up to now. Our interest in Markov entropy is twofold. First, it allows us to estimate growth properties of a language from statistics of experiments, if exact methods do not work. Second, it is related to a natural and efficient (at least theoretically) data compression scheme, which encodes the choices made during a walk in the prefix tree.

Our contribution is as follows. In Sect. 3 we define the order-n Markov entropy $\mu_n(L)$ of a language L in terms of length-n random walks in its prefix tree $\mathcal{T}(L)$ and the Markov entropy $\mu(L) = \lim_{n\to\infty} \mu_n(L)$. Then we relate Markov entropy to the exponential growth rate of L and to the parameter called branching frequency of a walk in $\mathcal{T}(L)$. In Sect. 4.1 we show how to compute Markov entropy for a regular language. Then in Sect. 4.2 we propose a model of random walk for an arbitrary factorial language through depth-first search and show how to recover branching frequency from observable parameters of a walk. Finally, in Sect. 5 we present algorithms used in the experimental study of Markov entropy for power-free and Abelian-power-free languages and the results of this study. All proofs are omitted; see arXiv:2105.02750 for the full version.

2 Preliminaries

We study words and languages over finite alphabets; Σ^* denotes the set of all words over an alphabet $\Sigma = \{0, \ldots, \sigma-1\}$. Standard notions of prefix, suffix, factor are used. We use the array notation $w = w[1..n]$ for a word of length $n = |w|$; thus $w[i..i+k-1]$ stands for the length-k factor of w starting at position i. In particular, $w[i..i] = w[i]$ is the ith letter of w and $w[i..i-1]$ is the empty word, denoted by λ. A word w is right extendable in a language L if L contains infinitely many words with prefix w; $\mathsf{re}(L)$ denotes the set of all words which are right extendable in L.

A word w has period p if $w[1..|w|-p] = w[p+1..w]$. For an integer $k > 1$, the k-power of a word w is the concatenation of k copies of w. For an arbitrary real $\beta > 1$, the β-power (resp., the β^+-power) of w is the prefix of length $\lceil \beta|w| \rceil$ (resp., $\lfloor \beta|w| + 1 \rfloor$) of the infinite word $w^\infty = ww\cdots w\cdots$. E.g., $(010)^{2^+} = (010)^{7/3} = 0100100$, $(010)^{5/2} = (010)^{(5/2)^+} = 01001001$. A word is β-power-free if it has no β-powers as factors; the k-ary β-power-free language $\mathsf{PF}(k, \beta)$ consists of all β-power-free words over the k-letter alphabet. The same definitions apply to β^+-powers. The crucial result on the power-free languages is the threshold theorem, conjectured by Dejean [7] and proved by efforts of many authors [3,6,16–18, 20]. The theorem establishes the boundary between finite and infinite power-free languages: the minimal infinite k-ary power-free languages are $\mathsf{PF}(3, \frac{7}{4}^+)$, $\mathsf{PF}(4, \frac{7}{5}^+)$, and $\mathsf{PF}(k, \frac{k}{k-1}^+)$ for $k = 2$ and $k \geq 5$. These languages are called threshold languages.

The Parikh vector $\psi(w)$ of a word w is a length-σ vector such that $\psi(w)[i]$ is the number of occurrences of the letter i in w for each $i \in \Sigma$. Two words with equal Parikh vectors are said to be Abelian equivalent. A concatenation of k Abelian equivalent words is an Abelian kth power. Abelian k-power-free words are defined in analogy with k-power-free words; Abelian square-free (resp., cube-free, 4-power-free) languages over four (resp., three, two) letters are infinite [8,12].

A language $L \subseteq \Sigma^*$ is *factorial* if it contains all factors of each its element. Power-free and Abelian-power-free languages are obviously factorial. The relation "to be a prefix (resp., a suffix, a factor)" is a partial order on any language. The diagram of the prefix order of a factorial language L is a directed tree $\mathcal{T}(L)$ called the *prefix tree*. Prefix trees are the main objects of study in this paper. For convenience, we assume that an edge of the form (w, wa) in $\mathcal{T}(L)$ is labeled by the letter a; in this way, the path from the root to w is labeled by w. For regular languages we use deterministic finite automata with partial transition function (PDFA), viewing them as labelled digraphs. We assume that all states of a PDFA are reachable from the initial state; since we study factorial languages, we also assume that all states are final (so a PDFA accepts a word iff it can read it). When a PDFA $\mathcal{A}$ is fixed, we write $q.w$ for the state of $\mathcal{A}$ obtained by reading w starting at the state q.

Combinatorial complexity (or *growth function*) of a language $L \subseteq \Sigma^*$ is a function counting length-n words in L: $C_L(n) = |L \cap \Sigma^n|$. The *growth rate* $\mathrm{gr}(L) = \limsup_{n\to\infty}(C_L(n))^{1/n}$ describes its asymptotic growth. The combinatorial complexity of factorial languages is submultiplicative: $C_L(m+n) \leq C_L(m)C_L(n)$; by Fekete's lemma [9], this implies $\mathrm{gr}(L) = \lim_{n\to\infty}(C_L(n))^{1/n} = \inf_{n\in\mathbb{N}}(C_L(n))^{1/n}$. A survey of techniques and results on computing growth rates for regular and power-free languages can be found in [27].

Infinite Trees. We consider infinite k-ary rooted trees: the number of children of any node is at most k. Nodes with more than one child are called *branching points*. The *level* $|u|$ of a node u is the length of the path from the root to u. A subtree $\mathcal{T}_u$ of a tree $\mathcal{T}$ consists of the node u and all its descendants. The tree $\mathcal{T}$ is *p-periodic* (resp., *p-subperiodic*) if there exists a function f on the set of nodes such that each subtree $\mathcal{T}_u$ is an isomorphic copy (resp., is a subgraph) of the subtree $\mathcal{T}_{f(u)}$ and $|f(u)| \leq p$. The prefix tree of any factorial language L is 0-subperiodic, since suffixes of elements of L are also in L. Furthermore, $\mathcal{T}(L)$ is p-periodic for some p iff L is regular (p-periodicity means exactly that L has finitely many quotients, which is equivalent to regularity).

There are two widely used parameters of growth for infinite trees; see, e.g., [15]. "Horizontal" growth is measured by the *growth rate* $\mathrm{gr}(\mathcal{T}) = \lim_{n\to\infty}(T_n)^{1/n}$, where T_n is the number of nodes of level n, whenever this limit exists. Hence, $\mathrm{gr}(\mathcal{T}(L)) = \mathrm{gr}(L)$. "Vertical" growth is measured by the *branching number* $\mathrm{br}(\mathcal{T})$, which is usually defined using the notion of network flow. However, Furstenberg's theorem [10] says that $\mathrm{br}(\mathcal{T}) = \mathrm{gr}(\mathcal{T})$ for subperiodic trees, so for prefix trees we have only one parameter. In Sect. 3, we propose one more parameter of growth using the notion of entropy.

Entropy. Let $\xi = (x_{1|p_1}, \ldots, x_{n|p_n})$ be a discrete finite-range random variable, where $p_i, i = 1, \ldots, n$, is the probability of the outcome x_i. The *entropy* of ξ is the average amount of information in the outcome of a single experiment: $H(\xi) =$

$-\sum_{i=1}^{k} p_i \log p_i$ (throughout the paper, log stands for the binary logarithm). Lemma 1 below contains basic properties of entropy, established by Shannon [23].

Lemma 1. *(1) For a random variable* $\xi = (x_{1|p_1}, \ldots, x_{n|p_n})$, $H(\xi) \leq \log n$; *equality holds for the uniform distribution only.*
(2) For a random vector (ξ, η), $H(\xi, \eta) \leq H(\xi) + H(\eta)$; *equality holds iff* ξ *and* η *are independent.*

3   Entropy Characteristics of Prefix Trees

Let $\mathcal{T} = \mathcal{T}(L)$ be a prefix tree. The entropy characteristics introduced below measure the expected uncertainty *of a single letter* in a random word from L. By *order-n general entropy* $H_n(L)$ we mean the entropy of a random variable uniformly distributed on the set $|L \cap \Sigma^n|$ (or on the set of level-n nodes of $\mathcal{T}$), divided by n. By Lemma 1(1), $H_n(L) = \frac{\log C_L(n)}{n}$. The fact that L is factorial guarantees the existence of the *general entropy* of L, which is by definition the limit

$$H(L) = \lim_{n \to \infty} H_n(L) = \lim_{n \to \infty} \log(C_L(n))^{1/n} = \log \mathsf{gr}(L).$$

A different notion of entropy stems from consideration of random walks in $\mathcal{T}$. As usual in graph theory, by *random walk* we mean a stochastic process (Markov chain), the result of which is a finite or infinite walk in the given graph. The process starts in the initial state (either fixed or randomly chosen from some distribution) and runs step by step, guided by the following rule: visiting the node u, choose an outgoing edge of u uniformly at random[1] and follow it to reach the next node. The walk stops if u has no outgoing edges. Note that all walks in $\mathcal{T}$ are directed paths; we refer to the walks starting at the root as *standard*. Let η_n be the random variable with the range $|L \cap \Sigma^n|$ such that the probability of a word $w \in L$ is the probability that a random standard walk in $\mathcal{T}$, reaching the level n, visits w. The *order-n Markov entropy* of L is $\mu_n(L) = \frac{H(\eta_n)}{n}$. The following lemma is immediate from definitions and Lemma 1(1).

Lemma 2. *For any factorial language L and any n, one has $\mu_n(L) \leq H_n(L)$.*

Similar to the case of the general entropy, the limit value exists:

Lemma 3. *Let L be a factorial language. Then there exists a limit $\mu(L) = \lim_{n \to \infty} \mu_n(L) = \inf_{n \in \mathbb{N}} \mu_n(L)$.*

We call $\mu(L)$ the *Markov entropy* of L. We want to estimate $\mu(L)$ for different languages; so our first goal is to relate $H(\eta_n)$, and thus $\mu_n(L)$, to the parameters of the tree $\mathcal{T}$. Let $\mathsf{ch}(w)$ denote the number of children of the node w in $\mathcal{T}$ and $P(w)$ be the probability of visiting the word w by a random standard walk.

---

[1] Non-uniform distributions are also used in many applications but we do not consider them here.

332   E. A. Petrova and A. M. Shur

Lemma 4. $P(w) = \left(\prod_{i=0}^{|w|-1} \mathsf{ch}(w[1..i]) \right)^{-1}$.

In general, $P(w)$ may underestimate the probability assigned to w by $\eta_{|w|}$; this is the case if some prefix of w has a child which generates a finite subtree with no nodes of level $|w|$. To remedy this, we consider trimming of prefix trees. By *n-trimmed version* of $\mathcal{T}$, denoted by $\mathcal{T}_{[n]}$, we mean the tree obtained from $\mathcal{T}$ by deletion of all finite subtrees $\mathcal{T}_u$ which have no nodes of level n (and thus of bigger levels). In other words, a node $w \in L$ is deleted iff L contains no length-n word with the prefix w.

Example 1. Let $L = \mathsf{PF}(2,3)$, $\mathcal{T} = \mathcal{T}(L)$. If $n \geq 9$, then $\mathcal{T}_{[n]}$ does not contain $u = 00100100$ because $u0, u1$ end with cubes; if $n \geq 15$, then $\mathcal{T}_{[n]}$ does not contain $v = 0100101001010$, because $v1, v00$, and $v01$ end with cubes.

The *trimmed version* of $\mathcal{T}$, denoted by $\mathcal{T}_{[]}$, is obtained from $\mathcal{T}$ by deletion of *all* finite subtrees. The next lemma follows from definitions.

Lemma 5. *(1)* $\mathcal{T}_{[]} = \bigcap_{n \in \mathbb{N}} \mathcal{T}_{[n]}$. *(2)* $\mathcal{T}_{[]}$ *is the prefix tree of* $\mathsf{re}(L)$.

We write $\mathsf{ch}_{[n]}(w)$ ($\mathsf{ch}_{[]}(w)$) for the number of children of w in $\mathcal{T}_{[n]}$ (resp., $\mathcal{T}_{[]}$) and $P_{[n]}(w)$ ($P_{[]}(w)$) for the probability of visiting w by a random standard walk in $\mathcal{T}_{[n]}$ (resp., $\mathcal{T}_{[]}$). As in Lemma 4, one has

$$P_{[n]}(w) = \left(\prod_{i=0}^{|w|-1} \mathsf{ch}_{[n]}(w[1..i]) \right)^{-1} \text{ and } P_{[]}(w) = \left(\prod_{i=0}^{|w|-1} \mathsf{ch}_{[]}(w[1..i]) \right)^{-1}. \quad (1)$$

Lemma 6. *Let* $w \in L$, $|w| = n$. *Then* η_n *assigns to* w *the probability* $P_{[n]}(w)$.

Definitions and Lemma 6 imply $H(\eta_n) = -\sum_{w \in L \cap \Sigma^n} P_{[n]}(w) \log P_{[n]}(w)$.

Given an arbitrary tree $\mathcal{T}$, we assign to each internal node u its *weight*, equal to the logarithm of the number of children of u. *Branching frequency* of standard walk ending at a node w, denoted by $\mathsf{bf}(\mathcal{T}, w)$, is the sum of weights of all nodes in the walk, except for w, divided by the length of the walk (=level of w). The use of branching frequency for prefix trees can be demonstrated as follows. For a language L, a natural problem is to design a method for compact representation of an arbitrary word $w \in L$. A possible solution is to encode the standard walk in $\mathcal{T} = \mathcal{T}(L)$, ending at w. We take $|w|$-trimmed version of $\mathcal{T}$ and encode consecutively all choices of edges needed to reach w. For each predecessor u of w we encode the correct choice among $\mathsf{ch}_{[|w|]}(u)$ outgoing edges. The existence of asymptotically optimal entropy coders, like the arithmetic coder [21], allows us to count $\log \mathsf{ch}_{[|w|]}(u)$ bits for encoding this choice. Thus w will be encoded by $\sum_{i=0}^{|w|-1} \log \left(\mathsf{ch}_{[|w|]}(w[1..i]) \right)$ bits, which is exactly $\mathsf{bf}(\mathcal{T}_{[|w|]}, w)$ bits per symbol.

Remark 1. The proposed method of coding generalizes the antidictionary compression method [4] for arbitrary alphabets. Antidictionary compression works as follows: given $w \in L \subseteq \{0,1\}^*$, examine each prefix $w[1..i]$; if it is the only child of $w[1..i-1]$ in the prefix tree of L, delete $w[i]$. In this way, the remaining bits encode the choices made in branching points during the standard walk to w. The compression ratio is the fraction of branching points among the predecessors of w: any branching point contributes 1 to the length of the code, while other nodes in the walk contribute nothing.

The following theorem relates branching frequencies to Markov entropy.

Theorem 1. *For a factorial language L and a positive integer n, the order-n Markov entropy of L equals the expected branching frequency of a length-n random walk in the prefix tree $T(L)$.*

4 Computing Entropy

4.1 General and Markov Entropy for Regular Languages

Let L be a factorial regular language, $\mathcal{A}$ be a PDFA, recognizing L. The problem of finding $gr(L)$, and thus $H(L)$, was solved by means of matrix theory as follows. By the Perron–Frobenius theorem, the maximum absolute value of an eigenvalue of a non-negative matrix M is itself an eigenvalue, called the *principal* eigenvalue. A folklore theorem (see [27, Th. 2]) says that $gr(L)$ equals the principal eigenvalue of the adjacency matrix of $\mathcal{A}$. This eigenvalue can be approximated[2] with any absolute error δ in $O(|\mathcal{A}|/\delta)$ time [24, Th. 5]; see also [27, Sect. 3.2.1].

Now consider the computation of $\mu(L)$. By Lemma 3 and Theorem 1, $\mu(L)$ is the limit of expected branching frequencies of length-n random standard walks in the prefix tree $T = T(L)$. Standard walks in T are in one-to-one correspondence with accepting walks in $\mathcal{A}$, so we can associate each node $w \in T$ with the state $\lambda.w \in \mathcal{A}$ and consider random walks in T as random walks in $\mathcal{A}$. We write $\deg^{\rightarrow}(u)$ for the out-degree of the node u in $\mathcal{A}$.

We need the apparatus of *finite-state Markov chains*. Such a Markov chain with m states is defined by a row-stochastic $m \times m$ matrix A (row-stochastic means that all entries are nonnegative and all row sums equal 1). The value $A[i, j]$ is treated as the probability that the next state in the chain will be j given that the current state is i. Any finite directed graph G with no nodes of out-degree 0 represents a finite-state Markov chain. The stochastic matrix of G is built as follows: take the adjacency matrix and divide each value by the row sum of its row (see Fig. 1 below). Recall some results on finite-state Markov chains (see, e.g., [11, Ch. 11]). Let A be the $m \times m$ matrix of the chain. The process is characterized by the vectors $\boldsymbol{p}^{(n)} = (p_1^{(n)}, \ldots, p_m^{(n)})$, where $p_i^{(n)}$ is the probability of being in state i after n steps; the initial distribution $\boldsymbol{p}^{(0)}$ is given as a part of description of the chain. The *stationary distribution* of A is a vector $\boldsymbol{p} = (p_1, \ldots, p_m)$ such that $p_i \geq 0$ for all i, $\sum_{i=1}^{m} p_i = 1$ and $\boldsymbol{p}A = \boldsymbol{p}$. Every row-stochastic matrix has one or more stationary distributions; such a distribution is unique for the matrices obtained from strongly connected digraphs. The sequence $\{\boldsymbol{p}^{(n)}\}$ approaches some stationary distribution $\boldsymbol{p}$ in the following sense:

---

[2] Note that it is not possible in general to find the roots of polynomials exactly.

(∗) there exists an integer $h \geq 1$ such that $\boldsymbol{p} = \lim_{n\to\infty} \frac{\boldsymbol{p}^{(n)}+\boldsymbol{p}^{(n+1)}+\cdots+\boldsymbol{p}^{(n+h-1)}}{h}$

(That is, the limit of the process is a length-h cycle and $\boldsymbol{p}$ gives the average probabilities of states in this cycle. In practical cases usually $h = 1$ and thus $\boldsymbol{p} = \lim_{n\to\infty} \boldsymbol{p}^{(n)}$.)

Theorem 2. *Let L be a factorial regular language, $\hat{A}$ be a PDFA accepting* re(L). *Suppose that $\hat{A}$ has m states $1,\ldots,m$ and $\boldsymbol{p} = (p_1,\ldots,p_m)$ is the stationary distribution for a random walk in $\hat{A}$, starting at the initial state. Then $\mu(L) = \sum_{i=1}^{m} p_i \log(\deg^{\to}(i))$.*

Example 2. Let $L \subset \{0,1\}^*$ be the regular language consisting of all words having no factor 11. Its accepting PDFA, the corresponding matrices and entropy computations are presented in Fig. 1. Note that re$(L) = L$.

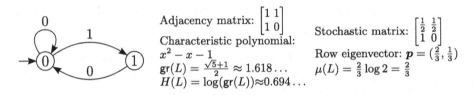

Adjacency matrix: $\begin{bmatrix} 1 & 1 \\ 1 & 0 \end{bmatrix}$

Characteristic polynomial:
$x^2 - x - 1$
gr$(L) = \frac{\sqrt{5}+1}{2} \approx 1.618\ldots$
$H(L) = \log(\text{gr}(L)) \approx 0.694\ldots$

Stochastic matrix: $\begin{bmatrix} \frac{1}{2} & \frac{1}{2} \\ 1 & 0 \end{bmatrix}$

Row eigenvector: $\boldsymbol{p} = (\frac{2}{3}, \frac{1}{3})$

$\mu(L) = \frac{2}{3}\log 2 = \frac{2}{3}$

Fig. 1. Accepting PDFA and entropy computations for the language L (Example 2).

Computational Aspects. Computing $\hat{A}$ from A takes $O(|A|)$ time, as it is sufficient to split A into strongly connected components and traverse the acyclic graph of components. The vector $\boldsymbol{p}$ can be computed by solving the size-m linear system $\boldsymbol{p}(\hat{A} - I) = \boldsymbol{0}$, where $\hat{A}$ is the adjacency matrix of $\hat{A}$ and I is the identity matrix. This solution requires $\Theta(m^3)$ time and $\Theta(m^2)$ space, which is too much for large automata. More problems arise if the solution is not unique; but the correct vector $\boldsymbol{p}$ still can be found by means of matrix theory (see [11, Ch. 11]). In order to process large automata (say, with millions of states), one can iteratively use the equality $\boldsymbol{p}^{(n+1)} = \boldsymbol{p}^{(n)}\hat{A}$ to approximate $\boldsymbol{p}$ with the desired precision. Each iteration can be performed in $O(m)$ time, because $\hat{A}$ has $O(m)$ nonzero entries. One can prove, similar to [26, Th. 3.1], that under certain natural restrictions $O(\delta^{-1})$ iterations is sufficient to obtain $\boldsymbol{p}$ within the approximation error δ.

4.2   Order-n Markov Entropy via Random Walks

Let $L \subseteq \Sigma^*$ be an arbitrary infinite factorial language such that the predicate $\mathcal{L}(w)$, which is true if $w \in L$ and false otherwise, is computable. There is little hope to compute $\mu(L)$, but one can use an oracle computing $\mathcal{L}(w)$ to build random walks in the prefix tree $\mathcal{T} = \mathcal{T}(L)$ and obtain statistical estimates of $\mu_n(L)$ for big n. We construct random walks by random depth-first search (Algorithm 1), executing the call DFS(λ, n). The algorithm stops immediately when level n is reached. When visiting node u, the algorithm chooses a non-visited child of u uniformly at random and visits it next. If all children of u are already visited, then u is a "dead end" (has no descendants at level n), and the search returns to the parent of u.

Algorithm 1. Random walk in $\mathcal{T}(L)$ by depth-first search

---

```
1: function DFS(u, n)                                    ▷ u=node, n=length of walk
2:   if |u| = n then break                               ▷ walk reached level n
3:   (a₁a₂ ... a_σ) ← random permutation of Σ
4:   for j = 1 to σ do
5:     if ℒ(ua_j) then DFS(ua_j, n)                       ▷ visit ua_i next
6:   return                                              ▷ u has no descendant at level n
```

Lemma 7. DFS(λ, n) *builds a length-n random standard walk in* $\mathcal{T}(L)$.

Consider the values of the counter j in the instances DFS(λ, n), DFS$(w[1], n)$, ..., DFS$(w[1..n-1], n)$ at the moment when the search reaches level n. We define *profile* of the constructed walk as the vector $\boldsymbol{r} = (r_1, \ldots, r_\sigma)$ such that r_i is the number of instances of DFS in which $j = i$. Note that different runs of Algorithm 1 may result in the same walk with different profiles (due to random choices made, depth-first search visits some dead ends and skips some of the others). Given a profile $\boldsymbol{r}$, one can compute the expected branching frequency bf$(\boldsymbol{r})$ of a walk with this profile: bf$(\boldsymbol{r}) = \frac{1}{n} \sum_{i=1}^{\sigma} c_i \log i$, where the parameters c_i are computed in Theorem 3 below.

Theorem 3. *Let* $\boldsymbol{r} = (r_1, \ldots, r_\sigma)$ *be a profile of a length-n random standard walk in a tree* $\mathcal{T}$. *For each* $i = 1, \ldots, \sigma$, *let* c_i *be the expected number of nodes, having exactly i children in the tree* $\mathcal{T}_{[n]}$, *in a random standard walk with the profile* $\boldsymbol{r}$. *Then*

$$(c_1, \ldots, c_\sigma)P = \boldsymbol{r}, \text{ where } P[i, k] = \frac{\binom{\sigma-i}{k-1}}{\binom{\sigma}{k-1}} - \frac{\binom{\sigma-i}{k}}{\binom{\sigma}{k}} \text{ for } i, k = 1, \ldots, \sigma. \quad (2)$$

Example 3. Let us solve (2) for $\sigma = 2$ (left) and $\sigma = 3$ (right):

$$(c_1, c_2) \begin{bmatrix} \frac{1}{2} & \frac{1}{2} \\ 1 & 0 \end{bmatrix} = (r_1, r_2) \qquad (c_1, c_2, c_3) \begin{bmatrix} \frac{1}{3} & \frac{1}{3} & \frac{1}{3} \\ \frac{2}{3} & \frac{1}{3} & 0 \\ 1 & 0 & 0 \end{bmatrix} = (r_1, r_2, r_3)$$

$c_1 = 2r_2, \ c_2 = r_1 - r_2$

bf$(\boldsymbol{r}) = \frac{r_1 - r_2}{r_1 + r_2}$

$c_1 = 3r_3, \ c_2 = 3r_2 - 3r_3, \ c_3 = r_1 - 2r_2 + r_3$

bf$(\boldsymbol{r}) = \frac{3(r_2 - r_3) + (r_1 - 2r_2 + r_3) \log 3}{r_1 + r_2}$

5 Experimental Results

With the goal of comparing general entropy and Markov entropy for power-free languages, we started with a side experiment. We took the ternary square-free language SF = PF$(3, 2)$, which is a well-studied test case. Its growth rate

$\mathsf{gr}(\mathsf{SF}) \approx 1.30176$ is known with high precision [27] from the study of its *regular approximations*. A kth regular approximation SF_k of SF is the language of all words having no squares of period $\leq k$ as factors. The sequence $\{\mathsf{gr}(\mathsf{SF}_k)\}$ demonstrates a fast convergence to $\mathsf{gr}(\mathsf{SF})$. So we wanted to (approximately) guess the Markov entropy $\mu(\mathsf{SF})$ extrapolating the initial segment of the sequence $\mu(\mathsf{SF}_k)$.

The results are as follows: we computed the values $\mu(\mathsf{SF}_k)$ up to $k = 45$ with absolute error $\delta < 10^{-8}$ using the technique from Sect. 4.1. We obtained $\mu(\mathsf{SF}_{45}) \approx 0.36981239$; the extrapolation of all obtained values gives $0.369810 < \mu(\mathsf{SF}) < 0.369811$. At the same time we have $H(\mathsf{SF}) = \log(\mathsf{gr}(\mathsf{SF})) \approx 0.380465$, so the two values are clearly distinct but close enough.

5.1 Random Walks in Power-Free Languages

To perform experiments with length-n random walks for a language L, one needs an algorithm to compute $\mathcal{L}(w)$ to be used with Algorithm 1. A standard approach is to maintain a data structure over the current word/walk w, which quickly answers the query "$w \in L$?" and supports addition/deletion of a letter to/from the right. The theoretically best such algorithm for power-free words was designed by Kosolobov [14]: it spends $O(\log n)$ time per addition/deletion and uses memory of size $O(n)$. However, the algorithm is complicated and the constants under O are big. We developed a practical algorithm which is competitive for the walks up to the length of several millions. For simplicity, we describe it for square-free words but the construction is the same for any power-free language.

We use arrays $\mathrm{repeat}_i[1..n]$, $i = 0, \ldots, \lfloor \log n \rfloor - 1$ to store previous occurrences of factors. If $|u| \geq j$ for the current word u, then $\mathrm{repeat}_i[j]$ is the *last* position of the previous occurrence of the factor $u[j-2^i+1..j]$ or $-\infty$ if there is no previous occurrence. To delete a letter from u we just delete the entries $\mathrm{repeat}_i[|u|]$; let us consider the procedure $\mathrm{add}(u, a)$ (Algorithm 2) which adds the letter a to u, checks square-freeness of ua and computes $\mathrm{repeat}_i[|u| + 1]$. The auxiliary array $\mathrm{last}[1..\sigma]$ stores the rightmost position of each letter in the current word.

Algorithm 2. Online square detection: adding a letter

```
1: function add(u, a)                                              ▷ u=word, a=letter to add
2:   repeat₀[|u| + 1] ← last[a]; last[a] ← |u| + 1      ▷ fill previous occurrence of a
3:   free ← true                                                   ▷ square-freeness flag
4:   for i = 0 to ⌊log n⌋ − 1 do
5:     x ← repeatᵢ[|u|+1]; p = |u| + 1 − x              ▷ p is the possible period of a square
6:     if p ≤ 2^{i+1} and repeatᵢ[x+2ⁱ] = x + 2ⁱ − p then free ← false; break    ▷ Fig. 2
7:     if i = ⌊log n⌋ − 1 then break                            ▷ no more arrays to update
8:     compute repeat_{i+1}[|u| + 1]                           ▷ from repeatᵢ
9:     if repeat_{i+1}[|u| + 1] = −∞ then break            ▷ all repeated suffixes processed
10: return free                                                    ▷ the answer to "is ua square-free?"
```

Correctness. Recall that u is square-free, so the occurrences of a factor of u can neither overlap nor touch. Assume that ua ends with a square vv, $p = |v|$, $2^i < p \leq 2^{i+1}$. Then p will be found in line 5 as $|u| + 1 - \mathsf{repeat}_i[|u|+1]$ (red arcs in Fig. 2 show the suffix of length 2^i and its previous occurrence). The

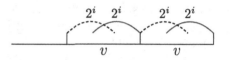

Fig. 2. Detecting a square by Algorithm 2.

condition in line 6 means exactly the equality of words marked by dash arcs in Fig. 2; thus, vv is detected and $\mathsf{add}(u,a)$ returns false. For the other direction, if $\mathsf{add}(u,a) = $ false, then the condition in line 6 held true and thus a square was detected as in Fig. 2. The *time complexity* is $O(\sqrt{n})$ on expectation; the experiments confirm this estimate.

Experiments. We studied the following languages: $\mathsf{PF}(2,3)$ and $\mathsf{PF}(3,2)$ as typical "test cases", threshold languages over $3,\ldots,10$, 20, 50, and 100 letters, and $\mathsf{PF}(2,\frac{7}{3}^+)$ as the smallest binary language of exponential growth. All languages from this list have "essentially binary" prefix trees: a letter cannot coincide with any of $(\sigma-2)$ preceding letters, and so a node of level at least $\sigma-2$ has at most two children. Hence we computed expected branching frequencies as in Example 3. For each language, we computed profiles of 1000 walks of length 10^5 and 100 walks of length 10^6. The tables with the data are available at [29]. We briefly analysed the data. The most interesting findings, summarized below, are the same for each of the studied languages. Some figures are presented in Table 1.

1. The profiles of all walks in $\mathcal{T} = \mathcal{T}(L)$ are close to each other. To be precise, assume that $\mathsf{bf}(r) = \mu_n(L)$ for all constructed profiles. Then the number r_2 computed for a length-n random walk is the number of heads in c_1 tosses of a fair coin (among c_1 nodes with two children, in r_2 cases the dead end was chosen first). Hence the computed values of r_2 form a sample from the binomial distribution $B(c_1, \frac{1}{2})$. And indeed, the set of computed r_2's looks indistinguishable from such a sample; see [29, stat100000]. This property suggests the mean value of $\mathsf{bf}(r)$ over all experiments as a good approximation of $\mu_n(L)$.
2. The 99% confidence interval for the mean branching frequency $\mathsf{bf}(\mathcal{T}_{[|w|]}, w)$ of the 1000 constructed walks of length 10^5 is of length $\sim 4 \cdot 10^{-4}$ and includes the mean value of $\mathsf{bf}(r)$ for the walks of length 10^6. For the language SF, this interval also includes the value $\mu(\mathsf{SF})$ conjectured from the study of $\mu(\mathsf{SF}_k)$. This property suggests that $\mu_n(L)$ for such big n is close to the Markov entropy $\mu(L)$.
3. As $\mu(L) \leq H(L) = \log(\mathsf{gr}(L))$, the value of $\mu(L)$ can be converted to the lower bound for the growth rate of L. The values $2^{\mathrm{mean}(\mathsf{bf}(r))}$ from our experiments differ from the best known upper bounds for the studied languages [27, Tbl. A1–A3] by the margin of 0.004–0.018. Such a bound is quite good for all

cases where specialized methods [13, 25] do not work. The results for threshold languages support the Shur–Gorbunova conjecture [28] that the growth rates of these languages tend to the limit $\alpha \approx 1.242$ as the size of the alphabet approaches infinity.

Table 1. Markov entropy for power-free languages: experiments

Language	Mean bf(r) (10^5)	Mean bf(r) (10^6)	$2^{\mu(L)}$	gr(L)
$PF(2, \frac{7}{3}^+)$	0.27221	0.27220	≈ 1.20766	≈ 1.22064
$PF(2, 3)$	0.52562	0.52553	≈ 1.43956	≈ 1.45758
$PF(3, \frac{7}{4}^+)$	0.30249	0.30251	≈ 1.23327	≈ 1.24561
$PF(3, 2)$	0.36988	0.36987	≈ 1.29223	≈ 1.30176
$PF(4, \frac{7}{5}^+)$	0.09137	0.09151	≈ 1.06535	< 1.06951
$PF(5, \frac{5}{4}^+)$	0.20279	0.20265	≈ 1.15092	< 1.15790
$PF(6, \frac{6}{5}^+)$	0.28536	0.28526	≈ 1.21871	< 1.22470
$PF(7, \frac{7}{6}^+)$	0.29753	0.29749	≈ 1.22903	< 1.23690
$PF(8, \frac{8}{7}^+)$	0.28881	0.28867	≈ 1.22163	< 1.23484
$PF(9, \frac{9}{8}^+)$	0.30716	0.30732	≈ 1.23727	< 1.24668
$PF(10, \frac{10}{9}^+)$	0.29674	0.29669	≈ 1.22836	< 1.23931
$PF(20, \frac{20}{19}^+)$	0.30002	0.29982	≈ 1.23099	< 1.24205
$PF(50, \frac{50}{49}^+)$	0.30006	0.29970	≈ 1.23089	< 1.24210
$PF(100, \frac{100}{99}^+)$	0.30047	0.29974	≈ 1.23093	< 1.24210

5.2 Random Walks in Abelian Power-Free Languages

Similar to Sect. 5.1, we need an algorithm checking Abelian power-freeness. Here we describe an algorithm detecting Abelian squares; its modification for other integer powers is straightforward. If a word $w[1..n]$ is fixed, we let $\psi_i = \psi(w[n-i+1..n]) - \psi(w[n-2i+1..n-i])$. A simple way to find whether w ends with Abelian square is to check $\psi_i = \mathbf{0}$ for all i. Since ψ_{i+1} can be obtained from ψ_i with a constant number of operations (add $w[n-i]$ twice, subtract $w[n-2i]$ and $w[n-2i-1]$), this check requires $\Theta(n)$ time. However, $\Theta(n)$ time per iteration appeared to be too much to perform experiments comparable with those for power-free languages, so we developed a faster algorithm. It maintains two length-n arrays for each letter $a \in \Sigma$: $d_a[i]$ is the position of ith from the left letter a in the current word w and $c_a[i]$ is the number of occurrences of a in $w[1..i]$ (i.e., a coordinate of $\psi(w[1..i])$). When a letter is added/deleted, these arrays are updated in $O(1)$ time (we regard σ as a constant). The function Asquare(u) (Algorithm 3) checks whether the word w has an Abelian square as a suffix.

Correctness: see full version. *Complexity:* in experiments, Algorithm 3 checked $\Theta(\sqrt{n})$ suffixes of a length-n word, but we have no theoretical proof for this.

Algorithm 3. Online Abelian square detection

```
1: function Asquare(u)                                            ▷ u=word
2:   l ← |u| − 1; i ← 1                                           ▷ two counters
3:   free ← false                   ▷ square-freeness flag; turns true when check finishes
4:   while not free do
5:     for a ∈ Σ do
6:       ψ[a] ← c_a[|u|] − c_a[|u|−i]              ▷ a-coordinate of ψ(u[|u|−i+1..|u|])
7:       if ψ[a] > c_a[|u|−i] then free ← true; break           ▷ no squares possible
8:     l ← min{l, d_a[c_a[|u|−i] − ψ[a] + 1]}
9:     if l = |u| − 2i + 1 then break        ▷ u[|u| − 2i + 1..|u|] is an Abelian square
10:    i ← ⌈(|u| − l + 1)/2⌉
11:  return free                      ▷ the answer to "is ua Abelian square-free?"
```

Experiments. The structure and growth of Abelian-power-free languages are little studied. We considered the 4-ary Abelian-square-free language ASF, the ternary Abelian-cube-free language ACF, and the binary Abelian-4-power-free language A4F; see Table 2. Our main interest was in estimating the actual growth rate of these languages. The upper (resp. lower) bounds for the growth rates are taken from [22] (resp., from [1,2,5]). For ASF and ACF we got profiles of 500 walks of length 10^5 and 100 walks of length $5 \cdot 10^5$; for A4F, 100 profiles of walks of length 10^5 were computed. The results suggest that the automata-based upper bounds for the growth rates of Abelian-power-free languages are quite imprecise, in contrast with the case of power-free languages. In addition, the experiments discovered the existence of very big finite subtrees on relatively low levels, which slow down the depth-first search. In fact, to obtain long enough words from A4F we modified the DFS function to allow "forced" backtracking if the length of the constructed word does not increase for a long time. Even with such a gadget, the time to build one walk of length 10^5 varied from 9 min to 4 h.

Table 2. Markov entropy for Abelian-power-free languages: experiments

Language	Mean bf(r) (10^5)	Meanbf(r) ($5 \cdot 10^5$)	$2^{\mu(L)}$	gr(L)
ASF	0.20475	0.20337	≈ 1.15138	<1.44435; >1.00002
ACF	1.08439	1.08418	≈ 2.12017	<2.37124; >1.02930
A4F	0.20736	−	≈ 1.15457	<1.37417; >1.04427

6   Conclusion and Future Work

In this paper we showed that efficient sampling of very long random words is a useful tool in the study of factorial languages. Already the first experiments allowed us to state a lot of problems for further research. To mention just a few:

- for which classes of languages, apart from regular ones, the Markov entropy can be computed (or approximated with a given error)?

- are there natural classes of languages satisfying $\mu(L) = H(L)$? $\mu(L) \ll H(L)$?
- how the branching frequencies of walks in a prefix tree are distributed? which statistical tests can help to approximate this distribution?

Concerning the last questions, we note that though our experiments showed "uniformity" of branching frequencies in each of the studied languages, the frequencies of individual words can vary significantly. For example, the language $\mathsf{PF}(2,3)$ with the average frequency about 0.525 contains infinite words $\mathbf{u}$ and $\mathbf{v}$ satisfying $\mathsf{bf}(\mathbf{u}) = 0.72$ and $\mathsf{bf}(\mathbf{v}) < 0.45$ [19].

References

1. Aberkane, A., Currie, J.D., Rampersad, N.: The number of ternary words avoiding abelian cubes grows exponentially. J. Integer Seq. **7**(2) (2004)
2. Carpi, A.: On the number of Abelian square-free words on four letters. Discrete Appl. Math. **81**, 155–167 (1998)
3. Carpi, A.: On Dejean's conjecture over large alphabets. Theor. Comput. Sci. **385**, 137–151 (1999)
4. Crochemore, M., Mignosi, F., Restivo, A., Salemi, S.: Data compression using antidictionaries. Proc. IEEE **88**(11), 1756–1768 (2000)
5. Currie, J.D.: The number of binary words avoiding abelian fourth powers grows exponentially. Theor. Comput. Sci. **319**, 441–446 (2004)
6. Currie, J.D., Rampersad, N.: A proof of Dejean's conjecture. Math. Comp. **80**, 1063–1070 (2011)
7. Dejean, F.: Sur un théorème de Thue. J. Combin. Theor. Ser. A **13**, 90–99 (1972)
8. Dekking, F.M.: Strongly non-repetitive sequences and progression-free sets. J. Combin. Theory. Ser. A **27**, 181–185 (1979)
9. Fekete, M.: Über der Verteilung der Wurzeln bei gewissen algebraischen Gleichungen mit ganzzahligen Koeffizienten. Math. Zeitschrift **17**, 228–249 (1923)
10. Furstenberg, H.: Disjointness in ergodic theory, minimal sets, and a problem in diophantine approximation. Math. Syst. Theor. **1**, 1–49 (1967)
11. Grinstead, C.M., Snell, J.L.: Introduction to Probability. American Mathematical Society, Providence (1997)
12. Keränen, V.: Abelian squares are avoidable on 4 letters. In: Kuich, W. (ed.) ICALP 1992. LNCS, vol. 623, pp. 41–52. Springer, Heidelberg (1992). https://doi.org/10.1007/3-540-55719-9_62
13. Kolpakov, R., Rao, M.: On the number of Dejean words over alphabets of 5, 6, 7, 8, 9 and 10 letters. Theor. Comput. Sci. **412**, 6507–6516 (2011)
14. Kosolobov, D.: Online detection of repetitions with backtracking. In: Cicalese, F., Porat, E., Vaccaro, U. (eds.) CPM 2015. LNCS, vol. 9133, pp. 295–306. Springer, Cham (2015). https://doi.org/10.1007/978-3-319-19929-0_25
15. Lyons, R., Peres, Y.: Probability on Trees and Networks, Cambridge Series in Statistical and Probabilistic Mathematics, vol. 42. Cambridge University Press, New York (2016)
16. Mohammad-Noori, M., Currie, J.D.: Dejean's conjecture and Sturmian words. Eur. J. Comb. **28**, 876–890 (2007)
17. Moulin-Ollagnier, J.: Proof of Dejean's conjecture for alphabets with 5, 6, 7, 8, 9, 10 and 11 letters. Theor. Comput. Sci. **95**, 187–205 (1992)

18. Pansiot, J.J.: A propos d'une conjecture de F. Dejean sur les répétitions dans les mots. Discrete Appl. Math. **7**, 297–311 (1984)
19. Petrova, E.A., Shur, A.M.: Branching densities of cube-free and square-free words. Algorithms **14**(4), 126 (2021)
20. Rao, M.: Last cases of Dejean's conjecture. Theor. Comput. Sci. **412**, 3010–3018 (2011)
21. Rissanen, J.J.: Generalized Kraft inequality and arithmetic coding. IBM J. Res. Dev. **20**, 198–203 (1976)
22. Samsonov, A.V., Shur, A.M.: On Abelian repetition threshold. RAIRO Theor. Inf. Appl. **46**, 147–163 (2012)
23. Shannon, C.E.: A mathematical theory of communication. Bell Syst. Tech. J. **27**(379–423), 623–656 (1948)
24. Shur, A.M.: Combinatorial complexity of regular languages. In: Hirsch, E.A., Razborov, A.A., Semenov, A., Slissenko, A. (eds.) CSR 2008. LNCS, vol. 5010, pp. 289–301. Springer, Heidelberg (2008). https://doi.org/10.1007/978-3-540-79709-8_30
25. Shur, A.M.: Two-sided bounds for the growth rates of power-free languages. In: Diekert, V., Nowotka, D. (eds.) DLT 2009. LNCS, vol. 5583, pp. 466–477. Springer, Heidelberg (2009). https://doi.org/10.1007/978-3-642-02737-6_38
26. Shur, A.M.: Growth rates of complexity of power-free languages. Theor. Comput. Sci. **411**, 3209–3223 (2010)
27. Shur, A.M.: Growth properties of power-free languages. Comput. Sci. Rev. **6**, 187–208 (2012)
28. Shur, A.M., Gorbunova, I.A.: On the growth rates of complexity of threshold languages. RAIRO Theor. Inf. Appl. **44**, 175–192 (2010)
29. Markov entropy of repetition-free languages–statistics (2021). https://tinyurl.com/2j36b6j7

A Linear-Time Simulation of Deterministic d-Limited Automata

Alexander A. Rubtsov[✉️] [ID]

National Research University Higher School of Economics, Moscow, Russia

Abstract. A d-limited automaton is a nondeterministic Turing machine that uses only the cells with the input word (and end-markers) and rewrites symbols only in the first d visits. This model was introduced by T. Hibbard in 1967 and he showed that d-limited automata recognize context-free languages for each $d \geqslant 2$. He also proved that languages recognizable by deterministic d-limited automata form a hierarchy and it was shown later by Pighizzini and Pisoni that it begins with deterministic context-free languages (DCFLs) (for $d = 2$).

As well-known, DCFLs are widely used in practice, especially in compilers since they are linear-time recognizable and have the corresponding CF-grammars subclass (LR(1)-grammars). In this paper we present a linear time recognition algorithm for deterministic d-limited automata (in the RAM model) which opens an opportunity for their possible practical applications.

1 Introduction

Context-free languages (CFLs) play an important role in computer science. The most well-known practical application of CFLs is the application of their deterministic subclass (DCFLs) to parsing algorithms in compilers, and the core of this application is connection between LR(1)-grammars that describe syntaxes of programming languages and deterministic pushdown automata (DPDAs) that implement linear-time parsing of LR(1)-grammars. In 1965 D. Knuth showed [12] that LR(1)-grammars generate exactly DCFLs, the class that is recognizable by DPDAs. So, DCFLs is a practically important subclass of CFLs that is linear-time recognizable and $LR(1)$-grammars are linear-time parsable, i.e. there is a linear time algorithm that constructs a derivation tree of an input word.

The best known upper bound for CFLs parsing is n^ω where $\omega \leqslant 2.373$ is the exponent of fast-matrix multiplication, and n is the length of the input word, was obtained by L. Valiant in 1975 [21]. It was shown in [13] and [1] why this bound is hard to improve. Some recent CFL studies were focused on subclasses that are hard to parse or at least to recognize [11], and on the subclasses that are linear-time recognizable [2]. In this paper, we show that a well-known subclass of CFLs is linear time recognizable. We move to the description of the subclass.

A.A. Rubtsov—Supported by Russian Science Foundation grant 20–11–20203.

N. Moreira and R. Reis (Eds.): DLT 2021, LNCS 12811, pp. 342–354, 2021.
https://doi.org/10.1007/978-3-030-81508-0_28

1.1 d-Limited Automata and d-DCFLs

Namely, we focus on d-DCFLs, as they were called by T. Hibbard who introduced this subclass of CFLs. To define this subclass, we define an auxiliary computational model. We provide here an informal definition, a formal definition could be found in the next section.

A d-limited automaton (d-LA) is a nondeterministic Turing machine (TM) that visits only the cells with the input word (and end-markers) and it rewrites a symbol in the cell (except end-markers) only in the first d visits. We focus only on the deterministic version of the model in the paper that is denoted by d-DLA. T. Hibbard showed [10] that for each $d \geqslant 2$ d-LAs recognize (exactly) the class of CFLs, 1-LAs recognize the class of regular languages [22] (Thm 12.1). Note that for $d = \infty$, (deterministic) d-LAs turns to (deterministic) linear-bounded automata that recognizes (deterministic) context-sensitive languages, so it is quite a natural computational model for the Chomsky hierarchy.

Pighizzini and Pisoni showed in [17] that deterministic 2-DLAs recognize DCFLs. T. Hibbard calls a subclass of CFLs, recognizable by deterministic d-DLAs, d-*deterministic* languages (d-DCFLs). He showed in [10] that for a fixed d, $(d + 1)$-DCFLs strictly contain d-DCFLs (there exists a $(d + 1)$-DCFL that is not a d-DCFL), so all d-DCFLs form a hierarchy.

We also mention that while DCFLs is a widely-used subclass of CFLs, it has the following practical flaws.

The languages $L_\# = \{\#a^n b^n c^m \mid n, m \geqslant 0\}$ and $L_\$ = \{\$a^m b^n c^n \mid n, m \geqslant 0\}$ are DCFLs, so as the language $L_\# \cup L_\$$, while the language $(L_\# \cup L_\$)^R$, consisting of the reversed words from $L_\# \cup L_\$$, is not a DCFL. If we allow deterministic pushdown automata (DPDAs) to process the input either from left to right or from right to left, the language $(L_\# \cup L_\$)^R$ could be recognized by the DPDA M_R that acts as a DPDA M_L recognizing $(L_\# \cup L_\$)$ but M_R processing of the input from right to left. A deterministic 3-DLA can shift the head to the rightmost cell and use the same approach of deterministic 2-DLA recognizing $(L_\# \cup L_\$)$ to recognize the language $(L_\# \cup L_\$)^R$.

Consider now the language $L_{\#,\$} = \{a^n b^n c^m \mid n, m \geqslant 0\} \cup \{a^m b^n c^n \mid n, m \geqslant 0\}$ which is a union of two DCFLs. It is a well-known fact (see [18]) that $L_{\#,\$}$ is an inherently ambiguous language. As is also well known, each DCFL is generated by an unambiguous (particularly LR(1)) CF-grammar. Hibbard has also proved in [10] that each d-DCFL is generated by an unambiguous CF-grammar, so the union $\cup_{d=1}^{\infty}$ d-DCFLs does not contain all CFLs. This fact implies that d-DCFLs share with DCFLs another practical flaw: they are not closed under the union operation, so one needs to apply parallel computation to parse such languages as $L_{\#,\$}$ in linear time via d-DLAs.

1.2 Our Contribution

The membership problem for d-DLAs takes on the input the d-DLA M and the input word w. The question of the problem, whether M accepts w. Denote by m the length of M's description and by n the length of w. We provide

$O(mn)$ algorithm in RAM for the membership problem that leads to a linear-time simulation algorithm if M is fixed. In fact, a more careful analysis leads to the bound $O(kn + m)$, where k is the number of M's states.

Hennie proved in [9] that each language recognizable in linear time by a (deterministic) TM is regular (a more general result holds for nondeterministic TMs [15,20]). So there is no linear-time TM that simulates a deterministic d-DLA for $d \geqslant 2$. B. Guillon and L. Prigioniero proved that each 1-DLA can be transformed into a linear-time TM [8] (and a similar result for 1-LAs). Their construction relies on the classical Shepherdson construction of simulating of two-way deterministic finite automata (2-DFAs) by one-way DFAs [19]. We also rely on this construction, but it cannot be applied directly due to the Hennie's result (in this case one could simulate a non-regular language by a linear-time TM).

So we transform a classical TM to a TM that operates on a doubly-linked list instead of a tape and transfer Shepherdson's construction to this model. This transformation allows us to obtain a linear-time simulation algorithm, but not an $O(mn)$ algorithm for the membership problem. To achieve this algorithm we transform Birget's algebraic constructions [3] into the language of graph theory, and construct a linear-time algorithm which computes a variation of the mapping composition.

Linear-time recognizable languages are used on practice for parsing, especially in compilers. We have already mentioned DCFLs, below we describe PEGs which are very popular now, while their predecessors, top-down parsing languages, were abandoned due to limitations of computers in 1960s. Maybe there will be no direct practical applications of our constructions, but the fact that a language recognizable by a deterministic d-DLA is linear-time recognizable can be used to prove linear-time recognizability of some specific languages and transform the construction to other models, especially PEGs.

From a theoretical point of view our results allow us to prove that some CFLs are easy (linear-time recognizable), while in general a CFL is recognizable in $O(n^\omega)$ and due to the conditional results hard languages (recognizable at least in superlinear time) "should" exist. We discuss the details in the following subsection.

1.3 Related Results

We begin with a description of linear-time recognizable subclasses of context-sensitive languages (CSLs) and CFLs. We start with a wide subclass of CSLs recognizable in linear time: the class of languages recognizable by two-way deterministic pushdown automata (2-DPDA). A linear time simulation algorithm of 2-DPDA was obtained by S. Cook in [5] and then simplified by R. Glück [7]. This class obviously contains DCFLs as a subclass, and it also contains the language of palindromes (over at least two-letters alphabet) that is a well-known example of CF-language that is not a DCFL. It is still an open question whether 2-DPDA recognize all CF-languages and the works of L. Lee [13] and Abboud et al. [1] proves that this is very unlikely due to theoretical-complexity assumptions: any CFG parser with time complexity $O(gn^{3-\varepsilon})$, where g is the size of the grammar and n is the length of the input word, can be efficiently converted into an algorithm to multiply $m \times m$ Boolean matrices in time $O(m^{3-\varepsilon/3})$. From our results naturally follows the question: can 2-DPDA simulate deterministic d-DLA for $d \geqslant 3$?

Another result is a linear-time parsing algorithm for a non-trivial subclass of CFLs: the regular closure of DCFLs, obtained by E. Bertsch and M.-J. Nederhof [2]. Each language from this class can be described as follows. Let us take a regular expression and replace each letter in it by a corresponding DCFL. This class evidently contains the aforementioned language $L_{\#,\$}$ (as a union of DCFLs), so it is a strict extension of DCFLs. Note that the language $L_{\#,\$}$ is also recognizable by a 2-DPDA.

Another interesting linear-time recognizable subclass of CSLs is the one generated by parsing expression grammars (PEGs). Roughly speaking, PEGs are a modification of CF-grammars that allow recursive calls (and returns from the calls), we do not provide the formal definition here. PEGs are an upgraded version of top-down parsing languages [4] developed by A. Birman and J. D. Ullman. They have been developed by B. Ford who has constructed a practical linear time parser for this model [6]. The class of languages generated by PEGs contains DCFLs, such CSLs as $\{a^n b^n c^n \mid n \geqslant 0\}$, and, as shown in [14] by B. Loff et al., the language of palindromes with the length of a power of 2. It is an open question, whether PEGs recognize palindromes. The situation with CFLs for PEGs is the same as for 2-DPDAs: there is no example of a CFL that is not PEG-recognizable, while according to conditional results such a language "should" exist. Another natural question that arises from our results: can PEGs generate all d-DCFLs?

d-LAs were abandoned for decades but then the formal language's community returned to their study. G. Pighizzini, who actively worked on this topic, made a survey of results on d-LAs and related models [16], focusing in part on state complexity.

We agree with the remark from [16] that T. Hibbard claimed in [10] that d-DLAs do not recognize palindromes for any d, while the formal proof is missing and would be interesting.

2 Definitions

We define Hibbard's model, introduced in [10], as it is defined today [16]. An equivalent definition in a more formal style could be found in [17].

2.1 Deterministic d-Limited Automaton

Fix an integer $d \geqslant 0$. A deterministic d-limited automaton (d-DLA) is a (deterministic) Turing machine with a single tape, which initially contains the input word bordered by the left end-marker $\triangleright$ and the right end-marker $\triangleleft$ with the following property. Each letter of the alphabet has the corresponding number from 0 to d called the *rank*, initially all the letters of the input word have the rank 0 and the end-markers have the rank d; when the head visits a cell with a letter with rank $r < d$ it rewrites it with a letter of the rank $r + 1$, and if the letter has the rank d the head does not change the letter.

A d-DLA $\mathcal{A}$ is defined by a tuple

$$\mathcal{A} = (Q, \Sigma, \Gamma, \delta, q_0, F),$$

where Q is the finite set of states, Σ is the input alphabet (each letter has the rank 0), Γ is the work-tape alphabet $\Sigma \cup \{\triangleright, \triangleleft\} \subseteq \Gamma$, we denote by $\Gamma_r \subseteq \Gamma$ the letters of the rank r, q_0 is the initial state, F is the set of accepting states and δ is the transition function

$$\delta : Q \times \Gamma \rightarrow Q \times \Gamma \times \{\leftarrow, \rightarrow\}$$

so that

- for $a_r \in \Gamma_r$, $r < d$ any transition has the form $\delta(q, a_r) = (q', a_{r+1}, m)$, where $a_{r+1} \in \Gamma_{r+1} \backslash \{\triangleright, \triangleleft\}$
- for $a_d \in \Gamma_d$ any transition has the form $\delta(q, a_d) = (q', a_d, m)$
- for $\triangleright, \triangleleft$ any transition has the form $\delta(q, \triangleleft) = (q', \triangleleft, \leftarrow)$, $\delta(q, \triangleright) = (q', \triangleright, \rightarrow)$

A d-DLA starts processing of the input word in the state q_0 with the head on the first input symbol. It consequently applies the transition function: being in a state q with a letter a under the head it computes $\delta(q, a) = (q', a', m)$, replaces the letter a by a', changes the state q to q' and moves the head to the right if $m = \rightarrow$ or to the left if $m = \leftarrow$. The automaton accepts the input if it reaches an accepting state $q_f \in F$ when the head arrives on the right end-marker $\triangleleft$. At this point it stops the computation. Note that since δ is totally defined, the automaton rejects the input only by entering an infinite loop.

In fact we have modified the original definition a little by adding two extra requirements. These modification does not change the class of recognizable languages. The first one is that the transition function is totally defined. The second one is the "continuous" growth of the rank. The first one costs of adding only one extra-state, and the second one is needed for the notation convenience; it blows up the length of the automaton description from m up to $O(dm)$, but this blow up can be avoided by a technical complication of the algorithm.

2.2 Deleting DLBA

We also construct an auxiliary modified model as follows. In this model there is no constrain on d-visits, the tape is replaced by a doubly linked list, so an automaton can delete an arbitrary cell between the end-markers (but not the end-markers). Formally we modify only the transition function as follows

$$\delta : Q \times \Gamma \rightarrow (Q \times (\Gamma \cup \{\bot\}) \times \{\leftarrow, \rightarrow\} \cup \{\uparrow\}),$$

where the symbol $\bot$ means that the cell would be deleted right after the head leaves the cell. After the deletion of the cell, the head moves from its left neighbour to its right neighbour when it moves to the right from the left neighbour and vice versa. If the transition function returns $\uparrow$ the computation is over and the input is rejected. We have no extra-requirements on the transition function.

We call the modified model the *deleting DLBA* since it is a modification of deterministic linear-bounded automata. Deleting DLBAs obviously recognize (exactly) deterministic CSLs. We use doubly linked lists in this model to achieve the linear time during the simulation of d-DLAs.

3   Linear-Time Simulation Algorithm

In this section we provide a linear-time simulation algorithm for d-DLAs. The main idea is as follows. If for all inputs each cell of a deleting DLBA is visited at most C times (for some constant C) then it works in linear time. It also works in linear time if the average number of visits per cell is at most C. Recall that Hennie's Theorem implies that both properties are impossible for a (non-deleting) DLBA recognizing a non-regular language. So we construct a deleting DLBA which satisfies the latter property from a d-DLA. When at some point the d-DLA has on its tape a maximal subword[1] with only letters of rank d, the deleting DLBA has only one cell with auxiliary information for this subword which it uses to simulate the behavior of the d-DLA on processing this subword. Deleting DLBA can be simulated by RAM in a straight-forward way, so we will provide the resulting linear-time algorithm for RAM in Subsect. 3.1.

Our simulation idea is similar to the Shepherdson's well-known simulation algorithm of a two-way DFA by a one-way DFA [19]. Note that in the case $d = 0$, d-DLA is a two-way DFA. The deleting DLBA writes in the cells that should contain letters of rank d the corresponding mappings of possible moves and if two mappings are written in adjacent cells it deletes one of the cells and replaces the mapping in the other cell by the (variation of) composition of the mappings. When the head arrives at the cell with a mapping

$$f : (Q \times \{\leftarrow, \rightarrow\} \cup \{\uparrow\}) \rightarrow (Q \times \{\leftarrow, \rightarrow\} \cup \{\uparrow\})$$

in the state q and the last move's direction was $m \in \{\leftarrow, \rightarrow\}$, the deleting DLBA computes $f(q, m) = (q', m')$ and moves the head in the state q' to the direction m'. If f returns $\uparrow$ it means that the d-DLA entered an infinite loop, so the deleting DLBA rejects the input in this case. We demand $f(\uparrow) = \uparrow$.

To simplify the notation we use the following shortcuts:

$$\overleftarrow{Q} = Q \times \{\leftarrow\}, \; \overrightarrow{Q} = Q \times \{\rightarrow\}, \; \overleftrightarrow{Q} = \overleftarrow{Q} \cup \overrightarrow{Q}, \; A_\uparrow = A \cup \{\uparrow\} \text{ for } A \in \{\overleftarrow{Q}, \overrightarrow{Q}, \overleftrightarrow{Q}\}.$$

We also use arrows to indicate the elements of these sets, i. e. $\overleftarrow{q} \in \overleftarrow{Q}$, and call elements of $\overleftrightarrow{Q}$ *directed* states. If $\delta(q, X) = (p, Y, m)$, where δ is the transition function of a d-DLA or a deleting DLBA, we denote $\delta(q, X) = (\overleftrightarrow{p}, Y)$, where the direction of p corresponds to the value of m.

---

[1] The subword that cannot be continued neither to the right nor to the left such that the resulting subword has only letters of rank d.

We start with the technical details. We refer to d-DLA as $\mathcal{A}$ and to deleting DLBA (that simulates $\mathcal{A}$) as M. We enumerate all cells (of each automata) from 0 to $n+1$, where n is the length of the input word w. The number of the cell is fixed during the whole computation, so it will not be affected by deletion. We denote the content of the i-th cell on the current M's step as $W_M[i]$; we refer to the content of the i-th cell right after the t-th step as $W_M^t[i]$. So $W_M^0[0] = \rhd$ and $W_M^0[n+1] = \lhd$. We refer to the content of $\mathcal{A}$'s tape as $W_{\mathcal{A}}$. Since a cell could be deleted we refer to the left (undeleted) neighbour of an i-th cell as $i.\mathsf{prev}$ and to the right neighbour as $i.\mathsf{next}$.

We say that an automaton (d-DLA or deleting DLBA) *arrives at a segment* $W[l,r] = W[l]W[l+1]\cdots W[r]$ *in the directed state* $\overleftrightarrow{q}$ if it arrives in the state q at the cell $W[l]$ in the case $\overleftrightarrow{q} = \overleftarrow{q}$ and at the cell $W[r]$ in the case $\overleftrightarrow{q} = \overrightarrow{q}$. Respectively, an automaton *departures from* $W[l,r]$ *in the directed state* $\overleftrightarrow{p}$ if it departures from $W[l]$ in the case $\overleftrightarrow{p} = \overleftarrow{p}$ and from $W[r]$ in the case $\overleftrightarrow{p} = \overrightarrow{p}$.

Now we describe M. We use indices $\mathcal{A}$ and M for the components of tuples that describe automata to make the notation clear. The working alphabet Γ_M is the union of the alphabet $\Gamma_{\mathcal{A}}$ and the set $\mathcal{F}$ of all mappings

$$f : \overleftrightarrow{Q}_\uparrow \to \overleftrightarrow{Q}_\uparrow, \text{ such that } f(\uparrow) = \uparrow.$$

We continue the description of M after we state auxiliary properties of $\mathcal{F}$. We also need a few auxiliary definitions.

We say that $f \in \mathcal{F}$ *describes the tape segment* $W_{\mathcal{A}}[l,r]$ that contains only symbols of rank d if it describes the behavior of $\mathcal{A}$ on this segment, i.e., the following condition holds. If $\mathcal{A}$ arrives at $W_{\mathcal{A}}[l,r]$ in the directed state $\overleftrightarrow{q}$, $f(\overleftrightarrow{q}) = \uparrow$ iff $\mathcal{A}$ enters an infinite loop, otherwise $\mathcal{A}$ departures from $W_{\mathcal{A}}[l,r]$ in the directed state $\overleftrightarrow{p} = f(\overleftrightarrow{q})$.

If a mapping f describes a segment $W_{\mathcal{A}}[L,r]$, and a mapping g describes a segment $W_{\mathcal{A}}[r+1,R]$. The *directed composition* $f \diamond g$ is the mapping h that describes the segment $W_{\mathcal{A}}[L,R]$.

Let f and g describe segments $W_{\mathcal{A}}[L,r]$ and $W_{\mathcal{A}}[r+1,R]$ and $\overrightarrow{q}$ be a directed state such that $\overrightarrow{q}$ means that the head arrives at $W_{\mathcal{A}}[r+1,R]$ (in the directed state $\overrightarrow{q}$ from $W_{\mathcal{A}}[L,r]$) and $\overleftarrow{q}$ means the arrival at $W_{\mathcal{A}}[L,r]$. We define the mapping $D : \mathcal{F} \times \mathcal{F} \times \overleftrightarrow{Q} \to \overleftrightarrow{Q}_\uparrow$ that returns the directed state $\overleftrightarrow{p}$ such that $\mathcal{A}$ departures from the segment $W_{\mathcal{A}}[L,R]$ in $\overleftrightarrow{p}$ (after arriving in the directed state $\overleftrightarrow{q}$) or $\uparrow$ if the head never leaves $W_{\mathcal{A}}[L,R]$. We call D the *departure function*.

A function $CF : \Gamma_d \to \mathcal{F}$ returns the mapping $CF(X)$ that describes a cell with the letter X of rank d. We call CF the *cell description function*.

In our algorithm we describe mappings from $\mathcal{F}$ via graphs as follows. A mapping $f \in \mathcal{F}$ that describes a segment L is represented via 4-parted graph with parts $\overrightarrow{L}_{\text{in}}$, $\overleftarrow{L}_{\text{in}}$, $\overrightarrow{L}_{\text{out}}$, and $\overleftarrow{L}_{\text{out}}$ as follows. Each part is a copy of the set $Q_{\mathcal{A}}$. The graph has an edge $\overleftrightarrow{q} \to \overleftrightarrow{p}$, $\overleftrightarrow{q} \in \overleftrightarrow{L}_{\text{in}}$, $\overleftrightarrow{p} \in \overleftrightarrow{L}_{\text{out}}$ iff $f(\overleftrightarrow{q}) = \overleftrightarrow{p}$. So, $f(\overleftrightarrow{q}) = \uparrow$ iff the vertex $\overleftrightarrow{q} \in \overleftrightarrow{L}_{\text{in}}$ has degree 0.

Proposition 1. *The directed composition* $\diamond$ *of mappings from* $\mathcal{F}$ *is well-defined and is always a computable and an associative mapping. The directed composi-*

tion, the departure function D and the cell description function CF are computable in $O(|Q_A|)$.

As we mentioned in Subsect. 1.2 our algorithm of computing $\diamond$, D, CF is an effective variant of the Birget's construction, so we do not go deep into details here, since one can find them in [3].

Proof. The CF function is evidently $O(|Q_A|)$-computable. Denote $CF(a_d)$ by f. So $f(\overleftarrow{q}) = \overleftarrow{p}$ iff $\delta_A(q, a_d) = (\overrightarrow{p}, a_d)$.

We provide effective algorithms for computing D and $\diamond$ mappings via graphs. Assume that f describes a segment L and g describes the segment R adjacent to L (to the right). In terms of graphs, the directed composition $\diamond$ and the departure function D are computable as follows. We glue the graphs for f and g so that $\overrightarrow{L}_{\text{out}} = \overrightarrow{R}_{\text{in}}$ and $\overleftarrow{L}_{\text{in}} = \overleftarrow{R}_{\text{out}}$ (Fig. 1) and obtain the *intermediate graph*. So $f \diamond g(\overleftrightarrow{q}) = \overleftrightarrow{p}$ iff there is a path from $\overleftrightarrow{q}$ to $\overleftrightarrow{p}$ in the intermediate graph (by the graph's construction). Note that the same holds for $D(f, g, \overleftrightarrow{q}) = \overleftrightarrow{p}$, the only difference between D and $\diamond$ is the initial vertex corresponding to $\overleftrightarrow{q}$.

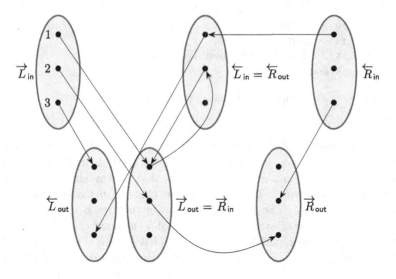

Fig. 1. Graph for computing the composition

Since the sets of vertices corresponding to domains of $f \diamond g(\overleftrightarrow{q})$ and $D'(\overleftrightarrow{q}) = D(f, g, \overleftrightarrow{q})$ do not intersect, we define the mapping h as follows:

$$h(v) = \begin{cases} f \diamond g(\overleftrightarrow{q}), \overleftrightarrow{q} \sim v, & \text{if } v \in \overleftarrow{L}_{\text{in}} \cup \overrightarrow{R}_{\text{in}} \\ D(f, g, \overleftrightarrow{q}), \overleftrightarrow{q} \sim v, & \text{if } v \in \overrightarrow{L}_{\text{in}} \cup \overleftarrow{R}_{\text{in}} \end{cases}$$

We compute the graph of h in $O(|Q_A|)$. Note that for $D(f, g, \overleftrightarrow{q})$ we need the result for the only state $\overleftrightarrow{q}$, but for the sake of simplicity we consider the general case. The algorithm is provided on Fig. 2. Denote by V the set of all vertices. Note that each vertex $u \in V$ has out degree at most 1, so we denote by u.next either the end of the edge $u \to u$.next or u.next $= \uparrow$ if u has out-degree 0. We store h in array (enumerate all vertices in the set $\overleftrightarrow{L}_{in} \cup \overleftrightarrow{R}_{in}$) and so we store the array of marks.

```
 1  marks[u] := NIL for each u ∈ V;
 2  h[v] := NIL for each v ∈ L⃡in ∪ R⃡in;
 3  for v ∈ L⃡in ∪ R⃡in do
 4      u := v.next;
 5      while u ∉ L⃡out ∪ R⃡out ∪ {↑} and h[v] = NIL do
 6          if m[u] = NIL then
 7              m[u] := v;
 8              u := u.next;
 9          else if m[u] = v then
10              h[v] := ↑;
11          else
12              h[v] := h[m[u]];
13          end
14      end
15      if h[v] = NIL then h[v] := u;
16  end
```

Fig. 2. Algorithm for computing h

The algorithm travels from the vertex v on the input of h until it either reaches an output state, or it reaches a marked vertex. If the vertex of the intermediate graph is marked by s it means that it was already used during traveling from the vertex s. If $s = v$, it means that we met a loop, so $h(v) = \uparrow$, otherwise $h(v) = h(s)$. The marking guaranties that we never visit any edge twice. Since out-degree of each vertex is at most 1 the number of edges $|E|$ in the graph is $O(|V|)$. So the algorithm runs in time $O(|V|+|E|) = O(|V|) = O(|Q_{\mathcal{A}}|)$. Recall that the vertex v is corresponding to the directed state $\overleftrightarrow{q}$ and $h(v)$ equals to either $f \diamond g(\overleftrightarrow{q})$ or $D(f, g, \overleftrightarrow{q})$ depending on the part containing v.   □

3.1   Simulation Algorithm

We provide the pseudocode of the simulation algorithm in Fig. 3 and now we also describe the algorithm. It provides a high-level description of M's transition function δ_M and the simulation of M in RAM. When we describe M's behavior and say "$\mathcal{A}$ moves", "$\mathcal{A}$ acts", etc., we refer to the result of the move $\delta_{\mathcal{A}}(q, a)$ where $a \in \Gamma$ is either the mentioned symbol or the symbol under M's head and q is the mentioned state or $\mathcal{A}$'s state corresponding to M's state. $\mathcal{A}$-moves described in lines 3...4 of the pseudocode. M has two kinds of moves: $\mathcal{A}$-moves

```
 1  ⃡q := ⃡q₀;  i := 1;
 2  while  no result returned do
 3      case  W_M[i] ∈ Γ_r ∪ {▷,◁}, r < d − 1 do              /* A-move */
 4        |   (⃖p, a_{r'}) := δ_A(q, W_M[i]);  W_M[i] := a_{r'};
 5      case W_M[i] ∈ Γ_{d−1} do                              /* Deletion scan */
 6        |   (⃖p, X) := δ_A(q, W_M[i]);
 7        |   g := CF(X) ;                      /* O(|Q|). See Proposition 1 */
 8        |   if i.prev > 0 and W_M[i.prev] ∈ F then
 9        |     |  f := W_M[i.prev];
10        |     |  if ⃖p = ⃗p then ⃖p := D(f, g, ⃖p);
11        |     |  if ⃖p =↑ then  return Reject;
12        |     |  g := f ◇ g;  i.prev := (i.prev).prev;        /* O(|Q|). */
13        |   end
14        |   if i.next < n + 1 and W_M[i.next] ∈ F then
15        |     |  h := W_M[i.next];
16        |     |  if ⃖p = ⃗p then  ⃖p = D(g, h, ⃗r);            /* O(|Q|). */
17        |     |  if ⃖p =↑ then  return Reject;
18        |     |  g := g ◇ h;  i.next := (i.next).next;         /* O(|Q|). */
19        |   end
20        |   W_M[i] := g;
21      case W_M[i] ∈ F do
22        |   f := W_M[i];
23        |   if f(⃡q) =↑ then  return Reject else ⃖p := f(⃡q);
24      end
25      if ⃖p = ⃗p then  i := i.prev  else i := i.next;
26      ⃡q := ⃡p;
27      if q ∈ F_A and W[i] =◁ then  return Accept;
28  end
```

Fig. 3. Simulation Algorithm

and technical moves. The A-moves correspond to moves of A, so M always has a state $q \in Q_A$ when it arrives at a cell after an A-move.

Since our algorithm depends on the first head's arrival to the cell of rank $d - 1$ (after which it becomes d), we have formal problems with the case $d = 0$. To avoid them, assume that in the beginning all cells have rank -1 (only for $d = 0$) and the d-DLA does not change the symbols of rank -1, but changes their rank.

The automaton M acts as A if M processes a letter of rank less than $d - 1$ (A-moves). When M visits a cell on the d-th time and A should have written a letter X of rank d in that cell (and X is not an end-marker), M writes to the corresponding cell the mapping $g = CF(X)$, recall that $g(\overleftrightarrow{q}) = \overleftarrow{p}$ iff $\delta_A(q, X) = (\overleftarrow{p}, X)$ for all $q \in Q_A, X \in \Gamma_d$. When M writes a mapping g in the cell i for the first time, it scans the cells i.prev and i.next and performs the following procedure that we call a *deletion scan*.

If only one of the cells i.prev and i.next contains a mapping (f or h respectively), then M writes to the cell i the mapping $f \diamond g$ for i.prev and the mapping

$g \diamond h$ for i.next and deletes the neighbouring cell. If both neighbours have the rank d, M writes to the cell i the mapping $f \diamond g \diamond h$ and deletes both neighbouring cells. After the deletion scan the cell i contains the result mapping g while the neighbours of i contain letters, so g describes the segment $W_{\mathcal{A}}[i.\text{prev}+1, i.\text{next}-1]$ and M moves the head to the same cell (i.prev or i.next) as $\mathcal{A}$ after $\mathcal{A}$ leaves the segment $W_{\mathcal{A}}[i.\text{prev} + 1, i.\text{next} - 1]$. This cell is computed via the departure function D during the deletion scan.

We described the cases when M arrives at a cell of rank $r < d$ from a cell of any rank and to a cell of rank d from a cell of rank d. So, it is left to describe M's action in the case when M arrives at a cell containing a mapping f in a directed state $\overleftarrow{q}$ from a cell with a letter of rank $r < d$ (lines 21...24). M computes $f(\overleftarrow{q}) = \overleftarrow{p}$ and moves the head to the left neighbour or to the right neighbour depending on the direction of $\overleftarrow{p}$ and arrives at the neighbour in the state p.

Lemma 2. *For each d-DLA $\mathcal{A}$ the described deleting DLBA M simulates $\mathcal{A}$, i.e., if on the t-th step $\mathcal{A}$ visits the cell i with the letter $W_{\mathcal{A}}^t[i]$ of rank less than $d-1$ or an end-marker then $W_{\mathcal{A}}^t[i] = W_M^{t'}[i]$, where t' is the corresponding step[2] of M, and $\mathcal{A}$ and M have the same states[3]; M accepts the input iff $\mathcal{A}$ does.*

Lemma 3. *M performs $O(|Q_{\mathcal{A}}|n)$ steps on processing the input of length n.*

We omit the proofs of Lemmata 2 and 3 due to space limitations. Informally, the correctness (Lemma 2) easily follows from the definitions and Proposition 1. Lemma 3 is based on amortized analysis, particularly the accounting method. We describe the budget strategy to provide the proof-idea. Each cell $i \in \{1, \ldots, n\}$ (on M's tape) has it's own budget $B[i]$ and we denote its value after the t-th step as $B^t[i]$. Since totally we have given $2dn$ "dollars" this strategy leads to the linear-bound on the number of operations each costs $O(|Q_{\mathcal{A}}|)$.

We account budgets according to the following rules (the budget $B^t[k]$ is defined for the cell k (either $k = i$ or $k = j$) at the step t if it satisfies the corresponding rule):

- $B^0[i] = 2d$ for all i
- $B^t[i] = B^{t-1}[i] - 1$ if the cell i is visited at the step t and contains a letter (i.e., has been visited less than d times)
- $B^t[j] = B^{t-1}[j] - 1$ if at the step t the head arrives at the cell i from the cell j and the i-th cell contains a mapping and the j-th cell contains a letter
- $B^t[i] = B^{t-1}[i]$ if the previous rules are not applicable

Theorem 4 (Main result). *For each d-DLA $\mathcal{A}$ the membership problem is solvable in time $O(nm)$, where n is the length of the input word w and m is the length of $\mathcal{A}$'s description. Algorithm 3 provides the simulation of $\mathcal{A}$ on w and runs in time $O(nm)$ provided that subroutines are performed via Algorithm 2.*

---

[2] We demand that each such step t has the corresponding step t' and if $t_1 < t_2$ then $t_1' < t_2'$.

[3] When M arrives at a cell (except during a deletion scan) it always has a state $q \in Q_{\mathcal{A}}$.

Acknowledgments. The author thanks anonymous referees for their helpful comments and Dmitry Chistikov for the discussion and suggestions of improvements.

References

1. Abboud, A., Backurs, A., Williams, V.V.: If the current clique algorithms are optimal, so is Valiant's parser. In: 2015 IEEE 56th Annual Symposium on Foundations of Computer Science, pp. 98–117 (2015)
2. Bertsch, E., Nederhof, M.J.: Regular closure of deterministic languages. SIAM J. Comput. **29**(1), 81–102 (1999)
3. Birget, J.C.: Concatenation of inputs in a two-way automaton. Theor. Comput. Sci. **63**(2), 141–156 (1989)
4. Birman, A., Ullman, J.D.: Parsing algorithms with backtrack. In: 11th Annual Symposium on Switching and Automata Theory (SWAT 1970), pp. 153–174 (1970)
5. Cook, S.A.: Linear time simulation of deterministic two-way pushdown automata. University of Toronto, Department of Computer Science (1970)
6. Ford, B.: Parsing expression grammars: a recognition-based syntactic foundation. In: SIGPLAN Notics, vol. 39, no. 1, pp. 111–122 (2004)
7. Glück, R.: Simulation of two-way pushdown automata revisited. In: Electronic Proceedings in Theoretical Computer Science, vol. 129, p. 250–258. Open Publishing Association, September 2013
8. Guillon, B., Prigioniero, L.: Linear-time limited automata. Theor. Comput. Sci. **798**, 95–108 (2019)
9. Hennie, F.: One-tape, off-line turing machine computations. Inf. Control **8**(6), 553–578 (1965)
10. Hibbard, T.N.: A generalization of context-free determinism. Inf. Control **11**(1/2), 196–238 (1967)
11. Jayaram, R., Saha, B.: Approximating language edit distance beyond fast matrix multiplication: ultralinear grammars are where parsing becomes hard! In: ICALP 2017, pp. 19:1–19:15 (2017)
12. Knuth, D.: On the translation of languages from left to right. Inf. Control **8**, 607–639 (1965)
13. Lee, L.: Fast context-free grammar parsing requires fast Boolean matrix multiplication. J. ACM **49**(1), 1–15 (2002)
14. Loff, B., Moreira, N., Reis, R.: The computational power of parsing expression grammars. In: Hoshi, M., Seki, S. (eds.) DLT 2018. LNCS, vol. 11088, pp. 491–502. Springer, Cham (2018). https://doi.org/10.1007/978-3-319-98654-8_40
15. Pighizzini, G.: Nondeterministic one-tape off-line turing machines and their time complexity. J. Autom. Lang. Comb. **14**(1), 107–124 (2009)
16. Pighizzini, G.: Limited automata: properties, complexity and variants. In: Hospodár, M., Jirásková, G., Konstantinidis, S. (eds.) DCFS 2019. LNCS, vol. 11612, pp. 57–73. Springer, Cham (2019). https://doi.org/10.1007/978-3-030-23247-4_4
17. Pighizzini, G., Pisoni, A.: Limited automata and context-free languages. Fundamenta Informaticae **136**(1–2), 157–176 (2015)
18. Shallit, J.O.: A Second Course in Formal Languages and Automata Theory. Cambridge University Press, Cambridge (2008)
19. Shepherdson, J.C.: The reduction of two-way automata to one-way automata. IBM J. Res. Dev. **3**(2), 198–200 (1959)

20. Tadaki, K., Yamakami, T., Lin, J.C.: Theory of one-tape linear-time turing machines. Theor. Comput. Sci. **411**(1), 22–43 (2010)
21. Valiant, L.G.: General context-free recognition in less than cubic time. J. Comput. Syst. Sci. **10**(2), 308–315 (1975)
22. Wagner, K., Wechsung, G.: Computational Complexity. Springer, Netherlands (1986). https://doi.org/10.1007/978-1-4614-1800-9

Carathéodory Extensions of Subclasses of Regular Languages

Ryoma Sin'ya[(✉)]

Akita University, Akita, Japan
ryoma@math.akita-u.ac.jp

Abstract. A language L is said to be regular measurable if there exists an infinite sequence of regular languages that "converges" to L. In [13], the author showed that, while many complex context-free languages are regular measurable, the set of all primitive words and certain deterministic context-free languages are regular *immeasurable*. This paper investigates general properties of measurability, including closure properties, decidability and different characterisation. Further, for a suitable subclass $\mathcal{C}$ of regular languages, we show that the class of all $\mathcal{C}$-measurable regular languages has a good algebraic structure.

1 Introduction

How can we measure the volume of an object with a very complex shape? If it can be wet, an easy way is to slowly and completely submerge the object suspended by a thread in a rectangular tank filed with water, pull it out, and calculate the amount of water that overflows from the reduced water level. The amount of water that overflows is needed to "cover" the object, so it will be a good estimation of the volume of the object. It is a standard way in measure theory to cover an object $X \subseteq \mathbb{R}^d$ with a set $Y \supseteq X$ with good properties, called a "basic set", and use the measure of Y as an estimation (from outer) of the measure of X.

For example, in the case of Lebesgue measure (*cf.* [15]), we define the length of an interval $I = [a, b], [a, b), (a, b], (a, b)$ as $|I| = b - a$, and call the direct product $B = I_1 \times \cdots \times I_d$ of d intervals as a box (with $|B| = |I_1| \times \cdots \times |I_d|$), and *regard a countable union of boxes as a basic set*. The Lebesgue outer measure of a set $X \subseteq \mathbb{R}$ is defined as

$$m^*(X) = \inf \left\{ \sum_{n=1}^{\infty} |B_n| \mid \bigcup_{n=1}^{\infty} B_n \supseteq X; B_n \text{ is a box for each } n \geq 1 \right\},$$

i.e., the lower bound on the volume required to cover X by a basic set $\bigcup_{n=1}^{\infty} B_n$. X is said to be Lebesgue measurable if it satisfies the following so-called *Carathéodory's condition* (where $\overline{X}$ is the complement of X):

$$\forall S \subseteq \mathbb{R}^d \qquad m^*(S) = m^*(S \cap X) + m^*(S \cap \overline{X}).$$

© Springer Nature Switzerland AG 2021
N. Moreira and R. Reis (Eds.): DLT 2021, LNCS 12811, pp. 355–367, 2021.
https://doi.org/10.1007/978-3-030-81508-0_29

Actually, for subsets of the set of natural numbers $\mathbb{N} (\ni 0)$, we can apply this measure theoretic approach. In [3], Buck defines the density of an arithmetic progression (AP for short) $A = \{pn + q \mid n \in \mathbb{N}\}$ where $p, q \in \mathbb{N}^1$ as $d(A) = 1/p$ ($d(A) = 0$ if $p = 0$), *regards a finite union of arithmetic progressions as a basic set,* and defines the outer density of $X \subseteq \mathbb{N}$ as

$$d^*(X) = \inf \left\{ \sum_{n=1}^{k} d(A_n) \mid \bigcup_{n=1}^{k} A_n \supseteq X; k \in \mathbb{N}, A_n \text{ is an AP for each } n \in [1, k] \right\}.$$

As like the Lebesgue measurability, $X \subseteq \mathbb{N}$ is said to be measurable if it satisfies the Carathéodory's condition

$$\forall S \subseteq \mathbb{N} \qquad d^*(S) = d^*(S \cap X) + d^*(S \cap \overline{X}),$$

and Buck called $d^*(X)$ *the measure density of X* in this case.

Regular measurability (REG-measurability) proposed in [13] is an adoption of the Buck's measure density for formal languages: we define the density of a language $L \subseteq A^*$, *regards a regular language as a basic set*, and define the measurability of a language via outer and inner density (precise definition appears in the next section). The main motivation of [13] is, not just to generalise Buck's measure density, but also to tackle a long-standing open problem so-called *primitive words conjecture*. Some non-trivial partial results can be found in [13], which we will briefly describe in the next section. Regular measurability is an emergent notion and hence its theory is not well developed yet. In fact, it is fair to say that very little is known about the class of all regular measurable languages (regular measurable context-free languages, respectively). This paper investigates fundamental properties of regular measurability (and $\mathcal{C}$-measurability for a general language class $\mathcal{C}$) like as closure properties, decidability and different characterisation. Moreover, as a "miniature" of regular measurability, for some subclass $\mathcal{C}$ of regular languages, we investigate $\mathcal{C}$-measurability. While the class of all regular measurable languages (regular measurable context-free languages) has a complex structure and it is somewhat hard to analyse, for some suitable subclass $\mathcal{C}$ (called *local variety*) of regular languages, we will show that the class of all $\mathcal{C}$-measurable regular languages has a good algebraic structure and more easier to analyse.

Our Contribution and the Organisation of the Paper In this paper, all theorems/corollaries without citation are new (as much as we know), and main results consist of three kinds: **(I)** Give some new examples of regular (im)measurable languages (Theorem 3 and 4, Corollary 1 in Sect. 2). **(II)** Show some closure properties, an undecidability result (modulo a certain conjecture), and a different characterisation via the Carathéodory's condition of $\mathcal{C}$-measurability for a general language class $\mathcal{C}$ (Theorem 5–8 in Sect. 3). **(III)** Examine Carathéodory extensions of some local varieties of regular languages (Theorem 11–14 in Sect. 4). We also discuss future work and pose few open problems in Sect. 5.

---

[1] Here p can be 0 and we call a singleton $\{q\}$ arithmetic progression in this case.

2   Density and Measurability

This section provides the precise definitions of density and measurability. In Sect. 2.3, we briefly describe results in [13], and also give some new examples of regular measurable/immeasurable languages.

2.1   Density of Formal Languages

For a set X, we denote by $\#(X)$ the cardinality of X. We denote by $\mathbb{N}$ the set of natural numbers including 0. For an alphabet A, we denote the set of all words (all non-empty words, respectively) over A by A^* (A^+, respectively). For a word $w \in A^*$ and a letter $a \in A$, $|w|_a$ denotes the number of occurrences of a in w. A word v is said to be a subword of a word w if $w = xvy$ for some $x, y \in A^*$. For a language $L \subseteq A^*$, we denote by $\overline{L} = A^* \setminus L$ the complement of L. We say that L is co-finite if its complement is finite. A language L is said to be *dense* if $L \cap A^* w A^* \neq \emptyset$ holds for any $w \in A^*$. L is not dense means $L \cap A^* w A^* = \emptyset$ for some word w by definition, and such word is called a forbidden word of L.

Definition 1. Let $L \subseteq A^*$ be a language. The *density* $\delta_A^*(L)$ of L over A is defined as

$$\delta_A^*(L) = \lim_{n \to \infty} \frac{1}{n} \sum_{k=0}^{n-1} \frac{\#(L \cap A^k)}{\#(A^k)}$$

if its exists, otherwise we write $\delta_A^*(L) = \perp$ and say that L *does not have a density.* L is called *null* if $\delta_A^*(L) = 0$, and conversely L is called *co-null* if $\delta_A^*(L) = 1$.

The following observation is basic. See Chapter 13 of [2] for more details.

Lemma 1. *Let* $K, L \subseteq A^*$ *with* $\delta_A^*(K) = \alpha, \delta_A^*(L) = \beta$. *Then we have:*

(1) $\alpha \leq \beta$ *if* $K \subseteq L$.
(2) $\delta_A^*(L \setminus K) = \beta - \alpha$ *if* $K \subseteq L$. *In particular,* $\delta_A^*(\overline{K}) = \delta_A^*(A^* \setminus K) = 1 - \alpha$.
(3) $\delta_A^*(K \cup L) \leq \alpha + \beta$ *if* $\delta_A^*(K \cup L) \neq \perp$.
(4) $\delta_A^*(K \cup L) = \alpha + \beta$ *if* $K \cap L = \emptyset$.
(5) $\delta_A^*(wK) = \delta_A^*(Kw) = \alpha/\#(A)^{|w|}$ *for each* $w \in A^+$.

Example 1. Here we enumerate a few examples of densities of languages.

(1) Consider $(AA)^*$ the set of all words with even length. Because $\frac{\#((AA)^* \cap A^n)}{\#(A^n)}$ is 1 if n is even otherwise 0, clearly $\delta_A^*((AA)^*) = 1/2$ holds.
(2) For each word w, the language $A^* w A^*$, *i.e.*, the set of all words that contain w as a subword, has density 1 (co-null). This fact is sometimes called *infinite monkey theorem*. A language L having a forbidden word w is always null; since $A^* w A^* \subseteq \overline{L}$ holds by definition, we have $\delta_A^*(A^* w A^*) \leq \delta_A^*(\overline{L})$ which implies $\delta_A^*(\overline{L}) = 1$ by infinite monkey theorem. Thus L is null.

(3) The following language

$$L_\perp = \{w \in A^* \mid 3^n \le |w| < 3^{n+1} \text{ for some even number } n\}$$

does not have a density ($\delta_A^*(L_\perp) = \perp$). It can be shown by a simple analysis that the value $\frac{1}{n} \sum_{i=0}^{n-1} \frac{\#(L_\perp \cap A^i)}{\#(A^i)}$ could be larger than 2/3 (when $n = 3^k$ for odd k) and smaller than 1/3 (when $n = 3^k$ for even k) for infinitely many n so that $\delta_A^*(L_\perp)$ diverges. See the full version [14] for details.

Example 1 shows us that, for some language, its density is either zero or one, for some, like $(AA)^*$, a density could be a rational number like 1/2, and for some, like $L_\perp$ a density may not even exist. However, the following theorem tells us that all regular languages *do* have densities.

Theorem 1 (*cf.* **Theorem III.6.1 of** [10]). *Every regular language has a density and it is rational.*

Also, for the class of regular languages, two notions "not null" (a measure theoretic largeness) and "dense" (a topological largeness) are equivalent.

Theorem 2 ([12]). *A regular language L is not null if and only if L is dense.*

2.2   C-measurability of Formal Languages

A *language class* $\mathcal{C}$ is a family of languages $\{\mathcal{C}_A\}_{A: \text{ finite alphabet}}$ where $\mathcal{C}_A \subseteq 2^{A^*}$ for each A and $\mathcal{C}_A \subseteq \mathcal{C}_B$ for each $A \subseteq B$. We simply write $L \in \mathcal{C}$ if $L \in \mathcal{C}_A$ for some alphabet A. We denote by REG and CFL the class of regular languages and context-free languages, respectively.

We now introduce the notion of $\mathcal{C}$-measurability which is a formal language theoretic analogue of Buck's measure density [3].

Definition 2 ([13]). Let $\mathcal{C}$ be a class of languages. For a language $L \subseteq A^*$, we define its $\mathcal{C}$-*inner-density* $\underline{\mu}_{\mathcal{C}_A}(L)$ and $\mathcal{C}$-*outer-density* $\overline{\mu}_{\mathcal{C}_A}(L)$ over A as

$$\underline{\mu}_{\mathcal{C}_A}(L) = \sup\{\delta_A^*(K) \mid K \subseteq L, K \in \mathcal{C}_A, \delta_A^*(K) \ne \perp\},$$
$$\overline{\mu}_{\mathcal{C}_A}(L) = \inf\{\delta_A^*(K) \mid L \subseteq K, K \in \mathcal{C}_A, \delta_A^*(K) \ne \perp\}.$$

A language L is said to be $\mathcal{C}$-*measurable* over A if $\underline{\mu}_{\mathcal{C}_A}(L) = \overline{\mu}_{\mathcal{C}_A}(L)$ holds, and we simply write $\overline{\mu}_{\mathcal{C}_A}(L)$ as $\mu_{\mathcal{C}_A}(L)$ in this case. We say that an infinite sequence $(L_n)_n$ of languages over A *converges* to L *from inner (from outer, respectively)* if $L_n \subseteq L$ ($L_n \supseteq L$, respectively) for each n and $\lim_{n \to \infty} \delta_A^*(L_n) = \delta_A^*(L)$.

Remark 1. Both density and $\mathcal{C}$-measurability depends on the alphabet. For example, any language $L \subseteq A^*$ is of density *zero* over $B \supsetneq A$. Also, any language $L \subseteq A^*$ is REG-measurable over $B \supsetneq A$: clearly $\emptyset \subseteq L \subseteq (B \backslash \{b\})^*$ holds for $b \in (B \backslash A)$ and hence $\underline{\mu}_{\mathrm{REG}_B}(L) = \overline{\mu}_{\mathrm{REG}_B}(L) = 0$ $((B \backslash \{b\})^*$ has a forbidden word b hence it is null over B by infinite monkey theorem), *i.e.*REG-measurable over B. Hereafter, we mainly consider density and $\mathcal{C}$-measurability over the *minimum* alphabet for each language L, *i.e.*, the minimum alphabet A satisfying $L \subseteq A^*$. We sometimes omit the subscript of $\underline{\mu}_{\mathrm{REG}_A}(L), \overline{\mu}_{\mathrm{REG}_A}(L)$ like $\underline{\mu}_{\mathrm{REG}}(L), \overline{\mu}_{\mathrm{REG}}(L)$, and we simply say "$L$ is of density one" or "L is $\mathcal{C}$-measurable". In this case the considered alphabet is always the minimum one.

The following basic lemmata will be used in the next section.

Lemma 2 (*cf.* [13]). *Let* $K, L \subseteq A^*$ *be two languages.*

(1) $\underline{\mu}_{\mathcal{C}_A}(K) \leq \delta_A^*(K) \leq \overline{\mu}_{\mathcal{C}_A}(K)$ *if* $\delta_A^*(K) \neq \bot$. *In particular,* $\delta_A^*(K) = \bot$ *implies* K *is* $\mathcal{C}$-immeasurable.
(2) $\overline{\mu}_{\mathcal{C}_A}(K) \leq \overline{\mu}_{\mathcal{C}_A}(L)$ *if* $K \subseteq L$.
(3) $\overline{\mu}_{\mathcal{C}_A}(K \cup L) \leq \overline{\mu}_{\mathcal{C}_A}(K) + \overline{\mu}_{\mathcal{C}_A}(L)$ *if* $\mathcal{C}$ *is closed under union.*
(4) $\overline{\mu}_{\mathcal{C}_A}(K) = \delta_A^*(K)$ *if* $K \in \mathcal{C}$ *and* $\delta_A^*(K) \neq \bot$.

Lemma 3 (*cf.* [13]). *Let* $\mathcal{C}$ *be a language class closed under complementation. A language* $L \subseteq A^*$ *is* $\mathcal{C}$-*measurable if and only if*

$$\overline{\mu}_{\mathcal{C}_A}(L) + \overline{\mu}_{\mathcal{C}_A}(\overline{L}) = 1. \tag{1}$$

2.3 Examples of REG-measurable/immeasurable Languages

In this subsection we describe several examples of REG-(im)measurable languages. In [13], it is shown that many complex context-free languages are REG-measurable, while the deterministic context-free language $\mathsf{M}_2 = \{w \in A^* \mid |w|_a > 2 \cdot |w|_b\}$ and the set Q of all primitive words (a word is said to be *primitive* if it can not be represented as a power of any shorter words) over $A = \{a, b\}$ are REG-immeasurable. In [13] the author originally conjectured that there is no context-free language like Q: if a context-free language L is co-null, then it can be somehow "approximated" by regular languages from inner, *i.e.*, $\underline{\mu}_{\mathrm{REG}}(L) > 0$. If this conjecture *was* true, then the primitive words conjecture "Q is not context-free" posed by Dömösi, Horváth and Ito [4] was true, too. However, the author found a counterexample $\overline{\mathsf{M}}_2$ and hence this naïve approach did not work (still, this approach has some possibility, see the last section of [13] for details).

Now we give three new examples of REG-(im)measurable languages. The following indexed language is not context-free, but REG-measurable.

Theorem 3. $L_{\exp} = \{a^{2^n} \mid n \in \mathbb{N}\}$ *is* REG-*measurable over* $A = \{a\}$.

Proof. Clearly, $\delta_A^*(L_{\exp}) = 0$ holds hence it is enough to construct a sequence of regular languages that converges to $L_{\exp}$ from outer. For each $k \geq 1$, a regular language $L_k = (a^k)^* \cup \{a^n \mid 0 < n < k\}$ satisfies $\delta_A^*(L_k) = 1/k$ ($\lim_{k \to \infty} \delta_A^*(L_k) = 0$, in particular). We show that $a^{2^n} \in L_{2^k}$ holds for each $k \geq 1$ and $n \in \mathbb{N}$ (*i.e.*, $L_{\exp} \subseteq L_{2^k}$). The case $2^n < 2^k$ is clear by definition thus consider the case $2^n \geq 2^k$. In this case, $2^n = 2^k \cdot 2^{n-k}$ holds hence a^{2^n} is the 2^{n-k} times repetition of a^{2^k} which means $a^{2^n} \in (a^{2^k})^* \subseteq L_{2^k}$. Thus the sequence $(L_{2^k})_{k \geq 1}$ converges to $L_{\exp}$ from outer. $\qquad\square$

The next theorem tells us that REG-measurable languages exist for each real number between 0 and 1 (see the full version [14] for the full proof).

Theorem 4. *Let A be an alphabet including at least two letters. For each real number $0 \leq \alpha \leq 1$, there exists a REG-measurable language L over A with density exactly α.*

Proof (sketch). Consider the case $A = \{a, b\}$ (a general case can be shown similarly). Let $(\alpha_n)_{n \geq 1}$ (where each $\alpha_i \in \{0, 1\}$) be the binary expansion of $\alpha \in [0, 1]$: $\alpha = \sum_{n=1}^{\infty} \alpha_n 2^{-n}$. Define $K_0 = \emptyset, M_0 = A^*$ and define K_n, M_n inductively as follows:

$$K_n = \begin{cases} b^{n-1}aA^* \cup K_{n-1} & \alpha_n = 1 \\ K_{n-1} & \alpha_n = 0 \end{cases} \qquad M_n = \begin{cases} M_{n-1} & \alpha_n = 1 \\ M_{n-1} \setminus b^{n-1}aA^* & \alpha_n = 0 \end{cases}$$

Clearly, each K_n, M_n are regular. One can formally show that the sequence $(K_n, M_n)_n$ converges to the language $L = \bigcup_{n \in \mathbb{N}} K_n = \bigcap_{n \in \mathbb{N}} M_n$ whose density is α. □

Finally, by Lemma 2-(1) we have the following REG-immeasurable language.

Corollary 1. $L_\perp$ *defined in Example 1-(3) is REG-immeasurable.*

3   Closure Properties and Carathéodory's Condition

In this section we investigate general properties of $\mathcal{C}$-measurability. First we show that $\mathcal{C}$-measurability is closed under Boolean operations and left-and-right quotients, with some density condition. This fact plays important role in the next section. Due to the space limitation, we omit the proof of Theorem 5, which is rather easier than Theorem 6. See the full version [14] for the proof.

Theorem 5. *Let $\mathcal{C}$ be a language class closed under Boolean operations. If L, K are $\mathcal{C}$-measurable, and if every language obtained by a finite Boolean combination of languages in $\mathcal{C} \cup \{L, K\}$ has a density, then the complement $\overline{L}$, the union $L \cup K$ and the intersection $L \cap K$ are also $\mathcal{C}$-measurable.*

Theorem 6. *Let $\mathcal{C}$ be a language class closed under left quotients (right quotients, respectively). If L is $\mathcal{C}$-measurable, and if the left quotient $a^{-1}L$ (the right quotient La^{-1}, respectively) has a density, then it is also $\mathcal{C}$-measurable.*

Proof. For a $\mathcal{C}$-measurable language L over A, we show that $a^{-1}L$ is also $\mathcal{C}$-measurable (La^{-1} can be shown by the same way). By definition, there is a convergent sequence $(K_n, M_n)_n$ to L. We show that $(a^{-1}K_n, a^{-1}M_n)_n$ converges to $a^{-1}L$.

For simplicity, we consider the case $A = \{a, b\}$ (a general case can be shown similarly). For each $a \in A$ we have $L \cap aA^* = aa^{-1}L$ and hence L can be written as $L = aa^{-1}L \cup bb^{-1}L \cup (L \cap \{\varepsilon\})$. By assumption $aa^{-1}L$ and $bb^{-1}L$

have density. Because $aa^{-1}L$ and $bb^{-1}L$ are mutually disjoint, by the additivity of δ_A^* (Lemma 1-(4)) we have

$$\delta_A^*(L) = \delta_A^*(aa^{-1}L) + \delta_A^*(bb^{-1}L). \tag{2}$$

$K_n \subseteq L$ holds for each n hence we have $a^{-1}K_n \subseteq a^{-1}L$ and $\delta_A^*(a^{-1}K_n) \leq \delta_A^*(a^{-1}L)$. Because $(K_n)_n$ is a convergent sequence to L from inner, for any $\epsilon/2 > 0$ there exists δ such that $\delta_A^*(L) - \delta_A^*(K_n) < \epsilon/2$ holds for every $n > \delta$. Thus from Equality (2) we can deduce that

$$\delta_A^*(L) - \delta_A^*(K_n) = \delta_A^*(aa^{-1}L) - \delta_A^*(aa^{-1}K_n) + \delta_A^*(bb^{-1}L) - \delta_A^*(bb^{-1}K_n) < \frac{\epsilon}{2}$$

holds for every $n > \delta$. We know $\delta_A^*(cc^{-1}L') = \delta_A^*(c^{-1}L')/2$ for any $c \in \{a, b\}$ and L' by Lemma 1-(5), the above inequality can be transformed as

$$\frac{1}{2}(\delta_A^*(a^{-1}L) - \delta_A^*(a^{-1}K_n)) + \frac{1}{2}(\delta_A^*(b^{-1}L) - \delta_A^*(b^{-1}K_n)) < \frac{\epsilon}{2}.$$

Hence we can conclude that $\delta_A^*(a^{-1}L) - \delta_A^*(a^{-1}K_n) < \epsilon$ for every $n > \delta$, i.e., $(a^{-1}K_n)_n$ is a convergent sequence to $a^{-1}L$ from inner. We can show that $(a^{-1}M_n)_n$ converges to L from outer by the same way. □

Corollary 2. *Let $C \subseteq D$ be language classes where C is closed under Boolean operations and left-and-right quotients and every language in D has a density. Then C-measurability in D is preserved under Boolean operations and left-and-right quotients.*

An application of Theorem 6 is a proof of the undecidability of REG-measurability for context-free languages, modulo the following conjecture.

Conjecture 1. If a context-free language L has a density, then its quotients $a^{-1}L$ and La^{-1} also have densities.

Theorem 7. *If Conjecture 1 is true, then it is undecidable whether a given context-free grammar generates REG-measurable language or not.*

Proof. The class CFL is closed under left-and-right quotients, hence by Theorem 6 the class $P = \{L \in \text{CFL}_A \mid L \text{ is REG-measurable}\}_A$ is also closed under left-and-right quotients. It is clear that REG $\subseteq P$ holds, and, as we explained in Sect. 2, there is REG-immeasurable context-free language M_2, i.e., $P \subsetneq$ CFL. Because the universality problem for CFL is undecidable, the REG-measurability is also undecidable for CFL by the well-known Greibach's theorem [7]. □

We conclude this section by giving the following Carathéodory's condition characterisation of REG-measurability. The proof is almost same with one of Lebesgue measurability (cf. [15]), albeit that requires some density condition which is formal language theoretic.

Theorem 8. *Let C be a class of languages closed under Boolean operations and let $L \subseteq A^*$ be a language. If every language obtained by a finite Boolean combination of languages in $C \cup \{L\}$ has a density, then L is C-measurable if and only if the following Carathéodory's condition holds:*

$$\forall X \subseteq A^* \qquad \overline{\mu}_C(X) = \overline{\mu}_C(X \cap L) + \overline{\mu}_C(X \cap \overline{L}). \tag{3}$$

Proof. If L satisfies the Carathéodory condition (3), then we obtain $\overline{\mu}_C(A^*) = 1 = \overline{\mu}_C(L) + \overline{\mu}_C(\overline{L})$ when $X = A^*$, thus by Lemma 3, L is C-measurable because C is closed under complementation by assumption.

Now we show the converse direction. Assume L is C-measurable. For any language $X \subseteq A^*$ and for any $\epsilon > 0$, by the definition of $\overline{\mu}_C$, there exists $K \in C$ such that $X \subseteq K$ and $\delta_A^*(K) \leq \overline{\mu}_C(X) + \epsilon$. Here L, K and $\overline{K}$ are all C-measurable, and by assumption $K \cap L$ and $K \cap \overline{L}$ have densities. Hence, by Theorem 5, $K \cap L$ and $K \cap \overline{L}$ are C-measurable. Because $K = (K \cap L) \cup (K \cap \overline{L})$ and $(K \cap L) \cap (K \cap \overline{L}) = \emptyset$,

$$\delta_A^*(K) = \delta_A^*(K \cap L) + \delta_A^*(K \cap \overline{L})$$

holds by the additivity of δ_A^* (Lemma 1-(4)). Hence we have

$$\overline{\mu}_C(X) \geq \delta_A^*(K) - \epsilon = \delta_A^*(K \cap L) + \delta_A^*(K \cap \overline{L}) - \epsilon$$
$$\geq \overline{\mu}_C(X \cap L) + \overline{\mu}_C(X \cap \overline{L}) - \epsilon.$$

Because $\epsilon > 0$ is taken arbitrarily, we can conclude that

$$\overline{\mu}_C(X) \geq \overline{\mu}_C(X \cap L) + \overline{\mu}_C(X \cap \overline{L})$$

holds. The reverse direction $\leq$ of the above inequality is directly obtained by the subadditivity of $\overline{\mu}_C$ (Lemma 2-(3)). $\square$

4   Carathéodory Extensions of Local Varieties

In this section, as a "miniature" of REG-measurability, we investigate C-measurability for some subclass C of REG. The considered subclasses of regular languages here are so-called local varieties, which enjoy good closure properties and have rich algebraic structure. First we introduce some background materials from algebraic language theory.

4.1   Local Varieties and an Eilenberg-Type Theorem

Due to the space limitation, we assume that the author has a basic knowledge of algebraic language theory (*e.g.*, syntactic monoids and morphism, *etc. cf.* [8,9]). For a language L over A, we denote its syntactic monoid by $\mathsf{Synt}(L)$ and its syntactic morphism by $\eta_L : A^* \to \mathsf{Synt}(L)$. A monoid M is said to be *aperiodic*, if there is $k \geq 1$ such that $x^k = x^{k+1}$ for any $x \in M$. M is called *zero* if it contains zero element 0: $0 \cdot x = x \cdot 0 = 0$ for all $x \in M$. Further, a zero semigroup S is called *nilpotent* if there is $k \geq 1$ such that $x^k = 0$ for any $x \in S$. A non-empty subset $I \subseteq M$ is called ideal if $M \cdot I \cdot M \subseteq I$. An ideal I is said to be minimal if no proper subset of I is an ideal. It is well-known that any finite monoid has a unique minimal ideal (*cf.* [9]).

The main targets in the next subsection are classes of regular languages with some *good* closure properties as follows.

Definition 3 (*cf.* [1]). *A family $\mathcal{C} \subseteq \mathrm{REG}_A$ of regular languages over A is called local variety if it is closed under Boolean operations and left-and-right quotients. A family V of finite monoids generated by A is called local pseudovariety if it is closed under quotients and subdirect products.*

Theorem 9 (Eilenberg-type theorem for local varieties [6]**).** *For each A, there is a lattice isomorphism between the class of all local varieties and the class of all local pseudovarieties.*

This Eilenberg-type theorem roughly states that: if a class of languages is somewhat "robust" (*i.e.*, enjoys good closure properties), then it could be characterised by an algebraic way (at least there should exist the corresponding local pseudovariety), and vice versa. We now enumerate three examples of local varieties and corresponding local pseudovarieties (see Fig. 1). A prominent example of a local variety is *star-free languages*. A language L is said to be star-free if it can be obtained by a finite combination of Boolean operations and concatenations of finite languages. The family SF_A of all star-free languages over A forms a local variety, and this class can be characterised in purely algebraic way as follows.

Theorem 10 (Schützenberger's theorem [11]**).** *The corresponding local pseudovariety of SF_A is the class of aperiodic finite monoids generated by A. Namely, $L \in \mathrm{SF}_A$ if and only if $\mathsf{Synt}(L)$ is aperiodic.*

Next we introduce two additional examples of local varieties. One is the family FIN_A of all *finite and co-finite languages* and another one is the family ZO_A of all regular languages with *density either zero or one*. FIN_A and ZO_A form a local variety, respectively. In his Volume B [5], Eilenberg showed that the class of all finite nilpotent semigroups form a pseudovariety (of semigroups) and its corresponding $+$-variety of languages is exactly the class of all finite and co-finite languages. The corresponding local pseudovariety of ZO_A is the family of all finite zero monoids (*cf.* [12]).

4.2   Extension as a Closure Operator

In this subsection we mainly consider "extensions" of local varieties. All results are summarised in Fig. 1. First we introduce necessary notation.

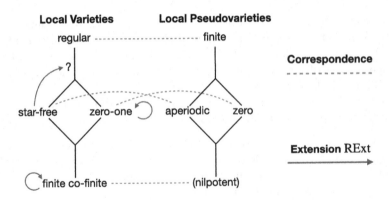

Fig. 1. Relation between local varieties, extensions and local pseudovarieties.

Definition 4. For a family $\mathcal{C} \subseteq 2^{A^*}$ of languages over A, we define its *(Carathéodory) extension* as

$$\mathrm{Ext}_A(\mathcal{C}) = \{L \subseteq A^* \mid L \text{ is } \mathcal{C}\text{-measurable}\},$$

and define its *regular extension* as

$$\mathrm{RExt}_A(\mathcal{C}) = \mathrm{Ext}_A(\mathcal{C}) \cap \mathrm{REG}_A.$$

Observe that this extension operator is a closure as follows (see the full version [14] for the proof).

Theorem 11. Ext_A *is a closure operator, i.e., it satisfies the following three properties for each $\mathcal{C}, \mathcal{D} \subseteq 2^{A^*}$.*

extensive: $\mathcal{C} \subseteq \mathrm{Ext}_A(\mathcal{C})$.
monotone: $\mathcal{C} \subseteq \mathcal{D}$ *implies* $\mathrm{Ext}_A(\mathcal{C}) \subseteq \mathrm{Ext}_A(\mathcal{D})$.
idempotent: $\mathrm{Ext}_A(\mathrm{Ext}_A(\mathcal{C})) = \mathrm{Ext}_A(\mathcal{C})$.

In the previous section, we showed that the $\mathcal{C}$-measurability is closed under Boolean operations and left-and-right quotients if $\mathcal{C}$ is closed under these operations and every language in $\mathcal{C}$ have a density (Corollary 2). Because every regular language have a density (Theorem 1), we have the following corollary.

Corollary 3. *For any local variety $\mathcal{C} \subseteq \mathrm{REG}_A$ over A, $\mathrm{RExt}_A(\mathcal{C}) \supseteq \mathcal{C}$ is also a local variety over A, i.e., RExt_A is a closure operator over the class of all local varieties.*

Clearly, any FIN_A-measurable language is either finite or co-finite. A similar argument can be applied for ZO_A. Thus RExt_A does not properly extend these two local varieties.

Theorem 12. $\mathrm{RExt}_A(\mathrm{FIN}_A) = \mathrm{FIN}_A$ *and* $\mathrm{RExt}_A(\mathrm{ZO}_A) = \mathrm{ZO}_A$ *for each A.*

Furthermore, for a unary alphabet $A = \{a\}$, it is well-known that $\mathrm{SF}_A = \mathrm{ZO}_A = \mathrm{FIN}_A$, hence we have the following as a corollary.

Corollary 4. $\mathrm{RExt}_A(\mathrm{SF}_A) = \mathrm{SF}_A = \mathrm{ZO}_A = \mathrm{FIN}_A$ *for* $A = \{a\}$.

The situation is different for the case $\#(A) \geq 2$. As we explained in Remark 1, if $\#(A) \geq 2$, $\mathrm{RExt}_A(\mathrm{SF}_A)$ can contain *any* regular language over $B \subsetneq A$ hence $\mathrm{RExt}_A(\mathrm{SF}_A) \supsetneq \mathrm{SF}_A$ ($\mathrm{RExt}_A(\mathrm{SF}_A) \ni (aa)^* \notin \mathrm{SF}_A$, in particular). The next theorem says, however, $\mathrm{RExt}_A(\mathrm{SF}_A)$ can not contain some regular languages over A like $(AA)^*$.

Theorem 13. *If a star-free language* $L \in \mathrm{SF}_A$ *satisfies* $\delta_A^*(L) > 0$, *then* L *contains words of even and odd length.*

Proof. Consider the syntactic monoid $\mathsf{Synt}(L)$, the syntactic morphism $\eta_L : A^* \to \mathsf{Synt}(L)$ and the syntactic image $S = \eta_L(L)$ of L. Because L is regular, $\mathsf{Synt}(L)$ is finite. Hence it has a unique minimal ideal $K \subseteq \mathsf{Synt}(L)$. Let w_x be a word whose syntactic image $\eta_L(w_x)$ is x for each $x \in \mathsf{Synt}(L)$.

The assumption $\delta_A^*(L) > 0$ implies $S \cap K \neq \emptyset$, because $\delta_A^*(\eta^{-1}(\mathsf{Synt}(L) \setminus K)) = 0$ holds; for each $k \in K$ and $x, y \in A^*$, we have $\eta_L(xw_k y) = \eta_L(x) \cdot k \cdot \eta_L(y) \in K$ and hence $\eta^{-1}(\mathsf{Synt}(L) \setminus K) \cap A^* w_k A^* = \emptyset$ which implies $\eta^{-1}(\mathsf{Synt}(L) \setminus K)$ is null by infinite monkey theorem. Thus L is not null implies its syntactic image S contains at least one element of K, say, $t \in S \cap K$.

Clearly, $\delta_A^*(\eta^{-1}(K)) = 1$ holds and hence $\eta^{-1}(K)$ contains some word w_{odd} of odd length. Let $m_{\mathrm{odd}} = \eta_L(w_{\mathrm{odd}})$ be its syntactic image. By Schützenberger's theorem (Theorem 10), $\mathsf{Synt}(L)$ is aperiodic thus there is some $i \geq 1$ such that $m_{\mathrm{odd}}^i = m_{\mathrm{odd}}^{i+1}$. By the minimality of the ideal K, there exist $x, y \in \mathsf{Synt}(L)$ such that $x \cdot m_{\mathrm{odd}}^i \cdot y = t$ (if not, the ideal $\mathsf{Synt}(L) \cdot m_{\mathrm{odd}}^i \cdot \mathsf{Synt}(L)$ generated by m_{odd}^i does not contain t hence it should be a proper subset of K). Then two words $w_x w_{\mathrm{odd}}^i w_y$ and $w_x w_{\mathrm{odd}}^{i+1} w_y$ has the same syntactic image

$$\eta_L(w_x w_{\mathrm{odd}}^i w_y) = x \cdot m_{\mathrm{odd}}^i \cdot y = t = x \cdot m_{\mathrm{odd}}^{i+1} \cdot y = \eta_L(w_x w_{\mathrm{odd}}^{i+1} w_y),$$

thus both belong to L. Because the length of w_{odd} is odd, the lengths of these two words are different modulo 2. □

The above theorem tells us that any star-free subset of $(AA)^*$ is null and any star-free superset of $(AA)^*$ is co-null, thus we have the following corollary.

Corollary 5. $(AA)^* \notin \mathrm{RExt}_A(\mathrm{SF}_A)$ *for any* A. *In particular,* $\underline{\mu}_{\mathrm{SF}_A}((AA)^*) = 0$ *and* $\overline{\mu}_{\mathrm{SF}_A}((AA)^*) = 1$. *Further,* $\mathrm{SF}_A \subsetneq \mathrm{RExt}_A(\mathrm{SF}_A) \subsetneq \mathrm{REG}_A$ *if* $\#(A) \geq 2$.

We are not aware what the associated local pseudovariety of this new local variety $\mathrm{RExt}_A(\mathrm{SF}_A)$ yet, but, we can say that $\mathrm{RExt}_A(\mathrm{SF}_A)$ always contains all zero-one regular languages.

Theorem 14. $\mathrm{RExt}_A(\mathrm{SF}_A) \supseteq \mathrm{ZO}_A$ *for any* A.

Proof. The case $\#(A) = 1$ follows from Theorem 4. We show this for a general alphabet A. Let $L \in \mathrm{ZO}_A$ and we can assume $\delta_A^*(L) = 0$ without loss of generality. By Theorem 2, L is null implies there is some forbidden word w of L: $L \cap A^* w A^* = \emptyset$. Hence $L \subseteq \overline{A^* w A^*}$ holds and $\underline{\mu}_{\mathrm{SF}_A}(L) = \overline{\mu}_{\mathrm{SF}_A}(L) = 0$. □

5   Future Work and Open Problems

We have investigated general properties of $\mathcal{C}$-measurability, and examine how the extension operator RExt_A extends certain local varieties of regular languages. An immediate future work is to give an algebraic characterisation of $\mathrm{RExt}_A(\mathrm{SF}_A)$. We are also interested whether we can characterise the associated extension operator of local pseudovarieties of finite monoids $\mathrm{MExt}_A(\mathsf{V}) = F(\mathrm{RExt}_A(F^{-1}(\mathsf{V})))$ in purely algebraic way, where F is the lattice isomorphism stated in Theorem 9. One of the ideal goals is to understand the class of REG-measurable context-free languages. However, it looks like a bit difficult since the theory of densities of context-free languages is not well developed yet (*e.g.*, Conjecture 1). Actually, we are not aware whether there is a context-free language that do not have a density ($L_\perp$ in Example 1-(3) is not context-free). More open problems related to REG-measurability and context-free languages were posed in [13].

Acknowledgements. This work was supported by JSPS KAKENHI Grant Number JP19K14582.

References

1. Adámek, J., Milius, S., Myers, R.S.R., Urbat, H.: Generalized Eilenberg theorem I: local varieties of languages. In: Muscholl, A. (ed.) FoSSaCS 2014. LNCS, vol. 8412, pp. 366–380. Springer, Heidelberg (2014). https://doi.org/10.1007/978-3-642-54830-7_24
2. Berstel, J., Perrin, D., Reutenauer, C.: Codes and Automata (Encyclopedia of Mathematics and its Applications). Cambridge University Press, Cambridge (2009)
3. Buck, R.C.: The measure theoretic approach to density. Am. J. Math. **68**(4), 560–580 (1946)
4. Dömösi, P., Horváth, S., Ito, M.: On the connection between formal languages and primitive words. In: First Session on Scientific Communication, pp. 59–67 (1991)
5. Eilenberg, S., Tilson, B.: Automata, languages and machines. In: Pure and Applied Mathematics, vol. B. Academic Press, New-York (1976)
6. Gehrke, M., Grigorieff, S., Pin, J.É.: Duality and equational theory of regular languages. In: Aceto, L., Damgård, I., Goldberg, L.A., Halldórsson, M.M., Ingólfsdóttir, A., Walukiewicz, I. (eds.) ICALP 2008. LNCS, vol. 5126, pp. 246–257. Springer, Heidelberg (2008). https://doi.org/10.1007/978-3-540-70583-3_21
7. Greibach, S.A.: A note on undecidable properties of formal languages. Math. Syst. Theor. **2**, 1–6 (1968)
8. Lawson, M.V.: Finite automata. Birkhäuser (2005)
9. Pin, J.E.: Mathematical foundations of automata theory (draft)
10. Salomaa, A., Soittola, M.: Automata Theoretic Aspects of Formal Power Series. Springer, New York (1978). https://doi.org/10.1007/978-1-4612-6264-0
11. Schützenberger, M.P.: On finite monoids having only trivial subgroups. Inf. Control **8**(2), 190–194 (1965)
12. Sin'ya, R.: An automata theoretic approach to the zero-one law for regular languages. In: Games, Automata, Logics and Formal Verification, pp. 172–185 (2015)
13. Sin'ya, R.: Asymptotic approximation by regular languages. In: Bureš, T., et al. (eds.) SOFSEM 2021. LNCS, vol. 12607, pp. 74–88. Springer, Cham (2021). https://doi.org/10.1007/978-3-030-67731-2_6

14. Sin'ya, R.: Carathéodory extensions of subclasses of regular languages (full version) (2021). http://www.math.akita-u.ac.jp/~ryoma/misc/caratheodory.pdf
15. Tao, T.: An Introduction to Measure Theory (Graduate Studies in Mathematics). American Mathematical Society, Providence (2013)

Parikh Word Representable Graphs and Morphisms

Nobin Thomas[1,2] (ID), Lisa Mathew[1] (ID), Somnath Bera[3] (ID), Atulya K. Nagar[4] (ID), and K. G. Subramanian[4(✉)] (ID)

[1] Department of Basic Sciences, Amal Jyothi College of Engineering, Kanjirappally 686 518, Kerala, India
[2] APJ Abdul Kalam Technological University, Thiruvananthapuram 695 016, Kerala, India
[3] School of Advanced Sciences-Mathematics, Vellore Institute of Technology, Chennai 600 127, Tamil Nadu, India
[4] School of Mathematics, Computer Science and Engineering, Liverpool Hope University, Hope Park, Liverpool L16 9JD, UK

Abstract. Study on numerical properties of words based on scattered subwords of words was initiated around the year 2000, introducing certain upper triangular matrices, called Parikh matrices. On the other hand, linking the areas of combinatorics on words and graph theory, a class of graphs, called Parikh word representable graphs ($PWRG$) of words, was introduced based on certain scattered subwords of words. Several properties of $PWRG$ have been investigated, especially corresponding to binary words. Here, we derive several structural properties of $PWRG$ of images of ternary words under certain morphisms.

1 Introduction

As an extension of the notion of Parikh mapping [13] of a word, Parikh matrix mapping was introduced by Mateescu et al. [10] associating certain upper triangular matrices called Parikh matrices, with words over an ordered alphabet, thus initiating a study of some numerical properties of words based on scattered subwords of words, which are also simply called subwords. Subsequently, many problems on words and subwords have been investigated (see, for example, [2,3,9,15,17,18] and references therein), establishing a number of interesting results. On the other hand studies on relating graphs and words have taken place (see, for example, [7,8]), thereby linking the two areas, namely graph theory and combinatorics on words. The concept of a Parikh word representable graph was introduced in [4] associating a graph with a word and several graph properties of Parikh word representable graphs, were studied recently [4,11,16]. In fact an important characterization that the Parikh word representable graphs are exactly the bipartite permutation graphs, is established by Teh et al. in [16] and a necessary and sufficient condition, besides other interesting and deep results, is

---

N. Thomas—Research Scholar, K. G. Subramanian—Honorary Visiting Professor.

© Springer Nature Switzerland AG 2021
N. Moreira and R. Reis (Eds.): DLT 2021, LNCS 12811, pp. 368–379, 2021.
https://doi.org/10.1007/978-3-030-81508-0_30

obtained in [16] for a Parikh ternary word representable graph to have a Hamiltonian cycle. In this paper, we study several structural properties such as graph isomorphism, Hamiltonian and Eulerian property of Parikh word representable graphs of images of words under certain morphisms. We also extend to a ternary alphabet certain known results such as connectivity and Eulerian property of Parikh word representable graphs of words over a binary alphabet.

2   Preliminaries

We recall certain needed notions related to words [12,14] and graphs [5]. For unexplained definitions and notations concerning words we refer to [9,14] and for unexplained concepts related to graphs, we refer to [5].

Let $\Sigma = \{a_1 < a_2 < \cdots < a_k\}, k \geq 1$ be an ordered alphabet with an order relation $<$ defined on it. We denote by Σ_2 and Σ_3, the binary ordered alphabet $\{a < b\}$ and the ternary ordered alphabet $\{a < b < c\}$ respectively. A word $w' = x_1 x_2 \ldots x_n$, $x_i \in \Sigma$ for $1 \leq i \leq n$, is a scattered subword or simply, a subword of a word w over Σ if and only if we can find words $y_0, y_1, \ldots, y_n$ over Σ, some of them possibly empty, such that $w = y_0 x_1 y_1 x_2 y_2 \ldots y_{n-1} x_n y_n$. The number of occurrences of a word u as a subword of w is denoted by $|w|_u$. The set of all words over an alphabet Σ, including the empty word λ, is denoted by Σ^*. We denote by $L(r)$, the language of a regular expression [14]. The mirror image of a word $w = a_1 a_2 \cdots a_{n-1} a_n$ over a given alphabet is the word $mi(w) = a_n a_{n-1} \cdots a_2 a_1$.

Definition 1. *[4] For each word $w = w_1 w_2 \ldots w_n, w_i \in \Sigma$ of length n over $\Sigma = \{a_1 < a_2 < \cdots < a_k\}$, we define a simple graph $\mathcal{G}(w)$ with n labeled vertices $1, 2, \ldots, n$ representing the positions of the letters $w_i, 1 \leq i \leq n$ in w such that corresponding to each occurrence of the subword $a_i a_{i+1}$ in w, for every $i, 1 \leq i \leq n-1$, there is an edge in the graph $\mathcal{G}(w)$ between the vertices corresponding to the positions of a_i and a_{i+1}. We say that the word w represents the graph $\mathcal{G}(w)$. A graph is said to be Parikh word representable if there exists a word w that represents it. We also say that vertex i is labeled with the symbol w_i.*

In Fig. 1, the Parikh word representable graph of the word *aababc* over Σ_3 is shown.

   Two words $w, w' \in \Sigma^*$ are said to be 1-equivalent [17] and we write $w \equiv_1 w'$ if there exist a series of words $w = v_0, v_1, \ldots, v_n = w'$ in Σ^* such that for $0 \leq i \leq n-1$, $v_i = x a_k a_l y, v_{i+1} = x a_l a_k y$, for some $a_k, a_l \in \Sigma$ with $|k - l| \geq 2$ and some $x, y \in \Sigma^*$.

Definition 2. *[17,18] Let $v, w \in \Sigma^*$. The core of w relative to v or simply v-core of w, denoted by $core_v(w)$, is the unique subword w' of w, satisfying the following conditions:*
(i) $|w'|_v = |w|_v$ and (ii) w' is a subword of every subword w'' of w satisfying $|w''|_v = |w|_v$.
We say that w is a v-core word if and only if $core_v(w) = w$.

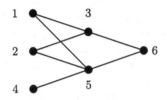

Fig. 1. The Parikh word representable graph $\mathcal{G}(aababc)$

If the alphabet is $\Sigma_2 = \{a < b\}$, the core of w, denoted core(w), is the unique subword w_0 of w with the smallest possible length such that $w \in b^* w_0 a^*$. A word $w \in \Sigma_2^*$ is said to be a core word if and only if core(w) = w.

3   Parikh Word Representable Graphs over a Ternary Alphabet

In [4], it was shown that the Parikh word representable graph of a binary word w is connected if and only if w is a core word. For ternary words this is not the case. In fact, $core_{cab}(w) = w$ for $w = cabb \in \Sigma_3$ but the Parikh word representable graph of w is not connected. In [16, Lemma 5.1, Page 13], besides several interesting general results, the authors have provided a sufficient condition for a Parikh word representable graph of a word over an ordered alphabet, to be connected.

Here we give in terms of regular expressions [14], a characterization for Parikh word representable graph of a word w over ternary alphabet, to be connected, but with w involving all three letters of the alphabet.

Theorem 1. *A Parikh word representable graph G of a word w over $\Sigma_3 = \{a < b < c\}$, having at least one a, at least one b and at least one c, is disconnected if and only if the word w is in the language of the regular expression*

$$r = \{a,b,c\}^* a\{a,c\}^* + \{a,c\}^* c\{a,b,c\}^* + \{b,c\}^* \{a,c\}^* \{a,b\}^*$$

Proof. It can be verified that if the word w belongs to the language $L(r)$ of the regular expression r, then the corresponding Parikh word representable graph is disconnected.

On the other hand if the Parikh word representable graph G is disconnected, then the corresponding word w representing G can be shown to be in $L(r)$ as follows: Consider any two vertices u and v in two different components of the graph G, where the label of u appears before the label of v in the corresponding word w. Note that we cannot have u and v respectively labelled a and b or respectively labelled b and c as otherwise there would be an edge between u and v. So we are left with the following cases to consider.

Case 1: If both u and v are labelled a and there is at least one b in the subword in w following the symbol corresponding to v, then there would be a path from u to v. Since the graph G is assumed to be disconnected, the word is in the language of the regular expression $\{a,b,c\}^*a\{a,b,c\}^*a\{a,c\}^*$.

If the word w has only one a, then it can be shown that the word must be in the language of the regular expression $\{b,c\}^*a\{c\}^*$.

Combining these two sub cases, it follows that the word w will be in the language of the regular expression $\{a,b,c\}^*a\{a,c\}^*$.

Case 2: Similarly if both u and v are labelled c and there is at least one b in the subword preceding the symbol corresponding to u, then there would be a path from u to v which is not possible. Hence the word is in the language of the regular expression $\{a,c\}^*c\{a,b,c\}^*c\{a,b,c\}^*$.

If the word has only one c, then it can be shown that the word must be in the language of the regular expression $\{a\}^*c\{a,b\}^*$.

Combining these two sub cases, it follows that the word will be in the language of the regular expression $\{a,c\}^*c\{a,b,c\}^*$.

Case 3: If both u and v are labelled b and there is at least one a in the subword preceding the symbol corresponding to u or one c in the subword following the symbol corresponding to v, then v would be reachable from u. Also, if there is a scattered subword abc between u and v, there would be a path from u to v. In order to avoid this, the corresponding word w is of the form $w = w_1 \alpha w_2$, for some $w_1 \in L(\{b,c\}^*)$, $w_2 \in L(\{a,b\}^*)$ and $\alpha \in L(b\{b,c\}^*\{a,c\}^*\{a,b\}^*b)$.

Case 4: If u is labelled a and v is labelled c, and there is a vertex labelled b in the subword between the symbols corresponding to u and v or if there is a scattered subword ab before u and a vertex labelled b after v or a symbol b before u and a scattered subword bc after v then v would be reachable from u. Therefore the corresponding word w is either as in Cases 1 or 2 or it is of the form $w = w_1 \beta w_2$, for some $\beta \in L(a\{a,c\}^*c)$, $w_1 \in L(\{b,c\}^*\{a,c\}^*)$, and $w_2 \in L(\{a,c\}^*\{a,b\}^*)$, since $|w_1|_{ab} = 0$ and $|w_2|_{bc} = 0$.

Case 5: If u is labelled c and v is labelled a, and there is a scattered subword ab among the symbols before the vertex u corresponding to c and a vertex labelled b after the vertex corresponding to v or a vertex labelled b before the vertex u and a scattered subword bc after v, then there would be a path from u to v. Therefore the corresponding word w is of the form $w = w_1 \gamma w_2$, for some $\gamma \in L(c\{a,c\}^*a)$, $w_1 \in L(\{b,c\}^*)$, and $w_2 \in L(\{a,b\}^*)$.

Case 6: If u is labelled b and v is labelled a, and there is a scattered subword bc after the symbol corresponding v or a scattered subword abc between the symbols corresponding to u and v and a symbol b after v we get a contradiction to the fact that u and v are in distinct components of the graph. Therefore the corresponding word w is of the form $w = w_1 \delta w_2$, for some $\delta \in L(b\{a,c\}^*a)$, $w_1 \in L(\{b,c\}^*)$, and $w_2 \in L(\{a,b\}^*)$.

Case 7: If u is labelled c and v is labelled b, and there is a scattered subword ab before u or a symbol b before u and a scattered subword abc between the symbols corresponding to u and v, then v would be reachable from u. Therefore the corresponding word w is of the form $w = w_1 \eta w_2$, for some $\eta \in c\{a,c\}^*b$, $w_1 \in L(\{b,c\}^*)$ and $w_2 \in L(\{a,b\}^*)$.

Simplifying the word w in each of the cases 3 to 7, we obtain w to be in the language $L(\{b,c\}^*\{a,c\}^*\{a,b\}^*)$.

Thus we find w is in the language of the regular expression

$$\{a,b,c\}^*a\{a,c\}^* + \{a,c\}^*c\{a,b,c\}^* + \{b,c\}^*\{a,c\}^*\{a,b\}^*$$

on combining the cases 1 to 7.   □

The notion of dual of a binary word was considered in [11]. Here we extend this to ternary words.

Definition 3. *A word $d(w) = y_1y_2\ldots y_n$ is said to be the dual of the ternary word $w = x_1x_2\ldots x_n$ over Σ_3 if*

$$y_i = \begin{cases} a, & \text{if } x_{n-i+1} = c \\ b, & \text{if } x_{n-i+1} = b \\ c, & \text{if } x_{n-i+1} = a \end{cases}$$

Definition 4. *A word w is said to be self dual if $d(w) = w$.*

Example 1. *accbac over Σ_3 is the dual of acbaac and abbcabbc is a self dual word.*

Isomorphism of graphs is a well-investigated problem in graph theory. We now recall the definition of isomorphism of graphs. Two graphs G and H are said to be isomorphic and we write $G \cong H$, if there is a bijection $f : V(G) \to V(H)$ between the vertex sets of the two graphs such that any two vertices u and v are adjacent in G if and only if $f(u)$ and $f(v)$ are adjacent in H.

Theorem 2. *Two Parikh word representable graphs $\mathcal{G}(w_1)$ and $\mathcal{G}(w_2)$, respectively corresponding to the words w_1 and w_2 over Σ_3, are isomorphic if any of the following conditions is satisfied:*

(i) $w_1 \equiv_1 w_2$
(ii) $w_2 = d(w_1)$
(iii) $w_1 = a^k u$ *and* $w_2 = uc^k$, *for some positive integer k, where $u \in \Sigma_3^*$.*

Proof. (i) Suppose $w_1 \equiv_1 w_2$. Then we can find a sequence of words $v_0, v_1, \ldots, v_k$ such that $v_0 = w_1, v_k = w_2$ and $v_i = xacy, v_{i+1} = xcay$. Then $\mathcal{G}(v_i)$ is obtained from $\mathcal{G}(xy)$ and by adding two vertices labelled a and c and connecting the vertex labelled a to each vertex labelled b in $\mathcal{G}(y)$ and the vertex labelled c to each vertex labelled b in $\mathcal{G}(x)$. Clearly $\mathcal{G}(v_{i+1})$ is also constructed in the same way except that the labels of the two vertices corresponding to a and c are interchanged. Hence $\mathcal{G}(v_i)$ and $\mathcal{G}(v_{i+1})$ are isomorphic which implies that $\mathcal{G}(w_1)$ and $\mathcal{G}(w_2)$ are isomorphic.
(ii) Suppose $w_2 = d(w_1)$ i.e., the two words w_1 and w_2 are duals of each other. Let $w_1 = x_1x_2\ldots x_i \ldots x_j \ldots x_n$. Then we have

$$w_2 = d(w_1) = d(x_n)\cdots d(x_j)\cdots d(x_i)\cdots d(x_2)d(x_1).$$

Let $\mathcal{G}(w_1) = (V, E), \mathcal{G}(w_2) = (V', E')$ with $V = \{1, 2, \ldots, n\}$ and $V' = \{1, 2, \ldots, n\}$. The mapping $\Phi : i \to n + 1 - i, (1 \leq i \leq n)$ gives a one-to-one correspondence between the vertices of $\mathcal{G}(w_1)$ and $\mathcal{G}(w_2)$, preserving adjacency and thus the undirected graph of w_1 is isomorphic to the undirected graph of w_2.

(iii) Suppose $w_1 = a^k u$ and $w_2 = u c^k$ where $u \in \Sigma_3^*$. Consider the graph corresponding to u. The graphs of both w_1 and w_2 are obtained from $\mathcal{G}(u)$ by adding k new vertices and adding edges between each of these vertices and each vertex labelled b in $\mathcal{G}(u)$. These new vertices are labelled a in $\mathcal{G}(w_1)$ and c in $\mathcal{G}(w_2)$. Hence the undirected graphs $\mathcal{G}(w_1)$ and $\mathcal{G}(w_2)$ are isomorphic.

$\square$

It is well-known that a graph is Eulerian if and only if every vertex of the graph has even degree. A necessary and sufficient condition for a connected Parikh word representable graph of a word over a binary alphabet to be Eulerian is provided in [11]. In the following result we extend this result for ternary alphabet.

Theorem 3. *A connected Parikh word representable graph over $\Sigma_3 = \{a < b < c\}$ is Eulerian if and only if it represents a word w of the form $w = a^{p_1} b^{q_1} c^{r_1} a^{p_2} b^{q_2} c^{r_2} \ldots a^{p_l} b^{q_l} c^{r_l}$ where*

(a) q_i is even for all i.
(b) p_i and r_{i-1} have the same parity for $2 \leq i \leq l - 1$, for $l \geq 3$.
(c) p_1 has the same parity as $\sum_{i=1}^{l} r_i$ and r_l has the same parity as $\sum_{i=1}^{l} p_i$.

Proof. Let $\mathcal{G}(w)$ be a graph representing $w = a^{p_1} b^{q_1} c^{r_1} a^{p_2} b^{q_2} c^{r_2} \cdots a^{p_l} b^{q_l} c^{r_l}$ over $\Sigma_3 = \{a < b < c\}$ satisfying given conditions. Then it can be verified that every vertex in $\mathcal{G}(w)$ has even degree. In fact, every vertex corresponding to each a in a^{p_1} has degree $\sum_{i=1}^{l} q_i$ which is even by condition (a) in the Theorem; every vertex corresponding to each b in b^{q_1} has degree $p_1 + \sum_{i=1}^{l} r_i$ which is also even by condition (c) in the Theorem; every vertex corresponding to each c in c^{r_1} has even degree q_1. The degrees of the other vertices can be found to be even in a similar manner. In fact the degrees of the vertices corresponding to the $a's$, $b's$ and $c's$ in an "intermediate" $a^{p_j} b^{q_j} c^{r_j}$, can be seen to be even using the conditions (b) and (c) in the Theorem. Hence $\mathcal{G}(w)$ is Eulerian.

Conversely, Suppose $\mathcal{G}(w)$ is Eulerian. Then all the vertices of $\mathcal{G}(w)$ have even degree. Considering the vertex corresponding to an a in the first a^{p_1} in w, the degree of this vertex is $q_1 + q_2 + \cdots + q_l$ which is even. Similarly, by considering the vertex corresponding to an a in a^{p_2} in w, the degree of this vertex is $q_2 + \cdots + q_l$ which is also even and therefore on taking the difference, we find q_1 is even. Proceeding in this manner, it can be proved that each q_i is even, establishing the condition (a).

Next consider two vertices corresponding to one b in each of the b^{q_i} and $b^{q_{i+1}}$. Then the degrees of these vertices are $p_1 + p_2 + \cdots + p_i + p_{i+1} + r_{i+1} + \cdots + r_l$ and $p_1 + p_2 + \cdots + p_i + r_i + r_{i+1} + \cdots + r_l$ are even which yield $r_i - p_{i+1}$ is even, proving condition (b).

By substituting $i = 1$ and $i = l - 1$ in the above case, we get condition (c). □

4 Morphisms on Words and Graphs

In this section, we study structural properties of Parikh word representable graphs of words under certain morphisms. We begin with the property of connectivity of the Parikh word representable graphs of the morphic images of words.

It is known that Parikh word representable graph of a core word over the binary alphabet Σ_2 is connected. We look for conditions for the Parikh word representable graph of the image of a word under a morphism to be connected.

The well-known Thue-Morse morphism [6] is a mapping $\mu : \Sigma_2^* \to \Sigma_2^*$ defined by

$$\mu(a) = ab, \mu(b) = ba.$$

Since a core word $w \in \Sigma_2^*$ starts with a and ends with b, $\mu(w)$ starts with b and ends with a. Therefore $\mu(w)$ is not a core word as it will end with a which means $\mathcal{G}(\mu(w))$ is disconnected, although $\mathcal{G}(w)$ is connected as $w \in \Sigma_2^*$. In fact, the following result which can be easily proved, gives a condition on a morphism such that the Parikh word representable graph of the morphic image of a core word over Σ_2 is connected.

Theorem 4. Let $\phi : \Sigma_2^* \to \Sigma_2^*$ be a morphism such that $\phi(a) = ax$ and $\phi(b) = yb$, for some $x, y \in \Sigma_2^*$. Then for any core word $w \in \Sigma_2^*$, $\mathcal{G}(\phi(w))$ is connected.

For a ternary alphabet Σ_3, we characterize the words such that the connectivity property of the Parikh word representable graphs is preserved under a special morphism, called Istrail morphism [6].

The Istrail morphism is a mapping $\iota : \Sigma_3^* \to \Sigma_3^*$ defined by

$$\iota(a) = abc, \iota(b) = ac, \iota(c) = b.$$

Theorem 5. Let $w \in \Sigma_3^*$ containing at least one a, at least one b and at least one c. Assume that $\mathcal{G}(w)$ is connected. Then $\mathcal{G}(\iota(w))$ is connected if and only if $w = core_{abc}(w)$.

Proof. Assume that $\mathcal{G}(\iota(w))$ is connected. From Theorem 1, it follows that $\iota(w)$ can not begin with c and or end with a. We have the following cases.

Case 1: If $\iota(w) = avb$ for some v in Σ_3^*, then it is clear that w begins either with an a or a b and ends with a c. However if $w \in L(b\{a, b, c\}^*c)$ we have, $i(w) \in L(ac\{a, b, c\}^*b)$ which is not possible since $\mathcal{G}(\iota(w))$ is connected. Moreover since $\mathcal{G}(w)$ is connected there is at least one b between a and c. Hence $w = core_{abc}(w)$.

Case 2: If $\iota(w) = avc$ for some v in Σ_3^*, then $w \in L(a\{a,b,c\}^*a+a\{a,b,c\}^*b+ b\{a,b,c\}^*a + b\{a,b,c\}^*b)$. Since $\mathcal{G}(w)$ is connected $w \notin L(a\{a,b,c\}^*a + b\{a,b,c\}^*a+b\{a,b,c\}^*b)$. If $w \in L(a\{a,b,c\}^*b)$ then $\iota(w) \in L(abc\{a,b,c\}^*ac)$ and as a result $\mathcal{G}(\iota(w))$ is not connected, a contradiction. Therefore this case is not possible.

Case 3: If $\iota(w)$ begins with b then $\iota(w) \in L(c\{a,b,c\}^*)$ and we have a contradiction to the fact that $\mathcal{G}(w)$ is connected.

To prove the converse, let w be a word over Σ_3 such that $w = $ core $_{abc}(w)$. Then $\mathcal{G}(w)$ is connected, by [16, Lemma 5.1]. If possible let $\mathcal{G}(\iota(w))$ be disconnected. Then by Theorem 1 we have,

$$\iota(w) \in L(\{a,b,c\}^*a\{a,c\}^* + \{a,c\}^*c\{a,b,c\}^* + \{b,c\}^*\{a,c\}^*\{a,b\}^*)$$

Case 1: If $\iota(w)$ is in $L(\{a,b,c\}^*a\{a,c\}^*)$ then $w = ub$ for some $u \in \Sigma_3^*$ and hence $w \neq$ core $_{abc}(w)$.

Case 2: If $\iota(w)$ is in $L(\{a,c\}^*c\{a,b,c\}^*)$ then $w = bu$ for some $u \in \Sigma_3^*$ and again $w \neq$ core $_{abc}(w)$.

Case 3: If $\iota(w)$ is in $L(\{b,c\}^*\{a,c\}^*\{a,b\}^*)$, then $w = cuc$ for some $u \in \Sigma_3^*$ and hence $w \neq$ core $_{abc}(w)$.

Thus our assumption is wrong and $\mathcal{G}(\iota(w))$ is connected. Hence the result.   □

Isomorphism of Parikh word representable graphs is studied in [4,11]. Here we discuss this problem in the context of morphisms. Before proceeding further, we obtain a result on the number of edges of the Parikh word representable graphs of the Istrail morphic images of two words.

Theorem 6. *If w and w' are two words over Σ_3 having the same Parikh vector, then $\mathcal{G}(\iota(w))$ and $\mathcal{G}(\iota(w'))$ have equal number of edges.*

Proof. The number of edges in $\mathcal{G}(w)$ for a ternary word $w \in \Sigma_3^*$ is given by $|w|_{ab} + |w|_{bc}$. It is known [1, Lemma 1] that

$$|\iota(w)|_{ab} = |w|_a + |w|_{aa} + |w|_{ac} + |w|_{ba} + |w|_{bc}$$

and

$$|\iota(w)|_{bc} = |w|_a + |w|_{aa} + |w|_{ab} + |w|_{ca} + |w|_{cb}$$

Hence

$$|E(\mathcal{G}(\iota(w)))| = 2|w|_a + 2|w|_{aa} + |w|_{ab} + |w|_{ba} + |w|_{bc} + |w|_{cb} + |w|_{ac} + |w|_{ca}$$
$$= |w|_a^2 + |w|_a + |w|_a|w|_b + |w|_b|w|_c + |w|_a|w|_c$$
$$= |w'|_a^2 + |w'|_a + |w'|_a|w'|_b + |w'|_b|w'|_c + |w'|_a|w'|_c = |E(\mathcal{G}(\iota(w')))|$$

□

Isomorphic graphs have the same number of edges but the converse is not true. Likewise, the graphs $\mathcal{G}(\iota(w)) = \mathcal{G}(abcabcac)$ and $\mathcal{G}(\iota(w')) = \mathcal{G}(abcacabc)$ have an equal number of (eight) edges but they are not isomorphic, where $w = a^2b$ and $w' = aba$ are over Σ_3 and have the same Parikh vector $(2,1,0)$. In fact $\mathcal{G}(abcacac)$ is disconnected where as $\mathcal{G}(abcacabc)$ is connected. On the other hand consider another word $w'' = ba^2$. Then $\mathcal{G}(\iota(w'')) = \mathcal{G}(acabcabc)$ also has 8 edges and $\mathcal{G}(\iota(w))$ and $\mathcal{G}(\iota(w''))$ are isomorphic.

Theorem 7. $\mathcal{G}(\iota(w))$ is isomorphic to $\mathcal{G}(\iota(mi(w)))$ for any word $w \in \Sigma_3^*$.

Proof. Let $w = w_1w_2\ldots w_{n-1}w_n$, $w_i \in \Sigma_3$, for $1 \le i \le n$. It follows from Theorem 2 that $\mathcal{G}(w) \cong \mathcal{G}(d(w))$ where $d(w)$ is the dual of w. Now

$$d(\iota(w_i)) = \begin{cases} d(\iota(a)) = d(abc) = abc = \iota(a) & \text{if } w_i = a \\ d(\iota(b)) = d(ac) = ac = \iota(b) & \text{if } w_i = b \\ d(\iota(c)) = d(b) = b = \iota(c) & \text{if } w_i = c \end{cases}$$

Hence $d(\iota(w_i)) = \iota(w_i)$ for $1 \le i \le n$. Therefore,

$$\begin{aligned} d(\iota(w)) &= d[(\iota(w_1)(\iota(w_2)\ldots(\iota(w_n)] \\ &= d(\iota(w_n))d(\iota(w_{n-1}))\ldots d(\iota(w_2))d(\iota(w_1)) \\ &= \iota(w_n)\iota(w_{n-1})\ldots\iota(w_2)\iota(w_1) = \iota(mi(w)) \end{aligned}$$

Hence the corresponding graphs are isomorphic. $\qquad\qquad\qquad\qquad\qquad\square$

Theorem 8. Let $\phi : \Sigma_2^* \to \Sigma_2^*$ be any morphism. Suppose w and w' are two binary core words such that $\mathcal{G}(w) \cong \mathcal{G}(w')$. Then $\mathcal{G}(\phi(w)) \cong \mathcal{G}(\phi(w'))$ if $\phi(b) = d(x)$ whenever $\phi(a) = x$ for some $x \in \Sigma_2^*$.

Proof. Let w and w' be two distinct words such that $\mathcal{G}(w) \cong \mathcal{G}(w')$ and $w = w_1w_2\ldots w_{n-1}w_n$, $w_i \in \Sigma_2$, for $1 \le i \le n$. Then w' is the dual of w [11, Theorem 3]. In fact $w' = d(w) = d(w_n)d(w_{n-1})\ldots d(w_2)d(w_1)$. Let $\phi : \Sigma_2^* \to \Sigma_2^*$ be a morphism defined by $\phi(a) = x$ and $\phi(b) = d(x)$, for some $x \in \Sigma_2^*$. In order to show $\mathcal{G}(\phi(w)) \cong \mathcal{G}(\phi(w'))$, it is enough to show that $\phi(w') = d(\phi(w))$. If $w_i = a$, for some $1 \le i \le n$, $\phi(d(w_i)) = \phi(d(a)) = \phi(b) = d(x) = d(\phi(a)) = d(\phi(w_i))$ i.e., $\phi(d(w_i)) = d(\phi(w_i))$. Likewise for $w_i = b$, we also have $\phi(d(w_i)) = d(\phi(w_i))$. Therefore

$$\begin{aligned} \phi(w') &= \phi(d(w_n))\phi(d(w_{n-1}))\ldots\phi(d(w_2))\phi(d(w_1)) \\ &= d(\phi(w_n))d(\phi(w_{n-1}))\ldots d(\phi(w_2))d(\phi(w_1)) \\ &= d(\phi(w_1)\phi(w_2)\ldots\phi(w_{n-1})\phi(w_n)) = d(\phi(w)) \end{aligned}$$

$\qquad\qquad\qquad\qquad\qquad\qquad\qquad\qquad\qquad\qquad\qquad\qquad\qquad\qquad\square$

Theorem 9. Let $\phi : \Sigma_3^* \to \Sigma_3^*$ be a morphism such that $\phi(c) = d(x)$ and $\phi(b) = y$ whenever $\phi(a) = x$ for some $x, y \in \Sigma_3^*$ such that $d(y) = y$. Suppose w and w' are two ternary words such that $w' = d(w)$. Then $\mathcal{G}(\phi(w)) \cong \mathcal{G}(\phi(w'))$.

Proof. Let w and w' be two words such that $\mathcal{G}(w) \cong \mathcal{G}(w')$ and $w = w_1 w_2 \ldots w_{n-1} w_n$, $w_i \in \Sigma_3$, for $1 \leq i \leq n$. Then we have $w' = d(w) = d(w_n) d(w_{n-1}) \ldots d(w_2) d(w_1)$. Let $\phi : \Sigma_3^* \rightarrow \Sigma_3^*$ be a morphism defined by $\phi(a) = x$, $\phi(c) = d(x)$, and $\phi(b) = y$ for some $x, y \in \Sigma_3^*$ such that $d(y) = y$. In order to show that $\mathcal{G}(\phi(w)) \cong \mathcal{G}(\phi(w'))$, it is enough to show that $\phi(w') = d(\phi(w))$. Now

$$\phi(d(w_i)) = \begin{cases} \phi(c) = d(x) = d(\phi(a)) & \text{if } w_i = a \\ \phi(b) = y = d(y) = d(\phi(b)) & \text{if } w_i = b \\ \phi(a) = d(x) = d(\phi(c)) & \text{if } w_i = c \end{cases}$$

Hence $\phi(d(w_i)) = d(\phi(w_i))$ for $1 \leq i \leq n$. Therefore

$$\begin{aligned} \phi(w') &= \phi(d(w_n)) \phi(d(w_{n-1})) \ldots \phi(d(w_2)) \phi(d(w_1)) \\ &= d(\phi(w_n)) d(\phi(w_{n-1})) \ldots d(\phi(w_2)) d(\phi(w_1)) \\ &= d(\phi(w_1) \phi(w_2) \ldots \phi(w_{n-1}) \phi(w_n)) = d(\phi(w)) \end{aligned}$$

$\square$

Theorem 10. *Let $\phi : \Sigma_2^* \rightarrow \Sigma_2^*$ be a morphism given by $\phi(a) = a^2 x$ and $\phi(b) = yb^2$, for some $x, y \in \Sigma_2^*$ such that all the prefixes of each of x and y have more number of a's than b's. Assume that the Parikh word representable graph of a word w over Σ_2 has a Hamiltonian cycle. Then $\mathcal{G}(\phi(w))$ has a Hamiltonian cycle.*

Proof. Let the Parikh word representable graph $\mathcal{G}(w)$ of the word w over Σ_2 have a Hamiltonian cycle. It was shown in [4, Theorem 7], that a Parikh word representable graph has a Hamiltonian cycle if and only if

(i) $w = a^2 w' b^2$, for some $w' \in \Sigma_2^*$ and
(ii) all the prefixes have more number of a's than b's.

Let ϕ be the morphism of the following form $\phi(a) = a^2 x$ and $\phi(b) = yb^2$, for some $x, y \in \Sigma_2^*$ such that all the prefixes of each of x and y have more number of a's than b's. It can be verified that the word $\phi(w)$ has the properties (i) and (ii). Hence $\mathcal{G}(\phi(w))$ has a Hamiltonian cycle. $\square$

Theorem 11. *Let $\phi : \Sigma_2^* \rightarrow \Sigma_2^*$ be a morphism such that*

$$\phi(x) = a^{2p_1} b^{2q_1} a^{2p_2} b^{2q_2} \ldots a^{2p_l} b^{2q_l},$$

for some $p_i, q_i \in \mathbb{N}$, $1 \leq i \leq l$, $x \in \{a, b\}$ and $p_1 \geq 1$, when $x = a$ and $q_l \geq 1$, when $x = b$. Then $\mathcal{G}(\phi(w))$ is Eulerian for every core word $w \in \Sigma_2^*$.

Proof. In [11, Theorem 7], it was shown that a Parikh word representable graph is Eulerian if and only if

$$w = a^{2m_1} b^{2n_1} a^{2m_2} b^{2n_2} \ldots a^{2m_l} b^{2n_l} , \text{ for } m_i, n_i \in \mathbb{N}, 1 \leq i \leq l, m_1, n_l \geq 1 \quad (1)$$

Since a core word over Σ_2^* starts with a and ends with b, it can be verified that for any core word $w \in \Sigma_2^*$, $\phi(w)$ is of the form (1). Therefore, $\mathcal{G}(\phi(w))$ is Eulerian. $\square$

Remark 1. There exists a morphism, say, $\psi : \Sigma_2^* \to \Sigma_2^*$ other than the morphism specified in the Theorem 11 and a word w such that $\mathcal{G}(\psi(w))$ is Eulerian. For example, take the morphism $\psi : \Sigma_2^* \to \Sigma_2^*$ defined by $\psi(a) = a^2b^3$ and $\psi(b) = b$ and the word ab. Then $\psi(ab) = a^2b^4$ and therefore, $\mathcal{G}(\psi(ab))$ is Eulerian.

Remark 2. The result in the Theorem 11 for the Parikh word representable graph of a morphic word to be Eulerian, cannot be extended for Σ_3 as can be seen from the following example.
Let $w = ab^2c$, $\phi(x) = ab^2c$, for $x \in \{a, b, c\}$. Then ϕ satisfies the above theorem and $\mathcal{G}(ab^2c)$ is Eulerian but $\mathcal{G}(ab^2cab^2cab^2cab^2c)$ is not Eulerian.

Theorem 12. *Let $\phi : \Sigma_3 \to \Sigma_3^*$ be a morphism such that $\phi(a)\phi(c) \equiv_1 \phi(c)\phi(a)$. Suppose w and w' are two words such that $w' \equiv_1 w$. Then $\mathcal{G}(\phi(w)) \cong \mathcal{G}(\phi(w'))$.*

Proof. Since $w' \equiv_1 w$, by the definition of 1-equivalence, we can find a series of words $w = w_0, w_1, w_2, \dots w_m = w'$ where w_{j+1} can be obtained from w_j by swapping two symbols c and a which appear consecutively. Suppose $w_j = a_1a_2 \dots ca \dots a_n$ for some $1 \le j \le m-1$. Clearly $w_{j+1} = a_1a_2 \dots ac \dots a_n$. Then

$$
\begin{aligned}
\phi(w_j) &= \phi(a_1a_2 \dots ca \dots a_n) \\
&= \phi(a_1)\phi(a_2) \dots \phi(c)\phi(a) \dots \phi(a_n) \\
&\equiv_1 \phi(a_1)\phi(a_2) \dots \phi(a)\phi(c) \dots \phi(a_n) \quad = \phi(a_1a_2 \dots ac \dots a_n) = \phi(w_{j+1})
\end{aligned}
$$

Hence $\phi(w) \equiv_1 \phi(w_1) \equiv_1 \phi(w_2) \equiv_1 \cdots \equiv_1 \phi(w')$. As a result, it follows from Theorem 2 that the corresponding graphs are isomorphic. $\quad\square$

5   Conclusion

We have established certain results on the properties of ternary Parikh word representable graphs and also studied the impact of word morphisms on Parikh word representable graphs corresponding to binary and ternary words. It will be of interest to examine other graph properties of this class of graphs.

Acknowledgement. The authors are grateful to the reviewers for their very useful and detailed comments which helped to revise and improve the contents and presentation of the paper, correcting the errors.

References

1. Atanasiu, A.: Parikh matrices, amiability and Istrail morphism. Int. J. Found. Comput. Sci. **21**(6), 1021–1033 (2010)
2. Atanasiu, A.: Binary amiable words. Int. J. Found. Comput. Sci. **18**(02), 387–400 (2007)
3. Atanasiu, A., Atanasiu, R., Petre, I.: Parikh matrices and amiable words. Theor. Comput. Sci. **390**(1), 102–109 (2008)
4. Bera, S., Mahalingam, K.: Structural properties of word representable graphs. Math. Comput. Sci. **10**(2), 209–222 (2016)

5. Bondy, G.A., Murty, U.S.R.: Graph Theory with Applications. North-Holland, Amsterdam (1982)
6. Istrail, S.: On irreducible languages and nonrational numbers. Bulletin mathématique de la Société des sciences mathématiques de Roumanie **21**, 301–308 (1977)
7. Kitaev, S., Lozin, V.: Words and Graphs, vol. 17. Springer, Cham (2015). https://doi.org/10.1007/978-3-319-25859-1
8. Kitaev, S., Salimov, P., Severs, C., Ulfarsson, H.: Word-representability of line graphs. Open J. Discrete Math. **1**(2), 96–101 (2011)
9. Mateescu, A., Salomaa, A.: Matrix indicators for subword occurrences and ambiguity. Int. J. Found. Comput. Sci. **15**(02), 277–292 (2004)
10. Mateescu, A., Salomaa, A., Salomaa, K., Yu, S.: A sharpening of the Parikh mapping. RAIRO - Theor. Inf. Appl. **35**(6), 551–564 (2001)
11. Mathew, L., Thomas, N., Somnath, B., Subramanian, K.G.: Some results on Parikh word representable graphs and partitions. Adv. Appl. Math. **107**, 102–115 (2019)
12. Lothaire, M.: Combinatorics on Words, Encyclopedia of Mathematics and its Applications, vol. 17. Addison Wesley, Boston (1983)
13. Parikh, R.J.: On context-free languages. J. ACM **13**(4), 570–581 (1966)
14. Rozenberg, G., Salomaa, A.: Handbook of Formal Languages. Springer, Heidelberg (1997). https://doi.org/10.1007/978-3-642-59136-5
15. Salomaa, A.: Parikh matrices: subword indicators and degrees of ambiguity. In: Böckenhauer, H.-J., Komm, D., Unger, W. (eds.) Adventures Between Lower Bounds and Higher Altitudes. LNCS, vol. 11011, pp. 100–112. Springer, Cham (2018). https://doi.org/10.1007/978-3-319-98355-4_7
16. Teh, W.C., Ng, Z.C., Javaid, M., Chern, Z.J.: Parikh word representability of bipartite permutation graphs. Discrete Appl. Math. **282**, 208–221 (2020)
17. Teh, W.C.: On core words and the Parikh matrix mapping. Int. J. Found. Comput. Sci. **26**(01), 123–142 (2015)
18. Teh, W.C., Kwa, K.H.: Core words and Parikh matrices. Theor. Comput. Sci. **582**, 60–69 (2015)

Author Index

Printed in the United States
by Baker & Taylor Publisher Services